Taiwan

the Bradt Travel Guide

Steven Crook

edition
2

www.bradtguides.com

Bradt Travel Guides Ltd, UK
The Globe Pequot Press Inc, USA

CHINA

East China Sea

Taiwan Strait

Fulong
Jinshan
Shimen
Yangmingshan National Park
Danshui
Keelung
H2
H2
H2A
H2
TAIPEI
F5
Taoyuan City
Banqiao
Xindian
F3
Yilan City
H7
Luodong
H2
H9
Sanxing
Dayuan
Zhongli
H4
H3
Daxi
H7
Lower Baling
Smangus
H7A
Nanshan
Mount Nanhu 3,742m
Hsinchu City
H1
F1
F3
H3
Qingquan
Mount Dabajian 3,490m
Snow Mountain 3,886m
Shei-Pa National Park
Lishan
Hehuanshan 3,422m
Taroko National Park
Xincheng
H8
H9
Hualien City
Miaoli City
H3
Taian
Fengyuan
Dayuling
H14A
Guguan
Puli
H14
H16
H11
Sanyi
F1
H3
H8
Taichung
H21
H21
H21
H16
H9
F3
H1
F6
Checheng
H14
F3
Changhua City
H17
Lugang
F1
Ershui
Douliu
H3
H1
H19
H17

Visit Taipei's National Palace Museum – home to the world's best collection of Chinese art and antiques
page 106

Shei-Pa National Park boasts excellent alpine hiking and is home to Snow Mountain, Taiwan's second-highest peak
page 198

Watch master woodcarvers in action in Sanyi
page 162

Lugang – see merchants' mansions and peer into artisans' workshops
page 180

Enjoy astounding vistas driving along the New Central Cross-Island Highway
page 206

Hike or drive through vertiginous Taroko Gorge
page 286

Go white-water rafting in the East Rift Valley
page 293

Tropic of Cancer

PACIFIC OCEAN

Penghu Islands

Look for nesting green turtles on the windswept beaches of the Penghu Islands
page 310

Tainan, the former capital — famous for its delicacies and ornate temples
page 207

Climb to the summit of Mount Jade — Taiwan's highest peak
page 204

Cycle along the Highway 11 coastal road admiring steep green hillsides and aboriginal villages
page 299

Look out for 1kg coconut crabs crossing the road on idyllic Green Island
page 335

Kenting National Park boasts superb beaches
page 274

Foguangshan — one of Taiwan's leading Buddhist monasteries
page 256

Little Liuqiu Island — this coral chunk makes an excellent day trip
page 332

South China Sea

Bashi Channel

Orchid Island

Green Island

Little Liuqiu Island

Yushan National Park

Mount Jade 3,952m

Xiangyangshan 3,603m

Guanshan 3,666m

Kenting National Park

Talijiang National Park

Chiayi City
Shizhuo
Meishan
Jiaxian
Yujing
Neimen
Qishan
Tainan
Gangshan
Qigu
Beimen
Kaohsiung
Pingtung City
Wutai
Daren
Checheng
Hengchun
Kending
Taitung City
Guanshan
Fuli
Yuli
Chenggong

H1
H9
H23
H11
H20
H9
H9
H26
H26
H9
H1
F3
H1
H17
H17
H1
H3
F1
F3
H1
H19
H17
F1
H3
F3
H3
H18

N

Bradt

0   50km
0   30 miles

Taiwan
Don't miss...

Raucous festivals
The annual Han Dan festival
in Taitung sees volunteers
take turns to have firecrackers
hurled at their bodies
(RM) page 307

Staggering mountains
Taroko National Park is a Mecca
for mountaineers, with peaks
such as the 3,740m Mount Nanhu
(TTB) page 286

Temple culture and architecture
Spectacularly made-up and attired *zhentou* troupes enliven temple events throughout Taiwan, but especially in the south
(RM) page 31

Biodiversity
Vinaceous rosefinch (*Carpodacus vinaceus*) can be seen at Snow Mountain
(TTB) page 199

Taiwanese food
Dihua Street, Taipei: Taiwan has an astonishing range of roadside stalls, cheap eateries and night markets
(TTB) page 63

Taiwan in colour

above The National Palace Museum houses one of the world's finest collections of art, much of which once belonged to the Chinese emperors (TTB) page 106

below left Kaohsiung's Formosa Boulevard KMRT Station contains *The Dome of Light*, claimed to be the world's largest piece of glass art (CF) page 254

below right Baoan Temple is Taipei's most fascinating shrine, featuring ornate carved screens and intricate murals (RM) page 103

bottom Taipei 101, once the world's tallest building at 509m, dominates the city skyline (CF) page 105

above Lugang's old streets offer up sights such as Japanese-era shops, 18th century wells, exquisite shrines and drying noodles (CF) page 180

right Dubbed 'Little Shanghai' in the 1930s, Jiufen's quaint streets retain much of their pre-World War II character (WC) page 131

below left A 'door god' at a temple in Tainan (RM)

below right Flowing through the heart of Kaohsiung and into the city's harbour, the Love River is ideal for an evening cruise or a riverside cycle (TTB) page 253

AUTHOR

Educated in the UK, Steven Crook was backpacking through Asia in 1991 when he decided to go to Taiwan. He was running out of money and needed a job. That wasn't the only reason, however. His geography teachers had never talked about the place and nobody he knew had ever been there. The prospect of visiting such an unfamiliar island was tantalising. He wasn't disappointed; he extended his stay and took up hiking. In 1996 he started writing about the country's mountains, temples and museums for newspapers and magazines. By 2009,  when he accepted Bradt's offer to write a travel guide to Taiwan, he'd seen most of the country – but because new museums, trails and other attractions keep opening, his 'to do and see' list doesn't seem to be getting any shorter.

AUTHOR'S STORY

Writing the first edition of this guidebook and updating it for a second edition has, on the whole, been a tremendous pleasure. The moments of confusion I've experienced are – possibly I'm rationalising here – key aspects of the Taiwan experience. The island's remarkable mountains and natural attractions are well known. But in the West, the incredible breadth and depth of Taiwan's cultures (I purposely use the plural) aren't so widely appreciated. There's nothing straightforward about the noisy parades which are central to folk-religion celebrations, no glib explanations why during such events men may cut themselves with swords or scantily clad young women pole dance. Trying to get to the bottom of things is an unending and sometimes frustrating journey, but underscores something I've felt every day for the past two decades: Taiwan may not always be beautiful and travelling here isn't without its niggles – but it's never dull.

When writing about Taiwan, it's hard not to fall back on clichés about 'east meeting west' and 'modernity blending with tradition'. After all, this is a country where businesspeople consult *feng shui* masters before laying out their offices and where high-school pupils pray to the god of education ahead of major exams. But the speed with which Taiwanese people adapt to change and the ease they show around imports of all kinds is striking. Most families have cars and new roads have shrunk the island. Riding the bullet train, I appreciate both its speed and impressive bilingual service. Slower forms of transport are bargains considering just how safe, reliable and comfortable they are.

Like many guidebook writers, I care deeply about the destination. Hopefully, some of my missionary zeal shows through. But really my job is an excuse, the best one yet invented, to go everywhere. I've always wanted to see what's over the next hill and around every corner. I'm fortunate to have Taiwan, where the hills are numerous and where each corner – both literal and figurative – leads to many others.

PUBLISHER'S FOREWORD *Adrian Phillips, Publishing Director*

My eyes were opened to the attractions of Taiwan a few years ago during a presentation at World Travel Market; we saw slides of wildlife and mountains, and folk traditions untouched by the 21st-century slickness often associated with the country. Taiwan certainly got its hooks into Steven Crook. After visiting during a backpacking trip through Asia, he decided to make the country his home, and over 20 years later he remains filled with what he calls a 'missionary zeal'. It's fantastic to bring this second edition of his book to the shelves so he can continue to spread the word, introducing travellers to the pleasures of Taiwan's festivals and landscapes.

Second edition published June 2014   First published 2010
Bradt Travel Guides Ltd
IDC House, The Vale, Chalfont St Peter, Bucks SL9 9RZ, England
www.bradtguides.com
Print edition published in the USA by The Globe Pequot Press Inc, PO Box 480, Guilford, Connecticut 06437-0480

Text copyright © 2014 Steven Crook
Maps copyright © 2014 Bradt Travel Guides Ltd
Photographs copyright © 2014 Individual photographers (see below)
Project Manager: Maisie Fitzpatrick
Cover image research: Pepi Bluck, Perfect Picture

ISBN: 978 1 84162 497 6 (print)
e-ISBN: 978 1 84162 794 6 (e-pub)
e-ISBN: 978 1 84162 695 6 (mobi)

British Library Cataloguing in Publication Data
A catalogue record for this book is available from the British Library

Photographs Craig Ferguson (CF); FLPA: Neil Bowman (NB/FLPA); Getty Images: Jung-Pang Wu (JPW/G); Rich Matheson (RM); Taiwan Tourist Board (TTB); Wikimedia Commons (WC): Patko Erika (PE/WC)
Front cover Picking orange day lilies, Sixty Stone Mountain, Hualien (JPW/G)
Back cover Door god, Tainan (RM); Wenshan Hot Springs (RM)
Title page Black-browed barbet (*Megalaima oorti*) (RM); a Rukai bride, Pingtung (RM); sticky rice dumplings (CF)

Maps David McCutcheon FBCart.S. The following maps were based on materials kindly supplied by Compass Media Group: Hsinchu City, Kaohsiung Main Station, Kaohsiung Love River, Taichung City Centre, Tainan City Centre, Taipei Eastern, Taipei Northwest and Taipei Southwest.

Typeset from the author's disc by Wakewing, High Wycombe
Production managed by Jellyfish Print Solutions; printed in India
Digital conversion by the Firsty Group

Acknowledgements

I never learned the names of many of those who helped me during the researching and writing of the first and second editions of this book. They were the friendly individuals who offered help when they spotted me studying bus-station timetables or taking notes from information boards. They had no idea what I was doing but were willing to spend time helping a stranger; it's folks like these who make travelling around and writing about Taiwan such a pleasure. I thank them wholeheartedly.

Several individuals working for Taiwan's Tourism Bureau helped by answering questions and setting up appointments. Among national park and national scenic area office staff who helped with information, transport, maps and materials, I'm especially grateful to Chen Chen-yu, Lisa Chen, Sandra Chen, Song Yi-ling and Hailing Hsing. A number of local government officials went out of their way to assist, notably Hou Ya-ting in Kaohsiung. In the private sector, Thomas Liao in Danshui and Charlies Liu near Fenqihu continue to do an excellent job of welcoming visitors (and explaining things to this writer).

The following Taiwan-based expatriates were particularly helpful: Stu Dawson and Neil Wade of Taiwan Adventures, Eddie Viljoen of Green Island Adventures, Doug Habecker and Donovan Smith of Compass Media, Richard Foster of Barking Deer Adventures and photographer Rich J Matheson. It was with Richard and Rich that I began exploring Taiwan's high mountains back in the 1990s.

I salute the guest contributors – John Boo (scuba diving), Richard Foster (birdwatching), Cheryl Robbins (indigenous people) and Robin Winkler (environmental issues) – for sharing their expertise.

At Bradt, I'd like to thank Adrian Phillips, Maisie Fitzpatrick, Claire Strange, Rachel Fielding, Anna Moores, Deborah Gerrard and Donald Greig for commissioning me to write this book and then guiding me through its completion with patience and wisdom.

Finally, much love and a thousand thank-yous to my wife Irene and son Conrad for accompanying me on several research trips and tolerating my absence for days at a time while I went solo.

This second edition is dedicated to my mother, Marceline Crook née Giddey (1941–2013), whose travels took her to four continents.

Contents

FEEDBACK REQUEST AND UPDATES WEBSITE

At Bradt Travel Guides we're aware that guidebooks start to go out of date on the day they're published – and that you, our readers, are out there in the field doing research of your own. You'll find out before us when a fine new family-run hotel opens or a favourite restaurant changes hands and goes downhill. So why not write and tell us about your experiences? Contact us on ☎ 01753 893444 or e info@bradtguides.com. We will forward emails to the author who may post 'one-off updates' on the Bradt website at www.bradtupdates.com/taiwan. Alternatively you can add a review of the book to www.bradtguides.com or Amazon.

LIST OF MAPS

NOTE ABOUT MAPS

Taiwan's cities are dense mazes of side streets, lanes and back alleys. For reasons of space and clarity, urban maps in this book do not show every single thoroughfare. For the same reason, regional maps leave out many minor roads. Roads labelled 'F' are freeways; those with an 'E' are expressways; those labelled 'H' are highways. Roads with a number but no letter are slower and often narrower.

KEYS AND SYMBOLS Maps include alphabetical keys covering the locations of those places to stay, eat or drink that are featured in the book. Note that regional maps may not show all hotels and restaurants in the area: other establishments may be located in towns shown on the map.

GRIDS AND GRID REFERENCES Several maps use grid lines to allow easy location of sites. Map grid references are listed in square brackets after listings in the text, with page number followed by grid number, eg: [91 A1].

Introduction

As a tourist destination, Taiwan has been flying under the radar. Other chapters of the Taiwan story, especially its economic success and its difficult relationship with China, are well known in the West. Businesspeople still come here in droves to source designed-in-Taiwan or made-in-Taiwan products. Relatively few, however, come to see what Taiwan is made of and the society Taiwanese people have created.

In a way, it's a shame Westerners no longer refer to this land as Formosa or Free China. The former name derives from a 16th-century description; Portuguese sailors bound for Japan are said to have called out *ilha formosa* – 'beautiful island' – when they glimpsed the towering cliffs and verdant hills of Taiwan's east. The main island, the size of Wales and Northern Ireland combined, retains a great deal of this natural beauty. There are so many mountains that the hundred peaks climbers try to bag – Taiwan's equivalent of Scotland's Munros – are all over 3,000m (9,842ft) high. And they're just the more accessible ones. In total, 258 summits top 3,000m. At 3,952m, Mount Jade is the highest peak in northeast Asia. Forests full of butterflies cover more than half the country. Coastal wetlands attract migratory waterbirds. Thanks to Taiwan's excellent transport system, it's possible to get from the latter to the former in a just few hours.

Many Taiwanese reject the 'China' label, even though the country's official name is the Republic of China. However, exploring Taiwan does give visitors an idea of what the giant on the other side of the Taiwan Strait could have been. Because certain traditions, in particular folk religion, have survived much better here than on the communist-ruled Chinese mainland, Taiwan is sometimes described as 'more Chinese than China'. There are Buddhist temples and Taoist clerics in every town and folk shrines in every village. Taipei's National Palace Museum remains the world's finest collection of Chinese artefacts. But I prefer to put it this way: Taiwan's society is much more than Chinese. The Han people who settled here from the 17th century onward found an island populated by Austronesian tribes. There was constant tension and frequent fighting but also trade and intermarriage. Between 1895 and 1945, Taiwan was ruled by Japan; Japanese food and architecture are still very evident. Taiwan was never colonised by a Western power yet there are smatterings of Americana, such as a love of baseball. If you're familiar with China, it's the differences between Taiwan and the mainland that'll strike you, not the similarities.

Some of the people browsing this book have been to Taiwan on business trips, possibly several times. Their memories may be of bleak industrial estates and heavy traffic. They may be sceptical when people talk of Taiwan's beautiful landscapes, biodiversity and cultural treasures. The country is a bit like an ex-boxer struggling to convince the world he's now a poet. But the poetry exists, I promise you, in its natural environment and extraordinary festivals. Come and see it for yourself.

Part One

GENERAL INFORMATION

Location Taiwan is an island in northeast Asia, separated from China by the Taiwan Strait and located on the western edge of the Pacific Ocean.

Neighbouring countries Taiwan has maritime borders with China, Japan and the Philippines.

Size/Area 36,191km^2

Climate Semi-tropical in the north, tropical in the south with wet summers and mild winters.

Status Republic

Population 23.3 million (2013). More than 96% of the population is of Han Chinese descent; around 2% is Austronesian.

Life expectancy 76.58 years (males), 83.06 (females)

Capital Taipei (population: 2.6 million)

Other main cities Kaohsiung (population: 2.8 million), Taichung (population: 2.6 million) and Tainan (population: 1.9 million)

Economy Free market with strong manufacturing and high-technology sectors.

GDP US$466 billion (2012)

Languages/official language Mandarin (official), Taiwanese, Hakka, aboriginal languages.

Religion Taoism and Buddhism with Christian and Muslim minorities.

Currency New Taiwan dollar. Banknotes with a value of 100, 200, 500, 1,000 and 2,000 NTD; coins with a value of 1, 5, 10, 20 and 50 NTD.

Exchange rate £1 = NTD50.7, US$1 = NTD30.7, €1 = NTD42.3 (March 2014)

National airline/airport China Airlines/Taiwan Taoyuan International Airport (IATA: TPE)

International telephone code +886

Time Taiwan is eight hours ahead of GMT (Greenwich Mean Time), 11 hours behind New York (Eastern Standard Time) and eight hours behind Los Angeles (Pacific Standard Time). It's in the same time zone as the PRC and one hour ahead of Singapore. Sunrise and sunset times are listed on English-language pages of the Central Weather Bureau's website (*www.cwb.gov.tw*).

Electrical voltage 110v/60Hz; two-pin plugs

Weights and measures Metric

Flag Red; the top left quarter is blue with a white star

National anthem San Min Chu I (Three Principles of the People)

National flower Plum blossom (*Prunus mei*)

National bird Formosan blue magpie (*Urocissa caerulea*)

National sports Baseball and basketball

Public holidays On the Gregorian calendar: 1 January (Founding Day of the Republic), 28 February (2-28 Peace Memorial Day), 5 April (Tomb-Sweeping Day), 1 May (Labour Day), 10 October (National Day). On the lunar calendar: January/February (Lunar New Year), June (Dragon Boat Festival), September (Mid-Autumn Festival).

1

Background Information

GEOGRAPHY

The country most outsiders and many of its own citizens call Taiwan, but which is officially the Republic of China (ROC), is in east Asia, southeast of the Chinese mainland and between Japan to the northeast and the Philippines to the south.

The ROC covers 36,191km², making it nearly twice as big as Wales but barely half the size of Tasmania. Compared with US states, it's a little larger than Maryland. What geographers define as Taiwan accounts for 95% of the ROC's land area. This main island is 394km long and 144km wide and shaped, Taiwanese often say, like a tobacco leaf. Taiwan includes the Penghu archipelago, Green Island, Orchid Island and a few other islets. In addition to these, the ROC controls three island clusters close to the Chinese coast (Kinmen, Matsu and Wuqiu) and the distant Pratas Islands. The Matsu Islands include the most northerly point of the ROC: Xiyin and Dongyin (two islands conjoined by a causeway) at 26°23'N. Pratas, three uninhabited atolls at 20°43'N and 116°42'E, is both the southernmost and westernmost outpost of the ROC. The Tropic of Cancer crosses Taiwan just south of the city of Chiayi.

It's Taiwan's mountains that stun visitors and create the most lasting impressions. Nearly one-third of the island is a kilometre or more above sea level. Some 10.3% reaches an elevation of 2,500m and 258 named peaks top 3,000m. Almost no humans live at these altitudes and only those willing to hike for days can properly experience this realm of alpine forests, wild animals and unique bird species.

There are five mountain ranges. The Central Mountain Range stretches four-fifths of the island's length. The Yushan Range, considered a separate entity because a river separates it from the Central Range, includes and is named after Taiwan's highest peak, Yushan or Mount Jade (3,952m). The Xueshan Range runs from the northeast coast to central Taiwan, a distance of 180km; its highest point is Taiwan's second-highest peak, Snow Mountain (3,886m). None of the peaks in the Alishan Range in Taiwan's southwest come close to 3,000m, but the area does include the famous resort from which it takes its name. The Coastal Mountain Range, which appeared when the Philippine Sea Plate collided with Taiwan, is just two million years old. The region between it and the interior mountains, the 180km-long East Rift Valley, is one of Taiwan's prettiest and most natural lowlands. There are extinct volcanoes near Taipei in Yangmingshan National Park. Several of Taiwan's outlying islands came into being because of undersea volcanic activity.

Because of the ongoing collision between the Philippine Sea Plate and the Asian Continental Plate, the entire island is rising at approximately four centimetres per year. Taiwan's location on the boundary of these two tectonic plates means it's vulnerable to earthquakes; 20th-century seismic events killed 8,000 people. There are benefits to being on the 'Pacific Ring of Fire', however – a string of beguiling mud volcanoes and an abundance of geothermal springs in which visitors can soak away stress.

Taiwan's population is about 23.3 million but its birth rate is now, by some reckonings, the lowest in the world. It's one of the most densely populated places on Earth. Nine out of ten Taiwanese live on the western plains and more reside in the north than the south.

The flattest and most fertile lands are the alluvial fans of rivers such as the 186km-long Zhuoshui (the island's longest waterway). Because of the island's topography and weather patterns – three-quarters of each year's total rain falls between May and October – Taiwan's rivers are short and often violent; only five waterways are more than 100km long. Natural lakes are few and tiny. Of Taiwan's six largest bodies of fresh water, five didn't exist at all until dams were built. Because of sedimentation and erosion, Taiwan is slowly gaining land along the west coast while losing it in the east. Climate change may lead to the inundation of parts of the western plains.

Considering almost every corner of the lowlands is used for agriculture, housing or industry, and that the camphor trade of the 18th and 19th centuries led to a massive felling of trees in the foothills, Taiwan has a remarkable amount of forest. Around 58% of the main island's land area is covered by trees or bamboo with hardwoods accounting for more than half of this area. While most of Taiwan's trees are in the highlands, in recent years there has been some reforestation on the western plains. Government efforts to preserve and expand tree cover have suffered setbacks. Landslides in the wake of 2009's Typhoon Morakot, for instance, swept an estimated 980,000 tonnes of branches, trunks and stumps into rivers.

CLIMATE

As you'd expect of a country that straddles the Tropic of Cancer, Taiwan is wet and warm. Seasons are distinct in terms both of temperature and the likelihood of rain. Daytime highs of 38°C have been recorded in urban areas during the summer. In December and January, northerners shiver as the mercury hovers around 10°C. The south doesn't get so cold, but jackets and gloves are essential if you're out early in the morning.

WHEN THE WIND BLOWS

The English word 'typhoon' is probably derived from one or another Chinese dialect; in Mandarin, these fearsome storms are called tái fēng. Typhoons form over the Pacific Ocean, hundreds of kilometres from land. Most then move due west, bringing heavy rain and dangerously strong winds to the islands (Taiwan, Okinawa, the Philippines) in their path. Typhoons tend to slow down when they hit land, but that doesn't make them any less deadly. In fact, because it's the rains they bring (and the consequent floods and landslides) that kill people and destroy property, some of the most destructive typhoons in Taiwan's recent history have been slow-moving storms that dumped immense quantities of water on fragile hillsides.

During a typical year there are 30 to 35 typhoons, of which three or four may hit Taiwan. Late July to mid-September is peak typhoon season, and even though Taiwan receives at least 72 hours' warning each time a typhoon approaches, the disruption to transport can still be severe. This is one reason why visitors do well to avoid Taiwan's summer.

Taiwan's annual average rainfall is 2,471mm. The north gets more than the south; the north's wet season is longer but less pronounced. A few places near Keelung receive close to 6,000mm of rain in a typical year. Taipei (an average of 170 rainy days per year) is noticeably wetter than central Kaohsiung (92 wet days each year). The ROC's outlying islands are relatively dry: Kinmen gets just 1,049mm of rain a year. Snowfall is uncommon below 2,000m in the northern half of Taiwan and below 3,000m in the south.

Taipei gets 1,408 hours of sunshine per year. Kaohsiung gets 2,082 hours, while in Tainan – where they used to produce salt by using sunshine to evaporate seawater – the annual average total is 2,264 hours. The days are relatively short, even in summer. In Taipei in early July, the sun rises about 05.10 and sets before 19.00. At the end of December, the times are around 06.40 and 17.20.

Taiwan's Central Weather Bureau publishes detailed English-language forecasts on their website (*www.cwb.gov.tw*).

NATURAL HISTORY

Taiwan has fantastic natural diversity in terms of topography, climate and soils. Of the world's 12 major soil types, 11 can be found in Taiwan. Consequently there's a wide range of habitats and these in turn nurture an astonishing variety of animals, birds, insects and plants. Rates of endemism are exceptionally high throughout the biosphere; a quarter of the country's 4,300 vascular plants are found nowhere else on Earth. A third of its reptile species and subspecies are unique, as are 36 of the 150-plus freshwater fish species, 11 of its 35 bats and 70% of its snails.

FAUNA One of the easiest animals to spot is Taiwan's only primate, the **Formosan macaque** (*Macaca cyclopis*). Also known as the Formosan rock monkey, this creature is distributed island-wide from sea level to at least 3,000m above sea level, but is most often spotted in foothills in the south and east. Macaques, who live in family groups usually numbering 20 to 40, have light brown fur often speckled with grey. Deep in the mountains there are larger animals such as **Formosan sambars** (*Rusa unicolor swinhoei*), a kind of deer, and **Formosan black bears** (*Ursus thibetanus formosanus*). The latter have distinctive V-shaped white marks on their chests and don't hibernate. Even though they've been known to steal food from hikers' packs while the humans are sleeping, they tend to keep a very low profile. Researchers fear this endemic subspecies will suffer the same fate as the **Formosan clouded leopard** (*Neofelis nebulosa brachyura*), a metre-long cat which hasn't been sighted since the late 1980s. Once hunted for its skin, it's now believed to be extinct.

Birds Thanks to its position on the East Asian–Australasian Flyway, Taiwan has fabulously varied birdlife. Fifty-three internationally recognised Important Bird Areas (IBAs) cover more than one-sixth of its land area. According to the most recent checklist issued by Taiwan's Chinese Wild Bird Federation (*www.bird.org.tw*), 608 avian species, including vagrants and migrants, have been recorded in Taiwan and its minor islands. At least 24 and perhaps as many as 29 are endemic species, while a further 59 are endemic subspecies. Many visiting birders have been able to add a dozen or more endemics, including the **Taiwan partridge** (*Arborophila crudigularis*) and the **mikado pheasant** (*Syrmaticus mikado*), to their 'life lists' during fortnight-long tours. Visitors who don't venture beyond the western lowlands will notice white-headed birds in parks and larger white birds near rice fields and rivers. The latter are egrets. The former, the **light-vented bulbul** (*Pycnonotus sinensis formosae*), is hybridising with and slowly causing the disappearance of the endemic variant, the black-capped **Taiwan bulbul** (*Pycnonotus taivanus*). The **Eurasian tree sparrow** (*Passer montanus*) is ubiquitous, and in foothills the **crested serpent eagle** (*Spilornis cheela hoya*) is an important predator.

FLORA Many of Taiwan's most common wild flowers are invasive species. Among them are **lantana** of various colours, especially white, yellow and orange, the daisy-like **cobbler's pegs** (*Bidens pilosa*) and the **flossflower** (*Ageratum houstonianum*). The former, an aggressive weed, is used by some Taiwanese as a folk treatment for diabetes. The last has delicate pink blooms. *Mimosa pudica* is also widespread; this species isn't very interesting to look at but it does have touch-sensitive leaves that curl up when brushed.

Taiwan is certainly a paradise for nature lovers – but a deeply troubled one.

CONSERVATION AND ENVIRONMENTAL ISSUES Robin Winkler

Taiwan's diplomatic isolation is often cited by government officials as a reason for its inability to take more effective measures to address environmental problems. No doubt, greater involvement in international organisations would probably induce Taiwan to take green issues more seriously. However, Taiwan's relative isolation from 'globalisation' until its entry into the WTO in 2002 saved much of its ecological wealth from exploitation. While a growing environmental awareness among the general public is evident throughout the country, since the nation first started legislating environmental protection in the 1970s, successive administrations have sent very mixed signals as to their commitment to improving Taiwan's environmental protection.

As readers will see from this guidebook, Taiwan has a spectacular range of habitats, making it one of the most biodiverse places on earth for its size. These are but relics of a much richer and not too distant past. Indigenous peoples were

NATIONAL PARKS IN THE ROC

The ROC has eight national parks of which four are alpine and four are maritime. Together, they account for almost 9% of the country's total land area. Admission is currently free for the seven national parks open to the public; at the time of writing, the authorities were weighing proposals to introduce admission and/or parking charges. Counting all types of conservation area, protected lands cover one-fifth of the ROC.

YUSHAN NATIONAL PARK (*www.ysnp.gov.tw*) Yushan, also known as Mount Jade, is Taiwan's highest peak and the national park that surrounds it is the country's largest land-based reserve. Land area: 105km². See page 202.

SHEI-PA NATIONAL PARK (*www.spnp.gov.tw*) More northerly and thus colder than Yushan National Park, this reserve is every bit as good in terms of high-mountain scenery. It's home to the Formosan land-locked salmon. Land area: 77km². See page 198.

TAROKO NATIONAL PARK (*www.taroko.gov.tw*) If Taroko Gorge isn't on your itinerary it should be. The park, however, is much more than the gorge – it boasts Taiwan's highest roads. Land area: 92km². See page 286.

YANGMINGSHAN NATIONAL PARK (*www.ymsnp.gov.tw*) Despite hordes of day trippers, the mountains northwest of Taipei offer excellent scenery and strenuous walks. Land area: 11km². See page 112.

KENTING NATIONAL PARK (*www.ktnp.gov.tw*) As popular as Yangmingshan but for different reasons. Kenting has beaches, tropical forests and marine ecology. Land and sea area: 33km². See page 274.

KINMEN NATIONAL PARK (*www.kmnp.gov.tw*) Comprising three parcels of coastline and one inland section, Kinmen's national park preserves the archipelago's architectural and military history as well as its natural allure. Land and sea area: 4km². See page 320.

TAIJIANG NATIONAL PARK (*www.tjnp.gov.tw*) Taiwan's newest national park embraces tidal areas and wetlands rich in birdlife plus historic sites connected to Koxinga's arrival in Taiwan. Land and sea area: 39km². See page 225.

DONGSHA ATOLL MARINE NATIONAL PARK (*http://marine.cpami.gov.tw*) This remote national park protects Pratas, the ROC's southernmost territory, and isn't open to tourists. The current emphasis is on conservation because the atolls have been damaged by fishing practices and global warming. Land and sea area: 3,537km².

simply unprepared for the demands of the modern world they faced from around 400 years ago. Deer hunting, camphor production and the abrupt modifications of agricultural traditions demanded by foreign and colonial ambitions, as well as a growing population, severely impacted on the indigenous peoples and the natural bounty on which they had depended for thousands of years.

The Chinese Nationalist (KMT) government that took power in 1945 and ruled Taiwan through to 2000 laid the foundations for rapid economic development. The island's poor environmental record can perhaps be attributed to an attitude promoted by the government and enshrined in the constitution – that the Republic of China is the legitimate government of all China and that someday it will retake the mainland. This 'temporary home mentality' manifested itself in little attention being given to taking care of the island's land, air, water and biodiversity. After World War II, unregulated industry spread throughout the country. Towards the end of martial law in 1987, one of the few forms of activism tolerated by the government was civic protests against factories causing water, air, noise and soil pollution. This tolerance was due more to the US-inspired model of letting the people fight amongst themselves rather than new-found environmental enlightenment, but there was growing unrest and the potential for major social disruption.

The 'Ten Major Construction Projects' begun in the 1970s are seen by many as the beginning of the end for Taiwan's natural environment. Freeways, power stations, airports and harbours were built. All this was important infrastructure, to be sure; the problem was that the government didn't know when to stop. Overdevelopment is apparent throughout Taiwan and one is likely to encounter a 'mosquito museum' (as white elephants are called in Taiwan) or two during travels around the nation.

Heavily polluted rivers, health problems and an environment in obvious decline led the government to establish an Environmental Protection Administration (EPA) in 1987. New laws, many of them modelled on laws in the United States, addressed air, surface water, groundwater, soil, marine and noise pollution. Biodiversity and species conservation became one of the responsibilities of the Council of Agriculture (COA), a central government agency that also oversees forestry but whose primary purpose according to its organic law is to support economic development. Until the felling of ancient trees was halted in 1990, the COA organised the harvesting of Taiwan's old-growth forests. It still manages large plantations of exotic tree species. The massive deforestation that began with the Japanese in the early 20th century was accelerated by the Chinese Nationalist regime after 1945. For a time, timber was a major source of foreign exchange; however, the money earned fell far short of compensating for economic losses due to destabilised hillsides, landslides and reduced life spans of reservoirs, not to mention the loss of diversity. The Formosan clouded leopard was finally declared extinct by a team of international scientists in 2013 following a 13-year study. Many of these problems could have been avoided had the roots of trees and the surrounding vegetation been left in place. Landslides where there were once healthy root systems are more common now that Taiwan is subjected to more frequent and stronger typhoons and heavier rainfall. The earthquake of 21 September 1999 also exacerbated the overall instability of mountain areas.

Taiwan introduced an environmental impact assessment (EIA) policy in the early 1980s. However, it has failed to stop major projects which continue to compromise the quality of Taiwan's environment such as the Fourth Nuclear Power Plant and one of the world's largest petrochemical plants. The latter, operated by Formosa Plastics Group, is located on central Taiwan's coast in the heart of a population of Indo-Pacific humpback dolphins (*Sousa chinensis*, popularly known as the Taiwan pink dolphin). If completed, the Fourth Nuclear Power Plant will mean six nuclear reactors of questionable safety located on a stretch of coastline vulnerable to tsunamis and within an hour's drive of Greater Taipei and its six million inhabitants. Many of those involved in the EIA process seem reluctant to apply the law in any way that could affect major projects supported by the central government. Indeed, government agencies – including the EPA itself – have proceeded with projects even after they were declared illegal by the courts. One outstanding exception where the EIA process seems to have been successful in meeting its purpose was the rejection in 2011 of the proposed Kuokuang Petrochemical Plant.

In 2005, a wake-up call arrived in a study produced by the World Economic Forum where Taiwan was ranked second to last out of 146 countries for environmental sustainability. Taiwan was placed 145th, behind China at 133rd. The only country ranked below Taiwan was North Korea. The survey was designed, as the joint authors from Columbia and Yale universities note, for the purpose of 'benchmarking national environmental stewardship'. It measured and assessed countries' land, water and air quality, management of consumption and waste, and threats to biodiversity, as well as those factors not always associated with the environment such as the rule of law and corruption, education, health care, plus vulnerability and responses to natural and anthropogenic disasters.

Taiwan's government did set up a Sustainable Development Commission in the 1990s to look into and deal with the many challenges and while the commission still functions, it has rarely if ever exercised any meaningful authority. The Basic Environment Act that came into law in 2002 incorporates the UN's definition of sustainable development, calls for a nuclear-free homeland and even reflects an enlightened view (when there is a conflict between economic development and the environment, the environment wins) but hasn't been effective at curbing excessive development. The latter provision was cited by Taiwan's president in the run-up to the announcement that the Kuokuang project wouldn't proceed. Even here, however, many academics have pointed out that pollution and other negative impacts resulting from the expansion of the existing Formosa Plastics Group exceed those expected from the Kuokuang plant.

The island's record on climate change is miserable. Taiwan's per capita carbon footprint is over 13 tonnes per year, one of the highest in the world and nearly four times the global average. Taiwan's emissions grew faster than those of any OECD country between 1990 and 2006. Government agencies continue to promote, and the EPA continues to approve, projects that will lead to massive rises in emissions. Taiwan has adopted some of the trappings of dealing with climate change, but the country isn't realistically committed to reducing greenhouse gas emissions. There has been very little scrutiny, discussion or criticism of the current government's emissions targets (to reach 2005 levels by 2020 and to cut CO_2 emissions to one-half of 2000 levels by 2050). There seems to be no willingness to address the factors that keep Taiwan's emissions so high. The current government supports building new coal-fired power stations, cement factories and gravel extraction facilities. During protests against the Kuokuang project, the main issue wasn't the amount of greenhouse gases the plant would emit but its impact on ecologically important wetlands.

Taiwan is an early victim of climate destabilisation. Already challenged by earthquakes and typhoons, the frequency and intensity of natural calamities is likely to grow. However, the government and industry seem quite complacent – or even welcoming the future with its 'opportunities' for rebuilding after disasters. So, when it comes to taking care of the environment that people and other living things inhabit, Taiwan has a long way to go. The bright spot is that travellers from other countries can help Taiwan's people see and appreciate what they have in the way of

1

natural beauty. This is often the first step in acting to preserve and restore Taiwan, so it can again live up to the name Ilha Formosa.

Robin Winkler is a lawyer and the founder of Taiwan Wild at Heart Legal Defense Association, Taiwan, a public-interest legal and advocacy organisation. He first came to Taiwan in 1977, and from July 2005 served as a commissioner on the Environmental Impact Assessment Committee of Taiwan's Environmental Protection Administration. He gave up his US citizenship in order to become an ROC national in 2003.

ENVIRONMENTAL CONTACTS IN TAIWAN

Citizen of the Earth, Taiwan 9th Flr 198 Boai 2nd Rd, Zuoying, Kaohsiung 813; ℡07 556 1585; f 07 556 1285; e citizenoftheearth.tw@gmail. com; www.cet-taiwan.org. One of the most active environmental groups in south Taiwan with a focus on issues of industrial structure, deforestation, habitat protection, climate change & ecology education.

Environment & Animal Society of Taiwan (EAST) 18, Lane 84, Hexing Rd, Taipei 116; ℡02 2236 9735; e eastfree@east.org.tw; www.east. org.tw. This animal welfare group has campaigned against the consumption of shark fin soup & Buddhist 'mercy release' (see box below).
Green Party 5th Flr 13 Zhongxiao E Rd Sec 1, Taipei 10049; ℡02 2392 0508; f 02 2392

BUDDHIST MERCY RELEASE

At ponds and lakes, visitors who read Chinese may notice signs prohibiting *fàng shēng*. This term, usually translated as 'mercy release', describes a Buddhist custom of releasing captured animals or fish into the wild. The pious believe that by doing this, they can not only bring themselves longevity and good luck in this life, but can also make amends for sins committed in their previous lives. The tradition began long ago with spontaneous acts of compassion. If a monk came across a creature about to be sold for food, he would buy it and set it free. However, the modern version of mercy release is completely different, the majority of creatures involved being raised or caught solely so they can be sold to religious individuals who plan to release them. The practice is commonplace in Asian countries with substantial Buddhist populations.

In Taiwan, both native and non-native species are used for mercy release ceremonies. Fish, turtles, birds and even insects have been released in events organised by temples. Non-native creatures often die soon after being freed because they're unsuited to the local environment; there have been instances where freshwater turtles have been released into the ocean. Animals that don't perish may thrive and become competitors for food or mate with native species, threatening their gene pools. The American bullfrog (*Lithobates catesbeianus*), a foreign species often used in mercy releases, preys on the native Taipei tree frog (*Rhacophorus taipeianus*). Almost all of Taiwan's major rivers are infested with exotic species, while Sun Moon Lake has been invaded by foreign species to the point where native species are close to extinction. When Lotus Pond was emptied for cleaning ahead of the 2009 World Games, 95% of the fish removed were exotics. They were turned into fertiliser while local species were saved and released into nearby creeks.

It seems the practice of 'mercy release' is now declining. Much of the credit should go to animal-rights groups which have worked hard to educate Buddhists about the likely consequences of actions.

0512; www.greenparty.org.tw. This small pro-environment group should not to be confused with the 'greens' who favour Taiwan's independence from China (see box, page 22).

Greenpeace, Taiwan Office 10, Lane 83, Roosevelt Rd Sec 1, Taipei 10093; ☏ 02 2321 2798; f 02 2321 3209; www.greenpeace.org/taiwan/zh/. Greenpeace has set up an office in Taiwan for volunteer training, fund-raising, publicity & work on their own & with local environmental groups on oceans/fishing & nuclear issues.

Society of Wilderness (SOW) 204 Zhaoan St, Taipei 100; ☏ 02 2307 1568; f 02 2307 2568; e sow@sow.org.tw; www.sow.org.tw. This conservation & nature education group also takes on plots of undeveloped land where nature can revive & manage itself.

Taiwan Academy of Ecology 685 Fuke Rd, Xitun, Taichung 407; ☏ 04 2463 4220; f 04 2463

4220; www.ecology.org.tw, http://taiwansousa.blogspot.com/. This central Taiwan group is involved in efforts to save Taiwan's highly endangered Indo-Pacific humpback dolphins (see page 8).

Taiwan Environmental Protection Union 2nd Flr 107 Tingzhou Rd Sec 3, Taipei 100; ☏ 02 2363 6419; f 02 2364 4293; e tepu.org@msa.hinet.net; tepu.org.tw. One of the very oldest registered associations dedicated to environmental issues; has a strong focus on anti-nuclear activities.

Wild at Heart Legal Defense Association 6th Flr 106 Huaining St, Taipei 10045; ☏ 02 2382 5789; f 02 2382 5810; www.wildatheart.org.tw. The 1st environmental advocacy organisation in Taiwan with full-time lawyers & specialising in policy & legal action on behalf of indigenous groups dispossessed of their land & on behalf of wildlife whose habitats are threatened.

TAIWAN'S HISTORY

PREHISTORY In the early 1970s, archaeologists digging in southwest Taiwan unearthed seven skull fragments and two molars. Three of the skull pieces, dated to 30,000 years ago, are the oldest human remains discovered in Taiwan. 'Zuozhen Man', so called because the discovery was made in what's now Tainan City's Zuozhen district, lived at a time when Taiwan was physically joined to the Eurasian landmass.

Around 18,000 years ago sea levels began to rise and within 6,000 years Taiwan had become an island. Local palaeolithic and neolithic cultures developed. In parts of western Taiwan the Iron Age began about 2,000 years ago, while tribes in the east and deep in the interior continued to depend on stone implements.

FORMOSA The captain – some say it was the navigator – of a Portuguese vessel sailing past Taiwan to Japan in 1544 gave the island the name by which it was known until well into the 20th century: *Ilha Formosa*, Portuguese for 'beautiful island'. In recent years a version of this name, rendered in Chinese characters and pronounced slightly differently, has become popular within the country.

Taiwanese were trading internationally long before the arrival of Westerners. Indigenous people of Austronesian origin (see *People*, page 24) bartered deer skins with Japanese merchants (who used them for harnesses and saddles) and sold deer meat to Chinese traders. Deer were hunted with snares, pitfalls and spears as well as bows and arrows.

DUTCH AND SPANISH RULE Having been refused permission to establish a commercial base on the Chinese coast or in the Penghu Islands, the Dutch East India Company (*Vereenigde Oost-Indische Compagnie*, VOC) was allowed in 1624 by the Ming Empire to found a small colony on Taiwan's southwest coast, at what is now Tainan. The Dutch called the location Tayouan, almost certainly a corruption of the aboriginal place name. This word eventually evolved into 'Taiwan' and came to be applied to the entire island. The VOC purchased locally grown sugar and rice for shipping to Japan. According to the company's records, in 1639 alone they collected almost 100,000 deer hides for export to Japan; not surprisingly, the vast herds seen by Dutch missionaries working in the interior soon disappeared. Wood, nutmeg, clove and pepper came in from southeast Asia; vessels arriving from Europe carried satin and linen and returned laden with silk and porcelain. To increase agricultural production, the Dutch encouraged peasants from the nearby Chinese province of Fujian to move to the Tainan area. Missionaries converted thousands of lowland aborigines to Christianity. Dutch-language schools were set up and several colonists married indigenous women.

The Spanish, rulers of the Philippines since 1565, had long hoped to expand northwards. In 1626, they established a base near what's now Keelung. Their motives were economic, strategic and religious; the Dominicans who were part of the Spanish expedition are thought to have been the first Christian missionaries to set foot on Taiwan. The Spanish occupied a site in Danshui in 1629 but abandoned it after less than a decade. Twelve years later the Dutch received intelligence that the Spanish garrison at Keelung had been weakened by redeployments and plague. They attacked and within days Taiwan's Spanish episode was over.

KOXINGA Were it not for one man, it's conceivable the Dutch would have retained Taiwan until World War II. That man was Zheng Chenggong, better known to Western historians as Koxinga. One of very few Chinese to figure in European histories written in the 17th century, he's been variously described as a ruthless pirate and an inept admiral. Born in Japan in 1624, his father was Chinese, his mother Japanese. He was fervent in his support for China's Ming Dynasty just as it was being overthrown by Manchu invaders from the north. The Manchus founded the Qing Dynasty in 1644 but Ming loyalists kept up the fight in China's south. Koxinga's father switched sides in 1646. China's new rulers ennobled him but because he failed to persuade his son to submit to the emperor, they executed him in 1661. Despite being awarded a prestigious title by the Qing in 1653 and occasionally negotiating with China's new rulers, Koxinga kept up a military campaign against the Manchus. The VOC knew of Koxinga because he traded with them to fund his struggle. When he fell sick, the Dutch colony sent its only physician to treat him. Koxinga refused to take the medicine the Dutchman prescribed.

In 1660, the VOC intercepted letters in which Koxinga made clear his desire to conquer Taiwan, which he'd never visited. On 2 April 1661, Koxinga's forces surrounded the Dutch strongholds, Fort Zeelandia and Fort Provintia in present-day Tainan. The garrison of the latter, caught unprepared and short of water, unconditionally surrendered on 4 April. Koxinga wasn't so lucky at Fort Zeelandia. Demands that the Dutch lay down arms were rebuffed; a series of cannon exchanges, Chinese efforts to storm the fortress and Dutch counter-raids followed. Although there was no prospect of a relief force arriving anytime soon, VOC Governor Frederik Coyett was determined to hold out. News of Koxinga's attack reached Batavia (now Jakarta in Indonesia) two months later, just after the VOC had sent Hermanus Clenk to replace Coyett. When Clenk arrived off the coast of Taiwan on 30 July, he realised the direness of the situation and made the less than admirable decision not to take up his new job. As Clenk fled back to Batavia, VOC reinforcements approached. The commander of this relief squadron was as cowardly as Clenk; promising to sail to Fujian and ask Qing generals there to come to the aid of the Dutch – something the former were showing a keen interest in doing – he instead headed directly for the safety of Batavia. By the end of the year there was little food left inside Fort Zeelandia and almost half of the 2,300

Europeans had died of wounds or disease. Several German mercenaries deserted; after one gave Koxinga information about the fort's layout, the Chinese made rapid military progress. Coyett signed the instrument of surrender on 1 February 1662. Under its terms the Dutch were allowed to leave with their personal possessions, VOC archives and sufficient provisions to reach Batavia. They left behind a substantial amount of money, merchandise and weaponry. But Koxinga's victory had been costly: more than one-third of the 25,000 men he'd led to Taiwan died in the battle for Fort Zeelandia.

Koxinga died suddenly on 23 June 1662, possibly of malaria. However, the anti-Manchu enclave was secure and the Kingdom of Dongning, as the mini-state styled itself, lasted another two decades. Koxinga's eldest son, Zheng Jing, ruled for most of this period. He continued his father's policies: skirmishing with imperial forces along the Chinese coast; smuggling so as to evade the Qing economic blockade; ordering his soldiers to fan out across the countryside and support themselves by farming; and trading with Japan. Like his father, he was committed to extirpating Christianity. Zheng Jing died in 1681 and was succeeded by his 12-year-old son, Zheng Keshuang.

CHINESE RULE Eager to finish off pro-Ming elements, the Qing Empire dispatched Shi Lang (1621–96) to retake the island. Shi, who had been planning the seizure of Taiwan since 1664, held a deep grudge against Koxinga's family. Initially a Ming loyalist, Shi went over to the Qing in 1646 after arguing with Koxinga; the latter responded to the defection by having Shi's father, brother and son put to death. A naval engagement near the Penghu Islands on 16–17 July 1683 was the only major battle in Shi's campaign. Within two months Zheng Keshuang had surrendered. He spent the rest of his life in comfortable captivity in Beijing.

The imperial court was divided over what to do with Taiwan. Some argued that the island's Chinese population should be evacuated back to the mainland. Others, including Shi, thought Taiwan should be retained. (He had a backup plan if the court rejected his advice: sell the island to the Dutch.) In 1684, Taiwan was made part of Fujian province. Officials were posted to the main settlements but they did little to develop the island's economy or improve the lives of its residents. Migration from the Chinese mainland to the island was illegal. This restriction, which large numbers of Fujianese ignored, wasn't eased until 1760.

For 150 years Taiwan's camphor forests were one of its main natural resources. The island was the world's foremost source of camphor, used for making balms and mothballs. This lucrative industry was an imperial monopoly; anyone caught felling a tree without permission was put to death. By 1811, at least two million people were living on the lowlands. Food was plentiful but disease killed so many people that, according to an idiom from the era, of every ten settlers 'just three remain; six are dead, and one has returned home'.

Banditry, clan warfare and ethnic strife plagued Taiwan until well into the 19th century. Different immigrant groups fought with each other and the island's indigenous inhabitants. Uprisings were common. In 1786, rebels led by Lin Shuang-wen (1756–88) took control of much of western Taiwan. Lin led a semi-religious secret society and proclaimed himself emperor. In 1788 he was captured, taken to Beijing and executed. Even though his movement caused thousands of deaths, the anti-Qing aspect of his campaign was regarded favourably by the Nationalists after World War II. A village in central Taiwan and two schools bear his name.

Most migrants were single men and gender imbalance was one cause of lawlessness. Because there were so few Han women, many settlers married aborigines. (DNA analysis suggests at least four out of five Hoklo and Hakka Taiwanese have some

Austronesian ancestry.) Also, Taiwan was different from other parts of the Chinese Empire in that divorced or widowed women easily found new husbands. But that didn't alter the traditional preference for sons over daughters; European residents noted female infanticide was still common in the 1860s.

If conditions were right junks could cross the Taiwan Strait in a day and a half, but gales sometimes blew ships off course and piracy was common until the second half of the 19th century. Boats were the only means of getting people or goods from one part of Taiwan to another; overland transport was unsafe and difficult on account of the lack of roads and the fast-flowing rivers that had to be crossed. Geographical obstacles meant few Han settlers made it to Taiwan's east. The indigenous tribes there were able to preserve their autonomy and culture until the Japanese occupation.

After yet another uprising was crushed in 1865, Taiwan gradually became more peaceful. A local gentry and scholar-literati class emerged in Tainan, Hsinchu and other settlements. Confucian academies were established. But corruption continued to be a massive problem. W A Pickering, a Briton who worked in Taiwan from 1863 to 1870, devoted an entire chapter of his book *Pioneering in Formosa: Recollections of Adventures among Mandarins, Wreckers and Head-hunting Savages* to the rapacity of the mandarins:

> The result of the misgovernment and oppression by the officials was that the resources of one of the most fertile islands in the world were being undeveloped or wasted, and instead of being a source of profit to the imperial government, Formosa was a drain upon its resources.

In December 1871 a ship from the Ryukyu Islands – then a semi-independent kingdom but soon annexed to Japan – was shipwrecked in south Taiwan. Three of those on board drowned. Of the 66 survivors, 54 were massacred by aborigines; the others escaped to a Han Chinese settlement and were repatriated. On behalf of the king of the Ryukyus, Japan demanded compensation. Beijing's response was curt: the Qing court bore no responsibility because the aborigines were beyond its jurisdiction. Tokyo then took matters into its own hands and dispatched a 3,600-strong expeditionary force. Near what's now called Mudan, they fought and won a battle against the tribesmen on 22 May 1874. Japanese battle casualties were minimal, but one in six of the Japanese soldiers died of disease during the seven months they spent in Taiwan. The invaders didn't leave until the Qing court had paid an indemnity. Afterwards, the Chinese took steps to strengthen Taiwan's defences, but later events proved that these were in vain.

In spring 1884 the Qing court clashed with France over Annam, now part of Vietnam. The French claimed it as a protectorate while China regarded it as a vassal state. To pressure the Qing court, in early October French forces occupied Keelung and attacked Danshui. But the French found it difficult to quarantine the island as junks would cross the Taiwan Strait during the night and then dodge between islets and sandbars where the waters were too shallow for French warships to pursue them. The war ended with China recognising France's claims.

Partly as a result of the French blockade, the Qing court began to pay much more attention to Taiwan. The island became a province in its own right in 1885; Liu Ming-chuan, who had led Qing forces in Taiwan during the Sino-French War, was the first governor. He achieved a lot during his six years in office. He ordered the building of a railroad between Taipei and Keelung, and in 1889 Taipei became the first city in the Chinese empire to have electric lights along its streets and inside major buildings. Liu also introduced a postal system, had a telegraph cable laid between Danshui and Xiamen and tried to reform taxation. He set up one government bureau to regulate the camphor and sulphur industries, and another to co-ordinate the search for oil. The creation of schools that taught foreign languages and science was encouraged; coastal fortifications were strengthened and soldiers given better training and equipment. After Liu was recalled to the mainland progress slowed. But Taiwanese hoping for another ruler who would shake things up didn't have to wait long.

CESSION TO JAPAN War broke out between China and Japan in August 1894 because of Korea. For centuries Korea's kings had been paying tribute to China, but Japan – then in the throes of radical reforms which would lead to its emergence as a powerful industrial nation – forced the country to open itself to external trade. In June 1894 a Japanese expeditionary force installed a puppet Korean government which immediately asked Japan to remove Chinese soldiers from Korean soil. The Chinese, who were already leaving, were no match for well-trained, well-equipped Japanese units. By February 1895 the Japanese were pressing on into Manchuria; the following month they seized the Penghu Islands. The war came to a formal end on 17 April with the signing of the Treaty of Shimonoseki. Even though the Qing Dynasty controlled no more than half of Taiwan, they ceded the entire island, plus Penghu, to Japan in perpetuity.

With the tacit encouragement of the imperial court – or at least a faction in it – Qing officials in Taiwan declared the island's independence. Between 24 May, when the Republic of Taiwan was proclaimed, and 23 October, when the Japanese Army occupied Tainan, the state designed its own flag, had two presidents and issued postage stamps (they're considered quite collectable). It was not, as often claimed, Asia's first republic, but it was certainly another step in creating Taiwanese identity. The takeover was expensive in human lives with over 10,000 soldiers and civilians on the Taiwanese side dying; 164 Japanese soldiers were killed in combat, and another 4,642 died in accidents or from disease. Prince Yoshihisa Kitashirakawa, nominal commander of the expeditionary force, succumbed to malaria in Tainan on 5 November.

JAPANESE RULE The deaths of Prince Yoshihisa and a third of the men under his leadership made it clear that, if the Japanese were ever to benefit from their conquest, public health would have to improve. Yoshitaka Mori, a professor at Tokyo National University of Fine Arts and Music, has argued that the Japanese gained political legitimacy through infrastructure and public health improvements, and that Goto Shinpei (1857–1929), chief of civilian affairs in the colonial government from 1898 to 1906, was one of the era's most important personalities. Mori comments:

> Goto was the first person who understood the importance of controlling the population not only by coercive force but also through a kind of consensus. By introducing a way of Western urban planning, in particular the idea of public sanitation, he established magnificent governmental buildings, hospitals and schools to display Japanese authority. New buildings... functioned to stabilise upheaval... while he ordered the destruction of old traditional buildings which might evoke memories of Taiwanese past.

Goto thought major public buildings should be 'soldiers in civilian clothes' that would impress upon the local population the wisdom and might of the Japanese.

He also established a system whereby opium could be sold only by licensed retailers and purchased only in limited quantities by registered smokers. There were 200,000 of the latter in 1904; by the end of 1922 that number had dwindled to fewer than 43,000. Goto's approach was both effective at curbing addiction and a way of aiding pro-Japan merchants, as the authorities made sure lucrative retail licenses went only to supporters of the colonial regime. Camphor, salt, alcohol and tobacco monopolies ensured the colonial government's finances stayed in the black. Many Taiwanese recognise that, when it came to modernising their island, Japan did much of the heavy lifting.

When Japanese forces arrived in 1895 they found an island almost totally bereft of roads. The new rulers got to work right away; between early 1896 and the end of 1897 the total length of Taiwan's roads more than tripled. Kaohsiung and Keelung harbours were dredged and connected to the north–south railroad; bridges were built and schools were established; the lowlands were surveyed for tax purposes. But despite the power of the Japanese government machine, the colonial regime had no control over the mountainous interior and much of the east coast.

To keep the aboriginal population under control, the Japanese decided in 1914 to confiscate the rifles used by indigenous people to hunt deer and other animals. Between hunting expeditions, all guns were to be kept under lock and key in police stations. This policy and the deceitful methods the Japanese used in executing it outraged a Bunun chief called Raho Ari. In 1915 he and his clansmen massacred a police platoon at Dafen and then went into hiding near the upper reaches of the Laonong River, in what's now Yushan National Park. Tamaho, the village they founded there, grew into a community of 266 people as disaffected Bunun from elsewhere joined the rebels. Raho Ari remained a thorn in the side of the colonial authorities for two decades; he was able at will to breach the 'guardline' (a network of police stations and electric fences separating those areas under Japanese control from the wild interior) and launch guerrilla attacks on police stations, to kill Japanese and seize weapons and ammunition.

Despite rapid economic and social progress, Han insurgencies were also frequent. This prompted some Japanese parliamentarians to urge the sale of the island to whomever would take it off Tokyo's hands. Two years after an uprising in Miaoli, anti-Japanese factions in the southwest launched a rebellion that led to the deaths of over 1,000 Taiwanese plus hundreds of Japanese policemen and civilians. Like the Boxers who murdered Westerners in China in 1900, many of those who participated in what came to be known as the Tapani Incident wore talismans which they believed made them invulnerable to modern weapons. The revolt marked the end of Han armed resistance, although fighting between Japanese forces and aborigines continued almost to the end of the colonial era.

Inspired by the emergence of newly independent countries in eastern Europe and a Korean movement that pushed for self-determination and national identity, Taiwanese intellectuals and gentry founded the Taiwanese Cultural Association on 17 October 1921. The establishment of the TCA is seen as a landmark in the island's intellectual development and the emergence of a distinct Taiwanese (as opposed to Chinese or Japanese) identity. The association was suppressed in the late 1930s.

By autumn 1930 Mona Rudao, the educated son of a Sediq chief, was seething with rage. One of his sons had been insulted by a Japanese official and his youngest sister had been abandoned by her Japanese husband. Many other aborigines felt aggrieved: the colonial regime had taken away their guns and some of their ancestral lands, felled sacred trees and compelled tribesmen to labour for low wages on government projects. Japanese officers were notorious for expecting sexual favours from aboriginal women. On 27 October 1930, Mona Rudao led a 300-strong band of warriors into the mountain town of Wushe where they attacked Japanese attending a school athletics event. The tribesmen were murderous but focused: 134 Japanese were killed but only two Han died. In response the Japanese assembled a massive force: 800 soldiers, 1,163 police officers and more than 1,300 paramilitaries recruited from other indigenous tribes. After two months of fighting, during which Japanese aircraft dropped poison gas on aboriginal holdouts, the rebellion petered out. Mona Rudao ordered his people to commit suicide rather than surrender. Some 290 killed themselves. Of those who didn't at least a hundred were put to death after laying down their arms. They were beheaded by other aborigines in the pay of the Japanese as the latter awarded a bounty for each head. To ensure his enemies wouldn't have his head as a trophy, Mona Rudao took his own life in a remote cave on 1 December. His remains were found four years later and put on public display in Taipei. He wasn't given a proper burial until 1981.

After the outbreak of the Second Sino-Japanese War in 1937, the Japanese government launched the 'Kominka Movement', an attempt to erase Han identity in Taiwan and promote loyalty to the emperor in Tokyo. Over a thousand shrines were demolished or confiscated as part of an ineffective effort to replace folk religion with Japanese beliefs. (Several had been destroyed earlier in the colonial period to make way for roads or public buildings.) Local periodicals were ordered to stop publishing Chinese-language supplements. The movement's promotion of the Japanese language and Japanese names was fairly successful: by 1945, two out of three Taiwanese could speak Japanese, and one in 14 had taken Japanese names. Among the latter was Lee Teng-hui, ROC president from 1988 to 2000, who until 1945 was known as Iwasato Masao.

WORLD WAR II Throughout the war in the Pacific, Japan treated Taiwan as a secure rear area where soldiers could be trained and POWs held (see box, page 133). Farmers were obliged to sell their rice to the colonial government, so taros and sweet potatoes became a major source of carbohydrates. Production of rubber and timber were increased. Thousands of Taiwanese civilians died in the final months of the war as the US Air Force bombed targets throughout the island. Just as war made British society more egalitarian, so the conscription of Japanese nationals and the rapid expansion of industry opened up skilled positions previously closed to Taiwanese. More than 200,000 Taiwanese joined the Japanese armed forces, some less willingly than others. Lee Teng-hui spent a short time in the Imperial Japanese Army; his elder brother was killed in the Philippines in 1945 while serving as a petty officer in the Imperial Japanese Navy. Several thousand aborigines served in combat units. One of them, an Amis tribesman called Attun Palalin, got separated from his unit during a battle in what's now Indonesia. He survived for decades by hunting and gathering. It wasn't until November 1974 that he learned the war was over and he could return to his home village.

NATIONALIST TAKEOVER At the end of the war, Taiwan became part of the Republic of China (ROC), the state created on the Chinese mainland when the last emperor was overthrown in 1911. On 25 October 1945, the last Japanese governor-general of Taiwan formally handed control of the island to Chen Yi, a Nationalist general whom Chiang Kai-shek had chosen to administer the island. Many Taiwanese were cautiously hopeful, but for some this optimism evaporated the moment they set eyes on the Nationalist army. Compared to the Japanese, KMT soldiers were slovenly and ill-disciplined. Taiwan's economy was already in a sorry state and Chen's mismanagement made the situation worse. He and his staff, whom many Taiwanese regarded as carpetbaggers, brought with them rampant corruption and hyperinflation.

Native Taiwanese were outraged by the favouritism Chen showed to his fellow mainlanders and by the looting of assets left behind by the Japanese. Public anger finally exploded on 27 February 1947 when Taipei citizens witnessed tobacco monopoly bureau agents beating an elderly widow whom they'd caught selling contraband cigarettes. The police responded to an impromptu demonstration with gunfire. Civilians were killed but the protests snowballed. As news of the violence spread there were uprisings across the island. It's said the majority of victims in the following week were mainlanders killed by native mobs.

Taiwanese leaders formed a committee and drew up a list of grievances. They met with Chen who requested ten days to consider their proposals. Secretly, the governor sent for extra troops to crush the rebellion. Taipei returned to semi-normality – but when Nationalist reinforcements arrived on 8 March, shooting began immediately. College students who'd formed peacekeeping teams surrendered their weapons as ordered and were then executed without trial. Hundreds of bodies were dumped in Keelung harbour. Up to 28,000 people died in what's known as the 2-28 Incident (after the date protesters began attacking government offices, assaulting and in some cases killing those inside).

Aware that Communists, Taiwan independence supporters and others were trying to undermine the regime, the Nationalist authorities cracked down on all forms of political dissent. In the wake of the 2-28 Incident, up to 80% of city- and county-level elites 'disappeared from the political field' (to use the words of a report produced for the government-backed 2-28 Memorial Foundation). According to another study, around 140,000 people were detained and at least 3,000 executed. Many were sent to Green Island. Among them were mainlanders who'd fled to Taiwan with the Nationalists, Japanese-educated Taiwanese intellectuals, aborigines and even high school students. Some had been trying to subvert the government. Some had campaigned peacefully for political reforms. Many, it's now known, were completely innocent and victims either of the regime's paranoia or ambitious officials.

RETREAT TO TAIWAN By late 1948 it was clear that Chiang Kai-shek was losing the civil war against Mao Zedong's Chinese Communist Party. On 10 December 1949, Chiang and his son, Chiang Ching-kuo, arrived in Taiwan. They brought with them the ROC's gold reserves and some of the regime's political prisoners. The following March the elder Chiang resumed the ROC presidency, which he'd stepped down from a year earlier in order to lead the Nationalist armed forces. At least 1.5 million mainlanders followed the Chiangs to Taiwan, almost half of them soldiers. Tens of thousands more arrived in the 1950s and 1960s via Hong Kong and Burma. These refugees weren't the only people cut off from their families and hometowns; some Taiwanese studying or doing business on the mainland in 1949 were stranded there until restrictions on travel were relaxed in the late 1980s. While Chiang consolidated his control of Taiwan, many observers predicted a communist invasion of the island. However, a few days after the Korean War broke out on 25 June 1950, President Harry S Truman ordered the US Navy to patrol the Taiwan Strait and prevent a resumption of the Communist-KMT conflict.

One of the reasons the Nationalists lost the Chinese Civil War was that they'd failed to address the needs of China's vast and impoverished rural population. Land reform efforts achieved little, and it was left to the Communists to seize and redistribute farmland. Apparently having learned a lesson – and no doubt keen to diminish the power of Taiwan's Japanese-influenced landed gentry – the KMT quickly implemented a 'land to the tiller' policy that revolutionised Taiwan's economy. The first step was to reduce rent, abolish the practice of paying rent in advance, and force landowners to grant six-year leases rather than the usual one or two years. Tenant farmers gained both income and security. Secondly, land that had previously belonged to the Japanese colonial government was sold off cheaply. Thirdly, major landowners were compelled to hand fields over to their tenants. The former were compensated: a little cash, some shares in state-owned companies and 'industrial revenue bonds' – government-backed vouchers that were worthless unless they were invested in some kind of business. A great many ex-landlords used these vouchers to set up factories making goods for export.

On 23 August 1958, communist forces began an intense bombardment of Kinmen, the KMT-held front-line island better known in the West as Quemoy. Planning to seize the island, the Communists fired 474,900 shells during the 44-day battle. There were four naval clashes and numerous dogfights between ROC and PRC jets. The exhausted Communists suspended their campaign on 5 October, but until 1979 the two sides made a habit of shelling each other on alternate days. Often the shells contained propaganda leaflets rather than high explosives.

INDUSTRIALISATION By 1940 manufacturing was contributing more to the economy than agriculture, yet it wasn't until the late 1950s that Taiwan ceased depending on exports of sugar and bananas. Factory-produced goods weren't just for foreign markets: refrigerators, rice cookers and electric fans were popular with domestic consumers. Clothes and shoes underpinned the economy in the 1960s; in the following decade Taiwan was the world's leading producer of tennis rackets and sunglasses. Economists have debated whether productivity was significantly enhanced or growth resulted mainly from greater capital investment and a larger workforce. Taiwan's population grew rapidly – from under eight million in 1950 to 14.6 million in 1970 – and women entered the labour market in record numbers. However, economic progress wasn't matched by democratic reforms. Peng Ming-min (b1923), a dissident who stood for the presidency in 1996, described political conditions in his 1972 book *A Taste of Freedom*:

> [The claim that Chiang's regime] represented a 'government of China' was an absurd fiction which amounted to a gigantic hoax. This fiction enabled the Nationalist government to maintain two levels of organisation, the so-called 'national government' in which all positions of effective power were reserved for [mainlanders]… and a subordinate provincial administration partially open to Formosan participation. Over 80% of the national budget was spent on military affairs, including elaborate secret police organisations… The Formosans who constitute 85% of the population [had] less than 3% representation in the national legislature… Advocates of birth control are considered defeatists, and a high birth rate is encouraged only to produce conscript soldiers for Chiang's armies twenty years hence.

1970S–2000 Chiang Kai-shek died on 5 April 1975 and was succeeded by Vice President Yen Chia-kan (1905–93). Like Chiang, Yen was a mainlander who'd retreated to Taiwan in 1949. When Yen's term ended in 1978, Chiang's only biological son, the Russian-educated Chiang Ching-kuo, became president. Throughout his premiership and presidency, the younger Chiang promoted several

THE SWEETENER IN TAIWAN'S DEVELOPMENT

According to Jack F Williams, an American geographer who wrote an academic paper titled *Sugar: The Sweetener in Taiwan's Development*, sugarcane was already growing in Taiwan when the Dutch set up their trading base in Tainan in 1624. The VOC recognised sugar's potential as a cash crop and encouraged Han migrants to plant more. Koxinga continued where the Dutch had left off and exported sugar to Japan. During Qing rule the industry grew but slowly; after 1895, however, production surged as Japanese entrepreneurs, backed by the colonial government, built modern refineries and expanded the area under cultivation. By 1920 sugar accounted for 65% of Taiwan's exports; by 1950 this figure was 80%. Since the late 1950s the industry has shrunk to a fraction of its former size because other countries are able to produce sugar more cheaply. Yet sugar has left a noticeable physical imprint on the landscape, and not only in the shape of imposing refinery buildings. Most of the large fields in the south used to be sugar plantations and Taiwan Sugar Corp remains one of the country's largest landowners.

Taiwan-born officials to high office. His first vice president, Hsieh Tung-min (1908–2001), was a Taiwanese who had moved to the Chinese mainland in 1925. Another of his protégés, agricultural economist Lee Teng-hui (b1923), had a very different background. Lee, who is still semi-active in politics, has never visited the Chinese mainland let alone lived there. He received a Japanese education and has often spoken of the affinity he felt for Japan.

On 15 December 1978, Washington and Beijing announced they were establishing formal diplomatic relations and that US military bases in Taiwan would close. The American move, intended to encircle the Soviet Union, left many Taiwanese feeling betrayed. The following year the US Congress passed the Taiwan Relations Act, a law stipulating that Washington–Taipei contact and co-operation – including arms sales – would continue, albeit on a semi-official basis.

Democracy activists launched a magazine called *Meilidao* (literally 'beautiful island', but in English sometimes called *Formosa*). The government, jittery after the rupturing of diplomatic ties with the US, had already decided to ban this publication when its Kaohsiung office applied for permission to hold a seminar marking Human Rights Day on 10 December 1979. The application was rejected but the organisers went ahead regardless. Demonstrators clashed with police and soldiers, and the authorities used the riot as a pretext to round up most of Taiwan's dissidents. More than 50 individuals were tried for their role in what was soon dubbed the 'Kaohsiung Incident' or the 'Meilidao Incident', or for harbouring fugitives. The trials were a watershed for Taiwan's democracy movement; not only were the accused able to make long speeches during proceedings attended by foreign reporters, but a second generation of activists – the lawyers defending them – caught the public eye. One of the latter, Chen Shui-bian (b1950), became Taiwan's first non-KMT president in 2000. The Meilidao Incident is commemorated in the Chinese name of Kaohsiung's Formosa Boulevard rapid-transit station.

For a long time 'Made in Taiwan' meant cheap and shoddy, but since the 1970s Taiwanese companies have been successfully 'moving up the chain', producing more sophisticated items and innovating rather than imitating. From the mid-1980s until the Asian Financial Crisis of 1997, exports of high-tech products such as computer peripherals and memory chips powered an economic boom. In 1950, living standards in Taiwan were on a par with those in India. Within two decades the island had overtaken Argentina in terms of real household incomes. In recent years international rankings of GDP per capita, adjusted for purchasing power parity, place Taiwan just ahead of the UK and Belgium.

During the final two years of Chiang Ching-kuo's presidency, Taiwan moved towards democracy. Martial law was lifted in 1987, as was a ban on the formation of new political parties (there are now well over 200, although Taiwan is essentially a two-party system). Opponents of the KMT established the Democratic Progressive Party. Taiwan's parliament ceased to be a rubber-stamp body, but proceedings were often marred by demonstrations and fights as lawmakers threw shoes and chairs at each other, smashed microphones or draped banners across the furniture.

Lee Teng-hui became the appointed mayor of Taipei in 1978 and vice president in 1984. When he took the top job after Chiang Ching-kuo's death on 13 January 1988 he wasn't expected to wield real power. But within a few years he'd skilfully sidelined his opponents within the KMT and the military, and brought like-minded people into his cabinet. Constitutional measures called 'Temporary Provisions Effective During the Period of Communist Rebellion' were cancelled. Old parliamentarians elected on the mainland in 1948 and 'frozen in office', representing districts they hadn't seen for decades, were finally pensioned off. For the first time in its history, those making Taiwan's laws had actually been elected by the island's people. While paying lip service to the ideal of unification, Lee embarked on a 'Taiwan First' path that riled Beijing but won him a landslide when the first direct presidential elections were held in 1996.

At 01.47 on 21 September 1999, people throughout Taiwan were roused from their sleep by a tremor measuring 7.3 on the Richter scale. Near the epicentre of what's often referred to as the 9-21 earthquake, in the central Taiwan township of Jiji, there was great devastation. Some 2,416 people died and 11,443 were seriously injured. Almost 100,000 buildings collapsed or were damaged beyond repair.

POST-MILLENNIUM EVENTS Barred by the constitution from seeking another term, Lee selected Vice President Lien Chan to be the KMT candidate in the 2000 presidential election. James Soong, a charismatic KMT heavyweight, bolted the party and ran as an independent. Lien's campaign failed to take off and Soong was harmed by corruption allegations. Chen Shui-bian, a former Taipei mayor running for the DPP, won with 39% of the vote. Chen's running mate, Annette Lu (a former dissident who'd spent over five years in jail), became Taiwan's first female vice president. Chen's election dismayed China, which has consistently claimed Taiwan as part of its territory and frequently blocks Taipei's efforts to take part in international organisations such as the United Nations. Many pan-greens (see box, page 22) thought a new era was about to unfold, but governing the country in the face of KMT opposition and obstruction wasn't easy. The KMT and its allies used their majority in parliament to thwart many of Chen's initiatives.

Chen's first term in office was choppy. His first prime minister lasted just five months. A sudden decision to cancel a partly built nuclear power station pleased environmentalists but angered business leaders; the stock market sank and unemployment rose. However, symbolic changes that underscored Taiwan's separate identity – such as adding the word 'Taiwan' to ROC passports – seemed genuinely popular. In the weeks before the 2004 presidential election, opinion polls showed Chen and Lien Chan (who'd recruited erstwhile rival James Soong as his running mate) neck-and-neck. The day before voting, Chen and Vice President Lu were campaigning in Tainan when a lone gunman fired from the crowd. Both were

THE BLUES AND THE GREENS

Politically, Taiwan is divided into two camps: the blues and the greens. The former faction is dominated by the Kuomintang (KMT), the Chinese Nationalist Party founded by Dr Sun Yat-sen and led for decades by Chiang Kai-shek. The greens (not to be confused with the environmentalist Green Party of Taiwan) are the Democratic Progressive Party (DPP) and other supporters of independence and localisation. Between 2008 and 2012, the DPP had a female leader, Tsai Ing-wen (b1957), who has a PhD from the London School of Economics. At the time of writing, the DPP's chairman was Su Tseng-chang (b1947), a lawyer and former premier. On most but not all issues, the DPP is backed by the Taiwan Solidarity Union (TSU), a party established in 2001 by supporters of former President Lee Teng-hui.

slightly wounded; the gunman escaped and committed suicide ten days later. Chen won the election by fewer than 30,000 votes out of almost 13 million cast. Some blue politicians insist the shooting was staged to generate sympathy votes, but none have shown how it could've been done.

During his term as Taipei mayor, Chen changed the name of Jieshou Road (which honoured Chiang Kai-shek) to Ketagalan Boulevard (after one of Taiwan's lowland aboriginal tribes). After reaching the presidency, he continued pushing for 'localisation' and 'name rectification'. The word 'China' was dropped from the names of government-owned companies and the post office. But Chen's approval ratings sank as first his wife, and then his son-in-law, were embroiled in corruption scandals.

Few people were surprised when the KMT's Ma Ying-jeou – like Chen a former Taipei mayor – won a decisive election victory over the DPP's Frank Hsieh in the presidential election on 22 March 2008. Ma, whose campaign had focused on economic issues and his own squeaky-clean image, got 58% of the vote. Within hours of his leaving office, prosecutors barred the outgoing president from leaving the country on the grounds he was suspected of corruption. Chen's fall from grace mesmerised the Taiwanese public; on 11 September 2009 he was sentenced to life in prison for money laundering, embezzlement and accepting bribes. (Following appeals and trials on related charges, his sentence was reduced to 19 years.) His wife, son, daughter-in-law and son-in-law also received jail terms. Many of his supporters believe there were political motives behind these court cases.

On the evening of 6 August 2009, local governments around Taiwan announced that schools and offices would not open the following day because of the approach of Typhoon Morakot. The rain began falling and didn't stop until some parts of the south had received an unbelievable 2,900mm (almost 10 feet) of precipitation in 72 hours. The village of Xiaolin in Kaohsiung was obliterated by a massive rock-slide. Dozens of mountain communities were cut off by landslides and thousands of people had to be rescued by helicopter. By the end of the week it was known that 700 people were dead or missing.

Despite Beijing's refusal to renounce the use of force against Taiwan, Ma's new government quickly signed several non-political agreements with the PRC. Scheduled direct flights between Taiwan and cities on the mainland got underway and PRC tourists began visiting Taiwan in large numbers. In mid-2010 the two sides inked the Economic Co-operation Framework Agreement (ECFA), a trade pact which supporters said would give Taiwanese companies greater access to the vast mainland market. However, critics argued it would make Taiwan even more dependent on China and erode the island's sovereignty.

Ma won a second term in office in early 2012, just before economic growth slowed again. By late 2013, anger over soaring house prices, stagnating wages, government land grabs and a wiretapping scandal pushed Ma's popularity ratings below 10%. Many Taiwanese are unhappy with their country's political and economic direction, yet civil society remains stronger here than almost anywhere else in Asia. Every day, newspapers embarrass the authorities and citizens protest without fear.

GOVERNMENT

Taiwan is a republic. The head of state is the president, directly elected by citizens aged 20 and above every four years. Presidents are limited to two consecutive terms. Taiwan's president since 2008 has been Ma Ying-jeou of the KMT (Chinese Nationalist Party). Ma was born in Hong Kong in 1950 to mainland Chinese parents.

The president appoints a premier (prime minister) who heads the cabinet. Unlike in the UK, cabinet members aren't members of parliament. The Legislative Yuan, as the parliament is called, has 113 members – 73 elected from single-member, first-past-the-post constituencies, 34 allocated proportionally to parties that obtain more than 5% of the national vote, and six reserved for indigenous people. Each citizen has two votes: one in his or her local constituency and one for a national party list. By-elections are held when lawmakers die or are removed from office. Lawmakers have been stripped of their seats after being convicted of buying votes; one was thrown out when it was discovered she held US citizenship. (Ordinary Taiwanese are allowed dual nationality, but all elected and senior appointed officials are forbidden from holding a second passport.) The greens (see box opposite) have never attained a majority in the Legislative Yuan.

ECONOMY

Taiwanese often say they work so hard and focus so much on business because the island has no natural resources. That's true in the modern industrial sense: Taiwan has no oil and only tiny amounts of natural gas; the north's coal, gold and copper mines closed decades ago; and the island's forests are no longer logged on any significant scale. Yet the influx of Han Chinese immigrants in the 18th and 19th centuries was due largely to the presence of camphor, plus enough water to make intensive agriculture possible.

Taiwan has moved on from its days as an island of manufacturers who export low-cost goods, although you'll still see plenty of factories. It has a well-developed capitalist economy; thousands of new companies emerge each year while thousands of old ones hit the wall. Barriers to entry are low so many Taiwanese try their hand at running a small enterprise. It isn't unusual for restaurants and shops to open without any kind of business license. Rules and regulations are often ignored until the business grows to a size where officialdom starts to take an interest.

Economic growth is now much slower than in the halcyon 1980s. In 2012, Taiwan's GDP was US$466.1 billion, making it the 27th largest economy in the world. When ranked by per capita GDP adjusted for purchasing power parity, Taiwan is just behind Germany and just ahead of the UK. In recent years, many of Taiwan's largest corporations have shifted manufacturing operations overseas (to China or other low-wage countries) while keeping their head offices and R&D

divisions in Taiwan. Services industries, including tourism, now employ more than half the working population. Agriculture accounts for less than 2% of GDP; most farmers are over 60 years old. The transition from a factory-based economy to a more diverse and advanced economy hasn't been easy for older, less educated individuals. As of late 2013, unemployment was above 4%.

Taiwan's reliance on the USA as an export market (it used to take almost half of its exports) has been replaced by economic dependence on the only country that threatens it militarily. In 2012 China, along with Hong Kong, took 42% of Taiwan's exports. The mainland has also absorbed over US$100 billion in Taiwanese investment (official figures, which don't include investments routed through third countries, are much lower).

PEOPLE

Travellers passing through Taiwan can be forgiven for assuming it's a homogeneous society. Compared to Japan or Hong Kong, Taiwan's Western and Asian expatriate populations are small and there are very few people of African origin. Taiwanese society has often and recently fractured along ethnic lines. The aborigines tried to defend their land against Han Chinese settlers. Within the Han majority, Hoklo from one county in Fujian fought Hoklo from another county. For decades after World War II, there was considerable friction between the Hoklo majority and the ruling class dominated by recent immigrants from the Chinese mainland.

Ethnic relations are now fairly harmonious and intermarriage, along with internal migration, is blurring the lines between population groups. However, children of 'mixed marriages' often fail to learn languages other than Mandarin and Taiwanese.

THE ABORIGINES Taiwan's original inhabitants number just over 520,000 and make up 2.2% of the population. The ROC government recognises 14 tribes, the largest being the Amis with around 192,000 members, the Paiwan (93,000) and the Atayal (83,000). Other groups, notably the Siraya in Tainan (see box, page 223) are lobbying for similar status, as recognition opens the door to subsidies and other benefits.

Taiwan's indigenous people are of Austronesian origin. In fact, some scholars claim Taiwan is where the Austronesian branch of humanity started out (see box, page 28). Formerly classified as 'mountain compatriots' – and still often stereotyped as hard-drinking, poorly educated but kind-hearted mountain-dwelling folk – the aborigines farmed and hunted on the lowlands until Han settlers forced them to relocate to the interior. There was a great deal of intermarriage between early settlers and indigenous people. Also, many of the latter abandoned their original names and languages to better fit into Han-dominated mainstream society.

The Japanese were intolerant of cultural practices they regarded as barbaric, such as the tattooing of faces and hands. A few very elderly Atayal, Sediq and Truku women still bear the traditional cheek tattoos of their tribes. Indigenous cultures survive in villages in mountain areas and in east Taiwan. However, few indigenous people under the age of 40 speak their ancestral tongue fluently, even among those who participate enthusiastically in the many and varied tribal festivals. Traditional clothing is worn only on special occasions and most aboriginal homes resemble the concrete boxes found in lowland towns.

Taiwanese who have indigenous ancestry are now less likely to hide the fact. Despite affirmative action and other government help, indigenous people continue to be considerably poorer and less well educated than other Taiwanese, although they're prominent in pop music and professional sport.

THE HOKLO PEOPLE A unified Hoklo ('Taiwanese') identity is a relatively recent thing. Well into the 19th century, Hoklo people identified themselves as being Quanzhou folk or Zhangzhou folk or from some other part of Fujian. During the Japanese occupation and the subsequent Nationalist dictatorship, these sub-ethnic groups coalesced. Taiwanese of Hoklo descent account for around 70% of the population. Some call themselves 'true Taiwanese' or even 'native Taiwanese' to the annoyance of aborigines.

THE HAKKA PEOPLE Like Hoklo Taiwanese, the Hakka are Han Chinese. Their origins are unclear but it's believed they emerged as a distinct sub-ethnic group, speaking their own language and following a unique set of customs, as they moved *en masse* from central China to the south in a series of migrations between the 4th and 17th centuries. Unlike most Han Chinese, the Hakka never practised foot-binding. Because they've had to relocate so often and they've sometimes faced persecution, the Hakka are often compared to the Jews. Like the Jews, they've a reputation for working hard, living frugally and encouraging their children to study hard. Hakka started arriving in Taiwan in the early 18th century.

Taiwan's Hakka are concentrated in the hilly region between Zhongli and the Dajia river, and in a few towns in the south, notably Meinong. Since the late 19th century many Hakka have migrated to the big cities or to east Taiwan.

THE MAINLANDERS About one-seventh of Taiwan's population is considered 'mainlander', although this includes many who were born on the island. In traditional Han thinking, one's ancestry and identity comes from one's father; for this reason, many ROC citizens who have a Taiwanese mother and have never visited the PRC are considered mainlanders.

When Chiang Kai-shek retreated to Taiwan in 1949, around 1.5 million people followed him. Among them were soldiers and Nationalist officials from every province, their wives and children, scholars, a large proportion of Shanghai's mercantile class, Buddhist monks and Muslims from China's west. Most settled in the larger cities but some ended up in remote mountain areas where they worked on road-building projects and farmed. Few mainlanders speak Taiwanese fluently.

ASIAN IMMIGRANTS For decades, ethnic Chinese from Malaysia, Myanmar and other countries have been coming to Taiwan to study. Many have stayed on, found jobs, married and had children. Since the 1990s, many Taiwanese men have sought wives abroad, especially from Vietnam. There are also contingents of Filipinos, Thais and Indonesians. Mainland Chinese who've relocated to Taiwan in recent years, usually because they've married an ROC citizen, are another minority. In recent years, one in 11 of the island's newborns has had at least one non-Taiwanese parent.

LANGUAGE

MANDARIN In theory, Taiwan and China share a common official language: Mandarin Chinese. In the PRC it's known as *Pǔtōnghuà* ('common language') while in Taiwan it's called *Guóyǔ* ('national language'). In reality, Taiwan Mandarin and mainland Mandarin are somewhat like American English and British English: people from one side usually have no problems communicating with folk from

COMMON SUPERSTITIONS

Taiwan is a highly educated society yet some ancient superstitions are showing incredible staying power. More than a few Taiwanese will tell you the future is sometimes foretold in dreams and that evil spirits threaten the well-being of the living.

The fear of ghosts is widespread among those of Fujianese descent. Because those who died suddenly – especially suicides, murder victims and those who drowned – are thought to haunt the spot where they died, estate agents are required by law to disclose details of any 'violent events' that took place in the properties they're trying to sell. If a murder victim is buried before his or her killer is brought to justice, the family of the deceased may inter that person with a knife in one hand and an axe in the other, so the dead person's spirit may better hunt down the killer.

Just as the number 13 is unlucky in the West, quite a few Taiwanese avoid renting or buying fourth-floor apartments because the Mandarin word for 'four' (sì) sounds similar to the word for 'death' (sǐ). Such homophones are central to several beliefs. Taoist priests who officiate at funerals sometimes present surviving relatives with nails. These are believed to help the younger generation beget sons and continue the family line because in Taiwanese the word for 'nail' sounds like the word for 'son' – both are pronounced *ding*. These nails aren't to be used, however, especially if there's a pregnant woman in the house. Hammering nails into the wall of a house where there's a mother-to-be may harm the unborn baby, it's said.

the other but there are differences in pronunciation and word use. The 'curled-tongue' accent so common in northern China is almost unknown in Taiwan except among people originally from certain parts of the mainland. Also, Taiwanese learn traditional ('long form') characters at school whereas mainlanders are taught simplified ('short form') characters. The latter are quicker to write but, say critics, much of the original beauty and nuance is lost.

In terms of grammar, Mandarin is beautifully simple. There are no cases or genders and verbs do not conjugate. Nouns stay the same whether they're singular or plural.

Pronunciation is difficult to master because the correct tone (pitch) must be used for each syllable. There are four tones plus a fifth, seldom-used neutral tone. Using an incorrect tone can convey a very different meaning to the one intended. For instance, *bēi* means 'cup' while *běi* means 'north'. Several words have both the same pronunciation and the same tone. Lǐ is a very common surname, for example, but one online dictionary lists 17 other words that sound exactly the same. Taken out of context, individual words are easily misunderstood, even by native Mandarin speakers.

With the exception of a few old people, everyone in Taiwan understands Mandarin, though not all are capable of or willing to speak it.

TAIWANESE The language many people call Taiwanese is a form of Hokkien, the language spoken in much of Fujian, the Chinese province from whence most of Taiwan's early Han settlers came. The language has various names in Taiwan including *Taigi, Holo, Táiwānhuà* and *Mǐnnányǔ*. It has eight tones. In rural areas, especially in the south, it's the most commonly used language.

Taiwanese and Mandarin are mutually unintelligible. However, there are several similarities, just as many English words are close to their German equivalents. Words borrowed from Japanese are frequently used; one you might hear is *o-to-bai*, meaning motorbike.

Between the 1950s and 1980s the KMT discouraged the use of Taiwanese. Students who spoke it in the classroom were punished and few Taiwanese-language TV shows were aired. Nowadays many soap operas, news reports and talk shows are entirely or mostly in Taiwanese. Some citizens still feel that speaking Taiwanese is low class. However, they're outnumbered by those who speak it proudly as an expression of their self or national identity. However, fluency in Taiwanese is no longer a clear marker of a person's ethnic or political affiliation. Some people with mixed mainlander/local parentage habitually speak Taiwanese. Also, quite a few young people who are 100% Taiwanese on both sides don't speak the language well. Nonetheless, those running for elected office must have some fluency in Taiwanese, whatever their politics.

HAKKA The language of Taiwan's Hakka minority isn't mutually intelligible with either Mandarin or Taiwanese. An archaic language that retains features of Chinese as it was spoken more than a thousand years ago, it's more closely related to Cantonese (Hong Kong's main language) than Mandarin. Taiwan's government subsidises a Hakka-language TV station and Hakka language courses in schools, yet the tongue is gradually losing ground to Mandarin and Taiwanese.

INDIGENOUS LANGUAGES Unlike the three Han languages commonly spoken in Taiwan (Mandarin, Taiwanese and Hakka), what are known as the Formosan Austronesian languages don't have tones. Nor, until the arrival of the Dutch in the 17th century, did they have any written form.

The amazing diversity of Taiwan's indigenous languages fascinates linguists and endows them with a significance far beyond the small number of speakers (perhaps 300,000 Taiwanese aboriginals and a handful of foreign Christian missionaries). Just as many researchers think Taiwan was the wellspring from which Austronesian peoples and cultures originated, many linguists believe Taiwan was the root of the entire Austronesian language family, a grouping that includes the national languages of Indonesia, Malaysia and the Philippines, plus hundreds more languages spoken in places as far apart as Madagascar, Hawaii and New Zealand. According to Robert A Blust, a professor at the University of Hawaii, Austronesian languages can be divided into ten branches, nine of which exist only in Taiwan, and that all Austronesian languages spoken outside Taiwan (including the language of Orchid Island's indigenous Tao people) belong to the Malayo-Polynesian branch, which embraces more than 1,200 languages spoken by over 350 million people.

Of the 26 Austronesian languages known to have been spoken in Taiwan, ten have died out. At least four more, including Thao and Pazeh (see box, page 198), are on the verge of extinction.

RELIGION

Religion in Taiwan is a bit like the island's politics: noisy, turbulent, inescapable and enlivened by a number of shady characters. However, unlike the hate-filled relationship between the blue and green camps, the various faiths, sects and cults seem to get along well. Many people are extremely pious, to be sure, but just as many seem to treat religion like they do life insurance – something that's so important they wouldn't do without it, but which needs to be attended to just once or twice a year.

No more than one in ten Taiwanese practices a religion that excludes other faiths, be it a 'pure' form of Buddhism, Christianity or Islam. The majority of pious Taiwanese follow a blend of Taoism, Buddhism and folk beliefs. The proportions vary from person to person and are impossible to estimate, even for a given individual, because, 'All three of these strains... have contributed heavily to [Taiwan's] religious life, and their interpenetration is so extensive as to prevent a thorough sorting of the elements one might associate with each in its "primal" state' (David K Jordan, *Gods, Ghosts & Ancestors*).

Taiwan has an estimated 30,000 non-Christian houses of worship. In these shrines you'll see effigies representing the Jade Emperor, Mazu and other deities of Chinese origin, plus icons of spirits propitiated only in Taiwan, such as the Yimin worshipped by Hakka people (see page 155). Guanyin, the Buddhist goddess of compassion, can be found in a great many folk shrines. However, Buddhist temples don't generally accommodate images of folk gods. Taoist rituals are conducted in folk shrines, before private altars and, as part of funerals or exorcisms, inside ordinary homes.

Popular religion in Taiwan includes thousands of divine or supernatural personalities; one tally puts the number of deities at approximately 36,000. Some have always been gods but many are like Christian saints in that they were ordinary humans who led exemplary lives. After death their reputations

TAIWAN: CRADLE OF AUSTRONESIA?

If some academics are right, millions of people in southeast Asia, the Pacific and New Zealand have some Taiwanese ancestry. The theory that Austronesian populations can trace their origins to Taiwan, first proposed a quarter of a century ago, gained credence in 2009 with the publication of two intriguing studies. One focused on words and languages, the other on germs.

It's not known when proto-Austronesians reached Taiwan, but most scholars are convinced they came from the Chinese mainland. According to a team at the University of Auckland, computer analyses of the core vocabularies of 400 Austronesian languages 'clearly show that the origin of the entire Austronesian language family can be dated back to Taiwan around 5,200 years ago'. A millennium on, the team concluded, Austronesians from Taiwan settled in the Philippines. From there, they spread rapidly across Polynesia. Several waves of migrants reached Hawaii and New Zealand between AD500 and 1300. Easter Island may have been reached as early as AD300, or as late as 1200.

A multi-national investigation of stomach bacteria reached very similar conclusions. Germs evolve like plants and animals, and by comparing gut bacteria taken from Taiwanese aborigines with samples from Polynesians and New Guineans, scientists were able to chart the way in which a certain microbe linked to various stomach ailments has mutated and diversified. This medical evidence correlates well with archaeological discoveries throughout the Pacific. However, studies of human DNA suggest the islands of southeast Asia were inhabited before Taiwan, and that climate change prompted proto-Austronesians to disperse in several directions, including north to Taiwan, within the past 10,000 years.

CALENDARS AND ZODIACS

Taiwanese companies, schools and government offices follow the Gregorian calendar. Most people work or go to school from Monday to Friday and have Saturday and Sunday off. However, official dates are counted from the establishment of the Republic of China in 1912. The year 2000 was therefore ROC year 89; 2014 is year 103.

What's often called the lunar calendar and sometimes referred to as the farmers' calendar is still very important, however. If you look closely at any diary or calendar made in Taiwan, you'll see the lunar date printed below the Gregorian date. The timing of many holidays and festivals depends on this calendar, which is actually lunisolar (in that it indicates both the moon phase and the time of the solar year). Certain religious practices, such as burning joss paper (see box, page 101) and not eating meat (see box, page 64), are observed on the first and 15th day of every lunar month. The lunar calendar is 354 days long. So it doesn't fall out of sync with the 365-day astronomical year, an intercalary (additional or 'leap') month is added to the lunar calendar about once every three years. The formula used to calculate when an extra month is required is very complex, so it's not as predictable as the quadrennial addition of February 29 to the Gregorian calendar.

The most important days on the lunar calendar are those at the very end of one lunar year and at the beginning of the next. This period, usually called Chinese New Year or Lunar New Year, is celebrated by ethnic Chinese communities throughout the world. The Chinese animal zodiac follows the lunar calendar, not the Gregorian calendar. Babies who came into the world on 28 January 2014 were born in the Year of the Snake; those born a week later are Year of the Horse kids. The other creatures in the 12-year cycle are: goat, monkey, rooster, dog, pig, rat, ox, tiger, rabbit and dragon.

grew as miracles were attributed to them. There are several instances of Chinese emperors issuing edicts stating that a certain deceased individual had become a god, a process more akin to ratification than promotion. In temples you'll also see depictions of supernatural individuals who aren't venerated – such as Mazu's two cohorts – and a few animals who are, such as Lord Tiger, whose effigy is usually on the floor beside an altar.

There are several explanations for the fantastic richness of the island's religious life. Firstly, most Taiwanese trace their ancestry to Fujian, a province regarded as the most superstitious part of China. The dangers faced by early migrants, such as the perilous sea crossing, epidemics and headhunting aborigines, made them cling even more tightly to their incense and icons. The Japanese colonial regime's Kominka Movement (see *History*, page 17) was a direct attack on folk beliefs, and the postwar Chinese Nationalist dictatorship discouraged what it branded 'excessive and wasteful' temple practices, but neither of these episodes can be compared to the decades-long vehement suppression of religion throughout the communist-ruled mainland. Rising income and better education since World War II hasn't led to growing secularism. If anything, temples have been a major beneficiary of Taiwan's prosperity. Not only do people have more money to donate, but it's said the pace and uncertainty of modern life induces them to seek answers from gods or gurus. Whatever the reasons, traditional religion in Taiwan shows no signs of decline.

As with churches and mosques, Chinese temples are laid out in accordance with certain architectural conventions. From the visitor's perspective, the first of these concerns the three doorways at the front.

The doors are always painted red – Taiwan's temples are dominated by shades of red and gold – and usually they're decorated with colourful full-body portraits of General Qin and General Yuchi. This duo, who lived in the Tang Dynasty, became 'door gods' because of their ability to repel demons. The lion statues in temple forecourts have a similar protective function; the lion pawing a ball is male, while the one with a cub is female. The door on the right, the 'dragon door', is the correct entrance to use. The one on the left, the 'tiger door', is the doorway by which you should leave. You shouldn't enter by the central portal as it's reserved for supernatural entities. The red wooden planks that lie across the bottom of each doorway are there to stop evil spirits from getting inside.

Larger temples have internal courtyards and small towers on either side. The tower on the right contains a bell; the one on the left has a large drum. These days, temple bells and drums are usually struck mechanically rather than by hand. In smaller shrines the bell and drum are within the main chamber, attached to the wall or the ceiling.

Most temples have at least three altars; some have a dozen. They're obvious and, as you'd expect, the central altar is dedicated to the temple's main deity. In front of each altar there's an offertory table on which you're likely to see joss paper, fruit, incense and candles. It may be difficult to get a really good look at the icons themselves as they're often behind steel bars or a Perspex screen. The bars prevent theft – precious idols have been stolen or kidnapped – while the screens keep them from getting sooty. Ancient temples typically also contain other important relics, among them carved stone censers (most modern censers are made of steel) and inscribed boards. The latter, rectangular boards hung from rafters, bear auspicious four-character slogans plus the name of the person (often an emperor or president) who donated it to the temple and the date the donation was made.

Many Buddhist houses of worship are beautiful in their simplicity. Folk temples, by contrast, are made as opulent as possible. In the eyes of those who build and decorate such shrines, less is never more. In many temples, the stone columns and wooden beams have been carved to resemble dragons and other creatures. The exteriors and roofs are often bedecked with ceramic figurines; many of the latter are mass-produced but some are superb examples of *koji* glazed earthenware (see page 234). Identifying the legendary characters and understanding the meaning of each animal greatly enhances a temple visit; a tour guide who can explain these things is worth his or her fee.

TAIWAN'S FOUR MAJOR RELIGIONS Taoism and Buddhism each have several million followers; providing accurate tallies is very difficult because of the overlap between the two.

Confucianism isn't a religion but rather a system of ethics which stressed propriety and respect for one's elders and betters. Confucian temples are best viewed as memorials to the philosopher and his most notable disciples. In them, Confucius is always represented by a tablet. In some folk shrines, however, statuettes of the sage are worshipped alongside mainstream deities.

Taoism This religion grew out of a philosophy. The putative founder, Chinese philosopher Laozi, lived in the fourth or sixth century BC; he's now one of the religion's deities. Tao (*dào* in Mandarin) means 'the path' or 'the direction', but in a religious context it's sometimes translated as 'the flow of the universe'; Taoism stresses going with that flow, not fighting the current. The three core principles can be summarised as kindness, frugality and modesty. The central Taoist text is the *Tao Te Ching*, attributed to Laozi. The Jade Emperor and Guan Gong are notable members of the Taoist pantheon.

Buddhism Buddhism spread from India to China more than 2,000 years ago and was brought to Taiwan by Han migrants in the 17th century. As in China, Buddhism in Taiwan is part of the Mahāyāna ('Great Vehicle') tradition. Until the 1960s Buddhism was less popular than Taoism and folk religion but recently it has enjoyed rapid growth. Dharma Drum Mountain, one of the island's major Buddhist associations, claims its membership increased tenfold between 1993 and 2008. The most prominent forms of Buddhism in Taiwan are Pure Land Buddhism (which scholars say appeals to those who grew up surrounded by Taoism) and Zen (*Chán* in Mandarin). In the 1930s and 1940s, the colonial authorities tried unsuccessfully to promote Shintoism in Taiwan; during that era Japanese Buddhism made some inroads. The Tibetan Tantric form of Buddhism has attracted followers in recent years, but it's tendency of Taiwanese Buddhists to engage in charitable acts around the world and social activism at home that gives them their high profile.

I-Kuan Tao Taiwan's third-largest religion has at least 800,000 adherents but is little known in the West. I-Kuan Tao, founded in China in the 1930s, draws on Buddhism, Taoism and Confucianism and requires followers to be non-smoking,

MAKE WAY FOR THE ZHENTOU!

Adding fantastic colour and vigour to Taiwan's religious life are the island's several hundred *zhentou* troupes. Some are highly trained professionals who tour for a living but most are amateurs with kinship ties to a particular temple. For many sightseers and all shutterbugs, these gaudily made-up, ornately dressed squads of young men (a few recently formed troupes are female) are the highlight of temple parades. During folk and Taoist religious celebrations, zhentou members strut, swagger and wave mock weapons. They're menacing yet fascinating; in the minds of many Taiwanese, they're synonymous with juvenile delinquency and gang culture – a perception which some cultural organisations, notably Ten Drum Art Percussion Group, are working hard to recast.

Of the many types of zhentou, perhaps the easiest to recognise are the *Bajiajiang* ('Eight Generals'). Four members of each octet play the role of 'infernal generals' while the others represent the gods of the seasons. In addition to fabulous headgear and face paint, they carry ritual items such as fans on which protective spells have been written. They're forbidden to smile, and some troupes traditionally require their members to avoid funerals, disease and menstruating women in the three days before they appear in public.

teetotal and vegetarian. I-Kuan Tao is notable for its stance on other religions: Christianity and Islam are regarded as valid equals; depictions of Jesus and Muhammad can be seen in some I-Kuan Tao shrines (such as Holy Glory Temple, see page 225) alongside the Maitreya Buddha and Guan Gong. Because of its secretive nature, the sect was illegal in Taiwan from the 1950s until 1987, although there was little active repression for most of this period.

Christianity Christianity arrived in Taiwan in the 17th century with the Dutch and the Spanish but it didn't put down deep roots. The British and North American missionaries who arrived after 1860, like George L Mackay (see box, page 140), had to start afresh. Thanks to their medical and educational work, within two decades they were accepted by society at large. However, the number of converts remains very small, something which many observers attribute to the emphasis in Han Chinese culture on filial respect and ancestor worship. Taiwanese who convert are sometimes accused of not respecting their elders and abandoning their ancestors. No more than 5% of Taiwan's Han population is Christian. Among indigenous people, conversion efforts have been much more successful – over half are Protestant and a significant minority are Roman Catholic.

GODS AND GODDESSES In addition to praying to their gods, many Taiwanese still offer sacrifices to their ancestors. In the traditional scheme of things, neglecting deceased relatives isn't just disrespectful to one's forebears but also dangerous to oneself. Dissatisfied ancestors, it's said, have the ability to inflict misfortune.

Mazu Taiwan's most prominent deity, Mazu (formerly spelled 'Matsu') is said to have been born Lim Vo'g Niu (in Mandarin, Lin Mo-niang) in Meizhou, a fishing community in Fujian, on the 23rd day of the third lunar month in AD960. Her birthday is celebrated throughout the ROC and there are especially large events in Dajia (see box, page 175) and Beigang.

By the time she was in her early teens, Mazu had an excellent grasp of Buddhist and Confucian texts. She used her powers to heal the sick and exorcise evil spirits but refused to marry. Her most famous achievement came at the age of 16 when her father and brothers, then far away on a fishing expedition, were caught in a tremendous storm. She slipped into a trance just as the storm was at its fiercest. After she regained consciousness her father and brothers returned home safely, swearing Mazu had projected herself out into the ocean to save them. An alternative legend has it that she saved her brothers, but because she was disturbed during her trance she let go of her father who then drowned. According to another version, she swam out to sea and searched for her father, but drowned and was washed ashore in the Matsu Islands. Many believe that when she was about 27, she told her family she was going to leave this world, climbed a nearby mountain and ascended to the heavens.

She was revered as a rainmaker and also persuaded two mischief-making demons to 'go straight' and become her servants. Altars dedicated to Mazu are very often flanked by human-sized statues of these two: Shunfeng Er ('ears that hear the wind') and Qianli Yan ('eyes that see a thousand leagues'). Mazu herself is often depicted with a rather plump face partially hidden by a veil of beads.

Fujianese migrants sailing to Taiwan often carried effigies of Mazu with them to ensure a safe crossing. Koxinga certainly brought with him a number of icons, as did Shi Lang, the Qing general who brought Taiwan into the imperial fold. Over time, Mazu has become much more than the patron saint of seafarers. Many Taiwanese who venture nowhere near the ocean seek her blessings in times of plenty and her aid in times of distress. More than 800 shrines around the ROC are dedicated to Mazu; many are named *Tiānhòu Gōng*, meaning 'Queen of Heaven Temple'.

Guan Gong Also known as Guan Di, this deity is traditionally depicted with a red face and wielding a *guandao*, a weapon somewhat like a halberd. He's one of the most prominent deities in Chinese religion and one of the highest-ranking former mortals in the pantheon. A general who lived more than 1,800 years ago, he's worshipped by police officers, gangsters, businesspeople and others who revere his steadfast loyalty and righteousness.

Land gods These lowly figures in the celestial hierarchy are the equivalent of village or borough chiefs. Like their human counterparts, their powers are limited to a particular place. There are tens of thousands of land-god shrines throughout Taiwan's countryside. Some are sizeable but many are no bigger than dog kennels. Most are quite basic and contain little more than a censer and a table or shelf where an idol has been placed. The land god is often depicted as wearing a mandarin's hat and robe. Sometimes he carries a staff (because he's believed to patrol his area of responsibility on foot) or a gold ingot (a symbol of prosperity).

Traditional graves incorporate small land-god shrines. These are at the front left as you face the gravestone. Land gods are also worshipped in major temples, almost always under the name *Fude Zhengshen*, which means 'Blessed and Benevolent Righteous God'. In Hakka districts, he's called 'Bo-gong'.

Land gods have birthdays, the most common dates being the second day of the second lunar month and the 15th day of the eighth lunar month.

City gods Just as there are thousands of land gods, there are numerous city and town gods. Each one is called *Chenghuangye*; *chéng* means city wall, *huáng* means moat and *yé* means lord. Every settlement in Taiwan that used to be walled – and a few such as Lugang that were not – has a city-god temple. In some places the city god is explicitly identified with a human official who once served in that locale and who was posthumously deified. Like land gods, city gods have no powers beyond their territory. They're worshipped by members of the public as well as local bureaucrats. Notable city-god temples can be found in Hsinchu, Chiayi and Tainan.

Wang Ye The words *wáng yé* mean 'royal lord' but this name is more honorific than accurate – the only royal connection is that the original 360 of the many hundreds of spirits in this category were musicians and scholars employed by Emperor Taizong (reigned AD626–649). They've been joined by, among others, Koxinga and a Japanese police officer who served in colonial-era Taiwan. That policeman, unwilling to follow orders to extort money from locals, committed suicide. Because he later appeared in a village chief's dream and warned of an impending epidemic, peasants in the area began worshipping him. He's a typical Wang Ye in the sense he's believed to possess plague-defeating powers.

The Wang Ye cult is stronger in Taiwan than elsewhere in Greater China because of plague-expelling customs in Fujian. Whenever coastal communities in that province were afflicted by disease, they'd place Wang Ye icons on boats and set them adrift. Prevailing currents carried many of these vessels to southwest Taiwan, which has more than two-thirds of the ROC's 1,200-plus Wang Ye shrines, including its best known, Nankunshen Daitian Temple. Knowing exactly what these boats were, Han people living along Taiwan's coastline received them with a mixture of fear and awe; they knew that ignoring the Wang Ye was to tempt fate, so they built shrines

1

CASTING BLOCKS, DRAWING LOTS

Divination has been an aspect of Chinese religious life since the beginning of the country's long history, when tortoise shells were heated and the resulting cracks 'read' in a process called pyromancy. In modern Taiwan, the most popular method of divination is the casting of pairs of blocks made of wood or bamboo. Because these blocks – known in Taiwanese as *poe* – are crescent shaped, they're sometimes called 'moon boards' in English. You'll see poe cast in folk temples (a process known as *pua-poe*) and before ancestor shrines in private homes. Typical blocks are 10–15cm long, painted red and placed on the altar when not in use. One side of each block is flat and the other is rounded. This difference is critical as casting these boards is somewhat like tossing a coin. The procedure is straightforward: a worshipper kneels, formulates his request (which he may whisper but is unlikely to utter aloud, and which is more often a statement than a question), cups the blocks in his hands, stands up and then lets the blocks drop from waist height. A moon board may land rounded side up or rounded side down. If only one lands rounded side up, this signals divine confirmation of the statement. If both land on their flat sides (rounded sides up), the deity is refuting the statement. If they both come to rest rounded side down, this shows the god is amused by the question. For a worshipper to be sure, he needs three consecutive confirmations. If he doesn't get them he may reformulate his request or give up.

Another common way of seeking supernatural advice is to draw lots. The lots are numbered bamboo slats – often 60 of them – placed in a cylinder on or beside an altar. Supplicants pick up the cylinder, give it a good shake and then pull out the slat sticking out the furthest. They read the number and, after casting poe to confirm it's correct, take a sheet of paper out of a drawer or off a numbered hook. Each sheet bears a message 30 to 60 characters in length. Because the language is frequently obscure or archaic, the volunteers who look after temples are often asked to assist with interpretation.

to house them and made offerings of incense. Rather than set icons on a vessel and push it out to sea, Taiwan's coastal communities have tended to construct elaborate votive boats and then set them ablaze. The most spectacular of these boat burnings is the triennial event in Donggang.

The Old Man Under the Moon One of Taiwan's most popular deities, the Old Man Under the Moon is a Cupid-like deity who helps lonely hearts. Each altar to this god has a bowl of short red threads which symbolise the traditional belief that each person is tied to and destined to eventually find his or her life partner; everyone who seeks his help takes a thread home. Shrines dedicated to the Old Man are especially busy ahead of Qixi, the traditional midsummer lovers' day.

The Jade Emperor Taoism's chief deity is like the chairman of the board – acknowledged to be the boss but seldom seen on the shop floor. Although he's said to reign over heaven, hell and humanity in the way the emperors of old used to rule China, the Jade Emperor is less prominent in Taiwan's folk temples than Mazu or Guan Gong. Icons of the Jade Emperor usually have him seated on a throne and wearing imperial robes and a flat-topped crown. The jade tablet he clasps before his chest is a symbol of his authority. His birthday is the ninth day after Lunar New Year.

The Yellow Emperor Not to be confused with the Jade Emperor, the Yellow Emperor was a legendary sovereign who ruled China 4,700 years ago. He's said to have refined the crop cultivation methods used ever since by Chinese people; the invention of chopsticks is attributed to one of his concubines. At the age of 100 he attained immortality. He's worshipped not only for his contributions to Chinese civilisation but also because he's considered the forefather of all Han people.

EDUCATION

Formal education is valued highly by Taiwanese and those who hold postgraduate degrees from famous universities are revered. The adult literacy rate is more than 98%; most of those who can't read or write are rural women over 60 years old.

Children are expected to study hard; many parents have an unhealthy obsession with their offspring's test results and class rankings. A generation or two ago, sons but not daughters were pushed hard. This is no longer the case; young females are under as much pressure to do well at school as males. Schooling is compulsory between the ages of six and 18. Most kids attend kindergarten for two or three years before entering primary school and the majority continue in full-time education until their early 20s. City kids aged ten and over spend several evenings per week in cram schools where they review, preview and supplement school lessons.

University courses last four years. Over the past 20 years, the number of universities has soared while the birth rate has plunged. Less well-known colleges are struggling to attract students. As a result, foreigners interested in studying in Taiwan can find some attractive scholarship opportunities. Information can be obtained from the Foundation for International Co-operation in Higher Education

STUDYING MANDARIN IN TAIWAN

Since China's emergence as an economic superpower, ambitious young Westerners have been travelling to the PRC to learn spoken Mandarin and written Chinese. This is a relatively recent phenomenon; before the late 1970s few outsiders, mostly elite students from China's allies in the developing world, were admitted by PRC colleges. Teaching Chinese is now big business, but China isn't necessarily the best place to go. Some of Taiwan's language schools, notably National Taiwan University's Mandarin Training Centre (*www.mtc.ntnu.edu.tw*) and the privately run Taipei Language Institute (*www.tli.com.tw*), have more than half a century of experience.

While it's true that many Taiwanese people habitually speak languages other than Mandarin, the same is true in many parts of the mainland. In the PRC, Chinese is taught using *hanyu pinyin* (a way of rendering Mandarin sounds in the Latin alphabet, now widely used in Taiwan for road and place names). In Taiwan, *zhuyin fuhao* (a set of 37 phonic symbols) is used to teach both foreign adults and local primary school pupils. Some individuals strongly prefer one system over another; you probably won't know which works best for you until you've tried both.

Students on a limited budget shouldn't rule out Taiwan, as the south of the island can be cheaper than Beijing or Shanghai. There's another reason why you may prefer living in Taiwan: you can say what you like about government policy and the country's politicians without having to worry about the consequences for yourself or those you associate with.

Michael Berry

An incredible array of unique and powerful cinematic voices have emerged from Taiwan over the past several decades. Hou Hsiao-hsien (b1947), Edward Yang (1947–2007), Malaysian-born Tsai Ming-liang (b1957), Chang Tso-chi (b1961), Cheng Wen-tang (b1958) and many others offer a rich series of perspectives on Taiwan's history and society, while, at the same time, using their films to provide broad and profound statements about the human condition. Many of these film-makers have also been innovators in terms of what they have brought to the art of film-making, such as Hou's aesthetic reinvention of the art form through his combined use of techniques such as the long-shot, long-take and the employment of non-professional actors.

Taiwan cinema is also a reflection of the country's dynamic journey in the modern era. Everything from the Japanese colonial period to the island's integration into the ROC in 1945, up to the incredible economic and democratic reforms witnessed over the past decades, has provided the landscape for cinematic reflection. At the same time, Taiwan cinema also serves as a fascinating counterpoint for other Chinese-language cinemas emerging from Hong Kong and mainland China. Taiwan's historical journey, unique mix of local dialects, stunning landscapes and political openness are all elements that have helped to forge a distinct cinematic identity.

For many years the local film industry faced great challenges, but a series of box-office triumphs, such as actor-turned-director Doze Niu's gangster melodrama *Monga* (2010) and writer-turned-director Giddens Ko's student romance *You are the Apple of My Eye* (2011), have contributed to the gradual reinvigoration of the local film market in Taiwan over the past decade. Some might argue that films like these might point to a 'dumbing down' of the industry, yet the simple reality is that film directors like Hou and Tsai are essentially art-house film directors whose work isn't expected to have widespread commercial appeal. While several New Wave

of Taiwan (*www.fichet.org.tw*) and the government's Study In Taiwan website (*www.studyintaiwan.org*).

CULTURE

Economic growth coupled with the lifting of martial law and the return of thousands of Taiwanese who've lived or studied abroad has led to an explosion in artistic endeavour and a proliferation of high-profile cultural events.

During the Chiang dictatorship (see *History*, page 18), the government's cultural policies were heavy-handed. Classical Chinese culture and ethics were promoted; local Taiwanese customs were ignored or derided as backward. Some allowance was made for indigenous Austronesian traditions but the overriding goal was to inculcate Chinese identity throughout the population and prepare the ROC's citizenry for the eventual defeat of Communism and the retaking of the mainland.

A massive shift began in the early 1990s. Political pluralism was matched by growing interest in local and minority customs. Museums, school books and television programmes began to focus on the truly local rather than the glories of old China. School curricula were rewritten to include a lot more of Taiwan's history, geography and literature and less of China's. Every city and county now has a cultural centre that hosts concerts, plays and other performances.

directors tasted some degree of commercial success in the early 1980s, the box-office has always been dominated by more commercial genres (such as martial arts films, romances and comedies) and for much of the past two decades foreign – especially Hollywood, Japanese and Korean – films have dominated. Art-house films like those produced by the leading voices of the New Taiwan Cinema should not be expected to be breakout commercial hits. Clearly, mainstream audiences want to see commercial fare like *Cape No. 7* (2008). However, the recent success of local commercial cinema does boost contemporary art-house cinema and there's a large degree of cross-pollination when it comes to the cast and crew producing these films. Different Taiwan films are often promoted side-by-side as examples of local film-making. It isn't uncommon to see a commercially successful genre film – like the gangster film *Monga* – displayed side-by-side with a more experimental film like Hou Chi-jan's *One Day* in stores.

The success of a few films has created an appetite for contemporary Taiwan cinema, opening a window of opportunity for a wider interest in different cinematic genres and styles coming from Taiwan. Equally important, the box-office success of these films helps crush entrenched stereotypes and misconceptions that Taiwan cinema is somehow synonymous with art-house film. Once funding sources return and the industry's infrastructure gets rebuilt, the entire film-making community, including art-house cinema, will reap the benefits.

Michael Berry, professor of Contemporary Chinese Cultural Studies at the University of California Santa Barbara, was a jury member at the 2010 Taipei Golden Horse Film Festival. He is a literary translator and author of several books on Chinese cinema, including Speaking in Images *(Columbia University Press, 2005), a collection of dialogues with 20 leading figures in the film industries of Taiwan, China and Hong Kong.*

Indigenous artists and performers are among those who have benefited from this paradigm shift.

Years ago, one writer described Taiwan as a 'cultural Titicaca', a lake into which many rivers flow but none leave. Nowadays, only the first part of this characterisation is true. Fujianese folk religion is still a massive influence. Japanese fashions, cartoons and comic books continue to be popular. Aspects of US popular culture – especially rap and hip-hop and the clothes and dance moves that go with them – are conspicuous. South Korean pop music and soap operas have made inroads. And just as the KMT toned down its efforts to promote a certain version of Chinese culture, exchanges with the mainland began exposing Taiwanese to trends on the other side of the Taiwan Strait. Also, the worldview of Taiwanese people is no longer dominated by the US and Japan. In recent years, tens of thousands of Taiwanese have studied in the UK. A great many Taiwanese have been abroad for business.

Many people in China's burgeoning middle classes regard Taiwan in the same way many Taiwanese view Japan – not a society to be emulated in every respect, but certainly a source of endearing fads and personalities. Cultural products are now one of Taiwan's major exports.

Taiwanese literature (see page 353) hasn't made much of an impact in the West. Nor has the island's music, although several Taiwanese pop singers have achieved stardom in the PRC. Cloud Gate Dance Theater (*www.cloudgate.org.tw*) has toured the world, as has the Ten Drum Art Percussion Group (*www.ten-hsieh.com.tw*). Sculptor Ju Ming (see page 139) has won critical acclaim. However, it's in cinema (see box, page 36) that artists from Taiwan have had the greatest international successes. Double Oscar-winner Ang Lee is perhaps the most famous Taiwanese person in the world.

2

Practical Information

WHEN TO VISIT

Even if you're sure you can endure the heat and humidity of a Taiwanese summer, avoid July, August and early September because of the typhoons that blow in from the Pacific. From late June to the end of August, thousands of local college students crowd Kenting National Park and Green Island. Yet for those who can handle the temperatures Taiwan's summers are wonderfully vivid. The skies are blue, the rivers are full and mountain peaks are clearly visible from the lowlands. Butterflies and flowers are abundant. Overall, October to March is the best period to visit because temperatures are comfortable and there's little chance of getting caught in a downpour. That said, it can get downright frigid in the mountains. Because of landslides, mountain areas are occasionally inaccessible during the summer wet season. The best times of year for high-altitude hiking – or any kind of mountain exploration – are October to November and the early spring. During the colder months, excursions to Penghu County and Orchid Island are less pleasant and more prone to delays. People with very sensitive respiratory systems should avoid Taiwan's southern lowlands during the winter because air quality declines during the season's long dry spells. Also, don't come around Lunar New Year – accommodation rates go through the roof, trains get booked out and the roads are jammed with sightseers and people visiting relatives.

HIGHLIGHTS

Your first impressions may be of bewildering urban chaos but with a little nudging (and this book) the door to the treasure house opens. Taiwan not only has a tremendous range of attractions – cultural, scenic and ecological – but also great depth in every category. Two weeks isn't nearly enough to do justice to its mountains, museums, minorities, temples or birds.

A PERSONAL TOP 6: NATURE AND THE OUTDOORS
East Taiwan Hualien to Taitung by Highway 11 is many cyclists' favourite but the inland route brings you closer to the region's indigenous population. See page 281.

Little Liuqiu Island This coral chunk is near enough to Kaohsiung to make an excellent day trip, yet far enough from 'mainland' Taiwan to have a completely different vibe. See page 332.

New Central Cross-Island Highway The high-altitude road that links Sun Moon Lake with Yushan National Park and Alishan more than justifies renting a car or hiring a driver. See page 206.

Penghu County Straight, empty roads link sandy beaches, crumbling coral houses and superb windsurfing spots. See page 310.

Snow Mountain Taiwan's number two peak in terms of height is a world-class three-day hike offering stunning vistas. See page 199.

Taroko Gorge You'll understand why this place is called a 'must-see' as soon as you reach Swallow Grotto or the Tunnel of Nine Turns. See page 286.

A PERSONAL TOP 6: CULTURE & MAN-MADE ATTRACTIONS
Folk religion and temple culture The fervour and colour of Taiwan's *tang-ki* (see box, page 228) and *zhentou* (see box, page 31) are unforgettable.

Kinmen County Staggeringly quaint villages scarred by Cold War battles. See page 318.

Lugang Get lost in the backstreets of Taiwan's living museum. See page 180.

National Museum of Taiwan History Whether you know nothing about Taiwan's past or have immersed yourself in the subject, you'll find this museum very satisfying. See page 222.

EXPLORING TAIWAN'S INDIGENOUS COMMUNITIES   *Cheryl Robbins*

There are several hundred indigenous communities in Taiwan. They're often close-knit, friendly places, with an average population of just a few hundred. Some are located high in the mountains and reached by narrow, winding roads. Some are located on the coast or near popular tourist areas. Many communities have limited or no bus service, so tourists have to drive themselves or join a tour.

One point is worth noting: Taiwan is a small, well-developed island. There are few places that can be considered truly remote. This means that indigenous people and communities have long had interactions with mainstream society. Thus, you shouldn't expect to see 'primitive' lifestyles. Taiwan's indigenous people wear contemporary clothing, except during special ceremonies, and most live in homes made of bricks and cement.

Although the very traditional way of life has all but disappeared, there are still a number of reasons to visit indigenous communities. Firstly, these communities are located in areas of natural beauty and offer ecotourism and sports opportunities such as hiking, white-water rafting, swimming, surfing and river tracing. Such places are often home to certified ecotourism guides who can lead challenging hikes or less taxing local ecological tours. In many indigenous villages, native Austronesian languages (see page 27) are still spoken. Chinese is spoken by almost everyone but few people speak English. This should not deter non-Chinese speakers, however, as indigenous people are generally very hospitable and a smile goes a long way.

Secondly, in indigenous areas there are often opportunities to interact with local people. Some have opened guesthouses, usually just a few spare rooms in or adjacent to their own homes. Guesthouse owners often serve as guides and can help tourists gain insights into the community's attractions and people. If

National Palace Museum The cream of the artistic output of one of the world's oldest and most accomplished civilisations. See page 106.

Tainan's Martial Rites Temple The most exquisite shrine in a city famous for temples, a place of supreme tranquillity and refinement. See page 218.

SUGGESTED ITINERARIES

Spend weekdays exploring the countryside, the mountains and little towns like Lugang and Danshui; spend weekends and national holidays in the major cities. Many scenic spots are all but deserted in the middle of the week; room rates are lower and there are some discounts on admission charges. Many museums close on Mondays.

A LONG WEEKEND As Asia-based Western expatriates are discovering, a long weekend in Taiwan is very feasible. Fly to Taipei for culture or Kaohsiung for outdoors adventure. The capital has more than enough shops, restaurants and museums to keep you out of mischief. For glimpses of tradition you needn't go beyond the city limits. Baoan and Longshan temples are among Taiwan's most interesting shrines. Dihua Street, where business is still done the way it was a hundred years ago, nicely counterpoints the city's department stores and boutiques. Central Kaohsiung has its attractions but if time's limited, speed away from the city,

you simply walk through the streets of the community, you'll often see residents chatting or barbecuing. Don't be surprised if you're invited to join in.

Thirdly, many indigenous community development associations are working to revive various aspects of their culture, such as the growing of millet, a traditional staple crop, or the production of handicrafts such as glass beads and wood carving. In addition, there are opportunities to see ceremonies that have been performed for centuries. During these times villages take on a festive atmosphere as those working and studying in urban areas return to join in. They wear traditional clothing and make use of traditional items, such as the Paiwan tribe's double drinking cup and the Saisiyat tribe's hip bells. Native-language ballads are sung and traditional dances performed. On the last night of some ceremonies, outsiders may be allowed to join the dance circle.

Fourthly, indigenous cuisine differs greatly from other cuisines in Taiwan. Traditionally, indigenous people hunted and fished and grew millet and taro root. They also gathered wild greens and flavoured their food with locally obtained herbs such as Aralia and mountain peppercorn. Restaurants in indigenous communities serve cuisine which includes local ingredients and is based on both traditional and modern preparation methods. All in all, indigenous villages offer unique experiences different from the rest of Taiwan, and are well worth adding to your itinerary.

Cheryl Robbins (e cheryl@tribe-asia.com) is a Taiwan-licensed tour guide originally from the US. She is the author of three guidebooks to Taiwan's indigenous areas and operates www.tribe-asia.com, which promotes local indigenous cultural products to international markets. Since 2013, she has been offering tour packages to Taiwan's indigenous areas.

2

either towards the hills, or down to the beaches and beautiful hinterland of Kenting National Park.

ONE WEEK Try to hit at least two but not more than three of the following: Taipei, Tainan, Taroko Gorge and somewhere in the high mountains. If you restrict yourself to the northwest, you'll probably be able to take in the woodcarving centre of Sanyi and possibly an indigenous village. Those staying in the south should get their own transport, and drive or ride towards Taitung on Highway 9. The return leg to Kaohsiung can be via Kenting National Park.

TWO WEEKS Ease yourself in with a full three days in and near your city of arrival, then rent a car or a motorcycle for a week so you can traverse the Central Mountain Range by whichever road is open and takes your fancy. When you reach the east coast stop at a hot springs if the weather's cool, a mountain creek if it isn't. Spend up to three days in Taroko Gorge. To find solitude or something close to it, arrive on Green Island or Orchid Island on a weekday. Consider hiking into the eastern part of Yushan National Park before heading back to western Taiwan by any mountain road you haven't already seen. If you've no intention of braving the roads, get to grips with the bus schedule or find a tour operator who can transport you to and around the hills. Do this because if you leave having seen only the places served by trains, you won't have seen the best of Taiwan.

TOUR OPERATORS

At long last, **tour companies in Western countries** are now realising what their counterparts in Japan and South Korea have known for years – that with a little explanation, Taiwan isn't a hard destination to sell.

Taiwan isn't always an easy country to explore. Language is often a problem and if you're going far from the major cities – which you should if you want to find the island's true flavours – comprehending bus schedules and finding food you like can be an exercise in frustration. Using a **local travel agent or tour guide** can smooth the way and will often save you money as well as time. Not only will they overcome the language barrier and steer you towards the best (but not necessarily most famous) attractions, they'll also know where in the back country you can find vegetarian food and even where there are toilets you can sit on as opposed to the kind you squat over.

The businesses listed under the 'Local travel agents and tour guides' heading cover several regions. Some can make arrangements for any part of the ROC. English-speaking tour guides specialising in one town or region are listed in the relevant chapters in the guide.

UK

Birdfinders Westbank Cheselbourne, Dorset DT2 7NW; ☎01258 839 066; e info@birdfinders. co.uk; www.birdfinders.co.uk. Their 13-day birdwatching trip (£3,495) includes Orchid Island, Kenting & high-altitude forests.
Black Tomato 1st Flr 40–42 Scrutton St, London, EC2A 4PP; ☎020 7426 9888; e info@blacktomato. co.uk; www.blacktomato.com. Offers 'Taipei Old & New' & 'Highland Adventures & Lakeside Retreat' plus options for foodies & art-lovers.

China Holidays 4 Glentworth St, London NW1 5PG; ☎020 7487 2999; e info@chinaholidays. co.uk; www.chinaholidays.co.uk. Offers a 15-day comprehensive tour (from £2,675) & can tailor itineraries for small groups.
Cox and Kings 6th Flr 30 Millbank, London, SW1P 4EE; ☎0845 564 8289; e sales@coxandkings.co.uk; www.coxandkings.co.uk. The 15-day/13-night 'Beautiful Island' tour includes the National Palace Museum & other Taipei sights, Alishan, Foguangshan & Zhiben. Prices start at £3,002.

Cultural Tours 320 Regent St, London W1B 3BB; ☎020 7636 7906; e info@culturaltours.co.uk; www.culturaltours.co.uk. Offers 4-day & 8-day itineraries that include rides on the bullet train & time in both Tainan & Kaohsiung.

Eastravel 79–81 Norwich Rd, Ipswich, Suffolk IP1 2PR; ☎01473 214 305; e reservations@eastravel. co.uk; www.eastravel.co.uk. Can tailor itineraries of various lengths inc self-drive trips.

Greentours Leigh Cottage, Gauledge Lane, Longnor, Buxton, Derbyshire SK17 0PA; ☎01298 83563; e enquiries@greentours.co.uk; www. greentours.co.uk. Organises tours which introduce Taiwan's fauna & flora.

The Oriental Caravan Dogwood Cottage, Brede, Rye TN31 6DY; ☎01424 883 570; e phil@ theorientalcaravan.com; www.theorientalcaravan. com. Small but highly rated outfit specialising in tours of Tibet, Japan & Taiwan. Their 14-day 'caravan' (from £1,845 excluding flights) is one of relatively few group tours to include Tainan.

Ours Travel 301 Euston Rd, London NW1 3AD; ☎020 7388 8955; e sales@ourstravel.com; www. ourstravel.com. Has a strong Taiwan focus & offers discounted air fares as well as tours & services to Taiwanese living or studying in the UK. Various options for those wanting short (2–5 days) tours of Taiwan.

US & CANADA

Absolute Travel 5th Flr 15 Watts St, New York, NY 10013; ☎212 627 1950; e info@absolutetravel. com; www.absolutetravel.com. Has itineraries for 4–9 days with an emphasis on culture & luxury.

All State Travel Inc 1608 S Nogales St, Rowland Heights, CA 91748; ☎626 854 1636; e customerservice@enjoyingtaiwan.com; www. enjoyingtaiwan.com. Offers cheap flights with stopovers in Beijing or Shanghai as well as tour packages lasting 5–9 days with an emphasis on Taiwan's eastern half.

Asia Classic Tours 481 8th Av, Suite 721, New York, NY 10001; ☎1800 717 7752; e sales@ asiaclassictours.com; www.asiaclassictours.com. Their 9-day 'Classic Taiwan' tour (from US$2,299 inc flights from Los Angeles or San Francisco) visits 7 very well-known sights.

Royal Scenic 750-5951 No 3 Rd, Richmond BC V6X 2E3; ☎604 270 1236; e info@royalscenic.com; www.royalscenic.com. Runs tours that combine Taiwan with Hong Kong, Shanghai or Tokyo.

AUSTRALIA

Formosa Travel & Holidays PO Box 2496, Bondi Junction, NSW 1355; ☎2 9369 1288; e info@ formosatravel.net; www.formosatravel.net. Offers various tours starting at AUS$860 for 6 days.

Taiwan Holidays Suite 92, 1st Flr 515 Kent St, Sydney, NSW 2000; ☎2 9267 1308; e sales@ taiwanholidays.com.au; www.taiwanholidays. com.au. Taiwanese-staffed agency with a wide range of transfers, stopovers & tours; other useful services include selling rail passes.

LOCAL TRAVEL AGENTS AND TOUR GUIDES

Barking Deer Adventures Richard Foster, PO Box 1452, Tainan 70499; m 0938 337 710; e barkingdeerinfo@gmail.com; www.barking-deer.com. Organises high-mountain hikes & less adventuresome tailor-made excursions.

Blue Skies Adventures (see advertisement, page 166) Mark Roche, 10th Flr 7, Lane 43, Jianan St, Kaohsiung; ☎07 389 0795; m 0982 858 316; e rochem@ksts.seed.net.tw; www. blueskiesadventures.com.tw. Has years of experience running high-mountain hikes & can help those wishing to join local triathlons & other events.

Cheryl Robbins m 0923 151 965; e cheryl@ tribe-asia.com. Originally from California, this ROC-licensed tour guide & travel writer specialises in Taiwan's indigenous areas & cultures.

Edison Travel Service 4th Flr 190 Songjiang Rd, Taipei; ☎02 2563 5313; f 02 2563 4803; e paul@ edison.com.tw; www.edison.com.tw. Regular tours with English-speaking guides. Can provide rentals with drivers & assist with hotel reservations & domestic & international flight bookings.

Golden Foundation Tours 5th Flr 142 Zhongxiao E Rd Sec 4, Taipei; ☎02 2773 3266; f 02 2772 3449; e gftour@gftours.com.tw; www.gftours.com.tw. This agency has partnered with some of Europe's major travel companies. Can help with hotel & public transport reservations, special-interest tours & conventions.

Hualien Outdoors (see advertisement, page 308) Matt Hopkins, 2-16 Guolian 5th Rd, Hualien; ☎03 833 9037; m 0989 512 380; e hualienoutdoors@ gmail.com; www.hualienoutdoors.org. This expat-run company runs river tracing & hiking trips in & around Hualien & Taroko Gorge National Park.

Life of Taiwan 9, Lane 38, Qianfong Rd, Tainan; ☎06 208 8173; m 0939 626 382; e contact@

lifeoftaiwan.com; http://lifeoftaiwan.com. Organises bespoke high-end tours for small groups interested in Taiwan's culture, food & natural attractions.

MyTaiwanTour 4th Flr 51 Changan E Rd Sec 2, Taipei; ✆ 02 2523 3881; e service@mytaiwantour. com; www.mytaiwantour.com. Professional English-speaking tour guides take you off the beaten path with 1- to 5-day packages that can be booked & paid for online.

RoundTaiwanRound 29 Fuyu 7th St, Hualien; ✆ 03 857 1005; m 0918 485 041; e service@ roundtaiwanround.com; http://rtaiwanr.com. Provides customised single- & multi-day trips with English-speaking guides throughout the country plus adventure tours, accommodation booking, car rental service & travel photography.

Taiwan Adventures (see advertisement, page 38) 9th Flr 628 Songshan Road, Taipei; ✆ 02 2346 5867; m 0983 212 499; e info@taiwan-adventures.com; www.taiwan-adventures.com. This Anglo-American company specialises in hiking, canyoning & rafting expeditions.

Taiwan Tea Tours 9, Lane 38, Qianfong Rd, Tainan; ✆ 06 208 8173; m 0939 626 382; e contact@ taiwanteatours.com; http://taiwanteatours. com. This sub-brand of Life of Taiwan (see above) specialises in tours for tea aficionados.

U-Dive Scuba Taiwan Club John Boo m 0913 388 065; e scuba_diving1@yahoo.com; www.udive.com.tw. Canadian-born PADI scuba instructor John Boo leads dives & teaches courses around the Kenting area.

WHOSE Travel Dale Mackie, 3rd Flr 106 Huamei W St Sec 1, Taichung; ✆ 04 2326 5191; e flights@ whosetravel.com; www.whosetravel.com. Very helpful English-speaking travel agent who can arrange local tours in Taiwan or assist if you're planning to go on to other countries in Asia after Taiwan.

TOURIST INFORMATION

Taiwan's **Tourism Bureau** (*www.taiwan.net.tw*) administers the country's 13 national scenic areas. The ROC's national parks are run by the Ministry of the Interior, while forest recreation areas come under the aegis of the Forestry Bureau, part of the Council of Agriculture. There's no official tourism representative in the UK.

Because **local visitor information centres and travel service centres** are run by various organisations, among them national scenic areas and local governments, service quality and information accuracy – not to mention English ability – is uneven. At a minimum, you should be able to get bilingual maps and leaflets about the area; at best they'll answer all your transport queries and even telephone homestays on your behalf. See page 90 for centres based in the capital.

OVERSEAS

⚑ Germany Taipei Tourism Office, Rheinstrasse 29, 60325 Frankfurt; ✆ +49 69 610 743; e info@ taiwantourismus.de; www.taiwantourismus.de

⚑ Hong Kong Taiwan Visitors Association, Room 1010, 10th Flr, Silvercord Tower 2, 30 Canton Road, Tsimshatsui, Kowloon; ✆ +852 2581 0933; e info@ tva.hk; www.welcome2taiwan.net

⚑ Japan Taiwan Visitors Association, 3rd Flr, Kawate Bldg, 1-5-8 Nishi-Shinbashi, Minato-Ku, Tokyo 105-0003; ✆ +81 3 3501 3591; e tokyo@ go-taiwan.net; www.go-taiwan.net

⚑ Malaysia Taiwan Visitors Association, Suite 25-01, Level 25, Wisma Goldhill, 67 Jalan Raja Chulan, 50200 Kuala Lumpur; ✆ +60 3 2070 6789; e tva@streamyx.com; www.welcome2taiwan.net

⚑ Singapore Taiwan Visitors Association, 30 Raffles Place, 10-01 Chevron House, Singapore 048622; ✆ +65 6223 6546; e tbrocsin@signet. com.sg; www.welcome2taiwan.net

⚑ US Tourism Representative, 9th Flr, 1 East 42nd St, New York, NY 10017; ✆ +1 212 867 1632; e tbrocnyc@gmail.com; www.go2taiwan.net

RED TAPE

Nationals of the UK, USA, Canada, Ireland, Japan, New Zealand and more than 20 other European countries can stay in the ROC for up to 90 days without a visa.

Australians, Malaysians and Singaporeans can stay for up to 30 days. As well as tourists, visa-free entry can be used by those coming for business reasons or to receive medical treatment. However, if you're intending to work, teach or engage in missionary activities, you should contact an ROC embassy or representative office well in advance to find out what kind of visa you should apply for. See the Bureau of Consular Affairs website (*www.boca.gov.tw*) for information about visa-free entry, visa fees and online application forms.

CUSTOMS REGULATIONS Taiwan's customs regulations are similar to those of other countries. Cold War-era rules barring visitors from bringing in newspapers or books printed in communist China were scrapped years ago. These days, the authorities are more worried about people returning from China with pirated goods or prohibited food items.

If you've more than a litre of alcoholic drinks, 200 cigarettes, 25 cigars or a pound of tobacco, declare it when you enter the ROC. You shouldn't bring in more than US$20,000 in gold or US$10,000 in cash (or the equivalent in travellers' cheques or other foreign currencies) or more than NTD60,000 in Taiwanese money. For Chinese currency, the limit is RMB20,000. Full details are available at www.customs.gov.tw.

There's a **tax-refund system** for foreign visitors who shop at participating stores. If you spend more than NTD3,000 in a single day at any of these shops no more than 30 days before your departure, and you take the items with you when you leave Taiwan, you can reclaim the 5% VAT at the airport prior to boarding your flight. The list of participating shops includes department stores and electronics shops.

DIPLOMATIC REPRESENTATION

Overseas Taiwan has formal diplomatic links with fewer than 30 countries, so just a handful of its overseas representative offices are called embassies or consulates. A complete list together with addresses & contact details is available at www.taiwanembassy.org. To placate Beijing, most countries call their diplomatic outposts in Taiwan 'trade offices' or similar.

Australia Taipei Economic & Cultural Office in Australia, 3rd Flr, Unit 8, 40 Blackall St Barton, Canberra, ACT 2600; +61 2 6120 2000; e tecoaus@gmail.com

Canada Taipei Economic & Cultural Office, Canada, 45 O'Connor St, Suite 1960, Ottawa, Ontario K1P 1A4; +1 613 231 5080; e teco@taiwan-canada.org

France Le Bureau de Représentation de Taipei en France, 78 Rue de l'Université, 75007 Paris; +33 1 44 39 88 20; e fra@boca.gov.tw

Germany Taipeh Vertretung in der Bundesrepublik Deutschland, Markgrafenstrasse 35, 10117 Berlin; +49 30 203 610; e roc.taiwan@gmx.de

Ireland Taipei Representative Office in Ireland, 8 Lower Hatch St, Dublin 2; +353 1 678 5413; e tpeire@eircom.net

UK Taipei Representative Office in the UK, 50 Grosvenor Gdns, London SW1W 0EB; 020 7881 2650; e tro@taiwan-tro.uk.net

US Taipei Economic & Cultural Representative Office in the US, 4201 Wisconsin Av, NW, Washington, DC 20016; +1 202 895 1800; e tecroinfodc@tecro.us

Taiwan (all in Taipei)

Australia Australian Commerce & Industry Office, 27th Flr 9–11 Songgao Rd; 02 8725 4100; www.australia.org.tw

Canada Canadian Trade Office, 1 Songzhi Rd; 02 8723 3000; e tapei@international.gc.ca; www.canada.org.tw

France French Institute, 10th Flr 205 Dunhua N Rd; 02 3518 5151; e taipei-ift.afe@diplomatie.gouv.fr; www.fi-taipei.org

Germany German Trade Office, Unit 9, 19th Flr 333 Keelung Rd Sec 1; 02 8758 5800; e info@taiwan.ahk.de; www.taiwan.ahk.de

⊖ Ireland Institute for Trade & Investment of Ireland, Room 12, 7th Flr 41 Nanjing W Rd; ☏02 2552 6101; e ititpe@ms8.hinet.net; www. idaireland.com

⊖ UK British Trade & Cultural Office, 26th Flr 9–11 Songgao Rd; ☏02 8758 2088; e info.

taipei@fco.gov.uk; http://ukintaiwan.fco.gov. uk/en/

⊖ US American Institute in Taiwan, 7, Lane 134, Xinyi Rd Sec 3; ☏02 2162 2000; e Taipei@mail.ait. org.tw; www.ait.org.tw

GETTING THERE AND AWAY

Taiwan makes for a good stopover if you're flying between Australia and Japan or South Korea or from North America to Singapore or Malaysia.

BY AIR The bulk of scheduled international flights land at Taiwan Taoyuan International Airport near Taipei or Kaohsiung International Airport. Some direct flights between Taiwan and the Chinese mainland (which are classed as neither full international flights nor domestic flights) land at Taichung and Taipei Songshan Airport.

Airlines
From the UK
✈ **Cathay Pacific** ☏020 8834 8800; www. cathaypacific.com. Flies Heathrow to Hong Kong 4 times daily, from where passengers have several options daily on to Taoyuan & Kaohsiung.

✈ **China Eastern Airlines** ☏020 7935 2676; www.chinaeastern.co.uk. At the time of writing, this PRC carrier was offering inexpensive tickets from London Heathrow to Taiwan, connecting in Shanghai.

✈ **EVA Air** ☏020 7380 8300; www.evaair.com. The better of Taiwan's airlines flies from London Heathrow to Taoyuan via Bangkok daily.

✈ **Malaysia Airlines** ☏020 7341 2000; www. malaysiaairlines.com. One of the cheaper carriers & with great stopover potential. Flights are non stop to Kuala Lumpur.

✈ **Singapore Airlines** ☏0844 800 2380; www. singaporeair.com. You'll arrive in Singapore from London Heathrow in the late afternoon & have to wait until the following morning to fly on to Taoyuan. At Singapore you could change to Taiwan's flag-carrier China Airlines if you want to arrive in Kaohsiung rather than Taoyuan.

From the Irish Republic
There aren't any direct flights to Taiwan from Ireland. An alternative to connecting at London Heathrow is KLM:

✈ **KLM** ☏0818 776 100; www.klm.com. Flies from Dublin with connections in Amsterdam

& Hong Kong. Return fares below €950 are sometimes available.

From the rest of Europe
✈ **China Airlines** www.china-airlines.com. Has about 20 flights each week between Taoyuan & Amsterdam, Frankfurt, Rome & Vienna.

✈ **EVA Air** www.evaair.com. Flies from Amsterdam, Paris (up to 4 times per week) & Vienna to Taoyuan.

From China
Direct flights across the Taiwan Strait are with PRC airlines or Taiwan's China Airlines, EVA Air & 3 minor carriers. The PRC airlines & related agents include:

✈ **Air China** ☏4008 100 999; www.airchina. com.cn

✈ **China Eastern Airlines** ☏8621 95530; www. ce-air.com

✈ **China Southern Airlines** ☏8620 95539; www.csair.com/en/

✈ **TravelZen** ☏+886 22546 6345; www. travelzen.com. This Taiwan-based agent has a good bilingual website through which tickets between the island & mainland can be booked.

From the US and Canada
✈ **China Airlines** ☏1800 227 5118; www.china-airlines.com. Flies from New York JFK, Los Angeles, San Francisco, Honolulu, Vancouver & Anchorage to Taoyuan.

✈ **EVA Air** ✆1800 695 1188; www.evaair.com.
Flies non stop from New York, Los Angeles, San
Francisco, Seattle, Toronto & Vancouver to Taoyuan.
✈ **United Airlines** ✆1 800 538 2929; www.
united.com. Flies from the US west coast to
Taoyuan via Tokyo.

**From Australia and New
Zealand** Cheaper options (below AU$1,000
return) include:

✈ **Garuda Indonesia** ✆02 9334 9900; www.
garuda-indonesia.com
✈ **China Southern Airlines** ✆02 9233 9788;
www.csair.com/en/

Main airports

Taiwan Taoyuan International Airport (TPE) Taiwan's busiest airport, 28km
due west of Taipei, is where long-haul flights land. It's a reasonably smart and well-
equipped airport and not intimidatingly huge. For details of transport to and from
the airport, changing money and car hire, see *Chapter 4*, page 115.

Kaohsiung International Airport (KHH) This modest-sized airport is
properly staffed so you can be sure of getting through customs and immigration
quickly and then on to Tainan or Kenting. For details see *Chapter 8*, page 244.

BY SEA The number of visitors arriving by sea has jumped and there are now
several regular ferry services between Taiwan and the Chinese mainland, including
from Keelung (see page 134), Kinmen (see page 319), Taichung Harbour and Bali
near Taipei. A number of cruise companies drop anchor in Keelung for a day when
sailing between Beijing or Shanghai and Hong Kong, among them:

Costa Cruises www.costacruise.com
Oceania Cruises www.oceaniacruises.com
Princess Cruises www.princess.com
Regent Seven Seas www.rssc.com

Royal Caribbean International www.
royalcaribbean.com
Yachts of Seabourn www.seabourn.com

HEALTH *with Dr Felicity Nicholson*

Taiwan is a healthy place but visitors should take some precautions, including
taking out adequate insurance before leaving home.

INOCULATIONS No vaccinations are required except yellow fever, and then only if
you're coming from an infected area such as sub-Saharan Africa or South America.
It is wise to be up to date with standard vaccinations including diphtheria, tetanus
and polio given in the UK as one vaccine (Revaxis), and also measles, mumps and
rubella. Vaccination against hepatitis A, typhoid and possibly hepatitis B and Japanese
encephalitis are advisable depending on your length of stay. Taiwan has a high
prevalence of hepatitis B in the population so vaccination would be recommended
for those working in medical settings and with children. It is also recommended for
those playing contact sports or indulging in risky behaviour. The course comprises
three vaccines given over a minimum of 21 days for those aged 16 and over. Younger
travellers require a minimum of 8 weeks to be vaccinated effectively. The Japanese
encephalitis vaccine (Ixiaro) consists of two doses ideally given one month apart, so
ensure that you have enough time if you need this vaccine. It's recommended for
those staying in rural parts of the country. Taiwan has one of the highest incidences
of hepatitis A in the world. One dose of hepatitis A vaccine will provide cover for one
year and can then be boosted to extend protection to around 25 years.

RABIES After half a century with no cases, rabies reemerged in Taiwan in 2013. Almost all recent cases have been in ferret-badgers (*Melogale moschata*), but there has been a case in a puppy that was bitten by a ferret-badger. So far there have been no human infections, but if you're bitten or scratched by any mammal do seek medical treatment as soon as possible.

MALARIA Mosquitoes can be a threat. Taiwan long ago eradicated malaria but there are sometimes outbreaks of dengue fever, usually in the south. Dengue fever is transmitted by day-biting mosquitoes and there is no vaccine or tablet to prevent it. DEET-based insect repellents (50–55% DEET) should be used on all exposed skin day and night.

FOOD PREPARATION AND DRINKING WATER Individuals with delicate stomachs should be OK if they exercise common sense. Night markets and roadside eateries

LONG-HAUL FLIGHTS, CLOTS AND DVT   *Dr Felicity Nicholson*

Any prolonged immobility, including travel by land or air, can result in deep-vein thrombosis (DVT) with the risk of embolus to the lungs. Certain factors can increase the risk and these include:

* Previous clot or a close relative with a history
* Being over 40, with increased risk over 80 years old
* Recent major operation or varicose-veins surgery
* Cancer
* Stroke
* Heart disease
* Obesity
* Pregnancy
* Hormone therapy
* Heavy smoking
* Severe varicose veins
* Being very tall (over 6ft/1.8m) or short (under 5ft/1.5m)

A deep-vein thrombosis causes painful swelling and redness of the calf or sometimes the thigh. It is only dangerous if a clot travels to the lungs (pulmonary embolus). Symptoms of a pulmonary embolus (PE) – which commonly start three to ten days after a long flight – include chest pain, shortness of breath, and sometimes coughing up small amounts of blood. Anyone who thinks that they might have a DVT needs to see a doctor immediately.

PREVENTION OF DVT
* Keep mobile before and during the flight; move around every couple of hours.
* Drink plenty of fluids during the flight.
* Avoid taking sleeping pills and excessive tea, coffee and alcohol.
* Consider wearing flight socks or support stockings.
* If you think you are at increased risk of a clot, ask your doctor if it is safe to travel.

aren't necessarily less sanitary than proper restaurants. If a place looks popular, that's usually a sign that the food is clean as well as tasty. Also, high turnover means food isn't left lying around.

Almost every hotel and homestay provides boiled tap water free of charge for guests. This is what most Taiwanese people drink, though it's debatable whether it's good for you long term. For short-term visitors, however, it's an acceptable alternative to buying mineral water.

ENVIRONMENTAL FACTORS Because of the high population density, coughs and colds sometimes spread quickly; this is why many Taiwanese wear masks on trains and in other crowded places. If you visit during the hot season, do always carry with you a long-sleeved shirt or cardigan. If you're sightseeing in a city you'll find yourself constantly entering and leaving air-conditioned areas and the temperature changes may give you a chill. In the countryside, be prepared for big differences between midday and late afternoon temperatures.

In regions with heavy industry and lots of motor vehicles, such as parts of Kaohsiung, **air quality** is often an issue, especially in the dry winter months. Secondhand smoke is a very minor problem; smoking is now barred in restaurants, pubs and other enclosed places.

CLINICS AND PHARMACIES In small towns and cities you'll find plenty of clinics (⊕ *09.00–12.00 & 15.00–20.00 daily*). Many doctors but few other health professionals speak English. In major hospitals they'll probably assign an English-speaker to see you to the right department. Prescription medicines are dispensed on site.

Major hospitals also have commercial pharmacies where you can buy over-the-counter medicines, aspirin, contraceptives and other items.

A full list of current **travel clinic websites** worldwide is available on www.istm. org. For other journey preparation information, consult www.nathnac.org/ds/map_world.aspx (UK) or http://wwwnc.cdc.gov/travel/ (US). Information about various medications may be found on www.netdoctor.co.uk/travel. All advice found online should be used in conjunction with expert advice received prior to or during travel.

PAYING FOR TREATMENT At clinics and hospitals you'll be expected to pay a registration fee before seeing the doctor, and for any medicines immediately afterwards. Bring your passport and cash as few places accept credit cards. Treatment is inexpensive by European standards and an absolute bargain compared with the US. You'll be given a receipt but it might be entirely in Chinese. At major hospitals they'll be able to provide you with a document in English which you can submit when making an insurance claim.

PUBLIC TOILETS The good news is that Taiwan has plenty of public toilets, they're almost always free and they're generally quite clean. You'll find them in parks, petrol stations, railway stations and temples. The bad news is that some toilets are marked in Chinese only and toilet paper and soap are seldom provided. Carry your own, like the Taiwanese do. Also, you should get used to using squat-style toilets, which are standard outside the major cities. Squatting is more hygienic and said to be better for your bowels. If you can't or won't use this kind of plumbing fixture, seek out a bathroom in a department store or fast-food restaurant. If there's a wastepaper basket next to the toilet, put used toilet paper and sanitary items in it, not in the toilet. In many older buildings the plumbing may get blocked if you toss paper down the toilet. Also, many guesthouses and hotels in the countryside have septic tanks instead of sewer connections, and these systems don't deal with paper well. Consider carrying alcohol swabs or some kind of sanitising gel. These are useful for cleaning your hands if you come across a tap that's run dry (this sometimes happens on trains) as well as wiping cutlery before eating or the tops of soda cans before drinking.

SAFETY

Taiwan is one of the world's safest countries for tourists. Street crime isn't a big issue, even late at night, and there's little danger of being harassed by a drunk. That said, homeowners do take precautions against burglary – hence the metal bars over windows and balconies – and pickpockets work festival and night-market crowds.

Traffic is the major threat to your well-being. Be very careful when crossing roads. Don't just look both ways, look in every direction as two wheelers often use the pavements or pedestrian crossings. There are two reasons why self-driving visitors should think twice before stopping at what appears to be the aftermath of a traffic accident: lawsuits and robberies. If you take an individual to hospital, you may later be held responsible for their death or injuries. Also, criminals have been known to stage fake-crash scenes on quiet country roads and beg passing drivers to stop. Good Samaritans have, for their trouble, been robbed and had their vehicles stolen.

The Foreign Office (*www.fco.gov.uk/travel*) is overcautious when it advises visitors to steer clear of political demonstrations. Such events are almost always good-natured. The main danger, if you can call it that, is being buttonholed by someone eager to expound on their cause.

NATURAL HAZARDS Taiwan suffers both earthquakes and typhoons but these shouldn't stop you visiting. If you cycle or hike in the lowlands or the foothills, keep an eye out for aggressive dogs. If you're confronted by one, pick up a stone or some gravel. In the countryside you should also be wary of but not paranoid about snakes (six poisonous species are fairly common) and hornets. The latter have been known to kill people.

POLICE Taiwan's police force (↘ *110*) doesn't have a stellar reputation for efficiency or enforcement but as a foreign visitor you can expect courtesy and assistance. All police stations are marked in English as well as Chinese. Few officers speak good English but if you go into a larger station you've a much better chance of finding someone who can communicate.

IN AN EMERGENCY Call ↘ 110 for police or ↘ 119 if there's a fire or an ambulance is needed. Operators may not understand English, so you may prefer to call the 24-hour 'information for foreigners' hotline (↘ *0800 024 111*).

WOMEN TRAVELLERS

Apart from being careful when taking taxis by themselves late at night, female tourists needn't take any exceptional precautions. Western women rate Taiwan highly in terms of hassle-free travelling.

GAY/LESBIAN TRAVELLERS

Attitudes to homosexuality have changed dramatically in the past two decades. Before the late 1990s most Taiwanese regarded it either as a psychiatric problem, something that occurs only in other countries or 'a phase' that a few mixed-up individuals go through when they're young. That said, gay-bashing has never been an issue and homosexuals seldom attracted police attention, even during the repressive martial-law period described by Pai Hsien-yung in his 1983 novel *Crystal Boys*. Nowadays there are gay venues in the major cities and an annual gay-pride parade in Taipei. However, gay men still face immense pressure from traditional parents to marry and continue the family line; the consequences of this form the basis of Ang Lee's 1993 film *The Wedding Banquet*. A bill allowing same-sex marriages has been drafted but not passed; discrimination in education or employment on the grounds of a person's sexual orientation is now illegal. However, very few prominent individuals have come out.

Local gay organisations include the Taiwan Tongzhi Hotline Association (*www. hotline.org.tw*). English speakers will find www.travelgayasia.com useful.

TRAVELLING WITH CHILDREN

Taiwan is a safe and welcoming destination for travellers with children. In restaurants, temples and shops, Taiwanese people show great tolerance towards kids who are noisy or fidgety. Children with Western features attract plenty of positive attention. Parents must, of course, take steps to protect their children against Taiwan's traffic, strong sunshine and mosquitoes, but in terms of food, cleanliness and general public health, Taiwan isn't a dangerous place.

If you plan to use a pushchair for any distance, be prepared for obstacle courses. In many places in urban Taiwan the pavement isn't flat or doesn't exist at all. Also, it isn't unusual for shopkeepers to pile so much merchandise on the pavement that pedestrians are forced to detour into the road. Parents with babies will find there are few diaper-changing stations except those at department stores, hypermarkets, mass rapid-transit (MRT) stations and some train stations.

Anyone with a young child knows it's essential to bring an extra set of clothes, including shoes, when going away from your base for more than a few hours. Taiwan's countryside has lot of places where kids can play safely – but they're likely to get dusty, muddy or sweaty. Making sure your children stay hydrated is also important, and this is another area in which Taiwan's 24/7 shopping culture is a boon for travellers. Even the smallest towns have convenience stores that stock milk and juices as well as mineral water, not to mention snacks that can help fill the stomachs of youngsters unimpressed by local cuisine.

Finding child-friendly accommodation is sometimes an issue. Five-star hotels and top-end resorts are invariably safe and comfortable, but may not match your budget and may not exist near your destination. Hotels in city centres are convenient but rooms are often small and sometimes noisy. Moreover, parents putting teenage children in a separate room may have cause for concern when they turn on the television: one or more channels may be devoted to hardcore pornography. The recent explosion in homestays is a boon for travellers with children. Unfortunately, many of these places are like ordinary Taiwanese homes in that they have tiled floors – hard surfaces for an infant to take a tumble on. Few homestays have elevators, which can be a problem if you're upstairs and your kids are still in pushchairs. Wherever you're staying, careful examination of your room

2

The steps visitors to Taiwan should take to minimise the environmental impact of their trip aren't so different from what travellers everywhere should be doing. When you make a purchase, refuse excess packaging. Separate your rubbish so as much as possible can be recycled; if you're unsure what kind of trash goes into which bin – few litter bins have bilingual labels – then ask. Use public transport wherever possible and, to save on 'food miles', eat local produce rather than imported foods. If you want to practise 'sustainable eating', you should avoid fish and sea creatures which are critical to reef ecosystems.

There are a few additional ways in which you can make a difference. Food and drink vendors in Taiwan tend to wrap every purchase in a fresh plastic bag. Energy is used to produce these and many of them end up on the roadside; if they do make it into the rubbish-processing system, more likely than not they'll be incinerated, a method of disposal that produces cancer-causing dioxins. Do reuse any bags you accumulate.

Carry your own reusable chopsticks and spoon (or knife and fork) rather than use disposable utensils made of bamboo or plastic. Environmentalists have been pleased to notice that in the past few years more and more restaurants have been providing proper cutlery that can be reused. Take your own cup to avoid the need for a new one every time you buy a drink from a roadside stall. In hot weather you should consume lots of liquids. Rather than buying several bottles of mineral water each day, bring a canteen and refill it at public water fountains. These can be found in most bus and train stations plus many temples. Not using more water than you need when bathing and washing clothes is especially important as – you may find this hard to believe if you're visiting during the wet summer months – Taiwan often suffers water shortages. Rainfall per square kilometre is more than three times the global average, but because of Taiwan's dense population, per capita precipitation is less than one-eighth of the world's average.

as soon as you get inside is advisable. Childproofing your hotel room is much the same as childproofing your home, and some parents may want to take along safety devices such as cupboard latches.

On both high-speed and conventional trains, very young kids can travel for free if they don't need a seat, and primary-school-age youngsters can get half-price tickets. Few taxis are equipped with child-safety seats, but car-rental companies say they can provide them if given some notice. If you do drive yourself, make use of the rest stations along the freeways. They're family-friendly places with playgrounds and other distractions.

DISABLED TRAVELLERS

Taiwan isn't the world's most wheelchair-friendly society, but it's come a long way in recent years. Public buildings and larger hotels almost always have ramp access. However, where pavements do exist, obstacles (parked cars, moving motorcycles, street vendors) often force wheelchair users out into the road. On the plus side, disabled people qualify for discounted train and bus tickets.

Physically challenged travellers are advised to take trains rather than buses wherever possible, as railway workers have been trained to give assistance to the disabled and visually impaired as they get on and off trains. Tipping for this service is not necessary or expected.

WHAT TO TAKE

There's very little you can't buy in Taiwan, but when deciding what and how many clothes to bring, bear in mind that Taiwanese people are generally shorter and thinner than Westerners, so you may not find something in your size. Even if you're coming during the hot season, do bring a light jacket, cardigan or shawl – something that's easy to put on and take off – as you'll probably be entering and leaving air-conditioned buildings several times a day. Winter visitors should be prepared for surprisingly low temperatures indoors as well as outside. Even in the mountains, there are plenty of hotels without any sort of heating. Bring multiple layers rather than thick sweaters, as between breakfast and early afternoon the mercury may rise by as much as 15°C.

Good walking shoes are essential for urban and rural exploring. Very few Taiwanese temples expect visitors to remove their footwear, so don't worry if your favourite boots require a lot of lacing. If you're not bringing sandals, consider buying a cheap pair while in Taiwan for evening trips to the convenience store and times when your feet need fresh air.

ELECTRICITY

Taiwan's domestic electricity supply is 110v/60Hz. Plugs are American-style and have two parallel flat prongs. Adaptors can be bought from electrical-goods shops or borrowed from hotels.

MONEY

Taiwan's currency is the New Taiwan dollar, abbreviated throughout this guidebook as NTD. In Mandarin, NT dollars are called *táibì*. When quoting a price, however, most people use the word *kuài*, as in *yī bǎi kuài* (NTD100).

The NTD comes in banknotes of 100, 200, 500, 1,000 and 2,000, and coins of 0.5, 1, 5, 10, 20 and 50. The NTD0.5, NTD1 and NTD50 coins are copper; the NTD20 has a bronze ring and cupro-nickel centre; the NTD5 and NTD10 coins are cupro-nickel. The NTD200 and NTD2,000 notes and NTD20 coin are seldom used and the NTD0.5 coin is extremely rare.

PEOPLE AND PEAKS IN YOUR WALLET

The head on the NTD1, 5 and 10 coins belongs to Chiang Kai-shek. The NTD20 coin shows aboriginal chieftain Mona Rudao (see *History*, page 16) and Tao canoes from Orchid Island. The NTD50 coin shows Sun Yat-sen, who also appears on the NTD100 note. The NTD200 note bears a likeness of Chiang Kai-shek together with the Presidential Office. The higher denomination notes have non-political images. The NTD500 features youngsters playing baseball, sika deer and Mount Dabajian. One side of the NTD1,000 shows a group of schoolchildren examining a globe; the other has a mikado pheasant in the foreground and the main peak of Mount Jade. The NTD2,000 note shows a locally made space satellite, the Formosan landlocked salmon (see box, page 200) and Mount Nanhu.

Keeping a pocketful of coins is a good idea as bus journeys usually have to be paid for with exact change, and sometimes taxi drivers aren't able to break large-denomination notes.

EXCHANGING MONEY AND TRAVELLERS' CHEQUES Outside of banks, major post offices and big hotels, your money-changing options are very limited. Unlike in some other Asian countries, money-changing kiosks are almost unknown in Taiwan. Some department stores are able to change US dollars, euros, Japanese yen and Chinese RMB. When buying NT dollars, you're likely to get a better rate of exchange in Taiwan than in your home country, so consider waiting until you've arrived and then changing money at the airport. The banks in Taoyuan and Kaohsiung airports keep very long hours for the convenience of international travellers.

CASH MACHINES Most of Taiwan's ATMs give you the option of Chinese or English instructions. Many but not all accept debit cards or credit cards issued overseas, so carrying enough cash to see you through the day is always a good idea. If you're heading somewhere remote – such as an island or a mountain village – take enough for that segment of your holiday.

CREDIT CARDS Do bring your credit cards as you'll find them very useful in major hotels, better restaurants and for buying train tickets. Credit cards tend not to be accepted in small eateries or homestays.

DISCOUNT CARDS If you have an International Student Identity Card, bring it. You'll get discounts at museums, forest recreation areas and other places.

BANKS Except for branches in the international airports, all banks keep the same opening hours, 09.00–15.30, Monday to Friday, and most offer foreign exchange services. If it's after 15.30 and you need to change money, try a major hotel or a department store. Differences in terms of exchange rates are minimal, so don't waste time walking from one bank to another comparing rates. Three of the largest local banks are: **Mega International Commercial Bank (Mega)** (*www.megabank. com.tw*), **Bank of Taiwan** (*www.bot.com.tw*) – not to be confused with Taiwan's central bank – and **First Bank** (*www.firstbank.com.tw*).

BUDGETING

Taiwan isn't nearly as expensive for travellers as destinations such as western Europe or Japan, but nor is it as inexpensive as southeast Asia. Public transport and eating out are bargains; accommodation will probably account for over half of your daily expenditure.

SCRIMPING If you take advantage of discounted intercity bus tickets, stay in cheaper hotels and hostels and eat what local people eat, a couple could spend less than NTD2,500 per day and still have a most enjoyable trip.

MODEST A daily budget of NTD2,000 per person is enough for reasonable hotel or homestay accommodation, transport that's convenient (such as occasionally renting a motorcycle), tickets to all the museums and other attractions you'd like to see, plus some upmarket meals.

At many attractions in Taiwan, including museums and forest recreation areas, senior citizens, full-time students (adults and children) and disabled people quality for half-price tickets. Throughout Part Two of this book, if more than one admission price is listed, the first is for standard entry while the second is the discounted rate for people in those categories. Sometimes a third, even cheaper ticket price is listed. This is unlikely to apply to foreign visitors; often it's for servicemen and police officers only. University students should show their student ID when asking for discounted tickets; seniors who look youthful should have their passports ready.

LUXURY Renting a car or paying a local tour operator to show you exactly what you want to see will greatly enhance your Taiwan experience. Jumping in and out of taxis in places like Tainan can save lots of time and isn't likely to add more than NTD800 to your day's spending. If you're happy to fork out NTD5,000 or more per night on hotels, you'll be able to stay in establishments which aren't just comfortable places to sleep but which add an extra layer of enjoyment and relaxation to your trip. Eating out is seldom expensive, so even gourmands and those who require Western meals are unlikely to spend more than NTD1,000 per person per day on food.

TIPPING There's very little tipping in Taiwan. Many visitors like this; others say the lack of incentive is a major reason why service is sometimes less than polished. When using a porter at an airport, it's usual to tip NTD100 per piece of luggage moved. Many upmarket restaurants and hotels add a 10% service charge; there's no need to add anything more.

GETTING AROUND

Public transport in Taiwan is safe, inexpensive, reliable and comfortable. Smoking is not permitted on buses or trains or inside stations. Foreign visitors may encounter language problems, but the information in this guidebook combined with the kindness of many Taiwanese (both transport workers and passing strangers) should ensure you get from one place to another smoothly. When taking any kind of bus or train, don't lose your ticket, as you'll need to show it – or run it through a machine – at your destination. Senior citizens holding discounted tickets on account of their age may be asked to provide ID showing their date of birth.

BY AIR Tourists are likely to fly only if they're heading to the east or one of the outlying islands. If weather conditions are right, flying Taipei–Taitung or Kaohsiung–Hualien is worth every penny of the fare for the stirring views you'll get of Taiwan's mountains and coastline. Flight times and ticket prices are listed in Part Two of this book; fares are likely to rise again early in 2014.

BY FERRY The boats that link Taiwan's mainland island with Penghu County, the Matsu Islands, Green Island and Orchid Island are a good option if you have plenty of time or dislike flying. There's no civilian boat service to Kinmen County. If you're heading to Little Liuqiu, the ferry from Donggang is your only option. Short-distance boat journeys include Danshui–Bali and the ferry to Kaohsiung's Cijin Island.

Vast amounts of energy have been devoted to the romanisation question: how should Taiwan render Chinese place names in the Latin alphabet? The issue boils down to this: should it use the system invented in the PRC and adopted by the UN, *hanyu pinyin*, or should it use a home-grown system called *tongyong pinyin*? The 'greens' (see box, page 22) favour tongyong pinyin whereas the 'blues' support the adoption of hanyu pinyin. However, the government hasn't gone the whole way. The names of major cities haven't changed even when the current spelling differs from the hanyu pinyin version. Taipei will remain Taipei; under hanyu pinyin it should be Taibei. Kaohsiung will stay spelled that way, even though in hanyu pinyin it's rendered Gaoxiong.

Throughout this book I've used hanyu pinyin except for those places already known outside Taiwan by another spelling (Taroko Gorge and Hsinchu, for instance) and a few places consistently spelled in a special way (such as certain aboriginal villages). The pronunciation guide that appears in parentheses after the name of each place or attraction is always hanyu pinyin.

Spelling mistakes sometimes appear on road signs and on leaflets given out to foreign tourists. Inconsistencies are rife: what one website labels Nanhu Big Mountain may elsewhere be spelled Nanhudashan (*dà* is Mandarin for big, *shān* means mountain). Common alternative spellings (such as Tamsui for Danshui) are noted in Part Two. Sometimes a little imagination helps: if you suspect that Banqiao, Banciao and Panchiao are the same place, you'd be right.

BY TRAIN Taiwan has two railway systems, TRA and HSR.

Taiwan Railway Administration (TRA) The TRA is the government-owned

conventional railway network. The Keelung–Kaohsiung line, by far the busiest part of the network, is divided into 'mountain' and 'ocean' routes. Just south of Hsinchu, the railroad splits: the Mountain Line goes inland via Miaoli and Sanyi, while the Ocean Line hugs the coast and bypasses Taichung. Trains to east Taiwan take the North Link via Yilan or the South Link via Pingtung. Branch lines serve Pingxi in New Taipei City, Neiwan near Hsinchu and Jiji in Nantou County. There are also useful short rail links between the TRA and HSR stations in Tainan and Hsinchu. Fares depend on distance and the type of train. A journey during rush hour is no more expensive than travelling off-peak but you may have to stand up. Over short distances TRA services are often quicker than buses. Over long distances, intercity buses are faster and cheaper.

Train types Trains are classed as Tze-Chiang (TC), Chu-Kuang (CK) or local services. TC and CK services are expresses covering long distances but making relatively few stops. Local trains stop at all or almost all stations along shorter routes. At the time of writing, the one-way fare between Taipei and Kaohsiung was NTD843 by TC (*typically takes 4¾hrs*) and NTD650 by CK (*takes 6–7hrs*). Local trains are considerably cheaper: Kaohsiung–Chiayi by TC (*takes 1¼hrs*) is NTD245; by local train (*takes 2hrs*) it's NTD158.

Getting tickets In many stations one ticket window (⊕ *usually 06.00–23.00 daily*) is marked 'For English'. Before approaching the clerk, it's a good idea to write down the romanised name of the station you want to go to and the departure time.

When you buy tickets for an express train, seat reservations are made automatically at no extra charge. If no seats are available, the clerk will tell you and may suggest a later train. If you stick to your original plan, your ticket will be marked 'no seat' but you can search for a space once you're on board.

You can buy tickets for express services up to 12 days in advance from any station, not only the station you'll be departing from. Buying tickets ahead of time is no cheaper than getting them at the last minute, but it's a good idea if you plan to travel at the weekend or on a national holiday. Getting a round-trip ticket is slightly cheaper than buying two one-way tickets. Credit cards are accepted. Tickets bought from a clerk have all the pertinent information in both English and Chinese.

Tickets bought from vending machines are in Chinese only and do not come with seat reservations. If you're in a rush and there's a long line for tickets, get a ticket from a vending machine. It doesn't matter if it's for a lower class of train or for only part of the journey; you can upgrade and/or extend it on board. To do this, find the ticket inspector and say *bǔ piào*. Confirm your destination and he'll issue a new ticket; you'll need to pay cash for the upgrade. If you get on a train without any kind of ticket, you may be asked to pay a surcharge.

There's no need to get fresh tickets if you miss a train for which you've reservations. Your tickets are valid on any train going to the same destination, but your seat reservation can't be transferred, and you may be required to pay for an upgrade.

Students can get a TR Pass (NTD599 for five consecutive days) entitling them to unlimited travel on all trains except TC expresses. Seven- and ten-day versions are also available; see www.youthtravel.tw for details. TR passes for non-students (NTD1,800 for three consecutive days) are worthwhile only if you plan to travel intensively.

Baggage Most stations now have lifts for disabled passengers and those with heavy bags. Major TRA stations have baggage services offices (⊕ *08.00–20.00 daily*) marked in English. This is where you go to ship your bicycle or motorcycle. You can also leave bags for a few hours or a few days – the charge is just NTD17 per item per day, regardless of size. The paperwork is straightforward and you'll be required to pay for the first day up front. You may be asked to show some ID, but the most important thing is to hold on to the receipt you're given. In Taipei Main Station and some other stations there are lockers, costing NTD50 for three hours or part thereof.

While your stuff is pretty safe on Taiwanese trains, do of course carry your valuables with you if you leave your carriage to visit the bathroom.

Food and drink On long-distance TRA trains there's a trolley service but the pickings are slim, so you're advised to stock up before you get on board. Drinking water is sometimes available on expresses but you'd do well to bring liquids.

High-speed Railway (HSR) Taiwan's bullet train covers the 339km between Taipei and Kaohsiung in as little as one hour 36 minutes. Currently there are eight stops: Taipei, Banqiao, Taoyuan, Hsinchu, Taichung, Chiayi, Tainan and Kaohsiung Zuoying. Four new stations will open in 2015: Nangang (in west Taipei), Miaoli, Changhua and Yunlin.

There are around four departures per hour in either direction between 06.30 and 23.00. Some services stop only at Taipei, Banqiao, Taichung and Kaohsiung Zuoying. Travelling by HSR isn't cheap but if you buy your ticket eight or more days in advance, you may be able to get as much as 35% off, bringing the price of a standard Taipei–Kaohsiung ticket down from NTD1,630 to NTD1,060. Business class (bigger seats, power outlet for your laptop, free coffee and newspapers) is 30%

2

more expensive. HSR tickets can be bought online and at stations (from staff or from vending machines that accept credit cards and cash).

BY BUS There are several bus companies and they compete on price and comfort level. All coaches are air conditioned; many are equipped with personal entertainment systems that show TV programmes and movies but these may not include English-language options. Major operators such as Kuo-Kuang and Ubus serve small towns such as Puli and Lugang as well as the big cities. Unfortunately, few companies have much English-language information on their websites, so you may need to go to the bus station and get timetable details in person. If heading from one big city to another there's usually no need to book ahead. Services are frequent and discount fares are often available midweek.

By tourist shuttle and tour bus
Two government-sponsored bus systems have made exploring some parts of Taiwan much easier for visitors who don't wish to drive. **Taiwan Tourist Shuttle** (*www.taiwantrip.com.tw*) services are much like regular buses except the routes were designed with sightseers in mind. On some, it's possible to get a one-day jump on/jump off ticket. **Taiwan Tour Bus** (*www. taiwantourbus.com.tw*) excursions last half or a whole day, with a guide on board who can introduce points of interest along the way. These tours can be a good way of seeing places like Taroko Gorge but you should review the information on the website carefully as reservations are necessary and English-speaking guides aren't available on all routes. Payment is usually made by credit card or Paypal.

By city bus
Useful local bus routes are mentioned throughout the guide. Buses are air conditioned and on most eating and drinking aren't allowed. Greater Taipei has a good bus network, as does Kaohsiung (in both cities most services operate ⊕ 06.30–20.30 daily; one-way fares NTD12–30). Compared to rapid-transit trains, urban bus travel is slow but you'll see much more (see box opposite).

BY CAR If you can deal with the way some Taiwanese people drive and can accept dense traffic in urban areas, consider getting your own vehicle for part of your stay.

Driving in Taiwan
Cars and motorcycles are supposed to drive on the right; outside the big cities, many two-wheelers use whichever side of the road is most convenient. Driving can be frustrating and stressful. At junctions, always observe what some call the 'lights plus one' rule – before moving forward, assume one more motorist or motorcyclist will try to rush across, despite the lights being against him. If an oncoming car flashes its headlights at you, it means you should give way, not (as in the UK) that the driver is letting you go first. Drivers and passengers are now required by law to wear seat belts at all times. Don't drink and drive; the alcohol limit for drivers in Taiwan is lower than in the UK.

Self-driving tourists should refer to the bus journey times listed in Part Two and not assume they can move significantly quicker.

Hiring a car
Car-rental businesses and their locations are listed in Part Two of this guidebook. Major hire companies include **Car Plus Auto Leasing** (✆ *0800 222 568; www.car-plus.com.tw*) and **Chailease Auto Rental** (✆ *0800 588 508; www. rentalcar.com.tw*). Both have good reputations and staff who can speak English; the latter has a specialist section for handling expatriates and tourists. Another rental

If you're footsore or it's simply too hot to stay outdoors, consider jumping on the first bus that comes your way. Wherever you go, you're sure to see plenty of interesting sights including vendors, tiny temples and apothecaries where practitioners of traditional medicine feel customers' pulses before dispensing herbs and roots. Funerals and wedding banquets are often held in marquees right beside main roads. At the former, participants wear white sackcloth and hoods. Nuptial celebrations are announced with firecrackers to welcome the bride and groom as they arrive in luxury cars decorated with red ribbons.

business with several branches is **IWS** (✆ *0800 200 414; www.iws.com.tw*). Expect to pay around NTD2,600 per day for a 1600cc Nissan Tiida and NTD3,700 per day for a 2000cc Mazda 5 which can take up to seven people.

When renting a car, a credit card is usually the only acceptable means of payment and you'll probably be required to sign a blank credit-card voucher to cover any fines that might be processed after your departure (they may not show up until three months later). You'll have to show both your passport and your international driver's license.

If your car or motorcycle disappears, go into any police station and give them the license number. If it was towed rather than stolen, they can find out very quickly and call you a taxi to where it's been impounded.

BY MOTORCYCLE It isn't easy to rent a real motorcycle as opposed to the step-through scooters used by many Taiwanese. These Vespa-type machines are fully automatic and come in a few different sizes, the most common being 50cc and 125cc. If you're on your own, neither large nor heavy, don't have much luggage and don't intend to stray far from the city, a 50cc scooter will do you fine. If you expect to cover more than 100km in a day, carry a passenger or climb serious hills, rent a 125cc. More powerful bikes are safer because you can accelerate out of trouble and use the engine as a brake when making long descents.

How to ride The fundamental rules are obvious but bear repeating: be careful, obey traffic laws regardless of what you see other people doing, don't ride when tired or intoxicated and always wear a helmet; rental businesses provide helmets for no additional cost. If dust and fumes bother you, do as the locals do and wear a mask. There are simple cloth masks which can be washed when they get grimy and hospital-style masks with carbon filters; the latter are said to be better at blocking nasty particulates. Even if bright sunshine isn't a problem for you, do wear some form of eye protection. Grit or insects – Taiwan has plenty of both – may get in your eyes.

Hiring a motorcycle Rental businesses are often found near train stations but tend not to have English signs. Get an international driver's license before leaving home as obtaining a license in Taiwan is a drawn-out process. Many motorcycle rental businesses will turn you away if you don't have an international license, while some places won't rent to a foreigner even if he or she has the necessary paperwork. This isn't always xenophobia; more often it's because the rental business doesn't want to get stuck with having to pay fines for traffic violations committed by customers they can't later track down. This problem wouldn't exist if motorcycle rental businesses accepted credit cards.

Before hitting the road, confirm whether the scooter takes 92 (as two-star petrol is called) or 95 (four-star). You'll be lucky if there's more than a tiny amount of fuel in the tank, so make the nearest petrol station your first objective. Renting a scooter for 24 hours typically costs NTD400. Read the *Driving in Taiwan* entry above for additional tips.

BY TAXI Although Taiwan's taxi industry has become more professional in recent years, very few drivers understand English (so carry your destination's name or address in Chinese) and women are advised against taking taxis by themselves late at night.

All legal taxis are yellow. Unless you're travelling a long distance, or from an airport or HSR station into the city centre – in which case the driver may ask for a flat fee – the fare is calculated by a clearly visible meter. At the time of writing, taxis in Taipei charged NTD70 for the first 1.25km, plus NTD5 for each additional 250m or one minute 40 seconds spent waiting. A 4km daytime journey in normal traffic therefore costs at least NTD125. There are small extra charges late at night, around Lunar New Year and if you have lots of luggage. In other cities, slightly different formulas are used to tot up taxi fares – you may see the meter starting at NTD100.

HITCHHIKING Hitchhiking isn't at all common in Taiwan, but solo foreign travellers will find it relatively easy to get a lift in more rural and mountainous areas. You may be expected to practise English with the driver's children, and you may have snacks and drinks forced on you, but you'll come away agreeing that Taiwanese people are some of the friendliest and most helpful in the world.

ON FOOT Look both ways before crossing the road and stay alert, even when you're on the pavement. Walking can be quite pleasurable in Taipei and Kaohsiung but in many other places the pavements are narrow and often cluttered with vendors, piles of merchandise and illegally parked motorcycles.

ROAD TYPES AND ROAD RULES

It's worth getting to grips with Taiwan's road-numbering system as there's potential for confusion. For instance, two separate north–south roads bear the number 3. On Freeway 3 you can cruise comfortably at over 100km/h; the other, Highway 3, is a winding country road on which you'd do well to average 50km/h.

Motorcycles and bicycles aren't allowed on freeways, which are like British motorways. The usual freeway speed limit is 110km/h; on other roads it's normally 50 or 60km/h. Speed traps are common and on freeways cameras also catch those driving too close to the vehicle in front. By law, cars travelling at 100km/h must be at least 50m behind the vehicle ahead. There are no traffic lights on freeways.

There are also several expressways which are almost as fast as freeways. Most of them run east–west and link the two north–south freeways. An exception is Expressway 61, which hugs the west coast between Bali in the north and Tainan in the south; some sections aren't yet open.

Some of the addresses in this guidebook look fearsomely complicated, as in addition to a street name and a building number there may well be a lane number, an alley number and a floor number. Fortunately the system isn't difficult to understand.

Most roads in most cities are marked with bilingual signs and long roads are often divided into sections which are numbered. Pay attention to these, as getting out of a taxi in the wrong section is likely to result in head-scratching confusion followed by a lengthy walk or another taxi journey. In some cities – Taipei, notably – roads are also divided into north and south sections or east and west sections.

Lanes are small thoroughfares that spur off roads or streets. Where's Lane 124? Between the buildings numbered 122 and 126. Alleys branch off lanes and are numbered in the same way. Alley 31, therefore, separates houses 29 and 33. Most lanes are one-car wide, and many alleys are too narrow for any kind of four-wheeled vehicle. Therefore if you're in a car and hunting for a place in the backstreets, you'd do well to park on the main road and set out on foot.

Whether you're heading for a hotel, restaurant or museum, carrying with you the address of your destination in Chinese characters is always a good idea. Armed with a Chinese address you can ask people for directions or hail a taxi.

BY BICYCLE Taiwan's cyclists have a lot to contend with: heat, unpredictable drivers and pollution (consider buying a disposable mask; supermarkets and convenience stores sell them). Despite these factors, Taiwan is an excellent place for a cycling vacation. Roads are well maintained and drivers are used to sharing the carriageway with two-wheelers. There's lots to see wherever you go and, in the lowlands at least, countless places where you can stop and buy a drink or a snack. At certain 7-Eleven convenience stores it's possible to borrow a bike pump (look for the bike-pump sign outside). If you can't find one of these, try a police station.

Folding bikes which have been properly bagged can be taken on any TRA local train and certain expresses at no extra cost. (Some cyclists get away with using large plastic trash bags.) Cyclists travelling with unbagged, non-folding bicycles are allowed only on particular trains and only if reservations have been made. What's more, they're not allowed to get on or off at some stations and an additional ticket must be purchased for each bicycle. Because this procedure is fearsomely complex, sending your bike ahead by train is often a better idea. To do this, take your bicycle to a major station (but not Taipei), remove lights and other items likely to fall off, fill in some paperwork and pay. It's cheap (Changhua–Kaohsiung costs NTD250) but slow: allow 24 hours between sending your bike off and collecting it at the destination.

Bagged non-folding bikes can be taken on HSR trains for free. Bagged and/or folding bicycles are allowed on rapid-transit trains in Taipei and Kaohsiung; this is free but unfeasible during rush hours. Folding bikes go for free on Kuo-Kuang intercity buses; non-folding bicycles are charged half price.

A good website for cyclists is www.taiwan-guide.org/david/cycling.html.

ACCOMMODATION

Compared with other travel expenses, accommodation in Taiwan isn't notably cheap. Hotel prices are almost always quoted in New Taiwan dollars (NTD). Credit cards are accepted by top- and mid-range hotels but often not by budget inns, homestays or campsites. Bargaining is occasionally possible at motels and mid-range places.

Rather than kettles in every room, in some establishments you'll find filtered-water machines in the lobby or corridor. These provide both room-temperature and piping-hot water. The buttons may be labelled in Chinese only, so be careful not to get scalded.

HOTELS Travellers willing to pay NTD3,000 or more per night will have plenty of options. In smaller towns and resorts you may struggle to find a hotel which has both personality and staff who have a good grasp of English. In all major towns, inexpensive hotels (often costing less than NTD1,000 per night) can be found near TRA stations. These places vary hugely in quality and you should be prepared to visit three or four before choosing one. Air conditioning and cable television are standard; if there's a deficiency it's likely to be the hot-water system. In cheaper inns, hot water is only available in the evening, as Taiwanese tend to bathe after dinner.

HOMESTAYS/B&BS The emergence of homestays (*mínsù*) throughout rural Taiwan is one of the most positive trends in the country's tourism industry. There are now thousands of guesthouses and in many you can learn a lot from the host family about local customs, lifestyles and ecology.

A huge variety of establishments call themselves homestays. Some, including several in Kinmen County and the Matsu Islands, occupy well-kept traditional buildings that would be tourist attractions even if they weren't bed-and-breakfasts. Some newer homestays were purpose-built and are very luxurious; a few places that call themselves B&Bs don't, oddly, offer breakfast. Many homestays in remote areas offer dinner to those who book it in advance but you may be expected to eat quite early. Even in low season rooms should be booked before arrival as many owners have farms to tend to and errands to run.

Foreign travellers face two language-related obstacles when it comes to homestays. Few homestay bosses speak English (exceptions are noted in Part Two) and some establishments are hard to find if you can't read Chinese signs. It's worthwhile looking through a homestay's website before making a reservation, even if the site has no English, as pictures of the guest rooms are useful when judging whether a place meets your standards.

ACCOMMODATION PRICE CODES

Accommodation listings are laid out in decreasing price order, under the following categories: Luxury, Upmarket, Mid-range, Budget and Shoestring. The following key (also on the inside front cover) gives an indication of prices. Prices are based on a double room per night in high season, including any taxes and service charges.

Luxury	$$$$$	NTD7,000
Upmarket	$$$$	NTD4,500–6,999
Mid-range	$$$	NTD2,500–4,499
Budget	$$	NTD1,000–2,499
Shoestring	$	<NTD1,000

MOTELS Locals will tell you motels prosper by providing places where people can conduct extramarital affairs. This perhaps explains why so many motels have large comfortable beds and are absolutely soundproof – just what you want for a good night's rest. For self-driving travellers, motels are a value-for-money alternative. They'd be an even better option if more were located in city centres or proper countryside rather than dull suburbs.

YOUTH HOSTELS Taiwan's hostelling scene includes 'youth activity centres' managed by the quasi-official China Youth Corps (an organisation which until 2000 bore the magnificent moniker, 'China Youth Anti-Communist National Salvation Corps') and establishments accredited by the Taiwan Youth Hostel Association (✆ 02 2331 1102; f 02 2331 1393; e ctyha@yh.org.tw; www.yh.org.tw), the local Hostelling International affiliate. In addition, www.hostels.com lists more than 200 establishments around the country. Church-run hostels in places like Tianxiang and Fenqihu are usually good options. Staying in one can be especially fascinating if you run into a missionary priest or nun who's spent decades in Taiwan and is willing to share some of his or her experiences.

MOUNTAIN SHELTERS If you do any serious hiking you'll probably stay in mountain shelters. In some you can sleep for free but bunk space should be booked ahead of time. For a few, such as Paiyun Lodge on Mount Jade, you pay when you make the booking. Comfort levels vary greatly and depend on how new the structure is and how many people you're sharing with. In many, no bedding is provided. The toilets may be grim and you shouldn't expect shower facilities. Many shelters have a water supply but this isn't always reliable; you may have to walk a considerable distance to fill your bottles.

CAMPSITES Well-organised campsites with shower facilities can be found throughout east Taiwan, in Kenting National Park, around Sun Moon Lake and several other places. Expect to pay around NTD200 per person per night. It's not worth dragging a high-quality tent all the way from your home country when a standard Taiwanese two-person tent, which you can buy from a hypermarket for less than NTD1,500, will do perfectly well. Some campsites rent out tents. It goes without saying that the drier, cooler winter months are the best time to camp. A useful website is www.taiwancamping.net.

EATING AND DRINKING

Taiwanese eat a lot and eat often, so it isn't surprising that around one in six is overweight. Many young women, however, are stick-thin. As in other east Asian countries, rice and noodles are staples. Sweet potatoes, taros and yams are secondary sources of carbohydrates. As you'd expect on an island, seafood (hǎi xiān) is common; much of the fish, however, is farmed rather than caught in the ocean. There's a good selection of vegetables, especially cabbage, carrots, turnips and cucumbers. Vegetables are often fried with crushed garlic rather than boiled or steamed. Sweetcorn and various beans are common.

Pork is the most frequently eaten meat and those following a kosher or halal diet should assume that meat sauces are pork-based unless stated otherwise. Chicken and mutton are also popular. Most of the beef eaten in Taiwan is imported, and part of the population – perhaps one in ten – never eats beef. This prohibition dates from pre-industrial times when cattle and water buffalo were protected because they were needed for ploughing and manure. Venison, goose and duck are easy to find. You may also have chances to try turtle, pigeon, frog, snake or snails – but not dog meat, the sale of which has been illegal since 2003.

TAIWANESE CUISINE Island cooking is a version of Chinese cuisine. It isn't especially spicy nor sour and doesn't much resemble the food sold by Chinese takeaways in the UK. Rice is thought to be very important indeed – few Taiwanese go 24 hours without eating a bowl or two of steamed polished white rice (*bái fàn*). Noodles (*miàn*) are common; they're usually served 'dry' with gravy (*gān miàn*) or with chunks of meat in a soup. Taiwanese cuisine has a vast range of broths and consommés. They differ from European soups in that the liquid is often clear and somewhat oily, and the ingredients (which may include large pieces of bone) aren't finely chopped.

Breakfast (*zǎo cān*) Few Western visitors find the traditional Taiwanese breakfast of rice gruel, pickles, peanuts and dried shredded pork appetising. If you're staying in an upmarket establishment you can expect a full breakfast buffet, but if you're not you may want to buy something the evening before. In towns and

RESTAURANT PRICE CODES

Restaurant listings are laid out in decreasing price order, under the following categories: Expensive, Above average, Mid-range, Cheap and Cheerful and Rock bottom. The following key (also on the inside front cover) gives an indication of prices. Prices are based on the cost of a main course (including tax) per person.

Expensive	$$$$$	NTD1,000+
Above average	$$$$	NTD500–999
Mid-range	$$$	NTD250–499
Cheap and cheerful	$$	NTD100–249
Rock bottom	$	<NTD100

cities there are plenty of breakfast eateries (⊕ *approx 05.30–11.00 daily*) that sell hot, inexpensive items like egg pancakes (*dàn bǐng*, you can ask to have bacon and/ or cheese added) and hamburgers (*hàn bǎo*, usually pork). Hot coffee is usually available, though it may come in a can. At least once during your stay try doughnut sticks and hot soy milk. Some find this type of food a little too greasy, but on cold mornings it's just the ticket.

Lunch (*wǔ cān*) and dinner (*wǎn cān*)
The foods eaten at lunchtime are very similar to those eaten at dinnertime. Lunchtime is usually 12.00–13.30, though many restaurants open earlier and close later, if at all. In small towns and mountain areas, you might struggle to get a hot meal after 19.30.

In many eating establishments the menu is either pasted on the wall or resembles a form with boxes that you tick. Because English-language menus (abbreviated EM throughout this guide) are rare, you'll be making good use of the food section of the *Language* appendix in this book (see pages 345–8). Pointing at what someone else is eating and holding up a finger or two to indicate quantity won't offend anyone.

Local-style buffets are especially convenient for those who don't speak Mandarin. They can be found throughout urban areas and vary considerably in terms of freshness and cleanliness. At one you'll see anywhere between a dozen and 50 different trays of food, with everything from meat to fish to vegetables. Because the food gets cold quickly and the choicest items go quickly, it pays to arrive early – 11.30 for lunch, 17.30 for dinner. Grab a paper plate (or box if you want to take the food away) and use tongs to pick up whatever takes your fancy. At the end of the line you'll be offered white rice; the cashier will then either weigh your plate or just take a look and come up with a figure. Unless you've really piled the food on, the meal shouldn't cost more than NTD100.

MAINLAND CUISINE
In Taiwan's bigger cities you'll find restaurants which specialise in Shanghainese, Cantonese, Hunanese and other mainland Chinese styles of cooking. Many were established by refugees who fled to Taiwan in the late 1940s. Restaurants inside major hotels often serve mainland cuisines and may be your best bet if you want English-speaking service

HAKKA COOKING
Hakka food isn't to everyone's liking because it's saltier, greasier and more vinegary than mainstream Taiwanese cuisine. As in other Chinese cuisines, Hakka meals are usually based around steamed white rice. However, one of the most popular dishes in Hakka regions is a kind of broad noodle made from rice flour and called ban-tiao (*bàn tiáo*). Fried with slivers of pork and carrot, or boiled and then served in soup or dry with a few slices of meat on top, a bowl of ban-tiao makes for a tasty lunch.

ABORIGINAL CUISINES
Visitors should seize any chance they have to try aboriginal foods. They're available nowhere else in the world and, in the opinion of many visitors, indigenous cooking tastes very good indeed.

Aboriginal feasts often include roasted or barbecued meat (some of it obtained by hunting), small fish and shrimp taken from mountain streams, and vegetables quite different from those seen in the lowlands. Until a few decades ago, millet was a staple food in many indigenous communities. To some extent it's been replaced by rice, but at festival time millet-based dishes are prominent. It's during such events that you'll see the most authentic aboriginal foods, including items not offered

2

In many local eateries condiments are available on every table, although salt and pepper aren't always among them. Vinegar, soy sauce and chillies are easy to recognise, but Western visitors shouldn't expect red plastic bottles to contain ketchup (often it's spicy sauce) or yellow ones to be filled with mustard (usually it's *jiàng yóu gāo*, a thick brown sauce made from soy sauce). Green bottles are likely to contain a liquid version of wasabi, a mustard-like condiment often used in Japanese cooking.

in restaurants. Among the Bunun tribe, raw pickled flying-squirrel intestines are considered a special delicacy, as is what's called 'stinky meat' – game that's begun to rot after being left in the trap a little too long. It's barbecued, fried with garlic and ginger, then served with a spicy sauce.

For aborigines living in mountain communities, hunting and gathering remain important ways of obtaining food.

EATING OUT Taiwan has an astonishing range of roadside stalls, cheap eateries, mid-range restaurants and pretentious dining establishments. In the listings in Part Two, rather than identify and describe Taiwan's best restaurants – a task that would take more than one lifetime – I've tried to present a cross-section of the dining scene, including the excellent, the typical-yet-tasty and what is to Western sensibilities downright bizarre.

Drinks In addition to the usual fizzy soft drinks and supermarket fruit juices, Taiwan has an excellent selection of fresh fruit and vegetable juices, plus milkshakes made with local fruit like papaya, pineapple and mango. Cold tea is drunk in huge quantities; a Taiwanese invention variously known as 'bubble milk tea' or 'pearl milk tea' (cold black tea mixed with milk and tapioca balls) has caught on overseas.

Taiwan Beer, a lager best drunk cold, is the most popular alcoholic tipple with more than 80% of the beer market. Popular imported brands include Heineken and Kirin (a Japanese brew). In many restaurants you'll see refrigerators full of

Nobody in Taiwan drinks tap water without first boiling or filtering it and neither should you. If you do drink some unboiled or unfiltered tap water by mistake – when brushing your teeth, say – don't worry too much about it. You won't be stricken with diarrhoea or something worse. The problem isn't so much nasty bacteria as industrial pollutants and the state of water tanks and pipes.

Some people drink only bottled water, but studies suggest some brands are no healthier than straight tap water. Almost all hotels and homestays will provide drinking water that's been boiled and/or filtered. There's no need to avoid the ice that comes with freshly squeezed juices and other drinks. If you do suffer from stomach problems while in Taiwan, it's likely to be a result of the kind of food you've been eating, not the cleanliness of the place where the food was prepared.

beer and other cold drinks. Just help yourself; the staff will add the cost to your bill. Red wine is far more popular than white wine and several local wineries have been launched. The best-known spirit is kaoliang – the Chinese name means 'sorghum', which is its main ingredient – and it's made in Kinmen County and the Matsu Islands.

Snacks In night markets (see pages 95 and 135) and alongside busy roads you'll find vendors who offer a vast range of tasty snacks, many of which are deep-fried and slathered with sauce. If you'd rather eat something healthier, buy fruit. Prices and availability vary according to the season, but local bananas seem to be sold year-round, as are imported apples, plus peaches and pears grown in the mountains. Taiwanese guavas, mangoes and pineapples are exceptionally good and quite unlike those sold in supermarkets in the West.

PUBLIC HOLIDAYS AND FESTIVALS

Banks and government offices close on national holidays. If a national holiday falls on a Saturday or Sunday, many private companies will take the following Monday off. If it falls on a Monday, museums and other attractions that normally close on Mondays will stay open and take Tuesday off instead.

Taiwan has hundreds of festivals. Many are strictly local affairs and more than a few were concocted by mayors looking to generate income and publicity for their townships. Many annual religious events are tied to the lunar calendar (see box, page 29). For indigenous festivals, the precise date may vary from one year to the next and from one village to another.

NATIONAL HOLIDAYS
Winter
Founding Day (*1 January*) Rather than marking the beginning of a new year on the Gregorian calendar, this holiday celebrates the establishment of the Republic of China on 1 January 1912.

Lunar New Year (*6 or more days including w/ends in late January or early February*) Chinese Lunar New Year is somewhat like the Christmas/New Year period in the UK. Most employers close for a week but for the retail and hospitality sectors it's a very busy time. Ahead of the Lunar New Year, people clean their homes and try to settle all their debts. Families dine together on New Year's Eve, then relax the following day. On the second day, married women visit their parents.

2-28 Peace Memorial Day (*28 February*) This day commemorates the massacre of 1947 (see *History*, page 18).

Tomb Sweeping Day (*5 April*) On this day many Taiwanese return to their home towns to clean their ancestors' graves, make offerings and burn joss paper.

Summer
Dragon Boat Festival (*fifth day of the fifth lunar month*) This festival usually falls in early June and celebrates Qu Yuan, a poet-politician who 2,300 years ago committed suicide as a protest against corruption. Highly competitive dragon-boat races are held in several cities and people eat sticky rice triangles called *zòng zǐ*.

Autumn

Mid-Autumn Festival (*15th day of the eighth lunar month*) This isn't so much a public celebration as a chance for families to get together, let off fireworks, admire the full moon, and share stodgy pastries called 'mooncakes'.

Double Ten Day (*10 October*) This holiday marks the beginning of the 1911 uprising in central China which toppled the Qing Dynasty and led to the founding of the ROC.

IMPORTANT NON-HOLIDAYS
Winter

Valentine's Day (*14 February*) Without any official encouragement whatsoever, Valentine's Day has become one of the most important days of the year for young Taiwanese.

Lantern Festival (*15th day of the first lunar month*) Traditionally the climax of the Lunar New Year festivities, Lantern Festival is now a major event in its own right featuring fireworks displays, the carrying of decorated lanterns through the streets and the release of lanterns into the night sky at various places including Pingxi near Taipei. Many of the lanterns are shaped or painted to resemble that year's zodiac animal (see box, page 29). Far more exciting are two events held on the same day as Lantern Festival but historically unrelated to it: Yanshui's Beehive Fireworks Festival and the Bombing of Han Dan in Taitung City.

Spring

Guanyin's Birthday (*19th day of the second lunar month*) The birthday of the Buddhist goddess of mercy is celebrated in temples with solemn prayers, in homes with vegetarian feasts and, incongruously, with displays of fighting skills in the town of Neimen (see page 258).

Bunun Ear-shooting Festival (*late April or early May*) This is one of Taiwan's most popular aboriginal festivals. The precise date varies from year to year and events are held in a number of locations including Lidao and Namasia. In addition to feasting and music, there are contests of skill and strength. Young males try to prove they deserve the respect accorded full adults by hitting animal ears hung on trees; bows and arrows are used, not guns.

Mazu's Birthday (*23rd day of the third lunar month*) The birthday of the sea goddess is celebrated with gusto at Dajia (see page 175) and other Mazu temples around the country.

Guan Gong's Birthday (*13th day of the fifth lunar month*) This god's birthday is marked by his devotees at major shrines including Tainan's Martial Rites Temple and Taipei's Longshan Temple.

Summer

Amis Harvest Festival (*July or August*) Indigenous villages in east Taiwan celebrate the abundance of harvest time with singing, dancing and feasting (see box, page 295).

Ghost Month (*seventh lunar month*) On the first day of the month the gates of Hell are believed to open and the spirits of the dead return to the human world.

Huge offerings are made to the wandering ghosts lest they cause mayhem. The living are concerned not only with their ancestors but with all inhabitants of the after-world. Because accidents and deaths that occur in Ghost Month are sometimes blamed on troublesome ghosts, during this period the traditionally minded avoid getting married, opening new businesses, moving house, going on long journeys or having non-emergency surgery. Ghost Month is important in Chinese communities throughout Asia. In Taiwan, Keelung is the best place to see the action.

Autumn

Pasta'ai Ceremony (*15th day of the tenth lunar month*) This biennial event, one of Taiwan's better-known indigenous traditions, is in effect an apology by the Saisiyat tribe to the spirits of those they massacred hundreds of years ago (see box, page 163).

SHOPPING

Taiwan has countless shops of all sizes and descriptions. Morning markets open before dawn and stay active until lunchtime. Many towns also have afternoon markets where you can find a similar range of fruit, vegetables, meat and fish (but not bread or dairy products). Department stores typically run 10.00–22.00 while supermarkets often open earlier. Family-run corner shops are usually open very long hours in cities, but may close soon after dinner in rural areas. Taiwan's bakeries are best visited late in the afternoon. All of these places tend to open seven days a week throughout the year, closing for no more than three days around the Lunar New Year. Convenience stores which stay open 24/7 are ubiquitous (see box below).

Taiwan's economic miracle was founded on manufacturing. The island's prosperity stems from making and exporting practical consumer goods, items which have found their way to every corner of the world. Taiwanese people are rightfully proud of this, but it does mean visitors are sometimes hard-pressed to find charming and distinctive mementos they can take home and share. Everything sold in Taiwan, it often seems, is available everywhere else. Even though a lot of electronic products are made in Taiwan or made in factories owned by Taiwanese

---

CONVENIENCE STORES

It's said Taiwan has the highest density of 24-hour convenience stores in the world and it's hard to imagine how the country would function without 7-Eleven and Family Mart, the two main chains. In addition to buying breakfast in the morning and beer at night (Taiwan has an admirably *laissez faire* approach to booze sales), locals stop by to pay their household bills, send parcels and buy concert tickets.

Many foreign visitors gain a profound appreciation of convenience stores. Can't face tepid rice gruel for breakfast? Get a bagel and a hot coffee from your nearest convenience store. Flat tyre on your bicycle? Look for a 7-Eleven displaying the bike-pump symbol and ask for help. Parking fees to pay? Something needs to be xeroxed or faxed? 7-Eleven or Family Mart. Looking for an English-language newspaper or imported beer? Convenience stores are often the best bet. Need hot water to make up a bottle for your infant or some tea for yourself? Any 7-Eleven will allow you to fill your Thermos or tin mug with piping hot water for free.

companies, don't expect huge savings on such goods. Also, English-language manuals and software may not be available.

Aboriginal art isn't widely available in the big cities but you'll come across it in places like Sandimen and throughout the east. Good options include glass-bead jewellery and textiles. Tribe Asia (*www.tribe-asia.com*) sells high-quality and authentic indigenous crafts via the internet.

If you can enlist the aid of a Mandarin-speaker, consider getting some personalised calligraphy banners made by a professional. Personal seals make excellent compact gifts if you can provide the seal-maker with the intended recipient's Chinese name. Calligraphers and seal-makers can be found in traditional business districts in every city, though very few of them speak English.

If you want to buy presents but are bereft of ideas, Taipei's Chinese Handicraft Mart (see *Shopping*, page 97) is an excellent place to start. The gift shops in major museums are also worth browsing. As befits a great repository, the National Palace Museum has an excellent on-site store with reproductions of paintings and other treasures exhibited in the museum.

ARTS AND ENTERTAINMENT

Like many other nationalities, Taiwanese spend much of their free time watching television, going to the cinema, playing computer games, shopping and listening to popular music. That said, substantial numbers of people pay to attend classes in traditional ink painting, oil painting (which took off during the Japanese occupation) or calligraphy. The last has no real parallel in the West; in Taiwan and China it's considered an art form in its own right and remains extremely popular.

The grassroots live music scene isn't as developed as it is in the West, but dramatic performances (including Taiwanese opera, see pages 127 and 129) and concerts are frequent in the major cities. Puppetry, modernised versions of which can be seen on local television, is often performed as part of religious celebrations.

Religious art continues to be a massive influence on stone carving, woodcarving and painting around the island. Many of Taiwan's most innovative artists, including sculptor Ju Ming, cut their teeth decorating temples. Exceptions include indigenous artists who work with ceramics, driftwood or glass beads (see *Shopping*, page 268).

To find out about gallery openings, museum exhibitions and live performances, scan the local English-language newspapers or ask at any visitor information centre.

MUSEUMS The number of museums, galleries and exhibition halls (⊕ *typically 09.00–17.00 Tue–Sun*) has rocketed in recent years thanks to government money and sponsorship from several large companies. An incomplete bilingual list can be found at http://museum.moc.gov.tw. Notable museums include:

Lukang Folk Arts Museum Many of the items come from one of Taiwan's richest families but they still count as folk artefacts.

National Museum of Taiwan History Covers every episode in the island's past.

National Palace Museum Rightfully regarded as one of the world's greatest collections.

National Taiwan Museum of Fine Arts A strong permanent collection and worthwhile rotating exhibitions.

Shung Ye Museum of Formosan Aborigines By far the best of the island's several indigenous-theme museums.

Taipei Fine Arts Museum Stresses modern artists and their works.

Taiwan Theatre Museum Has displays on opera and puppetry.

ARCHITECTURE

Sometimes it seems as if all of Taiwan's architectural energies and talent have gone into the design and construction of houses of worship. Urban areas are often bleak and untidy; many houses are drab concrete boxes. That said, architecture buffs will find a great deal to enjoy.

Until well into the 19th century, most Taiwanese lived in bamboo huts or wood-framed wattle-and-daub homes. Only in a handful of places, including some indigenous villages (see pages 265 and 270), were stone houses common. Following the Japanese takeover, reinforced-concrete European-Japanese buildings began appearing. After World War II, Chiang Kai-shek's regime emphasised 'Northern Palace' architecture (like Beijing's Forbidden City) featuring glazed roof tiles and elaborate *dougong* brackets. Local vernacular architecture was ignored and many historic structures were demolished during the postwar rush for development. Since the 1980s, however, preservation laws and civic organisations have saved a good number of Taiwan's heritage buildings.

TOP-RANK TEMPLES

Baoan Temple This feast for the eyes is Taipei's most interesting shrine.

Buddha Memorial Centre An imposing combination of Chinese, Indian and modern styles.

Chung Tai Chan Monastery Striking from afar and engrossing close up.

> ### DOS AND DON'TS WHEN VISITING TEMPLES
>
> Many temples are extremely wealthy thanks to their Taiwanese supporters. Very few charge admission; visitors are only expected to drop something in the donation box if they pray or throw divining blocks (see box, page 34).
>
> Don't hesitate to go into any temple if it looks interesting, even if you're dressed very casually and there are people praying inside. The caretaker may well have his feet up, his back to the altar and be watching baseball on television. There's no need to cover your head or your shoulders. Behave as you would in any other place of worship. Don't smoke, eat or drink; keep your voice down; don't point at people or effigies; and don't touch the offerings, which typically include fruit and glasses of rice wine. Be sensitive when taking photos. Removing your hat is a good idea but it isn't necessary to remove symbols of your own religion. In most temples you needn't take off your shoes.
>
> Don't take meat or fish into a place of worship that might be Buddhist; vegetarianism is a tenet of the religion. In folk temples you'll often see meat among the offerings. Women shouldn't enter a temple when they're menstruating.

Longshan Temple Not the busiest place of worship in Lugang but certainly the greatest in artistic terms.

Martial Rites Temple Perhaps the very finest shrine in Tainan, a city overflowing with classic temples.

Tzu Yun Temple With its Japanese-influenced shape and high-altitude location, Alishan's loveliest place of worship is a rarity among Taiwanese temples.

TRADITIONAL HOMES AND MANSIONS
Erkan Ancient Residences An almost-abandoned village located in windswept Penghu County.

Jinshi Mansion Dilapidated but still impressive, this is one of Hsinchu's most important relics (see page 153).

Kinmen's South Fujianese houses The county has preserved hundreds of alluring single-storey abodes.

Matsu's villages Qinbi and Jinsha are notable for their stone dwellings.

Xinhua Old Street A well-preserved and still lively 1930s commercial thoroughfare in Tainan.

JAPANESE-ERA LANDMARKS Angered by Tokyo's decision in 1972 to establish diplomatic ties with the PRC, Chiang Kai-shek's regime decreed that all colonial-era relics glorifying Japanese rule should be removed and that other remnants of the period should never be repaired. The policy was reversed in the late 1980s and colonial-era structures are now cherished.

The Japanese legacy in Tainan The colonists left a deep imprint on Taiwan's oldest city (see pages 221–2).

Put to new uses National Taiwan Museum, Futai Street Mansion, the Museum of Contemporary Art and the National Museum of Taiwanese Literature all date from the colonial period.

Shintoism Japan's state religion didn't make much headway in Taiwan but there's an intact former Shinto shrine in Taoyuan City and the ruins of another outside Jinguashi.

Railway stations The TRA stations in Hsinchu and Taichung date from before World War II.

NATIONALIST EDIFICES
Chiang Kai-shek Memorial Hall Whatever your feelings about the generalissimo, his memorial is unique.

Grand Hotel This Taipei landmark is a good example of 'Northern Palace' architecture rendered in rebar and concrete (see page 90).

National Revolutionary Martyrs Shrine This place was intended to be sober, even severe, and the architects succeeded.

21ST-CENTURY CONSTRUCTION
Beitou Branch of Taipei City Library This wooden structure is a model of style as well as sustainability.

Lanyang Museum Inspired by the slant of rock strata, this museum looks as if it's sinking into a wetland.

Taipei 101 What used to be the world's tallest building still pulls in shoppers and tourists.

Paper Dome A recycled building set in a place of great natural beauty.

SPORTS AND ACTIVITIES

Taiwan is a sports underachiever. Despite the achievements of Chi Cheng (a female sprinter who set three world records in one week in 1970) and baseball professionals playing in the USA, Taiwan's impact in the international sporting arena has been minimal. This isn't because Taiwanese teams and individuals are forced for political reasons to compete under the absurd moniker 'Chinese-Taipei'. Rather, it's the result of an education system that stresses test scores at the expense of overall development and an environment that until recently lacked sports facilities.

It wasn't until 2004 that the island's sports stars struck Olympic gold, winning two in the martial art taekwondo. At the Beijing Games four years later, Taiwanese athletes won two bronze medals in taekwondo and two bronzes in weightlifting. At the London Summer Games in 2012, one silver (women's weightlifting) and one bronze medal (taekwondo) were won.

Long term, things are looking up, thanks to government investment in training and infrastructure and a population that's becoming more outdoorsy. In 2009, Kaohsiung did an excellent job of hosting the eighth World Games, an Olympics-style event that features sports not on the Olympic roster such as karate and orienteering. Later the same year, Taipei was the venue for the 21st Deaflympics. In 2017, Taipei will host the 29th Summer Universiade.

BASEBALL Taiwan's national sport is baseball. Taiwanese players who've become stars in the US Baseball Major League are a source of immense national pride. However, Taiwan's own baseball league has been rocked by match-fixing scandals, and the national team's dismal performance in recent international competitions has led to great public disappointment. Taiwan finished eighth in the 2013 World Baseball Classic.

BASKETBALL Taiwan's foremost participation sport is played in schools and parks everywhere. There's a national league but some of its stars have joined better-paying teams in China. Jeremy Lin, an American of Taiwanese descent now playing for the Houston Rockets, became a Taiwanese hero after his stunning debut in the US National Basketball Association league in early 2012.

CAMPING Sleeping under canvas is popular in Kenting National Park as well as the mountains. See page 63 for details.

CLIMBING With the exception of some highly rated spots along the northeast coast, rock climbing isn't nearly as popular as you might expect given Taiwan's mountainous landscape.

COOKING Taiwanese are passionate about local and international food. Ivy Chen (*http://kitchenivy.com*), who speaks excellent English and some Japanese, teaches Taiwan and Chinese cooking in Taipei.

CYCLING AND MOUNTAIN BIKING In terms of rental and repair businesses, bicycle-only trails and ordinary roads suitable for bikers, Taiwan has excellent infrastructure for cyclists. See also *Getting around*, page 61.

ECOTOURISM Taiwan has a tremendous variety of butterflies, fireflies and other insects. Other curiosities you might see include freshwater scorpions, flying squirrels and landlocked salmon (see box, page 200). Whale watching is popular off the east coast (see box, page 302).

GOLF Golf has been played on the island since the Japanese occupation and several Taiwanese golfers have made a splash in international competitions, most recently Yani Tseng (b1989). For 109 consecutive weeks until early 2013, Tseng was the world's top-ranked female golfer. Taiwan has dozens of golf courses; www. golfworldmap.com lists nearly 60. The better ones charge non-members around NTD3,500 for green and caddie fees.

HIKING Taiwan is a hiker's dream. The island's mountains are numerous, steep and extremely scenic yet the vast majority of trails demand no technical climbing

SCUBA DIVING   *John Boo*

There are all sorts of different environments along Taiwan's coastline. The tropical south offers year-round diving with water temperatures of 21°C in winter and 29–30°C in summer. In the north, winter diving is only possible with a thicker wetsuit. Even then, it's not always enjoyable.

Taiwan's soft-coral sites are among the best in the world and there are healthy hard-coral sites in abundance. Whether on a shallow dive or a deep dive, a boat dive or a shore dive, you'll be able to find what every diver craves – the undersea world's natural beauty.

Before coming to Taiwan, I saw a headline that read: 'Taiwan is one of Asia's best-kept secrets in the diving community'. Not long after I moved to Kaohsiung. I completed all of my training as an Open Water Dive Instructor in and around Kenting, at Taiwan's southern tip, and then began to explore sites far away in north Taiwan such as Longdong Bay and Guishan Island.

After poking around in the north, I decided to turn back south and explore in greater detail. Little Liuqiu has fantastic undersea corals and is well known among Taiwanese divers for turtles. Out in the deep Pacific off the southeast coast, Green Island and Orchid Island offer some of Taiwan's best diving. The first time I visited Green Island I was amazed by the tallest bell corals I had ever seen, as well as both soft and hard corals in pristine condition.

Between January and March, Green Island also offers a hammerhead shark dive at depths of 30–35m. This is when the hammerheads are migrating in large schools;

skills. You'll have no problems finding a route that meets your requirements. Yangmingshan National Park has plenty of family-friendly paths while Yushan and Shei-Pa national parks offer multi-day treks through expedition country.

Before beginning any hike longer than a kilometre or two, take note of weather conditions and make sure you've snacks, water and sun protection. Don't leave the path; more than one Western tourist has disappeared without trace in recent years and others have got themselves into sticky situations. Rely on your eyes as well as your map; the fact that a route is clearly marked on a map doesn't mean it's survived recent typhoons and tremors. If it looks too dangerous to proceed, turn back.

If you're venturing deep into the interior or to peaks more than 3,000m high, check what permits are legally required and get them. Hikers who don't and later have to be rescued may well be billed for the rescue effort – and helicopters don't come cheap.

HOT SPRINGS Geothermal activity has given Taiwan more than 120 natural spas. Each spring has a slightly different mineral content, odour and colour. There are scalding sulphurous springs, cold bubbling springs, mud spas and clear-water springs. Some, like those at Xinbeitou and Zhiben, have become highly developed resorts. Others are more or less natural, and consist of nothing more than a riverside pool without changing rooms or other facilities.

The springs in Xinbeitou and on Yangmingshan are acidic and sulphuric. Natural spas in other parts of Taiwan tend to be carbonatic and rich in dissolved sodium, magnesium, potassium and calcium. The medicinal claims made for many hot springs should be taken with a pinch of sulphur but there's no doubt a soak can relieve stress and ease chronic body aches. At the end of a long hike, of course, a few hours in a hot spring is nothing short of blissful.

they come up to depths of around 30m during the day after hunting all night in deeper water. However, it isn't certain you'll see the sharks. It's also dangerous – divers have died after being caught in downward undersea currents that can keep a person submerged longer than his or her air can hold out. Green Island's other dive sites are far safer and very scenic. You can jump in almost anywhere and clearly see the bottom 30m below. There are tropical fish of all varieties. Orchid Island is a longer ferry journey from Taiwan's mainland but just as amazing.

After spending some time on these two islands I returned to Kenting, where I now live. There are at least 50 dive sites in this area. One, called Seven Stars, is 10km offshore. There's an old wreck and outstanding visibility. Kenting's soft-coral sites are among the best in the world, especially one at 6–10m depth near Houbihu called 'the flower garden'. Then there is Sand Island, which is not actually an island and not really made of sand. The powder is in fact crushed seashells, so fine it resembles sand. One side of the 'island' is off-limits because turtles come here to lay their eggs.

The waters around Kenting do suffer from overfishing, but enforcement is improving and environmental awareness is growing gradually. Taiwan's people are nice, the climate is nice and the diving just keeps getting better.

John Boo, who has lived in Taiwan since 1991, runs U-Dive Scuba Taiwan Club (m 0913 388 065; e scuba_diving1@yahoo.com; www.udive.com.tw).

As well as having a thriving local birdwatching scene, Taiwan has emerged as a key stop on the global birdwatcher's journey. Birders come with lists of species they hope to see, but leave impressed by much more than the island's avifauna. Taiwan's advantages include a hospitable population, good infrastructure, well-protected forests, no malaria or leeches, diverse habitats, great flora and butterflies – and all in a fairly compact area. It's possible to see most of Taiwan's 80-plus endemics and endemic subspecies, plus other outstanding birds, in just a few days.

The best places to see birds found only in Taiwan are the national forest recreation areas. For birding, the best-known of these is Dasyueshan where Swinhoe's pheasants (*Lophura swinhoii*) are often spotted right next to the road. For wintering wetland birds I suggest Yilan County, Jincheng Lake (part of Hsinchu City's 17km Coastline Scenic Area) and Aogu Wetland (see page 208) in Chiayi County.

There's good birding to be had even for visitors unable to get out of the lowland cities and into the high mountains. My favourite sites in central Taipei include the Botanical Garden – probably the easiest place in the world to spot the Malayan Night Heron (*Gorsachius melanolophus*) – and Daan Forest Park, where you should follow the bird photographers who are always there. At Chiang Kai-shek Memorial Hall, check the ponds and trees on the north, west, and south edges of the grounds. Huajiang Wild Duck Nature Park (see page 89) is less than 1km from the bustle of Longshan Temple in Wanhua. Further out, Guandu Nature Park (see page 84), further out but within walking distance of Guandu Station on the MRT's Red Line, has excellent facilities managed by the Wild Bird Society of Taipei (*http://wbst.org.tw*).

My favourite site near Taipei is Wulai. Lots of good birds can be spotted amid the mid-elevation mountains here, among them the Taiwan Blue Magpie (*Urocissa caerulea*), and the Maroon Oriole (*Oriolus traillii*). From the main village follow either of the two rivers east or south. Further afield, the main lower part of Taroko Gorge can be good in winter, especially the side road to Buluowan and the hiking trail to Lianhua Pond. If possible drive the road westwards and upwards from Taroko towards Hehuanshan as both the scenery and the birding are incredible.

Good birding can be done throughout the year. That said, spring is best with autumn and winter being almost as good. Summer is a bit tougher – not only is the weather hotter, but most migrant species are absent. Don't miss Kenting around 10 October for the raptor migration – birders should go to Sheding Nature Park in the morning, then Manzhou around dusk.

Taiwan's minor islands offer numerous opportunities. Matsu National Scenic Area, especially Dongyin Island, is excellent for spotting migrants between mid-April and mid-May and again from mid-September to mid-October. For a change of scene and good winter birding (which even non-birders will enjoy) check out Kinmen County.

Richard Foster, who in 2013 saw 388 of the 608 bird species recorded in Taiwan, is founder and chief guide of Taiwan EcoTours (m 0938 337 710; e taiwanecotours@gmail.com; http://taiwanbirding.com).

PARAGLIDING Taiwan has wind and hills and therefore paragliding. The best places are near Puli in the very centre of the island and Luye in the southeast.

RAFTING Letting the current sweep you through the white-water rapids of the Xiuguluan River is a fun way to cool off at the height of summer (see page 297).

WATERSPORTS Warm water and consistent winds make Penghu County a world-class windsurfing venue. Much of Taiwan's west coast is good for kitesurfing. The snorkelling and scuba diving around Green Island, Orchid Island and Kenting National Park is first-rate.

PHOTOGRAPHY

Taiwan is visually fascinating and there are very few laws or taboos limiting what a photographer is allowed to capture on film or a memory card. In addition to superb mountain and coastal landscapes, the cities are beehives of activity filled with memorable structures, signs and posters. Shutterbugs also adore Taiwan's many colourful festivals. Even if the weather isn't ideal, you'll find the warmth of Taiwan's people encouraging. Very few people will refuse permission if you ask to take snaps of their shops, their products or even themselves at work.

If people are kneeling under a roadside tarpaulin, they're attending a funeral. At other religious and semi-religious events, however, it's fine to shoot away. Almost certainly, you won't be the only one taking photos. You should always have your camera ready for immediate use. You never know what you'll find around the next corner. It could be a vendor selling vegetables you've never seen before, a dramatic display of religious fervour, or a family letting off firecrackers to celebrate their son winning a place at a top university.

Rich J Matheson (m *0912 760 624;* e *liefintaiwan@gmail.com; www. thetaiwanphotographer.com*), a Canadian professional photographer who has lived in Taiwan for the past 20 years, leads photo tours lasting from a half a day to one week. He provided many of the images for the colour section of this book.

MEDIA AND COMMUNICATIONS

PRINT The most popular Chinese-language newspaper in Taiwan is *Apple Daily* (*http://tw.nextmedia.com*), a sensationalist broadsheet packed with gory photos of road accidents and computer-generated graphics showing how crimes were committed. It also runs worthwhile travel articles and restaurant reviews. The same company owns *Next*, a weekly magazine that has uncovered some major scandals. Of the three main quality newspapers, *Liberty Times* supports the green camp (see box, page 22) while *United Daily News* and *China Times* back the blues.

English-language press Taiwan's two main English-language print dailies are the pro-green *Taipei Times* (*www.taipeitimes.com*) and the pro-KMT *China Post* (*www.chinapost.com.tw*). Both can be found in convenience stores and bookshops. The small ads in these newspapers are useful if you're looking for a job, a travel agent, or a place to rent, and also for restaurant and nightlife listings. The print edition of *Taiwan News* (*www.etaiwannews.com*) is much harder to find. Online alternatives include the business-orientated *Commonwealth Magazine* (*http:// english.cw.com.tw*) and *Want China Times* (*http://wantchinatimes.com*). The last focuses on business and cultural links with mainland China.

The Ministry of Foreign Affairs publishes a substantial English-language monthly called *Taiwan Review* (*http://taiwanreview.nat.gov.tw*). Sold in larger bookshops but free online, it's well worth seeking out if you've a serious interest in Taiwanese art or social issues. The ministry's daily news site is *Taiwan Today* (*www.taiwantoday.tw*). The American Chamber of Commerce in Taipei publishes a monthly, *Taiwan Business Topics*. This magazine ventures beyond dry business subjects; each year, one issue is devoted to travel and culture and another to fine dining. Some bookshops sell it and it's also online (*www.amcham.com.tw*).

TELEVISION Taiwan has dozens of television stations covering every demographic. Most broadcast a mix of Mandarin and Taiwanese-language programming; there are also government-supported Hakka and aboriginal channels. For years there's been talk of establishing a government-funded English-language channel. In many hotels you'll find CNN, HBO and ESPN alongside homegrown 24-hour news stations and channels devoted to Buddhism.

RADIO Turn the dial and you'll come across plenty of Mandarin and Taiwanese-language radio stations offering a blend of talk, music and news. The most popular mainstream stations include KISS (99.7 and 99.9FM; *www.kiss.com.tw*) and Hit FM (various frequencies; *www.hitoradio.com*). Pirate radio stations can be found throughout the spectrum; some have a political agenda while others make money advertising dubious products. The government-funded Radio Taiwan International (*www.rti.org.tw*) broadcasts in 13 languages including English on shortwave and the internet. Taiwan's only English-language FM station, ICRT (100.7FM; *www.icrt.com.tw*), plays mostly middle-of-the-road pop and rock. The hourly newscasts include weather and Taipei-centric traffic reports.

TELEPHONE AND FAX Public phones are easy to find in train and bus stations and outside convenience stores. Some take coins (NTD1 gets you a two-minute local call) but for most you'll need a stored-value card (at least NTD100) which you can buy from any convenience store. To call abroad, dial 002 then the country code:

Australia +61	**China** +86	**Ireland** +353	**UK** +44
Canada +1	**Hong Kong** +852	**New Zealand** +64	**USA** +1

City and county codes When calling Taiwan from overseas, drop the zero from the area code. When calling Taipei, you should thus dial 886 (Taiwan's country code) followed by 2 (area code, minus the zero), then the phone number.

Faxes You can send faxes from 7-Eleven shops; hotels charge considerably more.

Useful and emergency telephone numbers The government-run 24-hour Information For Foreigners hotline (✆ 0800 024 111) is free of charge, as is the 24-hour tourist information line (✆ 0800 011 765). Both are very useful; if they can't find the information you want immediately they'll call you back, usually within 30 minutes. The emergency services are at ✆ 110 (police) and ✆ 119 (fire and ambulance) but little English is spoken. Taipei's English-speaking police can be contacted at ✆ 02 2556 6007.

Cellphones Mobile telephone coverage throughout Taiwan is excellent, although you may encounter blind spots in the mountains. If you have an international 'roaming' account, bring your phone with you and it should work normally. If you don't, consider getting a temporary account (in the form of a SIM card to put in your phone) from one of the phone-company counters at Taiwan Taoyuan or Kaohsiung airports. Doing so at the airport is easier than doing so later on, elsewhere in the country. Alternatively, several days before leaving home apply for a **Digital Tour Buddy** (*http://youthtravel.tw*). Through this scheme travellers can borrow a 3G SIM card or 2G SIM card and phone for the duration of their visit; the cards contain useful phone numbers, a Chinese-English dictionary and other features.

POST OFFICES All post offices have green shopfronts. Most bear the single English word 'Post'. You'll find post offices on major roads in every city and small town. Most open 08.00–17.00 Monday–Friday; some also open 08.00–12.00 on Saturday. GPOs in major cities open for a few hours each Sunday and at many branches it's possible to change money (usually US dollars, euros and Japanese yen only). When sending mail within Taiwan, or from overseas to Taiwan, do ask a friend to write the destination and return addresses in Chinese. In theory, a letter bearing an address written entirely in romanised script should reach the intended recipient, but because of spelling inconsistencies this doesn't always happen. When sending something out of Taiwan, write the destination country in Chinese or English, not another language.

INTERNET Because Wi-Fi and broadband are now commonplace, internet cafés (*wǎng kā*) have become an endangered species. If you find one, expect to pay around NTD30 per hour; you may be required to buy a soft drink for a similar amount. If you're carrying a laptop, you're better off looking for a restaurant or coffee shop that offers wireless internet access. Many do but there isn't likely to be an English sign, so ask the staff if they have wireless (*wúxiàn wǎnglù*).

Foreign visitors carrying digital devices can get free Wi-Fi access by showing their passport at any Tourism Bureau-run information counter. They'll receive a password enabling them to go online at iTaiwan (*www.itaiwan.gov.tw*) hotspots at hospitals, bus and train stations, government offices and tourist attractions.

MAPS

Road maps of Taiwan go out of date quickly for two reasons. Typhoons sometimes close or destroy mountain routes, and the government is obsessed with road-building. If you plan to drive or ride any significant distance, go to a visitor information centre and grab the free regional maps covering the north, south, centre and east. If you have special interests, it's worth contacting the Tourism Bureau or one of its overseas offices before you arrive and seeing what they can come up with. A good source of maps in London is **Stanfords** (*12–14 Long Acre, London WC2E 9LP;* \ *+44 20 7836 1321;* e *sales@stanfords.co.uk; www.stanfords. co.uk;* ⊕ *09.00–20.00 Mon–Sat, 12.00–18.00 Sun*).

BUSINESS

Office workers are usually at their desks Monday to Friday 09.00–17.00, sometimes earlier, often later. Lunch lasts at least an hour, from midday, and is regarded by many as sacrosanct. If you wander into a company or a government office at that time you might find most people sleeping or absent. English and Japanese are widely spoken in Taiwanese business circles, and lots of Chinese tea is drunk. If you'd rather not drink tea, ask for water instead. Many companies operate as

2

normal on public holidays, but don't try to get any business done in the three or four days before the Lunar New Year or the week afterwards.

USEFUL CONTACTS/WEBSITES

American Chamber of Commerce in Taipei Suite 706, 7th Flr 129 Minsheng E Rd Sec 3, Taipei 10596; ☎+886 2 2718 8226; f +886 2 2718 8182; e amcham@amcham.com.tw; www.amcham.com.tw

Board of Foreign Trade www.trade.gov.tw

British Chamber of Commerce in Taipei 26th Flr 9–11 Songgao Rd, Taipei 11073; ☎+886 2 2720 1919; f +886 2 2720 9200; e info@bcctaipei.com; www.bcctaipei.com

European Chamber of Commerce Taipei 11th Flr 285 Zhongxiao E Rd Sec 4, Taipei 10692; ☎+886 2 2740 0236; f +886 2 2772 0530; www.ecct.com.tw

The Ministry of Economic Affairs www.moea.gov.tw

The Ministry of Foreign Affairs www.mofa.gov.tw

CULTURAL ETIQUETTE

Taiwanese people are open-minded and aware that people from the West do many things differently. You may get stared at during your trip but this doesn't mean offence has been taken.

GREETINGS Mandarin is quite straightforward when it comes to greeting people. Usually people say *nǐ hǎo* (literally 'you good?' but meaning 'hello'). Sometimes they'll use the more polite and formal *nín hǎo*. When entering a shop or restaurant, it's not necessary to do anything more than smile at whoever's behind the counter. Shaking hands is common in business circles. If you're from a culture where greeting a lady by kissing her cheek is normal, restrain yourself while in Taiwan.

DRUGS Taiwan has strict drugs laws and death sentences are possible for smugglers and dealers. The police are empowered to force those they suspect of using illegal drugs to take a urine test. If the test comes up positive for amphetamines, ecstasy or another controlled substance, the individual is sent to a detention centre for up to 30 days of compulsory detoxification. This is an administrative action, not a judicial procedure, so there's no appeal.

ALCOHOL Taiwan is quite free and easy when it comes to where and when you can buy and consume alcoholic drinks. Labourers can sometimes be seen drinking beer during the day; drinking in public places like parks and train stations is legal yet considered low class.

If drinking with Taiwanese friends, it's polite to top up their glasses before refilling your own. At formal events like wedding banquets, expect frequent toasts. You'll be expected to join in, but sipping tea or juice rather than an alcoholic beverage is perfectly acceptable.

Sometimes complete strangers will invite you to sit and drink with them; refuse politely if you don't wish to join them. The importance of not drinking and driving is now widely understood.

HOSPITALITY Taiwanese are extremely friendly to visitors from the West and Japan. If you're invited to a Taiwanese person's home, do bring a gift of some kind. Fruit is a good option but avoid cheaper varieties like bananas and guavas; go for whatever looks good in the supermarket. If you plan to bring alcohol, buy a bottle of decent whisky or red wine. Whatever you do, don't bring a clock as it implies you want the recipient to die! Don't be surprised if your host initially refuses your gift; he or she is being polite. Offer it again and eventually it'll be accepted. Say hello (in English or Mandarin) to everyone you see in the house but don't be surprised or offended if the very oldest or very youngest present doesn't seem to acknowledge your greeting. They may well be shy and unsure how to deal with a foreigner. However, it's just as likely that your hosts will ask you lots of questions about your work, your spouse or partner and what you think of Taiwan.

Take your shoes off when you arrive; you'll be offered a pair of plastic beach sandals (which English-speaking Taiwanese often call 'slippers') to wear inside the house. You'll probably be shown to the living room, which is where many families take their meals. Don't be shocked if old newspaper is used instead of a tablecloth and the TV stays on throughout the meal.

In most respects Taiwanese people aren't so different from Westerners, so it's hard to go wrong. Compliment your host's cooking (or choice of restaurant if you eat out), make sure everyone knows you've had a good time and make sure you don't stay too late if people need to work or attend school the next day.

TRAVELLING POSITIVELY

Taiwan isn't a conspicuously poor society, though you will see a few homeless people sleeping rough in the cities and families living in dilapidated houses. The worst social problems – which include poverty, unemployment, alcoholism and youngsters failing to complete high school – tend to be in the most remote parts of the country. For many visiting Westerners, the sorry state of Taiwan's animals is the most obvious and distressing issue.

Noordhoff Craniofacial Foundation www.lovemakeswhole.org. Founded by a now-retired American missionary-doctor who specialised in repairing cleft lips & palates, this foundation subsidises surgery & postoperative care for young children with facial deformities. Since 1989 more than 30,000 youngsters have been helped. Donations welcome.

Rangi Association e rangi.association@gmail.com. This informal group of expatriate volunteers works with indigenous groups; rangi means 'friend' in the language of the Atayal tribe. Donations are sometimes sought for specific projects.

Taiwan SPCA ☏ 02 2367 0317; e spca@spca.org; www.spca.org.tw. Taipei-based Taiwan SPCA is an expat-inspired animal welfare group which welcomes volunteers for rescues, CNR & educational events.

Woodpecker Life Association 223 Zhongshan Rd Sec 1, Guangfu, Hualien 97642; e bethanypeng@gmail.com. Woodpecker helps disadvantaged pupils stay in school & aims to broaden the horizons of youngsters in small towns in east Taiwan by encouraging travellers of all nationalities to visit schools. Welcomes donations of secondhand items that can be sold to raise funds & volunteers who can do a little teaching. Interested parties should contact Bethany via the email address listed above.

World Vision Taiwan 6th Flr 133 Minsheng E Rd Sec 4, Taipei 105; ☏ 02 2175 1995; e pr@worldvision.org.tw; www.worldvision.org.tw. This international Christian organisation matches Taiwanese sponsors with children in Taiwan (especially in aboriginal areas) & elsewhere, & does relief work in the wake of typhoons & other disasters. Donations welcome.

WWOOF Taiwan ☏ 02 8509 7056 ext 9; e info@wwooftaiwan.com; www.wwooftaiwan.com. Part of the WWOOF (World Wide Opportunities on Organic Farms) network, this group can arrange for you to stay & work on an organic farm. If you're not already a member you can join in Taiwan (NTD800 for a year), after which board & lodging is free.

Part Two

THE GUIDE

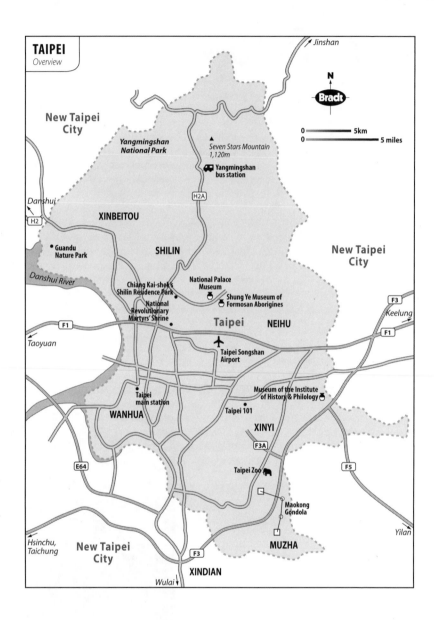

TAIPEI
Overview

Jinshan

N

Bradt

0 — 5km
0 — 5 miles

New Taipei City

Yangmingshan National Park

▲ *Seven Stars Mountain 1,120m*

🚌 **Yangmingshan bus station**

H2A

Danshui

H2

XINBEITOU

• **Guandu Nature Park**

Danshui River

SHILIN

New Taipei City

Chiang Kai-shek's Shilin Residence Park

National Palace Museum

Shung Ye Museum of Formosan Aborigines

National Revolutionary Martyrs' Shrine

Taipei

NEIHU

F3

Keelung

F1

F1

Taoyuan

✈ **Taipei Songshan Airport**

Museum of the Institute of History & Philology

• **Taipei main station**

WANHUA

• **Taipei 101**

XINYI

F3A

E64

Taipei Zoo 🐘

F5

Maokong Gondola

Yilan

Hsinchu, Taichung

New Taipei City

F3

MUZHA

XINDIAN

Wulai

3

Taipei 台北

Telephone code 02

Twenty-first-century Taipei is a delightful metropolis in which to spend time. It's safe and easy to get around and there's plenty to see and do in multiple categories including museums, temples, gastronomy, nature rambles and shopping.

Taiwan's capital, often compared with Hong Kong or Singapore and found lacking, is the nearest Greater China has to a renaissance city. The money-making here is avid, to be sure, but feels less visceral than in Hong Kong. Compared with Singapore, far less English is spoken but more genuine friendliness is expressed. There's greater freedom and civility here than in any other Han-majority metropolis. With 2.68 million people, Taipei will never rival London, Paris or Tokyo in artistic output or economic significance. However, it certainly holds its own when compared with Asian cities twice the size – and thanks to the mountains that limit Taipei's sprawl, getting lungfuls of fresh air and eyefuls of green forest isn't difficult.

Relatively few of Taipei's buildings are older than the Chiang Kai-shek Memorial Hall (completed in 1980) yet the city is streaked with veins of antiquity. The richest of these are in Wanhua, a down-at-heel, Taiwan-as-Formosa-used-to-be neighbourhood, and the riverside neighbourhood called Dadaocheng.

For many, the mere fact that Taipei has the world-class National Palace Museum justifies time in the capital. Visitors shouldn't, however, obsess about that stupendous repository to the exclusion of other attractions, such as the exquisite Baoan Temple. Nor should they pack their schedule with too much sightseeing. One of Taipei's most pleasurable pastimes is simply lingering on a busy street and watching passers-by: office workers in the latest fashions, retired Nationalist soldiers who speak with thick mainland Chinese accents, Buddhist nuns, Tibetan monks, southeast Asian labourers and swarms of college and high-school students.

HISTORY

Han migrants settled near the coast in the 17th century and gradually made their way upriver. In 1709, the imperial authorities – aware that population pressure in Fujian could lead to unrest – approved a scheme to develop the Taipei Basin. Migrants poured in and within half a century the area's native inhabitants, the Ketagalan tribe, were being forced to cede ground to Han Chinese settlers. As the latter increased in number, the former intermarried with the newcomers, assimilated or migrated. Within a century they'd disappeared as a distinct ethnic group.

Like London, modern Taipei is to some extent an agglomeration of villages and small towns. In the mid-19th century, one of these towns, Wanhua (now part of the capital's southwest), was a large, dynamic settlement. The merchants of Wanhua saw their counterparts in Dadaocheng (the area around Dihua Street) as upstarts and there was an ethnic component to this rivalry. Immigrants from different parts of Fujian had clashed violently in Wanhua in 1853. The losers, among them merchants, fled to the newer riverside community at Dadaocheng, which they called Twatutia. Tea was the commodity that powered Dadaocheng's growth and enabled it to overtake Wanhua.

The place name Taipei (*tái běi* in Mandarin, meaning 'north Taiwan') first appeared on maps in 1875 when the imperial court reorganised Taiwan's system of prefectures and subprefectures. The seat of the new Taipei prefecture was located between Wanhua and Dadaocheng for the same reasons Ottawa was chosen to be Canada's capital: it was a compromise between two powerful blocs and there was space to build.

In June 1895, the Japanese Army entered Taipei without firing a shot. The colonial regime set about tearing down the city's walls, widening and straightening roads and commissioning public buildings, among them the Japanese governor-general's office, which is now the Presidential Office. The National Taiwan Museum also dates from the colonial era. Taihoku (the city's Japanese name) quickly overtook Tainan and Taichung in terms of size and wealth, but it suffered substantial damage from American air raids in 1945.

In 1949, the influx of retreating Nationalists changed the face of Taipei society. Even now there are neighbourhoods dominated by mainlanders and their descendants, in which very little Taiwanese is spoken and where 'green' politicians (see box, page 22) stand no chance of electoral success. These mainlanders brought with them their customs and cuisines and turned the city into a microcosm of China.

For years, the Nationalist government regarded Taipei as a mere 'temporary capital' from which they would plot the retaking of the mainland. As a result little was spent on public works; well into the 1980s, the state of Taipei was an embarrassment. However, in the past two decades there's been great improvement. The sprawl (less than 40 years ago, the district where Taipei 101 now stands was mostly vegetable plots and graveyards) is criss-crossed by mass rapid-transit (MRT) lines. It's a testament to Taiwan's maturity and stability that in recent years, landmark events in the capital have not been protests or riots, but inaugurations of infrastructure projects and museum openings.

GETTING THERE AND AWAY

BY AIR What's officially known as Taipei Airport, but which most locals and expatriates refer to as **Songshan Airport** [map, page 84] (☏ 8770 3460; *www.tsa. gov.tw*), handles domestic flights to Hualien, Taitung, Penghu, Kinmen and Matsu (for one-way fares, see the entries on those destinations) as well as international flights to mainland China, Japan and Hong Kong. More than a dozen city bus lines stop right outside the airport. Songshan Airport is on the MRT's Brown Line.

BY HSR The high-speed rail system shares Taipei Main Station [89 F1] with TRA. Journey times are about one hour to Taichung (*NTD765*) and never more than two hours to Kaohsiung Zuoying (*NTD1,630*). There are three or more southbound bullet-train services per hour (⊕ *06.30–23.00 daily*), some of which don't stop at Taoyuan, Hsinchu, Chiayi or Tainan.

BY TRA From Taipei Main Station [89 F1], two or three expresses leave for Kaohsiung every hour between dawn and early evening every day of the week (*takes 4¾–7hrs; NTD650–843*). All southbound expresses on the Mountain Line (see *Getting around*, page 56) stop at Taichung (*takes 2–3hrs; NTD289–375*). There are very few southbound overnight trains and they're more expensive, slower and less comfortable than overnight coaches. Including local services, most of which go no further than Hsinchu (*takes 1–1¾hrs; NTD114–177*), there are five or more southbound departures per hour.

Heading north, there are four trains per hour to Keelung (*takes 45mins; NTD41–64*) and around 36 expresses per day to Hualien (*takes 2–3½hrs; NTD340–440*), of which a dozen continue on to Taitung (*takes 5–7hrs; NTD605–785*).

Left-luggage lockers (*NTD20–50 for 3hrs or part thereof*) are on the level below the ground floor.

BY BUS Direct buses link Taipei with every part of the island except the east coast. The most useful of the bus stations near the HSR and TRA stations is **Taipei Bus Station** [89 F1] (✆ *7733 5888; www.taipeibus.com.tw*). Tickets should be bought downstairs but buses are boarded upstairs. Around the clock there are several services per hour to major west-coast cities (typical journey times and one-way fares in parentheses): Hsinchu (*1½hrs; NTD130*); Zhudong (*1½hrs; NTD180*); Taichung (*2¾hrs; NTD260*); Changhua (*3¼hrs; NTD300*); Chiayi (*3½hrs; NTD330*); Tainan (*4¼hrs; NTD360*); and Kaohsiung (*5hrs; NTD530*). Prices are often 30% cheaper between Monday afternoon and Thursday night. You can also catch buses from this station to Yilan and Luodong (*#1915, #1916 & #1917; takes up to 1¼hrs; NTD104–135*).

Most Kuo-Kuang services use **Taipei West Bus Station** [89 E1], a pair of buildings a very short walk west of Taipei Main Station. Buses to Taiwan Taoyuan International Airport (*#1819; takes about 1hr; NTD125*) leave from Terminal A, the building nearer Taipei Main Station, around the clock. Service #1961 is cheaper (*NTD90*). Services to major west-coast cities, Puli (*#1832; takes 3½hrs; NTD385*) and Sun Moon Lake (*#1833; takes 4hrs; NTD460*) leave from Terminal B.

Taipei City Hall Bus Station [93 G1], accessed via the Blue Line MRT station of the same name, is convenient if you're staying in the eastern half of the city. As well as services to Taiwan Taoyuan International Airport (*#1960; departures at least hourly; ⊕ 04.00–23.00; takes 1¼hrs; NTD145*), during the day there are buses about every half hour to Tainan, Taichung, Hsinchu and Keelung. Services #1570, #1571 and #1572 leave for Yilan and Luodong (*up to 7 departures per hr; ⊕ 06.00–22.00 daily; takes 1hr; NTD90–120*).

GETTING AROUND

If you're going to be in the Taipei area for an extended period, get an EasyCard (*www.easycard.com.tw*). These 'touch and go' smart cards can be used for bus, taxi, TRA and MRT journeys throughout north Taiwan, to pay parking charges, and to pay admission charges to Taipei Zoo and some other places.

BY RAPID TRANSIT Taipei's mass rapid-transit (MRT) network (✆ *2181 2345; http:// english.trtc.com.tw/; ⊕ 06.00–midnight daily*), which has several colour-coded lines, is bilingual and disabled-friendly. With the exception of the Brown Line and the northern part of the Red Line, the system is underground. Tourists are most likely to use the Red, Blue and Orange lines. Departure frequency varies between one train every two minutes during peak hours to one train every 15 minutes late at night. Journey times and one-way fares are listed on the website; for example: Taipei Main Station to Taipei Zoo (*26mins; NTD35*) and Taipei Main Station to Longshan Temple

(*5mins; NTD20*). One-way tickets come in the form of reusable circular plastic tokens. If you plan to do a lot of sightseeing in one day, get an unlimited-distance day pass (*NTD200 including NTD50 deposit*). Each of the 100-plus stations has bathrooms, infant changing/feeding facilities and water fountains.

BY BUS Taipei's city bus system is comprehensive and user-friendly. Buses are far slower than rapid-transit trains, generally, but you get to see much more of the city. Stops are announced in English and Mandarin by audio recording and on an LED screen above the driver. During peak hours you may have to stand; if you're old or frail, however, someone will probably give up their seat for you. Bus journeys cost NTD15 per section with most journeys being a single section. On some buses you pay when you board; on others, you pay when getting off. Useful services starting out from Taipei Main Station include #260 to Yangmingshan and #295 to Taipei Zoo.

BY TAXI Few drivers understand English so whenever possible ask the staff at your hotel to write the name of your destination in Chinese. However, the **English Taxi Association** (✆ *2799 7997;* ⊕ *08.30–22.00 daily*) can send an English-speaking taxi driver to any place in the capital; they charge the same as standard taxis. Because the association doesn't have a lot of drivers, calling at least 30 minutes before you need the taxi is advised. Call a day or two in advance if you want a car and driver for a tour further afield, say to Wulai or Yangmingshan (*from NTD450 per hr*).

ON FOOT If the weather's on your side, Taipei is an excellent place for urban hiking. Unlike some other Taiwanese cities, the capital's pavements are broad and well maintained and the air quality isn't bad. There's zero risk of straying into a dangerous neighbourhood. You're never far from a convenience store if you need something cold to drink, and there are so many buses and taxis that you can switch to another mode of transport the moment you get tired.

BY BICYCLE Riverside bike paths go all the way from Xindian in the southeast to Danshui in the northwest. Bikes can be rented at various places close to the rivers; you'll be expected to leave a deposit and/or some form of ID. Some rental businesses allow you to borrow from one location and return the bike to another. Check closing times to avoid getting stuck with the bike until the next day. The city government's YouBike (*www.youbike.com.tw*) is inexpensive (*NTD10 for 30mins; pay by credit card or EasyCard*). There are 110-plus rental points but sometimes there are no bikes to be had at popular locations. You can carry bikes on to MRT trains at certain stations; look for the bicycle symbol on MRT maps.

BY HIRED CAR OR MOTORCYCLE There's no need to drive yourself around Taipei but you may want to rent a vehicle to explore north Taiwan.

🚗 **Car Plus Auto Leasing** 71-1 Jianguo N Rd Sec 1; ✆ 2502 1389; www.car-plus.com.tw; ⊕ 08.30–20.30 daily. General-use car rentals & long-term leasing; near Songjiang Nanjing MRT Station.
🚗 **Hotai Leasing** Ground Flr, Taipei Main Station; ✆ 2375 6000; www.easyrent.com.tw; ⊕ 07.00–23.00 daily. Can provide limousines with chauffeurs as well as conventional rentals.

🚗 **Bike Farm** m 0926 283 300; e bikefarmbikes@gmail.com; www.bikefarm. net. At least 24hrs' notice required for motorcycle/ scooter rentals. Min rental period 4 days & a deposit of at least NTD5,000 must be paid; vehicle will be delivered to your hotel.

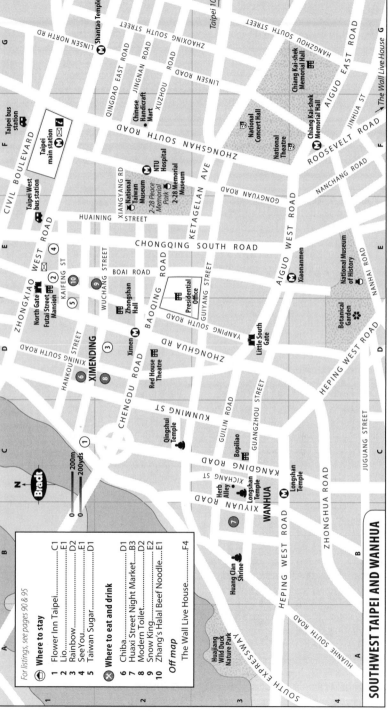

SOUTHWEST TAIPEI AND WANHUA

For listings, see pages 90 & 95

🛏 **Where to stay**
1 Flower Inn Taipei.........................C1
2 Lio...E1
3 Rainbow....................................D2
4 SeeYou......................................E1
5 Taiwan Sugar.............................D1

✕ **Where to eat and drink**
6 Chiba...D1
7 Huaxi Street Night Market.........B3
8 Modern Toilet............................D2
9 Snow King..................................E2
10 Zhang's Halal Beef Noodle..........E1

Off map
   The Wall Live House.....................F4

TOURIST INFORMATION

There are several visitor information centres, the most useful being those in Taipei Main Station [89 F1] (⏲ *08.00–20.00 daily*), Songshan Airport [map, page 84] (⏲ *08.00–20.00 daily*), Maokong Gondola Station (⏲ *09.00–18.00 Tue–Fri, 08.30–20.00 Sat–Sun*) and in the following MRT stations: Beitou (⏲ *09.00–18.00 daily*), Jiantan and Ximen [89 D2] (*both open* ⏲ *11.00–20.00 Mon–Fri, 11.00–21.00 Sat–Sun*). Try also **Taipei City Government's** tourism website: www.taipeitravel.net/en/.

⌂ WHERE TO STAY

SOUTHWEST TAIPEI All of the following hotels are shown on the map on page 89.

⌂ **SeeYou Hotel** (47 rooms) 18 Chongqing Rd Sec 1; ✆2388 7269; f 2388 2983; e seeyou. taipei@msa.hinet.net; www.taipeiseeyouhotel. com.tw. Rooms are on the small side but crammed with refrigerators, DVD players & other items, so you'll be able to make yourself comfortable. Most rooms have showers only; some have jacuzzis. Basic dbls priced under NTD2,300 at w/end. B/fast inc. **$$$**

⌂ **Taiwan Sugar Hotel** (68 rooms) 39 Zhonghua Rd Sec 1; ✆2388 5522; f 2311 7979; e taipeihotel@taisugar.com.tw; www.tscleisure. com.tw/tphotel/en/about.html. This 2013-opened hotel is the absolute antithesis of so many in Ximending which offer modish but rabbit-hutch rooms. Guestrooms are a very decent size. As you might expect of an establishment owned by the state-run sugar company, fixtures & fittings are solid if conservative. If the heavily discounted prices being offered at the time of writing are continued this will be one of the best accommodation bargains in central Taipei. B/fast inc. **$$$**

⌂ **Flower Inn Taipei** (6 rooms) 18-1 Kangding Rd; m 0923 777 993. Very clean & quiet for a hotel in this budget range & has a pleasant rooftop garden. No b/fast but you're close to restaurants & shops & each room has a refrigerator. Not especially close to MRT stations but within striking distance of both Ximending & Wanhua if you're happy exploring on foot. **$$**

⌂ **Lio Hotel** (37 rooms) 9 Yanping S Rd; ✆2314 5296; f 2314 8838; e lio.hotel@gmail.com; www. liohotel.com.tw. The sgl rooms here are probably the best deal in central Taipei for solo travellers who can do without windows & bathtubs, but want something better than a hostel environment. The rooms are clean, quiet & decorated in pastel

shades & soft golds. Wi-Fi & PC in lobby for guests' use. Surprisingly good b/fast inc. **$$**

⌂ **Rainbow Hotel** (70 rooms) 36 Hanzhong St; ✆2311 9193; f 2388 5011; e rainbow2009@kimo. com; www.rainbowhoteltaipei.com.tw. The décor is unimaginative but the Rainbow's location in the heart of Ximending, the size & cleanliness of its rooms & some very competitive prices make it an attractive option. Suites for 3, 4 & 5 ppl available. B/fast inc. **$$**

NORTHWEST TAIPEI All of the following hotels are shown on the map opposite.

⌂ **Ambassador Hotel** (416 rooms) 63 Zhongshan N Rd Sec 2; ✆2551 111; f 2531 5215; http://taipei.ambassadorhotel.com.tw. Thanks to recent renovations & an unswerving focus on friendly service, Taiwan's oldest 5-star hotel (established 1963) continues to be at the top of its game. Room décor is elegant rather than flashy & the beds are rated as among the city's most comfortable. In summer, request a room beside the small outdoor swimming pool. Long-running in-house restaurants offer Cantonese, Sichuan & other cuisines. For a blowout, try **A Cut Steakhouse** (✆2571 0389; ⏲ 11.30–15.00 & 18.00–22.30 daily; EM; **$$$$$**) which serves dry-aged US & Australian beef & has been praised by *Wine Spectator* magazine. All rooms inc buffet b/fast. **$$$$$**

⌂ **Grand Hotel** (490 rooms) 1 Zhongshan N Rd Sec 4; ✆2886 8888; f 2885 2885; e reservations@ grand-hotel.org; www.grand-hotel.org. Built at the behest of Madame Chiang Kai-shek, who wanted a hotel befitting ambassadors & world leaders, the Grand Hotel has had numerous ups & downs since its opening in 1952. Service standards are still a tad old-fashioned but the hotel has modernised extensively in recent years while retaining the conservative décor & massive lobby

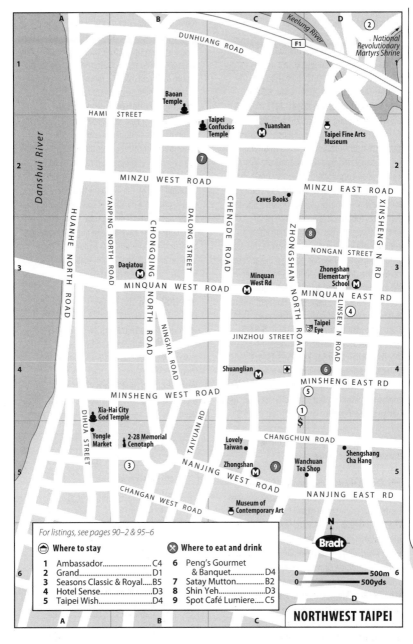

NORTHWEST TAIPEI

For listings, see pages 90–2 & 95–6

🏠 **Where to stay**

1	Ambassador	C4
2	Grand	D1
3	Seasons Classic & Royal	B5
4	Hotel Sense	D3
5	Taipei Wish	D4

❌ **Where to eat and drink**

6	Peng's Gourmet & Banquet	D4
7	Satay Mutton	B2
8	Shin Yeh	D3
9	Spot Café Lumiere	C5

that give this landmark considerable retro appeal. B/fast inc. **$$$$$**

🏠 **Hotel Sense** (79 rooms) 477 Linsen N Rd; 🕾 7743 1000; f 7743 1100; e info@hotelsense. com.tw; www.hotelsense.com.tw. The black & grey lobby of this new boutique hotel is a shrine to the

Art Deco movement. You'll immediately notice the low ceiling & high-backed armchairs. Fortunately, the styling in the guestrooms isn't quite so strong. The superior rooms are lovely but lack windows; all but one of the deluxe rooms (a very good option if you want accommodation for 3) boasts a large balcony. The 32-inch LCD TVs can be swivelled & watched from bed or the sofa that's in every room. The huge doors, distinctive bathtubs & high-tech toilets deserve mentioning. B/fast usually inc but you can save a little money by opting out. The nearest MRT station is 250m away. **$$$$**

🏠 **Seasons Classic & Royal** (113 rooms) 326 & 330 Nanjing W Rd; ☎2555 4288; f 2555 6499; e rsvn.tp.nw@royalseasons.com; www. taiwanseasonshotel.com. These 2 mid-range hotels, separated by a narrow lane, are managed by the same corporation. There are substantial differences in décor between the 2 so visit the website if you're particular about hand-painted furniture, cabinets inlaid with mother-of-pearl & flower motifs (an endearing effort to compensate for the lack of greenery in this oldish neighbourhood). Free tea, coffee & instant noodles around the clock plus friendly & efficient service. Wi-Fi & broadband throughout both buildings. Free shuttle bus to the Seasons Hot Spring Beitou & free tour of neighbourhood attractions such as Dihua St every afternoon. B/fast inc. **$$$$**

🏠 **Taipei Wish Hotel** (18 rooms) 17-3, Lane 77, Zhongshan N Rd Sec 2; ☎2563 3369; f 2567 7898; e wishotel@gmail.com; www.wishotel. tw. Very well priced considering its location. Some rooms lack windows but otherwise are more than adequate. Self-service laundry. B/fast inc. **$$**

EASTERN TAIPEI All of the following hotels are shown on the map opposite.

🏠 **Grand Hyatt** (853 rooms) 2 Songshou Rd; ☎2720 1234; f 2720 1111; e taipei.grand@ hyatt.com; www.taipei.grand.hyatt.com. One of the few hotels in Taiwan with special rooms for physically challenged guests, the Grand Hyatt is often filled with businesspeople because it's beside Taipei World Trade Centre. All guestrooms come with bathrobe, yoga mat, minibar, refrigerator & full-size safe. Rooms with views of Taipei 101 are no more expensive than those without so ask for one – or a mountain or poolside prospect – when booking. Residential apt-style suites with butler service available. 9 restaurants & bars. Fitness centres open ⊕ 24hrs daily. B/fast only inc with certain packages. **$$$$$**

🏠 **Rido Waikoloa Hotel** (73 rooms) 11 Xinyi Rd Sec 3; ☎2706 5600; f 2700 9923; e rido2000@ ms53.hinet.net; www.rido.com.tw. More upmarket

rooms in this almost eccentric establishment come with 4-poster beds & views over Daan Forest Park; spend time on the website as rooms come in very different styles. Vertigo sufferers may dislike the atrium & should ask for a room on a lower floor. B/fast inc & delivered to your room. **$$$$**

🏠 **Taipei Fullerton Fu-Xing South** (100 rooms) 41 Fuxing S Rd Sec 2; ☎2703 1234; e service2@taipeifullerton.com.tw; www. taipeifullerton.com.tw. This boutique hotel, which turns down tour groups so it can focus on its core market of international business travellers, is distinguished by the elegance that oozes from every corner & a narrow yet soaring atrium. Rooms at the back of the building have views of Taipei 101. Coffee & tea available to guests around the clock in the tremendously comfortable lobby lounge. Sauna & gym. 5mins walk from Daan MRT Station. For the best rates book directly through their website. Inc b/fast. **$$$$**

🏠 **Charming City Hotel** (90 rooms) 295 Xinyi Rd Sec 4; ☎0800 021 112; f 2707 6488; e service@ city-hotel.com.tw; www.city-hotel. com.tw. Often fully booked because of its proximity to Taipei World Trade Centre, this friendly establishment – part of a chain of 9 hotels around Taipei – sometimes discounts room rates to below NTD3,000 inc b/fast. If you need a bathtub say so when booking, otherwise

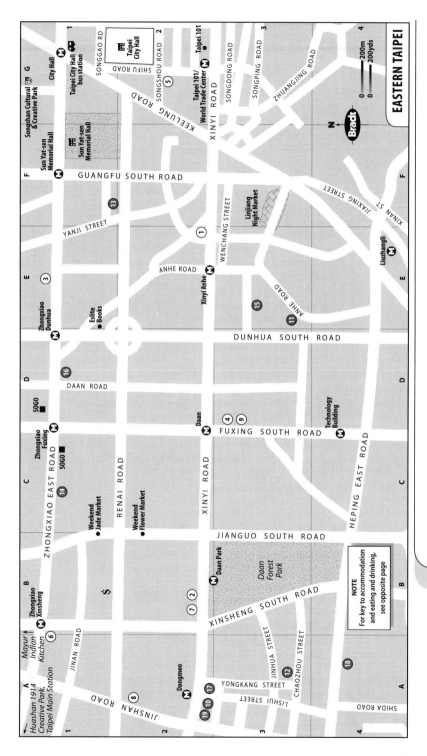

EASTERN TAIPEI

0   200m
0   200yds

NOTE
For key to accommodation
and eating and drinking,
see opposite page

you might be given a very slightly cheaper room without one. **$$$**

🏠 **Fu Hau City Hotel** (40 rooms) 9 Fuxing S Rd; ☎ 2325 0722; **f** 2702 8630; www.fuhauhotel. com.tw. This quiet, tasteful establishment, which appeals mainly to well-heeled locals, couldn't be any closer to the MRT's Brown Line. Thought has obviously been put not only into room design but also into making the corridors as attractive as possible. Discounts available through online booking system; NTD600 to add a 3rd bed. B/fast inc. **$$$**

🏠 **KDM Hotel** (70 rooms) 8 Zhongxiao E Rd Sec 3; ☎ 2721 1162; **f** 2711 9096; www. kdmhotel.com.tw. Despite its excellent location – a stone's throw from Zhongxiao Xinsheng MRT Station – this hotel has had some mixed reviews, so it pays to see more than 1 room before committing yourself. An extra bed can be added for just NTD300. B/fast inc. **$$$**

🏠 **Royal Biz Taipei** (48 rooms) 71 Jinshan S Rd; ☎ 2397 9399; **f** 2397 1399; **e** gm@ royalbiz. com.tw; www.royalbiz.com.tw. Growing in popularity due to its proximity to the Yongkang St dining district & an excellent choice if you want accommodation that's a cut above but won't break the bank. Rooms are spacious & plush with minibar, refrigerator, DVD player & broadband internet. Free tea & coffee in the lobby around the clock, free fruit & snacks in guestrooms. Buffet b/fast inc. **$$$**

🏠 **Dandy Hotel Daan Park** (73 rooms) 33 Xinyi Rd Sec 3; ☎ 2707 6899; **f** 2706 5777; **e** service.da@dandyhotel.com.tw; www. dandyhotel.com.tw. None of the rooms are large but this hotel is exceptionally family-friendly & guests can use the laundry room for free any time of day or night. A few rooms don't have windows & some lack bathtubs. Rates are slightly higher Fri–Sat. Buffet b/fast inc. **$$**

🏠 **Eastern Star Hotel** (25 rooms) 11th Flr 209 Zhongxiao E Rd Sec 4; ☎ 8773 6638; **f** 8773 6569 **e** east.hotel@msa.hinet.net; www.eaststarhotel.com.tw. Popular with businesspeople on a budget & travellers who want to be in the thick of the capital's shops & restaurants, Eastern Star offers modern rooms that are smallish but pretty well equipped for the price. B/fast inc. 300m from Zhongxiao Dunhua MRT Station. **$$**

XINBEITOU

🏠 **Villa 32 三二行館** (5 suites) 32 Zhongshan Rd; ☎ 6611 8888; **f** 6611 3000; **e** info@villa32. com; www.villa32.com. Separated from the outside world by walls & tall trees, this 5,000m^2 property is a place to pamper yourself. The interior features great amounts of teak & stone. Suites priced NTD16,000 & NTD25,000 plus 10% inc b/fast. Three are Western-style, inc the very spacious 2-floor Azure Room. The Japanese-style quarters have tatami mats & sliding paper doors. If you don't have money to burn, consider treating yourself to a daytime package that includes 4hrs in the public hot-spring pool & a meal; the Italian fusion cuisine is among the best in Taipei (*reservations required; EM & extensive wine list;* **$$$$$**). Admission to Villa 32's public pools (*no swimsuits allowed;* ⊕ *10.00–23.00 daily*) is by reservation only & costs for 4hrs NTD1,680 pp on w/days, NTD2,200 pp at the w/end. Private hot-spring rooms (*max 2 ppl for 1½hrs*) are NTD2,000 on w/days, NTD3,000 at the w/end. Pools closed first Mon each month; entire establishment closed for a week or more in Apr & Oct. No under-16s. **$$$$$**

🏠 **Seasons Hot Spring Beitou** (30 rooms) 26 Zhongshan Rd; ☎ 2555 4288; **f** 2896 9797; **e** rsvn.tp.bt@royalseasons.com; www.taiwanseasonshotel.com. This hotel's neoclassical look comes complete with shiny marble floors, white statues, chandeliers & solid yet graceful furniture. There are no public pools but the hot-spring rooms for short stays (*from NTD1,299 for 1½hrs*) are nicely appointed with tubs made of stone imported from China & cable TV. The in-house restaurant (⊕ *10.00–23.00 daily;* **$$$**) serves herbal stews & soups popular in cold weather, plus an excellent Japanese eel with rice. Free pick-up from Xinbeitou MRT Station. Overnight rates (*NTD4,200–11,000*) inc a choice of Western, Chinese or Japanese b/fast. **$$$$**

🏠 **I-Tsun Hotel 逸村飯店** (17 rooms) 140 Wenquan Rd; ☎ 2891 2121; **f** 2893 7129. This Beitou institution, just above Hell Valley, was founded in the 1920s. It's been repaired but not rebuilt, so it retains a lot of its original Japanese-era character. Technologically it's frozen in the fax era & very little English is understood. Some of the rooms have Western-style dbl beds; in others the guests sleep on tatamis. There are 2 indoor communal baths, one for each gender; from both you can gaze out into a garden featuring bonsai trees & a carp-filled pond. Japanese & Taiwanese food available; b/fast inc. **$$$**

✕ WHERE TO EAT AND DRINK

For additional ideas try **A Hungry Girl's Guide To Taipei** (*http://hungryintaipei. blogspot.tw*) and **Taipei Vegetarians** (*www.facebook.com/taipeivegetarians*).

SOUTHWEST TAIPEI All of the following establishments are shown on the map on page 89.

✕ **Chiba** 77 Wuchang St Sec 2 (inside Amba Hotel); ☎2375 2075; ⏰ 11.00–22.00 daily. Anyone wanting to escape Ximending's bustle for a bit will here find a restful, attractive environment plus an all-day menu of salads, panini, sandwiches & favourites such as spaghetti (*most around NTD300*) paired with a long list of hot & cold drinks (*from NTD110*). Alternatively, if you don't fancy your own hotel's b/fast offerings, come here for the morning buffet (⏰ 06.30–10.00 daily; *NTD400/280 plus 10%*) which inc eggs & noodles prepared to order. **$$$**

✕ **Huaxi Street Night Market** Huaxi & Guangzhou sts; ⏰ approx 17.00–24.00 daily. Dubbed 'snake alley' by the Western tourists who, decades ago, came to gawk as restaurateurs slaughtered, skinned & cooked limbless reptiles, this night market is still a place where you can drink snake-bile mixed with wine, a concoction said to be an aphrodisiac. The brothels that used to operate in the side alleys were closed down in the 1990s & the market itself is now pretty subdued. While it's still possible to order snake, turtle, rabbit & crocodile meat here, the butchering is now done out of sight. In addition to snake soup, you can try snake blood, snake urine & even snake semen. **$$**

✕ **Zhang's Halal Beef Noodles** 張家清真黃牛肉麵館 21 Yanping S Rd; ☎2331 2791; ⏰ 06.30–20.30 daily, closed 2nd Thu each month. Founded by a Muslim who relocated from mainland China to Taiwan with the KMT army, this restaurant is patronised mainly by non-Muslims eager to enjoy its famous meat-filled buns, fried dumplings (*jiān jiǎo*) & 12 kinds of beef noodles. Standard dishes like sesame-paste noodles are served with beef gravy instead of the ubiquitous pork. No English sign; look for the word 'Halal' in English. No EM. **$$**

✕ **Modern Toilet** 2nd Flr 7, Lane 50, Xining S Rd; ☎2311 8822; www.moderntoilet.com.tw; ⏰ 11.30–22.00 daily. When this chain launched several years back it attracted both local & overseas media attention & it continues to be much more gimmick than gourmet. Patrons sit on toilets & the food comes served in mock bedpans & surgical trays. The meals, which include pasta & mild curries, are fine but most come here for the novelty of eating chocolate ice cream from a bedpan, or sipping fruit juice from a portable urinal. **$**

✕ **Snow King** 雪王 65 Wuchang St Sec 1; ☎2331 8415; ⏰ 12.00–22.00 daily. A place for lovers of bizarre foods, Snow King has for more than 60 years been selling strangely flavoured homemade ice creams. Not just flavours that Westerners find odd, like fried peanut or green bean – we're talking beer, curry, wasabi & others. Most are priced NTD70–90 for a medium-sized bowl. **$**

♀ **The Wall Live House** Basement, 200 Roosevelt Rd Sec 4; ☎2930 0162; www.thewall. com.tw; ⏰ 15.00–02.00 Tue–Sun. The place to go for live rock & punk, inc bands from Japan, Europe & North America. Owned & managed by the American duo behind Spring Scream (*www. springscream.com*), an annual pop & rock festival held each year near Kenting. Gig tickets usually around NTD500. **$$$**

NORTHWEST TAIPEI All of the following establishments are shown on the map on page 91.

✕ **Peng's Gourmet & Banquet** 彭園 2nd Flr 380 Linsen N Rd; ☎2551 9157; www.pengyuan. com.tw; ⏰ 11.15–14.00 & 17.10–21.00 daily. Serving Hunanese food, a Chinese cuisine renowned for being spicy & aromatic, Peng's has grown into a chain of 8 restaurants over the past 30 years; the founder was the ROC vice-president's personal chef in the late 1940s. The interior is smart but somewhat old-fashioned. Most dishes on the EM are priced around NTD300 & best enjoyed by groups of 4 or more. Local beers & wines available. **$$$**

3

✕ **Satay Mutton** 241 Dalong St; m 0935 611 175; ⊕ 16.00–23.00 Wed–Mon. Smack in the middle of a street packed with eateries, this no-frills restaurant near Baoan Temple serves tasty mutton with rice (*NTD70 for 1 person*), noodles or in soups. The EM pasted on the wall doesn't tell the whole story – there's also fried sheep tripe (*NTD200*) & a few non-mutton dishes such as fried shrimps (*NTD200*). $$

✕ **Spot Café Lumiere** 18 Zhongshan N Rd Sec 2; ☎2562 5612; ⊕ 11.00–23.00 daily. This landmark building dates from 1925 & resembles an antebellum mansion in the south of the US, which is appropriate as the US ambassador lived here 1953–79. It's not just a good place to stop for a coffee or a beer – it doubles as a cinema showing art-house films. There aren't many meal options but the choice of sandwiches, desserts & teas is impressive & everything is tasty. Indoor & outdoor seating. EM. There's also a branch in Huashan 1914 (see *Entertainment*, page 98). $$

EASTERN TAIPEI All of the following establishments are shown on the map on page 93.

✕ **Alleycat's** Basement, 6 Lishui St; ☎2321 8949; www.alleycatspizza.com; ⊕ 17.00–23.00 Sun–Thu, 17.00–24.00 Fri–Sat. Alleycat's reputation was built on its stone-oven-baked pizzas, but the menu also lists *croccante*, *insalata* & *calzoni*. You may think the music's a bit loud or the crowd a bit young but you're unlikely to find fault with the food. EM. Details of other branches inc Ximending are on the bilingual website. $$$

✕ **HJS Fresh Grill** 139 Chaozhou St; ☎2322 5169; ⊕ 18.00–24.00 Mon–Fri, 12.00–14.00 & 18.00–24.00 Sat–Sun. Slightly hard to find but much loved, HJS serves items associated with the Turkic people of China's far west, inc grilled tofu & meats (*from NTD90*), substantial mains (*from NTD310*) & a lovely garlic, tomato & aubergine salad (*NTD220*). Come before 19.00 if you didn't reserve. Bar seats downstairs usually booked days ahead; upstairs there's seating for about 20. Soft drinks (*NTD35*) plus sake, shoju, vodka & local beer (*from NTD100*). Expect to spend NTD300 pp on food. EM. $$$

✕ **Kiki Restaurant** 47, Lane 280, Guangfu S Rd; ☎2781 4250; ⊕ 11.50–15.00 & 17.15–22.00 daily. The Szechuan cuisine served here isn't absolutely authentic – nor does it claim to be – but it's so good

reservations are a necessity. Most items are priced NTD200–300; mitigate the spiciness of meat & tofu dishes by ordering vegetables such as water-spinach flavoured with bean curd (*NTD150*) or fried bitter melon & egg (*NTD210*). EM. $$$

✕ **Mayur Indian Kitchen** 38 Xinsheng N Rd Sec 1; ☎2543 1817; ⊕ 12.00–14.30 & 17.00–22.00 Tue–Sun, 17.00–22.00 Mon. What's probably Taipei's best Indian restaurant was founded by a chef from the subcontinent whose experience in 5-star hotels shows through in both food & service. Both north Indian & south Indian dishes appear on the menu, which has à la carte dishes (*around NTD200*) inc an especially good lamb curry. Among drink options are Indian milk tea (*NTD45*) & 9 or more beers (*from NTD80 per bottle*) such as Kingfisher. The older, smaller branch near Taipei City Hall (*350-5 Keelung Rd Sec 1*; ☎2720 0011; ⊕ 12.00–22.00 daily*) has fewer menu options, slightly lower prices & outdoor seating only. EM. $$$

✕ **Shin Yeh** 2nd Flr 112 Zhongxiao E Rd Sec 4; ☎2752 9299; www.shinyeh.com.tw; ⊕ 11.00–15.00, 17.00–22.30 daily. Famous for its Taiwanese food, Shin Yeh is a restaurant best enjoyed by groups of 5 or more. Their other locations inc Taipei 101 (*85th flr*) & 34-1 Shuangcheng Street (marked on Northwest Taipei map). Of the more than 100 dishes listed on the EM (with pictures), the steamed crab roe on glutinous rice is one of the best. There's lots of seafood but relatively few vegetable options. Local & imported beers, wines & sakes. $$$

✕ **Thanh-Ky** 1, Lane 6, Yongkang St; ☎2321 1579; ⊕ 11.00–21.30 daily. Run by ethnic Chinese originally from Vietnam, Thanh-Ky is one of Yongkang Street's most popular eateries & for good reason. The pho (Vietnamese beef noodles) is excellent, as are the deep-fried starters. Vietnamese desserts such as jackfruit in coconut milk also available. Further down the same lane there's another branch (⊕ 11.30–14.00 & 17.30–21.30 daily). EM with pictures. $$

✕ **Vegetarian Heaven** 182 Heping E Rd Sec 1; ☎2363 8662; ⊕ 11.00–14.00 & 17.00–20.00 daily. A buffet-style restaurant where you help yourself from 30-odd dishes of vegetables & tofu-based items, then take your plate to the counter for weighing & payment, Vegetarian Heaven is a true paradise for non-meat eaters on a budget & others who prefer potato salad to rice. Bottomless bowls of free soup. A good feed costs about NTD130 pp. $$

✗ **Yong-Kang Beef Noodle** 17, Lane 31, Jinshan S Rd Sec 2; ✆2351 1051; ⊕ 11.00–21.30 daily. A prize-winning & often packed-to-the-gills beef noodle establishment, this restaurant also serves very popular steamed hogs' ribs (*fĕn rè pái gŭ*). EM with pictures. $$

♀ **Carnegie's** 100 Anhe Rd Sec 2; ✆2325 4433; www.carnegies.com.tw; ⊕ 11.00–02.00 or later daily. Now well into its second decade, Carnegie's once had a wild, dancing-on-tabletops kind of reputation but these days its appeal is thoroughly mainstream. Business lunches (*from NTD230*) are a good deal; homesick Brits may like some of the items on the à la carte menu such as steak & kidney pie (*NTD390*). There are also steaks (*NTD790–960*) & curries (*NTD420–480*). $$$$

♀ **On Tap** 21, Alley 11, Lane 216, Zhongxiao E Rd Sec 4; ✆2741 5365; www.ontaptaipei.com; ⊕ 17.00–02.00 Mon–Fri, 11.00–02.00 Sat–Sun. Serving ales & ciders as well as lagers, On Tap is as close to a British pub as you'll find in Taipei. Happy-hour specials until 20.00 every evening & all day at w/ends. Indoor & outdoor seating; live sports on a big screen. Salads (*from NTD180*), burgers (*NTD260–370*) & other Western staples plus finger foods. $$$

♀ **Ounce Taipei** 40, Lane 63, Dunhua S Rd Sec 2; ✆2708 6885; e info@ouncetaipei.com; http://ouncetaipei.com; ⊕ 19.00–02.00 Mon–Sat. A place for classic & cutting-edge cocktails, access to this speakeasy-style bar is through a coffee shop. For specials like barrel-aged cocktails & new acquisitions see their Facebook page; dozens of the liquors here are available nowhere else in Taiwan. Expect to pay around NTD400 per drink; reservations essential. $$$

SHOPPING

For fashions, tech toys and other mainstream items, shopaholics should head to Nanjing West Road (see *Northwest Taipei* map, page 91) or Zhongxiao East Road Section 4 (see *Eastern Taipei* map, page 93). For more traditional items, Wanhua and Dihua Street are good hunting grounds.

DEPARTMENT STORES Taipei's department stores follow the Japanese model, right down to lift operators who greet you with put-on smiles.

SOGO [93 C1 & D1] 300 Zhongxiao E Rd Sec 3 & 45 Zhongxiao E Rd Sec 4; ✆2776 5555; www.sogo.com.tw; ⊕ 11.00–21.30 daily. These 2 department stores, one on either side of Zhongxiao Fuxing MRT Station, have the usual brands & clean, well-lit food courts (but not much English on the menus).

Taipei 101 Mall [93 G2] Xinyi & Shifu rds ✆8101 7777; www.taipei-101.com.tw; ⊕ 11.00–21.30 daily. Five floors of shops to max out your credit card & a basement with some good-value eating options. Page One (*4th flr*) has perhaps the best selection of English-language books & magazines on the island.

SOUVENIRS

Chinese Handicraft Mart [89 F2] 1 Xuzhou Rd; ✆2393 3655; f 2393 7330; e thpc@handicraft.org.tw; www.handicraft.org.tw; ⊕ 09.00–17.30 daily. This government-sponsored not-for-profit organisation aids local handicraft industries by marketing their products. The mart has a massive inventory inc jade items, leather art, porcelain & hand puppets. The multilingual staff can arrange shipping, & goods can be ordered online or by telephone.

Lovely Taiwan Shop [91 C5] 18-2, Lane 25, Nanjing W Rd; ✆2558 2616; www.lovelytaiwan.org.tw; ⊕ 12.00–21.00 Tue–Sun. Run by a not-for-profit group which uses any surpluses to fund projects benefiting the villages & small communities from which it sources the craft items sold here.

Weekend Jade Market [93 B1] Jianguo S & Renai rds; ⊕ approx 09.00–17.00 Sat–Sun. Said to be one of the largest jade markets in the world, several hundred vendors gather here & sell not only jade items but also semiprecious stones, coral jewellery & Buddha statues. If you continue walking southwards you'll come to Taipei's main flower market, where you'll see orchids, bonsai & all kinds of cut flowers.

TEA Many tourists take boxes of Taiwan's excellent teas home with them. The capital's most famous tea dealers – among them shops which claim to have been in business since the 1840s – are concentrated in the city's northwest.

Shengshang Cha Hang [91 D5] 52 Changchun Rd; ☎2542 7205; www.shengshang.com.tw; ⏰ 09.30–23.00 daily. This shop's multilingual website is a good place to start for those who don't know much about Taiwanese tea.

Wanchuan Tea Shop [91 D5] 4, Lane 13, Nanjing E Rd Sec 1; ☎2521 4247; f 2511 5448; ⏰ 09.00–12.00 & 13.30–24.00 daily. Some English is spoken at this long-established shop, which has won awards for its oolongs & oriental beauty teas.

BOOKSHOPS The following have lots of English-language books & magazines:

Caves Books [91 C2] 54-3 Zhongshan N Rd Sec 3; ☎2599 1169; ⏰ 10.30–21.00 Mon-Sat, 10.30–19.00 Sun

Eslite Books [93 E1] 245 Dunhua S Rd Sec 1; ☎2775 5977; ⏰ 24hrs daily

Page One [93 G2] 4th Flr Taipei 101 Mall; ☎8101 8282; ⏰ 11.00–21.30 daily

OTHER PRACTICALITIES

POST

✉ **General Post Office** [89 E1] 114 Zhongxiao W Rd Sec 1; ⏰ 07.30–21.00 Mon–Fri, 08.30–16.30 Sat, 08.30–12.00 Sun

✉ **Taipei Main Station** [89 F1] (see page 86) ⏰ 08.00–18.30 Mon–Fri, 08.30–12.00 Sat–Sun

✉ **National Palace Museum** (see page 106) ⏰ 08.30–17.00 Mon–Fri, 08.30–20.30 Sat, 08.30–18.30 Sun

BANKS AND CHANGING MONEY Taipei
has scores of banks. Money can also be changed in major hotels & some department stores & in all 3 of the post office branches mentioned above.

$ **Changhwa Bank** 57 Zhongshan Rd Sec 2
$ **Land Bank** 29 Renai Rd Sec 3

MEDICAL
✚ **Mackay Memorial Hospital** [91 C4] 92 Zhongshan Rd Sec 2; ☎2543 3535; www.mmh.org.tw; ⏰ 24hrs daily

POLICE
Main police station 96 Yanping S Rd; ☎2381 8251; in emergencies call ☎110

ENTERTAINMENT

Taipei has no shortage of concert venues, exhibition halls and cinemas. The English-language newspapers are a good source of information about upcoming events, as are the leaflets you can pick up at MRT stations and visitor information centres. The following venues are of particular interest.

Huashan 1914 Creative Park 1 Bade Rd Sec 1; ☎2235 81914; www.huashan1914.com/en/; ⏰ 09.00–22.00 Tue–Sun. A century-old former winery (hence the '1914') originally slated for demolition, Huashan's empty warehouses were illegally taken over by a theatre troupe in the late 1990s. Now run by a foundation on behalf of the government, the park hosts concerts, workshops & art exhibitions. Exit 1 from Zhongxiao Fuxing MRT Station.

Songshan Cultural and Creative Park [93 G1] Lane 553, Zhongxiao E Rd; ☎2765 1388; www.songshanculturalpark.org; ⏰ indoors 09.00–18.00, outdoors 08.00–22.00 daily. The surviving part of a 1930s tobacco-processing complex (much was cleared to make space for Taipei Dome, a

baseball venue due to be completed by the end of 2015), this park hosts a range of cultural events & is the permanent home of the Taiwan Design Museum (☎2745 8199 ext 123; ⏰ 09.30–17.30 Tue–Sun; admission NTD50/30). From Taipei City Hall MRT Station's Exit 1 you'll need to walk 700m.

Taipei Eye [91 D4] 113 Zhongshan N Rd Sec 2; ☎2568 2677; www.taipeieye.com; admission NTD880; shows begin 20.00 Fri & Sat only. Of special interest to visitors from overseas, Taipei Eye offers 90-min-long performances featuring easy-to-digest portions of Beijing & Taiwanese opera, puppetry, local folk music & aboriginal dance. English & Japanese subtitles; after the show, the performers mingle with the audience. Enter Taiwan Cement Hall from Jinzhou St.

WHAT TO SEE AND DO

SOUTHWEST TAIPEI

Taipei's city gates Taipei's walls, completed in 1884 after the settlement was made capital of Taiwan province, enclosed an area south of the railway station. They were demolished in the first decade of the Japanese colonial era and the **North Gate 北門** (*Zhongxiao W & Yanping S rds*) is the only element to retain its original appearance. The **Little South Gate** [89 D3] (*Aiguo & Yanping S rds*) was heavily modified in 1966 on the orders of KMT leaders who thought the original wasn't 'Chinese' enough.

Futai Street Mansion [89 E1] (*26 Yanping S Rd; ⊕ 10.00–17.00 Tue–Sun; free admission*) Originally the headquarters of a Japanese-owned construction company, then the offices of a newspaper, this two-floor century-old stone building is now a small but engrossing museum devoted to aspects of Taipei's history.

Ximending 西門町 (Xīméndīng) [89 D1] The best place on the island to see Taiwan's Japanese-influenced youth culture, Ximending is a pedestrian shopping zone full of fashion shops, cinemas, tattoo parlours and places to eat. At the beginning of the Japanese colonial era Ximending ('west gate district') was an undeveloped area just outside the city's west gate; by World War I it had become Taipei's main entertainment district. The most elegant landmark is the octagonal **Red House 西門紅樓** [89 D2] (*www.redhouse.org.tw; ⊕ 11.00–21.30 Tue–Sun; free admission*). Built as a theatre in 1908, it's now billed as a 'market for artists and designers'. Inside there's a Chinese-only exhibition about the theatre (the website has plenty of English) plus several boutiques.

Zhongshan Hall [89 D2] (*98 Yanping S Rd; ☎ 2381 3137; www.csh.taipei.gov.tw; ⊕ 10.00–21.00 daily; free admission except during concerts*) Completed in 1936 to honour Japan's Emperor Hirohito (reigned 1926–89) but now named after Sun Yat-sen (see box, page 106), this Spanish Islamic building houses a quintessentially Taiwanese work of art: *Water Buffaloes*, a plaster relief executed by Huang Tu-shui (1895–1930). It depicts a rural scene of water buffaloes, banana trees and naked infants. The main hall, now a venue for concerts and conferences, is where the final Japanese governor-general of Taiwan surrendered to one of Chiang Kai-shek's generals on 25 October 1945. If you decide to eat at the plush **Fortress Café** (*2nd flr; ☎ 2381 9551; ⊕ 11.00–22.00 daily; EM lists Western dishes & desserts; $$$$*) you can sup indoors or on a balcony from which Chiang addressed supporters. Alternatively, get a coffee at **Director Tsai's Café Galerie** (*4th flr; ☎ 2331 2727; ⊕ 10.00–21.00 daily; EM also lists juices & meals; $$*). Named after film-maker Tsai Ming-liang (see box, page 36), it's decorated with old gramophone players and paintings of Tsai's favourite collaborator, actor Lee Kang-sheng.

National Taiwan Museum 國立台灣博物館 [89 E2] (*2 Xiangyang Rd; ☎ 2382 2566; www.ntm.gov.tw; ⊕ 10.00–17.00 Tue–Sun, closed first week every Dec; admission NTD20/10*) Made partly of stone imported from Japan, this impressive edifice was built 1913–15 to commemorate the achievements of colonial governor Kodama Gentaro and his right-hand man, Goto Shinpei (see *History*, page 15). It now contains a mix of permanent and temporary exhibitions, with especially strong natural history and aboriginal-artefact sections; look out for the Bunun calendar etched on a piece of wood. The museum has expanded across the road into what used to be a bank (keep your ticket so you don't have to pay again). This annex has lots of information about dinosaurs, fossils and land reform after World War II.

2-28 Peace Memorial Park 二二八和平紀念公園 [89 E2] (⊕ *24hrs daily*) But for the Japanese-era National Taiwan Museum and the starkly modern **2-28 Memorial Monument**, this is a very Chinese park, full of ponds and pavilions. It's actually Taiwan's oldest city park, dating from 1908, and its historical and social significance goes beyond urban planning. The former radio station in the southeastern corner was seized by protesters just after 28 February 1947 and now houses the **2-28 Memorial Museum** [89 F2] (✆ *2389 7228; ⊕ 10.00–17.00 Tue–Sun; admission NTD20/10*). The museum, which doesn't contain much English, is strictly for history mavens. In the 1960s and 1970s the park was one of the few places in the capital where gay men could gather in safety.

Chiang Kai-shek Memorial Hall 中正紀念堂 (Zhōngzhèng Jìniàntáng)
[89 G4] (✆ *2343 1100; www.cksmh.gov.tw; ⊕ 09.00–18.00 daily*) There's much more to this complex – inaugurated on 5 April 1980, the fifth anniversary of the dictator's death – than quasi-classical Chinese architecture and spit-and-polish military policemen. Taipei citizens come here to attend cultural events (the two brown-roofed buildings are the National Theatre and National Concert Hall), to practise martial arts or hip-hop dance moves, or to find a secluded park bench they can share with a lover or a good book. The blue-roofed, white-sided tower at the eastern end of the site is the memorial proper; the materials in exhibition rooms directly beneath the immense bronze image of the generalissimo (he's seated, very much like Daniel Chester French's statue of Abraham Lincoln) are predictably hagiographic. There's plenty about the high points of Chiang's career (the Northern Expedition that unified China in the late 1920s, defeating communist attempts to seize Kinmen in the 1950s), but the loss of first the mainland and then China's seat in the UN are skated over. Other topics that get hardly a look in are the generalissimo's Methodism and his first two wives. Among the relics displayed are documents, flags, furniture, an armour-plated limousine and medals pinned on Chiang's chest by presidents, monarchs and tin-pot tyrants. Visitors are requested to dress respectfully but this rule doesn't seem to be enforced. If you'd like a Chiang Kai-shek doll, check out the souvenir shop.

Taipei Botanical Garden 台北植物園 (Táiběi Zhíwùyuán) [89 D4] (*corner of Nanhai and Heping W rds; http://tpbg.tfri.gov.tw; ⊕ 04.00–22.00 daily; free admission*) Established at the very beginning of the colonial era, these gardens cover just 8ha but have almost 2,000 different tree and plant species, not to mention birds like the Japanese white eye (*Zosterops japonicus*). The resident avians are remarkably tolerant of human admirers and photographers. The garden's very detailed bilingual website will engross the green-fingered. At the adjacent **National Museum of History** 國立歷史博物館 [89 E4] (*www.nmh.gov.tw; ⊕ 10.00–18.00 Tue–Sun; admission NTD30/15*) the focus is on China, not Taiwan, and you'll find a decent collection of millennia-old artefacts from the mainland. Take the MRT to Xiaonanmen (change at Ximen on the Blue Line) and leave by Exit 3.

WANHUA 萬華 Many Taiwanese toponyms have been dragged through multiple languages. Wanhua is the Mandarin pronunciation of two characters chosen by the Japanese colonial authorities because, when pronounced in standard Japanese, they came close to imitating the name actually used by the area's inhabitants, *Mangka*

(sometimes spelled Manka, Monga or Bangkah). That 19th-century place name, which has been revived in recent years, was itself derived from an indigenous term meaning 'canoe'. In the early days of Han settlement, Ketagalan tribesmen would bring their boats downstream and barter vegetables and charcoal for Chinese products.

These days, Taipei citizens consider Wanhua a less than ideal district in which to live. Coming here from east Taipei, you'll notice the people are less fashionably dressed, the cars are older and the buildings scruffier. For tourists, however, Wanhua is very rich – rich in history, architecture and traditional culture. Longshan Temple, best accessed from the MRT station of the same name, is a logical place to start.

Longshan Temple 龍山寺 (Lóngshān Sì) [89 C3] (⊕ 06.00–22.00 daily) Named after a shrine in Jinjiang County, Fujian – the ancestral district of many of those who settled in Wanhua in the 18th century – Longshan Temple is the only place of worship in Taipei City that comes close to Baoan Temple in terms of art, history and ongoing religious action. It's a folk temple that leans towards Buddhism,

MONEY TO BURN

Many Taiwanese honour their gods and ancestors by burning incense and joss paper, especially the small sheets of yellow paper many Westerners call 'ghost money'. Taoists do it more often and in greater quantities than Buddhists and for slightly different reasons. According to both religions, the living have an obligation to take care of the deceased by making offerings of fruit and other foods, and by sending them spirit currency (the dead have living expenses, it's believed). Adherents of folk religion have an additional motive. Because it's widely believed that burning joss paper brings a person good luck, businesspeople often place tables of offerings in front of their shops or offices and order their employees to *bài bài* (pray) and burn bundles of spirit currency in portable braziers.

During the annual Ghost Festival, huge quantities of ghost money are sacrificed to keep troublesome spirits at bay. Just as there are several types of incense, there are different kinds of joss paper for different rituals. Paper which is to be burned for a funeral is folded in a special way, sometimes to resemble a lotus, sometimes into the shape of a ship. Joss paper used to be made by hand from rice straw. It's now mass-produced in factories and lots of chemicals are used – so many, in fact, that the government has warned that those who burn joss paper risk inhaling dangerous quantities of nitrogen oxide, benzene and toluene.

Environmentalists have promoted online 'virtual ghost-money burning' services and the burning of 'spirit credit cards' which the dead can use in the after-world instead of banknotes. Some shrines, including Longshan Temple (see above) no longer permit the on-site burning of joss paper, while a handful of others have installed wet scrubbers, devices which force smoke through a dense particle-capturing mist. Unfortunately, at least one study has found these scrubbers make no significant difference to the quantity of carcinogenic emissions. Master Cheng Yen, founder of the Buddhist Compassion Relief Tzu Chi Foundation (see page 285), has said that sincerity and virtue are far more important than burning joss paper. However, these reforms have yet to make much of a dent in the tradition. Each year an estimated 90,000 to 200,000 tonnes of joss paper go up in smoke in Taiwan.

Guanyin having been the centre of attention since the temple was established in 1738. Guan Gong, who as usual has a red face, is on the left at the back and Mazu is the main deity in the rear chamber. She was installed here in 1793 at the behest of a merchants' guild whose members often made the dangerous voyage between Taiwan and the Chinese mainland. If you visit in the evening you'll see a queue of young people at the back on the left, waiting to pray to the Old Man Under the Moon (see *Religion*, page 34).

There used to be a pond in front of the temple's main entrance because a *feng shui* expert determined the temple was the abode of a beautiful female spirit and that she should have a 'mirror' in which she could gaze at her own countenance. In 1923 the Japanese colonial authorities decided the pond was a health hazard and ordered it filled in and turned into a park. The current main structure, completed in 1959, replaced a building wrecked by American bombs during World War II.

The section of Xiyuan Road nearest Longshan Temple has 20-odd shops selling Buddha statuettes and religious accoutrements.

Herb Alley 青草巷 [89 C3] (*Lane 224, Xichang St*) At least seven of the businesses (⏰ *approx 08.00–20.00 daily*) here have been dealing in medicinal and culinary herbs for over a hundred years. In the 18th and 19th centuries, when people fell sick they were as likely to consult a spirit medium as a physician. The shaman would ask a deity for a 'prescription' which would be filled here. Wandering through this lane is an olfactory and visual pleasure.

MACKAY IN WANHUA

Nowhere did the missionary work of George L Mackay (see box, page 140) face greater opposition than in Wanhua. Referring to the settlement by its Holo name, he described his forays into the city in his book *From Far Formosa*:

> Bangkah was the Gibraltar of heathenism in north Formosa… thoroughly Chinese and intensely anti-foreign in all its interests and sympathies. The citizens… are materialistic, superstitious dollar-seekers. At every visit, when passing through their streets, we are maligned, jeered at and abused. Hundreds of children run ahead, yelling with derisive shouts; others follow, pelting us with orange peel, mud and rotten eggs… the authorities of Bangkah issued proclamations calling on all citizens, on pain of imprisonment or death, not to rent, lease or sell either houses or other property to the barbarian missionary.

In December 1877, Mackay did find a place he could rent – but xenophobic local merchants paid lepers and beggars to harass the missionary and his associates. After a mob invaded the premises, tore tiles from the roof and bricks out of the walls, the British consul rushed to the scene and demanded the local mandarin meet the Chinese Empire's treaty obligations and ensure Mackay's safety. Protected by Chinese soldiers, Mackay built a mission station on the same site. Nevertheless, active opposition continued: Taiwanese who dared attend meetings were boycotted, and in 1879 Mackay's wife was almost blinded when a man taking part in an 'idolatrous procession' shoved a burning torch into her face. It was another decade before Christians were to feel safe in Wanhua, but by 1893 Mackay was being carried through the streets in a sedan chair and presented with honorary parasols by civil and military officials.

Bopiliao 剝皮寮 (*Lane 173, Kangding Rd*) The name of this recently renovated neighbourhood, one of Taipei's oldest, gives a clue as to what used to be the main industry. Bopiliao means 'the hut where bark is peeled off', and two centuries ago this was where tree trunks imported from China were stripped of their bark so they could be used for building. Taiwan didn't lack for trees in that era, but Han settlers considered logging in the headhunter-dominated foothills far too dangerous. Step inside the **Heritage and Culture Education Centre of Taipei** [89 C3] (*101 Guangzhou St; ☎2336 1704; ⏰ 09.00–17.00 Tue–Sun; free admission*), the home of a doctor during the Japanese colonial era, to learn about the area's past. In 1966, just after Taiwan's baby boom peaked, the adjacent elementary school had more than 11,000 students!

Qingshan Temple 青山宮 [89 C2] (*218 Guiyang St Sec 2; ⏰ 05.30–21.20 daily*) Named after and dedicated to the King of Qingshan, a general in Fujian almost 1,800 years ago who was promoted to godhood in the 12th century, this house of worship was founded in 1854. In that year, an icon of the king was being carried through this neighbourhood by fishermen when the statue suddenly became too heavy to move. By divination the king's followers determined he wished to stay in this place, so a shrine was built. The king's birthday, the 22nd day of the tenth lunar month, is one of Wanhua's most important annual events. The ground floor of this temple has a tremendous collection of effigies notable for their fearsome countenances and collar-length eyebrows. Seek out one on the right as you enter. One half of his face has a normal Chinese complexion but the other half is black with a red eyebrow; his title is given as *sī yáng yīn* 司陽陰, literally 'controller of yin and yang'. The Jade Emperor commands centre stage on the top floor where, on the right, there's an idol of the Lord of the South Pole Star. On the left you'll find the Lord of the North Pole Star.

NORTHWEST TAIPEI Start by taking the MRT to Yuanshan on the Red Line then follow the signs to Baoan and Confucius temples, which are almost side-by-side and less than 500m from the station.

Baoan Temple 保安宮 (Bǎoān Gōng) [91 B1] (*61 Hami St; www.baoan.org.tw; ⏰ 06.00–22.00 daily*) In artistic terms, this 200-year-old temple is without doubt one of Taiwan's finest places of worship. The quality of its 1995–2002 restoration received international recognition in the form of an honourable mention in the 2003 UNESCO Asia-Pacific Heritage Awards for Culture Conservation. Come at dusk if you can, and spend time appreciating the door gods, the fabulously ornate carved screens and the large murals on the outside of the central shrine painted by Pan Li-shui (see box, page 104). The main shrine in the centre of the courtyard is dedicated to Baosheng Dadi ('the life-guarding emperor'), a god of justice, sustenance and medicine. Baosheng Dadi was born Wu Dao in Fujian in AD979; a Taoist physician, it's said he once brought a skeleton back to life. Deified by a local cult soon after his death, he was fast-tracked for full godhood during the Ming Dynasty (1368–1644) after his intercession cured an emperor's concubine of cancer. His prominence in Taiwan dates from 1699 when he was credited with bringing an epidemic under control. The god's birthday falls on the 15th day of the third lunar month and is celebrated with the Baosheng Cultural Festival. The temple's name isn't derived from the deity's title. Instead it means 'keeping Tongan folk safe', the founders having come from Fujian's Tongan County. Other deities worshipped include Shennong, the god of farming and putative inventor of the hoe, plough and irrigation. You'll recognise this chubby fellow because he holds rice stalks. Near the temple, bilingual information panels explain how this neighbourhood came to be called Dalongdong and why Hami Street used to be known as Sishisikan Street (literally 'street of 44 thresholds').

Taipei Confucius Temple 台北孔廟 [91 B2] (*275 Dalong St;* ☎ *2592 3934; www. ct.taipei.gov.tw;* ⏰ *08.30–21.00 Tue–Sat, 08.30–17.00 Sun & national holidays; exhibition rooms close 17.00*) After the warmth and embellishment of Baoan Temple, the capital's Confucian shrine comes across as grand but a little desolate. Within, the sage is represented by a simple tablet; in Baoan Temple he gets a small statue. Built 1925–39 on the site of an earlier Confucian shrine, the complex contains various multimedia displays and static exhibitions. An especially good one explains the traditional instruments and ceremonial music heard each 28 September during the grand rites which mark Confucius's birthday. To learn more, take a look at the temple's thorough website before visiting, or take the 60-minute English-language audio tour (*free; NTD1,000 deposit*).

Taipei Fine Arts Museum 台北市立美術館 (Táiběi Shìlì Měishùguǎn) [91 D2] (*181 Zhongshan N Rd Sec 3;* ☎ *2595 7656; www.tfam.museum;* ⏰ *09.30–17.30 Tue–Fri & Sun, 09.30–20.30 Sat; free admission to basement galleries; admission to other floors NTD30/15, free 17.00–20.30 Sat only*) Exhibitions at TFAM lean towards the modern and usually highlight Taiwanese artists, including some who live abroad.

Dihua Street 迪化街 (Díhuà Jiē) A hub of traditional commerce, Dihua Street is where local families go in the run-up to Lunar New Year to buy ritual items and special treats. In recent years the street has seen quite a bit of gentrification, a good thing as several of the oldest, grandest merchant homes were on the verge of collapse a couple of decades ago. You'll soon find and smell the dried fruits, medicinal herbs and other goods associated with the street. **Yongle Market 永樂市場** (*21 Dihua St Sec 1;* ⏰ *09.30–18.00 daily*), housed in an ugly building near the southern end of the street, is one of the best places in Taiwan to get clothes tailor-made, including a kind of dress the Taiwanese call a *qípáo*, but which Westerners know as a cheongsam. Walking north, you'll come across baroque features such as shields, laurels and even minarets; the façade of the herbal medicine clinic at number 71 bears ginseng embossments. Dihua Street isn't easy to reach by public transport; consider taking a taxi from Zhongshan MRT Station.

XiaHai City God Temple 霞海城隍廟 [91 A4] (*61 Dihua St Sec 1;* ⏰ *06.10–19.30 daily*) Even if you're not much into folk shrines, the modest size and excellent bilingual labelling within Taipei's best-known city-god temple make for a highly

digestible stop. The city god himself is a generalist who can bestow peace, prosperity, happiness and good weather. He's kept company by effigies representing his wife (note the offerings of cosmetics), Mazu, the Old Man Under the Moon and others. This representation of the Old Man is thought to be particularly efficacious: the temple claims that more than 20 couples tie the knot each day thanks to his efforts. The city-god icon arrived in Mangka from China in 1821. During ethnic clashes in 1853, the effigy was evacuated to its current location. It was a bloody retreat and the 38 men who died while protecting the god are enshrined here as *Yiyonggong* ('brave guards').

Museum of Contemporary Art 台北當代藝術館 [91 C5] (*39 Changan W Rd;* ✎ *2552 3720; www.mocataipei.org.tw;* ⊕ *10.00–18.00 Tue–Sun; admission NTD50/0, free for families 10.00–12.00 Sat–Sun & national holidays*) Housed in what used to be a school during the Japanese colonial era, MOCA is Taiwan's only contemporary arts museum. As with TFAM, visits to MOCA can be hit-or-miss affairs depending on your tastes and what's showing. The website lists current and upcoming exhibitions.

2-28 Memorial Cenotaph [91 B5] (*Lane 185, Nanjing E Rd*) This simple bilingual plaque is a dignified reminder that the 2-28 Incident of 1947 (see *History*, page 18) erupted at this very spot.

EASTERN TAIPEI

Taipei 101 台北101 (Yī Líng Yī) [93 G2] (*www.taipei-101.com.tw*) Formerly the world's tallest structure at 509m including antenna, Taipei 101 is surely memorable if not especially beautiful. Divided into segments each of eight floors, architect C Y Lee was inspired by the shape of bamboo, which not only grows well throughout Taiwan but is also a symbol throughout the Chinese world of longevity and resilience. Much has been written about the meaning of the motifs that can be seen on the side of the tower, how *feng shui* considerations influenced the design and how the structure was made typhoon- and earthquake-proof. Tickets for the Observatory on the 91st floor (*admission NTD500/450;* ⊕ *09.00–22.00 daily*) can be bought on the fifth floor of the mall. Security has been tight since 2007, when Austrian BASE jumper Felix Baumgartner (who now holds the world skydiving record) leapt from the viewing deck, landed safely in a nearby car park and fled the country before he could be arrested. The adjacent mall (⊕ *11.00–21.30 daily*) has five floors of fancy shops and an impressive range of eating options.

Sun Yat-sen Memorial Hall 國父紀念館 (Guófù Jìniànguǎn) [93 F1] (✎ *2758 8008; www.yatsen.gov.tw;* ⊕ *09.00–18.00 daily*) This memorial to the Republic of China's founding father, completed in 1972, is less ostentatious than the Chiang Kai-shek Memorial Hall, the roof being less than half the height of the Chiang edifice. Architect Wang Da-hong purposely avoided both Western conventions and Chinese palatial architecture to invoke Sun's belief that neither a return to China's past nor slavish imitation of the West could solve the nation's problems. The historical displays inside barely touch on Taiwan – which isn't surprising as Sun made just three brief visits to the island – but among the heirlooms and photographs you're sure to find some things of interest. Exit 4 of Sun Yat-sen Memorial Hall MRT Station leads to the northwestern corner of the 11.5ha grounds; work your way around to the front entrance facing Renai Road where, each hour on the hour,

Sun Yat-sen (1866–1925), born to a Hakka family in south China and educated in Hawaii and Hong Kong, is revered by both Chinese Nationalists and the PRC government. He spent years fomenting revolution and was in exile when China's last emperor was overthrown. Rushing back, he became the ROC's first president on 1 January 1912 but stepped down just ten weeks later.

Sun married for the third time in 1915. His bride was Soong Ching-ling (1893–1981), elder sister of Soong May-ling, who later became Madame Chiang Kai-shek. Sun died long before Taiwan was incorporated into the ROC and was interred in Nanjing, the mainland city that was the ROC's capital. In the 1940s, Soong Ching-ling sided with the Communists. Sun's ideology, *San Min Chu I* ('Three Principles of The People'), provides the lyrics to the ROC national anthem and was a compulsory subject for college students until the late 1990s.

the changing of the military police detachment draws a small crowd. The guards are there to protect a larger-than-life bronze statue of Sun.

TAIPEI SUBURBS

SHILIN

National Palace Museum 國立故宮博物院 **(Gù Gōng)** (☏ 2881 2021; *www.npm. gov.tw;* ⊕ *08.30–18.30 Sun–Thu, 08.30–21.00 Fri–Sat; admission NTD250, free for preschool children & disabled, free for everyone on 1 Jan, 18 May, 27 Sept, 10 Oct & Lantern Festival*) Rightly considered to have one of the world's finest collections, the NPM is colossally rewarding for anyone interested in east Asian art. It derives its name from the fact that much of this magnificent accumulation used to be the personal collection of the Chinese emperors. Collecting was an imperial habit from the Song Dynasty (AD960–1279) onward. When the Qing Dynasty gave way to the Republic of China in 1911, the last emperor was permitted to remain in the Forbidden City for more than a decade. During this period numerous items were pilfered and sold by the eunuchs in his employment. After the last emperor was expelled from his palace in 1924, the original NPM was established in the Forbidden City. However, because Japan was expanding its sphere of influence in north China, in 1933 the most valuable artefacts were packed up and moved away. These crates and boxes were then moved several more times during World War II and the subsequent civil war. By the beginning of 1949 most had been transported to Keelung. Only in 1965, with the opening of the current building, were the treasures put on display once again.

The NPM collection is growing as a result of purchases and donations. At the end of 2012 the museum held 694,223 items (the British Museum has eight million), among which were 610,051 rare books and documents (the vast majority from the Qing Dynasty), 69,092 antiquities plus 12,970 paintings and works of calligraphy. Fewer than 1% are on public display at any one time. Some artefacts have never been displayed because they're too fragile or they've not yet been sufficiently researched. An expansion project, approved in 2012 and due to be completed by 2024, will more than triple the exhibition space.

Many of the prettiest pieces in the collection were gifts from Chinese officials hoping to curry favour with the emperor. Others were tributes from vassal states such as Tibet. A few, such as the timepieces cherished by Qing rulers, were gifts from

Western diplomats. And not all of the works executed in China were undertaken by Chinese artists. A number of paintings, the most famous being *A Hundred Steeds*, are the accomplishments of Giuseppe Castiglione (1688–1766), an Italian Jesuit missionary who became a court painter in Beijing.

Getting a general idea of what's here and lingering over displays that catch your eye requires at least three hours inside; don't be surprised if the museum ends up taking over the day. Those with special interests would do well to look at the NPM's very thorough website before they arrive. The museum spells Chinese words and names according to hanyu pinyin (see box, page 56). This may confuse those who read up before leaving home: the Ch'ing Dynasty is now rendered Qing; Sung is Song; Ch'in is Qin; Hsia is Xia. Also, many emperors' names are spelled differently.

Free English-language tours are conducted twice daily (⏰ *10.00 & 15.00*). To join one you should sign up online (look for 'Gallery Tours' on the museum's website) three days beforehand. If this isn't possible, ask when you get to the museum if there are any spaces for that day's tours. Tours last between one and two hours and most guides are amenable to requests and very willing to answer questions. They're especially good at explaining the symbolism of shapes and motifs. Presenting someone with an object that incorporates the 12 animals of the Chinese zodiac, for instance, signified that you wished him or her a long life. Paintings that depicted travel implied scholarship, because one had to go far afield to acquire knowledge. When the tour has finished you're free to revisit any galleries which looked particularly interesting. If you'd rather explore at your own pace, rent an English-language audio guide (*NTD100 for adults' version, NTD50 for children's version; deposit ID or NTD1,000*). The audio files can be downloaded for free from the museum's website so there's no need to rent a player if you have a suitable device. If you've time to kill before the start of a tour, spend it in the coffee shop to the left of the ticket office (⏰ *09.00–17.00 daily;* $) or in the gift shop one floor below. The latter has an excellent range of souvenirs from cheap 'Jadeite Cabbage' bottle openers to exquisite reproductions of paintings and calligraphy works. Many of the latter are excellent value at NTD3,000 or less.

Once you enter the museum proper, the Orientation Gallery, on the same level as the entrance, is a logical place to begin. Timelines put China's various dynasties and kingdoms in chronological order and relate those eras to what was happening in other parts of the world. On the same floor, you'll notice that the icons and statues in 'Compassion and Wisdom: Religious Sculptural Arts' are exclusively Buddhist; you won't find any folk or Taoist effigies like those that populate most Taiwanese temples. Some of the most striking pieces in this gallery are of Tibetan origin. Elsewhere on the first floor there's Qing Dynasty furniture, curio boxes with their contents, plus rare books.

One of the principal displays on the second floor is 'The Ancient Art of Writing: Selections from the History of Chinese Calligraphy'. Calligraphy remains

IN LIEU OF A SIGNATURE

Personal seals have been used by Han people for more than 2,500 years. Even in 21st-century Taiwan, documents and cheques are more often sealed than signed. Most of the name stamps you'll see being used in banks and offices are machine-carved and made of wood, bamboo or even plastic, but the NPM has a number of exquisite seals (or 'chops' as they're sometimes called) carved from jade or cast from bronze. Bat motifs, a symbol of luck, are a common feature. Some fist-sized seals bear dragon sculptures or excerpts from poems.

a popular art form; in modern Taiwan, when a couple is engaged to marry or a family has a happy event to celebrate, a calligrapher is often commissioned to write a congratulatory banner. For many of the scrolls in the NPM, the meaning of the characters matters less than the beauty of the brushwork (proper calligraphy is always done with an animal-hair brush and ink made from soot). On some you'll notice 60 or more red imprints – the names of personages who have, at one time or another, owned the scroll and used their personal seals to mark their property. In the China of yore such additions were thought of as enhancements, not defacements. In the margins, you may even see short comments written by previous owners.

There are often queues for one of the most popular permanent exhibitions, 'Dazzling Gems of the Collection: Famous Pieces from the Qing Dynasty Palaces' (third floor). The best known of the 16 items here is the 19cm-long Jadeite Cabbage; look closely for the katydid and the locust and read the information panel to discover the meaning of these symbols. The cabbage is thought to have arrived in the imperial household as part of a concubine's dowry. You may also have seen photos of the Meat-shaped Stone, a chunk of jasper carved to resemble a portion of fatty pork.

Those interested in the role of bronze should make their way to two galleries on the third floor, 'Classical Civilisation: The Bronze Age' and 'The Mystery of Bronzes'. The former includes bronze vessels used in ancestor-worship rituals. The latter explains techniques of smelting and casting, and also that a fad for ancient bronzeware in the late Ming and early Qing dynasties prompted craftsmen to develop ways of faking the patina of rust that's found on truly ancient pieces.

The three restaurants in the museum's East Wing (all ⊕ 09.00–19.30; EM; $$) serve set meals, soups, dim sum, hot drinks and snacks.

For information about the yet-to-open NPM Southern Branch, see page 236.

Getting there

By bus Most visitors take the MRT's Red Line to Shilin (*from Taipei Main Station takes 11mins; NTD25*) then one of the frequent #304, #255 or R30 buses to the museum (*takes about 15mins; NTD15*). Bus #304 goes all the way to the museum from Zhonghua Road near Ximending (*takes 40mins; NTD30*).

By taxi From Shilin MRT Station it shouldn't cost more than NTD170.

Shung Ye Museum of Formosan Aborigines (*282 Zhishan Rd Sec 2;* ☎ *2841 2611; www.museum.org.tw;* ⊕ *09.00–17.00 Tue–Sun, closed Jan 20–Feb 20; admission NTD150/100*) Taiwan's foremost collection of indigenous artefacts is less than 200m from the NPM and the English throughout is impeccable. English-language tours for groups and specialists can be arranged if the museum is given at least a week's notice. The core of the collection was donated by C F Lin, a Han Taiwanese businessman who over many years acquired 800-plus aboriginal artefacts, most of them from the Atayal, Paiwan and Tao tribes. The museum, which opened in 1994, now has a collection of almost 2,000 ethnological items, among them canoes from Orchid Island and finely woven clothes. One absorbing section about tattooing features tools and describes the process in detail. Men earned arm, chest and back tattoos by hunting; women were tattooed on the face or hands if they could weave well. There are also smoking pipes (several tribes grew their own tobacco), a Paiwan bronze dagger, pots in which Paiwan people believed their ancestors dwelt, and carved wooden twin-cups used by southern tribes to toast deals or seal alliances. By drinking from the same utensil, chiefs could show they trusted each other.

Chiang Kai-shek's Shilin Residence Park 士林官邸 (Shìlín Guāndǐ)

(*60 Fulin Rd; www.culture.gov.tw/frontsite/shilin/; grounds ⊕ 08.00–19.00 daily, residence ⊕ 09.30–12.00 & 13.00–17.00 Tue–Sun; free admission to grounds, admission to residence NTD100/50*) After 1949 Chiang appropriated or had built for himself at least 20 grand houses and villas in various parts of Taiwan. The 9.3ha of gardens that surround this abode – the dictator's main residence in the 1960s and early 1970s – were opened to the public in 1996; the house remained off-limits until after Madame Chiang Kai-shek (1898–2003), who regarded it as her personal property, passed away. The interior is hardly palatial but you'll see the living room where the Chiangs relaxed and some of the antiques which decorated their home as well as the upstairs bedroom where the generalissimo died. The residence is closed on many national holidays and for two weeks each September. Only small numbers of visitors are admitted so reserve a ticket in advance if you plan to come at the weekend. Midweek it's usually possible to roll up and join a tour within an hour; while waiting, take a look at the Methodist chapel where the ROC's first couple often prayed.

Getting there Buses between Shilin MRT Station and the National Palace Museum stop near the residence. Walking from Shilin MRT Station takes around 10 minutes.

National Revolutionary Martyrs Shrine 忠烈祠 (Zhōngliè Cí) (*139 Beian Rd; http://afrc.mnd.gov.tw/faith_martyr/English/index.aspx; ⊕ 09.00–17.00 daily; free admission*) This shrine, consecrated in 1969, is sacred ground for hardcore Chinese Nationalists. In architectural terms it's cut from the same cloth as the Chiang and Sun memorial halls; it has the same kind of entrance gate as the former and a sanctuary topped with the same glazed tiles as the latter. The approach to the sanctuary is lined with ROC flags. Once there, you'll notice an ornate entranceway, the main hall (off-limits to visitors), one shrine for civilians on the right and another for soldiers on the left. Of the 401,196 martyrs commemorated here all but 2,540 were military personnel, and more than three quarters of them died fighting the Japanese during World War II. The KMT launched sporadic military operations

JADE IN OLD CHINA AND PREHISTORIC TAIWAN

Some of the oldest pieces in the NPM's collection are made of jade, a material which in ancient times was believed to have semi-magical properties and so was often turned into ritual or ceremonial items. In terms of colour, jade may be white, green, brown or even reddish. Carved into blades, discs, dragons or figurines of humans or gods, several of the pieces in the museum have endured for 7,000 years. Jade artefacts were also highly valued by the indigenous Beinan culture which thrived in southeast Taiwan over 2,000 years ago (see page 306).

Jade was treasured for its toughness and beauty and valued more highly than gold. Jade thumb rings were popular during the Ming and Qing dynasties as wearing them showed one didn't engage in physical labour. In 21st-century Taiwan, jade is a popular material for making bracelets and pendants. However, some of what was considered to be 'jade' in the China of old doesn't fall into the modern definition. According to geologists, 'true' jade is either nephrite and jadeite. Both are semiprecious stones. The former used to be mined in considerable quantities in China itself; the latter was imported from what's now Burma. Ancient Chinese regarded any beautiful stone as jade, and faux-jades included serpentine, soapstone, topaz and quartz.

against the communist mainland for years following their retreat to Taiwan and among those enshrined here are spies, saboteurs and reconnaissance pilots. Martyrs are listed on wooden tablets, each one carrying up to 75 names. Some died before the establishment of the ROC in anti-Qing uprisings, others perished fighting the Communists. Some of the photos are prison mugshots; at least one was taken after the firing squad had done its work. The profiles, many of which are bilingual, make for interesting reading. Memorial tablets are grouped according to era and region, but unfortunately these categories aren't labelled in English. One such section is devoted to 251 Taiwanese who died resisting Japan's 1895–1945 colonial rule of the island. If the history doesn't interest you, the hourly changing of the guard might. The slow-motion goose-stepping and rapid twirling of rifles is done with absolute and engrossing precision. These young men deserve the round of applause they get at the end of each ceremony.

Getting there Buses from the Red Line's Yuanshan MRT Station include #247 and #287 (*departs every 20–30mins; NTD15*), which stop outside the shrine.

XINBEITOU 新北投 (XĪN BĚITÓU) Called Xinbeitou ('New Beitou') to distinguish
it from older neighbourhoods closer to the Danshui River, Xinbeitou is pressed up against the southwestern edge of Yangmingshan National Park. It's a geothermal hotspot: super-hot sulphur-tainted acidic water spews out of the rocks and into public pools and the bathtubs of dozens of hotels. The Ketagalan people, the lowland tribe that dominated the Taipei Basin until the 1700s, knew about and made good use of the scalding waters. They called this area Paktaaw. This word, which meant 'witch', eventually morphed into the current place name. It was outsiders who spotted the tourist potential of the springs: a German businessman who enjoyed a soak during an 1893 visit returned the following year to open a clubhouse. A Japanese entrepreneur followed suit in 1896.

Exploring Xinbeitou on foot is enjoyable as there's plenty of shade, not much traffic, fine mountain views and good walkways on both sides of the stream that gurgles down the hill. The sights described here can be seen in a leisurely few hours if you do a loop, proceeding up Zhongshan Road as far as Hell Valley, then returning to the MRT station via Wenquan Road and Guangming Road. It's hard to get lost.

Tourist information about the area is available from the Taipei Hot Springs Association website (*www.taipeisprings.org.tw*).

Getting there Take the MRT Red Line to Beitou then change trains for Xinbeitou (*25mins from Taipei Main Station; NTD35*). Bus #230, which runs between the Yangmingshan stop and Beitou MRT Station, goes through Xinbeitou.

What to see and do
Ketagalan Culture Centre 凱達格蘭文化館 (*3-1 Zhongshan Rd; www.ketagalan. taipei.gov.tw;* ⊕ *09.00–17.00 Tue–Sun, closed national holidays; free admission*) Cross the road in front of Xinbeitou MRT Station and walk towards the park. If you follow Zhongshan Road for a bit more than 100m, you'll see this centre on your left. Supported by the city government, it's named after the long-gone lowland tribe. There are brief but worthwhile displays about Taiwan's aboriginal groups and temporary exhibitions of indigenous art.

Beitou Branch of Taipei City Library 台北市立圖書館北投分館 (⊕ *08.30–21.00 Tue–Sat, 09.00–17.00 Sun–Mon, closed first Thu each month*) If you were hoping to pop into this attractive wooden building across the park from the Ketagalan Cultural Centre, and browse magazines in frigid comfort, you might be disappointed. There's very little air conditioning because the library is one of Taiwan's most energy-efficient buildings and has won prizes for sustainable design. Large windows let natural light and breezes in; the roof collects rainwater for flushing toilets and watering plants. However, it isn't as green as it could be: the timber was shipped all the way from North America and there are no bike racks (because, the architect has said, the library is inside a park and bikes are banned from Taipei's parks).

Beitou Hot Springs Museum 北投溫泉博物館 (\ *2893 9981;* ⊕ *09.00–17.00 Tue–Sun, closed national holidays; free admission*) Continue walking along Zhongshan Road to find this small museum, a 1913 replica of one of Japan's most famous bathhouses. The displays inside include lots of geological information about Taiwan's natural spas. The original bathing pool can be seen downstairs, though no-one has soaked here for decades. The columns and arches are akin to those in a Turkish bath, but the stained-glass windows come as a surprise. Just up the road there's an open-air bath that's still in use: **Millennium Hot Spring** (*6 Zhongshan Rd;* ⊕ *05.30–22.00 daily; closes briefly for cleaning every 2hrs; admission NTD40/20*). Bathers are required to wear swimsuits and shower caps.

Hell Valley 地熱谷 **(Dìrè Gǔ)** (⊕ *24hrs daily; free admission*) About 300m beyond Millennium Hot Spring is one of Taipei's most impressive natural sights, a cloudy blue-green pond that emits dense miasmas of steam. The fence is there to stop people getting too close, as falling in would probably be fatal – the water temperature is seldom lower than 90°C. There's no mention of hell in the Chinese place name which means simply 'geothermal gully', while some signs use a dull English-language alternative: 'Hot Spring Valley'.

Puji Temple 普濟寺 (*112 Wenquan Rd;* ⊕ *08.00–17.00 daily*) One of Xinbeitou's hidden treasures, this exquisite Japanese-style temple is obscured by trees and accessed via stone steps. The gate near the road is to keep out stray dogs; human visitors are welcome to tour the grounds but shouldn't enter the shrine, which is dedicated to Guanyin. The temple was founded in 1905 by the Shingon sect, a form of Japanese Buddhism. The current structure, a picture of grace, dates from the early 1930s. The frame and walls are juniper; the roof is hip-and-gable style.

Longnai Hot Springs 瀧乃湯 (*244 Guangming Rd;* ⊕ *06.30–21.00 daily; admission NTD90/50*) Almost lost amid much taller and newer buildings, Longnai offers a thoroughly traditional bathing experience. There are two pools inside this slightly decrepit pre-World War II bungalow, one for each gender. No swimsuits are needed but you should have your own towel. There are no toilets inside so go before you get here. The water temperature is usually 40–42°C. From Longnai it's less than 500m back to Xinbeitou MRT Station.

NANGANG
Museum of the Institute of History and Philology 歷史文物陳列館
(*130 Academia Rd Sec 2;* \ *2652 3180; http://museum.sinica.edu.tw;* ⊕ *09.30–16.30 Wed & Sat only; free admission*) The small but excellent MIHP is on the campus of Academia Sinica, Taiwan's national academy and the country's leading research establishment in several fields. The Taiwanese Materials section has Koxinga-era maps and memorials relating to the island, plus paintings of aboriginal lifestyles.

Among the documents selected from the Qing imperial archives (rescued by researchers in the 1920s from a Beijing paper-recycling merchant) are records of negotiations between Koxinga and the Manchu usurpers before the former retreated to Taiwan. Even if you've no great interest in China, you'll find intriguing the 2,000-year-old letters, reports and weather records written on bamboo slips by soldiers and officials posted to the empire's northwest, not to mention the even older skulls and weapons.

If you've made the trek out to this corner of Taipei, you may want to also visit the **Museum of the Institute of Ethnology** (*www.ioe.sinica.edu.tw;* ⊕ *09.30–16.30 Wed & Sat only; free admission*). It's next door to the MIHP and engrossing for aficionados of aboriginal culture. Elsewhere on the campus, **Lingnan Fine Arts Museum** (✆ *2789 9937;* ⊕ *12.00–17.00 Tue–Fri & 10.00–17.00 Sat; free admission*) displays ink-wash paintings which combine a Western approach to detail with ancient Chinese brush painting techniques.

Getting there Take a Blue Line MRT train to Kunyang (*15mins from Taipei Main Station; NTD25*) then bus #212, #270 or Blue 25 (*frequent departures; takes 15–20mins; NTD15*). Get off when you see on your left the Latin words 'Academia Sinica'. Bilingual maps will then guide you around the campus.

MUZHA 木柵

Taipei Zoo (*www.zoo.gov.tw;* ⊕ *09.00–17.00 daily except Lunar New Year's Eve; indoor areas close some Mon, see website for details; admission NTD60/30*) This zoo has some of Taiwan's best-known animals, including Formosan black bears, and a superb insectarium.

Getting there Take the Brown Line to Taipei Zoo MRT Station (*from Taipei Main Station takes 26mins; NTD35*).

Maokong Gondola (*http://gondola.trtc.com.tw; operates* ⊕ *09.00–21.00 Tue–Sun; NTD50/25 one-way*) This highly recommended 4.03km-long cable-car journey takes 25 minutes one-way and in good weather the views are excellent; in bad weather (such as when typhoons are in the vicinity) service is suspended. Passengers board near Taipei Zoo's ticket office and the second of the four stations is inside the zoo. The final stop, Maokong, is 299m above sea level and in the heart of one of Taiwan's oldest tea-growing areas. As well as dozens of places where you can enjoy a brew and snacks, there are short hiking trails. You can get maps of the vicinity from the visitor information centres at both terminus stations.

YANGMINGSHAN NATIONAL PARK 陽明山國家公園
(Yángmíngshān Guójiā Gōngyuán)

If you've seen Taiwan's Central Mountain Range, the hills and dormant volcanoes of this 11,455ha national park – almost equally divided between the cities of Taipei and New Taipei – are unlikely to leave you gasping in awe. However, if you're here for birds and butterflies you'll certainly enjoy the park. Twitchers have a good chance of ticking off one of Taiwan's endemic species, the Formosan magpie (*Urocissa caerulea*). Lepidopterologists, if they come in late spring, will have a field day with the park's 150-plus butterfly species.

Because of its proximity to Taipei, convenient public transport and user-friendly bilingual signage, parts of the park get overrun at weekends. Midweek you'll still

Tea is Taiwan's traditional beverage. Despite the growing popularity of coffee and herbal infusions, annual per capita tea consumption climbed from 344g in 1980 to 1,540g in 2007. Domestic production, however, is now much lower than in the 1970s, even though the island still has around 15,000ha of tea plantations. Now more than half of the tea drunk in Taiwan is imported from low-wage countries. Cheap tea is turned into packaged drinks for supermarkets and convenience stores; locally grown tea tends to be much more expensive. Demand from China has driven up prices and growers of prize-winning teas have been able to sell their harvests for more than £10,000 per kg.

Because of climatic and topographical variations, Taiwan grows a wide range of different teas. In addition to black teas and green teas (increasingly popular throughout the world because of their perceived health benefits), there are various oolongs which are somewhere between green teas and black teas. Unlike their Japanese counterparts, Taiwanese tea aficionados don't follow any rigid ceremonies when brewing and sipping the beverage. They do, however, discard the very first brew each time as a matter of course.

From the 1870s to the 1890s, north Taiwan saw an export-driven tea boom. North America and southeast Asia were the major markets; beneficiaries included Western businessmen living in Danshui, Han merchants in Dadaocheng (that part of Taipei near Baoan Temple) and plantation owners in Maokong and elsewhere. There were losers, too. In an early example of globalisation having dire effects on indigenous peoples, the demand for tea led to aborigines being pushed off their ancestral lands.

To learn more about Taiwan's tea, see www.teafromtaiwan.com or www.taiwanteaguy.com.

meet plenty of hikers, but there's an upside to this – you needn't worry about getting lost or stranded. During the colder months, many Taiwanese drive up so they can enjoy the park's hot springs. In addition to the hotels near Yangmingshan Bus Station, where you can soak for a few hours if you'd rather not stay overnight, there are public pools on the eastern slopes of the park's highest mountain. Each year, usually from late February, there's a month-long flower festival.

Yangmingshan's original name was Grass Mountain, a reference to the tall grasses that cover many of the slopes and summits. After World War II it was renamed in honour of Wang Yang-ming (1472–1529), a Confucianist philosopher.

GETTING THERE, AWAY AND AROUND

By bus The two main services to Yangmingshan Bus Station are #230 from Beitou via Xinbeitou (*departs every 30mins before 17.00, approx hourly after 17.00; ⊕ 06.00–22.10 daily; takes 20mins; NTD15*) and #260 (*departs every 7–10mins; ⊕ 05.10–22.30 daily; takes at least 35mins; NTD30*) from Taipei Main Station via Jiantan MRT Station. There's also the Red 5 from Jiantan MRT Station (*departs every 7–13mins; ⊕ 06.00–00.15 daily; NTD15*). The first bus of the day is often packed with retirees going hiking. At weekends you'll probably have to queue for a spot on a bus heading back to the city. Leisure Bus #108 is a shuttle service between various points in the national park (*departs every 5–8mins Sat–Sun, every 15mins Mon–Fri; ⊕ 07.00–17.30; NTD15*). Details of other buses can be found on the national park's website. Free shuttle services are often arranged during festivals.

By car or motorcycle Before driving into the park, ask the tourist hotline (📞*0800 011 765*) if traffic controls are in place because of festivals or other special events.

TOURIST INFORMATION

ℹ️ **Yangmingshan National Park** www.ymsnp.gov.tw

ℹ️ **Headquarters/Main Visitor Centre** 10mins walk from Yangmingshan Bus Station; 📞2861 5741; ⏰ 08.30–16.30 daily, closed last Mon each month. Here you can buy Richard Saunders' excellent *Yangmingshan: The Guide*; it details 41 different hikes within the park.

WHAT TO SEE AND DO Yangmingshan's peaks may be tiddlers by the standards of the Central Mountain Range but hikers should be properly prepared in terms of footwear, clothing, snacks and water.

Grass Mountain Chateau (*89 Hudi Rd;* 📞*2862 2404; www.grassmountainchateau. com.tw;* ⏰ *10.00–17.00 Tue–Sun; admission NTD30*) Yet another of Chiang Kai-shek's hideaways, this single-story chateau was built in 1920 by a Japanese sugar corporation. Three years later, Crown Prince Hirohito (later Japan's emperor) spent a few hours here during a tour of Taiwan. The original chateau was destroyed by arson in 2007 but the replica is faithful in every detail and incorporates stones and timbers retrieved from the ruins. The four adjacent buildings, which used to house Chiang's bodyguards and assistants, are occasionally open for exhibitions. The restaurant (⏰ *11.00–21.00 Tue–Sun; EM;* $$$$) commands magnificent views. Set meals with Taiwanese dishes are just over NTD500; waffles and other treats are also available.

Getting there Walking here from Yangmingshan Bus Station takes about 20 minutes; it's level most of the way. Take Hushan Road rather than the highway towards Jinshan. The Little 8 and Little 9 minibuses (*both depart every 20mins; NTD15*) stop near the chateau and go to/from, respectively, the Red Line's Shipai MRT Station and Beitou.

Seven Stars Mountain 七星山 (Qīxīngshān) The tallest point within the park, the 1,120m-high peak of Seven Stars Mountain is a fine spot from which to gaze over Taipei City and the mouth of the Danshui River. The ascent begins at the park's main visitor centre. No map is required – all you need are reasonably strong legs. Allow four hours to reach the top, take in the spectacular view and make your way down. Energetic hikers can continue northwest to Xiaoyoukeng or eastward to Lengshuikeng. Both descents take no more than an hour.

Xiaoyoukeng 小油坑 The fumaroles of Xiaoyoukeng have been spewing steam and sulphur for millennia, staining the land yellow-green and creating the park's single most striking sight. As long ago as the early 16th century, Ketagalan aborigines were mining the sulphur and bartering it with Han Chinese merchants. If you take a #1717 bus (see *Getting there, away and around*, page 137), you'll see the main vent on your right. Hikers coming from Seven Stars Mountain often use this bus service to get back to Taipei.

Lengshuikeng Public Hot Springs 冷水坑溫泉 (⏰ *09.00–17.00 daily; free admission*) Lengshuikeng means 'cool water hole' and it's true that the water doesn't scald like some other natural spas. However, at approximately 40°C it's a pleasant temperature for bathing after a hike. The sulphur content is very high, hence the water's milky appearance. There is a pool for each gender. Swimsuits are not required.

4

North Taiwan

Most of Taiwan's international visitors fly into Taoyuan and head directly to Taipei or other parts of the country, bypassing a region which deserves at least three days in any two-week itinerary. For the purposes of this guidebook, north Taiwan consists of New Taipei City (sometimes called Xinbei; land area: 2,053km²; population: 3.95 million), Keelung City (133km²; 376,000 people) and the counties of Taoyuan (1,221km²; 2.04 million people) and Yilan (2,143km²; 458,000 people).

New Taipei City, formerly known as Taipei County, is a microcosm of Taiwan. It has densely populated urban areas, steep uplands dotted with tiny aboriginal villages and everything in between. Danshui and Sanxia are rich in history while Wulai is an indigenous enclave conveniently close to the capital. The rugged north and northeast coasts abound in memorable landscapes. You'll either love or hate Keelung, a place so bustling it makes Taipei look sleepy. As the statistics above suggest, Taoyuan and Yilan are very different places. The lowland portion of Taoyuan is heavily industrialised while the inland half has the attractive old town of Daxi, indigenous villages and scenery that's more than pleasing. Yilan, by contrast, was largely spared the small-factory revolution that powered Taiwan's economic miracle but damaged its environment. Long regarded as one of Taiwan's most liveable places, it's popular with cyclists and birdwatchers.

The opening of Freeway 5 means Yilan is being tied ever more closely to Taipei – yet it doesn't mean you have to approach it from the capital. The beautiful but little-used North Cross-Island Highway links Yilan with Taoyuan; this mountain route, certainly one of north Taiwan's highlights, deserves to be taken slowly.

TAOYUAN AIRPORT 台灣桃園國際機場 (Táiwān Táoyuán Guójì Jīchǎng) Telephone code 03

Almost all long-haul flights into Taiwan land at Taiwan Taoyuan International Airport. Inaugurated in 1979 and originally known as Chiang Kai-shek International Airport, the facility was renamed in 2006 as part of the Chen administration's localisation policy. Ironically, the pan-greens' decision brought Taiwan into line with PRC practice, which has always been to refer to the airport in media reports as 'Taoyuan International Airport', so as to avoid mentioning the late Nationalist leader.

GETTING THERE AND AWAY

By air There are currently two terminals at Taiwan Taoyuan International Airport (*IATA code: TPE;* ✆ *398 3728; www.taoyuan-airport.com*). Most Hong Kong and southeast Asian carriers use T1 (✆ *398 2143*) while long-haul and mainland Chinese airlines use the newer and nicer T2 (✆ *398 3274*). Don't worry if you arrive at the

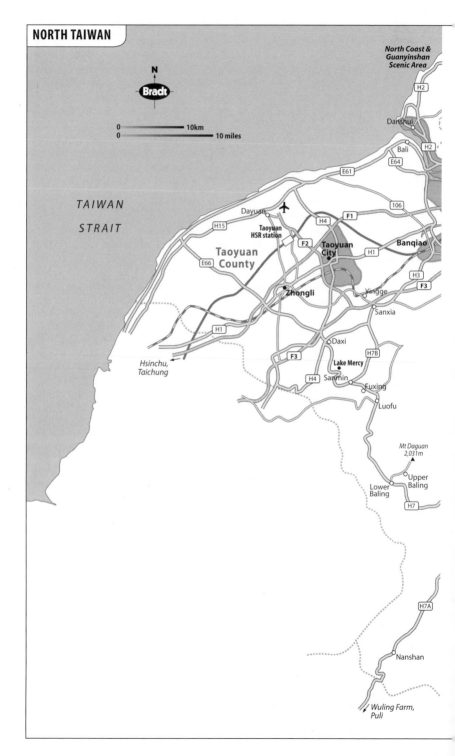

NORTH TAIWAN

N

Bradt

0 ——— 10km
0 ——— 10 miles

North Coast &
Guanyinshan
Scenic Area

H2

Danshui

Bali

H2

E64

E61

106

TAIWAN

STRAIT

Dayuan

Taoyuan
HSR station

H15

H4

F1

F2

Taoyuan
City

H1

Banqiao

Taoyuan
County

E66

H1

H3

F3

●Zhongli

Yingge

Sanxia

●Daxi

H1

H7B

F3

Lake Mercy

H4

Sanmin

Fuxing

Hsinchu,
Taichung

Luofu

Mt Daguan
2,031m ▲

○Upper
Baling

Lower
Baling

H7

H7A

Nanshan

Wuling Farm,
Puli

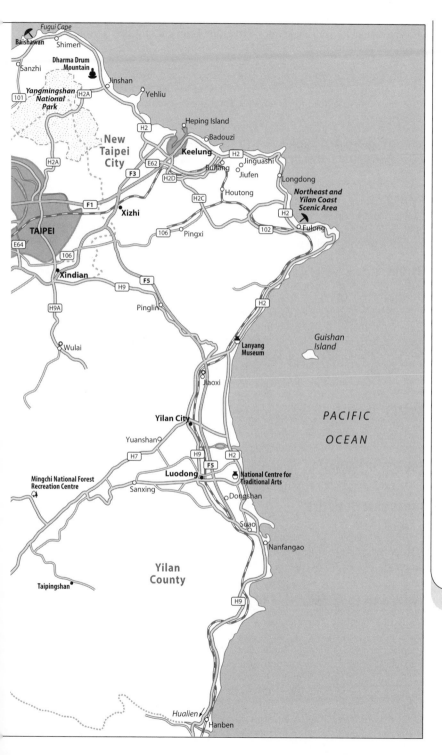

wrong terminal for your flight out – a free mini-train links the two. Terminal 3 will open in stages between 2014 and 2018.

By car Freeway 2, which links to both Freeway 1 and Freeway 3, leads directly to the airport. Freeway 1 is preferable if your initial destination is Taipei or Hsinchu; otherwise head for Freeway 3. There are two **vehicle-rental offices** inside the airport:

🚗 **Hotai Leasing Corp** Arrivals, T1; 📞 398 3636; www.easyrent.com.tw; ⏰ 05.00–24.00 daily

🚗 **Ching Bing Auto Leasing** Arrivals, T2; 📞 398 2989; www.chingbing.com.tw; 📧 order@ chingbing.com.tw; ⏰ 06.00–00.30 daily

By HSR Taoyuan HSR Station is 11km from the airport, 18km from the centre of Taoyuan and 10km from Zhongli. Regular buses (*NTD20–30 one-way*) connect the HSR station with all three places. To/from Taipei by HSR takes 22 minutes (*NTD175 one-way*); to/from Kaohsiung Zuoying takes 1¾ hours (*NTD1,455 one-way*).

By bus Various services link the airport with central Taipei (*takes about 1hr*) including #1819 to Taipei Main Station (*departs every 15–20mins; from the airport* ⏰ *24hrs daily; NTD125*). If you're aiming for a specific part of the capital, ask before buying your ticket as there are several routes and one may stop right outside your hotel. There are also good links to Taichung, the most frequent service being #1623 (*departs every 30–60mins from the airport;* ⏰ *06.10–00.10 daily; takes 2¼hrs; NTD240*). Until mid-evening, local buses set off for Taoyuan (*#5059, every 30mins; takes 40mins; NTD53*) and Zhongli (*#5089, about every hr; takes 40mins; NTD59*). In both cities these buses leave from and terminate at stops very near the TRA stations.

By MRT The MRT line linking the airport to Taipei Main Railway Station should be operational by the end of 2015. It will eventually be extended to Taoyuan HSR Station and Zhongli.

TOURIST INFORMATION Airport tourist information counters (*both* ⏰ *07.00– 23.30 daily*) can be found in T1 (📞 *398 2194*) and T2 (📞 *398 3341*).

OTHER PRACTICALITIES
$ **Bank of Taiwan** Both terminals; ⏰ 06.00– 21.20 daily in Departures, 24hrs daily in Arrivals
$ **Mega** Both terminals; ⏰ 06.00–23.00 daily in Departures, 07.00–23.00 daily in Arrivals

✉ T1 Departure Hall; ⏰ 08.00–17.00 Mon–Fri, 08.30–12.00 Sat

TAOYUAN CITY 桃園市 (Táoyuán Shì)   *Telephone code 03*

It's hard to picture Taoyuan as an orchard full of blossoming peach trees. Yet that's how it looked two centuries ago, and that's why this manufacturing centre (population: 415,000) has a name that strikes 21st-century visitors as perversely bucolic: *táo* (peach) *yuán* (garden). The pioneers who settled hereabouts in the late 1700s dubbed it Humaozhuang, meaning 'the terrace covered by plants with leaves as sharp as tigers' teeth'. They cleared the land to grow rice, vegetables and – of course – peaches.

Since World War II, agriculture has taken a back seat to car-making and electronics. There's no compelling reason for travellers heading to or emerging from the airport to get embroiled in the city, and those planning to drive across the North Cross-Island Highway may well prefer to stay on the freeway and follow the signs to Daxi.

GETTING THERE AND AWAY

By car Take Freeway 1. Taoyuan is 24km south of Taipei and 153km north of Taichung.

By TRA and HSR Every day dozens of trains link Taoyuan with Taipei (*departs* ⊕ *05.00–23.30 daily; most take 35mins; NTD42–66*). See the airport entry on page 115 for HSR information.

By bus Long-distance buses leave from various stops on Fuxing Road, 100m north of the TRA station. Airport bus #5059 (*departs every 30mins;* ⊕ *05.50–21.30 daily; takes 40mins; NTD42*) can be caught at 85 Fuxing Road. From the bus station near the back of Taoyuan TRA Station (take the tunnel under the tracks and walk about 200m), #5005 heads to Sanxia (*departs every 20mins;* ⊕ *06.10–21.30 daily; takes 40mins; NTD42*) via Yingge, while #5096 serves Daxi (*departs every 15mins;* ⊕ *05.50–21.30 daily; takes 30mins; NTD40*).

🏠 WHERE TO STAY

🏠 **City Suites Gateway** (153 rooms) 442 Zhongzheng Rd, Dayuan; ✆ 385 3017; f 385 3031; e reservation@citysuites.com.tw; www.citysuites. com.tw. Smallish rooms but very quiet & the location outside Taoyuan City can't be beaten if you want to minimise travel time before a morning flight. Not as remote as you might first think; turn left as you leave the lobby & in 5mins you're on a busy shopping/eating street. Buffet b/fast inc, served 06.00–10.00. **$$$**

🏠 **Harazuru Hotel** (50 rooms) 122 Shuangfeng Rd; ✆ 355 8833; f 357 2096; e harazuru@ ms15.hinet.net; www.harazuru. com.tw. A good option if you want to be on the airport side of the city but near enough to downtown to have dinner & drinks there. Popular with businesspeople who like the location & multilingual service. All rooms have broadband internet, refrigerators & cable TV. Extra beds can be put in a room for NTD300. PC in the lobby. Buffet b/fast inc. **$$$**

🏠 **Hsin Tao Hotel** (60 rooms) 8th Flr 180 Fuxing Rd; ✆ 333 1131; f 333 1139. Smack between the Shinkong & Tonlin department stores, this hotel can be found quickly if you walk from the TRA station to Fuxing Rd. Turn left & look for the hotel sign high up on the building's side. It's clean, but few rooms have windows & none have refrigerators. Couples can sometimes get a room for under NTD1,000 & rooms sleeping 4 for less than NTD1,500. Wi-Fi. **$$**

🍴 WHERE TO EAT AND DRINK

🍴 **Ali Baba's Indian Kitchen** 2nd Flr 86 Minsheng Rd; ✆ 336 0882; www.ali88.com.tw; ⊕ 11.30–15.00 & 17.30–23.00 daily. A branch of a well-liked Taipei halal Indian restaurant, Ali Baba's is a 10-min walk from the TRA station. Minsheng Rd runs parallel to Zhongzheng Rd, on the right if you're coming from the station. The founder is a Pakistani married to a Taiwanese; the menu he's designed is mutton-heavy but also has a good number of vegetarian options. W/end lunch is all-you-can-eat for NTD450 pp. EM. **$$$**

🍴 **Beiping Dagezi Knife-Cut Noodles** 北平大個子刀削麵 7 Datong Rd; ✆ 335 6678; ⊕ 11.00–20.00 daily. On the face of it just another brightly lit eatery with a TV turned up loud, this restaurant sells food usually associated with China's Muslim northwest. When an order is placed, the cook picks up a big slab of dough & skilfully carves off inch-wide strips. The tomato pig-rib noodles (*fān qié pái gǔ miàn*) are extremely popular. Help yourself to side dishes of tofu or pickles. Alternatives to knife-cut noodles include ramen, steamed dumplings & beef soup. Datong Rd crosses Zhongzheng Rd very near the TRA station. If you're coming from the former, turn right when you reach Datong Rd. Local beer available. No EM. **$$**

WHAT TO SEE AND DO The main attraction in Taoyuan City is an important relic from the Japanese colonial era.

Martyrs' Shrine 忠烈祠 (Zhōngliè Cí) (*200 Chenggong Rd Sec 2; ⊕ 08.30–16.30 daily; free admission*) Very few Shinto places of worship survived Nationalist rule and this is certainly the largest and most accessible. Bilingual information boards explain the functions of the buildings and the meanings of the statues. Completed by the Japanese in 1938 as a temple worshipping Amaterasu, the mythical ancestress of Japan's royal family, it also honoured Prince Yoshihisa Kitashirakawa, the imperial relative who died of malaria while leading Japan's 1895 takeover. Made largely of cypress, the structure is classically Japanese in that it reflects the strong cultural influence on Japan of China's Tang Dynasty. During the 1970s it was the subject of a long dispute between preservationists and those who wanted it demolished because they saw it as a hated reminder of Japanese rule. The compromise eventually reached saw the buildings saved but converted into a shrine for heroes from Taiwan's past. Koxinga is here, as are Liu Yong-fu (the second and final president of the Republic of Taiwan in 1895) and Qiu Feng-jia, who led local soldiers in trying to repel the Japanese. Every 29 March there's a memorial ceremony. For the other 364 days it's a place where people go to stroll among cherry trees and enjoy fine views of what is, alas, an unattractive city. To get here, take city bus #105 (*departs every 10–20mins; NTD18*) from the stop very near the corner of Zhongzheng and Fuxing roads. Get off about ten minutes later at the hospital and follow the main road as it curves uphill. Very soon you'll see a broad stairway on the right.

SANXIA 三峽 AND YINGGE 鶯歌 *Telephone code 02*

Twin towns separated by the broad wadi of the Dahan River, Sanxia (population: 109,000) and Yingge (population: 88,000) are associated, respectively, with traditional architecture and ceramics.

Sanxia means 'three gorges', but if you arrive on a clear day it's the nearby mountains rather than the narrow streams that will impress you. An abundance of natural resources – camphor, coal, tea and timber – powered the town's growth. Indigo dyeing was a major industry. By 1930, however, trains and lorries had replaced riverboats as the main means of shifting goods around north Taiwan and Sanxia was soon eclipsed by upstart towns like Taoyuan.

Yingge is to Taiwan what Stoke-on-Trent used to be to England. Most of the pottery produced here these days is decorative rather than practical.

GETTING THERE AND AWAY
By TRA Yingge is well served by trains. From Taipei takes about half an hour (*NTD31–37*), from Taoyuan takes less than 10 minutes (*NTD15–18*).

By bus Options include #908 (*departs every 8–20mins; ⊕ 06.00–22.00 daily; takes 40mins; NTD30*) to/from Jingan MRT Station on the Orange and soon-to-open Circular lines; and #916 (*departs every 10–20mins; ⊕ 06.00–23.30 daily; takes 45mins; NTD30*) to/from Yongning MRT Station on the Blue Line. From Taoyuan, bus #5005 (*departs every 20mins; ⊕ 06.10–21.30 daily*) follows a winding route to Sanxia (*takes 40mins; NTD42*) with stops *en route* very near Yingge Ceramics Old Street, Yingge TRA Station and the ceramics museum.

By car Take Freeway 3 to the Sanxia-Yingge exit at km50.

By motorcycle or bicycle Approach by Highway 3. If you're bound for the east coast, follow the signs from Sanxia to Dapu and then Sanmin. This road, Highway 7B, joins up with the North Cross-Island Highway near Sanmin.

✗ WHERE TO EAT AND DRINK

✗ **Changfu Restaurant** 長福飲食店
17 Changfu St, Sanxia; ☏ 2671 9543; ⏱ 09.00–19.30 daily. A good place to scoff down a lunch of fish, Changfu also does very popular deep-fried chicken rolls 雞捲 (*jī juǎn*), fried noodles, tofu & gravy rice. The menu (no English) also lists beef & fish. Get here before 17.00 or you might find some items have sold out. **$$**

WHAT TO SEE AND DO Finding your way around Sanxia is a cinch thanks to bilingual map boards and signposts.

Sanxia Historical Relics Hall 三峽歷史文物館 (⏱ *09.00–17.00 Tue–Sun; free admission*) This small museum is in the heart of Sanxia. Skip the ground floor and head upstairs to see photos of the town as it used to look.

Zushi Temple 祖師廟 (Zǔshī Miào) (⏱ *04.00–23.00 daily*) The shrine that many regard as the very pinnacle of religious art in Taiwan is, you may think at first, grossly overrated. Patches of crudely painted concrete are visible, as is messy wiring. But if you go over the wood and stone carvings column by column and inch by inch you'll be won over. In addition to the usual dragons and sages, there are crabs and other crustaceans, fish, owls, pangolins, elephants and a whole orchestra of musicians. The gold-leaf-bedecked ceiling of the central chamber, where incense is offered to Zushi, is breathtakingly ornate. Zushi, which means 'divine progenitor', is the godly name of Chen Zhaoying, a 13th-century government official honoured for his bravery at a time when the Mongols were invading China. The temple was established in 1769, rebuilt in 1833 and flattened during fighting between Japanese forces and Taiwanese militia in 1895. Rebuilt again in 1899, a major renovation effort was begun in 1947 under the supervision of Li Mei-shu (1902–83), a local politician and acclaimed painter. Since Li's death progress on the temple has been stymied by a dispute between the management committee, which has preferred to use cheaper semi-finished decorations imported from the Chinese mainland, and those who back Li's policy of employing local master carvers and artists.

Li Mei-shu Memorial Gallery 李梅樹紀念館 (*10, Lane 43, Zhonghua Rd; ☏ 2673 2333; f 2673 6077; www.limeishu.org; ⏱ 10.00–17.30 Sat–Sun & national holidays; groups can visit Mon–Fri if reservations are made 10 days before; admission NTD100*) This gallery, managed by Li's family, showcases several of the artist's finest works. It's within walking distance of the temple; look at one of the map boards and then set off across the river.

Sanjiaoyong Street 三角湧老街 Sanxia's oldest thoroughfare and former business hub has been reborn as a touristy 'old street' and reverted to its pre-1945 name. By far the largest building on the 260m-long street is a hangar-like temple, but it's the redbrick Baroque-style shop-houses that catch the eye. Several of them are more than a century old, although the street's distinctive look didn't appear until around 1915, when the colonial authorities ordered gutters to be added for reasons of public health. The declared doctrine of the 2004–06 renovation was 'original architecture, original materials'. This meant firing hundreds of mud bricks for internal partitions and straightening sagging roofs. However, residents were

permitted to build additional floors so long as façades were preserved and the classical appearance of the street maintained. Embellishments of vases (a symbol of peace – in both Mandarin and Taiwanese the word for vase sounds similar to the word for peace), lotuses, dragons and lions were redone. The street and the alleyways that lead off it have been paved with chiselled (rather than machined) granite slabs. Unavoidable modern features such as manhole covers and house numbers have been made to look as traditional as possible.

Yingge Ceramics Old Street 陶瓷老街 (*shops* ⊕ *approx 10.00–20.00 daily*) Don't attempt to walk the 4km between Sanxia and Yingge. Because of heavy traffic it's an unpleasant and not terribly safe hike, so take a bus or taxi. Once you've got to the seaward side of the Dahan River, you'll find a cluster of ceramics vendors near Yingge TRA Station; the street isn't especially old but it is a good place to pick up Chinese teapots and other fragile souvenirs.

Yingge Ceramics Museum 鶯歌陶瓷博物館 (**Yīnggē Táocí Bówùguǎn**) (*200 Wenhua Rd;* \ *8677 2727; www.ceramics.ntpc.gov.tw;* ⊕ *09.30–17.00 Tue–Fri, 09.30–18.00 Sat–Sun, closed first Mon each month; free admission*) Externally bleak but highly rated, this museum covers everything from the production of roof tiles in 17th-century Taiwan and ceramic art to the use of ceramics in electronics and medicine. The English wording outside the museum is tiny, so keep your eyes peeled if you're driving or approaching by bus.

WULAI 烏來 (WULÁI) *Telephone code 02*

Wulai covers more land than Taipei City but because over 90% of the district is mountainous it has just 6,000 residents. A third are Atayal (alternative spellings of Wulai, such as *Urai* and *Ulay*, are closer to the indigenous pronunciation than the current place name) and their culture is evident in the restaurants that line Wulai's main street, as well as in the small tribal museum.

Wulai's hillsides are covered by mixed forest and separated by boulder-filled azure rivers. Unfortunately this beautiful backdrop is spoiled somewhat by the foreground, a mishmash of homes, shops and small hotels. The riverside public hot-springs pools are surrounded by concrete and spaghetti-like pipework. Still, it isn't difficult to enjoy yourself here. In addition to the springs – the waters are colourless and don't have a strong smell – there are excellent opportunities for ecotourism. Wulai is one of the best year-round butterflying areas in north Taiwan and birdwatchers will find plenty of reasons to twitch.

GETTING THERE AND AWAY

By car or motorcycle Highway 9A from Xindian. Headlights must be kept on between Xindian and km13, just before Wulai.

By public transport Take the MRT's Green Line to Xindian (*from Taipei Main Station takes 20mins; NTD30*) then board bus #849 or #1601 (*departs every 15mins;* ⊕ *05.30–21.30 daily; takes 30mins; NTD40*) to the busiest part of Wulai.

TOURIST INFORMATION There are visitor information centres in Xindian MRT Station (⊕ *09.00–17.30 Mon–Fri, 08.00–19.30 Sat–Sun & national holidays*) in Wulai Village and at Wulai Waterfall (*both* ⊕ *09.00–17.30 daily*).

WHERE TO STAY AND EAT Mid-range hotels and typical Taiwanese eateries can be found in and around the main village.

🏠 **Pause Landis** (30 rooms) 61 Yanti, Wulai; ✆2661 8000; f 2661 8080; e service@pauselandis. com.tw; www.pauselandis.com.tw. Room & meal or pool & meal packages can save a good amount of money so get in touch with this swish establishment ahead of time. The various designs of the private hot-spring rooms (*from NTD1,800 for use 08.00–22.30*) show imagination & great taste; in one, the tub resembles a gigantic wok. Use of popular, gender-segregated public pools (⏲ *08.00–22.30 daily*) is NTD800 pp. No under-12s. **$$$$$**

🏠 **Volando Urai Spring Spa & Resort** (23 rooms) 3 Yanti, Wulai; ✆2661 6555; f 2661 6559; e fo@volandourai.com.tw; www. springparkhotel.com.tw. Slate, granite & some delicate examples of Atayal weaving lend this place an air of quiet refinement. Staying here isn't by any standards cheap – during the winter busy season the smallest suite will set you back NTD16,000 & you may want to spend a little more for 'Grand View' rooms which are both grand & perfectly positioned for views over the river. Inc

b/fast, a gourmet French dinner & midnight snack. No under-12s. Coming from Taipei, the Spring Park is on the right 1km before Wutai's main village, just past the 13km marker on Highway 9A. Free shuttle buses pick up guests from Xindian MRT Station if booked beforehand. **$$$$$**

✖ **Taiya Popo** 泰雅婆婆美食店 14 Wulai St; ✆2661 6371; ⏲ 10.00–21.00 daily. Located beside Wulai Atayal Museum – look for this restaurant's bamboo-bedecked walls – Taiya Popo is the best known of Wulai's indigenous eateries thanks to local & international media coverage. Like many of the eateries around here, seasoned rice in a bamboo tube 竹筒飯 (*zhú tǒng fàn*) is a popular offering. Mountain boar 山豬 (*shān zhū ròu*) can be quite delicious, while vegetable options include bamboo shoots & yams. To prove your manhood, order a portion of *damamian* – a mixture of raw pork, rice & salt that's been fermented in a jar for 2 weeks at room temperature. No EM but some English understood. **$$**

WHAT TO SEE AND DO If nature takes priority over hot springs, turn right at km13.5 on Highway 9A instead of driving into Wulai Village. As soon as you cross the bridge you'll find bilingual information boards about nearby hiking and birding trails.

Wulai Atayal Museum 烏來泰雅民族博物館 (12 Wulai St; ✆ 2661 8162; www. atayal.ntpc.gov.tw; ⏲ 09.30–17.00 Tue–Fri, 09.30–18.00 Sat–Sun, closed 1st Mon every month; free admission)
In addition to clothes, tools and model houses there are bilingual displays which touch on local indigenous history, religion, festivals and ecological practices – all of which are endangered in Wulai, in large part because outsiders dominate the local tourist trade. If you've arrived by bus, the museum is on the main street, on the right-hand side of the road. Look for the huge carved face above the entrance.

Public hot springs 公用溫泉 (⏲ 24hrs daily; free admission)
Go to the end of the main street, cross the little bridge and look for the steps going down to the river on the right. Given that the pools are free and unsupervised, the surroundings are as clean (or as messy) as you'd expect. Before spending lots of money to use a private pool in a hotel, bear in mind that a few of Wulai's establishments have been caught using recycled spring water, or even ordinary tap water adulterated with powdered sulphur.

Wulai Waterfall 烏來瀑布
Some 80m from top to bottom, this is the highest waterfall in north Taiwan and pretty if not breathtaking. Getting here is a

4

25-minute walk from Wulai's main street, or a 1.6km, six-minute ride on the mini-train, or 'log cart' as bilingual signs refer to it; departures are according to demand (⏰ *09.00–17.00 daily; NTD50 one-way*). The visitor information centre here can give directions to further-flung attractions.

Neidong Forest Recreation Area 內洞森林遊樂區 (⏰ *08.00–17.00 daily; admission NTD80/40 Sat–Sun, NTD65/40 Mon–Fri*) If you walk upstream beyond Wulai Waterfall, after around 45 minutes you'll come to this 1,191ha forest recreation area. The falls here are lower but prettier than Wulai's main cascade. On the hiking trails, the longest of which is 2.2km, you may spot creatures such as the endemic Meintein tree frog (*Kurixalus idiootocus*) as well as lots of birds. Flora includes wild ginger and begonias.

NORTH CROSS-ISLAND HIGHWAY 北橫公路 *Telephone code 03*

Inland of Daxi Highway 7 is known as the North Cross-Island Highway. While not as breathtaking as its equivalents in central Taiwan and the south, it's at least reliably open and a very pleasant way for self-driving tourists to get to Yilan County.

GETTING THERE, AWAY AND AROUND

By bus There are several options but none go all the way across the North Cross-Island Highway. Buses going inland of Daxi will stop at Lake Mercy if you tell the driver when boarding. Service #5096 links Daxi with the bus station behind Taoyuan TRA Station (*departs every 15mins;* ⏰ *05.50–21.30 daily; takes 30mins; NTD40*). #5104 connects Daxi with Fuxing (*at least 7 departures daily;* ⏰ *06.40–21.15; takes 45mins; NTD64*). There's also an unnumbered Daxi–Luofu service (*departs 09.10 & 18.00 daily*) which stops in Fuxing. #5093 (*departs from Daxi 13.10, 15.00 & 17.00*) terminates at Lower Baling (*NTD137*). #5090 is a daily service from Taoyuan to Lalashan/Mount Daguan (*departs at 06.50; takes at least 2hrs; NTD204*) via Daxi (*NTD40*), Lake Mercy (*NTD57*) and Fuxing (*NTD91*).

By car Take Freeway 3 to the Daxi exit at km62. If you head inland on Highway 7, you're required to keep your headlights on at all times between km7 and km84.

By motorcycle or bicycle Take Highway 4 from Sanxia or Highway 3 if you're approaching from the south.

TOURIST INFORMATION

☑ **Taoyuan County Tourism Bureau** http://travel-taoyuan.tycg.gov.tw
☑ **Cihu Tourist Service Centre** km6 Hwy 7; ⏰ 08.00–17.00 daily

☑ **Lalashan Visitor Centre** Between Lower Baling & Mount Daguan; ⏰ 08.30–17.30 daily

🏠 **WHERE TO STAY AND EAT** There are several homestays in the vicinities of Sanmin and Upper Baling but few are signposted in English. Sanmin and Fuxing have plenty of eating options but English-language signs and menus are the exception.

🏠 **Mingchi Mountain Lodge** 明池山莊 (111 rooms) km68 Hwy 7; 📞 989 4104; 📠 980 1723; www.yeze.com.tw/mingchih/homepage.htm. Across the road from Mingchi National Forest

Recreation Area (to which guests get free entry), the accommodation here is in wood cabins & the main building. The former are nicer than the latter but getting to some of them involves more than a few steps. Rooms & suites for 2, 4 or 8 ppl priced NTD3,900–8,200 w/ends & national holidays, slightly more in Jul–Aug; website has photos of rooms but very little English. Reasonable Taiwanese food available ($$$). B/fast inc only with certain packages. $$$$

🏠 **Fusing Youth Activity Centre** (57 rooms) Fuxing Village; 📞382 2276; 📠382 2789; www.cyh. org.tw. There's no missing this place, the largest building in Fuxing. Situated at the end of a road chock-a-block with eateries, the centre has relatively few rooms for couples & tends to fill up with school groups at w/ends & throughout summer. The VIP rooms on the corner (*NTD6,000*) have spectacular views over the valley but some might feel the wall-to-ceiling windows don't provide enough privacy. Room rates are 20% lower on w/days. Wi-Fi, English spoken & b/fast inc. There are superb views over the river from the restaurant-coffee shop (🕐 *07.00–22.30 daily; EM; $$*). $$$

🏠 **Baling Mountain Villa** (1 room, 1 dorm) Lower Baling; 📞391 2126; www.cyh.org.tw. This building is very close to Hwy 7 & near Lower Baling's shops & eateries. Beds in the 12-person dorm are excellent value at NTD420 pp. Up to 4 ppl can sleep in the only other room. Bookings must be made through Fusing Youth Activity Centre, either by phone or in person. Inc b/fast. $$

WHAT TO SEE AND DO This section assumes visitors are starting from Daxi on the western side.

Daxi 大溪 (Dàxī)
A major inland port shipping tea and camphor throughout the Qing era, Daxi (literally 'big stream') hasn't been the same since the construction of a nearby dam in the 1960s left the Dahan River barely deep enough for a kayak. Goods now arrive and leave in lorries rather than boats, but the town's old quarter still reflects the good old days. Before World War II, **Heping Road** was known as Lower Street and **Zhongyang Road** was Upper Street. Together they formed the business hub of the town and its hinterland, and the century-old Baroque-style merchant houses along these roads incorporate Greek, Roman and Taiwanese elements. You're unlikely to find much that's truly traditional beneath the redbrick archways; the shops selling various kinds of dried tofu, a local speciality, perhaps come closest. The neighbourhood makes for pleasant strolling, however, and inside the 200-year-old **Furen Temple** 福仁宮 (*100 Heping Rd;* 🕐 *06.00–20.00 daily*) you'll find a collection of 'whipping tops', traditional spinning tops larger than basketballs and weighing up to 100kg. If you continue past the temple to where Heping Road makes a 90-degree turn you'll get good views of the river and the stone steps up which stevedores used to lug cargo.

Lake Mercy 慈湖 (Cíhú)
Chiang Kai-shek said he adored the scenery just inland of Daxi because it reminded him of his hometown on the Chinese mainland. However, it was more than just a holiday retreat – the generalissimo had it fitted out as an emergency command centre from which he could direct operations against Mao's Communists. The tourist service centre is the best place to park; it's also a good starting point for those arriving by bus because inside there are dozens of captioned historical photos of the two Chiangs, their wives and other notables. The coverage is uncritical yet educational. From the centre, walk first to **Cihu Mausoleum** 慈湖陵寢 (🕐 *08.00–17.00 daily; free admission*). This is where Chiang Kai-shek's remains still lie in state; at the time of writing, there seemed little impetus to give him a permanent burial – something he said shouldn't happen until China is unified under a non-communist government. Visitors are expected to behave respectfully but the atmosphere isn't too strict. Do also visit **Cihu Sculpture Memorial Park** (🕐 *08.00–17.00 daily; free admission*), a repository for more than 150 Chiang Kai-shek statues 'donated' ('discarded' would be a more accurate word) by various cities and towns. Just two decades ago almost every campus and park in Taiwan had a

4

life-size or larger bronze, stone or cement representation of Chiang. In districts run by the Democratic Progressive Party many of the statues have been removed, along with other relics of the Chiang era. **Daxi Mausoleum** (⊕ *08.00–17.00 daily; free admission*), the resting place of Chiang Ching-kuo, is 25 minutes' walk from the elder Chiang's mausoleum. The younger Chiang is a far more popular figure than his father, yet his temporary tomb draws far fewer visitors.

Sanmin Bat Cave 三民蝙蝠洞 If you've your own transport you'll be able to get within 20 minutes' walk of this impressively big cave, the adjacent waterfall and some very lush forest. The turn-off is very near km12; look for the English sign reading 'Tuba Church'. The church itself is hard to find, but if you follow the road to the very end (about 3km) you'll come to the trailhead.

Fuxing 復興 (Fùxīng) If you're heading all the way across the North Cross-Island Highway, this sizeable village (elevation: 410m) is the last place you can enjoy any semblance of urban 'bustle', and then only at the weekend. The main drag has a post office and plenty of restaurants, some of which serve Atayal food and sell bottles of sweet, cloudy millet liquor 小米酒 (*xiǎo mǐ jiǔ*). Fill up at the petrol station here (⊕ *07.00–17.00 daily*) as you won't see another one until km99. You'll notice that many of the signposts around Fuxing are bilingual – Chinese and romanised Atayal.

Luofu 羅浮 More a series of scattered hamlets than a proper village, Luofu has a prominent church and, near km22.5, a 36km-long back road which goes on to Guanxi near Beipu. For about 13km beyond Fuxing, the highway hardly climbs at all. Between Luofu and Lower Baling (*km47.5*) the landscape is defined by high cliffs and a river that never runs straight.

Beyond Lower Baling 下巴陵 Coming from the western side of the island, the traffic thins out a lot as soon as you pass Lower Baling because the bulk of tourists head for Mount Daguan or the peach-growing area of Upper Baling 上巴陵. Lower Baling is a tiny place but it has a couple of places to eat; from there it's 72km to Yilan City. The eastern half of the North Cross-Island Highway is a journey through sublime temperate forest; when you stop, you're likely to hear only birdsong. There are no villages and, apart from the road, few signs of humanity. The road's highest point, 1,140m above sea level, is where it crosses the boundary between Taoyuan and Yilan.

Mount Daguan Nature Preserve 達觀山自然保護區 (Dáguānshān Zìrán Bǎohùqū) (⊕ *08.00–18.00 daily; admission NTD100/50*) Still widely known and signposted by an alternative name, **Lalashan 拉拉山**, this reserve encompasses a grove of monster trees. An easy-to-follow 3.7km trail passes 22 of these ancient cypresses. The oldest has been here for 2,800 years; the tallest is 55m. The climate is often wet, misty and cold so bring an umbrella and a jacket.

Mingchi National Forest Recreation Area 明池森林遊樂區 (Míngchí Sēnlín Yóulèqū) (*km67 Hwy 7;* ✆ *989 4106;* ⊕ *08.00–17.00 daily; admission NTD120/60/10*) Located in the most beautiful section of the North Cross-Island Highway, this forest reserve takes its name, literally 'shining pool', from a small lake. The surrounding woodlands deserve much more of your time than that body of water; they're full of strange ferns, curious herbs and wild orchids. The highest part of the recreation area is 1,700m above sea level.

YILAN COUNTY 宜蘭縣 (YÍLÁN XIÀN) *Telephone code 03*

Almost all of Yilan County's residents live on the Lanyang Plain. Named after the Lanyang River, a waterway that broadens into an impressive torrent as it makes its way from Mount Nanhu (3,742m, Taiwan's ninth-highest peak) to the Pacific Ocean, the plain is a fertile flatland where rice, watermelons and spring onions grow well.

The region is thick with rural homestays. If you prefer an urban base there's not much to choose between Yilan City 宜蘭市, north of the river, and Luodong 羅東, to the south. The two are similar in size (populations 96,000 and 72,000, respectively), facilities and distractions. The latter is near the National Centre for Traditional Arts. The former is closer to Jiaoxi 卓溪, a hot spring resort, and Lanyang Museum.

HISTORY What's now called Yilan County has seen a succession of human inhabitants. The Atayal were driven from the lowlands into the mountains by another indigenous tribe, the Kavalan. The latter were themselves displaced by Han settlers from the 1790s onward and now cling to their culture in a handful of settlements further south. A British adventurer named James Horn appeared on the coast in 1868. Bankrolled by Western merchants who hoped he could recover the bodies of Europeans lost in a shipwreck, he married the daughter of an aboriginal chief and attempted to establish a colony. China protested this incursion and pressured the British consul to order Horn to leave. Horn agreed to do so but drowned while trying to board the boat set to take him to Danshui.

Until well into the 20th century, the county was quite isolated from the rest of Taiwan. Some very local customs appeared, including the performing art now known as Taiwanese opera. Even today, many Yilan natives speak Taiwanese with a distinctive accent. Thanks to Freeway 5, most of the county is now less than an hour from Taipei, a fact that draws second-homers and day trippers.

TAIWANESE OPERA

Taiwanese opera, which is said to have originated in Yilan County, isn't an especially accessible art form. Visitors who stumble across productions usually find them baffling, garish and over the top. Shrine performances, which often celebrate the birthdays of local deities, are typically low-budget affairs. The stage is the back of a customised flatbed truck, and usually just two or three actors are on it at any one moment. There's no orchestra, nor even any live vocals; the performers mime to a recorded soundtrack. The music may be ear-splittingly loud and the actors obviously jaded. The lyrics are entirely in Taiwanese and rich in slang and idioms. Like Beijing opera, Taiwanese opera is properly performed to the accompaniment of traditional instruments such as three-stringed banjos and bamboo flutes, plus the various gongs and drums that punctuate dialogues and provide fierce backing for the sessions of acrobatics that represent combat.

Much of the movement on a Chinese opera stage – be it Beijing, Taiwanese or another regional variant – is symbolic rather than realistic. The audience understands what these standard gestures represent: purposeful striding in circles means the actor is undertaking a long journey, whereas hands clasped behind one's back is a show of bravery.

Taiwan's best-known opera troupe is Ming Hwa Yuan (*www.twopera.co*). Extracts from their performances can be found on YouTube.

GETTING THERE, AWAY AND AROUND

By TRA Most Taipei–Yilan City expresses take less than 1½ hours (*over 30 departures ⊕ 06.10–22.10 daily; NTD168–218*). There's at least one train per hour to Hualien (⊕ *05.38–23.46 daily; takes no more than 1hr 40mins; NTD143–223*). Within the county, three or more trains per hour link Yilan City with Luodong (*departs ⊕ 05.38–23.51 daily; takes 10mins; NTD15–23*).

By bus Services #1570, #1571 and #1572 link Yilan, Luodong and Jiaoxi with Taipei City Hall Bus Station (*up to 7 departures per hr; ⊕ 06.00–22.00 daily; takes 1hr; NTD90–120*). The last of these also makes stops in Jiaoxi. Buses #1915, #1916 and #1917 (*very frequent departures ⊕ 24hrs daily; takes up to 1¼hrs; NTD104–135*) go to/from Taipei Bus Station. Kuo-Kuang's #1751 Yilan–Lishan service runs twice a day (*departures from Yilan at 07.00 & 12.40, from Lishan at 08.30 & 13.30; takes 4hrs; NTD337*), stopping at Wuling Farm on the way.

By car Freeway 5 is by far the quickest way of driving from northwest Taiwan to Yilan County, but the North Cross-Island Highway offers better scenery.

By motorcycle Before the opening of Freeway 5 cars and lorries had to choose between a long coastal route and Highway 9, a slow-but-scenic road through the mountains via Pinglin, a pretty tea-growing region. The freeway has taken the great bulk of traffic, leaving Highway 9 for drivers with time on their hands, motorcyclists and determined cyclists.

TOURIST INFORMATION

🛈 Northeast and Yilan Coast National Scenic Area www.necoast-nsa.gov.tw
🛈 Yilan TRA Station Visitor Information Centre ⊕ 09.00–20.00 daily

🛈 Wushi Harbour Visitor Centre Between Lanyang Museum & Wushi Harbour; ✆ 978 9078; ⊕ 09.00–17.00 Tue–Sun & national holidays that are Mon

WHERE TO STAY AND EAT

🏠 **Grand Boss Hotel** (40 rooms) 366 Yixing Rd Sec 1, Yilan City; ✆ 931 2999; f 931 2899; http://grandboss.hotel.com.tw/eng/. Less than 400m north of Yilan TRA Station & much better than most of the hotels in the city centre, Grand Boss has rooms that seem a little plain after the sumptuous 17th-century French-style lobby. However, everything's in working order even if the windows are a bit small. All guests have free access to the fitness room inc snooker table & children's room with games & toys. Free car parking; guests can use hotel's bikes for free. Standard rooms sometimes available for under NTD2,500; all rates inc b/fast. The in-house restaurant (⊕ *11.30–14.30 & 17.30–22.00 daily; EM;* $$) serves Western food & there are several cheap eateries within walking distance. $$$
🏠 **The Dew Bed & Breakfast** (9 rooms) 363 Wuhan 5th Rd, Dongshan; ✆ 956 8492; m 0910 058 080; www.thedew.com.tw; e thedew363@

yahoo.com.tw. Yilan County has an unbelievable number of homestays but The Dew stands out for being exceptionally clean & having English-speaking owners who can help book tickets for whale-watching trips & other activities. The family has 3 locations, all near Luodong; guests can borrow bikes for free. Inc b/fast & unlimited tea/coffee. $$$
✖ **Cangjiu Winery** Next to Toucheng Farm, near km129 Hwy 2; ✆ 977 8555; www.cjwine.com; ⊕ 09.00–18.00 daily, reservations required after 18.00. Several of the wines produced here are non-grape, made instead with kumquat or grains. Many of the ingredients are grown in the valley & among problems faced by English-speaking founder Jack Cho are wild pigs who butt trees (to make ripe fruit fall to the ground) so violently the trees sometimes topple over. Typical prices are NTD280 (for 400ml of golden date wine) to NTD580 (for 750ml of Canjiu's classic red) & all can be enjoyed

alongside lamb chops, steaks, chicken, grilled salmon & other dishes (*NTD350–600*) served with local vegetables. If you drink too much, stay at **Toucheng Farm** (*82 rooms inc some for groups;* ✎ *977 2222; f 977 8688; www.tcfarm.com.tw; inc b/fast $$$*), owned by the same family & a shortish downhill walk from the winery. To reach the farm & winery, turn inland just north of km129 on Hwy 2. The entrance to the farm is on the left;

continue up the hill to find the winery (admission NTD100/50 but visitors get this money back if they buy wine or order food). **$$$**

✘ **Luodong Night Market** Minsheng & Gongyuan rds, Luodong; ⊕ approx 17.00–24.00 daily. Considered a must-see by all Taiwanese & many Asian visitors, this night market offers a good selection of snacks from all over Taiwan but gets very crowded. **$**

WHAT TO SEE AND DO

Lanyang Museum (*km134 Hwy 2;* ✎ *977 9700; www.lym.gov.tw;* ⊕ *09.00–17.00 Thu–Tue; admission NTD100/50*) Unless you wish to delve deep into the past of Yilan County, you're likely to find the award-winning design of this museum, situated next to Wushi Harbour, more exciting than the displays inside, which cover the region's nature, history and culture.

Guishan Island 龜山島 From many points along the coast you can see this 2.9km² islet. The name means 'turtle mountain island' and it does somewhat resemble a south-facing turtle. Home to a tiny fishing community until 1977, when the population was evacuated to Yilan proper so sensitive military equipment could be installed, Guishan Island is now open to limited numbers of ecotourists who come to see the lizards, birds and plants. Just offshore, there are active undersea volcanic vents. The island is open each year 1 March–30 November. Overnight stays are not permitted and visitors must apply in advance for permits through the Northeast and Yilan Coast National Scenic Area Administration (*www. necoast-nsa.gov.tw*).

Taiwan Theatre Museum (*101 Fuxing Rd Sec 2, Yilan City;* ✎ *932 2440;* ⊕ *09.00–12.00 & 13.00–17.00 Tue–Sun; free admission*) This little-known museum (within walking distance of Yilan City's bus and train stations) provides an excellent introduction to Taiwanese opera (see box, page 127) and other performing arts. Local troupes rehearse in costume on the third floor from 15.00 on the second and fourth Saturday each month. The second floor has a collection of more than 100 traditional glove and string puppets that will have photographers drooling; the ones dressed as ROC soldiers featured in anti-communist propaganda shows during the 1950s and 1960s.

National Centre for Traditional Arts 國立傳統藝術中心 (**Guólì Chuántǒng Yìshù Zhōngxīn**) (✎ *970 5815; f 960 5237; www.ncfta.gov.tw;* ⊕ *09.00–18.00 daily; admission NTD150/100/75; parking NTD50*) One of the county's most popular attractions, this theme park endeavours to preserve and transmit local customs and art forms. Stages, exhibition halls and replica buildings are spread over 24ha and visitors will enjoy the short performances given at frequent intervals each day; typically you'll be able to take in shadow and glove puppetry, acrobatics, a 19th-century wedding procession, dance and Taiwanese opera. Most of the schedules and displays are in Chinese only, so reserve an English-speaking guide (✎ *950 7711 or send a fax*) a week or more in advance. The Folk Art Boulevard is lined with craft showrooms worth investigating even if you're not an ardent shopper. To escape the crowds, cross one of the small bridges and head to Scholar Huang's House. This traditional courtyard abode was built in 1877 in what's now Yilan City, and it was dismantled and reassembled here some years back; the displays inside are very worthwhile. The food court (⏰ *09.00–19.00 daily*) has a good selection of reasonably priced meals and snacks; there's also a convenience store and a coffee shop. On-site accommodation is available at **Forte Dong-shan Villa** (*78 rooms;* ☎ *960 2121;* f *960 2020;* e *reservations-yl@fortehotels.com.tw; www.forte-hotel.net;* **$$$** *b/fast inc*), which has especially attractive family rooms.

Every half hour, a bus leaves the back of Luodong TRA Station for the NCFTA (*departs* ⏰ *08.30–17.30 daily; takes 20mins; NTD25*). If you're driving, follow the signs from Luodong; the centre is on the inland side of Highway 2. It's 8km and flat all the way from Luodong so cycling is feasible.

THE NORTHEAST   *Telephone code 02*

Taiwan's richest coal, gold and copper deposits lay beneath the hills east and southeast of Keelung. The old mining towns of Jiufen and Jinguashi are now well and truly on the tourist map and make for good excursions, while the Pingxi Branch Railway connects a string of man-made and natural attractions.

GETTING THERE, AWAY AND AROUND
By car, motorcycle or bicycle If you're approaching on either freeway, Expressway 62 allows you to bypass Keelung and head straight for Ruifang. Road 102 leaves central Keelung for Ruifang and then Jiufen and Jinguashi. An extremely steep, twisting short cut connects Jinguashi and Highway 2, which stays very close to the ocean all the way to Yilan County. Expect to share the coast road with quite a few lorries.

By TRA From Taipei, many local trains and occasional expresses stop at Ruifang (*departs* ⏰ *05.12–23.00 daily; takes 45mins; NTD49–76*) from where you can take a bus to Jiufen or Jinguashi or another train to Houtong or along the Pingxi Branch Line. There are 16 services each way daily on the branch line; Ruifang to Jingtong takes 45 minutes (*NTD29*). Jump-on/jump-off day passes (*NTD52/28*) can be purchased at Ruifang and from counter 12 on the ground floor in Taipei Main Railway Station. Each day, nearly 30 Yilan-bound trains stop at Fulong (*takes 1¼hrs from Taipei; NTD83–128*).

By bus #788 leaves from the stop at 18 Zhong 1st Road near Keelung TRA Station (*departs every 15mins;* ⏰ *05.55–21.55 daily*). This local service stops at Ruifang and Jiufen with most services terminating at Jinguashi (*takes 40mins; NTD30*). Kuo-Kuang bus #1811 has five departures per day (⏰ *08.20–20.20; takes about 3½hrs*) from Taipei West Bus Station Terminal A to Yilan and then Luodong (*both destinations NTD230*). Also from Terminal A, #1812 is a daily service which sets out at 14.20 and follows Highway 2 all the way to Nanfangao (*takes 3¼hrs; NTD230*). The bus leaves Nanfangao for Taipei at 06.35.

TOURIST INFORMATION There are visitor information centres in Ruifang TRA Station (⏰ *09.00–18.00 daily*), Fulong (⏰ *08.00–17.30 daily*) and Jinguashi (⏰ *09.00–17.00 daily*). If you're planning to spend a few days in this part of Taiwan, Richard Saunders' *Taipei Escapes 1: Sights and Hikes around Northeastern Taiwan* (Community Services Centre, NTD500) is an excellent resource. Also try the website of the **Northeast and Yilan Coast National Scenic Area** (*www.necoast-nsa.gov.tw*).

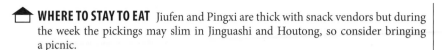

WHERE TO STAY TO EAT Jiufen and Pingxi are thick with snack vendors but during the week the pickings may slim in Jinguashi and Houtong, so consider bringing a picnic.

Sunny Room (7 rooms) 56 Shuci Rd, Jiufen; ☎ 2497 0956; e sun5657@gmail.com. www.sunnyroom.tw. Much raved-about with justification, this homestay is a little difficult to find & only suitable for those willing to tackle steps when going to/from the heart of Jiufen. Upstairs rooms have especially good views. If arriving in Jiufen by bus, be prepared to walk a bit & tackle some steps before reaching this B&B so consider a

taxi from Ruifang if you've much luggage. Healthy b/fast inc. **$$$**

Windsor Castle 溫莎堡 (7 rooms) 62 Jishan Rd, Jiufen; ☎ 2406 3709; m 0920 076 336; http:// windsor.idv.tw. Take a look at the website to get an idea of the very fine views that can be had from this clean, comfortable establishment, 5mins walk from Jiufen's main tourist street. English spoken; room rates inc b/fast & afternoon tea. **$$$**

WHAT TO SEE AND DO

The northeast coast Allow an hour to drive from Yilan County to Keelung on Highway 2, not including sightseeing and bathroom breaks. **Fulong Beach** 福隆海水浴場 (⊕ *08.00–18.00 daily May–Sep; admission NTD100/80*) is a long, broad stretch of sand where people swim, canoe, surf and windsurf. Expect crowds during summer weekends, the annual Hohaiyan Rock Festival and sand-sculpture competitions. The town of Fulong doesn't lack for eating and accommodation options. Beside the unmissable white buildings near km88, child-friendly **Longdong South Ocean Park** 龍洞南口海洋公園 (⊕ *09.00–17.30 daily; admission NTD100/80/50*) has saltwater pools of varying sizes and depths good for swimming, paddling and searching for starfish and crabs. Visitors can rent snorkelling gear and there's an on-site restaurant (*EM; meals from NTD70*). Parking a car here costs NTD50, a motorcycle NTD20. The 70m-high sandstone cliffs around Longdong offer excellent rock climbing and bouldering with 500-plus routes. At km78.5, look inland and you'll see immense black cement pipes snaking up the mountainside; they discharged noxious gases from a 13-storey copper refinery, the remains of which are now known as the **Thirteen Levels** (*not open to the public*). Minerals washed out from the area's abandoned mines have stained the nearby creek orange-gold and colour part of the sea. The **'Bats Crossing'** sign at km75 asks drivers to take care because each summer over half a million female common bent-wing bats (*Miniopterus schreibersii*) gather in two nearby disused mines to give birth. During the season, mighty swarms of bats emerge at dusk to feed on insects.

Jiufen 九份 **(Jiǔfèn)** So bustling in the 1930s that outsiders nicknamed it 'Little Shanghai', this former mining town went through hard times before it was rescued from obscurity by the 1989 film *A City of Sadness* (see box, page 135) and from economic oblivion by the tourists who've been pouring in ever since. The quaint streets retain a fair bit of its pre-World War II character but if anything wins you over, it'll be the superb views down towards the sea. If you prefer exercise to crowds, hike up **Mount Keelung**. Reaching the top of this 587m-high mountain takes healthy folks less than half an hour. The trailhead, just beyond the centre of Jiufen on Road 102, is clearly marked; the path itself is mainly stone steps. Unless the weather's poor, from the top you'll enjoy tremendous views of Heping Island and other points on the coast.

Gold Ecological Park 黃金博物園區 ☎ *2496 2800; www.gep.ntpc.gov.tw;* ⊕ *09.00–17.00 Mon–Fri, 09.00–18.00 Sat–Sun, closed first Mon every month; free* *admission*) Like Jiufen, **Jinguashi** 金瓜石 lost much of its population when mineral extraction ceased in the early 1980s. The GEP now embracing most of the town preserves a great deal of industrial infrastructure; those fascinated by economic history will want to spend half a day touring the two museums (in one you can touch a 220.3kg gold ingot worth around £5.9 million), Japanese-era dormitories and other sites. The section of mine shaft open to the public (*admission NTD50*) is too clean and well lit to be convincing but that's the only criticism that can be made of the park. Particularly appealing are the windswept ruins of a Shinto shrine, perched on a mountain ledge 15 minutes' walk above the town. During World War II, Jinguashi was the site of a prisoner-of-war camp (see box opposite). A memorial was unveiled in 1997 and Remembrance Day events are held there each year.

Houtong Coal-Mine Ecological Park (\ *2497 4143;* ⊕ *08.00–18.00 Tue–Fri; free admission*) If you liked Jinguashi, take a local train to **Houtong** 猴硐 (*departures from Taipei every hr; takes 55mins; NTD56–67; from Ruifang every 30mins; takes 6mins; NTD15*) for an extra dose of industrial archaeology. Get a leaflet from the information centre near the station and start walking – the **Geology House** and **Commemorative House of Miners** are the most distant sights but especially absorbing.

Pingxi Branch Railway 平溪支線 Like Taiwan's other branch railways, this 12.9km-long spur was built so the resources of the interior could be more easily exploited. Coal deposits were discovered in 1907 near Jingtong, the terminus of the branch line, but large-scale mining didn't begin until 1918. At one point 14 collieries employed 80% of the area's adult males. The track, completed in 1921, goes through six tunnels and over 15 bridges. There's good scenery along the way but if you want to enjoy it, avoid summer weekends when trains are so packed you'll be lucky see anything let alone get a seat. Midweek is best; for good views of dense forest and pretty streams sit on the right when setting out from Ruifang, after which there are eight stops. In the tiny town of **Shifen** 十分, the railroad doubles as the main street. The waterfall 20 minutes' walk away (⊕ *08.00–17.30 daily; admission NTD100/50*) is one of Taiwan's widest.

The penultimate stop of **Pingxi** 平溪 is synonymous with sky lanterns – bamboo or wire frames covered with paper which are propelled upwards by the heat of the wick burning inside. Originally used in the bandit-ridden 19th century by remote households wanting to tell their neighbours all was well, the custom is now popular with young couples who paint their wishes on the sides of a lantern (*from NTD100 each*) then watch it float into the distance. Romantic, to be sure, but bad for the environment as lantern remnants end up in trees and streams. The custom has spread to many parts of Taiwan, including nearby Shifen. If you'd rather not backtrack through Ruifang, take bus #795 (*departs every 40mins;* ⊕ *04.50–22.40 daily; takes 1¼hrs; NTD45*) from Shifen, Pingxi or Jingtong to Muzha MRT Station in southwestern Taipei.

KEELUNG 基隆 (JĪLÓNG) *Telephone code 02*

Before setting aside time for north Taiwan's most important port, know this: Keelung is much like any other Taiwanese city, only more so. Noisier, messier, more crowded and more confusing. Squashed between the ocean and craggy mountains, the city gets notorious amounts of rain. As a result the concrete is stained, there's mould in dark corners and moss on the rooftops. Near the TRA station, sleazy bars and karaoke parlours alternate with brightly lit arcades where pachinko, a Japanese pinball-type game, is played. Keelung is neither quaint nor pretty, but it does have a wealth of abandoned fortifications and rich local culture.

HISTORY Keelung has had as much history as precipitation. The first outsiders to show an interest were the Spanish, who in 1626 established an outpost on a nearby islet and began trading with the indigenous population. After losing their Tainan base to Koxinga, the Dutch attempted a comeback here in 1663; they gave up after a profitless half-decade. Relatively few Han Chinese came this way until the late 18th century as established sea routes led them instead to the southwest or what's now Wanhua. During the First Opium War (1839–42), Royal Navy and British East India Company vessels shelled the port but all three British attempts to land troops were fought off.

Two Fujianese communities dominated the Keelung area: those who traced their origins to Zhangzhou and others whose ancestors came from Quanzhou. In addition to minor cultural and linguistic differences, these two groups sacrificed to different Taoist deities. In 1851, disputes between the two sides over stray cattle and access to fresh water escalated into full-scale ethnic warfare. Local worthies finally brokered a peace deal which included burying the hundreds of dead and joint rites each Ghost Month to propitiate the deceased. In recent decades the event has grown into a joyous, raucous festival that encompasses parades and folk-art performances as well as food, drink and entertainment for the ghosts. If you happen to be in the north at the right time, it's worth diverting to Keelung to take in what's now called the Mid-Summer Ghost Festival.

Keelung was opened to foreign trade in 1860 and the arrival of coal-burning steamships jump-started the hinterland's mining industry (see opposite). French marines and foreign legionnaires occupied the town for nine months during the Sino-French War. Chinese forces successfully contained the French, who during the stalemate lost far more men to cholera and typhoid than enemy action. The French cemetery is perhaps the city's most anomalous sight.

ALLIED POWS IN WARTIME TAIWAN

During World War II, more than 4,300 Allied prisoners-of-war were detained in Taiwan, then part of the Japanese Empire. The majority were British soldiers who surrendered when Singapore fell on 15 February 1942. As in other parts of Asia, many POWs suffered neglect and cruelty at the hands of the Japanese.

Kinkaseki – as Jinguashi was known before 1945 – was the most notorious of the 16 sites in Taiwan where POWs were held. Prisoners were forced to descend 800 steps into a sweltering mine shaft each morning, work hard through the day and then return to a camp where they were often beaten or tortured. Of the first 523 POWs sent to the mine, more than 400 succumbed to tropical diseases, rockfalls and exhaustion. One survivor, Cardiff-born Jack Edwards (1918–2006), wrote a moving book about his experiences called *Banzai You Bastards!*

The Taiwan POW Camps Memorial Society (*www.powtaiwan.org*) organises visits to Kinkaseki by former prisoners and maintains an online directory with the names, ranks and other details of those held in Taiwan. In recent years, the society has unveiled memorials at the sites of several other POW camps around the island.

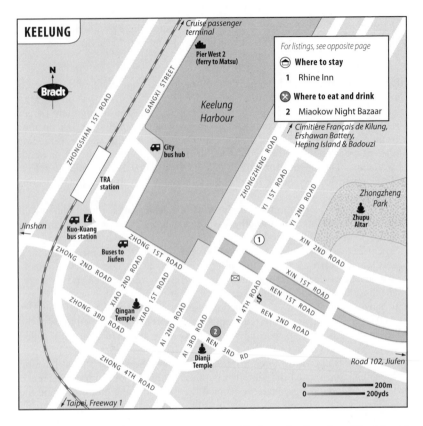

For listings, see opposite page

KEELUNG

Cruise passenger terminal

Pier West 2 (ferry to Matsu)

Keelung Harbour

City bus hub

TRA station

Jinshan

Kuo-Kuang bus station

Buses to Jiufen

Qingan Temple

Dianji Temple

GANGXI STREET

ZHONGSHAN 1ST ROAD

ZHONGZHENG ROAD

YI 1ST ROAD

YI 2ND ROAD

Zhongzheng Park

Zhupu Altar

XIN 2ND ROAD

XIN 1ST ROAD

REN 1ST ROAD

REN 2ND ROAD

REN 3RD RD

AI 4TH ROAD

AI 3RD ROAD

AI 2ND ROAD

XIAO 1ST ROAD

XIAO 2ND ROAD

ZHONG 1ST ROAD

ZHONG 2ND ROAD

ZHONG 3RD ROAD

ZHONG 4TH ROAD

Cimitière Français de Kilung, Ershawan Battery, Heping Island & Badouzi

Road 102, Jiufen

Taipei, Freeway 1

Where to stay
1 Rhine Inn

Where to eat and drink
2 Miaokow Night Bazaar

0 ——— 200m
0 ——— 200yds

During and after the Japanese occupation, Keelung developed rapidly. It's still very much a working harbour, but in the past few years the authorities have begun transforming it into a cruise-ship destination.

GETTING THERE AND AWAY

By TRA Few northbound expresses reach Keelung but local services from Taipei (*takes 45mins; NTD41–64*) are frequent. If you're coming from the east coast, change trains at Badu or Qidu, minor stations between Keelung and Taipei. The branch line between Ruifang and the National Museum of Marine Science and Technology at Badouzi is now running again (*departs every 30mins; ⊕ 08.35–17.55 daily; takes 10mins; NTD15*).

By bus Kuo-Kuang's #1813 service sets out from Taipei's West Station Terminal A (*departs every 20mins; ⊕ 06.00–24.00 daily; takes around 45mins; NTD55*). Outside of rush hours, Kuo-Kuang buses are more frequent and quicker than trains. There are also services from Taipei City Hall Bus Station (see page 87). Coastal services include #862 to/from Danshui (*departs every 30mins; ⊕ 05.50–20.30 daily; takes 2hrs; NTD120*) and #790 to/from Jinshan (*departs every 15mins; ⊕ 05.45–22.00 daily; takes 40mins; NTD45*) via Yehliu.

By boat The *COSCO Star* (✆ 2778 9678 ext 153 or 156) links Keelung's Pier West 3 and Xiamen on the Chinese coast (*departs from Xiamen 18.00 Thu; departs from*

Keelung 19.00 Sun). Both arrive the following morning around 09.00; one-way fares start at NTD3,500. A Chinese-only schedule can be found at www.coscotw. com.tw. The overnight ferry to the Matsu Islands leaves from Pier West 2 near the TRA station; see page 326 for details. A new passenger terminal is being built on the northwestern side of the harbour and it's possible that, after 2015, all ferry departures will be handled there.

By car Both Freeway 1 and Freeway 3 will take you into the heart of the city but because of parking issues and traffic density you're strongly advised to use public transport.

GETTING AROUND
By bus Keelung's most useful city bus services are #101 to Heping Island (*takes 20mins*) and #103 to Badouzi (*takes 30mins*). Both depart about every 20 minutes (⊕ *06.00–23.00 daily; NTD15 one-way*) from near the TRA station. Less frequent services between the railway station and Badouzi include #107, #108 and #1051.

TOURIST INFORMATION
🗾 **Keelung City Government** www.klcg.gov.tw ⊕ 08.30–12.00, 13.30–17.00 Mon–Fri; 09.00–
🗾 **Keelung Visitor Information Centre** On 16.00 Sat–Sun & national holidays
the right as you leave the TRA Station;

🏠 **WHERE TO STAY AND EAT** Both of the following establishments are shown on the map opposite.

🏠 **Rhine Inn** (67 rooms) 17th Flr 177 Xin 1st Rd; ☎ 2425 7766; f 2425 9669; www.rhineinn. com.tw. Occupying several floors of Keelung's tallest building (there's a cinema downstairs), the Rhine's rooms aren't huge but they are comfortably appointed & several have excellent harbour views. The décor is dominated by creamy shades of brown. B/fast inc. **$$$**
✘ **Miaokow Night Bazaar** 廟口夜市 Ren 3rd Rd between Ai 3rd & Ai 4th rds; ⊕ 24hrs daily. 'Miaokow' means 'temple's entrance' & this night market is now much more famous than the shrine around which vendors began gathering in the late Qing Dynasty. Its success means the 60-odd stalls in the 'official' section are joined each evening by at least 100 others around the end of Ai 4th Rd nearest the river. Almost every one of the former has a bilingual sign, but some of these leave you none the wiser. For instance, 'salted porridge' is more usually called congee. Few have EMs or English-speaking workers. Following your nose would be a good idea but for all the competing smells; if you look around you're bound to find a soup or snack that you'll enjoy. **$**

North Taiwan KEELUNG

4

MOVIES SHOT ON LOCATION

A City of Sadness, which depicts the political turmoil of the late 1940s and its impact on one family living in Jiufen, isn't the only Taiwanese movie to have given the economy of the place where it was filmed a shot in the arm. *Cape No. 7*, a 2008 romance which eventually became the most commercially successful Taiwanese film ever, inspired thousands to visit places in and around Kenting National Park. Two years later, the gangster film *Monga* spurred people to explore the Taipei's old Wanhua neighbourhood. *Cape No. 7*'s director, Wei Te-sheng, went on to make 2011's *Warriors of the Rainbow: Seediq Bale*, filming outdoor scenes in the mountains of central Taiwan and around Wulai near Taipei.

OTHER PRACTICALITIES

✉ **General Post Office** 130 Ai 3rd Rd; open: 08.00–19.00 Mon–Fri, 08.30–16.30 Sat, 08.30–12.00 Sun

$ **Changhwa Bank** 60 Ai 4th Rd

WHAT TO SEE AND DO If you're using public transport, it makes sense to begin at Badouzi or Heping Island and then move towards the city centre. Richard Saunders' *Taipei Escapes 1* has details of day trips and hikes in the Keelung area.

Badouzi 八斗子 There's a lot of tourism-related development going on around this fishing town, including the new **National Museum of Marine Science and Technology** (*km70 Hwy 2;* ☎ *2469 6000; www.nmmst.gov.tw;* ⊕ *09.00–17.00 Tue–Sun; admission NTD200/140*). Several colour-coded walking routes have been marked out for visitors to follow; taking the blue route from Highway 2 near the museum and then the green route over the headlands is recommended. City bus #103 terminates outside the museum and from here you can catch buses on to Longdong and Fulong.

Heping Island 和平島 Formerly called Sheliao Island, this is where the Spanish established their first base in Taiwan (see *History*, page 12). Nowadays much of this 4km² island, reached by city bus #101 and linked to the city by a causeway, is crowded with drab houses. However, if you keep walking and enter **Ho-Ping Island Hi Park** (⊕ *08.00–17.00 daily, until 19.00 Apr–Oct; admission NTD60/40*) you'll find peculiar rock formations, saltwater swimming pools (⊕ *Jun–Oct*) and a cave where graffiti left by 17th-century Dutch sailors has been discovered. The cave is underwhelming but it's still easy to spend a few hours in the park and kids will enjoy themselves immensely. The castle-like structure inside the park is an unconvincing replica of a Spanish fort; inside you can get meals and soft drinks.

Cimetière Français de Kilung 法國公墓 (*101 Zhongzheng Rd;* ⊕ *24hrs daily; free admission*) The graves of French servicemen who died in the Keelung area during the Sino-French War (see *History*, page 14) were moved to this spot, about 100m north of the stairs leading to Ershawan Battery, in 1909. A handful of tombs originally in the Penghu Islands were relocated here in 1953. Many of the 600-plus French soldiers interred here were North Africans and presumably Muslims, yet none of the ten gravestones or memorials acknowledge religions other than Christianity.

Ershawan Battery aka Haimen Tianxian 海門天險 (⊕ *24hrs daily; free admission*) At km64 on Highway 2 you'll see steps going up the forested hillside. Take these and within ten minutes you'll find yourself at Ershawan Battery, a ridgetop defence post established by the Qing authorities during the First Opium War (1839–42). Little remains of the original encampment but the views over the harbour are good and bilingual information boards provide some history. Continue on to **Zhongzheng Park 中正公園**, 20 minutes' gentle strolling away, where there's a seven-storey-high Guanyin statue and **Zhupu Altar 主普壇** (⊕ *07.00–19.00 daily*). This building resembles a thousand other Taiwanese shrines but is an important venue for ceremonies during the Mid-Summer Ghost Festival. Both the altar and the small on-site museum devoted to the festival stay closed during Ghost Month.

Dianji Temple 奠濟宮 (⊕ *06.00–22.00 daily*) The shrine that gives Miaokow Night Bazaar its name isn't worth more than a quick look unless you come on the 15th day of the second lunar month, the birthday of Kaizhang Shengwang, a revered ancestor and patron deity of the those who trace their origins to Zhangzhou. The temple was founded in 1873 on land donated by Lin Ben-yuan, one of the era's most successful merchants.

Qingan Temple 慶安宮 (*1 Zhong 2nd Rd;* ⊕ *05.30–20.00 daily*) The Zhangzhou community's most important place of worship has stood on this site since 1815. Renovated in 1999, the temple has a large stone statue of Guanyin out front and door gods which, rather than the usual portraits, are painted wood reliefs. If you find someone who speaks English, ask him or her to point out the land god, the Jade Emperor, Confucius and Laozi. Mid-Summer Ghost Festival rites are held here, including the chanting of sutras by monks on the 14th day of the seventh lunar month to beckon and soothe roaming ghosts.

THE NORTH COAST *Telephone code 02*

The coastline between Keelung and Danshui is as green and rugged as that of Ireland. None of the towns are large (or special) and in winter the weather is often like Ireland's – cold, wet and blustery. However, fans of strange landforms will enjoy themselves at Laomei and Yehliu, while those into culture and art can look forward to a major monastery and a museum. Brace yourself for heavy traffic at weekends and on national holidays.

GETTING THERE, AWAY AND AROUND

By bus Bus #1717, which goes from NTU Hospital MRT Station to Jinshan via Jiantan MRT Station and Yangmingshan (*departs about hourly;* ⊕ *06.30–18.30 daily; takes 1¼hrs; NTD150*) is one of north Taiwan's most scenic bus rides. The buses that ply Highway 2 (see the Keelung and Danshui *Getting there and away* sections on pages 134 and 141 respectively) are frequent and can drop you within walking distance of most attractions. Getting a one-day pass (*NTD100*) for the Crown Northern Coastline Tourist Shuttle (*8 departures daily Mon–Fri, 18 daily Sat–Sun; timetable at www.taiwantrip.com.tw*) will save you money and is a good way of getting to Juming Museum. Kuo-Kuang's #1815 service from Taipei West Station Terminal A (*departs about hourly;* ⊕ *06.20–20.15 daily*) makes stops at Yehliu (*NTD96*), Jinshan (*NTD120*) and Dharma Drum Mountain (*takes 1¾hrs; NTD135*).

By car or motorcycle Highway 2A will take you over Yangmingshan from central Taipei, but call the tourist information hotline (✆ *0800 011 765*) in advance as sometimes there are traffic controls. Away from the coast, there are some pretty back roads (Road 101 near Danshui is one) on which it's easy to get lost.

TOURIST INFORMATION

☑ North Coast and Guanyinshan National Scenic Area www.northguan-nsa.gov.tw
☑ Baishawan Visitor Information Centre
⊕ 09.00–17.00 daily

☑ Yehliu Visitor Information Centre
⊕ 08.00–17.00 daily

🏠 **WHERE TO STAY AND EAT** There are homestays between Danshui and Jinshan and the latter town has a good range of hot-springs hotels.

🏠 **Calla Young Garden Resort** (22 rooms) 33 Linkou, Chonghe Village, Jinshan; ✆ 2408 0001; f 2408 0066; e calla.mail@msa.hinet.net; www. calla.com.tw. Pricey but worth it for 3 reasons –

there's space to really stretch out in the rooms, the food is very good (*NTD850–990 pp for non-guests*) & there's every kind of hot-spring facility. The saltwater pool comes as a surprise, the hotel being 6km from the sea. Private spa suites are NTD2,000 for 2hrs; access to the public springs (some are single-sex, no-clothes-worn pools; others are mixed, swimwear-compulsory pools) costs NTD400 pp with no time limit. Staying overnight at the w/end will set a couple back by close to NTD7,000 but that inc b/fast & dinner. #1717 buses (see page 137) stop nearby. **$$$$**

La Casa (3 rooms) Near Sanzhi Junior High School; m 0931 131 383; e chgodbout@yahoo.com.tw; http://tw.myblog.yahoo.com/la-casa/. Less than 10mins' drive from Baishawan, La Casa is a rustic little homestay with a colourful exterior & interior décor that some might find just a bit too cute. Room rates start at NTD1,500 for a dbl midweek. Owner Charlene Lee has done lots of travelling herself & sometimes accommodates backpackers for a bargain NTD600. Inc brunch, dinner sometimes available. **$$**

WHAT TO SEE AND DO Attractions are listed in the order you'll encounter them if starting out from Keelung.

Yehliu Geopark 野柳地質公園 (Yěliǔ Dìzhì Gōngyuán) (↘ 2492 2016; www.ylgeopark.org.tw; ⊕ 07.30–17.00 daily daily; admission NTD50/25) The single most popular tourist destination on the north coast, this natural wonderland is a place geologists and kids adore. There are sometimes queues to see the park's most famous sight, the Queen's Head, so named because it resembles the famous bust of Nefertiti. Just as engrossing are the caves, hoodoos, pot-holes, overhangs, honeycombed outcrops, and rocks marked with swirls or concentric ripples. All of these features are the result of wind and wave erosion. The peninsula is 1.7km long, so be prepared for some walking.

Jinshan 金山 (Jīnshān) This pleasant little town isn't quite on the coast. After getting off the bus, you'll need to walk for the better part of an hour if you want to see the ocean from the end of the cape, but the hike is recommended. Follow the signs to the **Twin Candlesticks**, a pair of unwieldy-looking 60m-high rock columns just offshore. The Yehliu promontory is clearly visible 5km to the southeast. When returning to the town centre, a convenient and enjoyable place to try Jinshan's iron-rich hot springs is **The Governor-General's Hot Spring** (*196 Minsheng Rd;* ↘ *2408 2628; www.warmspring.com.tw;* ⊕ *09.00–24.00 daily, meals available* ⊕ *11.00–22.00 daily*). Built in 1939 on the orders of the Japanese viceroy as a place for entertaining dignitaries, it was used for much of the postwar period as an army outpost. As well as an outdoor hot spring and cold pool (*NTD300/180, swimsuits required*), there are private rooms and gender-segregated ocean-view pools on the fourth floor (*swimsuits not required*).

Dharma Drum Mountain 法鼓山 (Fǎgǔshān) (↘ 2498 7171; www.ddm.org.tw; ⊕ 09.00–16.00 daily) One of Taiwan's religious landmarks, DDM was established in 1989 and grew out of a monastery led by the Venerable Chan Master Sheng-Yen (1930–2009). The complex now includes two universities, a college, a memorial hall, exhibition rooms and a network of walking paths. Free half-day and one-day English-language tours, recommended for those interested in religion and/or meditation, can be arranged if notification is made at least ten days ahead (e vedus@ddmf.org.tw). Casual visitors are welcome and will find plenty of English-language signs and leaflets. Smoking or consuming meat or alcohol isn't allowed in the complex and photography isn't permitted indoors.

Bus #1815 picks up passengers at Taipei West Bus Station Terminal A and Taipei City Hall Station and terminates at DDM (see *Getting there and away* on page 137). Allow half an hour if you're walking between the bus stop on Highway 2 and DDM.

Juming Museum 朱銘美術館 (Zhūmíng Meǐshùguǎn) (☎ 2498 9940; www.juming.org.tw; ⏲ Tue–Sun 10.00–18.00 May–Oct, 10.00–17.00 Nov–Apr; admission NTD250/220)

Ju Ming (b1938) is Taiwan's most famous sculptor and this sprawling indoors-and-outdoors gallery showcases many of his finest works. His creations are, at first glance, massive and crude but it's not unusual for collectors to shell out US$250,000 for one of his signature bronze figures. Also on display are works by Warhol, Picasso, Henry Moore and others from Ju's personal collection. The museum's website has comprehensive travel information including details of free shuttle vans from Jinshan.

Laomei Algal Reef 老梅海岸

Laomei is a rather forlorn seaside village but if it's low tide, head down to the beach and turn left – you'll be able to see something rather odd and very photogenic. Wave erosion has cut deep grooves into a large patch of bedrock and the humps that run down to the water are covered with multiple layers of dark green algae. When the algae die, their limestone skeletons remain in place and new algae grows on top of them. Imagine rows of boulders covered with moss, emerging from the ocean. Tide times can be checked on the internet (www.cwb.gov.tw). Click on 'forecast', then 'fishery' then 'tidal forecast'. Find 'New Taipei City, Shimen' on the list to see tide details for 30 days ahead. Walking from Laomei's bus stop to the reef, then around Fugui Cape and back to Highway 2 takes around an hour.

Fugui Cape 富貴角 (Fùguì Jiǎo)

Taiwan's most northerly point – the ROC controls territory significantly further north in the Matsu Islands – is about 30 minutes from Danshui by bus. *Fùguì* is a Mandarin derivation of a Taiwanese transliteration of a 17th-century Dutch term meaning 'small peninsula'. This gorse-covered promontory was created millions of years ago when volcanism in what's now Yangmingshan National Park hurled lava and rocks as far as the coast. Among them are windkanter boulders recognisable by their sharp edges, the result of erosion by sand-bearing northeasterlies. Neither the peninsula's radar base nor its lighthouse are open to the public. On the western side of the cape, take a look at the small harbour where just-caught lobsters and crabs try to escape from plastic tubs outside seafood restaurants (*no EMs; confirm prices before taking a seat*).

Baishawan 白沙灣

Come here in the summer and you'll find hundreds of people enjoying this beach, one of the nicest in north Taiwan. Baishawan means 'white sandy bay' and the name is spot on – the sand is fine, clean and pale. There are places to eat, drink coffee and rent surfboards.

DANSHUI 淡水 (DÀNSHUǏ) *Telephone code 02*

Nowadays a suburb of the capital with 130,000 inhabitants, but for much of its history a town bigger and more important than Taipei, Danshui (government departments prefer the old spelling, 'Tamsui') has been able to retain a good amount of its identity and historic character. The attractions – among them schools, graves and a fortress-turned-consulate – are clustered more or less within walking distance of each other. There's no need to venture out to the modern housing estates which fill the flatlands between the old town and the ocean.

GEORGE L MACKAY (1844–1901)

George Leslie Mackay, the first Canadian to serve overseas as a Christian missionary, entered Taiwan's history when he disembarked at Takao (now Kaohsiung) on 29 December 1871. The eldest son of Scottish Highlanders, Mackay had studied at seminaries in Canada, the United States and Scotland. He was only 27 when he was dispatched to Taiwan by the Canadian Presbyterian Church.

Within days of his arrival Mackay was picking up Taiwanese words from a British Presbyterian. From Takao, he sailed north to Danshui, reaching the town on 9 March 1872. There he worked day and night to master the Taiwanese language. As soon as he became semi-proficient, he began to preach to whoever was willing to listen, and to debate ethics and religion with the educated elite. 'The proud, conceited literati would enter my room, open my Bibles and other books, throw them on the floor and then strut out with a grunt of contempt', he recalled in *From Far Formosa*, the 1896 book he wrote about his missionary experiences. But it was from among this group that he made his first convert, a young man who went on to play an important role in the spreading of Christianity in north Taiwan.

Among non-Christian Taiwanese, Mackay is revered for his educational and medical work. While touring the countryside he offered his services as a dentist, pulling more than 21,000 teeth. These he always returned to their owners, lest he be accused of sorcery. Two of Danshui's landmark schools were founded by Mackay: Aletheia University (until 1999 known as Tamsui Oxford College after Oxford County in Ontario, Mackay's birthplace) and Tamkang High School. Mackay Memorial Hospital, which he established in 1880, now has more than a thousand beds.

Mackay's name will always be linked with Danshui (which in *From Far Formosa* he described as 'a smoky, dirty town'), but during his first seven years in Taiwan he stayed there a total of just 175 days. The rest of the time was spent travelling, usually on foot. He became something of a polymath. As well as a preacher, doctor and dentist, he became an architect who designed 60 churches and a civil engineer who supervised the building of them.

There can be no doubt that Mackay was incredibly courageous and physically very tough. He survived bouts of malaria and meningitis. *From Far Formosa* suggests a man absolutely convinced he was doing God's work, and who believed non-Christian Taiwanese were 'hopelessly blinded' by Taoism's 'spirit-superstition and wretched incantations'. Yet in some ways Mackay was ahead of his time. His married a Taiwanese woman in an era when miscegenation was frowned upon in the West; and he publicly denounced as 'unjust and un-Christian' the head-tax levied on Chinese (and only Chinese) entering Canada. Mackay's evident love for Taiwan continues to endear him to Taiwanese and his life story features in primary school textbooks.

HISTORY By the late 18th century, Danshui (meaning 'fresh water', also the name of the river that drains the Taipei Basin and flows past the town) was growing fast thanks to strong trade links with the Chinese mainland. Between 1859 and 1895, when Japan took control of Taiwan, the Treaty of Tientsin gave traders from the British Empire, Russia, the United States and France special rights and protections in Danshui. Among them was John Dodd, an English merchant who arrived in 1864 and who played a key role in the development of Taiwan's tea industry (see page 113). He was living in the town when it was blockaded and shelled by the French during the Sino-French War of 1884–85. He wrote extensively about that period and also about Taiwan's indigenous people and flora. However, his life and achievements are overshadowed by those of another Danshui-based expatriate, Canadian-born missionary George L Mackay (see box opposite). Like many harbours on the west coast, Danshui's port suffered from silting. By the 1920s, almost all ships bound for north Taiwan anchored instead in Keelung's deep-water harbour.

GETTING THERE, AWAY AND AROUND

By car or motorcycle You're unlikely to drive to Danshui, but if you do, start your search for a parking spot on Wenhua Road. If that fails, try west of Fort San Domingo.

By MRT The Red Line links Taipei Main Station with Tamsui MRT Station (*services ⊕ 06.00–23.24 daily; takes 40mins; NTD50*).

By bus Danshui's bus stops are on both sides of the main road just outside the MRT station. Buses to Keelung (*#862, departs every 30mins; ⊕ 05.50–20.30 daily; takes 2hrs; NTD120*) and Jinshan (*#863, departs every 30mins; ⊕ 05.40–21.30 daily; takes 1¼hrs; NTD75*) are convenient for touring the north coast. Within Danshui, the Red 26 bus goes westward from the MRT station, down Zhongshan and Wenhua roads, stopping very near Fort San Domingo.

By boat Small ferries cross the Danshui River to Bali at least every 15 minutes (*⊕ 06.15–20.00 daily; takes 10mins; NTD20 one-way, return NTD39*). By the time you read this, construction of a road/MRT bridge between Danshui and Bali should have begun.

By bicycle Decent mountain bikes are available from **Outdoor Bike Leisure Base** (☏ *2625 9802; ⊕ 11.30–19.00 Mon–Fri, 10.30–19.00 Sat–Sun & national holidays*) for NTD100 per hour or NTD200 per day. From Danshui, bike-only trails follow the riverbank southeast into the heart of Taipei.

TOURIST INFORMATION

🛈 **North Coast and Guanyinshan National Scenic Area** www.northguan-nsa.gov.tw

🛈 **Danshui Visitor Information Centre** Tamsui MRT Station ⊕ 08.30–18.30 daily

🏠 **WHERE TO STAY** All of the following hotels are shown on the map on page 142.

🏠 **Hotel Solar** (74 rooms) 35 Zhongzheng E Rd; ☏ 2621 3281; f 2623 7788; e hotel.solar2@msa.hinet.net; www.hotel-solar.com.tw. This place is clean & very central but as soon as you see the furnishings you'll know it isn't a modern establishment. Rooms on the 7th flr have excellent river views. English spoken. Inc b/fast. **$$**

🏠 **Thomas Homestay** (1 apt) 3rd Flr 3, Lane 28, Zhongzheng Rd; m 0953 860 788; e thomas@thomashomestay.com; www.thomashomestay. com. This place is a little different from other homestays in that the host family does not live here (so call or email at least a day before) & they accept just one group at a time, be it a couple or even 6 or 7 ppl. This means you'll have the place to yourself & you're welcome to use the kitchen or washing machine (soap powder provided). You can see the river from the living room. Cable TV & DVD player. Thomas & his wife, a Danshui native, speak excellent English & are used to visitors from all parts of the world. **$$**

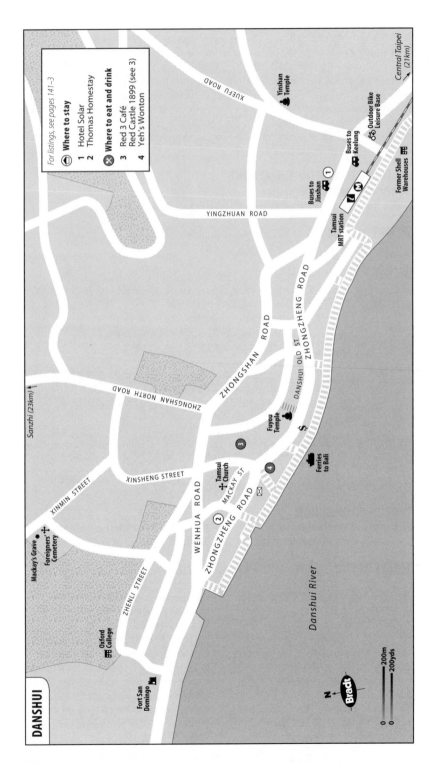

DANSHUI

For listings, see pages 141–3

Where to stay
1 Hotel Solar
2 Thomas Homestay

Where to eat and drink
3 Red 3 Café
  Red Castle 1899 (see 3)
4 Yeh's Wonton

Central Taipei (21km)

Yinshan Temple

Buses to Keelung

Outdoor Bike Leisure Base

Former Shell Warehouses

Buses to Jinshan

XUEFU ROAD

YINGZHUAN ROAD

Tamsui MRT station

ZHONGZHENG ROAD

ZHONGSHAN ROAD

DANSHUI OLD ST

ZHONGSHAN NORTH ROAD

Sanzhi (23km)

Fuyou Temple

Ferries to Bali

XINSHENG STREET

XINMIN STREET

Mackay's Grave

Foreigners' Cemetery

Oxford College

ZHENLI STREET

Fort San Domingo

Tamsui Church

MACKAY ST

WENHUA ROAD

ZHONGZHENG ROAD

Danshui River

N

Bradt

0   200m
0   200yds

✕ WHERE TO EAT AND DRINK Zhongzheng Road, the riverside pedestrian zone and the alleyways in between are packed with vendors selling deep-fried delights. There's a night market every evening on Yingzhuan Road. All of the following establishments are shown on the map on page 142.

✕ Red 3 Café 3rd Flr 6, Lane 2, Sanmin St; 📞2625 8855; www.rc1899.com.tw; ⏱ 11.00–23.00 Sun–Thu, 11.00–24.00 Fri–Sat. The '3' in the name signifies the 3rd flr (2nd flr if you're British) & if it's views across the river you want, rather than the ambience of a 110-year-old building, this is a better option than the more obvious **Red Castle 1899** (*EM, Taiwanese cuisine;* ⏱ *12.00–16.00 & 17.00–21.00 daily;* $$$). The latter restaurant occupies the 2-floor renovated landmark on top of which Red 3 Café was built a decade ago. Red 3's EM lists Western standards such as spaghetti & steak priced NTD200–520. Red 3 has a very wide selection of teas, coffees, juices, smoothies, cocktails, liquors & imported beers. Accessible from Zhongzheng Road Lane 14. $$$

✕ Yeh's Wonton Restaurant 177 Zhongzheng Rd; 📞2621 7286; www.wenchou.com.tw; ⏱ 09.00–21.00 daily. Expect queues for takeout food at this tiny (3 tables only) eatery. According to their website, they've served more than 2 million people over the past 30-odd years. In addition to wonton dishes, there's roasted chicken leg, pork chops & savoury breads flavoured with radish or green onions. No EM but the picture menu makes ordering easy. $

OTHER PRACTICALITIES

✉ 203 Zhongzheng Rd; ⏱ 08.00–18.00 Mon–Fri; 08.30–12.00 Sat–Sun

$ **Cooperative Bank** 119 Zhongzheng Rd

WHAT TO SEE AND DO Danshui abounds in physical reminders of the past. Some, like the temples, were established by Han settlers and their descendants, but there's a whole slew of locations associated with Mackay and the other Westerners who made Danshui their home. The restored warehouses southeast of Tamsui MRT Station, for instance, date from the 1860s and were owned by Shell Petroleum (now Royal Dutch Shell) between 1897 and 2001 and now contain a small museum.

What's called Danshui Old Street 淡水老街 is a stretch of Zhongzheng Road that isn't especially old or interesting. It does, however, lead to several of the town's main sights and many of its eateries.

Yinshan Temple 鄞山寺 (⏱ *05.00–19.00 daily*) Danshui's most beautiful shrine, Yinshan Temple is especially worth visiting after dark when the exterior is illuminated. It's one of two shrines in Taiwan dedicated to Dingguang Buddha, a 10th-century deified Chinese monk, and the effigy of a meditating monk presents quite a contrast to the fearsome-looking bearded gods seen in most temples.

Fuyou Temple 福佑宮 (*200 Zhongzheng Rd;* ⏱ *05.00–20.45 daily*) This atmospheric Mazu shrine has a notable relic – a battered-looking inscribed board which hangs from a ceiling beam in the middle of the main chamber. Conferred by order of Emperor Guangxu just after the Sino-French War (see *History*, page 14), it makes public his recognition of and appreciation for Mazu's apparent intercession on behalf of the Chinese side during the conflict. It reads (from right to left, which is often but not always the case with written Chinese) *Yì tiān chāo yòu*, meaning 'bright heaven's blessing'.

Mackay Street 馬偕街 One of very few roads in Taiwan named after someone not of Han Chinese descent, this short thoroughfare has a number of places related to the eponymous missionary, among them a brass statue at the eastern end of the street; **Mackay's original clinic** (*6 Mackay St;* ⊕ *11.00–18.00 Tue–Thu, 11.00–21.00 Sat–Sun; free admission*); **Tamsui Church** (*8 Mackay St;* ⊕ *for services only*), designed by his son, who followed in his father's footsteps and served as a missionary here before and after World War II; and the old single-floor **house** which Mackay Sr rented for a while (*20 Mackay St; closed to the public*).

Foreigners' Cemetery 外僑墓園 (⊕ *during school hours; free admission*) At least 75 and perhaps as many as 81 Westerners were interred in this graveyard, about the size of two tennis courts, between 1867 and 1974. Among the 19 Americans and 15 Britons buried here are missionaries, infants, soldiers, sailors and a diplomat. There are also Germans, Spaniards, Portuguese and French. The tombs are now well cared for but for much of the 1980s, after the US Embassy in Taipei closed down, the plot was ownerless and neglected. If you enter via the school gates on Xinmin Street, you'll pass the memorial to George L Mackay and the tombs of the missionary and some of his family members.

Oxford College 牛津學堂 (⊕ *10.00–16.00 Mon–Fri, campus* ⊕ *07.00–22.00 Mon–Fri; free admission*) The original 1882 redbrick building, now surrounded by the modern buildings of Aletheia University, is an attractive blend of Taiwanese residential and Western ecclesiastical architecture. One part has been designated the **Mackay Memorial Hall** in honour of the college's founder (see box, page 140) while another displays photos and documents about the Presbyterian Church. A side gate links the university with Fort San Domingo.

Fort San Domingo 紅毛城 (Hóngmáo Chéng) (⊕ *09.30–18.00 Tue–Sun & all national holidays except Lunar New Year's Day; free admission*) With its miniature turrets and red walls, Danshui's most popular attraction resembles a Victorian folly, but this square fortress has been around since 1646. It was built by the Dutch East India Company and some sources refer to it by its Dutch name, Fort Antonio. In that era Taiwanese referred to Europeans as 'red-haired barbarians', so locals dubbed the building *hóngmáo chéng*, meaning 'castle of the red-haired folk'. The current Western moniker is actually the name given by the Spanish to the stockade that stood here in the 1630s. For much of the 18th century, imperial troops were stationed in the building. In 1867, the British government turned the site into their main Taiwan consulate, having agreed to pay an annual rent of 10 taels of silver (equivalent to 12 Troy ounces). They renovated the fort and built a lovely two-floor consular residence next door; the latter has several bricks marked 'VR 1891', VR being Queen Victoria.

There's quite a bit to see inside these buildings, including wall safes, a stove for burning documents and cells for detaining British nationals (who were immune to local laws but could be punished by UK courts). The consulate was closed 1941–46 because of World War II. In 1950, the British government recognised the communist regime in Beijing but kept the Danshui consulate open. This put the British diplomats based here in an awkward situation; they had to avoid contact with officials of the ROC's central government, and communicated only with Taiwan's provincial authorities. The consulate was closed in 1972 as part of a deal whereby the UK upgraded its Beijing mission to embassy status.

Bali 八里 (Bālǐ) Even if you've no time to explore this township opposite Danshui, consider taking the boat (see *Getting there, away and around*, page 141) across the

estuary for the views you'll get of Yangmingshan National Park to the east and Guanyinshan 觀音山 to the south. The latter mountain is 612m high and the loftiest of the eight peaks in Taiwan named after the Buddhist goddess. If it's low tide, take a close look at the mudflats near Bali's ferry dock – you'll notice hundreds of fiddler crabs and dozens of finger-length mudskippers.

Bike-rental businesses (*from NTD60 per hr*) can be found near the dock; a pleasant 3.5km-long bike trail path passes mangrove swamps on its way to **Shisanhang Museum of Archaeology** 十三行博物館 (↘ *2619 1313; www.sshm.tpc.gov. tw;* ⊕ *09.30–17.00 daily, closed first Mon every month; free admission*). This museum preserves artefacts of the prehistoric Shisanhang culture, which smelted iron and buried their dead hereabouts 500 to 1,800 years ago. Alternatives to cycling include the Red 13 bus from Guandu MRT Station (on the Red Line) to the museum via Bali's ferry dock.

5

Hakka Country

The northwestern counties of Hsinchu and Miaoli (combined population 1.51 million, land area 3,351km²) form Taiwan's Hakka heartland. Because much of the land is unsuitable for growing rice, Fujianese migrants preferred to go elsewhere. As a consequence, the interior remained undeveloped until Hakka settlers began to arrive in the late 18th century. These days you won't hear the Hakka language spoken very much in Hsinchu City, a prosperous place whose historic side isn't well known. It was never a purely Hakka settlement and its booming high-tech industries have drawn migrants from every corner of the ROC, as well as thousands of foreigners. However, if you venture into the hilly townships that characterise this part of Taiwan, you'll have plenty of chances to meet Hakka people who still use their mother tongue on a daily basis and whose lives, like those of their grandparents, revolve around extended families, farming, the local temple and traditional festivals like the annual celebration of the Yimin militiamen's bravery. English-language information about Hakka culture can be found at www.hakka.gov.tw.

Just as they struggled against an unfavourable natural environment, Hakka settlers also faced indigenous opposition. They traded with, competed against and often fought Atayal and Saisiyat aborigines, eventually pushing them deeper into the highlands. Beipu, once a fortified frontier town, is popular now for its quaintness. Sanyi has become a renowned woodcarving centre, while Nanzhuang offers an appealing blend of Hakka and indigenous cultures and natural attractions. Aboriginal clans cling to their way of life in the eastern third of the region; their villages are rewarding but somewhat difficult places to visit.

HSINCHU CITY 新竹市 (XĪNZHÚ SHÌ) *Telephone code 03*

When it comes to attracting domestic tourists, Hsinchu faces the same perceptional disadvantage Taiwan has been battling against in its national effort to draw international visitors. Just as Taiwan is still better known for making things than its rich culture and natural beauty, this city's recent economic achievements – evidenced by the semiconductor foundries, optoelectronics companies and computer-peripheral makers hosted by Hsinchu Science-based Industrial Park – have been so impressive that few outsiders know about its long history and alluring colonial-era buildings, or that the local government has succeeded in translating its prosperity into tangible quality-of-life improvements. This is a shame: in my book, Hsinchu (population: 429,000) is the most interesting west-coast city between Taipei and Tainan.

HISTORY Fujianese, who've been settling hereabouts since at least 1711, called the town Tek-kham (in Mandarin, Zhuqian), meaning 'bamboo barricade'. There was no barricade and the presence of bamboo was nothing more than a coincidence because –

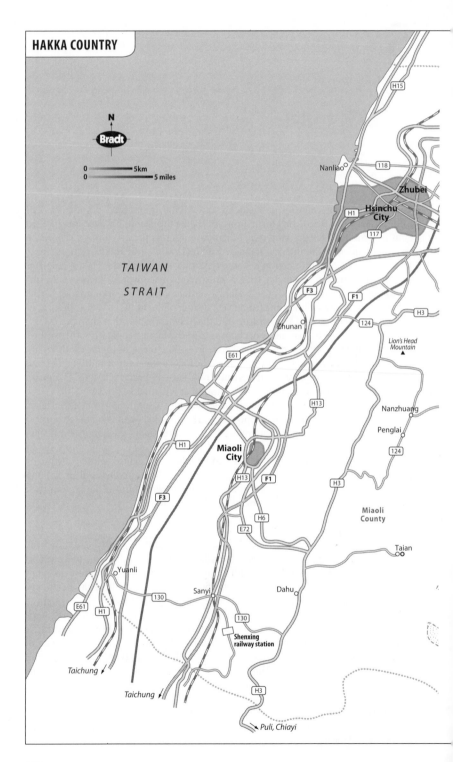

HAKKA COUNTRY

N

Bradt

0 ———— 5km
0 ———— 5 miles

TAIWAN

STRAIT

Nanliao

118

Zhubei

H15

Hsinchu
City

H1

117

F3

F1

H3

124

Zhunan

Lion's Head
Mountain ▲

E61

H13

Nanzhuang

Penglai

124

H1

Miaoli
City

H13

F1

H3

F3

H6

Miaoli
County

E72

Taian

H3

Yuanli

Dahu

E61

130

Sanyi

H1

130

**Shenxing
railway station**

Taichung

Taichung

H3

↘ *Puli, Chiayi*

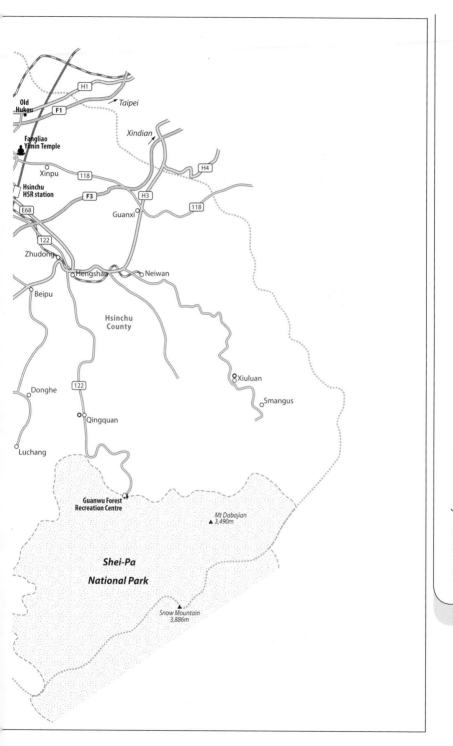

Old
Hukou

F1

H1

Taipei

Xindian

Fangliao
Yimin Temple

Xinpu

118

H4

Hsinchu
HSR station

F3

H3

118

E68

Guanxi

122

Zhudong

Hengshan

Neiwan

Beipu

Hsinchu
County

Xiuluan

Donghe

122

Smangus

Qingquan

Luchang

Guanwu Forest
Recreation Centre

Mt Dabajian
▲ 3,490m

Shei-Pa

National Park

Snow Mountain
3,886m

like many 17th- and 18th-century place names – Tek-kham was a simply loose Chinese rendering of the name used by the area's indigenous inhabitants. In the language of the local Taokas tribe it meant 'seashore'. The Taokas moved away or assimilated as the Han town developed. Then, as now, the population was a mix of Fujianese and Hakka. In the first quarter of the 19th century, when Taipei was still a brusque frontier community, Tek-kham had several schools and an active group of literati. One of the latter, Zheng Yong-xi (1788–1858), became in 1823 the first Taiwan-born candidate to pass the highest-level imperial examination for scholar-bureaucrats, thus gaining the title *jinshi*. Zheng and his clan left their mark on Hsinchu, as the city was renamed in 1880. In 1826, Zheng successfully lobbied the Qing court for permission to construct a 2.7km-long brick-and-stone wall around the town, promising it would be financed entirely by citizens' donations. Visitors can still see a small part of that wall (most was torn down during the Japanese colonial era), the house where Zheng lived and the shrine where his descendants worship their ancestors.

GETTING THERE AND AWAY

By HSR Trains to/from Taipei take just over half an hour (*NTD315*). To Kaohsiung Zuoying they take 1½ hours (*NTD1,310*). Hsinchu HSR Station is 11km east of Yingxi Old East Gate; the quickest way to get to the city centre is by the TRA branch line (*departs every 30mins;* ⊕ *06.17–23.17 daily; takes 20mins; NTD20*) from Liujia Station next to the HSR Station. Bus #1782 (*2 or 3 departures per hr;* ⊕ *07.15–23.45 daily; takes 25mins; NTD32*) runs between the HSR station and the city centre, stopping near the Image Museum.

By TRA Expresses from Taipei (*NTD137–177*) or Taichung (*NTD152–197*) take a bit over an hour.

By bus Kuo-Kuang and other companies link Hsinchu's South Bus Station with Taipei (*service #1822 departs every 20mins;* ⊕ *05.20–22.30 daily; takes 1½hrs; NTD130*). The South Bus Station is also where you can board a bus to Zhudong if you're headed for Beipu. From the North Bus Station there are services to Zhongli via Hukou, Fangliao and other small towns in Hsinchu's hinterland.

By car By Freeway 1, Hsinchu is 70km south of Taipei and 83km north of Taichung.

GETTING AROUND

By bus Most of the sights marked on the map are within 20 minutes' walk of the TRA station. To get to Nanliao on the coast, take city bus #15 (*departs every 25mins;* ⊕ *06.20–22.00 daily; takes 20mins; NTD15*) from the stop on Minzu Road near the TRA station.

By taxi Andrese Yann (m *0963 321 049*) speaks English and Spanish and is available for airport and countryside trips.

By hired car

🚗 **Car Plus Auto Leasing** [151 G2] 156 Zhonghua Rd Sec 2; ☏ 515 3528; www.car-plus. com.tw; ⊕ 08.30–20.30 daily. General-use car

rentals & long-term leasing. Car Plus also has a counter inside Hsinchu HSR Station.

By train Branch lines link the city centre with the HSR station and Neiwan (see page 157).

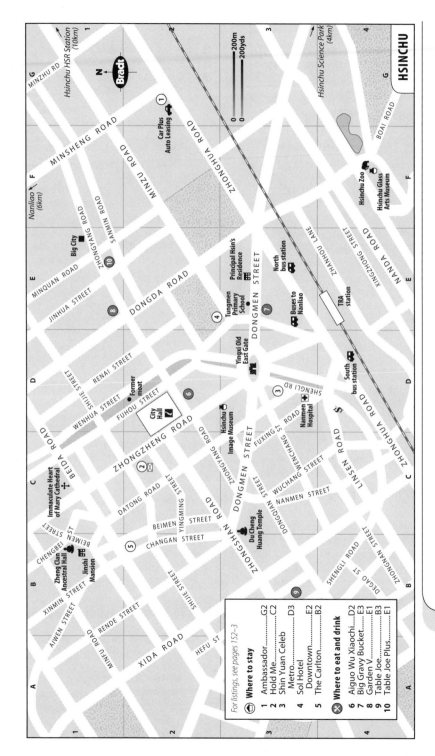

Hsinchu HSR Station (10km)

MINZHU RD

MINSHENG ROAD

MINZU ROAD

ZHONGHUA ROAD

Car Plus Auto Leasing ①

Hsinchu Science Park (4km)

BOAI ROAD

Hsinchu Zoo

Hsinchu Glass Arts Museum

Nanliao (6km)

MINQUAN ROAD

ZHONGYANG ROAD

SANMIN ROAD

JINHUA STREET

Big City

DONGDA ROAD

⑩

⑧

Principal Hsin's Residence

DONGMEN STREET

North bus station ⑦

Buses to Nanliao

ZHANHOU LANE

XINGZHONG STREET

NANDA ROAD

TRA station

RENAI STREET

Former moat

FUHOU STREET

Tungmen Primary School

④

Yingxi Old East Gate

DONGMEN STREET

FUXING ST

South bus station

WENHUA STREET

WENHSIIE STREET

BEIDA ROAD

City Hall 𝑖

⑥

ZHONGZHENG ROAD

Hsinchu Image Museum

ZHONGYANG ROAD

③

SHENGLI RD

Nanmen Hospital

WUCHANG STREET

DONGQIAN STREET

LINSEN ROAD

ZHONGHUA ROAD

Immaculate Heart of Mary Cathedral ✝

BEIDA ROAD

DATONG ROAD

②

YINGMING STREET

BEIMEN STREET

NANMEN STREET

SHENGLI ROAD

CHENGBEI

BEIMEN ST

Zheng Clan Ancestral Hall

Jinshi Mansion

⑤

CHANGAN STREET

Du Cheng Huang Temple

ZHONGSHAN ROAD

DECAO ST

ZHONGNAN STREET

XINMIN STREET

AIWEN STREET

RENDE STREET

SHIJIE STREET

XIDA ROAD

HEFU ST

⑨

MINZU ROAD

N

Bradt

0   200m
0   200yds

Hakka Country HSINCHU CITY

For listings, see pages 152–3

① Where to stay

1	Ambassador	G2
2	Hold Me	C2
3	Shin Yuan Celeb Metro	D3
4	Sol Hotel Downtown	E2
5	The Carlton	B2

✕ Where to eat and drink

6	Aiguo Wu Xiaochi	D2
7	Big Gravy Bucket	E3
8	Garden V	E1
9	Table Joe	B3
10	Table Joe Plus	E1

5

TOURIST INFORMATION

Foreigner Assistance Centre [151 D2] Hsinchu City Hall; http://foreigner.hccg.gov.tw/en/; 08.00–12.00 & 13.00–17.00 Mon–Fri; 521 6121 ext 564 or 565

Liujia Visitor Information Centre Liujia TRA Station; 09.00–17.00 daily

Nanliao Tourist Information Centre 261 Nanliao St; 09.30–17.30 Tue–Sun

 WHERE TO STAY All of the following hotels are shown on the map on page 151.

Ambassador Hotel (257 rooms) 188 Zhonghua Rd Sec 2; 515 1111; f 515 1216; e reservations@ambassador-hsinchu. tw; http://hsinchu.ambassadorhotel.com.tw. With rooms on the top 12 floors of a 24-storey building, the Ambassador gets rave reviews from businesspeople impressed with the service & range of rooms & suites. The hotel has the only presidential suite between Taipei & Taichung, plus a swimming pool & sauna; in-house restaurants offer Chinese, European & other cuisines. Inc b/fast. $$$$$

Sol Hotel Downtown (152 rooms) 10 Wenhua St; 534 7266; f 533 5750; www. solhotel.com.tw. Aimed very much at business travellers but good for tourists on account of its central yet quiet location & reasonable prices, Sol's rooms were decorated by someone who understands that less is more & restraint shows good taste. Gym & self-service laundry. Inc b/fast. $$$$

The Carlton (117 rooms) 225 Beida Rd; 525 9999; f 525 5999; www.carlton-hotel. com.tw. Ever so slightly old-fashioned, as befits a hotel within walking distance of the Cheng Huang Temple, the Carlton has an excellent location for those wanting to explore the city centre on foot. Rooms are spacious & well equipped. Extra beds can be added for NTD700. Guests can use the small gym & there's a Taiwanese restaurant on the 2nd flr. Inc b/fast. $$$$

Shin Yuan Celeb Metro Hotel (35 rooms) 20 Datong Rd; 521 1888; f 526 8877; e shinyn. cmh@msa.hinet.net; www.shinyuan-hotel.com. tw. The glitzier yet quieter sibling of the 75-room Shin Yuan Hotel (*11 Datong Rd*), the Celeb Metro branch has guestrooms awash with shiny golds & yellows. Chic bathrooms (white pebble floors, traditional wooden buckets), DVD players, internet access & newspaper in your preferred language are standard. B/fast inc. $$$

Hold Me Hotel (21 rooms) 11th Flr, 107 Zhongzheng Rd; 521 3333; f 522 2206; e holdmehotel@yahoo.com.tw; www.hmhotel. com.tw. Very quiet, very central & by Hsinchu's relatively expensive standards very good value, although the rooms aren't overlarge. B/fast inc. $$

WHERE TO EAT AND DRINK The Foreigner Assistance Centre's website (*http://foreigner.hccg.gov.tw/en/* – click on 'Sightseeing and travel' then 'Dining') has details of more than 60 traditional eateries in the Hsinchu area. The 50-plus food vendors clustered around the front of the Cheng Huang Temple serve a good range of Taiwanese snacks and hot, filling dishes; specialities include the city's excellent pork meatballs 新竹摃丸 (*xīnzhú gòng wán*) in a clear soup and rice noodles. The lane immediately left of Tungmen Primary School's 東門國小 main gate is full of bars, coffee shops and inexpensive eateries.

All of the following establishments are shown on the map on page 151.

Garden V 136 Dongda Rd Sec 1; 543 8898; 11.30–14.00 & 17.00–21.00 daily. This classy Shanghainese restaurant – soft lights & a clientele who know to keep their voices low – has a menu & layout which best suits small groups of gourmands. Dishes priced NTD180–780; decent selection of European wines from NTD1,200 per bottle. EM; parking nearby isn't difficult. $$$

Aiguo Wu Xiaochi 1001 Dongmen Market; 524 9612; 11.00–19.00 Mon–Fri. Eat here & market-goers will assume you're a long-term resident who knows where some of the city's best Hakka/Taiwanese home cooking is served. Now run by the founder's grandson; no EM so enlist a Chinese speaker or this book's language appendix. Only 2 tables so you may have to wait for a seat. $$

✘ **Table Joe** 102 Hefu St; ✆527 8150; ⌚ 10.00–22.00 daily. Probably the best place in the city for burgers, onion rings & other Western staples, Table Joe attracts a youngish crowd & offers tourists home-from-home hospitality. **Table Joe Plus** (*25 Sanmin Rd;* ✆*535 6070*) keeps the same hours but has a slightly different menu. EM. **$$**

✘ **Big Gravy Bucket** 大滷桶 32-2 Minzu Rd; m 0966 662 558; ⌚ 15.30–23.00 Mon–Sat, 12.00–21.00 Sun. If you've a mind to try *lǔ wèi* –

the category of food items that includes chickens' feet, ducks' hearts, tempura, various soy products & unidentifiable animal organs – this is a good place to do it. No language skills are needed; simply grab a pair of tongs & put the sausages, meatballs etc you want in a plastic basin, then wait while they're cut up, heated & sprinkled with spring onion. This kind of food goes very well with beer. None is sold but the staff say it's OK to bring in drinks from outside & there's no corkage. **$**

SHOPPING

Big City [151 E1] 229 Zhongyang Rd; ✆623 8000; www.fecityonline.com; ⌚ 11.00–21.30 daily. Reasons to visit Hsinchu's biggest mall include a hypermarket & gourmet deli (both in the basement), a cinema (4th flr), English-language books & magazines (5th flr) as well as 20-odd places to get a meal (4th & 7th flrs).

OTHER PRACTICALITIES

$ **Bank of Taiwan** 29 Linsen Rd
✚ **Nanmen Hospital** 20 Linsen Rd; ✆528 6456; ⌚ 24hrs daily

✉ **Post office** [151 C2] 2 Yingming St; ⌚ 08.00–17.30 Mon–Fri

WHAT TO SEE AND DO

Yingxi Old East Gate 迎曦東門城 [151 D3] Most of the city wall was torn down in 1902; this gate, the only remnant, is now treasured as an emblem of Hsinchu. A double-eave structure that looks best at night when floodlit, it's sometimes used as a concert venue. After being pressed into service as a sewer, a long section of what used to be Hsinchu's moat has been cleaned up and beautified with banyans, flowerbeds and stepping stones. As an urban creek it's now every bit as attractive as Seoul's famous Cheonggyecheon – and it cost the taxpayer far less.

Du Cheng Huang Temple 都城隍廟 (**Dū Chéng Huáng Miào**) [151 C3] (*75 Zhongshan Rd; www.weiling.org.tw;* ⌚ *04.30–22.30 daily*) Since 1889 the deity venerated here has been seen as the divine equivalent of a provincial governor, thus outranking every other city god in Taiwan. He's also unique in having two sons; effigies of them are at the very back of the temple, on the left of the city god's wife, while fertility goddess Zhusheng Niang Niang is on her right. Established in 1748, the temple also features a huge iron abacus (to remind people that the gods tally their righteous deeds and sins), but the real stars are the statues – the Six Generals, the Two Judges and others. Pick up a bilingual leaflet from the supervisors' desk to find out who's who. If you can, come in the early evening when the temple is full of families who pray and burn joss paper before eating at the food stalls which surround the temple.

Beimen Street [151 C2] Not long ago this thoroughfare was an authentic 'old street' lined with two-floor colonial-era merchant houses behind which stood even older structures. The neighbourhood has suffered from neglect and piecemeal development but it's still worth walking north from Cheng Huang Temple to get whiffs of old Taiwan. Antique wooden beams and doors retrieved when a traditional building was demolished add character to the boutique at number 95. At number 109, you'll find a shop selling *bùdàixì* puppets, while at number 156 there's a timeworn herbal apothecary. Across the road from the latter stand a pair of small yet photogenic shrines, **Changhe Temple** and **Shuixian Temple**; information boards out front have all the facts. The main part of **Jinshi Mansion** 進士第, the residence commissioned by Zheng Yong-xi in 1838, is numbered 163; at the time of writing it was covered by a steel frame to prevent further deterioration. Other segments bear numbers 167 to 179 and one reason why proposals to renovate this five-courtyard complex have come to nothing is that ownership is divided among scores of Zheng's descendants. Damaged by fire during World War II, the mansion – classed as a national relic but never opened to the public – is now in a very poor state. Nonetheless, intricate stone-lattice windows and exquisite woodcarvings of dragons and flowers can be appreciated from the street. The adjacent **Zheng Clan Ancestral Hall** 鄭氏家廟 [151 B1] (*185 Beimen St*), which dates from 1853, is where descendants of the scholar-official worship their illustrious ancestor and other forefathers. It's in far better condition than the mansion yet invariably locked up. The two stone banner-holders outside show the clan produced not one but two *jinshi* (see page 186).

Immaculate Heart of Mary Cathedral [151 C1] (*156 Zhongzheng Rd;* ☎ *525 6057;* ⏲ *for services only*) Many of Taiwan's Catholic churches incorporate elements of Chinese 'Northern Palace' architecture, but the design of this 1957 landmark is emphatically Western.

Hsinchu Image Museum 影像博物館 [151 D3] (*65 Zhongshan Rd;* ☎ *528 5840;* ⏲ *09.30–12.00, 13.30–17.00, 18.30–21.00 Wed–Sun; admission to museum or film NTD20/10*) Built in 1933 as the city's first modern cinema, the displays about Taiwan's film industry aren't half as appealing as the opportunity to watch a movie in stylish Art Deco surroundings.

Principal Hsin's Residence [151 E3] (*32 Dongmen St;* ⏲ *09.00–17.00 Tue–Sun; free admission*) Almost a century old and formerly the home of a noted educator, this bungalow is a good example of colonial-era Japanese architecture.

Hsinchu Glass Arts Museum 新竹市玻璃工藝博物館 [151 F4] (⏲ *09.00–17.00 Wed–Sun; admission NTD20*) Located in the same park as the city's zoo and Confucian shrine, this museum celebrates Hsinchu's tradition of glass-making. At one point, 80% of the lights decorating North American Christmas trees were made in the Hsinchu area. Displays focus on modern glass art rather than industrial processes.

17km Coastline Scenic Area Even though it abuts the coast, Hsinchu is seldom thought of as a maritime city. It's about 7km from Hsinchu TRA Station to the sea and the old fishing settlement of **Nanliao** 南寮 in the city's north feels like a separate town. There are still a few ice-making factories which supply ice used for packing the catch. Fresh-air freaks (Hsinchu is nicknamed 'the windy city') and birdwatchers may want to rent a bicycle at the port and pedal south; bike trails continue beyond the city limits into Miaoli County. The entire scenic area is an Important Bird Area on account of the Kentish plovers (*Charadrius alexandrinus*) and Saunders's gulls (*Chroicocephalus saundersi*) that winter here.

NORTH OF HSINCHU *Telephone code 03*

Those driving from Hsinchu City to the North Cross-Island Highway may find these two places worth a digression.

HUKOU OLD STREET 湖口老街 (HÚKǑU LǍOJIĒ) Popular with domestic

sightseers, Hukou Old Street is of limited appeal unless you've a special interest in urban conservation. Almost all the 200-plus houses are two-floor shop-house combinations dating from around 1915. Most are family homes, although a few businesses sell souvenirs or meals. The street owes its existence to the north–south railroad; a station used to stand where there's now a Catholic church. When the tracks were shifted seaward after World War II, businesses moved out or withered away. As in Lugang, there was neither the incentive nor the money to rebuild. A comprehensive government-funded renovation has restored aspects of the street's original appearance. Power, telephone and TV cables are underground and neither air-conditioning units nor rooftop water tanks are visible from the street. Many houses have traditional wooden sliding doors rather than vertical metal shutters.

Getting there
Cars should take Freeway 1 to the Hukou exit then drive north on Highway 1 for 3km. Buses from Hsinchu include #5622 (*departs every 30mins;* ⏰ *06.45–22.20 daily; takes 40mins; NTD43*) and #5300 (*departs at least hourly;* ⏰ *07.20–20.10 daily*). The latter takes about 40 minutes whether you start from Hsinchu (*NTD56*) or Zhongli (*NTD65*). All buses stop on Highway 1, a few minutes' walk from the old street.

FANGLIAO YIMIN TEMPLE 枋寮義民廟 (FĀNGLIÁO YÌMÍN MIÀO) (*Yimin & Baozhong rds, Xinpu;* ⏰ *07.00–21.00 daily*) The most important place of worship for

many of Taiwan's Hakka citizens, this temple differs from the majority of shrines in that it isn't dedicated to an individual who lived and was deified in China centuries ago, or to a legendary figure like the Jade Emperor, but rather to men who died fighting to protect Hakka settlements here in Taiwan during the 18th and 19th centuries. When Lin Shuang-wen's rebels (see *History*, page 13) moved to seize granaries in the region, 1,300 Hakka volunteers took up arms. They called themselves the 'Yimin Army', *yìmín* meaning 'upholding faithfulness and honesty'. After repelling Lin's men they fought alongside Hoklo Taiwanese and aborigines to liberate nearby towns.

There's a reason why Taiwan's most important Yimin shrine is in a backwater. The bodies of 200-plus Yimin killed fighting Lin's forces were loaded on to ox carts so they could be interred in their home villages. After stopping to rest where the temple now stands, the oxen (themselves commemorated by stone sculptures in front of the temple) refused to go any further. Through prayer and divination, the convoy's leaders determined the dead Yimin wished to be buried at this very spot. They set about building a tomb and a makeshift shrine. A second tomb was added in the 1860s after more than 100 Yimin soldiers died battling another major uprising; these two mass graves are in the garden behind the temple. The shrine's original memorial tablets were destroyed in 1895 when Japanese troops clashed with Taiwanese irregulars. The temple is unusual in that it lacks effigies of deities; even Guan Gong is represented by a simple tablet.

Thousands of people come here between the 18th and 20th of the seventh lunar month each year for the Hakka Yimin Festival, during which it's traditional to sacrifice minced chicken or duck (not whole fowl as is usual in Taiwanese folk rites) or sliced pork. If you attend, you're likely to witness a highly controversial religious practice: the display of 'divine pigs'. These enormous swine are fed (often forcibly and sometimes with sand and iron-filings, critics allege) until they're so big they're unable to walk. The root cause of this cruelty is vanity – the heavier the pig, the greater the prestige of the family which raised it. Inside the temple, on the left, there are photos of pigs which have won prizes in recent years.

Getting there and away If you're driving or riding from Hsinchu City, take Road 118 inland to the junction with Road 117, then head north for just over 1km. Bus #5621 (*9 departures per day;* ⏱ *06.50–19.05; takes 35mins; NTD33*) sets out from Hsinchu's North Station and stops right outside the temple.

EAST OF HSINCHU *Telephone code 03*

Winning scenery and appealing villages make this region a delight to explore if you've your own transport, and more than justify getting to grips with bus schedules and routes.

GETTING THERE, AWAY AND AROUND
By car or motorcycle Arrive via Highway 3. Minor roads linking Beipu with Lion's Head Mountain and Nanzhuang are clearly signposted in English.

By bus If you're interested only in Beipu, go first to Zhudong by #5608 or #5673 from Hsinchu's South Bus Station (*NTD53*) or #1820 from Taipei (*NTD140*). In Zhudong board #5610 (*NTD26*) for the final stage of the journey. There are buses every 30–45 minutes on these routes. Alternatively, take one of the Taiwan Tourist Shuttle services. The Lion's Head Mountain route (*departures hourly, on the hour* ⏱ *08.00–15.00 Mon–Fri, every 30mins* ⏱ *08.00–16.00 Sat–Sun*) links Zhubei TRA Station, Hsinchu HSR Station and central Beipu with the visitor centre at Lion's Head Mountain. Journey time from the HSR station to the visitor centre is an hour; a one-day pass is NTD100 and can be purchased on the bus. The last bus back to the HSR and TRA stations leaves at 17.00. The Lion's Head Mountain–Nanzhuang route sets out from the latter place and stops at Cyuanhua Temple and Lion's Head Mountain Visitor Information Centre only (*departures hourly* ⏱ *09.30–15.30 Mon–Fri, 14 departures* ⏱ *08.00–17.00 Sat–Sun & national holidays; takes 30mins; one-day pass NTD50*).

By train Sixteen trains per day serve Neiwan of which six start from Hsinchu (*journey time 1hr; NTD42*). The others begin from Zhuzhong (*journey time 42mins; NTD29*) near Hsinchu HSR Station.

TOURIST INFORMATION
🛈 **Tri-Mountain National Scenic Area** www.trimt-nsa.gov.tw

🛈 **Lion's Head Mountain Visitor Information Centre** ⏱ 08.30–17.30 daily

⌂ WHERE TO STAY
⌂ **Daai Mountain Villa** 大隘山莊 (6 rooms) 14, 8 Div, Dalin Village, Beipu; ☎580 3663; f 580 4725; e il0596@yahoo.com.tw; www.daaihill.com.tw. One of the area's best-known homestays & a good cut above most of the competition, Daai Mountain Villa is a classical-style 2-storey building furnished with antique & near-antique furniture & fine replicas. Great views, too. Look for Dahu Rd south out of central Beipu & be ready to turn left after about 3km. Inc b/fast. **$$$**

⌂ **Jing Yuan Bed & Breakfast** (5 rooms) 96, 4 Div, Ruifong Village, Zhudong; ☎580 4951;

f 580 4718; www.scenically.com.tw. Lots of wood in the rooms, some of which sleep 4. Hakka meals, coffees & fruit teas also available. Getting here is a little complicated. Take Road 122 inland past Hwy 3 & turn right at km30. After 2.8km turn left & it's another 800m to the homestay. It's also possible to approach from Beipu Cold Spring. Inc b/fast. **$$$**

⌂ **Cyuanhua Temple Shishan Building** 勸化堂獅山大樓 (72 rooms) ☎037 822 563. The main accommodation option on Lion's Head Mountain, the Shishan Building is next to & operated by Cyuanhua Temple. Across the border in Miaoli County, so you'll need to add the area code 037 if calling from Hsinchu or further afield. The rooms (some take 3, 4 or 6 ppl) aren't 5-star but not nearly so austere as the monastic surroundings might have you expect. Simple but filling vegetarian meals (**$**) available if booked a few hours in advance. A bit of a walk from the nearest car park/bus stop so don't carry too much luggage. **$$**

✗ WHERE TO EAT AND DRINK

✗ **Brick & Mortar House** 113 Changchun St, Beipu; ☎580 2299; ⏰ 10.30–20.00 daily. Located outside the old town centre, so parking is easy. The sprawling 1-floor building is mostly redbrick but mud-brick & river stones are visible in parts. Coming from the north, turn right just before km82 on Hwy 3 & you'll see it almost immediately. Popular with natives who've moved to the big city & are returning to visit relatives, which surely means something. Dishes include Hakka stir-fry & chicken for NTD200–300. **$$$**

✗ **Hundred Years Old Store Hakka Dishes** 百年老店客家菜 23 Beipu St, Beipu; ☎580 2213; ⏰ 10.00–21.00 daily. Just short of a century old, this restaurant's food wins plaudits but the white-tile walls & bright lights do nothing for ambience. Lots of fish & seafood on the menu. If you're translating character by character, be aware that the meat in '3-cup field chicken' 三杯田雞 (*sān bei tián jī*) is frog flesh. **$$$**

✗ **The Well** 水井茶堂 1 Zhongzheng Rd, Beipu; ☎580 5122; ⏰ 10.00–18.00 daily. Run by a true local & a magnet for tourists wanting to try their hand at pounding tea (see box, page 151), The Well is an old single-storey house that's been alluringly done out externally & internally. The meal sets win no prizes for originality but you won't leave hungry. **$$$**

✗ **Old Street Flat Rice Noodles** 老街粄條 31 Miaoqian St, Beipu; ☎580 3871; ⏰ 08.00–17.00 Mon–Thu, 07.00–17.00 Fri–Sun. Some Beipu restaurants fake old; this one doesn't have to as its photogenic home has been around for a century. Within, sections of wall have been stripped of plaster to show the original daub, bricks & stones. The menu features Hakka staples inc ban-tiao noodles (*portion of fried noodles NTD60*) & eggs fried with basil (*small portion NTD50*). Some English is spoken & the staff, aware that many Westerners dislike internal organs, can advise when ordering. Local beer available. **$$**

WHAT TO SEE AND DO

Neiwan Branch Railway Built to serve industry but now used by commuters, this 27.9km-long branch line links Hsinchu with the little riverside town of **Neiwan** 內灣, 258m above sea level. Travel on a weekday if you can, as at weekends the railway is often crowded with local sightseers. The scenery around Neiwan is pleasant and in late spring if you stay after dusk you're likely to see fireflies.

Beipu 北埔 (**Běipǔ**) Like Tainan and Lugang, Beipu (population 10,000, 98% Hakka) is a place where the past can still be seen and touched, though it's actually much younger than those two bastions of tradition. Given the circumstances in which the town was founded in 1835 – armed Hakka settlers forced out the original Atayal inhabitants – it's not surprising that for decades afterwards the townsfolk didn't feel safe at night. In addition to the usual walls and gates, Beipu's pioneers deployed a guileful way of protecting the settlement. The town's streets were covered with stone slabs, most of which were fixed in place. A few weren't, however, and made a loud 'clunk' when stepped on. Locals knew where to step, of course, but intruders trying to infiltrate couldn't help but set off these 'alarm stones'. During the colonial era, coal turned Beipu into a boom town where miners blew their wages in wine shops and brothels. These days the businesses that thrive are altogether more salubrious and, as often as not, aimed squarely at incoming tourists. **Citian Temple** 慈天宮 (*1 Beipu St*; ⊕ *05.30–19.00 daily*) is at the heart of Beipu's historic quarter. Local folk come to this shrine to worship Guanyin and the Three Mountain Kings. The latter, represented by a tablet on the left, are deities revered by Hakka people throughout east and southeast Asia. To the right, at 14 Miaoqian Street, you'll find a shop (⊕ *08.00–18.00 daily*) selling camphor oil, a key product in the 18th and 19th centuries. Making 3,600cc of oil requires 100kg of wood; these days many of the shop's customers are dog-owners who rub it into their pets' fur to repel insects. Make a point of exploring the lanes and streets behind and beside the temple. You'll find decaying brick walls and ancient wells, as well as an exquisitely photogenic mansion called **Tianshuitang** 天水堂 (*1 Zhongzheng Rd; not open to the public*). If you're getting about by car or motorcycle, do explore the hills southeast of the town – the scenery is gorgeous.

Lion's Head Mountain 獅頭山 (Shītóushān)

Excursions to Beipu can easily be combined with a visit to this segment of the Tri-Mountain National Scenic Area. None of the mountain's five hiking trails are especially challenging, but they do offer a chance to get close to nature and see picturesque Buddhist shrines and monasteries established more than a century ago. The best known, **Cyuanhua Temple** 勸化堂 (**Quànhuà Táng**) (⊕ *05.00–19.00 daily*), offers food and accommodation. The visitor information centre can provide a very thorough English-language map-leaflet with distances and altitudes (the highest point is 492m above sea level) and can help with arranging accommodation at Cyuanhua Temple. If you arrive at the information centre before lunch you'll be able to hike southwest to Cyuanhua Temple, dally a little at the sights, and still make it to the bus stop on Road 124 in plenty of time to either return to Hsinchu or continue on to Nanzhuang.

THE ABORIGINAL INTERIOR

Adventurous self-drivers may want to visit indigenous communities located deep in the mountainous interior of Hsinchu and Miaoli counties.

GETTING THERE, AWAY AND AROUND You'll need your own car and strong nerves because road conditions are often poor. Only highly experienced riders should attempt to reach these places by motorcycle. Having lots of time is essential as distances on maps and signposts are deceptive; the final 16km to Smangus, for instance, often takes an hour. None of these destinations can realistically be done as day trips from the lowlands.

For Qingquan, take Highway 3 to Hengshan then Road 122 south. To reach Xiuluan and Smangus, follow Highway 3 northeast away from Hsinchu City until you see signs to Neiwan; beyond Neiwan the route is clearly signposted. The turn-off to Taian is north of Dahu.

Just as Hakka people have a distinctive way of cooking, they also have a special way of preparing tea. In several of Beipu's restaurants, tourists can try their hand at making *léi chá* (literally 'pounded tea'). This involves a lot of elbow work but it's also good fun. If you order a set you'll be brought the ingredients on a tray plus a mortar and pestle with which to grind them. The recipe varies from one establishment to the next but often includes sesame seeds, pine nuts, peanuts, sunflower seeds, crispy rice and peppermint as well as dried tea leaves. Once you've reduced everything but the rice to a fine paste, added piping hot water and a spoonful of soybean powder, and stirred the resulting concoction, you'll have something that looks like pea soup. Throw in the rice and it's ready to drink. The taste is very different from tea you're used to, of course, and it isn't to everyone's liking – but it'll be a cuppa you'll remember for quite some time.

WHAT TO SEE AND DO

Qingquan 清泉 This mostly Atayal village is best known among Taiwanese for being the place where Zhang Xueliang (1901–2001), a Manchurian warlord, was kept in detention between 1946 and 1959. Arrested in 1936 on the orders of Chiang Kai-shek, whom he had kidnapped and coerced into an alliance with China's Communists, Zhang was variously a soldier, politician, opium addict and womaniser (Mussolini's eldest daughter was one of his lovers). He endured more than half a century under house arrest in various locations before spending his final years in Hawaii. **Zhang Xueliang's Former Residence** (⊕ *09.00–17.00 daily; free admission*) is a beautiful reconstruction of the house where Zhang and his wife stayed. In addition to hot springs and homestays, Qingquan has an inexpensive hostel operated by the local Catholic church. The priest is an American who's lived here since the 1970s and speaks Atayal.

Xiuluan 秀巒 The toponym means 'elegant mountain ranges' but the nearby peaks are often lost in fog. The village's free, 100% natural hot-spring pools are beside the river. To go beyond this tiny settlement you'll need to obtain a mountain permit at the police checkpoint; the procedure is straightforward but you'll need to show your passport.

Smangus 司馬庫斯 This village, which lies at an elevation of around 1,600m, hasn't been on the tourist map for very long, although Atayal have been living here off and on for well over a century. Like many other indigenous groups, the clan that regard this as their ancestral land were forced by the Japanese colonial regime to move to a lower elevation so they could be more easily controlled. After 1945 they returned, but living conditions were extremely tough until just a few years ago. Electricity didn't come to the village until 1979 and there wasn't a proper road before 1995. Villagers have responded to the recent tourism boom by establishing a church-affiliated co-operative that shares homestay and restaurant revenues in a way that's designed to encourage young people to remain part of the community. Get a Chinese-speaker to contact the visitor centre (☎ *03 584 7688; www.smangus. org*) in advance if you want to arrange accommodation and/or meals. Smangus's main attraction is a grove of giant trees, one of which is an estimated 2,500 years old. Because the villagers are Christians they don't, unlike their forebears, consider the trees to be sacred. Reaching the grove and then returning to the village is a proper hike that takes the better part of a day.

Taian Hot Springs 泰安溫泉 Between Dahu and Nanzhuang, Road 62 leads inland from Highway 3 to where there's a range of hotels and some challenging day hikes. The springs themselves are clear, odourless, carbonic and weakly acidic.

NANZHUANG 南庄 (NÁNZHUĀNG) *Telephone code 037*

Well and truly discovered by domestic tourists, the Nanzhuang area has a slew of scenic, cultural and ecological attractions. The town itself is really no more than a large village. It's a good spot to explore on foot and get a meal, but Penglai and the tiny aboriginal villages beyond Donghe are more attractive places to spend the night. The valleys inland of Nanzhuang are home to a branch of one of Taiwan's smallest aboriginal tribes, the 6,100-strong Saisiyat.

GETTING THERE, AWAY AND AROUND
By car, motorcycle or bicycle Take Highway 3 then Road 124. Cyclists should know that coming from the south involves far more hill climbing than approaching from the north.

By bus #5804 leaves Hsinchu every hour (⊕ *06.50–19.50 daily; takes 1¼hrs; NTD155*). The stop is on Zhongzheng Road, about 50m from Hsinchu TRA Station and on the left if you're walking away from the railway station. From Nanzhuang there are three #5824 services per day to Xiangtian Lake (*departs 06.20, 11.30 & 14.00; takes 25mins; NTD44*). One way of getting from Nanzhuang to Lion's Head Mountain is by a Tourist Shuttle service (*departs hourly* ⊕ *09.30–15.30 Mon–Fri, 14 departures* ⊕ *08.00–17.00 Sat–Sun & national holidays; takes 30mins*). It stops at Cyuanhua Temple and Lion's Head Mountain Visitor Information Centre only; a one-day pass is NTD50.

TOURIST INFORMATION
🄘 **Miaoli County Culture and Tourism Bureau** www.miaolitravel.net

🄘 **Nanzhuang Visitor Centre** Near Nanzhuang Market; ⊕ 08.30–17.30 daily

🏠 **WHERE TO STAY** Very little English is spoken in the area's homestays, so get a Chinese-speaker to call and make reservations if you plan to arrive at the weekend.

🏠 **Good-Mountain Good-Water Cabins & Homestay** 好山好水景觀木屋民宿 (17 rooms) km33.5 Rd 124; ☎825 789; www.gmgw.com.tw. The accommodation here is far neater & much more comfortable than the front office suggests & every evening the manager leads a Chinese-language (yet highly enjoyable even if you don't speak a word) ecotour of the grounds. You can expect to see various moths, frogs (Penglai has 17 of Taiwan's 32 amphibian species), freshwater crabs & shrimp & possibly flying squirrels. The creek that runs through the grounds is clean enough for children to play in & there are camping

spots with electricity. Good Mountain is on the left if you're coming from Nanzhuang, less than 100m down a side road. Basic b/fast inc, no other meals. **$$$**

🏠 **Lily Village** (12 rooms) km31 Rd 124; ☎825 822; f 825 821; www.lilyvillage.com.tw. Popular with well-off Taiwanese & surrounded by farmland, Lily has largish modern rooms & is equidistant between Penglai & Nanzhuang; look for the fake windmill on the right if you're coming from the latter. B/fast inc; the in-house restaurant offers a good range of meals but these must be booked at least a day in advance. **$$$**

🛏 **Moon B&B** (6 rooms) Via km35.5, Rd 124; 📞 825 681; http://moonmate.idv.tw/. A modern 2-floor building with an excellent mountain setting 540m above sea level, Moon B&B is very popular with families but isn't especially easy to find. Groups of around 14 ppl can book the entire establishment for NTD10,000 per night. Coming from Nanzhuang, look for the small blue bilingual sign on the right, just past the police station. Turn off Road 124 there & ignore the narrow farm roads that branch off. B/fast inc. **$$**

🛏 **Raisinay Guest House** (6 rooms) 21 Shibi, Donghe; 📞 821 255; f 823 109; www.raisinay.com. Above the weaving-&-dyeing workshop of the same name, Raisinay's guest rooms feature tasteful aboriginal décor. The most attractive room is the 4-person slate-floored family 'Banana' chamber (*NTD4,200 at w/ends*). No AC but none needed at this altitude. B/fast inc. **$$**

✗ **WHERE TO EAT** Several vendors on Nanzhuang Old Street sell traditional snacks.

✗ **Market Delicacies** 市場小吃 📞822 435; ⊕ 06.00–17.00 daily. The best of the eateries inside Nanzhuang's retail market, this friendly establishment (located at the back on the right) serves up typical Hakka goodies inc ban-tiao, Hakka stir fry & congee. Their signature dish is pig-skin rice 豬皮飯 (*zhū pí fàn*). Local beer available. **$$**

🧋 **Yongliang Ice Factory** 永涼製冰廠 47 Zhongzheng Rd; 📞822 207; ⊕ 07.00–20.00 daily. A 1950s-style ice-lolly maker that has counted presidents among its patrons (photographic proof is proudly displayed on the wall), Yongliang is a good place to grab something cooling while wandering around Nanzhuang. Step inside to see how popsicle-making used to be done, as the original equipment is still utilised on a daily basis. The boss runs a small homestay around the corner. **$**

WHAT TO SEE AND DO Road 124 leads right through Nanzhuang. You'll have no problems finding the pedestrians-only Old Street across the road from the visitor centre and market building.

Nanzhuang Old Street 南庄老街
Before joining the herd as it shops, photographs and eats its way through the alleyways, there are a couple of distractions you should locate. The function of the first is obvious if someone happens to be using it when you arrive. It's a place where in the olden days townsfolk would come to do their laundry. The water, which is said to be very clean, comes from the hill above. The rutted stone slabs serve as washboards. A few residents still use it for its original purpose but you're more likely to see tourists washing their kids' sticky fingers. In the compound above there's a small shrine dedicated to the local land god; in Hakka areas like Nanzhuang the deity is called *bo-gong*. Little English is spoken along Old Street and few of the local specialities are labelled in anything other than Chinese. This matters not one jot. If something looks good and you're offered a morsel-sized sample, accept it – there's no obligation to buy. The most picturesque building along the street is a wooden former post office over a hundred years old.

Penglai Stream Biological Tour Area 蓬萊溪自然生態園區
(⊕ *24hrs daily; free admission*) South of Nanzhuang, Road 124 passes through nondescript Nanjiang before reaching Penglai 蓬萊. In the middle of the village, look for a temple that's on the right if you're coming from Nanzhuang. If you park there and walk down towards the river, you'll soon find the entrance to a nature reserve where fishing has been banned since 2001. Following the wooden walkway downstream takes at least an hour; along the way you will probably spot grey herons and clusters of butterflies. Peer into the water and you've an excellent chance of seeing schools of fish, among them two endemic species: *Acrossocheilus paradoxus*, sometimes

5

known as the Taiwan stone minnow, and *Candidia barbata*. The former is a silvery dark-grey colour and grows up to 10cm in length. The latter is greenish and of a similar size.

Donghe 東河 (Dōnghé)
Having finished your nature ramble at Penglai, double back to the bridge just south of Nanzhuang. Road 21, a 14.5km-long dead end, veers eastwards here. Donghe, the most substantial settlement on the road, is intriguingly multi-cultural: in addition to Taiwanese of Hakka and Fujianese descent, there are Atayal and Saisiyat households. Just past the elementary school, behind which there's a basic eatery, a former logging-company office has been renovated and turned into the **Walo Industrial Culture Gallery** 瓦祿產業文化館 (✆ 823 050; ⊕ 09.00–17.00 Wed–Mon; free admission). Local artisans exhibit and sell their work here. There's also a café inside.

Xiangtian Lake 向天湖 (Xiàngtiān Hú)
Some 738m above sea level, this indigenous settlement is where you'll find the absorbing **Saisiyat Folklore Museum** 賽夏族民俗文物館 (✆ 825 024; ⊕ 09.00–17.00 Tue–Sun; free admission). There's a replica of a traditional Saisiyat home plus lots of information about the Pasta'ai Ceremony. The last bus back to Nanzhuang leaves at 14.30.

Shibi 石壁
A few minutes beyond Donghe on Road 21, Shibi is notable for the rough cliffs that line both sides of the valley and the **Raisinay Dyeing and Weaving Workshop** 石壁編織工作坊 (*same location & contact details as Raisinay Guest House, page 161*; www.raisinay.com; ⊕ 09.00–17.00 Tue–Sun). Short classes taught in Chinese can be taken at Raisinay – which means 'rocky cliff' in Atayal – if arranged in advance. High-quality pieces made from hemp, such as waistcoats and pencil cases, can be bought off the shelf and make for top-notch keepsakes.

Shensian Valley 神仙谷
The main attraction between Shibi and Luchang is the confluence of three streams where rushing torrents have cut and smoothed a series of gullies far too dangerous to swim in. Nature makes quite a racket here; in addition to the non-stop crash of water on rock, birds babble and cicadas buzz. The footbridge across the river leads to a trail that goes 2.2km downstream; this path has been closed in the past due to typhoon damage, so you may have to retrace your steps rather than complete a loop.

Luchang 鹿場 (Lùchǎng)
Formerly a thriving mining-and-logging settlement, few people now live here and there's little to do but enjoy superb views down the valley and buy locally grown high-mountain produce. The old police station, a remnant of the colonial government's efforts to control the indigenous population, has been renovated.

SANYI 三義 (SĀNYÌ) *Telephone code 037*

Taiwan's foremost woodcarving centre and its surroundings make for an excellent day trip from Taichung or Hsinchu. If possible, stay overnight so you can give the area the time it deserves.

The woodcarving industry got its start during the early part of the Japanese colonial period when the local camphor forests were heavily logged. Roots and stumps were plentiful and carvings made by local artisans were popular with Taiwanese and Japanese Buddhists. Americans were important customers after

One element of Saisiyat culture has become well known within Taiwan: the biennial Pasta'ai Ceremony. Held in the middle of the 10th lunar month of each even-numbered year, the four-day/three-night festival is intended to appease the spirits of an extinct tribe called the 'short people'. According to Saisiyat tradition, these dwarfs taught the Saisiyat how to farm. Relations between the two groups were harmonious until, it's said, a Saisiyat woman was raped by one of the dwarfs. A brief war followed; the victorious Saisiyat exterminated their enemies but soon suffered a series of grave misfortunes. Tribal leaders, believing the spirits of the short people were wreaking revenge, decided to hold the Pasta'ai. The importance of the festival to the tribe can be seen from what happened when local clergy urged Christian tribespeople not to participate. The majority, it's reported, have stopped attending church services. An especially impressive version of the event, which features rites to welcome the spirits, offerings, prayers and dancing, is held every ten years. The next super-Pasta'ai will be in the autumn of 2016.

World War II: Catholics commissioned sculptures of the Virgin Mary while soldiers based in Taiwan picked up souvenirs. Each summer there are exhibitions and competitions.

Gorgeous valleys and forest-covered hills lie to the east of Sanyi. To explore them you'll need your own car or motorcycle or to be a determined cyclist.

GETTING THERE, AWAY AND AROUND

By car By Freeway 1 Sanyi is 125km south of Taipei, 28km north of Taichung. As soon as you come off the freeway you'll see bilingual signs to Shuimei Street and the museum.

By motorcycle or bicycle If possible arrive or leave by the splendidly scenic Road 130 (see page 165).

By TRA Sanyi is never more than 48 minutes from Taichung (*NTD50–60*) and less than an hour from Hsinchu (*NTD77–92*). There's at least one train in either direction per hour. Shuimei Street and the Wood Sculpture Museum are both about 2km from Sanyi TRA Station. A taxi to the museum shouldn't cost more than NTD150.

By bus Compared to the train, bus #5664 from Miaoli (*departs every 40mins ⊕ 06.15–21.40 daily; takes 40mins; NTD58*) gets you a bit closer to the woodcarving part of town.

TOURIST INFORMATION
⛑ Miaoli County Culture and Tourism Bureau www.miaolitravel.net

 WHERE TO STAY
⌂ 101 Restful Hotel (30 rooms) 28 Xihu Village; ☎ 872 299; f 875 599; www.101hotel. com.tw. So close to the freeway exit you'll hear the rumble of traffic in the distance – but it won't keep you awake – this motel has well-appointed rooms for 2 or 4 with large beds & deluxe massage

showers. 20% discounts Mon–Thu & a couple won't pay more than NTD3,000 at w/ends. Basic b/fast inc. **$$$**

⌂ **Hall of Hearts** (5 rooms) km17.2 Rd 130; ☎879 996; f 879 821; http://037879996. mmmtravel.com.tw. Not many homestays on Road 130 have English signs but Hall of Hearts – on the right coming from Sanyi – is an exception. Rooms are boxy but well-priced (a couple may pay just NTD1,600 inc b/fast). Some English spoken & Western meals available in the evening; the herbs used in the kitchen come from the owners' garden. **$$**

✗ WHERE TO EAT AND DRINK

✗ **Shanzhong Chuanqi** 山中傳奇 Across the tracks from Shengxing Station; ☎870 818; ⊕ 10.00–21.00 Mon–Fri, 09.00–22.00 Sat–Sun & national holidays. Built largely of recycled railway sleepers, this restaurant has dozens of tables on various levels & a menu full of good, solid Taiwanese fare. Good views over the station & village; in firefly season it often stays open until midnight. Coffees & teas (inc DIY *léi chá*, 'pounded tea') from NTD100; hot pots & meal sets are priced around NTD400. **$$$**

✗ **Jinbang Noodle Restaurant** 金榜麵館 (**Jīnbǎng Miànguǎn**) 170–7 Zhongzheng Rd, Sanyi; ☎873 567; ⊕ 07.30–20.00 daily. So popular with locals you might have trouble finding a table, Jinbang serves up Hakka dishes inc rice noodles with pork & ban-tiao with pork or beef. Many dishes priced under NTD80. The menu also features pig's head meat 豬頭肉 (*zhū tóu ròu*) & ducks' heads 鴨頭 (*yā tóu*) plus safer bets like wonton soup. **$$**

WHAT TO SEE AND DO Well over a hundred shops sell woodcarvings and they range from stores packed with cheap, mass-produced souvenirs to exclusive galleries. Two neighbourhoods are dominated by workshops and showrooms and you'll have no problems finding either. One, Shuimei Street, is a stretch of Highway 13 just north of the freeway exit. The other, Guangsheng Village 廣聲新城, is a newer part of town where you'll also find Sanyi's popular museum.

Sanyi Wood Sculpture Museum 三義木雕博物館 (Sānyì Mùdiāo Bówùguǎn)

(☎876 009; http://wood.mlc.gov.tw/; ⊕ 09.00–17.00 Tue-Sun; admission NTD80/50/ free) Not a place to be rushed, this museum has galleries on four floors and is permeated by woody aromas. Among the hundreds of religious, practical, decorative and abstract carvings are exquisite prize-winning works by local artists. The most interesting sections are those devoted to the history of the art in China, aboriginal woodcarving and temple carving (look out for the 11-faced Guanyin statue). If you're familiar with his style, you'll be able to pick out works by Ju Ming. Displays are labelled in Chinese only, but an English-language audio tour is available (leave your ID as a deposit), as is a 15-minute introductory video.

Snow Path If you face the museum, you'll see the start of this short hiking trail – so named because each spring white Tung-tree blossoms make it look as though snow has fallen on the hillside – to your right. After 20 minutes of uphill walking you'll reach a tea plantation.

Shengxing Railway Station 勝興火車站 At 402m above sea level, this station used to be the highest point on the north–south railroad. This stretch of railway hasn't been used by scheduled services since 1997 – trains now take a straighter route nearer the sea – but the colonial-era wooden station building remains in place. Special trains pulled by steam locomotives can be ridden between May and August; ask at Sanyi's visitor centre or call the tourist hotline (☎0800 011 765). The village here is very quaint and makes the most of its rustic appeal. It does get packed

The deadliest earthquake in Taiwan's history struck at 06.02, 21 April 1935 and Hsinchu, Sanyi and Nanzhuang were among the worst-hit districts. Measuring 7.1 on the Richter scale, the quake left 3,422 people dead, 11,833 injured and over 60,000 buildings in ruins. Traditional construction methods were blamed for many of the deaths. At that time many countryside homes had adobe walls and heavy tiled roofs. The former crumbled easily when damp, causing the latter to fall in on the occupants and prompting one academic to name the event 'the adobe quake'.

with people at times, in particular during the Hakka Tung Blossom Festival (*http://tung.hakka.gov.tw*). Vehicles can be parked in one of the village's car parks or on the main road (*NTD50; no time limit*).

Longteng Broken Bridge 龍騰斷橋 To reach this bridge drive through Shengxing Village and follow the road for 5km. Hikers have the option of a slightly shorter and much flatter route: tramp along the railway tracks through the 725m-long tunnel by the station and you'll reach the bridge in about an hour. Longteng Bridge was completed in 1909 but damaged beyond repair in the terrible earthquake of 1935. The only arch to survive that disaster collapsed during 1999's big quake, after which the site was declared a national monument. It's hard to explain the attraction of this ruin, which from a distance resembles a row of giant mushrooms, yet it and the surrounding hills are certainly appealing.

Road 130 This route connects Yuanli on the coast with Highway 3, meeting the latter south of **Dahu**, a town famous for its strawberries. The inland section of Road 130 is exceptionally pretty and at least a dozen homestays (most signposted in Chinese only) can be found between km17 and km22 on Road 130. Near km17.5 a turn-off on the right goes uphill for approximately 1km to **Fodingshan Chaosheng Temple** 佛頂山朝聖寺 (⏲ *06.00–18.00 daily*). The architecture of this very new Buddhist place of worship shows strong Japanese influences; the gardens are delightful and there's an intriguing collection of Buddhist-themed statuary as well as nice views of the nearby hills. A little further along Road 130 there are spots where, if you come in the middle of spring, impressive clusters of fireflies can be seen. From the highest point on the road it's often possible to see both 3,530m-high Mount Daxue and the Dajia River, 14km to the south.

6

Central Taiwan

Cleaved by powerful rivers and rippled with hills, central Taiwan didn't see much development before the arrival of the Japanese. The first few waves of Han migrants stayed close to the coast. Lugang, where they traded and prayed, remains one of Taiwan's most fascinating towns. Changhua, a Qing prefectural capital for a century and a half, has preserved a good part of its history. Economically, the region is now dominated by the modern metropolis of Taichung.

Most of the region's other attractions are deep in the interior. Sun Moon Lake has long been one of Taiwan's most popular tourist destinations. Around Hehuanshan, mountain scenery can be enjoyed without having to get out of your car or off your motorcycle. If you feel the need to lace up your boots and do some serious hiking, there are few better places in east Asia than Yushan and Shei-Pa national parks. The former embraces Taiwan's highest peak, Mount Jade, and an expanse of expedition country that will have experienced trekkers salivating. Shei-Pa National Park includes Snow Mountain, the island's second-highest peak. Visit either reserve and you'll agree that made-in-Taiwan alpine views are world class.

Central Taiwan, which covers 8,685km², consists of the municipality of Taichung and the counties of Nantou, Changhua and Yunlin. A quarter of the region's 5.21 million people live in central Taichung.

TAICHUNG 台中 (TÁIZHŌNG) *Telephone code 04*

Ever so briefly Taiwan's capital, Taichung is often overlooked by travellers, despite having worthwhile museums and international eating options. This makes it a good place to be when the weather's bad, but that seldom happens as the city is blessed with an equitable climate. Some visitors base themselves here while exploring Sanyi, Lugang and other small towns.

HISTORY For more than a century from the 1720s, the plot of land that's now Taichung Park was an army training ground called Datun ('big mound'). In 1885, Liu Ming-chuan's proposal that the site be developed into the administrative centre of the new provincial government was approved by the Qing court. However, little progress was made before Liu left Taiwan six years later, and Taipei's role as interim capital was eventually formalised. Under Japanese rule Taichung, then known as Taichu, grew rapidly. Buildings from that era dot the city, but apart from the railway station there are few grand structures. From the 1960s onward, Taichung prospered as thousands of local entrepreneurs set up small factories making clothes, electric fans and other common consumer goods. These days, in terms of being aspirational, fashion-conscious and outward looking, Taichung's people aren't far behind the citizens of Taipei.

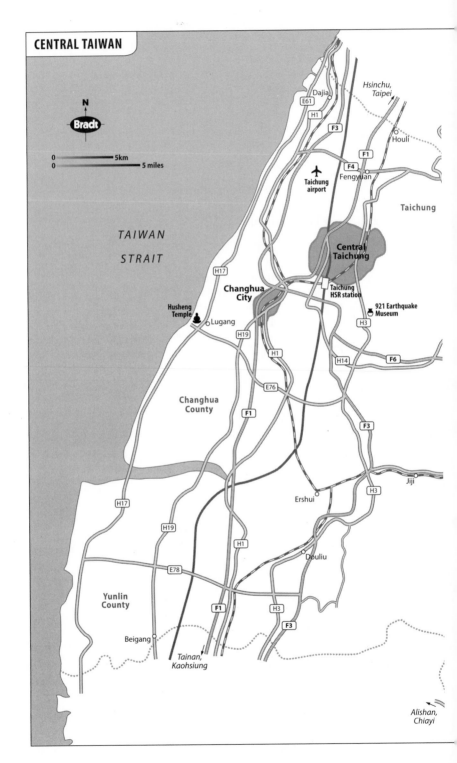

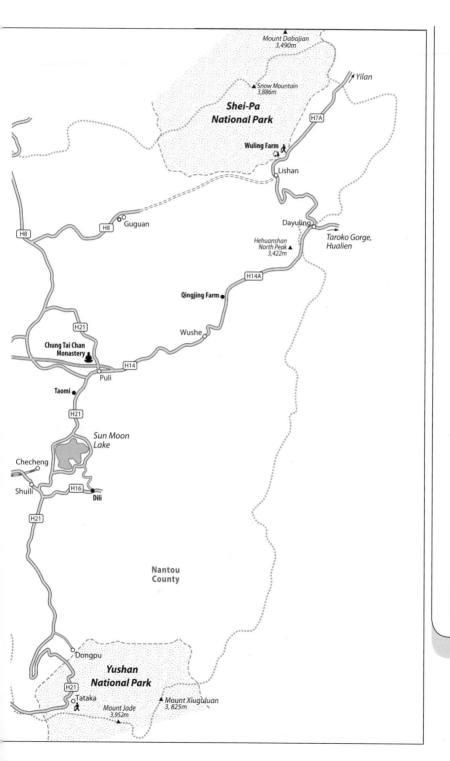

Mount Dabajian
3,490m

Snow Mountain
3,886m

*Shei-Pa
National Park*

H7A

Yilan

Wuling Farm

Lishan

Guguan

H8

H8

Dayuling

Taroko Gorge,
Hualien

*Hehuanshan
North Peak* ▲
3,422m

H14A

Qingjing Farm

H21

Wushe

Chung Tai Chan
Monastery

H14

Puli

Taomi

H21

*Sun Moon
Lake*

Checheng

Shuili

H16

Dili

H21

Nantou
County

Dongpu

*Yushan
National Park*

H21

Tataka

Mount Xiuguluan
3,825m

Mount Jade
3,952m

GETTING THERE AND AWAY

By air Flights to and from Hong Kong and several mainland Chinese cities plus domestic services to the outlying islands are based at **Taichung Airport** (*IATA: RMQ; ⟍ 2615 5000; www.tca.gov.tw*). The airport, 20km northwest of the city centre, can be reached by bus #115 from the TRA station (*11 departures per day ⊕ 06.00–21.50; takes at least 1hr; NTD49*) or #69 from the HSR station (*16 departures per day; ⊕ 06.20–21.10; takes almost 1hr; NTD57*). A taxi from either station will cost around NTD500. There's a visitor information centre (⊕ *09.00–17.00 daily*) in the airport but no car-rental outlet.

By HSR Taichung HSR Station is 11km south of the city centre. Trains to/from Taipei take an hour (*NTD765*), a little less to/from Kaohsiung Zuoying (*NTD860*). As well as free shuttle and city bus services to various parts of the metropolis and Taichung's airport, frequent direct buses link the HSR station with Lugang, Puli and Sun Moon Lake. The bus stops are downstairs and labelled in English. To get from the HSR station to central Taichung, take a local train from Xinwuri 新烏日 TRA Station (*takes 10mins; NTD15*).

By TRA There's at least one express per hour to/from Taipei (*takes 1¾–3hrs; NTD289–375*), Hsinchu (*1–1½hrs; NTD152–197*) and Kaohsiung (*2½–3½hrs; NTD361–469*).

By bus Kuo-Kuang has four services to/from Taipei per hour (*departures ⊕ 05.00–23.40 daily; takes 3hrs; NTD260*). Buses run every half hour to Tainan (*departs ⊕ 06.10–21.45; takes 2½hrs; NTD170*) and almost as frequently to Chiayi (*departs ⊕ 06.00–22.00; takes 1¾hrs; NTD165*). During the same period, there's at least one bus per hour to/from Kaohsiung (*NTD300*), Pingtung (*NTD345*) and Hsinchu (*NTD150*). Nine services per day go directly to Taoyuan Airport (*departs ⊕ 05.00–18.30; takes 2½hrs; NTD240*). Other bus companies offer similar services near the TRA station, so shop around as cheap promotional fares are often available.

Buses arriving from Taipei and other cities usually stop at Chaoma Bus Station very near Freeway 1 and then at various points along Taiwan Boulevard before terminating near the TRA station. Direct buses to/from Lugang, Sun Moon Lake and Puli leave from other stops near the TRA station; for details ask at the visitor information centre.

By car, motorcycle or bicycle Freeway 1's Taichung Interchange at km178 is the most convenient way for cars to approach central Taichung. Taichung is 153km south

---

TAICHUNG PORT ROAD IS NOW TAIWAN BOULEVARD

In mid-2012, the main thoroughfare running northwest from Taichung TRA Station to Freeway 1 was renamed Taiwan Boulevard. What used to be Zhongzheng Road is now Taiwan Boulevard Section 1. The stretch formerly known as Taichung Port Road (sometimes written Taichunggang Road) Section 1 is now, officially, Taiwan Boulevard Section 2, while Taichung Port Road Section 2 has become Taiwan Boulevard Section 3. Some hotels and restaurants have been slow to update their websites and business cards, so you may come across the old road names.

of Taipei and 189km north of Kaohsiung. If you're heading for the mountains from Taichung, consider taking Road 136; beyond the suburbs, it's scenic and rather steep.

GETTING AROUND

By bus Taichung's bus system is extensive but confusing, so many visitors rely on taxis. City buses #71 and #75 will get you from Taichung TRA Station [173 F4] to the National Taiwan Museum of Fine Arts [173 D3]. One-way fares start at NTD20/11.

By hired car General-use car rentals and long-term leasing are available from **Car Plus Auto Leasing** (*826 Taiwan Bd Sec 3;* ☎ *2703 2912; www.car-plus.com.tw;* ⏰ *08.30–20.30 daily*). Car Plus also has a counter inside Taichung HSR Station.

By rapid transit The first part of Taichung's rapid transit network, the Green Line between Wenxin Road and the HSR station, should be up and running during the lifetime of this guide.

TOURIST INFORMATION

🛈 **Taichung City Government** http://eng. taichung.gov.tw

🛈 **Taichung TRA Station Visitor Information Centre** [173 F4] ☎2221 2126; ⏰ 09.00–17.00 daily

LOCAL TOUR OPERATOR

Green Island Adventures 📱 0972 065 479; 📧 greenislandreservations@yahoo.com; www. greenislandadventures.com. This Taichung-based tour operator can help book discounted accommodation & offers tailor-made city tours plus excursions to Lugang, Sun Moon Lake & other destinations.

🏠 **WHERE TO STAY** All of the following hotels are shown on the map on page 173.

🏠 **Tempus Hotel** (334 rooms) 9 Taiwan Bd Sec 3 (lobby accessed from Dongxing Rd); ☎2326 8008; f 2320 0106; 📧 tempus@tempus.com.tw; www.tempus.com.tw. Many of the rooms & even some of the bathrooms in Taichung's plushest hotel have huge windows. Subdued colours & excellent service make for a true 5-star experience. Guests have free use of the fitness centre, swimming pool & sauna in the adjacent Mandara Life Club & needn't pay to join aerobics & yoga classes. The club also has a children's play area. The hotel has a bar, a bakery & 2 restaurants, the best of which is La Mode (*ground floor;* ⏰ *06.30–22.30 daily; EM;* **$$$$**), which serves consistently excellent European cuisine & offers a good choice of European & New World wines. Lunch & dinner are semi-buffet (*main course & salad bar from NTD880 pp*). Buffet b/fast inc. **$$$$$**
🏠 **Mulan Spa Motel** (45 rooms) 245 Shizheng Rd; ☎2252 7878; f 2252 8686; 📧 mulan@swmall. com.tw; www.mulan.com.tw. One of several plush motels in the district bordered by Taiwan Bd,

Wenxin Rd & Freeway 1, Mulan Spa's suites feature private patios, lots of greenery & mini swimming pools. In-room indulgences include massage chairs & steam rooms. B/fast inc. **$$$$**
🏠 **Kao Yuan Hotel** (40 rooms) 392 Taiwan Bd Sec 1; ☎2226 1566; f 2226 1568; 📧 services@ kaoyuan.com.tw; www.kaoyuan.com.tw. This hotel has 2 strikes against it: the staff don't speak much English & the immediate surroundings, while safe, aren't very attractive. However, the rooms are perfectly maintained & surprisingly good for the price. A few rooms have 2 dbl beds. B/fast inc. **$$**
🏠 **Kiwi Express Hotel** (43 rooms) 441 Taiwan Bd Sec 1; ☎2229 4466; f 2220 9725; www.rs-kiwihotel.com. This decent budget inn has a good location & helpful English-speaking staff. The rooms, which have new fittings & furnishings, lack character – hardly an issue with rates sometimes below NTD1,300. When making a reservation, specify if you require a window or a bathtub; at the time of writing the online booking system was

6

Chinese only. Guests can borrow bikes from the hotel & use the PC in the lobby. B/fast inc. **$$** ⌂ **Corner Backpacker Hostel** (3 dorms) 113 Xitun Rd Sec 1; m 0973 331 020; www. corner-backpacker.hostel.com. Opened by an avid Taiwanese traveller & fluent English-speaker, Corner is a good place to meet other travellers.

Characterful & well-equipped air-conditioned dorms each have 6 beds (*NTD600 pp, discounts on w/days*). 1 dorm is men-only, another women-only & the 3rd is for groups. No smoking; guests should be quiet after 22.00 but can return to the hostel anytime before midnight. Free Wi-Fi; shared bathrooms. **$**

✗ **WHERE TO EAT AND DRINK** All of the following establishments are shown on the map opposite.

✗ **Bollywood** 1026 Jianxing Rd; ☎2319 2828; ⏲ 11.00–14.00 Tue–Sun, 16.30–22.00 daily. Widely regarded as the best of the city's Indian restaurants, Bollywood offers traditional dishes from the subcontinent plus novelties like Bombay fish & chips. Main courses are priced around NTD300. This place also does roaring bar business with a full range of cocktails & bottled beers, plus a choice of draught beers. Among those who've eaten here is Suraj Sharma, star of 2012 Oscar-winner *Life of Pi* – many of the film's special effects were created in a Taichung studio. This neighbourhood is Taichung's 'Little India,' so if you don't like the look of Bollywood, nose around the other restaurants nearby. EM. **$$$**

✗ **La Pala Pizzeria** 165 Zhongxing St; ☎2301 3996; ⏲ 11.30–22.00 daily. An excellent mid-range choice (you may have to wait for a table & reservations are essential at the w/end) with several antipasti options (*NTD90–380*), pasta (*from NTD280*) & 10-inch pizzas which start at NTD190. Other recommended dishes inc *fettuccine ai porcini* (*NTD310*); the wine & beer list is impressive but not cheap. EM. **$$$**

✗ **Gulu Gulu** 2, Lane 13, Wuquan W 4th St; ☎2378 3128; ⏲ 11.00–24.00 daily. Not many indigenous restaurateurs have enjoyed consistent success in a big city market. Chiu Jin-ming, a member of the Paiwan tribe, is an exception. Since 2004 he's been drawing healthy numbers of customers with a range of dishes that include boar & a version of *ah-vai*, a Paiwan delicacy made with

fermented millet, pork & vegetables. Many of the ingredients & sauces are made & sent weekly by Chiu's mother in Taitung. Decorated with driftwood sculptures, animal jawbones & garlands of dried millet, Gulu Gulu also offers live indigenous music every night & vegetarian dishes. As well as beer there's aboriginal millet wine & punch made with beer & passion-fruit juice. The street it's on is lined with interesting restaurants. EM. **$$**

✗ **Toong Yuan Bean Jelly** Jincheng Rd & Jingcheng 2nd St; ☎2319 5757; ⏲ 12.00–23.00 daily. If you're craving dessert, try instead a popular local dish – a bowl of soft, sweetened soy-bean jelly (*dòu huā*). The menu is only in Chinese, but the workers can show you some of the optional ingredients, such as kidney beans, azuki beans & mung beans & will ask you if you want the concoction hot or cold. If this sounds a bit too foreign, ask for a scoop of ice cream to be added. If you're willing to explore, you'll find lots of coffee, alcohol & food options within 200m of this establishment, inc some well hidden in back streets. **$**

✗ **Zhonghua Night Market** Corner of Zhonghua & Gongyuan rds; ⏲ dusk–approx 03.00 daily. Not Taichung's largest night market (that would be the unbelievably crowded Fengjia Night Market, far out in the northwestern suburbs) but certainly the one easiest to reach, this maze of stalls & vendors should satisfy anyone's need for good-natured hubbub. There's more than food here; those with a taste for the cheap & cheerful will leave with bagfuls of clothes, accessories & shoes. **$**

SHOPPING

Top City [173 B1] 251 Taiwan Bd Sec 3; ☎3702 2168; www.fecityonline.com; ⏲ 11.00–22.00 daily. Eating options inside this department store cover much of Asia & there's also a cinema.

Sogo [173 D2] 459 Taiwan Bd Sec 2; ⏲ 11.00–22.00 daily. A useful landmark with the usual brands.
Caves Books [173 D2] 12 Guanqian Rd; ☎2326 5559; ⏲ 10.30–22.00 daily. Four floors of books & magazines plus a coffee shop.

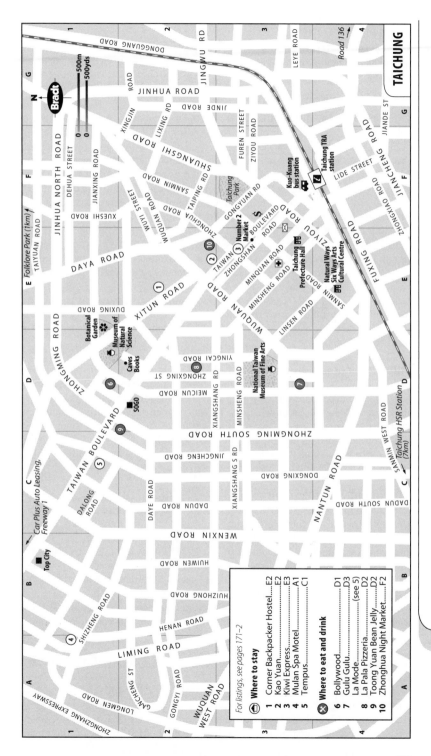

TAICHUNG

Where to stay

1 Corner Backpacker Hostel	E2
2 Kao Yuan	E2
3 Kiwi Express	E3
4 Mulan Spa Motel	A1
5 Tempus	C1

Where to eat and drink

6 Bollywood	D1
7 Gulu Gulu	D3
La Mode	(see 5)
8 La Pala Pizzeria	D2
9 Toong Yuan Bean Jelly	D2
10 Zhonghua Night Market	F2

For listings, see pages 171–2

OTHER PRACTICALITIES

$ **Bank of Taiwan** [173 F3] 144 Taiwan Bd Sec 1
✚ **Taichung Hospital** 台中醫院 [173 E3] 199 Minquan Rd; ✆ 2229 4411; ⊕ 24hrs daily

✉ **General post office** [173 E3] 86 Minquan Rd; ⊕ 07.30–21.00 Mon–Fri, 08.30–16.30 Sat, 08.30–12.00 Sun

WHAT TO SEE AND DO

Japanese-era heritage buildings Architecture aficionados will find three colonial-era landmarks in the old city centre worth a look. **Taichung TRA Station** [173 F4] is a 1917 renaissance-style beauty that's easily the most impressive of the five surviving 'classical' railway stations in Taiwan. It's being preserved even while the tracks themselves are being elevated as part of a project to eliminate level crossings. Designed by Moriyama Matsunosuke and resembling in form and original function Moriyama's National Museum of Taiwan Literature, **Taichung Prefecture Hall** [173 E3] (*99 Minquan Rd;* ⊕ *09.00–17.30 daily; free admission*) was built in stages between 1913 and 1934. Bureaucrats still work here, so if you want to look around inside – the grassy courtyard is attractive – you'll need to sign in with the security guard. The whitewashed frontage is the main attraction, however, and it's often used as a backdrop by local couples taking pre-wedding photos. The **Natural Ways Six Arts Cultural Centre** [173 E4] (*33 Linsen Rd;* ✆ *2375 9366;* ⊕ *09.00–17.00 Tue–Sun; free admission*) is a reconstruction of the dojo and an office which formed part of Taichung's prison between 1937 and 1992. The name alludes to the six disciplines Confucius regarded as key to a good education.

Number 2 Market 台中第二市場 [173 E3] (*Sanmin & Zhongzheng rds;* ⊕ *24hrs daily*) Clothing is the main line of business here; you can get your shoes resoled or your jacket patched and one tiny shop advertises 'handmade underwear'. There's also a 'wet' market, a section where the floor is permanently wet because butchers are cutting meat and grocers are washing vegetables. You may see a shopper buy a live chicken, have its neck wrung and then wait while it's thrown into a device like a washing machine that removes the feathers. More than a dozen food stalls, including a few that operate dusk-to-dawn, sell cheap Taiwanese dishes.

Museum of Natural Science 國立自然科學博物館 [173 D1] (*1 Guanqian Rd;* ✆ *2322 6940; www.nmns.edu.tw;* ⊕ *09.00–17.00 Tue–Sun; admission NTD100/50*) Themes explored in this high-quality and child-friendly museum go beyond straightforward geo-science and biology to embrace local spiritual life and herbal medicine. Separate tickets are sold for the 3D (*NTD100/50*) and IMAX (*NTD70/30*) cinemas; the website has details of film showings as well as current and upcoming exhibitions. The museum manages the adjacent **Botanical Garden** [173 E1] (⊕ *06.00–22.00 daily; free admission*) which covers 4.5ha and hosts 800 plant species. Allot some time for the garden's 31m-high hothouse (⊕ *09.00–17.00 Tue–Sun; admission NTD20/10*) where there's an indoors rainforest ecosystem complete with waterfall.

National Taiwan Museum of Fine Arts 國立台灣美術館 (**Guólì Táiwān Měishùguǎn**) [173 D3] (*2 Wuquan W Rd Sec 1;* ✆ *2372 3552; www.ntmofa.gov.tw;* ⊕ *09.00–17.00 Tue–Fri, 09.00–18.00 Sat–Sun; free admission except for special exhibitions*) Check the website ahead of time to see if any special exhibitions match your interests. If not, head for the third floor and the 82 visual artworks displayed there. All were executed in Taiwan or by Taiwanese artists overseas. The range of styles and materials is broad; amid the oil paintings, gouache, ink on paper and acrylic works are landscapes and abstract images. If you've already been to Kaohsiung's Lotus Pond, you'll probably find Li Ming-tse's huge (31.7m²) and mischievous depiction of it – nudes, ninjas and superheroes flit between landmarks – utterly enchanting. Visitors are welcome to borrow an English-language audio guide (*free; show ID*). Important works by Chen Cheng-po (see page 231), Li Mei-shu (see page 121) and Richard Lin (1933–2011), a minimalist who spent his most productive years in the UK, are included.

Taichung Folklore Park 台中民俗公園 (Táizhōng Mínsú Gōngyuán)

(*73 Lushun Rd Sec 2;* 2245 1310; 08.30–22.00 Tue–Sun; free admission) Featuring depictions of Taiwanese lifestyles before industrialisation, this recently renovated park contains photogenic reproductions of two 18th/19th-century buildings and the **Taiwan Folklore Museum** (*09.00–17.00 Tue–Sun*). The museum is in the basement of the four-sided courtyard building on the right and has a collection of folk artefacts which includes classy mother-of-pearl furniture, porcelain pillows, agricultural implements and a carpenter's ruler with special markings to ensure the items he makes are auspiciously proportioned. Among the religious paraphernalia on display are censers, josses and doll-sized robes and headgear used to adorn icons.

HEADING SOUTH

CHANGHUA CITY 彰化市 (ZHĀNGHUÀ SHÌ) *Telephone code 04*

Best known for the Buddha statue atop Mount Bagua, Changhua comes as a pleasant surprise to many people. There are more Qing-era relics in this city of a quarter of a million people than in nearby Taichung. It also has one of Taiwan's three most

---

THE WORLD'S BIGGEST BIRTHDAY PARTY

What's claimed to be the largest regular religious event in the world outside India begins and ends each spring in Dajia, a town of 78,000 people in the northwestern part of Taichung. To celebrate Mazu's birthday, an immense procession sets out on foot from Jenn Lann Temple 大甲鎮瀾宮 and makes its way southwards. Over the course of eight days, a palanquin bearing the shrine's revered Mazu icon is carried 300km through towns and villages, stopping to accept offerings at dozens of shrines and roadside altars on the way. When the parade reaches Fengtian Temple, 14km northwest of Chiayi City, the palanquin turns around and begins the return leg.

Up to 200,000 people attend the start of the procession and a million or more watch or join in over the following days. Many are fervent believers. Others are hoping to gain good luck, or simply want to enjoy the spectacle, which includes puppet and opera performances, dragon and lion dances, children's games and martial-arts demonstrations. Each year a handful of devotees walk the entire distance. Some people push their way through the crowd and try to touch the palanquin; every day hundreds prostrate themselves on the road ahead of the procession so the icon is carried over them. Both are ways of winning the sea goddess's blessing.

In recent years, the pilgrimage has been heavily promoted as the Taichung City Mazu International Festival.

important Confucian temples, but it's the massive seated Buddha, a relatively recent addition to the landscape, which really pulls in the tourists.

History Changhua rose to prominence in 1723 when it was made capital of one of Taiwan's three prefectures. Half a century later, Lin Shuang-wen (see *History*, page 13) launched his rebellion just north of here and proclaimed himself emperor after seizing the town.

The decisive engagement of Japan's takeover of Taiwan was fought around Mount Bagua on 27 August 1895. The Taiwanese, who had modern artillery dug in on the slopes of the hill, were unable to hold back the invaders. Two senior commanders and more than 1,000 local soldiers died in the fighting. But rather than press the advantage the Japanese paused for more than a month to regroup and await reinforcements. It proved a costly delay. September is always hot and wet; diseases, notably malaria, killed more than 2,000 Japanese. Seventy years later a mass grave containing 679 bodies – presumably Taiwanese casualties – was unearthed and turned into a memorial park.

Getting there, away and around
By TRA Almost all north–south expresses stop in Changhua. Trains to/from Taichung take less than half an hour (*NTD26–40*) with most stopping *en route* at Xinwuri (*NTD15–23*) for Taichung HSR Station. Changhua TRA Station has a baggage services office (⊕ *08.00–20.00 daily*) where you can store luggage while exploring Changhua or Lugang.

By bus Every half hour, Kuo-Kuang bus #1829 leaves Taipei West Station Terminal B for Yuanlin via Changhua (⊕ *06.00–22.00 daily; takes 3½hrs; NTD300*). Services linking Changhua with Lugang include #6909, #6933 and #6934 (*departs every 15mins;* ⊕ *06.20–22.50 daily; takes 40mins; NTD53*).

By car By Freeway 1 Changhua is 20km south of Taichung, 173km south of Taipei and 169km north of Kaohsiung. Parking in central Changhua isn't easy so consider finding a spot on Mount Bagua and walking from there.

By bicycle or motorcycle For ambitious cyclists willing to tackle some hills, Road 139 is an excellent way to approach the city from the south via Mount Bagua. To hire a motorcycle in Changhua City, try rental businesses such as **Zheng Jie** (*576 Zhongzheng Rd Sec 1;* \ *725 5052;* ⊕ *06.00–01.00 daily*) on the left as you exit the TRA station.

Tourist Information
ℹ Changhua City Government www.changhua.gov.tw
ℹ Changhua Visitor Information Centre Inside the TRA station; ⊕ 08.30–17.30 daily

ℹ Mount Bagua Visitor Information Centre Guashan Rd; ⊕ 08.30–17.30 daily

⌂ Where to stay and eat
⌂ **Taiwan Hotel** (45 rooms) 48 Zhongzheng Rd Sec 2; \ 722 4681; f 724 6474; e hoteltaiwan047@gmail.com; www.hoteltaiwan.com.tw. Thoroughly renovated since the last edition of this book, Taiwan Hotel is clean, friendly & very central. 3-person rooms can often be had for less than NTD3,000.

Cable TV, but not every room has a window. Good location if you find Changhua's nightlife dull – you can either jump on a train to Taichung or go to the cinema next door. Inc b/fast. **$$**
✕ **Ah-Chang's Meat Circles** 阿璋肉圓 **(Azhāng Ròu Yuán)** 144 Changan St; \ 722 9517;

06.00–21.00 daily. Changhua's most famous eatery is on the corner of Changan St & Chenling Rd & serves the city's best-known local delicacy, something that's often translated as 'meatballs' but which bear little resemblance to the equivalent in Italian cooking. For a start, they're not spheres so much as thick discs, so glutinous you'll need a fork to break them apart. One meat circle 肉圓 (ròu yuán, NTD35) is usually enough unless you're exceptionally hungry. Add a dash of spicy sauce & order a bowl of dragon-marrow soup 龍骨髓湯

(lónggǔ suǐ tāng, NTD35). Despite its name, this is a consommé poured over steamed egg, slivers of mushrooms & a few medicinal herbs. AC, no EM. $
✗ **Changhua Vegetarian Food 彰化素食 (Zhānghuà Sù Shí)** 117 Changan St; ☏723 6427; 07.30–20.30 daily. Good noodle dishes, tofu & fake meat. Unlike many restaurants in this price range, the interior has AC; no EM. There are lots of good, inexpensive eateries in this neighbourhood, 300m southeast of the TRA station. Changan St runs south from Guangfu Rd. $

Other practicalities
✉ **General Post Office** 130 Guangfu Rd; 08.00–21.00 Mon–Fri, 08.30–16.30 Sat, 08.30–12.00 Sun

$ **Hua Nan** 152 Guangfu Rd

What to see and do
To begin a walking tour, turn your back on the TRA station, cross the road and walk down Guangfu Road.

Dingguang Buddha Temple 定光佛寺 (*140 Guangfu Rd;* 06.00–21.00 daily) Forgive yourself if you accidentally walk past this 18th-century shrine as what faces the street resembles a run-down commercial building rather than a house of worship. Built to honour Dingguang Buddha, the 10th-century monk also sanctified at Danshui's Yinshan Temple, it's a sombre yet popular place of worship. The interior is lit by hundreds of candles; amid the gloom, you may be able to make out smoke-blackened inscribed boards conferred by the Qing emperors Jiaqing, Qianlong and Daoguang. The pious don't think of this kind of grime as dirt but as proof the resident deities have received thousands of prayers over the years. From here, stay on Guangfu Road and continue walking away from the railway station until you reach Minsheng Road. Turn right at that junction.

Yuanqing Hall 元清觀 (*207 Minsheng Rd;* 06.30–21.00 daily) On 9 April 2006 the main chamber of this 1763 temple, dedicated to the Jade Emperor, was gutted by a fire so ruinous many Changhua folk feared the shrine would lose its status as a national relic. The principal icons survived the blaze and were placed on makeshift altars so the faithful wouldn't be inconvenienced during reconstruction. Inaugurated at the beginning of 2012, the temple has several new beams and panels easily distinguishable by clean, bright colours and expert brushwork. Across the junction from the temple there's a traditional tatami-maker on the corner (*202 Minsheng Rd;* 08.00–20.00 daily). Tatamis are hard straw mattresses 7–8cm thick; the word is Japanese but has been part of the local vocabulary since the colonial era.

Confucius Temple 孔子廟 *(Kǒngzǐ Miào)* (*30 Kongmen Rd but enter from Minsheng Rd; open: 08.00–17.30 daily, closed national holidays*) The entrance to Changhua's most stately edifice is a few doors down from the tatami store. Peeling paint and faded decorations give this place an aura of genuine antiquity that's appealing yet melancholy. Founded in 1726, it was expanded in 1830, partly dismantled during the Japanese occupation and then restored to its 1830 dimensions in 1978. There's almost nothing in the way of labels or information panels, but hunt around and you should find a bilingual booklet that explains the history and meaning of every memorial tablet and architectural feature. To continue the walking tour, on leaving the Confucius Temple turn left and left again, past the main doorway which is opened only on 28 September, the sage's birthday.

Red-haired Well 紅毛井 Follow Kongmen Road east to Zhongshan Road then turn left. Within a minute or two you'll spot an off-white Japanese-era Art Deco building, **Changhua Arts Museum** 彰化美術館 (⊕ *13.30–21.00 Tue–Fri, 09.00–21.00 Sat–Sun; free admission*). Set back from the road, squeezed between the museum and a sprawling hillside grave, you'll see what's now a land-god shrine. The sealed well in front of it gets its name because it's said to have been dug in the 17th century by employees of the Dutch East India Company – in that era, Europeans were referred to as 'red-haired barbarians'. To get to Mount Bagua, backtrack a little then take the stairway behind the library to the top; it's a short but invigorating walk with plenty of shade.

Mount Bagua 八卦山 **(Bāguàshān)** This isn't much of a mountain, the peak being just 97m above sea level, but the ridge extends south for more than 30km and often you can see as far as the wind turbines that dot the coast. Named after the 'Eight Diagrams' that feature prominently in Taoist cosmology, the mountain's best-known landmark is **The Great Buddha** 八卦山大佛 (*exhibition* ⊕ *08.00–20.00 daily, surrounding park* ⊕ *24hrs daily; free admission*). Up close it's more attractive than a simple written description – 23m high, made of concrete and painted a very dark brown – might suggest. There's paid and free parking nearby. Each spring this segment of the Tri-Mountain National Scenic Area (*www.trimt-nsa.gov.tw*) is a birdwatching location of note, thanks to migrating grey-faced buzzard-hawks (*Butastur indicus*) and other raptor species. In May and June, you can also expect to see an impressive variety of butterflies.

BEIGANG 北港 (BĚIGĂNG) *Telephone code 05*
Beigang hasn't changed much in recent decades. The town functions as a marketplace and religious centre for the surrounding countryside. The population has been shrinking since the early 1980s, and even now relatively few of the town's 42,000 people work in factories or offices. Traditional businesses that supply what conservative country folk need and desire (funerary articles, ritual items used in weddings, and huge pastries given out to friends and relatives whenever a youngster passes a major exam) form the backbone of the economy. Following a dispute over temple precedence in the late 1980s, the annual Dajia Mazu parade (see box, page 175) no longer stops off in Beigang. But even without the parade, worship of the sea goddess remains a major industry, and the 300-year-old Chaotian Temple is one of Taiwan's busiest.

Among Beigang's founders were buccaneers, rebels and lowland aborigines. Lin Daoqian, a pirate leader who later achieved notoriety in southeast Asia, is said to have dropped anchor here in 1563. More than half a century later, Yan Siqi arrived leading 13 ships. A Chinese trader who had moved to Japan in 1613, Yan was forced to leave his adopted home because of his involvement in an armed struggle against the shogun. After his group had established itself at Beigang, emissaries were sent to Fujian to recruit more settlers. Nowadays Yan is celebrated as a pioneer of Han settlement in Taiwan; an obelisk honouring him stands in centre of Beigang.

By the second half of the 18th century Beigang had grown into a town worth fighting over. Lin Shuang-wen's attempt to seize Beigang failed (see *History*, page 13); another band of rebels was seen off in 1862. Since then things have been quiet, save for market days when farmers come to trade peanuts, garlic and sesame oil – and the drums, gongs and firecrackers that accompany religious celebrations. Now a good 20km from the sea, Beigang's name ('north harbour') alludes to the fact that, well into the 19th century, ocean-going vessels sailed this far inland before disgorging their passengers and cargo. Before the Japanese occupation, the town had a slightly different name: Bengang. The literal meaning is 'stupid harbour', but most likely it's derived from the old aboriginal place name, Ponkan.

Getting there and away

By bus Several services link Chiayi City with the town (see *Getting there and away*, page 231); get off as soon as the bus crosses the Beigang River. From the north, service #9015 connects Beigang with Taichung (*departs every 30mins ⊕ 06.05–21.40; takes 2½hrs; NTD230*).

By car or motorcycle Take Highway 19 from north or south. There's paid parking between where Highway 19 crosses the Beigang River and the red pedestrian bridge.

Tourist information The visitor information centre (*6 Zhongshan Rd; ⊕ 09.00–17.00 daily*) is above the post office.

What to see and do Everything you'll want to see lies within the old riverside neighbourhood and small bilingual signs on street corners will help you navigate. If you've arrived on a bus from Chiayi, it makes sense to visit the Militia Shrine first.

Militia Shrine aka Yimin Temple 義民廟 (*20 Jingyi St; ⊕ 07.00–21.00 daily*)
This shrine exists to venerate militiamen who died fighting Lin Shuang-wen and one singularly brave dog. Inside there are delicate engravings of owls plus ornate plaques presented by visiting worthies to commemorate the martyrs. The militiamen themselves are interred in concrete-covered mass graves beside the temple's main chamber. The dog, which is credited with foiling several night-time sneak attacks by Lin's forces before it was poisoned by an enemy infiltrator, lies in a separate tomb that's big enough for three humans. This grave is at the back of the building, and in the chamber to the left there's an engraved stone tablet praising the 'righteous dog general'. Nearby, inside a plastic case atop an altar, a statue of a small dog (wearing an embroidered cape, much like deities of human origin) waits for offerings. Oddly, these usually consist of crackers, fruit or other kinds of food living dogs don't enjoy. If you visit the temple on the 30th day of the fifth lunar month, you'll see rites to honour the human martyrs. A bilingual information panel in front of the temple provides some background, but makes no mention of the dog.

Chaotian Temple 朝天宮 (*Cháotiān Gōng*) (*⊕ 04.30–24.00 daily*) Here you'll find everything you'd expect to see in a major Mazu temple – icons historic and revered, crowds of worshippers, clouds of incense smoke and curiosities like an iron nail embedded in a stone step. The nail would be very easy to miss were it not for the dab of faded red paint that surrounds it and the railings that cordon off this section of steps. It remains firmly lodged precisely where it was hammered, more than 200 years ago, by 'a filial son surnamed Xiao, a native of Quanzhou in Fujian province'. Xiao, a Chinese-language plaque continues, was desperate to know if his parents had survived a voyage across the Taiwan Strait. He asked Mazu to prove to him that they hadn't perished. When the soft nail penetrated the stone, Xiao took that as a sign his mother and father were still alive – which in fact they were.

Mingli Buddha Shop (*47 Zhongshan Rd;* ⏰ *approx 09.00–18.00 daily*) One of the few non-food businesses on Zhongshan Road, this is both a workshop where Buddha and folk-god effigies are carved by the friendly Mr Tsai and a store dealing in secondhand/antique religious items and souvenirs.

Jhengsing Theatre 振興戲院 (*42 Zhongshan Rd;* ⏰ *08.00–21.00 daily*) Zhongshan Road links Chaotian Temple and Beigang's pedestrian bridge. In addition to being a good place to find lunch, it's chock-full of shops which sell pastries, sesame oil, peanut concoctions and deep-fried broad beans. Now home to a biscuit-and-candies business, the building at number 42 is still widely known by the name it bore when it was a cinema. Films were shown here until the 1960s and tourists are free to wander around the small auditorium at the back and the rooms upstairs where antique furniture is on display.

LUGANG 鹿港 (LÙGǍNG) *Telephone code 04*

Touristy yet crammed to the gills with genuine culture and antiquity, Lugang (often spelled 'Lukang') is rightfully one of Taiwan's most popular lowland destinations. It's hard to believe now but, from the mid-18th century to the last quarter of the 19th century, this out-of-the-way town (population now 85,000) was Taiwan's second largest city. In that era, Tainan and Lugang were like Taipei and Kaohsiung now – the former focused on politics and government, the latter obsessed with commerce. While not quite frozen in time, Lugang has preserved enough of its physical past to make it a worth an entire day. The town is easy to reach by bus and almost every sight is within walking distance of the core.

HISTORY The characters *lù* and *gǎng* together mean 'deer harbour' and the most often given explanation of this town's name is that it was a place where the indigenous Babuza people hunted for deer. However, some think Lugang is a corruption of the aboriginal place name, Rokau-an. Lugang already had a well-established Han population in 1685, the year Qing authorities began posting coastguards at the mouth of the Lugang river to combat piracy and smuggling.

The settlement enjoyed rapid growth after the completion in 1719 of a huge privately financed irrigation system in the town's hinterland. Rice production rose dramatically and Lugang's merchants began shipping the surplus to Fujian. Soon more than 3,500 ships were using the port each year. The harbour here was never very good – larger sailing ships could enter only at high tide and it was inaccessible to the steamers which replaced them – but it was the best in central Taiwan. Donald R DeGlopper, an American anthropologist who did fieldwork in Lugang, describes a bustling commercial centre:

> Lugang's prosperity and indeed its very existence depended on a trading system that exchanged the rice, sugar and fibre (hemp, ramie) of central Taiwan for the cloth, crockery and other manufactured goods of southern Fujian... During the 19th century Lugang was a city of wholesalers and middlemen, with many large firms devoted to trade in rice, sugar, cloth, timber, pottery, fish and other commodities. Oxcarts and gangs of porters moved through its narrow streets and hundreds of workers loaded and unloaded the bamboo rafts and small boats that were rowed or poled into its shallow inner harbour. The merchants lived in solid, multi-storey houses, the very bricks and tiles of which had been imported from Fujian.
>
> Donald R DeGlopper, *Lukang: A City and Its Trading System*

LUGANG FOLK AND THEIR MUSLIM ANCESTORS

The Muslim cemetery is long gone and it's extremely unlikely you'll see anyone wearing a burqa, but a number of Lugang's most eminent families, among them the original owners of the Ding Mansion (see page 186), were of Muslim origin. Their ancestors arrived in the 17th and 18th centuries from Quanzhou in Fujian, where Arab and Persian merchants had been living for centuries before the opening of Taiwan.

Many were already partly assimilated into Han society before reaching Taiwan where, isolated from the large Muslim communities on the Chinese coast, they gradually lost their traditions. However, a few households still possess Korans which they can't read, but which they recognise as sacred. It's said they wash those who've just died in an Islamic manner and wrap the deceased in simple white shrouds, rather than the multiple layers of clothing decreed by Han custom. Moreover, when making offerings to their ancestors, they purposely exclude pork. Aware that their house of worship stands where there was once a mosque, this taboo is also observed by some of those who make offerings at Xincuo Changan Temple, a small folk shrine 5km north of the Queen of Heaven Temple.

So many Fujianese lived in Lugang that locals nicknamed it Little Quanzhou. Business and politics were dominated by eight *jiāo*, groupings somewhat like medieval European guilds. One consisted of merchants who imported stone, wood and silk from Quanzhou; another comprised those who exported rice and sugar to, and imported timber from, the Kinmen archipelago and the Fujian towns of Xiamen and Zhangzhou. A third guild imported salted fish products from Guangdong and Penghu; the others focused on peanut and sesame oil, cloth, dye, sugar and groceries. Produce from Taiwan's interior reached Lugang by oxcart or on the backs of porters.

The shape-shifting nature of Taiwan's coastline caused serious problems. In 1717, the harbour was narrow and choked with silt, but by 1740 it had become broad and deep again. The town's fortunes began to decline precipitously before the 19th century ended, partly as a result of sediment blocking the port but also because the growth of Taiwan's population left little surplus rice to export. The Japanese colonial regime reorganised the island's economy to meet the needs of its new masters. Trading links with Fujian were disrupted; roads and trains replaced coastal shipping as the principal means of moving goods from one part of Taiwan to another. Many of the town's entrepreneurs packed their bags for Taipei and other arriviste settlements.

One of Lugang's most interesting customs died out before World War II but DeGlopper was able to interview some who had participated:

The men of Lugang would gather every year on one day in the early spring, line up by surname, and throw rocks at their fellows of other surnames. They were thus throwing rocks at and dodging rocks thrown by men who were in other contexts their in-laws, mother's brothers, business partners, old school friends [etc]… The rock fight was a festive public occasion; women and children watched and cheered; vendors sold snacks. Blood was shed and teeth lost, but… no one was ever killed. [Some people said] folks back then had different thoughts and believed that if blood was not shed in the spring, then the community might suffer bad luck during the coming year.

Donald R DeGlopper, *Blood, Luck and Clanship:
The Annual Rockfight at Lukang, Taiwan*

GETTING THERE AND AWAY

By car Expressway 76 links Lugang with both north–south freeways and Expressway 61. Driving around the town itself isn't advisable as the streets are narrow and often packed with pilgrims and vendors, but finding a free parking space near the Queen of Heaven Temple or Wenkai Academy usually isn't difficult.

By motorcycle or bicycle Highway 17, which approaches Lugang from both north and south, is flat and takes you through typical lowland scenery.

By bus Ubus service #1652 leaves Taipei Bus Station at least seven times per day for Lugang (⊕ 08.20–20.20; takes 3½hrs; NTD350). Plenty of services link Changhua City with central Lugang including #6909, #6933 and #6934 (*departs every 15mins;* ⊕ *06.20–22.50 daily; takes 40mins; NTD53).* The Taiwan Tourist Shuttle Bus Lukang Route (*departs from Taichung HSR Station 5 times per day* ⊕ *10.00–18.00 Mon–Fri, departs every hour on the hour* ⊕ *09.00–18.00 Sat–Sun*) covers some of Changhua City's sights and terminates at Taiwan Glass Gallery near Husheng Temple (see page 187). A timetable, list of stops and fare details are at www.taiwantrip.com.tw.

GETTING AROUND With the exception of Husheng Temple all sights can be reached on foot. Bicycles can be borrowed (*free but buy a souvenir to show your appreciation*) from the visitor centres. The Presbyterian Church manages what it calls a 'tourism tricycle' service (☎ 776 2567; ⊕ 09.00–18.00 daily). The usual charge for two passengers to be brought to eight tourist spots is NTD600. Don't expect an English-speaking driver.

TOURIST INFORMATION

☑ Lugang Township Government www.lukang.gov.tw
☑ North Area Visitor Centre 488 Fuxing Rd; ⊕ 10.00–18.00 daily

☑ South Area Visitor Centre 110 Changlu Rd Sec 8; ⊕ 09.00–17.00 daily

LOCAL TOUR OPERATOR

Yuyun Lin m 0932 680 147; e meilkbnb@gmail.com. This English-speaking guide (also owner of LK Bed & Breakfast) does 3-hr tours for NTD2,000.

🏠 **WHERE TO STAY** Both of the following hotels are shown on the map opposite.

🏠 **LK Bed & Breakfast** (14 rooms) 46 Chunhui St; ☎777 4446; m 0932 680 147; e meilkbnb@gmail.com; www.lkbnb.com.tw. This 6-storey building was Lugang's tallest when it was built in 1976 as an industrialist's wedding gift to his son. The latter's sister, Yuyun Lin, has turned the house into a tasteful homestay with wooden floors, sparkling bathrooms & a wonderful roof space where guests can enjoy late afternoon breezes. Rooms for 2, 3, 4 or 6 ppl. Check out the 1950s-meets-1980s upstairs living room. Spacious garden & free car parking. Free bike loan & b/fast inc. **$$$**

🏠 **Quanzhong Hotel** 全忠旅社 (10 rooms) 104 Zhongshan Rd; ☎777 2640. An old budget establishment but the owners keep it clean & the location is excellent. All rooms have en-suite bathrooms & cable TV. No English sign. **$**

✖ **WHERE TO EAT** Lugang doesn't have many proper restaurants worth investigating but it does have dozens of intriguing food stalls and hole-in-the-wall eateries.

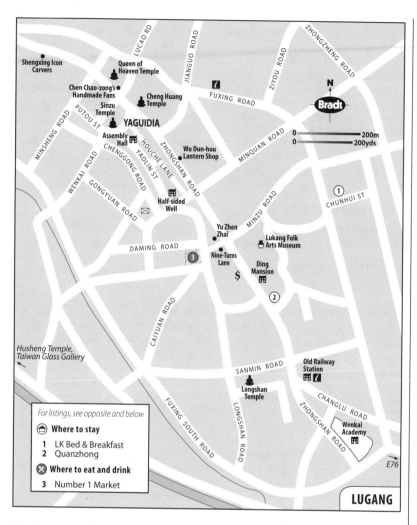

For listings, see opposite and below

🏠 **Where to stay**

1 LK Bed & Breakfast
2 Quanzhong

❌ **Where to eat and drink**

3 Number 1 Market

LUGANG

The hungry and the intrepid should head for the **Number 1 Market** 第一市場 where there are plenty of hot traditional foods from dawn until dusk every day. For snacks like oyster omelettes, hunt around the front of the Queen of Heaven Temple. There you'll also find several vendors hawking one of Lugang's best-known specialities, called 'cow's tongue' 牛舌餅 (*niú shé bǐng*). It's actually a flat sweetbread stuffed with a sugary paste and sprinkled with sesame seeds. If you'd like to try one before committing yourself to a whole packet, several shops sell individual biscuits (*NTD10*).

SHOPPING

Shengxing Icon Carvers 勝興神像雕刻社

517 Zhongshan Rd; ⏰ 08.30–19.30 daily. The area around the Queen of Heaven Temple is thick with woodcarvers, lantern-makers, tinsmiths & other craftsmen. Of the 65-plus workshops in central

Lugang, at least a dozen were founded or are still run by artisans who've won national prizes. The pious come here from all over southern & central Taiwan to commission josses. Shengxing Icon Carvers is a fairly typical business in that it caters to the genuinely religious, not tourists. There's not much to see save some unpainted samples in the window.

Chen Chao-zong's Handmade Fans 陳朝宗手工扇 400-1 Zhongshan Rd; ☎777 5629; ⏰ 08.00–17.00 daily. Mr Chen has been making & hand-painting fans like those favoured by the ladies of yesteryear for decades; prices start at NTD400.

Wu Dun-hou Lantern Shop 吳敦厚燈鋪 312 Zhongshan Rd; ☎777 6680; ⏰ 09.00–12.00 & 14.00–22.00 daily. This shop showcases the hand-painted bamboo-framed paper lanterns which have earned the eponymous Mr Wu (b1925) an international reputation. Aleksandr Solzhenitsyn & Lady Gaga are among those who've left Taiwan with one of his lanterns in their luggage. These days, the award-winning artisan seldom visits his shop but you've a good chance of seeing someone he trained putting the finishing touches to a lantern.

Yu Zhen Zhai 168 Minzu Rd; ☎777 3672; ⏰ 08.00–22.30 daily. Lugang's best-known bakery sells traditional pastries in colourful presentation boxes. Flavours include pineapple, mung bean, vanilla, chocolate & sesame. Prices start at NTD80.

OTHER PRACTICALITIES

✉ **General post office** 1 Chenggong Rd; ⏰ 08.00–17.30 Mon–Fri; 08.30–12.00 Sat–Sun

$ **Changhwa Bank** 137 Zhongshan Rd

WHAT TO SEE AND DO Lugang has plenty of bilingual signs so finding your way around isn't difficult.

Queen of Heaven Temple 天后宮 (Tiānhòu Gōng) (⏰ 06.00–22.00 daily) Like

other super-popular shrines, this temple – which some English signs refer to as 'Tien-hou Temple' – isn't a place for the nervous of disposition. It's riotously lively at weekends; the temple's mechanised drums are extremely loud and pilgrims set off strings of firecrackers in the forecourt. A second or two after each outburst, you'll see a mini-mushroom cloud rising skyward. Don't let the people or noise distract you, and remember to look up as you enter – there are some splendid woodcarvings above the doors. The shop near the back of the complex sells a range of practical Mazu-themed souvenirs including T-shirts, mugs and baseball caps. The claim often made that this temple was established in 1590 isn't quite accurate. Lugang residents were certainly worshipping Mazu at that time, but it was another half-century before any kind of permanent structure appeared. The temple's small, black-faced Mazu icon is especially valued as it's said to have been brought to Taiwan by Shi Lang (see *History*, page 13). At weekends the stretch of Zhongshan Road nearest the temple becomes an open-air market. Vendors sell amulets, CDs of Buddhist chanting and bronze statuettes of figures from Chinese mythology, as well as basic groceries like vegetables.

Cheng Huang Temple 城隍廟 (366 Zhongshan Rd; ⏰ 06.00–21.00 daily) Locals

come to this ornate shrine for various reasons, one being that the city god and other resident deities are said to be exceptionally good at resolving cases of theft. One of their greatest successes was the recovery of valuable proprietary items lost by a major Taiwanese computer company. The stone lions just outside the temple, you'll notice, are secured to the pavement by welded iron bars. According to temple staff, this is because they're 'valuable relics, many hundreds of years old', and liable to be stolen. The town god may be a superb detective, it seems, but he isn't much of a security guard.

Across the street from the temple there used to be a small plaza called **Yaguidia**, which in Taiwanese means 'courtyard of the hungry ghosts'. The name didn't come about because of any supernatural activity. Rather, it's where at the end of long voyages sailors and fishermen would come to enjoy their first proper meal in days.

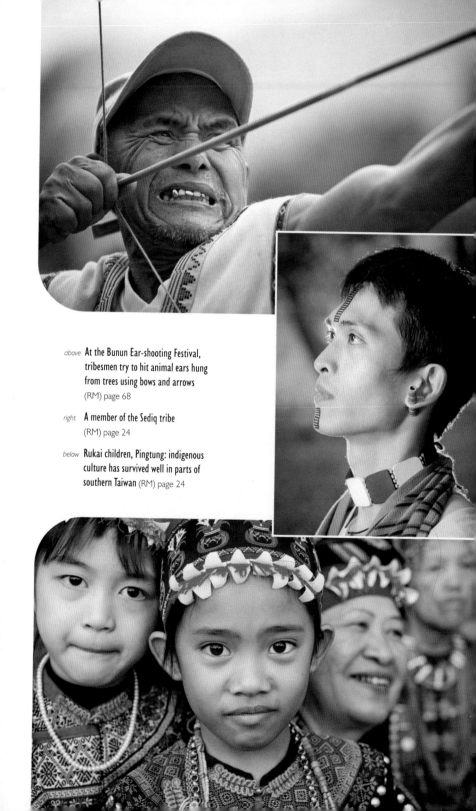

above At the Bunun Ear-shooting Festival, tribesmen try to hit animal ears hung from trees using bows and arrows (RM) page 68

right A member of the Sediq tribe (RM) page 24

below Rukai children, Pingtung: indigenous culture has survived well in parts of southern Taiwan (RM) page 24

above   Meinong is renowned for its painted oil-paper parasols (TTB) page 262

left   Taiwanese opera performances typically feature bright make-up and costumes, traditional instruments and symbolic gestures (CF) page 127

below   Guan Gong is one of the most important deities in Chinese religion, and is revered by police officers, businesspeople and gangsters alike (RM) page 33

bottom   Foguangshan is Taiwan's leading monastery and runs a TV station, several publishing houses and a children's home (RM) page 256

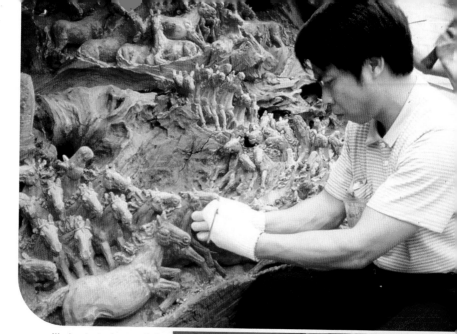

above Woodcarving has been practised in Sanyi since the Japanese colonial period (TTB) page 162

right Yingge has long been the country's foremost producer of ceramics; these days the town's output is decorative rather than practical (TTB) page 120

below The annual Beehive Fireworks Festival, Yanshui, takes the Taiwanese love of explosions to new extremes, with tens of thousands of rockets let off in every direction (RM) page 229

above left   Eternal Spring Shrine is precariously positioned near the bottom of the vertiginous Taroko Gorge (TTB) page 290

above right   Further into Taroko Gorge, Wenshan Hot Springs have a backdrop of beautiful striated rock (RM) page 292

below   Alishan Forest Railway, a century old, is one of the highest in the world (TTB) page 235

right   Caoshan Moonscape World is a uniquely desolate area of badlands; in certain lights the eroded hillocks and steep ravines look truly lunar (RM) page 224

below left   Set amid mountains, its shores punctuated by temples, Sun Moon Lake is popular for bike rides and boat trips (CF) page 190

below right   Mount Jade is the country's highest peak and a favourite with mountaineers (TTB) page 204

bottom   All but one of Penghu County's 90 islands were formed by volcanic activity, and they feature striking basalt columns (TTB) page 310

left   Today Guishan Island is a haven for lizards, birds and plants, and accessible only to limited numbers of ecotourists (TTB) page 129

below left & right   Yehliu Geopark is a natural wonderland, with an array of curious rock formations (including the Queen's Head) caused by wind and wave erosion (NB/FLPA and TTB) page 138

bottom   Xinbeitou, on Taipei's outskirts, is a geothermal hotspot and best explored on foot or by bike (CF) page 110

Taiwan is a haven for birdwatchers, with over 25 endemic avian species.

above Greater painted snipe (*Rostratula benghalensis*) (TTB)

above right Black-browed barbet (*Megalaima oorti*) (RM)

right Steere's babbler (*Liocichla steerii*) (TTB)

below left Malayan night heron (*Gorsachius melanolophus*) (NB/FLPA)

below right Taiwan blue magpie (*Urocissa caerulea*) (NB/FLPA)

The Heart of Cycling

Ready to roll

From exhilarating peaks and lush valleys to perfect lakes, Taiwan offers cyclists some of the world's most spectacular scenery for two-wheeled discovery, all accessible on hundreds of miles of smooth road, protected cycle trails and off-road routes. For relaxed riders or athletic adventurers, there's no better place to explore pristine nature and breathtaking vistas – there are even bike-friendly hotels and restaurants where bikers can pause for refreshment, all while enjoying the nation's famously warm welcome and fabulous food.

Taroko Gorge
Hundreds of feet above water, this gorge crossing is just one of the thrilling moments cycling through Taroko National Park.

www.taiwan.net.tw

The seafarers ate with such gusto locals nicknamed them 'hungry ghosts'. There's nothing to be seen nowadays but a Chinese-language information board.

Lugang's old streets Putou and Yaolin streets, along with several nearby lanes, have never been widened for cars. During Lugang's heyday, many of the town's shipping agents and merchants lived hereabouts. Several of the homes are now souvenir shops but what must have been one of the most imposing mansions is uninhabited and crumbling at 8 Houche Lane. Hoping their sons would be as academically successful as the man who built Ding Mansion (see page 186), the first few generations living at 8 Yaolin Street would order the youngsters to take their books and brushes to the attic, then remove the ladder that provided the only access. One of Lugang's most popular photo opportunities is **Half-Sided Well 半邊井** (*12 Yaolin St*). In the 18th and 19th centuries, it wasn't unusual for rich households to dig private wells; the family here wanted the convenience of a water source near their front door but were public-spirited enough to have it straddle the boundary of their land so neighbours could also draw water.

Sinzu Temple 新祖宮 (*96 Putou St;* ⏱ *07.00–20.00 daily*) Also known as the Official Queen of Heaven Temple, this shrine's name doesn't imply that the main Queen of Heaven Temple is illegitimate or that the Mazu worshipped there is an impostor. Instead, it reflects the official shrine's unique background. It's the only Mazu temple in Taiwan founded by order of the authorities, the edict being issued by the imperial court in 1788 because the general who crushed Lin Shuang-wen's revolt (see *History*, page 13) believed Mazu had aided his campaign. For several decades only government officials could worship here but it was later opened to the public.

Assembly Hall 公會堂 (*74 Putou St;* ⏱ *09.00–17.30 daily*) This 1928 landmark is a whitewashed anomaly amid the neighbourhood's red and brown bricks. Local artists' works are sold inside.

Zhongshan Road's traditional shops Once called 'See-No-Sky Street' because it was so narrow and shops' awnings blocked the sunlight, Zhongshan Road was widened during the colonial era. There are several well-preserved Japanese-era shops with Art Deco features, the most impressive of which is Yu Zhen Zhai's three-storey flagship store (see opposite) on the corner of Minzu Road. The shop at number 232 sells fishing nets of all sizes and types. At number 196 there's a traditional pharmacy but the proprietor doesn't allow photography. Even more special is the rumpled hardware store at number 149. Step inside and look up; you'll see stairs and beams that haven't been replaced in the building's near-200 years of existence. When it was new, seawater was less than 100m away. The ocean is now about 3km away.

Lukang Folk Arts Museum 鹿港民俗文物館 (*Access via Lane 74, Zhongshan Rd;* ☎ *777 2019; www.lukangarts.org.tw;* ⏱ *09.00–17.00 daily; admission NTD130/70*) This museum is housed in a beautiful Baroque mansion built 1913–19 for the Koo family. Major landowners during the Japanese era, the Koos branched out into cement and other industries after World War II and remain one of Taiwan's most important business clans. In 1973 the family donated the house and many of the 6,000 items inside to establish the museum. There are books, documents, portraits, musical instruments, antique pieces of furniture and traditional garments. There's plenty of English inside and while the museum is certainly worthwhile, it's been criticised for presenting a version of Taiwan's history that stresses migration from China while neglecting indigenous, Japanese and other influences.

Nine-Turns Lane 九曲巷 This backstreet, which doesn't merit more than a quick look, can be accessed from near the Number 1 Market; the entrance is on the right of the florist's at 163 Minzu Road. It's said the curves and sharp corners were intended to block harsh, sand-bearing winter winds. But there's an unintended and unpleasant consequence: in summertime it's often stifling.

Ding Mansion 丁家古厝 (*132 Zhongshan Rd; free admission; ⊕ 09.00–17.00 Tue–Sun*) The façade is 1920s but behind it stands a sensitively restored residence built in the 1880s by Ding Shou-quan, who'd just passed the highest level of China's imperial civil-service examinations to become a *jinshi* ('presented scholar'). The red and gold tablet high above the doorway to the central chamber bears those two characters, symbolising the status he'd achieved. The mansion is just 4.5m wide but 77m deep; there are three courtyards and a back door that leads to the entrance of Lugang Folk Arts Museum.

Old Railway Station (*110 Changlu Rd Sec 8; ⊕ 09.00–17.00 daily*) It's often said that Lugang's great and good lobbied against a rail connection early in the colonial period and so condemned the town to backwater status. However, no-one seems to have objected in 1911 when a Japanese-owned sugar company laid narrow-gauge tracks and built a station within 150m of one of the town's holiest sites, Longshan Temple. After World War II, Taiwan Sugar Corporation (see box, page 20) operated passenger services from this point. The building stood empty between the 1970s and 2011, when it was revamped as a visitor centre and tourist attraction; children will enjoy clambering over the preserved locomotive. There's free parking here plus bike racks.

Longshan Temple 龍山寺 (Lóngshān Sì) (*⊕ 05.30–21.30 daily*) Undoubtedly one of Taiwan's most inspiring places of worship and probably the oldest Buddhist shrine on the island, Longshan Temple (founded 600m north of its current location in 1653) is a splendid example of traditional religious architecture. Like the finest European cathedrals, construction took generations. Despite serious earthquake damage in 1795, 1848 and 1999, the temple retains a tremendous sense of antiquity as well as considerable beauty.

The original seated Guanyin icon was over 1,200 years old when it was destroyed in a fire in 1921. Its replacement, now in the main hall, was for years relegated to a side chamber at the behest of Japanese Buddhists backed by the colonial authorities. The complex boasts 99 doorways of all shapes yet its most famous feature is neither a portal nor an effigy, but rather a sublime octagonal ceiling in the front pavilion. Designed to fool malign spirits into thinking the temple is in fact underwater (and thus impervious to arson), a mass of carved and painted wood converges on the whiskery face of a dragon. Do also pay attention to the temple's windows – several, especially those at the front, are wooden screens of exceptional delicacy and embellishment.

Wenkai Academy 文開書院 (Wénkāi Shūyuàn) (*⊕ 09.00–17.30 daily; free admission*) Whether it's the starting point of your tour or the final sight, this educational-religious complex deserves to be taken in slowly. There's little in the way of labelling so you won't learn much but it's a delightful place to linger and much loved by photographers. The academy was established in 1827 to prepare students for imperial civil-service examinations, success in which brought tremendous prestige for candidates' families.

Husheng Temple 護聖宮 (Hùshèng Gōng) (30 Lugong S 4th Rd; ☏ 781 1299; ⊕ 08.00–18.00 daily; free admission) Jaded tourist sit up: this is no McTemple. Built 2007–12 using over 70,000 pieces of coloured glass, this house of worship cost Taiwan's leading glass-maker more than £1.5m but has generated massive publicity. And rightfully so, you'll agree, if you visit around dusk when LEDs illuminate the translucent walls. Inside, the stunning image of Mount Jade (consisting of over 1,400 glass pieces) is a highlight.

The temple is located in an industrial zone 7km from central Lugang, next to **Taiwan Glass Gallery** (⊕ 08.00–18.00 daily; free admission). The latter is worth a quick look and sells appealing if fragile souvenirs.

HEADING INLAND

9-21 EARTHQUAKE MUSEUM 九二一地震教育園區 (JIŬÈRYĪ DÌZHÈN JIÀOYÙ YUÁNQŪ) (46 Zhongzheng Rd, Wufeng, Taichung; ☏ 04 2339 0906; www.921emt. edu.tw; ⊕ 09.00–17.00 Tue–Sun; admission NTD50/30, free before 10.00 Wed) This museum, a good stop on the road between Taichung and Sun Moon Lake, was built on the site of a high school campus wrecked by the strongest tremor to strike Taiwan in the 20th century (see History, page 21). The quake left the school's running track corrugated with ridges which made for one of the disaster's most enduring images. These, together with several devastated classrooms, have been preserved as part of an engrossing yet sobering exhibition. There's a great deal of information about why and how earthquakes occur, as well as specific details of the 1999 disaster. If you've never felt a temblor, head for the Quake Experience Theatre. Kids will enjoy the 3D film presentations.

Getting there The nearest freeway interchange is Wufeng at km211 on Freeway 3. Turn right on to Highway 3 and proceed to km197 where you'll see signs to the museum. Several buses from central Taichung stop nearby, the most convenient from Taichung TRA Station being #50 (departs every 10–15mins; takes 40mins; NTD35) which terminates right outside the museum.

JIJI BRANCH RAILWAY 集集線火車 Telephone code 04 or 049
This 29.7km-long branch line was built in 1920 to transport materials and machinery for hydro-electric plants into the interior, and to carry sugar and timber out to the lowlands. A long-established tourist attraction, the branch railway veers inland from the main north–south line at Ershui and follows the course of Taiwan's longest river, the Zhuoshui (literally, 'turbid water'). Jiji, the town served by the fourth of the line's six stops, has been rebuilt since 1999's earthquake, but not entirely – one of its most memorable attractions is the semi-collapsed Wuchang Temple. On the edge of town, the Endemic Species Research Institute is a must for ecotourists.

Even if you're too lazy to get off the train and explore, you'll find the railway journey an agreeable way to spend a few hours. In addition to mountain and river views, you'll catch sight of farms and forests before arriving at the ex-logging village of Checheng. The railway can be done as a day trip from Taichung or Chiayi. Note there's nowhere to change money along the line.

6

Getting there, away and around

By TRA Ershui 二水 is well served by mainline services. Expresses to/from Taipei take three to four hours (*NTD376–487*); to/from Kaohsiung is under three hours (*NTD275*). Trains from Taichung take less than an hour (*NTD72–87*). Ershui has a baggage office (⏰ *08.00–20.00*). On the branch railway there are 13 services in each direction daily between Ershui and Checheng (*departing from Ershui* ⏰ *04.56–21.35*), several of which set out from Taichung and also serve Taichung HSR Station. Ershui–Checheng takes under an hour. A one-way ticket costs NTD44; a one-day jump on/jump off pass for the branch line is NTD80.

By bus #6333 links Taichung with Shuili (*departs every 15mins;* ⏰ *05.00–22.00 daily; takes 1¼hrs; NTD150*), stopping right outside the the the Endemic Species Research Institute in Jiji (*NTD130*) *en route*. From Shuili's bus stops on Minquan Road – turn left if you're coming from the TRA stop – there are infrequent local buses to Sun Moon Lake, Puli and Dongpu.

By car or motorcycle Drivers in a hurry should take Freeway 3 to the Mingjian exit at km236, then Highway 16. Motorcyclists are spoiled for choice as the region has several attractive roads including 131 and 139.

By hired bicycle There's one rental business (*NTD50/hr or NTD100/day;* ⏰ *08.00–18.00 daily*) right outside Ershui TRA Station and at least four between Jiji TRA Station (*bicycles NTD100/day, electric scooters NTD350/day*) and the town's visitor information centre.

Tourist information The website of Tri-Mountain National Scenic Area (*www. trimt-nsa.gov.tw*) has information about Ershui and around under the 'Baguashan Scenic Area' heading; click on 'Songboling Recreational Area'. There are information centres in Ershui (*TRA station;* ⏰ *09.00–17.00 Mon–Fri, 08.00–17.00 Sat–Sun & national holidays*), Jiji (*100m from the TRA station; walk straight down Minsheng Rd;* ⏰ *09.00–17.00 daily*) and Checheng (*next to the log pond;* ⏰ *09.00–17.00 Mon–Fri, 09.00–17.30 Sat–Sun & national holidays*).

⌂ Where to stay

⌂ **Mountain Fish Water Boutique Hotel**
(29 rooms) 205 Chenggong Rd, Jiji; ☏049 276 1000; f 049 276 4767; e mfw0492761000@ hotmail.com; www.mfwhotel.com.tw. This modern hotel is a good deal, having chic rooms with good views over the valley & midweek rates sometimes below NTD2,300. Those on the 6th flr (1 is for 8 ppl, the other for 6) also boast high ceilings, 180-degree-panorama windows & massive square bathtubs. The website lacks English but if you call, email or show up unannounced you'll have no communication problems. To find this hotel, leave the TRA station, pass the information centre & keep going until you see a swimming pool on your left (which guests can use) & a high school straight ahead. Turn left & you'll see it; it isn't far. B/fast inc. **$$$**

⌂ **My Cafe House** 我的咖啡屋民宿
(13 rooms) 206 Wenhua St, Jiji; ☏049 276 0934; e mycafehouse@yahoo.com.tw. This slickly run but monolingual homestay offers large rooms (inc 1 taking up to 9 ppl) within walking distance of Jiji TRA Station. Putting a third person in a normal suite costs NTD400. Wi-Fi throughout, b/fast inc. Meals & hot drinks available to non-guests. Get a Chinese-speaker to help you book. To find My Cafe House, walk past Jiji's visitor information centre & cross the stream. On the left, look out for signs bearing the phone number. **$$$**
⌂ **Chun Feng Homestay** 春風民宿 (6 rooms) Longquan; ☏049 278 1392; f 049 278 1731. Less than 50m from Longquan TRA Station if you're walking away from the main road, Chun Feng is fairly basic but has important advantages: good

prices, a spacious balcony from which you can gaze at the hills & a small back garden filled with caged birds & driftwood sculptures. Only one room has its own bathroom. The 7-person room functions as a dormitory (*NTD350 pp*). Guests are welcome to use the refrigerator in the hall. On w/days solo travellers can get a room for as little as NTD800. **$$**

✖ Where to eat
Plenty of snack vendors and small eateries can be found close to Ershui and Jiji TRA stations.

✖ **A-Xia Beef Noodles** 阿霞牛肉麵 **(Axiá Niú Ròu Miàn)** Longquan; ☎049 278 1320; ⏰ 11.00–14.00 & 16.00–21.00 Sun–Fri. Locals speak reverently of this externally nondescript eatery, which is just across the railroad from the main road in Longquan, & you'll notice appetising aromas the moment you step inside. The Chinese-only menu lists wonton soup, steamed dumplings & other dishes in addition to beef noodles. **$**

🍦 **Blue Cloud Ice Shop** 碧雲冰城 **(Bìyún Bīng Chéng)** 130 Bazhang Rd, Jiji; ☎049 276 2957; ⏰ 07.00–19.00 daily. This prize-winning ice-lolly maker near Wuchang Temple serves up some interesting flavours inc pineapple, taro milk (*yùtóu niúnǎi bīng*) & milk with sweetcorn (*yù mǐ niú nǎi bīng*). You won't complain about the prices – the most expensive lollies are NTD12. **$**

What to see and do
There's plenty to keep you occupied around Ershui if you have your own vehicle or hire a bike. The visitor information centre beside the TRA station can provide maps and explain routes.

Shoutian Temple 受天宮 *(Shòutiān Gōng)*
(⏰ *06.00–21.00 daily*) Even if you've no interest in the Lord of the North Pole – the martial god worshipped here – or his followers, the view over the plains from this ridgetop shrine (2.4km from Ershui TRA Station as the crow flies) will likely hold your attention. Hikers, who should get directions before setting out, are almost certain to encounter macaques which are neither aggressive nor scared of humans. Driving up is also an option.

Formosan Macaque Ecosystem Education Hall 台灣獼猴生態教育館
(*km43.2 Rd 152*; ☎ *04 879 7640*; ⏰ *09.00–17.00 Tue–Sun; free admission*) To reach this hall, which has good English-language displays about Taiwan's only monkey species, you'll need to drive or cycle east from Ershui, shadowing the branch railway beyond Yuanquan TRA Station, for 7.5km. The butterfly conservation area behind the hall has pretty insects, but for real macaques you're better off heading for the hills near Shoutian Temple.

Jiji TRA Station
(⏰ *24hrs daily*) Few visitors get off at the three stops between Ershui and Jiji: Yuanquan 源泉 is attractively bucolic; Zhuoshui 濁水 is less interesting than quaint, compact Longquan 龍泉. On reaching Jiji 集集, the done thing is to take photos of the 1933 station building. It fell down in the big earthquake but was carefully reassembled using the original beams and planks, plus roof tiles salvaged from Japanese-era ruins elsewhere. If you follow Minsheng Road past the bicycle-rental businesses, you'll see the visitor information centre on your left.

Wuchang Temple 武昌宮
(*building closed to the public, grounds open* ⏰ *24hrs daily*) Much more famous now than it ever was when intact, the ground floor of this house of worship collapsed during the September 21 earthquake, but much of the rest survived intact. It's an odd and much-photographed sight. By the time you read this, a brand new edition of the temple, directly in front of the ruin, will probably have been inaugurated.

Endemic Species Research Institute 特有生物研究保育中心 *(Téyǒu Shēngwù Yánjiū Bǎoyù Zhōngxīn)* (☏ *049 2761 331; www.tesri.gov.tw*) This government-run centre is on the right if you're driving out of Jiji on the main road to Shuili. Much of it is off-limits to the public, but the **Conservation Education Centre** (☉ *09.00–16.30 Tue–Sun, closed 1–10 Jun & 1–10 Dec; admission NTD50/30*) provides an excellent introduction to Taiwan's astonishing biodiversity. Taiwan's endemic birds receive a lot of attention but rates of endemism are much higher in other parts of the biosphere. The displays describe the threats these special creatures face and what ordinary people can do to help preserve the environment. Almost everything inside is bilingual. If a criticism can be made, it's that the centre highlights conservation laws and regulations while hardly touching on the crucial issue of enforcement. The adjacent **Ecological Park** (☉ *08.30–16.30 daily; free admission*) is divided into various sections including aquatic plants, grassland, broad-leaf forest and butterfly-food plants. The fern section has more than one third of Taiwan's 560-plus fern species. Expect to see a good variety of insects and lizards.

Mingsin Academy of Classical Learning 明新書院 (☉ *08.00–20.00 daily; free admission*) Founded in 1878 and moved to its present location next to ESRI in 1908, the academy was endowed by businessmen who made fortunes from camphor. Literacy and Confucianism were among the subjects taught here. Like the train station, it was a casualty of the September 21 earthquake and had to be rebuilt. It's a pretty little complex of single-storey buildings and shrines which deserves a quick look.

Shuili 水里 *and* **Checheng** 車埕 There's little reason to stop in Shuili unless you want to board a bus. From here, Highway 21 leads north to Sun Moon Lake and south to the New Central Cross-Island Highway. Checheng is the final stop on the Jiji Branch Railway and has preserved some of its timber-handling facilities.

SUN MOON LAKE 日月潭 (RÌYUÈ TÁN) Telephone code 049

What's often but incorrectly described as Taiwan's largest natural lake (its current dimensions are a result of human engineering) falls into the 'touristy-but-pretty' category. It's a lovely place to visit but if you don't make it here, don't feel you've missed something unique.

The lake, which covers 8km², assumed its modern shape and size in the early 1930s when the Japanese colonial regime dammed the basin as part of a hydro-electricity project. Supposedly, the eastern part is round like the sun while the southern section resembles a sickle moon. The surface is 748m above sea level and the waters up to 30m deep. Rising waters forced members of the Thao, a tiny indigenous ethnic group, to leave Lalu Island in the southwestern quarter of the lake they call Zintun. This islet, which shrank further as a result of the 21

SUN MOON LAKE TICKET PACKAGES

All-in-one tickets (*NTD330 pp*) including the cable car, round-the-lake buses and tourist boat services, plus discounts on bicycle rental, were available at the time of writing. Details of these and more expensive packages extending as far afield as Alishan can be found on the scenic area's website (*www.sunmoonlake.gov.tw*).

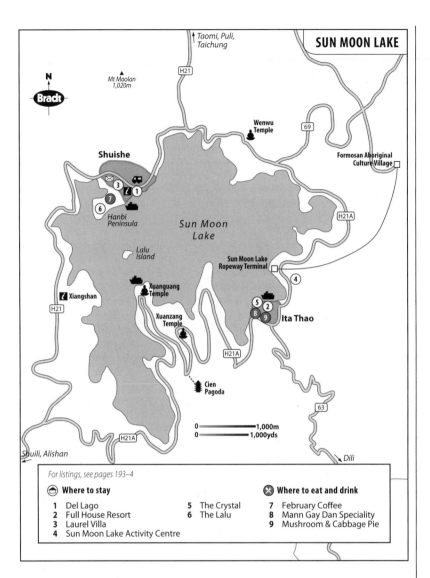

SUN MOON LAKE

Taomi, Puli, Taichung

H21

Mt Maolan
1,020m

N

Bradt

Wenwu
Temple

69

Shuishe

Formosan Aboriginal
Culture Village

3
7
1

6

Hanbi
Peninsula

H21A

Sun Moon
Lake

Lalu
Island

Sun Moon Lake
Ropeway Terminal

4

Xuanguang
Temple

Xiangshan

5 2

H21

8
9

Ita Thao

Xuanzang
Temple

H21A

Cien
Pagoda

63

0 ━━━━━ 1,000m
0 ━━━━━ 1,000yds

H21A

Shuili, Alishan

Dili

For listings, see pages 193–4

⌂ **Where to stay**

1 Del Lago
2 Full House Resort
3 Laurel Villa
4 Sun Moon Lake Activity Centre

5 The Crystal
6 The Lalu

✕ **Where to eat and drink**

7 February Coffee
8 Mann Gay Dan Speciality
9 Mushroom & Cabbage Pie

September earthquake, is where Thao people believe their ancestral spirits dwell. Nowadays the tribe's main home is Ita Thao, a settlement on the southeastern shores of the lake.

Sun Moon Lake is good to visit any time of year, but unless you're planning to take part it's best to avoid the area on the day of the annual mass cross-lake swim, usually held in late September. Swimming is prohibited at all other times.

GETTING THERE AND AWAY

By car, motorcycle or bicycle Drivers in a hurry can use Freeway 6 to Puli then Highway 21. Two-wheelers may want to avoid Highway 21 because the traffic can be heavy. A scenic but steep alternative is Road 131 from Puli then Local Road 69, which joins Highway 21A near Wenwu Temple.

By bus All buses arrive and depart from beside the visitor information centre in Shuishe. Each day Kuo-Kuang has at least six #1833 services (⏱ *07.00–17.00; takes 4hrs; NTD460*) from Taipei West Station Terminal B. From Taichung TRA Station via Taichung HSR Station, more than 20 #6670 services per day go to Sun Moon Lake via Puli (*departs* ⏱ *07.25–19.50; takes about 1½hrs; NTD217*). The Tourist Shuttle service follows a similar route (*9–11 departures daily; timetable at www.taiwantrip. com.tw; NTD190*). From Puli there's at least one #6668 service each hour (*departs* ⏱ *06.05–21.00 daily; takes 40mins; NTD62*). Leaving Sun Moon Lake, the final bus back to Taichung departs at 19.25 and to Puli at 21.30. The #6739 Sun Moon Lake–Alishan bus leaves Shuishe at 08.00 and 09.00 (*takes 3½hrs; NTD350*).

GETTING AROUND

By bus Download the timetable of the 'Lake-Surroundings Bus' (#6669) from the scenic area website or get a copy from the visitor centre. Jump on/jump off tickets are NTD80 and valid for one day (*8 buses daily Mon–Fri; 10 buses daily at w/ends and national holidays;* ⏱ *07.30–18.00*). Before each stop a multilingual announcement is made; press the bell or the driver may not stop.

BAD FOR THE BODY AND THE ENVIRONMENT

From whichever direction you approach Sun Moon Lake, you'll see hillside plantations of thin palm trees 5–6m tall. These are betel-nut trees (*Areca catechu*), though the 'nuts' are in fact dark green, walnut-sized fruit. If chewed, betel nut is a stimulant. For this reason it's popular with lorry and taxi drivers and others who work long hours. It warms the body and sometimes causes the chewer to break out in a sweat. Masticating on a nut causes the mouth to salivate. This fluid should not be swallowed; the red splotches sometimes seen on roads are betel-nut expectorations. In aboriginal cultures, betel nut has long had a ritual as well as recreational role.

Preparing the nuts for sale (each one has to be slit open, filled with lime paste and wrapped in a leaf that comes from a different kind of plant) is a major industry that employs tens of thousands of people, women mostly. Of the estimated 70,000 roadside stands around the island that sell betel nut, the ones most likely to catch your eye are those staffed by 'betel-nut beauties', skimpily dressed young women who sit in brightly lit glass cubicles waiting for customers. Many of these stands also sell cigarettes, soft drinks and mineral water.

Compared to the general population, heavy users of betel nut suffer very high rates of oral cancer. Non-users also have good reasons to worry about the nut's popularity. Compared to woodlands, betel nut plantations retain very little moisture, partly because their leaves are too small to shade the topsoil. Consequently, whenever there's a heavy downpour, the run-off is sudden and massive. Moreover, the palms have shallow roots and are thus easy to dislodge. During typhoons and tropical storms, groves on steep slopes quickly turn into landslide zones. Successive governments have vowed to crack down on illegal betel-nut plantations in mountain areas, and according to official data some progress has been made. In 2011, the island grew 129,316 tonnes of the nut, 11% less than in 2008. In terms of total betel-nut production, Taiwan is second only to India, and betel nut remains Taiwan's number two cash crop – rice is number one.

By boat Tourist boats cruise between Shuishe, Ita Thao and Xuanguang Temple (*departs every 15–30mins;* ⊕ *approx 09.00–17.30 daily*). The official price is NTD100 per journey but discounts are often available.

By bicycle The scenic area website has details of bike paths. Going all the way around the lake (total distance: 33km) can be done very comfortably in a day but heavy traffic means weekends are best avoided. Giant (*in the visitor centre basement;* ⊕ *06.00–19.00 May–Oct, 07.00–18.00 Nov–Apr, closed Thu*) has the best bicycles. Weekday rentals begin at NTD150 per day; on weekdays, you'll pay NTD200 for two hours. Unlike at some other Giant rental stations, all bikes hired here must be returned here. Cheaper bikes can be rented from shops near the waterfront.

By hired motorcycle 125cc and electric scooters can be rented in Shuishe and Ita Thao. Typical rates for the former are NTD500 per day, NTD600 per 24 hours. The latter are slightly cheaper.

By cable car The Sun Moon Lake Ropeway (⊕ *10.30–16.00 Mon–Fri, 10.00–16.30 Sat–Sun & national holidays; takes 10mins; round trip NTD300/250*), a 1.87km-long cable-car system, is a spectacular way of arriving on the lake's eastern shore a short walk from Ita Thao. Those holding tickets for the Formosan Aboriginal Cultural Village (see page 194) can park at the village and travel on the cable car for free.

TOURIST INFORMATION Sun Moon Lake National Scenic Area (☎ *285 5668; www. sunmoonlake.gov.tw*) runs visitor information centres in Shuishe, Ita Thao and Xiangshan (*all* ⊕ *09.00–17.00 daily*).

WHERE TO STAY There's plenty of accommodation in Shuishe and Ita Thao. The former has several inexpensive if nondescript hotels near the visitor information centre. The following hotels are shown on the map on page 191.

Shuishe

🏠 **Hotel Del Lago** (88 rooms) ☎ 285 6688; f 285 6463; e dellago@dellago.com.tw; www. dellago.com.tw. Close to the lake & close to the action, Del Lago's rooms are more than adequate in terms of facilities & near unbeatable in terms of lake views. Tea-tasting sessions are held in the lobby; ask the staff for details. Each morning, if the weather is good, staff members lead a hike to the top of nearby Mount Maolan (*1,020m; return trip 1½hrs*). Buffet b/fast inc. $$$$$

🏠 **Laurel Villa** (9 rooms) 28 Mingsheng St; ☎ 285 5551; f 285 5552; e laurel.villa@gmail. com; www.laurelvilla.com.tw. Straightforward, well-maintained rooms & a super-helpful bilingual host family have made this homestay a big hit with visitors from the West & Singapore. Most mornings, early-bird guests are led to a superb sunrise-viewing spot. Meals served here include organically grown vegetables from the owner's

parents' nearby farm; drinking water is sourced from a spring on the same land. If you've arrived in Shuishe by bus, turn left down Mingsheng St & look for the English sign at number 28. B/fast inc. $$$

Ita Thao

🏠 **The Crystal** (20 rooms) ☎ 700 8188; f 700 8189; www.thecrystal.com.tw. This boutique hotel has a waterfront location & rooms that are strikingly designed, spacious & extremely comfortable. All beds are king-size plus. Broadband & Wi-Fi. Includes b/fast & dinner (*restaurant open to non-guests; Western & Chinese options; EM;* $$$$). There's a smallish gym (⊕ *09.00–22.30 daily*) & an observation deck that's especially pleasant just after dawn. Rooms without a lake view are 30% cheaper. $$$$$

🏠 **Full House Resort** 富豪群渡假民宿 (10 rooms) ☎ 285 0307; f 285 0001; e a2850307@

yahoo.com.tw; www.fhsml.idv.tw. Ita Thao has two large, chalet-type hotels; Full House is the one that's smaller & set back from the water's edge. The English sign is small & little English is spoken within, but if you're sick of concrete & tiles, you'll adore the wooden walls, floors & ceilings here. Comfortable, distinctive rooms & a lobby that's filled with artworks collected by the owner. The lobby doubles as an eating area but many of those eating here (⊕ *11.00–22.00 daily; EM;* $$$) prefer the lush garden. The menu is geared to groups; teas, coffees & beers from NTD150. Inc b/fast. $$$

✖ WHERE TO EAT   The following establishments are shown on the map on page 191.

✖ Mann Gay Dan Speciality Restaurant
瑪蓋旦 Inside the Thao Chasing-White-Deer Tribe Fair, Ita Thao; ☎291 8656; ⊕ 11.20–18.20 Mon–Fri, 10.20–19.20 Sat–Sun & national holidays. This long-standing aboriginal restaurant is a big hit with local tourists who wolf down platefuls of freshwater shrimp, barbecued meat & high-mountain vegetables. Ordering is by sets designed for 2–8 ppl that work out NTD350–500 pp. No EM but the menu has pictures. Local beers & liquors available; indoor & outdoor seating. If you're facing the water's edge, the restaurant is on the far left. The newer building, back from the water's edge, has AC but no view & may be closed on w/days. $$$

✖ February Coffee   Between Mingsheng St, Shuishe & the Hanbi Trail; ☎285 5471; ⊕ 10.00–22.00 Wed–Mon, meals available 11.30–21.00 Wed–Mon. A good bet if you want Western food but don't want to pay 5-star-hotel prices for it. Choice of pastas plus snacks like French fries. Coffees, teas & beers. Indoor & outdoor seating. EM. $$

✖ Mushroom & Cabbage Pie   111 Wenhua St, Ita Thao; ☎285 0082; ⊕ approx 10.00–19.00 daily. A few tables under a tarpaulin & just 2 or 3 deep-fried items, but this vendor is perhaps Ita Thao's best. Point to order a round cabbage & mushroom pie &/or a cylindrical boar-meat & cheese pie. Both are NTD40 each & delicious. No EM. $

OTHER PRACTICALITIES   There is a post office in Shuishe (*36 Mingsheng St, Shuishe; ⊕ 08.30–12.30 & 13.00–16.30 Mon–Fri*).

WHAT TO SEE AND DO   At Sun Moon Lake, the whole is very much more than the sum of its parts. The temples where tourists congregate are modern structures and Ita Thao is a typical Taiwanese village. Nonetheless, spending a sunny day circumnavigating the lake is highly recommended. Because there's relatively little to be seen south of Shuishe, visitors starting from there tend to look at the Hanbi Peninsula first before moving clockwise.

Hanbi Peninsula 涵碧半島   Chiang Kai-shek spent a lot of time in a villa on this small finger of land immediately southwest of Shuishe. The dictator's retreat is long gone, replaced by one of Taiwan's swankiest hotels, **The Lalu** (*96 rooms;* ☎ *285 5311; www.thelalu.com.tw;* $$$$$ *inc b/fast, meals available*). However, the church where Chiang worshipped still stands. The waterside hiking trail takes around 30 minutes.

Wenwu Temple   Dedicated to both Confucius (the *wén,* or literary, part of its name) and Guan Gong (the *wǔ,* or martial, element), this sizeable house of worship replaced two temples which were inundated when the water level rose. The interior has several superbly decorated beams but you'll find the view over the lake from the roof far more alluring. Do explore some of the hiking trails near here as you can get away from the road and down to the water's edge. None is longer than 600m.

Sun Moon Lake Ropeway 日月潭纜車   This very scenic cable-car ride (see *Getting around,* page 193) links the lake with **Formosan Aboriginal Culture Village** 九族文化村 (☎ *289 5361; www.nine.com.tw; ⊕ 08.00–17.00 daily; admission NTD780/680/390*), where indigenous heritage is presented in an amusement park setting. The terminal, within walking distance of Ita Thao, includes a coffee shop (*EM; $*) and a restaurant (*EM; $$*); there are lots of tables where you can sit and take in the view. Across the road from the terminal is **Sun Moon Lake Youth Activity Centre** 日月潭青年活動中心 (*45 rooms & 24 cabins;* \ *285 0070;* f *285 0037; http://sun. cyh.org.tw/eng/;* **$$** *inc b/fast, meals available for groups $$*).

Ita Thao 伊達邵
Were it not for the souvenir sellers who don pseudo-aboriginal clothing during peak season, you'd never guess this village is the 'capital' of the Thao people (see box, page 198). About 60 of the households here are registered as members of the tribe; as in other parts of Taiwan, many of the businesses are run by lowlanders of Han descent. For details of the Thao's history and culture, see www.dmtip.gov.tw/Eng/Thao.htm.

Just south of Ita Thao police station, Local Road 63 heads into the mountains to and beyond Tannan, a Bunun settlement. Minor landslides are frequent – watch out for rocks on the tarmac – but this very scenic and little-used route is almost always open all the way to Dili on Highway 16. Total distance is 11.5km; being mostly downhill it's ideal for cyclists. East of Dili, Highway 16 is in terrible disrepair. West to Shuili the going is usually fine.

Xuanzang Temple 玄奘寺 and Xuanguang Temple 玄光寺
(*both* ⏰ *05.30– 19.30 daily*) Linked by an 850m-long hiking trail, these two shrines hold relics associated with Xuan Zang (AD602–664), a Buddhist monk revered for travelling to India and translating religious texts. Between the fourth and seventh centuries AD at least 3,000 Chinese Buddhists set out for the subcontinent. Perhaps 80 reached their destination and Xuan Zang was one of just 15 known to have survived the return journey. Nine hundred years after his death, his adventures were retold in a classic Chinese novel, *Journey to the West*, which inspired a 1970s Japanese television series shown in English-speaking countries under the title *Monkey*.

Cien Pagoda 慈恩塔
(⏰ *24hrs daily; free admission*) Commissioned by Chiang Kai-shek as a memorial to his mother, Cien Pagoda never gets as crowded as the temples on the north side of the lake, and the panoramic views from the upper floors more than justify climbing the stairs. The top of the pagoda is exactly 1,000m above sea level.

PULI TO LISHAN *Telephone code 049*

The busy town of **Puli** 埔里 is an important transport hub but lacks major attractions. Within striking distance, however, is a monumental Buddhist shrine as well as some of the island's most captivating mountain scenery.

Because a key section of Highway 8 is closed to non-residents, getting to Lishan usually involves a spectacular detour over Highway 14A. This, the highest stretch of tarmac in the country, climbs above the treeline to an elevation of 3,275m. From it you'll see excellent landscapes and perhaps even some snow. If there is snowfall, expect traffic jams as lowland Taiwanese rush to the hills for a once-in-a-lifetime snowman-making experience. At Dayuling, you can proceed to Lishan and then Wuling Farm or turn east towards Taroko Gorge.

GETTING THERE, AWAY AND AROUND
By car or motorcycle It's 100km from Puli to Lishan. Expect the going to be slow and keep your headlights on at all times. There are petrol stations in Wushe, at km11 on Highway 14A and in Lishan (*all open* ⏰ *approx 08.00–18.00 daily*).

By bus Over 20 services per day link Puli with Wushe (*#6658, 6659 & 6664; departures 06.00–20.00 daily; takes 40–50mins; NTD89*). Several continue on to Qingjing Farm (*from Puli takes 1¼hrs; NTD127*), meaning you can savour the mountains for a couple of hours before boarding #6506, a daily service to Lishan. This bus sets out from Fengyuan Bus Station, less than 100m from Fengyuan TRA Station, at 08.50 and follows Highway 8 then Highway 21, where the good scenery begins. The bus, which can be boarded at Puli at 10.45, reaches Dayuling at 12.50 (*NTD464*) and Lishan at 14.00 (*NTD564*). It's possible to board this bus at Qingqing Farm or Hehuanshan but only if you get a Chinese-speaker to call the bus company (✆ *04 2287 7732*) during office hours the day before. In the opposite direction, the bus leaves Lishan at 08.00, stops in Dayuling an hour later and gets back to Fengyuan at 13.20. For Lishan–Wuling Farm services, see page 200.

🏠 **WHERE TO STAY AND EAT** Entrepreneurs have opened dozens of homestays – including a few mock Tudor mansions – between Wushe and Qingjing Farm. Several offer lavish mountain views, sumptuous comfort and reasonable midweek prices. Carry provisions as between Qingjing Farm and Lishan there's nothing but a few vendors on Hehuanshan. For accommodation in Lishan, see page 200.

🏠 **Herblife Homestay** (7 rooms) Taomi Village; ✆ 291 3551 m 0913 809 823; http://herblife.okgo.tw. If you're driving or walking into Taomi, go past the elementary school & you'll immediately see this homestay's butterfly-motif sign on the right, directly opposite the km9 marker on Local Road 68. The gorgeous garden & pristine interior more than make up for a lack of English. Inc b/fast & dinner. Non-guests can eat here (*dishes NTD180–500; no EM*). **$$$**

🏠 **Minglan Farmstead** (9 rooms) ✆ 280 2251; www.minglan.com.tw. Popular with birders, Minglan is situated 1,100m above sea level, about 1km before Wushe if you're approaching from Puli (look for a side road on the right just where the main road swings left). Minglan's common balcony & most of its rooms look over the valley where the owners grow medicinal herbs, vegetables & bamboo. Bookings seldom needed midweek when rooms can often be had for NTD1,960. For w/ends (*from NTD2,800*) get a Chinese-speaker to make a reservation. Groups may like the 8-person & 12-person rooms. B/fast inc. The same family operates a good-value Taiwanese-style restaurant, also called Minglan, in the centre of Wushe (🕐 *11.00–20.30 daily; no EM; $$*). **$$$**

TOURIST INFORMATION There's a visitor information centre in Lishan (*near the bus stop*; 🕐 *08.30–17.30 daily*). Hehuanshan is part of Taroko National Park (*www.taroko.gov.tw*) but Lishan falls under the Tri-Mountain National Scenic Area (*www.trimt-nsa.gov.tw*).

OTHER PRACTICALITIES There are banks in Puli and a post office in Wushe (🕐 *08.00–16.30 Mon–Fri*) where you can change money.

WHAT TO SEE AND DO The first sight is actually south of Puli. Lishan is described on page 201.

Paper Dome 埔里紙教堂 (*http://paperdome.blogspot.com*; 🕐 *09.00–20.00 Sun–Fri, 09.00–21.00 Sat & national holidays; admission NTD100/50*) Almost two-thirds of the buildings in Taomi were destroyed in the 21 September earthquake but the village has successfully reinvented itself as an ecotourism destination and now has over a dozen B&Bs. Contrary to its Chinese name, which means 'Puli's paper church', the Paper Dome isn't now a place of worship. What makes it special are the materials used in its construction and the fact it's a recycled building in the truest sense of the word. Its original owners, a Catholic church in Japan, decided it was no longer big enough for their purposes. Some years after dismantling it, they donated the pieces – principally 58 columns, each 32.5cm in diameter and 5m high, made from laminated and fireproofed layers of recycled paper – to this village. A Taiwanese charity reassembled it and added an exterior membrane of steel and waterproof polycarbonate. It's quite special and best seen around dusk. The site includes artificial wetlands, a coffee shop, a restaurant and a craft shop.

Taomi Village is between Puli and Sun Moon Lake at km51.5 on Highway 21. Coming from Puli, turn right off the highway, then left and you'll very soon see the dome and places where you can park. Buses between Puli and Sun Moon Lake will stop here if you forewarn the driver.

Chung Tai Chan Monastery 中台禪寺 (Zhōng Tái Chán Sì) (*Turn west at km39 Hwy 21;* \ *293 0215;* e *ctworld@mail.ctcm.org.tw; www.ctworld.org.tw;* ⊕ *08.00–17.30 daily*) Designed by C Y Lee, the architect behind Taipei 101, this edifice is especially impressive if you come in the middle of the afternoon and stay until it gets dark, when the exterior is lit up. Casual visitors usually see only the **Hall of the Four Heavenly Kings** (dominated by 12m-high black granite statues of a quartet of guardian deities) and the adjacent **Great Majestic Hall**. Call or email several days in advance for a guided tour (*free, donations welcome*) of the entire complex and an explanation of the sect's brand of Chan (better known in the West as Zen) Buddhism. Within the complex, **Chung Tai Museum** (*www.ctmuseum.org;* ⊕ *09.30–17.30, closed 2nd & 4th Mon each month but open all national holidays; admission NTD100/70*) displays Buddhist art and artefacts. Driving here from Puli is a cinch but if you're coming from the north the turn-off is less obvious.

Wushe 霧社 (Wùshè) This small town, 1,180m above sea level and known to Sediq tribespeople as Paran, is where Mona Rudao launched his uprising against the Japanese in 1930 (see *History*, page 16). If you're coming from Puli, you'll see the white archway of the Wushe Incident Memorial Park on the left just before reaching the town centre.

Qingjing Farm 清境農場 (*km10 Hwy 14A; www.cingjing.gov.tw*) Established by the KMT regime in the early 1960s as a place where veterans of the Chinese Civil War could settle down, Qingjing Farm's current inhabitants include descendants of anti-communist guerrillas who waged war in the mainland's southwest long after Chiang Kai-shek retreated to Taiwan. The farm's sheep and pastures are a big hit with Taiwanese tourists. Western visitors go for the scenery and birdlife; for the latter, ask a guide to take you to the pheasant-rich **Blue-Gate Trail**.

Sanjiaofong Trail (*km17.3 Hwy 14A*) It's easy to miss the entrance to this 780m-long trail but if you're in the mood for a jaunt, look for a brown-and-white sign on the right as you're heading toward Dayuling. You'll want a hat for the first bit as there's no shade but soon you'll be ascending through forest. Allow an hour to do this spot justice.

Hehuanshan 合歡山 Hikers with good legs can knock off the main peak of Taiwan's 34th highest mountain (oddly, at 3,416m it's very slightly lower than

the north and east peaks) and return to the trailhead near km30.8 on Highway 14A in around two hours. Getting to the north peak, which many regard as more worthwhile, takes up to four hours; the scenery is good in every direction and in April and May the mountain's rhododendrons are in bloom.

SHEI-PA NATIONAL PARK 雪霸國家公園
(XUĚBÀ GUÓJIĀ GŌNGYUÁN) *Telephone code 037 or 04*

With 51 mountain peaks above 3,000m, Shei-Pa National Park features some of Taiwan's very best alpine scenery. Because this 76,850ha park is entirely in the subtropics and the lowest spot is 760m above sea level, temperatures often go very low. Typically, the mornings are gloriously clear but the weather in the afternoons is often cloudy or wet. Blizzards are a possibility in wintertime.

The park gets its English name from peculiar renderings of its two most notable peaks: Snow Mountain (variously known as Syueshan, Hsuehshan and Mount Xue) and Mount Dabajian (sometimes Dabajian Mountain). The former is Taiwan's second-highest mountain; at 3,886m (12,749ft) it's just 66m shorter than Mount Jade. The latter, which reaches 3,490m, has – from some directions at least – a distinctive cylindrical appearance.

Mount Dabajian is considered a holy spot by Atayal and Saisiyat aborigines. The first recorded ascent was by a team of Japanese climbers in 1927; one of them, Numai Tetsutaro, later described the crest-line between Mount Dabajian and Snow Mountain as a 'holy ridge'. This name has stuck and serious hikers may want to consider spending up to ten days doing what's now called the Holy Ridge 'O' Route. Another popular trek is Snow Mountain West Ridge Trail, which takes six days.

Because the park sprawls across county boundaries, telephone codes are included in the listings.

TOURIST INFORMATION The headquarters of Shei-Pa National Park (*www. spnp.gov.tw*) doubles as **Wenshui Visitor Centre** (*Fuxing Village, Dahu, Miaoli*

DISAPPEARING LANGUAGES

They've been renowned since the Japanese colonial era for their unique music, built around rhythms pounded out with pestles, yet the 700-strong Thao tribe wasn't officially recognised as an indigenous ethnic group until 2001. Since then activists have been trying to make up for lost time and save the tribe's language. At the time of writing fewer than ten people, all of them elderly, were able to speak it proficiently. Robert A Blust, professor of linguistics at the University of Hawaii and author of a Thao–English dictionary sponsored by Taiwan's government, has written: 'The present situation of the Thao can be described as one of terminal assimilation.'

Not everyone is so pessimistic, however. Peter K Austin, Marit Rausing Professor of Field Linguistics at the University of London's School of Oriental and African Studies, who in an August 2008 *Guardian* newspaper article listed Thao as one of the world's 'top ten endangered languages', has praised the efforts of those trying to revitalise the language. Other indigenous tongues in Taiwan are even closer to outright extinction – the last surviving native speaker of Pazeh, a lowland aboriginal language, died in October 2010 yet activists in Puli are endeavouring to keep the tongue alive.

County; ☎ *037 996 100;* ⊕ *09.00–16.30 Tue–Sun, open on national holidays that fall on Mon).*

LOCAL TOUR OPERATOR Taiwan Adventures (see advertisement, page 38) ☎ *02 2346 5867;* **m** *0983 212 499;* **e** *info@taiwan-adventures.com; www.taiwan-adventures.com*) organises regular group/private trips to Snow Mountain and other peaks in the national park.

SNOW MOUNTAIN 雪山 (XUĚSHĀN) Even if you're here only because you couldn't get permits for Mount Jade, there's absolutely no reason to feel you're settling for second best. Hiking up Snow Mountain is far too good an experience to be considered a consolation prize; in terms of scenic and ecological variety – not to mention pleasurable exertion – it's every bit as good as its taller compatriot. By Taiwan's standards it does snow fairly often here but that's not how the mountain got its name. The Atayal named it Sekoan, meaning 'broken cliffs'; it's a toponym you'll understand if you get close to the summit. The first Han people to know about the mountain adapted the indigenous name, then shortened it.

The trailhead is located within Wuling Farm (see page 201); hikers need to pay admission even if they stay in their vehicle until the service station (elevation: 2,140m) where permits are inspected. The station's bathrooms are the last ones until Chika Cabin (2,463m), a good hour's walk away. It takes five or more hours to get from Chika Cabin to 369 Cabin (3,100m) and the trail passes very close to Snow Mountain's east peak (3,201m). Many hikers set out from 369 Cabin well before dawn and try to reach the top, four hours' walk away, before sunrise.

Along the trail bilingual information boards introduce the fauna and flora, and explain various phenomena, such as why the rocks on one side of the valley are smaller than those on the other side. Birds include Taiwan flamecrests (*Regulus goodfellowi*), tiny but colourful warblers, and vinaceous rosefinches (*Carpodacus vinaceus*). The latter hang around the cabins, picking up crumbs left by humans.

Climbing to and returning from the peak can be done in two days if you get an early start, but spending three days on the mountain is usual and advisable. Proper equipment and provisions are essential as the cabins (both are free) lack bedding and cooking facilities. Both national park and police permits are required and enforcement is strict. Beds in the two cabins must be booked in advance, so don't change your itinerary on a whim.

MOUNT DABAJIAN 大霸尖山 (DÀBÀJIĀNSHĀN) This mountain is accessed via **Qingquan** (see page 159) and **Guanwu National Forest Recreation Area** (⊕ *24hrs daily; free admission*); there's no public transport anywhere near the trailhead. Some call the mountain 'Taiwan's Matterhorn', but in terms of shape it's more akin to an immense plinth than a pyramid. Like the Matterhorn, Mount Dabajian should not be underestimated; allow three full days and don't go if you're not in good shape. Permits are required and hikers aren't allowed through the checkpoint after 11.00 because the first day involves a 19km march to Jiujiu Hut (2,700m above sea level) where there are dormitories and kitchen facilities. To make the first day less brutal, many groups camp near the 15km point, saving a gruelling ascent for the following morning. From Jiujiu Hut, approaching Mount Dabajian involves skirting or going over four 3,000m-plus peaks. The actual summit is off-limits, as the rock layer is too unstable to support the ladders and chains hikers would need to reach the very top. That may put off peak-baggers, but in clear weather the superb views to be had along the way more than make up for any lack of bragging rights.

LISHAN TO WULING *Telephone code 04*

Before the September 21 earthquake ravaged the area, it was possible to drive from Guguan to Taroko Gorge on the high-altitude section of Highway 8, a route also known as the Central Cross-Island Highway. At the time of writing the road had been repaired but was open only to residents of nearby mountain villages, everyone else having to travel via Wushe and Hehuanshan (see page 197).

Getting there, away and around

By car or motorcycle It's 24km from Lishan to Wuling and 57km from Wuling to Qilan where you can continue on to Yilan City or turn right on to the North Cross-Island Highway. Thick mists are very common between Wuling and Nanshan so keep your headlights on. There are petrol stations at Lishan and Nanshan (*both* ⊕ *08.00–18.00 daily*).

By bus Bus #6508 leaves Lishan at 16.50 each day, arriving at Wuling Farm around 17.30 (*NTD85 one-way*). It sets out from Wuling Farm to Lishan at 06.30. Kuo-Kuang's #1751 Yilan–Lishan service (*departs from Yilan at 07.00 & 12.40, from Lishan at 08.30 & 13.30; takes 4hrs; NTD337*) stops at Wuling Farm. Lishan-bound buses take almost three hours to reach Wuling Farm (*NTD285*). Yilan-bound buses take less than an hour (*NTD76*).

Where to stay and eat For budget lodgings, try the small hotels on the main road in Lishan. Information about Wuling Farm's campsite is at www.wuling-farm. com.tw/en/camp/index.php. Meals are available in all of the hotels listed here and there are shops in Lishan, but it would be wise to bring some supplies.

🏠 **Hoya Resort Hotel Wuling** (143 rooms) ☎2590 1399; f 2590 1118; e service@hoyaresort. com.tw; www.hoyaresort.com.tw. Well-managed & offering good food but some guests have complained of a confusing layout & having to take 2 separate lifts to reach their rooms. **$$$$**

🏠 **Lishan Guest House** (97 rooms) ☎2265 3939; f 2265 2353; www.lishanguesthouse.com. tw. One of Chiang Kai-shek's country retreats (he had at least 20), this impossible-to-miss complex

SALMON THAT NEVER JOURNEY TO THE SEA

Scientists are fascinated by *Oncorhynchus formosanus* not because it's one of the world's few landlocked salmon species but because it lives so near the tropics. It's a relict species which strayed into Taiwan's rivers during a glacial age 800,000 years ago. Limited in range by its inability to survive in water warmer than approximately 18°C, the species would perhaps already be extinct were it not for human intervention.

In recent years, wild salmon numbers have recovered from below 300 to over 5,000 – largely, it's thought, because several weirs have been dismantled and agricultural activities near the Qijiawan Creek have been scaled back. However, spreading the fish to other waterways is proving very difficult. Of hatchery-bred salmon released when they're about a year old, very few survive post-typhoon floods. Scientists have discovered that salmon numbers are not much influenced by the number of fish-eating birds or food supply, as there are few predators and Wuling's streams have an abundance of aquatic insects. The species continues to face two dire threats: a very narrow genetic base and global warming.

near Lishan's petrol station was converted into a hotel in late 2012. Externally it's a low-rise version of Taipei's Grand Hotel – red columns hold up a glazed-tile roof – but the guestrooms are modern & spacious, although not all have bathtubs.

Located at the western end of the town, a stone's throw from the visitor information centre & bus stop, this hotel isn't a bad deal given that English is spoken & room rates (*NTD4,000 midweek/ NTD5,000 at w/ends for a standard 2-person room*) inc buffet b/fast & hot pot dinner (you choose your flavour & type of meat). **$$$$**
⌂ **Hoya Inn Wuling** (24 rooms) ☎2590 1288; e inn@hoyaresort.com.tw; www.hoyaresort. com.tw/inn/. Alternatively known as Wu Ling Village, this inn is cosier than Wuling Hotel, slightly cheaper & in a much better location – a stone's throw from the trail to Taoshan Waterfall – for

those planning to explore on foot. Outside of the summer & Lunar New Year peak seasons, solo travellers can get a bed in one of the 6-person dorms for NTD700 (*NTD900 at w/ends*). B/fast inc. **$$$**
⌂ **Wuling Hotel** (111 rooms) ☎2590 1259 ext 2001 & 2003; f 2590 1355; www.wuling-farm.com.tw/en/room/index.php. An institution with many names, among them Wuling Guest House & Wuling National Hostel, this place offers accommodation in cabins & a 1980s building just inside Wuling Farm. The pricing system is complex & the online reservation page is Chinese-only but midweek discounts mean 2 ppl can often stay for around NTD3,000 & a family of 4 for less than NTD4,500. Most deals inc b/fast & dinner. **$$$**

Tourist information There are visitor information centres in Lishan (*near the bus stop;* ⊕ *08.30–17.30 daily*) and Wuling Farm (*between Hoya Resort Hotel & the bus station;* ⊕ *09.00–16.30 Tue–Sun*). Lishan is part of the Tri-Mountain National Scenic Area (*www.trimt-nsa.gov.tw*).

What to see and do

***Lishan* 梨山 (*Líshān*)** (*km86 Hwy 8*) The smartest structure in this spread-out little town is the Presbyterian Church; many other buildings look as though they were hastily assembled using sheets of corrugated metal. Also, the frames that support thousands of apple and pear trees on the hillsides hereabouts do nothing to enhance the area's appearance. However, if you decide to stay you'll find some pleasant trails (one starts right behind Lishan Guest House) and very pleasing views over the surrounding area.

***Wuling Farm* 武陵農場 (*Wǔlíng Nóngchǎng*)** (*3km from the turn-off at km54 Hwy 7A*) (☎ *2590 1020; www.wuling-farm.com.tw;* ⊕ *08.00–17.00 daily; admission NTD130/80 Mon–Fri, NTD160/80 Sat–Sun & national holidays; parking NTD50/10*) Also known as **Wuling National Forest Recreation Area**, this area's history is similar to that of Qingjing Farm (see page 197) but it's seen far less development. Many of the peach and apple orchards established in the 1960s have been taken back by the national park and planted with native trees. The lower parts of the recreation area (1,740–2,100m above sea level) have lots of red and green maples, oaks and gum trees. There are also vast clusters of pine trees. Cherry and plum blossoms appear around the end of winter and are a magnet for domestic tourists.

Wuling is the starting point of some truly excellent hikes, including the ascent of Snow Mountain (see page 199). Even if the mountain isn't on your itinerary, consider driving up to the trailhead for the views you'll get over the area. For those without their own vehicles, the two-hour minibus tour (*NTD150 pp*) is a good way of seeing the recreation area. There's also a free guided walking tour; for details see the farm's website. Bicycles can be rented from a shop (⊕ *08.00–17.30 daily*) next to the bus station. Prices range from NTD100 for a bike for two hours to NTD400 per hour for a three-person electric tricycle.

Tourists are barred from approaching Qijiawan Creek, the main waterway, to protect its population of Formosan landlocked salmon (see box, page 200) from human disturbance. Artificially propagated salmon can be seen near the bus station in the **Taiwan Salmon Eco Centre** (⊕ *09.00–12.00 & 13.00–17.00 Tue–Sun; free admission*). The displays here cover their feeding and breeding habits but don't include much English. The only place where visitors are allowed close enough to the creek to glimpse wild fish is 2.4km beyond the visitor centre, at what maps call the **Salmon Observatory**. Distinguishing salmon from the other three fish species that inhabit the creek is close to impossible, however.

No permits are required for the 4.3km hike to **Taoshan Waterfall** 桃山瀑布. The concrete footpath, shaded by pine trees, climbs gradually to 2,250m above sea level. Allow at least three hours to get to the fall and back, and set out before breakfast to beat the crowds. Very near the start, you'll get lovely views of Qijiawan Creek and the forest from a footbridge.

YUSHAN NATIONAL PARK 玉山國家公園
(YÙSHĀN GUÓJIĀ GŌNGYUÁN) *Telephone code 049*

Taiwan's largest national park covers 1,055km², 3% of the country's land area, and is named after the island's highest peak. Both the park and the mountain are called *yù* (jade) *shān* (mountain) in Mandarin. The park's official English name is Yushan but many English-language publications refer to the mountain itself as Mount Jade (3,952m); for the sake of clarity this guidebook does the same.

Large tracts of the park are totally unspoiled. Roads don't penetrate beyond the northwest and southwest corners, and it's only in the past few years that ordinary hikers (as opposed to fully equipped expeditions) have been able to cross the park from west to east. Those who get into the core of the reserve, which takes three or four days of walking, have an excellent chance of seeing some of the park's 28 mammal species. Black bears aren't easy to spot, but Formosan serows (*Capricornis swinhoei*) and Formosan sambars gather near water sources, and Reeves's muntjacs can be heard yapping after dark.

The park's only permanent human settlements are the mainly Bunun communities of Dongpu and Meishan. The former, a well-developed hot-springs resort in the park's northwest, is 1,120m above sea level. The latter is accessed by the South Cross-Island Highway. Much of the park is traditional Bunun stomping ground and it's from this tribe that the mountain porters who work on Mount Jade are recruited.

For all kinds of visitors – not just tourists who don't want to stray far from their vehicles – Tataka is a highlight. The New Central Cross-Island Highway crests here at 2,610m above sea level and there are truly stunning views of Taiwan's highest uplands. If you're climbing Mount Jade, you'll almost certainly start from here. For details of the eastern segment of Yushan National Park, see page 297.

GETTING THERE AND AWAY
By car or motorcycle Tataka is 21km from Alishan via Highway 18 and 71km from Shuili via Highway 21. The nearest petrol stations are those in Alishan and in Heshe 和社 at km102 on Highway 21. Dongpu is reached by Highway 21 to Heshe, then Local Road 60.

By bus The #6739 Sun Moon Lake–Tataka–Alishan bus service sets out from Sun Moon Lake at 08.00 and 09.00 and reaches Tataka about three hours later.

From Alishan, buses depart at 13.00 and 14.00. Sun Moon Lake's Shuishe bus stop to Tataka costs NTD276 one-way; Alishan to Tataka is NTD73 (*takes about 30mins*).

By minibus Several of Alishan's hotels offer to take guests to Tataka (*NTD300 return*) to see the sunrise there instead of Zhushan.

TOURIST INFORMATION

☑ Yushan National Park Headquarters 國家公園管理處 515 Zhongshan Rd Sec 1, Shuili; ☏277 3121; www.ysnp.gov.tw; ⏱ 09.00–16.30 daily. Collect maps & information, & apply for mountain permits in person at this office.

☑ Tataka Visitor Centre km145 Hwy 21; ⏱ 09.00–16.30 daily. Birders & butterfly enthusiasts should check out the exhibition upstairs.

TOUR OPERATORS

Barking Deer Adventures m 0938 337 710; e barkingdeerinfo@gmail.com; www.barking-deer.com. Has organised ascents of Mount Jade & treks all the way across the park.
Blue Skies Adventures (see advertisement, page 166) ☏07 389 0795; e info@ blueskiesadventures.com.tw; www.

blueskiesadventures.com.tw. Another experienced hiking outfit.
Taiwan Adventures (see advertisement, page 38) ☏02 2346 5867; m 0983 212 499; e info@ taiwan-adventures.com; www.taiwan-adventures. com. Runs regular group/private trips to Mount Jade.

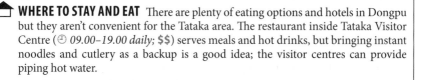

WHERE TO STAY AND EAT There are plenty of eating options and hotels in Dongpu but they aren't convenient for the Tataka area. The restaurant inside Tataka Visitor Centre (⏱ 09.00–19.00 daily; $$) serves meals and hot drinks, but bringing instant noodles and cutlery as a backup is a good idea; the visitor centres can provide piping hot water.

⌂ Dongpu Hostel (3 dorms) km108 Hwy 18; ☏270 2213. With 106 tightly packed beds (*NTD300 pp*), those who opt to spend the night here shouldn't expect a fabulous night's rest. However, the location is perfect for exploring Tataka & enjoying the sunset & sunrise views. You may be sharing with a hiking group that rises

before dawn to tackle Mount Jade; you might have the place all to yourself. Bedding provided. The shower facilities are rudimentary & seldom used. Call ahead if you want a meal cooked for you; guests who bring their own food are welcome to use the kitchen. **$**

WHAT TO SEE AND DO It's 15km from Alishan to the park's western boundary.

Lulin Sacred Tree 鹿林神木 (*km102 Hwy 18*) This tree, a 2,700-year-old, 43m-high Formosan cypress (*Chamaecyparis formosensis*) is very close to but almost invisible from the road. Look for the sign and stairs on the left as you're coming from Alishan.

Shishan 石山 (*km104.2 Hwy 18*) Just past the national park boundary marker there's a service centre that's only sporadically open. At the km105 marker you'll see a net strung across the road, put there to help macaques cross safely. What park literature calls 'inappropriate interactions' between the animals and human visitors have caused changes in the former's behaviour, including incidents in which macaques have vandalised cars when the occupants didn't give them food.

Mount Lulin 鹿林山 (*Trailhead at km106.5 Hwy 18*) A good option if you lack the time or permits for Mount Jade but have plenty of energy, the hike to the top of Mount Lulin (elevation: 2,845m) is likely to strengthen your resolve to return to this place and go all the way to the top of Taiwan. It's possible to then hike northeast to Mount Linjhih 麟趾山 (2,854m) without returning to the highway.

Tataka 塔塔加 **(Tǎtǎjiā)** (*km145 Hwy 21*) Highways 18 and 21 meet at this point, 2,610m above sea level. Parking, dropping into the visitor centre and then exploring the various trails – or simply strolling along the main road – are highly recommended. The botanically minded will enjoy the bilingual information boards which introduce tree and plant species. One, the Formosan pieris (*Pieris taiwanensis hayata*), is an endemic evergreen shrub with leaves which aborigines used to mash and use as an organic pesticide.

Mount Dongpu 東埔山 (*Trailhead at km144.2 Hwy 21*) Allow 30 minutes to reach the summit of this 2,782m-high mountain and plenty of additional time for taking in the wondrous panoramas. Mount Jade is clearly visible to the southeast.

Mount Jade 玉山 **(Yùshān)** This is the peak everyone wants to bag. Consequently permit applications often exceed the fixed daily quota by a ratio of 10:1. Visitor numbers are kept down to protect the mountain's fragile ecology and also because there isn't much space in **Paiyun Lodge** 排雲山莊 (*92 beds in 8 dorms; NTD480 pp*). Apart from limited camping options, the lodge is the only accommodation between the trailhead and the peak. It's much easier to get permits for midweek dates than for weekends. Applications must be submitted well in advance. The process can be completed online but it's best to get a hiking outfit to do the 'paperwork' for you, or to join an organised hike. Mount Jade and some other trails in the national park are closed to the public for a month each year, sometime between January and March. The precise dates vary from year to year and may be brought forward or extended because of weather conditions.

Most hikers spend two days and one night on Mount Jade and scale the main peak only. Before beginning the walk to Paiyun Lodge it's necessary to go to the

---

THE NAME(S) OF TAIWAN'S HIGHEST PEAK

Is it Mount Jade, Jade Mountain, Mount Yu or Yushan? To the Tsou tribe, it's *Pattonkan* – but the official toponym Batongguan actually refers to a different place, a high-altitude meadow where hikers on multi-day treks often camp.

The mountain would surely have been seen by the Dutch from their base in 17th-century Tainan, yet there's no record of it acquiring a Dutch name. From the 1860s until after World War II, English speakers referred to the mountain as Mount Morrison, although it's unclear whether this name honoured Robert Morrison (1782–1834), a Scotsman and pioneering missionary in China, or a ship's captain who recorded sighting the mountain while anchored near Tainan. Between 1900 and 1945, the mountain's official name was *Niitakayama*, Japanese for 'new high mountain' and an admission that Taiwan's highest peak was taller than Japan's beloved Mount Fuji. The phrase *Niitakayama nobore* ('Climb Niitakayama') has been notorious since 1941 – it was the code sent out by Imperial Japanese Navy headquarters on 7 December 1941, instructing its fleet to attack Pearl Harbour the following day.

police checkpoint (🕐 *06.00–18.00 daily*) to have your permits inspected. You're advised to fill your water bottles there, especially if you're tramping the 2.8km to the actual trailhead at **Tataka Anbu**. Private vehicles are not allowed past the checkpoint; the only alternative to walking is to jump on one of the minibuses that shuttle between the highway, the checkpoint and the saddle (*NTD100 pp one-way*). From Tataka Anbu (2,600m) it's 8.5km to Paiyun Lodge. The track to Mount Jade is to the left. The surfaced road dropping down to the south is only open to scientific researchers. Soon after stepping on to the trail, you may see Taiwan laughing thrushes (*Garrulax morrisonianus*) scampering ahead of you; they've become totally unafraid of humans.

Up to 20 people per day are permitted to attempt a one-day ascent of the mountain. To be allowed to proceed on to the summit they must reach Paiyun Lodge before 10.00. They should return to the Tataka trailhead by 17.00.

The hike to Paiyun Lodge is straightforward and very enjoyable. Along the way there are two toilets and a few shelters where you can rest. At km2.7 you'll see the trailhead for **Yushan Front Peak** (3,236m). This side trail is steep so allow up to three hours to get to the top and come back down to the main path. In a few places along the main trail, wooden walkways have been built and there are precipitous drops on the right side. These sections are quite safe so long as you pay attention to where you're putting your feet.

When you reach Paiyun Lodge (3,415m), find the warden and show him your permit. He'll show you to your bunks; if you don't have a sleeping bag you can rent one for NTD300. The lodge has a reliable water supply but the electricity may not be on 24 hours so have your torch handy through the night. Hikers aren't permitted to cook for themselves; meals should be ordered a week in advance (📞 *04 2217 5127*; **e** *yushan.sky@msa.hinet.net*; *NTD150–300*). Boiling hot water is available very early in the morning so you can make coffee before going up to the peak.

If you've arrived at the lodge with time and energy to spare, **Mount Jade West Peak 玉山西峰** (3,528m) awaits. The round trip takes two to three hours; carry a torch and extra clothing as you might not make it back before dusk. Once the sun has set there's nothing to do at Paiyun Lodge and it gets very cold very quickly. Even if you don't feel sleepy you should turn in early as a courtesy to the majority who hope to reach the summit before sunrise.

The 2.4km from the lodge to the summit takes even the fastest hikers well over an hour. Most people rise early enough to eat some breakfast before heading out into the darkness. Watch out for ice on the path. In the dark it isn't difficult to lose the trail as it zigzags between trees and juniper bushes. If the ground feels unusually rough you may have blundered off the track. If that happens, retrace your steps carefully. Some 700m beyond Paiyun Lodge the trail forks. Keep left if you're aiming for the summit; going right will take you to **Mount Jade South Peak 玉山南峰** (3,844m). It's another 1.7km to the main peak. Take it slowly; where chains have been fixed in place you should pay careful attention to your footing and stick to the established route. There's a caged section where a metal frame protects hikers from falling rocks. The trail splits just before the summit. Left goes to the weather station on **Mount Jade North Peak** (3,858m), right leads to the peak. It can be extremely windy at this point, as it often is on the peak itself. Whatever the conditions, the mood among hikers who make it to the top is invariably exuberant. Expect yelping, shouting and singing as the sun makes its appearance. Don't rush down the mountain afterwards. Search out a sheltered spot a little below the summit where you can enjoy views over scores of high mountains – and pat yourself on the back for reaching east Asia's highest point.

New Central Cross-Island Highway 新中橫 Between Tataka and Shuili, Highway 21 is known as the New Central Cross-Island Highway. This road, which you'll take if you visit the hot-springs resort of **Dongpu** 東埔, doesn't in fact go across the island. It offers one of Taiwan's finest mountain driving experiences but make sure you have enough petrol, food and drinks before setting out. Also, ask about road conditions as the highway is sometimes damaged by landslides.

Batongguan Cross-Island Old Trail 八通關越嶺古道 This 90km trek, from Dongpu in the west to near Yuli in the east, is neither the longest nor the most difficult in Taiwan. It is, however, an incredible way to spend a week (or more, if you choose to tack on an ascent of Mount Jade from the north) in true wilderness. The trail, blazed in 1920–21 by the Japanese authorities so they could better monitor and control the aborigines, wasn't the first formal route through the Central Mountain Range. A previous path, established in 1875 on the orders of the Qing imperial court, has long been unusable. Tents aren't needed as there are shelters along the route. Self-sufficiency in terms of provisions is essential, and you shouldn't contemplate tackling this route unless you've plenty of hiking experience.

7

Southwest Taiwan

Most of the Han migrants who sailed for Taiwan in the 17th and early 18th centuries landed on the island's southwest coastline for three reasons: prevailing winds, flat land suitable for rice cultivation and a modicum of established civilisation. Tainan, renowned for its shrines and other antiquities, has the lion's share of points of interest. If you've any curiosity about Taiwan's past, this old city is a must-visit deserving a minimum of two whole days.

There are yet more historic buildings and lively temples in Chiayi City. The former, however, is more often used as a launch pad for trips to Alishan and other places in the mountainous interior. A tourist destination since the Japanese colonial era, Alishan's cool weather and temperate woodlands are profoundly soothing. From the resort it's possible to make forays into Yushan National Park.

Southwest Taiwan comprises Tainan, Chiayi City and Chiayi County (combined land area: 4,153km²; population: 2.69 million). The municipality of Tainan embraces both the ancient city and a hinterland of small towns and farming villages. Chiayi City is surrounded by a county of the same name; the latter stretches from the fishing port of Budai to the western face of Mount Jade. The region enjoys mild winters, the weather being dry and almost always sunny between October and March.

TAINAN 台南 (TÁINÁN) *Telephone code 06*

Visiting Tainan is essential if you hope to learn about Taiwanese history, religion or traditional life. Comparisons to Kyoto are often made and aren't far off the mark. Taiwan's former capital has more government-recognised first-grade relics than any other city; on every street there are signs of the pre-industrial past. However, Tainan is easier to navigate than Japan's cultural treasure house – most of the sights can be walked to – and a good deal less expensive. It's a place where temples don't charge admission and where sightseers often find themselves far outnumbered by those visiting for reasons of piety. Among Taiwanese, Tainan is almost as famous for its snack foods as it is for traditional culture. Westerners find many of these delicacies rather odd but the brave and the gluttonous will have a field day. About three-quarters of a million people live in Tainan's urban core.

HISTORY The history of Tainan is largely the history of Taiwan. Small numbers of Han Chinese, among them traders, fugitives and pirates, were living alongside the indigenous inhabitants when the Dutch arrived in the area in 1624 (see *History*, page 11). The trickle of Han settlers turned into a flood when the VOC began offering incentives – oxen, seeds and tools – to Fujianese willing to cross the Taiwan Strait and work the land. The Dutch used thoroughly modern methods

207

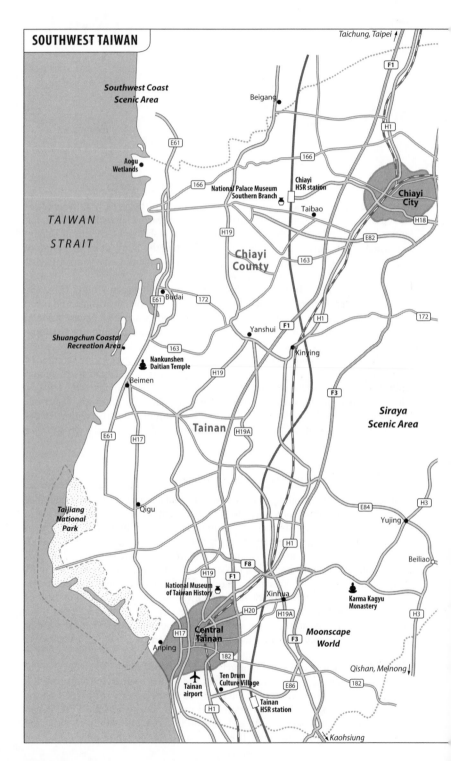

SOUTHWEST TAIWAN

Taichung, Taipei
F1

Southwest Coast
Scenic Area

Beigang
H1

E61

Aogu
Wetlands

166

National Palace Museum
Southern Branch

Chiayi
HSR station

Chiayi
City

H18

Taibao

H19

E82

TAIWAN

STRAIT

Chiayi
County

163

E61 Budai

172

Shuangchun Coastal
Recreation Area

163

Yanshui

F1

H1

172

Nankunshen
Daitian Temple

Xinying

H19

Beimen

F3

Tainan

H19A

Siraya
Scenic Area

E61 H17

Taijiang
National
Park

Qigu

E84

H3

Yujing

H1

Beiliao

H19

F8

F1

National Museum
of Taiwan History

Xinhua

Karma Kagyu
Monastery

H3

H20

H19A

H17

Central
Tainan

Anping

182

Moonscape
World

F3

Qishan, Meinong

Tainan
airport

Ten Drum
Culture Village

E86

182

H1

Tainan
HSR station

Kaohsiung

208

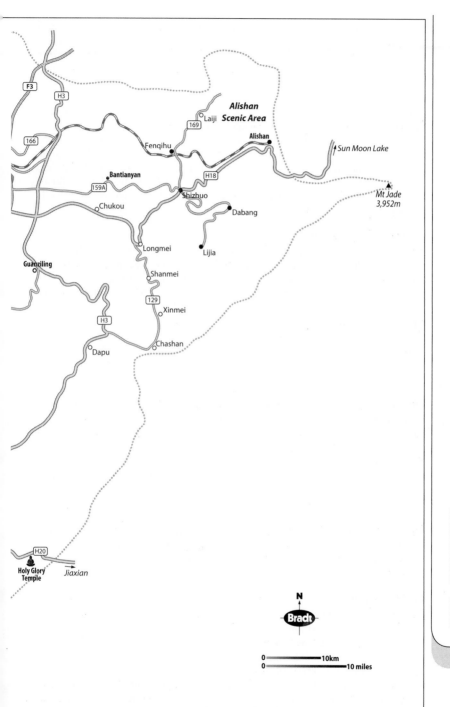

to attract immigrants: they promised tax holidays and advertised through local entrepreneurs on the Chinese coast. While the 38 years of VOC control set economic patterns that lasted well into the 18th century (sugar and rice exported in large quantities, tobacco and ginger in smaller amounts), it was the subsequent regime, Koxinga's Kingdom of Donging, that turned Tainan into a centre of Han civilisation.

By the early 1700s Chinese settlers had established themselves along most of Taiwan's west coast, but Tainan remained the most developed part of the island until well into the 19th century. For almost all of the 212 years the Qing Dynasty ruled Tainan it was known as *Táiwǎnfǔ* (Westerners spelled it 'Taiwanfoo'), meaning 'Taiwan's capital'. The city acquired its current name, which means 'south Taiwan', when the provincial capital was shifted to the north in 1885. Since World War II, Tainan has lagged behind Taipei, Taichung and Kaohsiung in terms of economic development but succeeded in preserving a great deal of its character.

GETTING THERE AND AWAY

By air Daily flights to Magong and Kinmen leave from **Tainan Airport** (*IATA code: TNN;* \260 1016; *www.tna.gov.tw*), 6km south of the city centre. In mid-2013, thrice-weekly flights to Hong Kong were launched and by the time you read this there could be scheduled flights to more than one destination in mainland China.

By HSR There are at least two trains to Taipei per hour and they take about one hour 40 minutes (*NTD1,480*) while to Taichung takes 45 minutes (*NTD710*). Tainan HSR Station is an inconvenient 13km southeast of the city centre but a TRA branch line (*departs every 30mins;* ☉ *06.35–23.52 daily; takes 24mins; NTD25*) links Shalun Station next to the HSR station with the city centre.

By TRA Expresses to/from Taipei take 4¼ to six hours (*NTD569–738*) while to/from Taichung they take 2 to 2¾ hours (*NTD280–363*). Trains to/from Kaohsiung take about an hour (*NTD68–106*).

By bus Kuo-Kuang's #1837 service goes to Taipei (*departures at least hourly;* ☉ *06.00–24.00 daily; takes 4¼hrs; NTD360*) while #1871 goes to Taichung (*departs every 30mins;* ☉ *06.10–21.50 daily; NTD170*). Other bus companies have offices on the same stretch of Beimen Road.

By car or motorcycle By Freeway 1 Tainan is 302km south of Taipei and 40km north of Kaohsiung. Two-wheelers may want to approach via Highway 17, a road which runs near the coast south to Kaohsiung and north through Beimen into Chiayi County.

GETTING AROUND

By bus City bus #2 links the TRA station with Anping (*departs about every 20mins;* ☉ *06.20–22.00 daily; takes 25mins; NTD18*) and stops very close to Confucius Temple, the Great South Gate and Five Concubines Temple. Two Tourist Shuttle services pick up passengers on the west side of Tainan Park: #88 to Anping (*departs every hour* ☉ *09.00–18.00 Mon–Fri, every 30mins* ☉ *08.30–19.00 Sat–Sun*) and the less frequent #99 to Qigu. Some of the latter go as far afield as the Black-faced Spoonbill Area in Taijiang National Park. Single journeys on #88 and #99 are NTD18; a one-day pass for the tourist shuttles and conventional city buses is NTD80.

By rented bicycle

🚴 **Dragon Bike** 120 Anbei Rd; ☎228 5472; Ⓢ 10.00–20.00 Mon–Fri; 09.00–20.00 Sat–Sun. Standard bikes from NTD100 per day.

🚴 **Cozy Bike Rental** [212 C3] 43 Nanmen Rd; ☎221 5166; Ⓢ 10.00–18.30 daily. Bikes with baskets for NTD120 per 4hrs, or NTD300 for 24hrs.

By hired car or motorcycle

🚗 **Car Plus Auto Leasing** [212 C1] 113 Beimen Rd Sec 2; ☎223 5566; www.car-plus. com.tw; Ⓢ 08.30–20.30 daily. General-use car rentals & long-term leasing. Car Plus also has a counter inside Tainan HSR Station.

🚗 **Songxing Scooter Rental** [212 D2] 2 Beimen Rd Sec 2; ☎200 6302; Ⓢ 06.00–24.00 daily. Located just outside Tainan TRA Station. Other rental businesses are clustered around the back of the station.

TOURIST INFORMATION

ⓘ **Tainan City Government Tourism Bureau** http://tour.tainan.gov.tw. Covers every part of the municipality inc Beimen, Yanshui & other far-flung districts. The bilingual walking-guide maps & information boards around the city centre are exceptionally useful.

ⓘ **Tainan City Guide** http://tainancity. wordpress.com. An unofficial but excellent resource.
ⓘ **TRA Station Visitor Information Centre** [212 D2] Ⓢ 09.00–18.00 daily
ⓘ **Anping Visitor Information Centre** 790 Anping Rd; Ⓢ 10.00–18.00 Tue–Sun

🏠 **WHERE TO STAY** The following hotels are shown on the map on page 212.

🏠 **Shangri-La's Far Eastern Plaza Hotel** (333 rooms) 89 Daxue Rd West Sec; ☎702 8888; **f** 702 7777; **e** reservations.sltn@shangri-la.com; www.shangri-la.com. Located in the steel & glass cylinder behind Tainan TRA Station, guestrooms (11th to 37th flrs) in this 5-star offer excellent city views & are a pleasing change from the boxiness of many hotels, thanks to the curve of the outer wall. Black-&-white photos of the city add a local touch to each room. The largest suites are 50m^2. Health club inc sauna & gym; the heart-shaped swimming pool is outdoors but heated in the winter (Ⓢ 06.00–23.00). Inc buffet b/fast. Golf & wedding packages are especially good deals, as are family packages which inc Sun brunch & late check-out. Book either of the in-house restaurants online for a discount. **Shanghai Pavilion** (*38th flr;* Ⓢ *11.30–14.30 & 18.00–21.30 daily; à la carte menu & set meals from NTD1,500 + 10% service charge; EM* $$$$$) offers a range of Huaiyang, Cantonese & Taiwanese dishes. Café at Far Eastern (*10th flr; EM* $$$$) is a multi-national buffet. $$$$

🏠 **Tayih Landis Hotel** (315 rooms) 660 Ximen Rd Sec 1; ☎213 5555; **f** 213 5599; **e** pr@ tayihlandis.com.tw; www.tayihlandis.com.tw. The city's 1st 5-star hotel, the Tayih Landis has guestrooms decorated in dark, almost sombre

colours. For a more uplifting style – but one that keeps with the Art Deco, chevrons-&-all approach evident elsewhere in the hotel – opt for a deluxe king room. Guests sleep on floors 8–22 & when making a reservation can request a view towards the ocean or inland over the Old Tainan Martial Arts Academy. Standard superior rooms are 43m^2 & often go for around NTD4,000. All room deals inc internet & free use of the indoor heated swimming pool, jacuzzi, fitness centre, sauna & steam room (Ⓢ *06.00–22.00 daily*). B/fast inc. The hotel's restaurants offer Chinese, Japanese & international buffet but perhaps the best in-house eating option is **New Asia Teppanyaki Restaurant** (*2nd flr;* ☎*213 5555 ext 6341;* Ⓢ *12.00–14.30 & 18.00–21.30 daily; EM;* $$$$$) where lunch sets start at NTD880; wines from NTD1,100. $$$$

🏠 **JJ-W Culture Hotel** (27 rooms) 11 Zhengxing St; ☎220 9866; **f** 220 9867; **e** service@ jj-whotel.com.tw; www.jj-whotel.com.tw. One of the most characterful new hotels to have appeared in south Taiwan in recent years & convenient for exploring Tainan's old commercial district, JJ-W is in fact a radical reimagining of a hotel built in 1970. Large windows flood the interior with natural light & there's a theme for each room's décor. Furnishings are a mix of traditional pieces

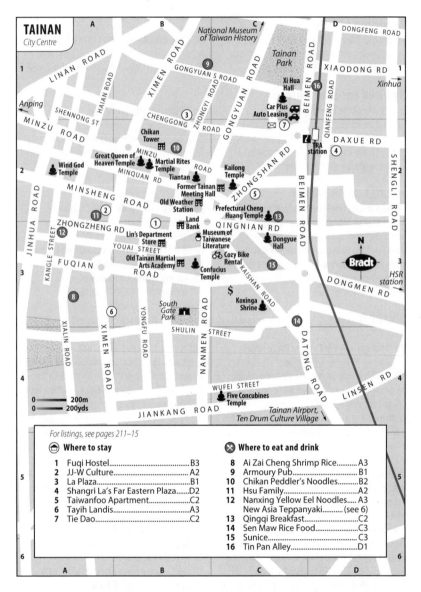

TAINAN
City Centre

National Museum
of Taiwan History

DONGFENG ROAD

XIAODONG RD

Xinhua

Tainan
Park

Anping

Xi Hua
Hall

Car Plus
Auto Leasing

DAXUE RD

TRA
station

Chikan
Tower

SHENGLI ROAD

Great Queen of
Heaven Temple

Wind God
Temple

Martial Rites
Temple

Tiantan

Kailong
Temple

Former Tainan
Meeting Hall

Old Weather
Station

Prefectural Cheng
Huang Temple

Land
Bank

Museum of
Taiwanese
Literature

Dongyue
Hall

Lin's Department
Store

Old Tainan Martial
Arts Academy

Cozy Bike
Rental

Confucius
Temple

South
Gate
Park

Koxinga
Shrine

Bradt

HSR
station

SHULIN STREET

Five Concubines
Temple

Tainan Airport,
Ten Drum Culture Village

JIANKANG ROAD

0 — 200m
0 — 200yds

For listings, see pages 211–15

🛏 **Where to stay**

1 Fuqi Hostel...B3
2 JJ-W Culture..A2
3 La Plaza...B1
4 Shangri La's Far Eastern Plaza.......D2
5 Taiwanfoo Apartment.......................C2
6 Tayih Landis...A3
7 Tie Dao..C2

✴ **Where to eat and drink**

8 Ai Zai Cheng Shrimp Rice...........A3
9 Armoury Pub....................................B1
10 Chikan Peddler's Noodles...........B2
11 Hsu Family..A2
12 Nanxing Yellow Eel Noodles.....A3
New Asia Teppanyaki...........(see 6)
13 Qingqi Breakfast.............................C2
14 Sen Maw Rice Food........................C3
15 Sunice...C3
16 Tin Pan Alley....................................D1

& ultra-modern fittings. The upstairs lounge area has a PC for guests' use plus unlimited tea & coffee. Artists were given carte blanche with a number of rooms: Tsai Ming-liang's (see page 36) has unplastered walls, a bathtub on a mezzanine & portholes in the sleeping area. The same owners also operate the women-only 28-room **JJ-S Hotel** (*74, Lane 158, Zhongyi Rd Sec 2;* ☎ *223 1666;* f *223 3666; www.jj-shotel.com.tw;* **$$$**). B/fast inc. **$$$**

🏠 **La Plaza Hotel** (103 rooms) 202 Chenggong Rd; ☎ 229 0271; f 221 1133; e laplazahotel@ yahoo.com.tw; www.laplaza.com.tw. The popularity of this hotel (with Japanese business travellers in particular) is entirely understandable. The rooms are absolutely spotless & well appointed. Broadband & Wi-Fi throughout the building. There's a fitness centre & guests can borrow bikes for free. Some of the 3-person rooms are especially good value as they have balconies

& small living rooms. Additional bed in the room for NTD500. B/fast inc, served in the 8th-flr restaurant that also serves steaks, salads & other dishes (⏱ 11.30–14.00, 17.30–20.30 daily; EM; $$$). **$$$**

🏠 **Taiwanfoo Apartment** (1 apt) 90 Zhongshan Rd; **m** 0932 041 915; **e** taiwanfoo. apt@gmail.com; www.tainanhomestay.com. Owned by the author of this guidebook, who also leads informal tours of south Taiwan, this super-central & quiet apt is ideal for small parties (up to 5 ppl) who want a place to themselves. Refrigerator, cable TV, internet & washing machine (soap powder provided). Call or email at least 3 days in advance. **$$**

🏠 **Fuqi Hostel** (3 dorms) 76 Zhongzheng Rd; 📞703 4543; **e** fuqi.tainan@gmail.com. www.fuqi.

hostel.com. While offering 28 beds, for as little as NTD450 pp per night, the English-speaking owners of this hostel have succeeded in keeping some of this building's 1940s character but that also means narrow, steep stairs (cyclists hoping to bring their bikes indoors might struggle). Reception ⏱ 09.00–22.00 daily. **$**

🏠 **Tie Dao Hotel** (130 rooms) 2 Chenggong Rd; 📞221 3200; www.tie-dao.com.tw. 'Tie Dao' means railroad & this is the best of the cheapies near Tainan TRA Station. If you don't mind curving corridors that seem to go on forever it's a good bet. Because of the building's unusual shape, a few of the 4-person corner rooms have huge amounts of redundant space. Internet & basic b/fast inc. **$**

✗ WHERE TO EAT

City centre The following establishments are shown on the map on opposite.

✗ **Chikan Peddler's Noodles** 赤崁擔仔麵 180 Minzu Rd Sec 2; 📞220 5336; www.chikan. com.tw; ⏱ 11.00–02.00 daily. The emphasis here is on traditional recipes cooked with high-quality ingredients. The eponymous danzai noodles (served

with minced pork & a single shrimp) are extremely tasty but portions are small so order some extra items. The wooden ceiling beams aren't original but not everything here is artifice: the tables & chairs downstairs are genuinely time-worn & look like they were retrieved from a primary school. Long-legged diners will feel more comfortable upstairs; both floors have AC. Among the furnishings there's a radio

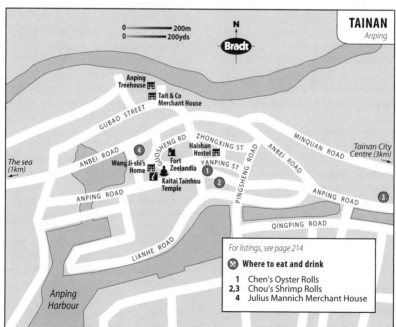

& a telephone from the first half of the 20th century. Even the kid's high chair is an old wooden model. Not all the menu is bilingual; desserts include bean curd & shaved ice. **$$**

✖ **Nanxing Yellow Eel Noodles** 南興鱔魚意麵 92 Kangle St; ☎229 2979; ⏰ 12.00–03.00 daily. This tiny eatery has no English sign or menu & only 3 tables but local gourmets say it's the best in its field. The eel is neither fishy nor greasy; non-eel dishes include fried noodles, fried vegetables & various kinds of offal. **$$**

✖ **Ai Zai Cheng Shrimp Rice** 66 Haian Rd Sec 1; ☎220 1897; ⏰ 07.00–17.30 daily. In business since 1922, this simple eatery serves up portions of rice topped with shrimps cooked on a charcoal grill (*NTD40*), a delicious duck broth which also contains dried fish & strips of pork (*NTD30*), & side dishes such as sausages & soups (*from NTD10*). AC & EM; pay when you order at the counter. Soft drinks available. **$**

✖ **Hsu Family Restaurant** 許家芋粿 8 Guohua St Sec 3; ☎228 8897; ⏰ 09.30–22.30 daily. The owners like to keep things simple. There are but 3 dishes, none priced over NTD50. The meatballs here contain shrimp as well as pork. The thick mushroom soup (*xiāng gū gēng*) is glutinous & tasty. The signature dish is the delightful savoury taro cake 芋粿 (*yù guǒ*). Naturally the owners won't say what they add to the taro paste to give it such a mild yet memorable flavour. **$**

✖ **Qingqi Breakfast** 清祺早餐 135 Qingnian Rd; ☎228 5781; ⏰ 04.30–11.30 & 13.30–22.00 daily. Name notwithstanding, this long-established eatery serves excellent vegetarian dim sum throughout the day. Help yourself from what's kept warm in the circular bamboo steamers out front, order noodles if you're especially hungry & take your selection to the counter inside where you pay. The bright lights & white-tile walls may remind you of an old hospital but for many the cleanliness is a draw. **$**

✖ **Sen Maw Rice Food** 317 Kaishan Rd; ☎214 3389; ⏰ 07.00–19.00 Thu–Tue. Going since the early 1980s, Sen Maw specialises in the savoury pudding-type dish known in Taiwanese as *waguei*. Add spicy sauce or crushed garlic according to your preference & wash it down with a bowl of meatball soup. **$**

✖ **Sunice** 太陽牌冰店 41 Minquan Rd Sec 1; ☎225 9375; ⏰ 08.00–20.00 daily. The only English on the front of this nondescript outlet reads 'Tarra Ice Brick'. What they serve up is not quite high-calorie ice cream nor the crushed ice that's so popular during Taiwan's summers but something in between. It's very refreshing & 19 flavours are available, among them conventional tastes like mango & strawberry. More radical options inc walnut & egg yolk, yam & rice cake. They've been doing this for half a century & have it down pat. **$**

Anping The following establishments are shown on the map on page 213.

✖ **Julius Mannich Merchant House** 東興洋行 3, Lane 233, Anbei Rd; ☎226 4573; ⏰ 10.00–21.00 daily. For Western visitors, this 19th-century house, built to house a German trading company, isn't much of a tourist attraction. Rather than explain Taiwan's interactions with Western traders, the displays focus on German heritage. As a place to eat & drink, however, it's worth considering as the menu lists pork knuckle, sausages, sauerkraut & typical snacks. Meal sets start at NTD200. Bottled & draught German beers from NTD90. Soft drinks priced NTD30–130. **$$$**

✖ **Chen's Oyster Rolls** 陳家蚵捲 786 Anping Rd; ☎222 9661; ⏰ 10.00–20.00 daily. Chens uses modern technology to crank out delicious yet inexpensive traditional food. In addition to the signature oyster omelettes, there are shrimp rolls (best with a squirt of wasabi) & soups. EM but you may have to hunt for it. Portions are snack-sized, so order 2 or 3 items pp if you've a serious appetite. **$**

✖ **Chou's Shrimp Rolls** 周氏蝦捲 408-1 Anping Rd; ☎280 1304; http://chous.com.tw; ⏰ 10.00–22.00 daily. Don't expect much olde-worlde atmosphere at Anping's best-known seafood eatery, where it seems every aspect of preparation & serving has been optimised by efficiency experts. The good thing is you won't have to wait long & the food is consistently excellent, especially the signature rolls. A single portion of the famous shrimp rolls (*xiā juǎn*) doesn't make a meal, so also order meatballs or soup. There's a small branch near Fort Zeelandia at 125 Anping Rd (☎229 2618; ⏰ *07.00–19.30 daily*). **$**

WHERE TO DRINK The following establishments are shown on the map on page 212.

♀ **Armoury Pub** 82 Gongyuan S Rd; ☏226 9520; www.armorypub.com.tw; ⏰ 20.00–03.00 daily. Likely the most successful pub in Tainan's history but not quite the expat-magnet or artist-hangout it was in its heyday, the Armoury still draws lots of young locals. DJs & bands often perform & the bar (which gets its name because it's next to what used to be an arsenal) offers a good range of imported beers (*from NTD100*), cocktails (*from NTD150*) & hot meals. **$$**

♀ **Tin Pan Alley** 28 Beimen Rd Sec 2; ☏223 1123; www.facebook.com/tinpanalleytaiwan; ⏰ 11.00–02.30 daily. Beer from NTD100 (*NTD70 in happy hour*), bottled & draft ciders from NTD150 plus cocktails for similar prices mean this is a good place to wet your whistle. It also has some of the city's best pizzas (*NTD200 & up*), sandwiches & Mexican items. Check their Facebook page for details of quiz nights & food specials. **$$**

OTHER PRACTICALITIES

$ Bank of Taiwan [212 C3] 155 Fuqian Rd Sec 1
✉ **General Post Office** [212 C2] 6 Chenggong Rd; ⏰ 08.00–20.00 Mon–Fri, 08.30–16.30 Sat, 08.30–12.00 Sun. Money can be changed in the banking section next door ⏰ 08.00–17.30 Mon–Fri.

✚ **National Chengkung University Hospital** 138 Shengli Rd; ☏235 3535; www.hosp.ncku.edu. tw; ⏰ 24hrs daily

WHAT TO SEE AND DO Because there's so much to take in, major attractions have been arranged as four tours.

ANPING 安平 The cradle of Han Chinese civilisation in Taiwan and the first European base on the island, Anping – the name means 'place of peace' and was chosen by Koxinga himself – has a wealth of physical remains from the 17th, 18th and 19th centuries. After the Dutch were expelled, the English East India Company cut a deal with Koxinga's son and set up a trade base. The venture didn't prosper, however, and so between 1682 and 1864, when Anping was opened to foreign trade, the port handled coastal and cross-Strait shipping only.

Fort Zeelandia aka Anping Old Fort 安平古堡 *(Ānpíng Gǔbǎo)* (⏰ 08.30–17.30 daily; admission NTD50/25) What you see here is very different from what existed during the Dutch era. The original bastion – completed in 1634 and named after the ship on which the first VOC governor arrived – had a much larger footprint than the current site. Inside the fort you'll find models showing the original layout and features such as the Protestant chapel (Catholics had to worship in secret), the governor's residence and the execution ground just beyond the outer wall. Typhoons, earthquakes and the appropriation of building materials meant that, by the beginning of the 20th century, little was left of the Dutch structure.

The excellent museum in the building on the left gives a thorough overview of both the fort's history and technical aspects of its construction. Pottery shards – some Dutch, others Chinese – retrieved during archaeological excavations are displayed, and the ultimate fate of Frederik Coyett, the Swedish-born governor who surrendered to Koxinga in 1662 (see *History*, page 12), is described. On his return to Batavia he was blamed for the loss of the Taiwan colony, arrested and imprisoned. (In fact he had repeatedly warned his superiors that Koxinga was a threat; just prior to Koxinga's attack, the VOC had resolved to replace him with someone less 'alarmist'.) When Coyett finally made it back to Europe, he tried to clear his name by authoring a self-serving account of his governorship and the siege.

Right behind the museum stands the largest surviving section of the original fortress. A massive brick-and-coral wall, it looks weathered and truly battered yet ready to survive another few centuries. Climb the steps inside the watchtower (a 20th-century addition) for views towards the city and the coast. None of the cannon arrayed near the watchtower date from the Dutch era, although the least corroded one is almost 300 years old and could in its day fire a small cannonball 2km.

Kaitai Tianhou Temple 開台天后宮 (*33 Guosheng Rd;* ⏰ *05.00–22.00 daily*)
The green glazed roof tiles of this shrine can be seen from Fort Zeelandia and the current structure, completed in 1976, is exceptionally intricate and colourful. It's claimed the main Mazu icon inside is more than a millennium old and was brought to Taiwan by Koxinga himself. If so, the statuette has been lucky to survive. Since its founding in 1668 the temple has moved more than once, caught fire and been demolished on the orders of the Japanese colonial authorities.

Wang Ji-shi's Home 王雞屎洋樓 (*2, Lane 35, Guosheng Rd; not open to the public*)
Possibly Wang wanted a house that would distract attention from his given name, which literally meant 'chicken droppings'. The fact his parents named him thus suggests he was a sickly baby; they possibly believed – as many did in Taiwan at that time – that a more grandiose name would arouse the jealousy of disease-spreading spirits. As an adult Wang did well in the salt trade, and his 1937 two-storey abode continues to excite architecture buffs. Octagonal windows face the fort, but to see the façade you'll have to duck down the tiny alley on the building's left. For another view and a quick look at a quaint bungalow from the same era, take the lane on the right. Since his death in 1948, Wang has been venerated as a land god in the dingy shrine just around the corner at 12, Lane 35, Guosheng Road. Look for a small soot-black effigy on the right of the front altar, just in front of a horse, smoking a real cigarette through a holder.

Anping's old streets Budget some time for **Yanping Street**, said to be the oldest road in Taiwan, and nearby lanes. For the past two centuries there's been a small temple at 106 Yanping Street, but during the Dutch era this site signified segregation – only Europeans were allowed to reside between this spot and Fort Zeelandia; Chinese, Japanese and aborigines were kept on the inland side. Some alleyways are so narrow wandering tourists risk grazed elbows. You'll stumble across piles of wood salvaged from collapsed houses and stone slabs which likely came from the mainland as ballast aboard cargo junks. The oldest houses are modest L-shaped structures with tiny courtyards. Above the doorways of some sword-lion motifs keep evil at bay; often blue-faced and green-whiskered, each lion grips a blade between its teeth while staring down at passers-by. One of the most photogenic sword lions belongs to a ruin at 44 Zhongxing Street. Nearby **Haishan Hostel** 海山館 (*7, Lane 52, Xiaozhong St;* ⏰ *09.00–17.00 daily; free admission*) was built in the late 17th century as a dormitory and gathering place for soldiers from Haitan in Fujian.

Tait & Co Merchant House 德記洋行 (*194 Anbei Rd;* ⏰ *08.30–17.30 daily; admission NTD50/25*) The Victorian businessmen who lived and worked in this elegant two-floor, 130-year-old building dealt mainly in tea, but also provided banking and insurance services to fellow Western merchants. The museum on the ground floor, one of the best in Anping, focuses not on the 19th century but on the 17th. Extracts from VOC archives record the arrival of Chinese junks loaded with migrants, salt and iron cooking pots. The utensils were bartered with aborigines for deer skins and meat. The Dutch were fond of making laws: neither indigenous people nor Chinese settlers were allowed to own a dog without a licence (dogs were used for hunting fowl); a license was needed for snaring deer; and gambling was forbidden. It's thought some of the bricks used to build the ruined warehouse behind the Tait office were purloined from the ruins of Fort Zeelandia. The warehouse is now known as **Anping Treehouse 安平樹屋** (*admission inc in the Tait ticket*) on account of the huge banyans that have grown through the roof. The way in which roots have climbed walls and grown across openings is almost surreal; make a point of exploring every corner of the building.

Koxinga's capital

Confucius Temple 孔子廟 *(Kǒngzǐ Miào)* [212 B3] (*2 Nanmen Rd; http:// confucius.culture.tw; inner courtyard ⊕ 08.00–17.30 daily, grounds ⊕ 24hrs daily; closed Tomb Sweeping, Dragon Boat and Mid-Autumn festivals; admission to the grounds free; admission to the inner courtyard NTD25*) Possibly the most sublimely beautiful historical building in Taiwan, Tainan's Confucius Temple is a genuine must-see. Founded by Koxinga's son in 1665 and central to the Ming loyalists' efforts to preserve and transmit classical Chinese values, the temple functioned as both a school and a shrine where the sage was – and each 28 September continues to be – venerated. Calligraphy tablets donated by all six of Taiwan's presidents hang in the inner sanctum, and every year on the seventh day of the seventh lunar month, teenagers in traditional garb ride here on horseback and offer incense to Confucius as part of the Qixi rite (see box, page 220). Sadly, many of the massive and ancient banyan trees in the temple's grounds have reached the ends of their lives. By the main gate on Nanmen Road, note the inscription on your right as you face the temple. It orders visitors on horseback to dismount before entering. It's in both Chinese and Manchurian; the latter, an official language of the Qing court, resembles written Tibetan. The stone archway across the road dates from 1777 and celebrates the role of the Confucius Temple in cultivating literati.

Koxinga Shrine 延平郡王祠 *(Yánpíng Jùnwángcí)* [212 C3] (*152 Kaishan Rd; ⊕ 09.00–17.30 daily*) Koxinga died before the mini-state he established was a year old. Like many other Chinese historical figures, his spirit was worshipped not only by his descendants but also by those convinced such a great man must have godly powers. The manicured grounds that surround the shrine are very attractive even for those with no interest in the man or the cult. History buffs should spend their time inside the shrine itself rather than the adjacent museum (⊕ *09.00–17.00 Tue– Sun; free admission*) as the information panels contain some fascinating snippets: Koxinga's Japanese mother committed suicide in 1646 rather than suffer the indignity of being captured by the Manchus (his father, however, defected to the invaders); the Qing authorities moved Koxinga's grave to Fujian in 1699; and, for the first few decades of Qing rule, local people worshipped the Ming loyalist under the pseudonym 'Prince Zhu' to avoid angering the island's new rulers. His birthday is still celebrated on the 16th day of the first lunar month. In time Koxinga was rehabilitated. In 1874, an imperial official on an inspection tour of Taiwan noted how this long-dead enemy of the Qing was still revered by Tainan residents. He recommended to the court that permission be given to upgrade the existing shrine. The emperor gave his consent the following year and at the same time ratified Koxinga's status as a god. The Japanese, keen to stress Koxinga's connections to their country, converted the site into a Shinto *jinja*. This was unacceptable to the Chinese Nationalists and in the early 1960s they replaced it with the current building. A statue of Koxinga, seated as if on a throne, takes centre stage; offerings of incense and fruit are made each day. More than a hundred of his most loyal and trusted lieutenants are also commemorated here.

Dongyue Hall 東嶽殿 [212 C3] (*110 Minquan Rd Sec 1;* ⊕ *05.30–21.30 daily*)
When 19th-century missionary George L Mackay described religion in Taiwan
as being 'of the same kind and quality as the heathenism of China… the same
poisonous mixture, the same dark, damning nightmare', he was likely thinking of
places like this – a cramped and spooky place of worship named after Emperor
Dongyue, a god whose job description includes making sure sinners get their just
deserts. Other deities worshipped here include underworld generals and ministers,
but the main object of veneraton is King Dizang (Sanskrit name *Ksitigarbha*), the
Buddhist bodhisattva of those in hell. Because King Dizang is believed to have
power over monsters and mischief-making demons, disaster victims sometimes
beg him for relief. However, the majority of those praying here are relatives of the
recently deceased, petitioning the emperor in an effort to minimise their loved
ones' suffering in the after-world.

Some of the posthumous torments wrongdoers can anticipate are depicted in
the temple's graphic wall murals. These show terrified prisoners being chopped into
pieces and fed to wolves or dropped on spikes. The first version of this temple shrine
was a thatched hut built in 1673. Early followers included some of Koxinga's soldiers
who would offer incense to the emperor and then wear packets of incense ash as
amulets for protection against the pestilence then rife in Taiwan. This temple's special
atmosphere is heightened by a lack of direct natural light. The interior is awkward
because the Japanese colonial authorities – no fans of Taiwanese folk religion –
ordered the demolition of part of the shrine when they decided to widen Tainan's
roads in the 1930s. On the right as you exit the shrine there's a workshop that turns
out paper models of houses, cars and other items which are burned during funerals to
ensure the dead do not lack for shelter or furniture in the next world. This stretch of
Minquan Road is where the pious do their shopping. Several stores sell indispensables
such as votive money, incense sticks and stainless steel ghost-money burners. You
may browse, but be respectful when taking photos or handling items.

Martial Rites Temple aka Official God of War Temple 祀典武廟 *(Sìdiăn Wŭ
Miào)* [212 B2] (*229 Yongfu Rd Sec 2;* ⊕ *07.00–21.00 daily*) If you've time for
only one of Tainan's major shrines, make it this gorgeous edifice. The temple used
to be part of Prince Ning Jing's palace, but in 1674 the Ming pretender agreed to
convert it into a shrine dedicated to Guan Gong. Walk through the main chamber
to find a pavilion dedicated to Guanyin on the left (note the delicate but weathered
woodcarvings of dragons). Behind it there's a delightful little rock garden. The little
temple opposite at 200 Yongfu Road Section 2 honours an equine spirit – Guan
Gong's steed.

Qing Taiwanfoo
Great Queen of Heaven Temple 大天后宮 *(Dàtiānhòu Gōng)* [212 B2]
(⊕ *05.00–21.00 daily*) When leaving the Martial Rites Temple, sightseers usually
head next door to this timber-framed Mazu shrine. Established in 1684 by Shi
Lang, the general who masterminded the defeat of the Kingdom of Dongning
(see *History*, page 13), it was also formerly part of Prince Ning Jing's mansion. Shi
attributed his victory to the Mazu icons he carried with him during the campaign;
he may have been sincere, but it's possible his conspicuous piety was contrived to
win over Taiwan's Mazu-adoring population. Inside the temple a gold-skinned and
sour-faced Mazu is flanked by the two demons she tamed. On the right as you face
the goddess there's an antique set of 21 votive handbells. At the back of the complex,
behind a red fence, stands Ning Jing's memorial tablet – he committed suicide here

in 1683, aged 65 – but even if you read Chinese it's near-impossible to pick out amid the clutter of tablets and icons.

The alleyway which links the Martial Rites Temple and the Great Queen of Heaven Temple, Lane 227 of Yongfu Road Section 2, is known as 'fortune-tellers' alley' because at least three residents ply this trade in their front rooms. None of them speak English, so bring a bilingual friend if you want your fortune told.

Chikan Tower 赤崁樓 **(Chìkǎn Lóu)** [212 B2] (*212 Minzu Rd Sec 2;* ⊕ *08.30–21.00 daily; admission NTD50/25*) Located across the road from the Martial Rites Temples, this is where the Dutch built their second stronghold in 1653. The Chinese appellation, which means 'red-roofed tower', is derived from an aboriginal name. Little remains of that bastion, which the VOC called **Fort Provintia**, although an exposed remnant will give you an idea of just how robust it was. In reality, Chikan Tower is a small complex of traditional Chinese buildings set in a Chinese classical garden; think moon gates, carp-filled ponds and manicured mini-trees. As such it works well, especially in the evening when the on-site coffee shop (*EM; non-alcoholic drinks; $*) draws a relaxed crowd. Two pagodas and a school were built on the Dutch ruins in the 19th century. Only a small part of the school still exists, but the pagodas have been kept up in good condition. The front tower was built in 1886 at the urging of local officials who credited the Sea God with protecting Taiwan during the Mudan Incident of 1874 and the Sino-French War of 1884–85. The Sea God's services are no longer required but the other tower still has a religious function. It's known as the Wenchang Pavilion, and in addition to honouring Wenchang Dijun, visiting students climb the creaking wooden stairway to petition a statue of Kueixingxiang, the god of literature.

Haian Road [212 A1] This broad boulevard is lined with car parks, coffee shops and boutiques. The widening of the road in the 1990s, together with an aborted shopping-centre project, left several empty buildings and irregularly shaped plots of land. Artists were given a free hand to remodel the extensive frontage; the results have been widely hailed as a successful example of art transforming a public place and helping to regenerate a neighbourhood. While here, make a point of wandering down **Shennong Street**, Tainan's most traditional thoroughfare. Some of the old two-storey merchant houses have been turned into shops or bars and retain the original steep wooden staircases.

Wind God Temple 風神廟 [212 A2] (*8, Lane 143, Minquan Rd Sec 3;* ⊕ *07.00–21.00 daily*) This is the only temple devoted to the Wind God in Taiwan, which is surprising given the frequency of typhoons. The Wind God, represented by effigies in the centre of the shrine, is believed to have influence over the five elements of earth, fire, metal, water and wood. On the right, the Thunder God holds a hammer in one hand and a nail in the other. His wife, the Lightning Mother, carries a pair of circular mirrors on the left. At the time of the temple's founding in 1739, the ocean was a stone's throw away and the **Government Reception Archway** 接官亭 was where VIPs arriving from the mainland would disembark. Take a close look at this stone archway and you'll find carvings of dragons, lions and sages.

Great South Gate 大南門 [212 B3] (*Nanmen Rd & Shulin St; gate* ⊕ *08.00–17.00 daily, surrounding park* ⊕ *24hrs daily*) Served by bus #2, the South Gate is the best preserved of Tainan's four remaining city gates (there used to be 14). There's a segment of wall and even a pair of cannons, though presumably the latter were originally installed on top of the wall rather than pointing at it. The two-storey building in the centre of the park dates from 1932 and features a slightly unusual combination: Art Deco windows and a tiled exterior. At the end of the park furthest from Nanmen Road there's a collection of stelae, inscribed stone tablets from the mid-18th to mid-19th century. These stelae, each the size of a very large tombstone, served various official functions. Some promulgated new laws, others recorded the visit of a high official or the suppression of a rebellion. Information panels beside each slab summarise the text in both English and modern Chinese. They're fascinating snapshots of Qing society: one decree, dating from 1767, stipulates that beggars shall not display corpses when soliciting alms; there's also a directive that people should not commit suicide as a way of repudiating their debts.

Five Concubines Temple 五妃廟 [212 C4] (*Between Wufei St & Jiankang Rd;* ⏲ *08.30–21.00 daily*) This shrine, founded in 1748 and located in a small park full of gnarled trees, commemorates the ladies who, when the Kingdom of Dongning was destroyed in 1683, decided to accompany their lord Prince Ning Jing to the next world rather than take his advice to remarry or flee to a nunnery. Instead of the usual door gods, the entrance bears body-length portraits of two of the concubines. Inside, all five are represented by doll-sized josses. Beside the tomb where the concubines are said to be buried there's a tiny shrine devoted to two eunuchs who also killed themselves rather than submit to the island's new rulers.

Altar of Heaven aka Tiantan 天壇 [212 B2] (*16, Lane 84, Zhongyi Rd Sec 2;* ⏲ *05.00–22.00 daily*) Hidden in the backstreets but unmissable thanks to its egg-yolk yellow walls, this is said to be where Koxinga prayed to the Jade Emperor and where, in the 18th century, local folk celebrated that god's birthday on the ninth day of the first lunar month. The temple, which was built in 1854, continues to be

---

QIXI: BECOMING A GROWN-UP IN TAINAN

Taiwanese can drive when they're 18 and vote when they're 20. But according to one of Tainan's most popular customs, they become adults when they turn 16. In Qing-era Tainan, a child reaching that age was a cause for celebration because 16-year-olds working on the docks and in workshops were entitled to adult wages, not the half-salaries younger employees received. Since the 1740s, 16-year-olds and their parents have been going to the **Kailong Temple** 開隆宮 (*56, Lane 79, Zhongshan Rd;* ⏲ *05.30–21.00 daily*) on the seventh day of the seventh lunar month to celebrate this coming of age. The event is called *qīxī* in Mandarin because it coincides with a traditional lovers' day. In 2014, the principal rite will be on the morning of 2 August. In 2015, it'll be on 20 August.

Until quite recently those wishing to take part in the ceremony, which involves crawling under an altar three times, had to purchase special gowns, shoes and hats and prepare specific offerings to honour Qiniangma, the goddess believed to protect children under the age of 16. Nowadays the clothing can be rented and offerings need not adhere to custom so closely. The city government has been promoting the event as a way to bring visitors to Tainan. Even if watching teenagers wave joss sticks while their parents try to cram offerings on to tables already buckling under the weight of fruit, rice and seaweed doesn't appeal to you, some of the associated folk performances and concerts might.

very popular. There's a good chance you'll run into some kind of religious event and see a Taoist priest crack a thick whip to scare off ghosts. These rites are invariably accompanied by deafening pipe-and-drum music; there are no hymns or requiems in folk religion, just lengthy jams. Unusually, there's no effigy on the main altar, but rather an ornate tablet bearing the emperor's title: *Yùhuáng Shàngdì*. The shrine's most famous calligraphy tablet bears the character *yī* ('one'), which is written with a single left-to-right horizontal stroke.

Prefectural Cheng Huang Temple 都城隍廟 [212 C2] (*133 Qingnian Rd;* ⏰ *05.30–21.00 daily*) While not as large as its counterparts in Chiayi or Hsinchu, Tainan's city-god shrine is to be seen as much for the serene back garden with its huge spirit-money furnace as for the interior art. Before going inside look at the corners of the frontage – the largest and highest of the figurines on both sides depict Europeans, although their attire looks more Chinese than Western. If you come here on or around the 11th day of the fifth lunar month, you'll see lively celebrations for the city god's birthday. The faithful confer offerings on the deity and get free sacks of rice in return.

Xi Hua Hall 西華堂 [212 C1] (*92 Beizhong St, also accessible from 65 Xihua St;* ⏰ *06.30–18.00 daily*) A small 260-year-old Buddhist nunnery that's an oasis of peace despite its city-centre location, Xi Hua Hall is less than 50m from **Tainan Park** 台南公園 (⏰ *24hrs daily*). Inside the park there's a memorial archway venerating literature and learning; it was erected during the reign of Emperor Jiaqing (1796–1820).

Japanese Tainan
The city is rich in Japanese-era architecture and the highlights can be seen by taking a leisurely two-hour walking tour. To begin, head southwest from the station.

Former Tainan Meeting Hall 原台南公會堂 [212 C2] (⏰ *08.00–22.00 daily; free admission*) This 1911 French-influenced structure hosts occasional exhibitions while the adjacent wood building functions as a coffee/souvenir shop. The lawn, pond and rockery behind date from the 1820s and together are known as **Wu Garden** (⏰ *24hrs daily; free admission*) after Wu Shang-xin (1795–1848), a salt tycoon who owned a major chunk of this neighbourhood. Wu's gravestone is now displayed in Great South Gate Park.

Old Weather Station 台南氣象站 [212 B2] (*21 Gongyuan Rd;* ⏰ *09.00–17.00 Mon–Fri; free admission*) Likely the oldest Japanese government building surviving in Taiwan, locals nicknamed this 1898 structure 'the pepper-pot' on account of its unusual shape. The displays inside lack English labels but you'll have no difficulty recognising the old seismographs.

National Museum of Taiwanese Literature 國立台灣文學館 (*Guólì Táiwān Wénxuéguǎn*) [212 B3] (*1 Zhongzheng Rd;* ☎ *221 7201; www.nmtl.gov.tw;* ⏰ *09.00–21.00 Tue–Sun; free admission*) Externally and internally charming, Tainan's former city hall was built in 1916 and is distinguished by a European façade and a fine mansard roof. When the city government relocated in 1997, the structure was converted to a museum that has bilingual displays about the lives and works of both local and foreign writers. If you plan to spend a while inside, get an English-language audio guide from the cloakroom on the right as you enter (hand over your passport or NTD1,000 as a deposit).

Old Tainan Martial Arts Academy 原台南武德殿 [212 B3] (*Youai St; usually closed to the public*) If you're leaving the literature museum, head south and turn right just before the Confucius Temple to see the back of the Martial Arts Academy, a voluptuous piece of classical Japanese architecture. The original was erected in 1936; the current structure serves as an elementary-school auditorium.

Land Bank 土地銀行 [212 C3] (*28 Zhongzheng Rd;* ⊕ *09.00–15.30 Mon–Fri*) This massive Art Deco edifice was built in 1937 as a branch of Japan's Kang Gyo Bank. The interior is worth a very quick look; you can change money upstairs.

Lin's Department Store 林百貨店 [212 B3] (*Zhongzheng & Zhongyi rds;* ⊕ *10.00–17.00 Wed–Sun*) Known during the colonial era as Hayashi Hyakkaten, this department store won great public attention when it opened in 1932 because it boasted Taiwan's first passenger elevator. After a thorough renovation visitors can once again ride that lift, which seems very small by modern standards, and admire its unique mosaic floor. Do go up to the rooftop to see the restored Shinto shrine plus bomb damage and bullet holes from an American air raid in the last few months of World War II. By the time you read this, shops and perhaps a restaurant are likely to be operating inside.

THE OUTSKIRTS

National Museum of Taiwan History 國立台灣歷史博物館 *(Guólì Táiwān Lìshǐ Bówùguǎn)* (*250 Zhanghe Rd Sec 1, Annan District;* ☏ *356 8899; www.nmth.gov. tw;* ⊕ *09.00–17.00 Tue–Sun; free admission*) The permanent exhibits in this excellent museum go all the way back to 'Zuozhen Man' (see *History*, page 11). Of the many vivid models and images, most memorable is the full-size replica of a single-mast junk, the kind of vessel that transported goods between Taiwan and the Chinese mainland during the Qing era. Several of the museum's 200 fibreglass human figures are in or around the boat; crew members negotiate with an imperial official who wears a mandarin's gown while stowaways hoping to start a new life in Taiwan cower in the hold. Elsewhere, dozens more waxworks-style figures form a religious parade or work on the land. These mock-ups do a superb job of pushing one's imagination back to the Taiwan of yore. Other displays explore the 19th-century tea trade and the adoption of Alid, a deity revered by the indigenous Siraya people (see box opposite), by Han Taiwanese who now worship him as Alizu.

The museum is 10km northeast of the city centre and is linked to Tainan TRA Station by bus #18 (*12 departures per day Mon–Fri; 22 departures per day Sat–Sun;* ⊕ *07.05–18.40; takes 30mins; NTD18*).

Ten Drum Culture Village (☏ *266 2225 ext 777; www.ten-hsieh.com.tw;* ⊕ *09.00–17.00 daily; admission NTD300/280*) Lauded at home for the way in which it has lifted *zhentou* culture (see box, page 31) to a new level, the Grammy-nominated Ten Drum Art Percussion Group has won a reputation overseas for electrifying performances which feature flutes, gongs and martial-arts moves as well as sensational drumming. The parent organisation is now based at this former sugar refinery where troupe full-timers give at least four performances every weekend (*10.30 & 15.00 Sat–Sun*). Drum groups from around Asia are invited to play here every summer. Also on site there's a workshop where an artisan makes buffalo-hide drums the traditional way.

An easy way to get here is to take a local train to Baoan. From Tainan there are around four departures each hour (*takes 6mins; NTD15*). Turn right when leaving

Baoan TRA Station and walk 1km towards the refinery's chimney stack – it's the tallest structure for some distance around and on it you'll see the English words 'Ten Drum'. Baoan TRA Station will also provide access to **Chi Mei Museum** (*www. chimeimuseum.com*) when this depository for a local tycoon's eclectic art collection opens to the public sometime in 2014.

A FORGOTTEN TRIBE CAMPAIGNS FOR RECOGNITION

On the face of it, Tainan is ethnically homogeneous. Almost everyone, it seems, is descended from Han Chinese who came to Taiwan two or more centuries ago. That's what most people believe, anyhow. The leaders of the Xinhua-based Siraya Culture Association think otherwise, arguing that many Tainan folk are indigenous even if they don't know it. When the Dutch arrived in the 1600s, Taiwan's southwest was the stomping ground of the Siraya people, an Austronesian tribe. This ethnic group didn't simply disappear as Han settlers poured into the region, the SCA argues. Elements of its culture and language live on, and since the SCA's formation in 1999 the association has been striving to 'energize the Siraya tribe' and reconstruct the Siraya language, the last native speaker having died circa 1908.

Siraya had no written form until the 1630s, when Dutch missionaries devised a romanisation system to aid their conversion efforts. One pastor wrote: 'Their language sounds pleasant, modest, measured, and extraordinarily graceful, so that judging them in this respect you would not think them to be savage but to be outstandingly wise men, filled to the brim with modesty and virtue.' Working from gospel fragments and contracts (for at least 150 years after the Europeans left, the Siraya used the Dutch-designed writing system when drawing up lease agreements and other transactions) the SCA has compiled and published a 3,500-word Siraya glossary. You won't hear Siraya spoken in Xinhua, but here are a few words to impress – or baffle – the locals: *tabe* is hello; *tatalag* means welcome; *alid* means god, while *alilid* means to thank.

According to a Han traveller who visited the region in 1603, Siraya society was matriarchal. There were no tribal chiefs or kings as such, and everyone was considered equal. Rather than cultivate rice in paddy fields, the Siraya subsisted on dry or 'upland' rice. Deer were hunted, but only in winter; skin and horns were bartered with Han settlers in exchange for cloth and other goods. Siraya homes were bamboo framed and the roofs were thatched with straw. Doors were left unlocked, he wrote, because society was so orderly. Unlike Han people, who have traditionally preferred to bury their dead at times and in locations they considered auspicious, when a Siraya died, his or her body was first preserved by smoking, then buried under the floor of the family home. Compulsory abortions were another unusual feature of traditional Siraya society; couples weren't allowed to live together or have children until the husband ceased being a warrior and became a community elder.

We have a good idea what the Siraya looked like before they became assimilated, thanks to the artists working for the VOC and Scotsman John Thomson (1837–1921). Thomson, later the British royal family's official photographer, toured Taiwan's southwest in 1871 and took some of the very first photos of the region. His images are preserved at the Wellcome Library in London and can be viewed online at http://images.wellcome.ac.uk.

HEADING INLAND FROM TAINAN *Telephone code 06*

Once you've got past the suburbs, Highway 20 is a good introduction to the south's countryside and foothills.

GETTING THERE, AWAY AND AROUND

By bus Green Line buses set out from Tainan TRA Station for Yujing every half hour (⏱ *06.00–22.00 daily; takes 1hr; NTD119*) via Xinhua (*takes 30mins; NTD43*). From Yujing there are infrequent buses to Jiaxian (see page 265) via Holy Glory Temple.

By car, motorcycle or bicycle Highway 20 gets busy during rush hours. Weekends see heavy traffic eastwards in the mornings and westwards around dusk. From Yujing, it's possible to take Highway 3 north past Zengwen Reservoir and on to Alishan via Local Road 129 (see page 239). From Beiliao, Highway 3 leads south, skirting Moonscape World before reaching Qishan.

TOURIST INFORMATION

ℹ Siraya National Scenic Area Administration 西拉雅國家風景區 ☏699 0335; www.siraya-nsa.gov.tw

WHAT TO SEE AND DO References are to distance markers on Highway 20.

Xinhua Old Street 新化老街 (*km12*) A stretch of Zhongzheng Road remains Xinhua's commercial heart but to see it you'll need to leave Highway 20. Turn right when you see the sign to Guanmiao and after 250m you'll be on the old street. After the road was widened in 1920, the authorities encouraged local merchants to build new homes. Most of these two-floor abodes are in splendid condition and have baroque and Art Deco features typical of the era, such as pebble-dash façades, shield motifs and plaster laurel wreaths. This kind of architecture isn't especially rare in Taiwan but Xinhua Old Street is almost unique in that the buildings' finer details aren't hidden behind advertising hoardings. Also, the businesses along it are largely traditional. Redundant husking machines can be seen inside the rice shops at numbers 425 and 439 while other businesses sell fabrics or herbal medicines. If you arrive before lunch, dive down Lane 369 and explore the morning market that fills several alleyways. Parking on the old street isn't advised; continue south and you'll soon find a spot.

Moonscape World 草山月世界 (*near km22.5*) The English name makes it sound like a theme park, but Caoshan Moonscape World is in fact an area of badlands, a striking exception to the tropical lushness found elsewhere in Taiwan. It gets more than enough rain but because the terrain consists of crumbly brown stone, vegetation tends to get washed away or drowned in slurry. Late afternoon is a good time to visit as the setting sun makes the eroded hillocks and steep ravines look truly lunar. Despite the desolation, the area is rich in birds and insects. A few families grow bananas and bamboo between the gullies and ridges. Best explored by motorcycle or bicycle (the roads are narrow but those on four wheels will do fine if they drive slowly and cautiously), Moonscape World can be entered via several roads – look for bilingual signs on Highway 20 or continue past Yujing to Beiliao 北寮, then take Highway 3 southwards until you see signs for Hill 308 **308高地** where you'll find restaurants with good views over the badlands.

Karma Kagyu Monastery (*km24.9;* ☎ *573 2103; www.lopon.org.tw;* ⏰ *08.00–16.30 daily*) In recent years Tantric Buddhism has gained ground in Taiwan and this modern monastery blends Tibetan and Chinese elements. It serves as the Taiwan seat of Ogyen Trinley Dorje, the young man accepted by most but not all Tibetan Buddhists as the 17th Karmapa Lama, the religion's third-most-senior figure. The white stupa can be seen from the highway but more interesting is the main hall with its *thangkas* (Tibetan devotional scroll paintings) and Buddha statues. The largest of the latter has a head of blue curls, such hair being one of the Buddha's 32 distinguishing physical characteristics.

Holy Glory Temple 寶光寺 (**Bǎoguāng Sì**) (*km45;* ☎ *577 2229; www.yiguandao. com;* ⏰ *05.00–19.00 daily*) The hillside headquarters of one of Taiwan's main I-Kuan Tao sects is impressive in terms of size and setting. Ceiling paintings inside the principal shrine depict Christ and Muhammad alongside figures from Chinese mythology. Incense but not joss paper is burned here and visitors should take off their shoes before entering any of the shrines. The on-site buffet (⏰ *11.30–13.00 daily; free, donations accepted*) is vegetarian. A short distance east of the temple, Highway 20 crosses into Kaohsiung.

TAINAN'S COAST *Telephone code 06*

TAIJIANG NATIONAL PARK 台江國家公園 (**TÁIJIĀNG GUÓJIĀ GŌNGYUÁN**) The wetlands and river mouths just north of Tainan offer some of Asia's best birding. Sicao, which is near Anping, and Qigu, the district immediately north of the Zengwen River, are Important Bird Areas; together they form the core of Taiwan's newest national park, a reserve that stretches across the ocean all the way to the southeastern corner of Penghu County. The name 'Taijiang' refers to a lagoon which appeared in 1817 after a powerful typhoon shifted huge amounts of silt.

Getting there and away To drive to the Black-faced Spoonbill Area, take Highway 17 north from central Tainan and follow the bilingual signs. Just after crossing the Zengwen River at km162 you'll need to turn right and then right again. From there it's 8km to the management centre; the first birdwatching platform is another 900m down the road. The only public transport to this spot is the occasional #99 bus; you can get a schedule from the Tainan TRA Station Visitor Information Centre.

Tourist information
🛈 **Taijiang National Park Headquarters**
2 Chengping Rd, Anping; ☎ 391 0000; www.tjnp.
gov.tw; ⏰ 08.30–17.30 Mon–Fri.

What to see and do
Sicao Wildlife Refuge 四草野生動物保護區 (***Sìcǎo Yěshēng Dòngwù Bǎohùqū***) This 515ha reserve predates the establishment of the national park and is relatively close to the city. In late spring the refuge is crowded with black-winged stilts (*Himantopus himantopus*).

Black-faced Spoonbill Area 黑面琵鷺保育區 (***Hēimiànpílù Bǎohùqū***) Surrounded by mudflats, fish farms and abandoned salt pans, this reserve focuses on one particular migratory species. The spoonbills gather here between late September and early spring and spend most of their time foraging on the

The black-faced spoonbill (*Platalea minor*) has caught the public imagination like no other bird in Taiwan. Because of its handsome appearance and an avalanche of media coverage, it's now better known among local people than most of the island's endemic species. Black-faced spoonbills breed along the Korean coast in late spring. The majority spend the winter in the Tainan area; those who don't head for Hong Kong or Vietnam. The birds start their lives with black feathers; some take six years to become fully white. Their bills change from brown to black and their irises become fully red. During the breeding season both males and females grow golden decorating feathers on their breasts, necks and heads. The adults are large, averaging 75cm in length.

On the face of it, efforts to protect the bird seem to be working. The number of black-faced spoonbills counted in east Asia has climbed from 288 in 1988 to more than 2,000 in recent years. A January 2013 survey found 1,533 of the birds in Taiwan, the vast majority in Tainan. The species still faces threats, however. Construction projects are cutting into feeding areas and causing disturbance. Also, of course, the birds' stardom brings legions of birders and photographers to the area.

mudflats. The **management centre** (⊕ *09.00–17.00 Tue–Sun*) has useful bilingual presentations plus some specimens preserved by taxidermy. Waterbirds are plentiful all year round and often-seen avians include Caspian terns (*Hydroprogne caspia*), brown shrikes (*Lanius cristatus*) and common greenshanks (*Tringa nebularia*).

BEIMEN 北門 (BĚIMÉN) The heart of an area devoted to the growing of shallots and muskmelons, Beimen is so small that you'll have no problems finding your way around. There are two useful landmarks: the canal and the white telecoms office, one of the tallest buildings in town. The Presbyterian church is beside the former while the Southwest Coast National Scenic Area headquarters are near the latter.

Getting there and away

By car or motorcycle From north or south take Expressway 61 or Highway 17 and follow the signs. It's almost always possible to park for free in central Beimen or in the grounds of Nankunshen Daitian Temple.

By bus From Tainan TRA Station buses #7600 (*13 departures per day;* ⊕ *06.10–20.20*) and #7602 (*7 departures per day;* ⊕ *07.10–19.15*) go to Nankunshen (*takes 1¾hrs; NTD121*) via Beimen (*NTD111*). For details of buses between Xinying and Nankunshen, see *Getting there and away*, page 229.

Tourist information

☑ **Southwest Coast National Scenic Area** www.swcoast-nsa.gov.tw

☑ **Beimen Visitor Centre** 200 Beimen Li; ⊕ 09.00–17.30 daily

What to see and do

Taiwan Black-foot Disease Socio-Medical Service Memorial Hall 台灣烏腳病醫療紀念館 (*27 Yonglong Li;* ☏ *786 2012; www.blackfoot.org.tw;* ⊕ *09.00–17.00 Tue–Sun; free admission*) This museum occupies an elegant Japanese-style bungalow in the heart of Beimen, between the church and the telecoms office. You'll see a two-storey building with these words on its façade: 'Pak-Mng Mercy's Door Free Clinic'. Pak-Mng is the Taiwanese pronunciation of Beimen. The memorial hall is on the same side of the road, a few houses further from the canal. The clinic operated 1960–86 and was run by King-ho Wang (1916–2014), a local doctor and lay preacher who received logistical and financial help from American missionary Lillian Dickson (1901–83). The museum celebrates their efforts to combat a peculiar local health problem: black-foot disease (BFD), which doctors describe as 'a chronic progressive arteriosclerotic vascular disease of the extremities'. The disease was caused by drinking well-water which contained a high concentration of arsenic, and BFD victims were more often men than women. The selective nature of the problem, coupled with Buddhist notions of rebirth and accumulated merit, caused many (including some of the sufferers) to assume it was punishment for bad deeds in a previous existence. Even when BFD was properly understood by doctors, some locals persisted in believing it was contagious (it was not), caused by evil spirits, or the result of being cursed.

Visitors to the memorial hall can view a short film (English subtitles) about the clinic and Wang's work, which went beyond treating sufferers' physical symptoms. With his late wife he ran a straw-mat workshop to provide employment. When an indigent patient died, he bought wood and made the coffin himself. Displays in the hall are labelled in Chinese only but the amputated hand and feet preserved in formaldehyde need no explanation. It's usually possible to also have a look inside the original clinic building, which at the time of writing still contained old medical equipment including cases of scalpels and saws, an X-ray machine and a gurney for operations.

Shuangchun Coastal Recreation Area 雙春濱海遊憩區 (⊕ 24hrs daily; free admission)

Variously called a recreation area and an ecology park, this is one of very few places in Taiwan where all four local mangrove species can be seen. A boardwalk takes visitors through the mangroves and over mudflats rich in crabs and mudskippers. The latter are fish that, when out of water, use their pectoral fins to propel themselves across the land. A few grow as long as a man's finger but most are less than half that size. There are thousands more mangroves between the park and the southern bank of the Bazhang, the river that divides Tainan from Chiayi County.

Nankunshen Daitian Temple 南鯤鯓代天府 (Nánkūnshēn Dàitiānfǔ)

(km139.5 Hwy 17; www.nkstemple.org.tw; ⊕ 06.00–21.00 daily) One of the island's liveliest places of worship with an estimated four million visitors each year, Daitian Temple is a must-see for anyone curious about Taiwanese religion. It's also one of the country's oldest religious sites. According to a leaflet published by the temple, its history goes back to the first quarter of the 17th century:

One night the moon was full and bright and silence reigned supreme. Suddenly, there were sounds of bells, drums, pipes and strings passing from the sea. The sounds were clear and sweet. The fishermen on the island were very surprised. They went out to investigate the source of the sounds. There was a resplendent and magnificent yacht with three masts sailing slowly towards the port. Those fishermen guessed […] it was an official's boat […] and perhaps it had lost its direction and sailed to this port by mistake. Early the next day they wanted to find out what had happened to the boat. However, they couldn't find any large vessel, only a broken little boat lying against the coast. On the boat there were five statuettes of gods and a banner [bearing the names of the gods and the temple in mainland China they had come from].

The fishermen were delighted with their find. Convinced of the idols' efficacy (how could an unmanned vessel make it across the Taiwan Strait without divine protection?), they pulled the boat ashore and placed the effigies in a straw hut. They weren't disappointed: they enjoyed record catches, and prayers to the five gods, also known as the Five Kings, cured the sick better than any medicine. The gods' fame spread and in the 1660s a proper temple was built. Ever since, it's been a centre of the Wang Ye cult (see *Religion*, page 33). Since 1818, a sixth god has been worshipped in a poky little temple to the right of the main hall of worship. Wanshanye ('ten thousand goodness lord') is a home-grown addition to the pantheon, a local orphan who had attained enlightenment a century earlier.

Great amounts of spirit money are burned at this temple and each day thousands of joss sticks are lit and sacrificed to the resident deities. It's often very noisy indeed and the constant announcements may remind you of a busy airport. You might see a gaudily decorated truck park in front of the main shrine so a bikini-clad singer at the back can belt out standards through a karaoke machine – an everyday expression of folk beliefs in rural Taiwan. Visit on a Sunday morning and you'll see a constant stream of processions as effigies from affiliated temples arrive to pay tribute. The 26th and 27th days of the fourth lunar month – the birthdays, respectively, of the Great King and the Fifth King – are especially festive. During these events, don't be embarrassed to gawk or take photos; you'll be rubbing shoulders with plenty of agnostic locals who've turned up for the spectacle alone.

Many processions feature *tang-ki*, men possessed by gods. These spirit mediums wear nothing from the waist up; to show how their patrons protect them from injury, they cut themselves on the face, chest and back with swords, small axes and other sharp instruments. Some pierce their cheeks with long needles. Others speak in tongues. In the past, *tang-ki* (the term is Taiwanese) were sometimes asked to drive away phantoms or intercede when a relative fell sick. They weren't paid for such work but many accepted gifts. No one chooses to be a spirit medium and there are stories of anointed individuals refusing to serve, then suffering great misfortune until they accept their extraordinary role.

The complex has grown in recent years with the opening of **Da-kun Garden Hall of Culture and History** (⏱ *08.00–17.00 daily; admission by donation*), in which you'll find a classical Chinese garden and some Chinese-language displays about the temple, and the **Lingxiaobao Hall** (⏱ *07.30–17.20 daily*). The latter, an annexe to the rear of the main hall, was built to house a very special depiction of Taoism's chief deity, the Jade Emperor, a solid-gold tablet weighing 405kg and worth over £10 million. This icon is impressive but shouldn't distract you from dozens of fabulous beam and panel paintings. Some are truly top-notch, a few merely well-intentioned. Rather than repeat the myths and legends shown in many houses of worship, these pictures celebrate Taiwanese scenery, culture and heroes, including Jeremy Lin (see *Sports and Activities*, page 000), even though Lin himself is an evangelical Christian.

YANSHUI 鹽水 (YÁNSHUǏ)

YANSHUI 鹽水 (YÁNSHUǏ) Simply put, Yanshui is a charming old town. It's also a good size for exploring on foot; one can stroll from the Martial Temple on the northern edge of the town to Qiaonan Old Street in less than half an hour. Yanshui's side streets and alleyways are full of quaint houses, small shrines and old-fashioned shops. You wouldn't think it from the town's current size (population: 27,000) and relaxing somnolence, but as recently as the mid-19th century it was one of Taiwan's four most important settlements, a ranking expressed in a local idiom: 'First, Tainan; second, Lugang; third, Mangka [the old name for Taipei's Wanhua district];

fourth, Yuejin [the name of Yanshui's port]'. Yuejin harbour suffered from silting and closed for good in 1900.

Getting there and away

By car or motorcycle Yanshui is 3km from the Xinying Exit on Freeway 1, 263km south of Taipei, 79km north of Kaohsiung. If you're on two wheels, approach by Highway 19 or Highway 19A. Parking near the centre isn't difficult except during the Beehive Fireworks Festival, when police bar non-residents from bringing vehicles into the town.

By public transport Xinying, the nearest TRA station, is well served by expresses. Trains take less than half an hour to/from Chiayi (*NTD33–52*) and around 50

THE BEEHIVE FIREWORKS FESTIVAL 鹽水蜂炮

Fireworks and firecrackers are part of the Taiwan soundtrack, but just after each Lunar New Year the citizens of Yanshui takes things to an extreme. If you have a taste for huge crowds, mild danger and sensory overload, the Beehive Fireworks Festival is a not-to-be-missed experience. It isn't a fireworks display in the conventional sense, although there are plenty of colourful explosions high in the sky. It's an audience participation event, and it's every bit as dangerous as running with the bulls at Pamplona. Those who aren't prepared risk serious injury. Each year dozens of people suffer burns, eye injuries or temporary deafness. Don't go anywhere near the front line without a full-face motorcycle helmet, gloves, multiple layers of clothing and a towel or scarf to prevent stray rockets from getting under your visor. Don't worry if you're travelling light; you can buy everything you need in Yanshui on the night.

The festival has its origins in a cholera outbreak. Around 1885, a seemingly unstoppable epidemic had the townsfolk panic-stricken. They besought Guan Gong, the deified general regarded as the god of brotherhood and righteousness, to expel the evil spirits they blamed for the pestilence. They carried an effigy of the god through the town, burning piles of spirit money and igniting firecrackers at every turn. This exorcism by fire and noise worked and the epidemic soon receded. Each year, coinciding with the Lantern Festival, there's a re-enactment of this plague-expulsion parade. The event is sponsored by businesses and temples; participation is free. Residents cash in by selling snacks, soft drinks and protective attire.

The festival now includes folk arts performances and other activities spread over two or more days. The fireworks parade begins around dusk on the 15th day of the first lunar month, and continues until dawn the following day. It features a series of 'beehives' – freight container-sized arsenals which fire tens of thousands of rockets over and into the crowd. Like angry bees, the fireworks scream in every direction, ricocheting off the tarmac and houses. When they hit, they hurt – even through two or three layers of clothing. The experience isn't quite the same as being in combat, perhaps, but those caught on the front line may feel they've been pelted with stones by an angry mob.

For some participants, the parade continues to be a demonstration of religious devotion and gratitude. Most of those who attend, however, are thrill-seekers 'pursuing experience and sensation', to use the words of a former culture minister.

minutes to/from Tainan (*NTD56–87*). Xinying TRA Station has a baggage office (⏰ *08.00–20.00 daily*). Xinying's bus station is just across the roundabout from the TRA station; from it Brown Line buses leave every half hour for Yanshui (*departs* ⏰ *06.05–20.05 daily; takes 20mins; NTD26–34*). Eight services per day continue on to Nankunshen (⏰ *07.00–19.45; takes 50mins; NTD82–91*). Yanshui doesn't have a bus station; get on/off near the junction of Zhongshan and Zhongzheng roads.

Tourist information

☒ Xinying TRA Station Visitor Information Centre ⏰ 10.00–18.00 Mon–Fri, 09.00–18.00 Sat–Sun & national holidays

☒ Yanshui Streets Visitors Centre 21 Zhongshan Rd; ⏰ 08.00–17.00 Mon–Fri, 09.00–18.00 Sat–Sun. There's no English sign but it's easy to find being opposite Yanshui's post office. Books, postcards & some souvenirs, but very little in English.

✗ **Where to eat** A good place to find straightforward local food, including Yanshui's trademark comestible, *yì miàn* – an unpretentious but satisfying and tasty noodle dish – is on the corner of Kangle and Zhongshan roads. Several eateries operate under awnings (⏰ *approx 08.00–18.30 daily; no EMs; $*) and options include seafood and vegetarian fare.

What to see and do The shortest route from the centre of Yanshui to Qiaonan Street is via Zhongzheng Road, a thoroughfare lined with 1920s shop-house combinations.

Martial Temple 武廟 (*87 Wumiao Rd;* ⏰ *05.00–20.30 daily*) This 320-year-old shrine is dedicated to Guan Gong – there's a huge statue of him on the right as you approach the front of the temple – but it isn't nearly as interesting as the Beehive Fireworks Festival (see box, page 229) Guan Gong's devotees organise each year.

The Octagon 八角樓 (*1, Lane 4, Zhongshan Rd;* ⏰ *09.00–16.30 daily; free admission*) The town's most distinctive structure is all that remains of a sprawling mansion built in 1847 for Ye Kai-hong, the town's leading merchant. Ye made his fortune exporting sugar to the Chinese mainland, and many of the materials used in the construction of this two-floor wood-and-stone residence – including the fir columns, roof tiles and limestone slabs – came to Taiwan from the mainland as ballast on his ships. The ground floor is open to the public; inside you'll see the original partitions and a portrait of Ye's son. The lanes behind the Octagon are among Yanshui's most photogenic.

Yanshui Catholic Church (*19 Ximen Rd;* ⏰ *10.00–11.30 & 13.00–15.30 Wed–Sun*) Of Taiwan's Christian places of worship, this is perhaps the one which most resembles a Chinese temple. The depiction of the Last Supper features men with Asian faces and hairstyles wearing traditional Chinese clothes; they eat steamed buns with chopsticks. The crucifixion scenes are also thoroughly 'localised'.

Qiaonan Old Street 橋南街 The name of Yanshui's oldest thoroughfare means 'south of the bridge', and the bridge in question spans a small body of water that once formed part of Yuejin harbour. Around a dozen of the street's single-storey wooden-framed houses were built in the 1880s or earlier. At number 8, a sixth-generation blacksmith still plies his trade, but these days he turns out decorative items for tourists rather than farmers' tools.

CHIAYI CITY 嘉義市 (JIĀYÌ SHÌ) *Telephone code 05*

Chiayi (population: 271,000) will never rival Tainan in terms of visible history, nor will it ever have the sophistication of Taichung. But spending a slow 24 hours here just after an energetic excursion into the mountains isn't a bad idea, especially if you want to see lifestyles somewhere between the frenetic metropolitan existence of Taipei and rural languor.

HISTORY The written history of Chiayi begins in the 1640s, when Dutch East India Company officials passed through an aboriginal village here, collecting taxes and searching for potential exports. The Dutch spelled the village's name Tilaossen. Han settlers, who were already arriving in some numbers, called it Tirosen and rendered it in characters which Mandarin speakers pronounce Zhuluoshan. In 1734 the settlement got its first city wall, a palisade of sharpened bamboo stakes. It earned its current name – which means 'right, fitting and proper' – from the emperor himself in 1787 when it defied Lin Shuang-wen's army (see *History*, page 13).

After an earthquake flattened the city in 1906, Chiayi gained the straight but somewhat narrow roads it has today. The following year saw work begin on the famous logging railroad to Alishan. The timber trade had a big impact on Chiayi; buildings made of wood taken from the mountains can still be seen throughout the city. It also became a centre of art and scholarship. In 1926, Chiayi-born Chen Cheng-po (1895–1947) became the first Taiwanese painter to have a work included in Japan's most prestigious art exhibition. One of the city's most famous sons, he's now remembered as much for his grisly end (during the 2-28 Incident he was executed at the railway station by KMT soldiers) as for his pictures, which embodied both Chinese landscape-painting conventions and Modernism. Chen's works are still very popular – one fetched €1.48m when auctioned in 2011 – and reproductions have been set on steel easels at various points around the city.

GETTING THERE AND AWAY
By car By Freeway 1 Chiayi is 239km south of Taipei and 103km north of Kaohsiung. From the Chiayi exit at km264 it's a longish drive into the city centre.

By HSR Chiayi HSR Station is 15km west of the city centre. High-speed trains to/from Taipei take 1½ hours (*NTD1,180*); to/from Kaohsiung Zuoying they take 35 minutes (*NTD450*). At least two buses per hour link the HSR station with the back of the TRA station (*takes 25mins; NTD50*) and Chiayi Park.

By TRA Expresses take 3½ to five hours to/from Taipei (*NTD461–598*), between 1¼ and two hours to/from Kaohsiung (*NTD189–245*) and as little as 1¼ hours to/from Taichung (*NTD172–224*). Trains to/from Tainan take about an hour (*NTD90–139*).

By bus Chiayi's long-distance bus station is at the back of the TRA station. Kuo-Kuang has departures every half hour to Taipei (⊕ *05.00–23.00 daily; takes 3½hrs; NTD240–350*) and every 40 minutes to Taichung (⊕ *06.00–22.00 daily; takes 1¾hrs; NTD165*). Other companies based in the same terminal have round-the-clock services to Taipei (*NTD240–450*) and Kaohsiung (*takes 1½hrs; NTD260*).

Buses leave for nearer destinations from two stations. **Station A**, right outside the TRA station, is where you should go to catch a bus to Alishan (*10 departures per day*; ⊕ *06.10–14.10; takes 2½hrs; NTD250*), Fenqihu (*departs* ⊕ *07.10 & 15.10 daily; takes 1¾hrs; NTD181*) or Bantianyan. This station also has services about every half-hour to Beigang (⊕ *06.30–22.00; takes 50mins; NTD73*). **Station B**, a few minutes' walk down Zhongshan Road, has 60 departures per day to Beigang (⊕ *06.00–22.00; takes 45–55mins; NTD73*) and buses set out from there to Yanshui about once an hour (⊕ *06.00–19.00 daily; takes 1¼hrs; NTD111*).

By Alishan Forest Railway At the time of writing, the railway (see box, page 235) was running daily between Chiayi TRA Station and Fenqihu (*departs from Chiayi 09.00, from Fenqihu 14.00; takes 2¼hrs; NTD240 one-way*) and there was talk of restoring services all the way to Alishan before the end of 2014. Extra services are laid on at weekends and national holidays. Children and seniors get half-price tickets.

By air Chiayi Airport (*IATA: CYI;* ☎*286 7886; www.cya.gov.tw*), 5km southwest of the city centre, has daily flights to Magong and Kinmen.

GETTING AROUND

By bus There's a skeleton city bus network but considering the infrequency of the buses, you're best off walking, biking or taking taxis.

By hired car or motorcycle

🚗 **Car Plus Auto Leasing** 576 Zhongshan Rd; ☎227 8855; www.car-plus.com.tw; ⊕ 08.30–20.30 daily. General-use car rentals & long-term leasing. Car Plus also has a counter inside Chiayi HSR Station.

🚗 **168 Vehicle Rental** 719 Zhongzheng Rd; ☎216 6689; ⊕ 06.30–01.30 daily. One of several motorcycle rental places across the road from the TRA station.

By bicycle Bikes can be borrowed for free at the front and back of the TRA station. Show photo ID at one of the information counters (⊕ *06.00–17.00 daily*) and bring the bike back within 24 hours.

TOURIST INFORMATION

🏛 **Chiayi City Government** www.chiayi.gov. tw

🏛 **Chiayi TRA Station Visitor Information Centre** ☎225 6649; ⊕ 08.30–12.00 & 13.00–17.00 daily

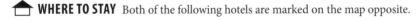

🏠 **WHERE TO STAY** Both of the following hotels are marked on the map opposite.

🏠 **Yuh Tong Hotel** (120 rooms) 7 Weixin Rd; ☎275 6111; f 278 0222; www.yuhtonghotel.com. tw. This recent addition has the city centre's most comfortable rooms, most boasting high ceilings, wooden floors & large windows. In keeping with local tradition, the lobby is decorated with koji figurines & wood sculptures. Guests have free use of the fitness centre & can borrow bicycles. In-house restaurants serve Chinese cuisine (*dishes NTD160–500*) & passable French/Italian food (*meal sets NTD300–700; both* ⊕ *11.30–14.00 &*

17.30–22.00 *daily*). Promotions sometimes push room rates under NTD4,000. Buffet b/fast inc. **$$$$**

🏠 **Hotel Shin Kao** (47 rooms) 581 Zhongshan Rd; ☎227 2252; f 216 0960; e shinkao.hotel@ gmail.com. All rooms are basic (hairdryers have to be borrowed from the lobby) & most are small but the whole building is well maintained. Rooms can often be had for NTD900; 4-person rooms go for NTD1,300. No b/fast. **$$**

✕ **WHERE TO EAT AND DRINK** The following establishments are marked on the map opposite.

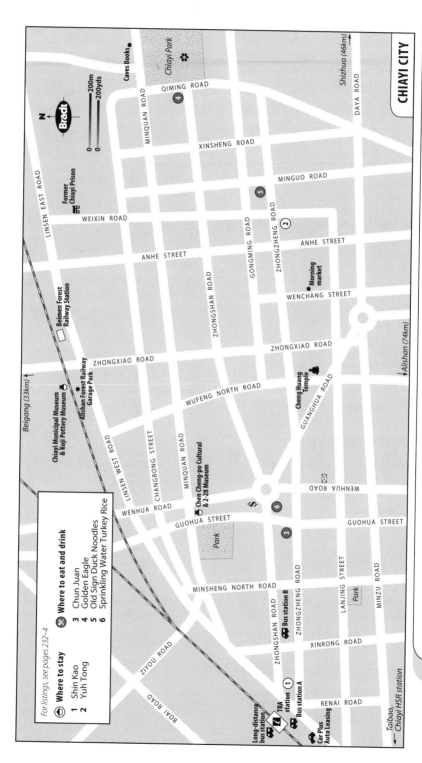

CHIAYI CITY

For listings, see pages 232–4

Where to stay
1 Shin Kao
2 Yuh Tong

Where to eat and drink
3 Chun Juan
4 Golden Eagle
5 Old Sign Duck Noodles
6 Sprinkling Water Turkey Rice

Golden Eagle 243 Qiming Rd; ✆277 5277; ⏰ 17.30–12.30 Mon–Fri, 18.00–02.00 Sat–Sun. Another of Taiwan's faux-British pubs, the Golden Eagle has a decent selection of German, Japanese & American beers & some good Western food inc burgers & sandwiches (*most dishes NTD160–360*). The music is never too loud & they'll only turn on the TV if customers request it. English-speaking staff, EM, AC but no outdoor tables. $$

Chun Juan 春卷 468 Zhongzheng Rd; ⏰ approx 10.00–17.00 daily. In Chinese restaurants in the West, spring rolls (*chūn juǎn*) are often finger-sized fried appetisers. Traditional Taiwanese spring rolls are bigger & healthier, being non-fried wraps packed with slivers of cold pork, egg & green vegetables sprinkled with crushed peanuts & sugar. This street-corner vendor is an excellent place to try them; just gesture if you don't want one of the ingredients. Eat on the spot (there are stools & tables) or take away. With a cup of broth, a single, quite filling roll costs NTD45. $

Old Sign Duck Noodles 老牌鴨肉麵 181 Minguo Rd; ✆275 6676; ⏰ 10.30–19.30 daily. After operating for more than 50 years in the nearby town of Minxiong (renowned for its duck & goose cuisine), owner Mr Hsu relocated to Chiayi in 2005. Portions of duck noodles (*yāròu miàn*) or duck with rice (*yāròu fàn*) are small but inexpensive. Side orders inc seasonal greens & soups. No EM or English sign, just simple, excellent Taiwanese food. $

Sprinkling Water Turkey Rice 325 Zhongshan Rd; ✆222 2433; ⏰ 10.00–21.00 daily. More than any other dish, Chiayi is associated with what locals call *huǒjī ròu fàn*, shredded turkey & gravy served on white rice. The turkey served in this chain is sourced locally & reliably excellent. The Chinese-only menu lists 15-plus side dishes inc tofu, soups & vegetables. Soft drinks & beer (*NTD70 per bottle*) available. $

OTHER PRACTICALITIES

$ **Bank of Taiwan** 306 Zhongshan Rd

Caves Books 28 Minquan Rd; ✆278 5798; ⏰ 10.30–21.00 daily

Yang Ming Hospital 252 Wufeng N Rd; ✆228 4567; www.ymhospital.com.tw; ⏰ 24hrs daily

General Post Office 134 Wenhua Rd; ⏰ 08.00–19.00 Mon–Fri, 08.30–16.30 Sat, 08.30–12.00 Sun

WHAT TO SEE AND DO

Chen Cheng-po Cultural and 2-28 Museum (*228-12 Guohua St; ✆ 222 4525; ⏰ 09.00–17.00 Mon–Fri; free admission*) The front section of this small museum has reproductions of 32 of Chen's paintings with bilingual commentaries, while the back room is given over to Chinese-only information about the 2-28 Incident in Chiayi. More copies of Chen's works can be found in the park across the road, at the Wenhua/Zhongshan roundabout and online at http://chenchengpo.org.

Chiayi Municipal Museum (*275 Zhongxiao Road; www.cabcy.gov.tw/cymm; ✆ 278 0303; ⏰ 09.00–12.00 & 13.30–17.00 Wed–Sun; free admission*) This museum has sections devoted to fossils, local geology and Chen Cheng-po. More interesting is the collection in the basement of a building nearer Zhongxiao Road: the **Koji Pottery Museum** (*⏰ 09.00–17.00 Tue–Sun; free admission*) introduces the gorgeously colourful ceramic art which decorates many of Taiwan's finest temples as well as some of the form's leading artists. It's well worth an hour of your time.

Alishan Forest Railway Garage Park (*⏰ 24hrs daily; free admission*) Here railway enthusiasts can get a close look at some of the forest railway's locomotives and carriages as well as the sheds in which they were repaired. This entire neighbourhood has been transformed in recent years. Slum housing has been cleared and buildings associated with the logging industry have been refurbished. **Chiayi Motive Power Wood Sculpture Museum** (*⏰ 08.30–12.00 & 13.00–16.30*

Wed–Sun; free admission) is a former power station where prize-winning wood carvings are now displayed. A cluster of Japanese-style bungalows built for forestry executives and their families on Linsen East Road has been refurbished and named **Cypress Forestry Life Village** (⏰ *10.00–18.00 Tue–Sun; free admission*). Inside there are several art spaces but you'll likely find the exteriors more appealing.

Former Chiayi Prison (*140 Weixin Road;* ✆ *276 9574;* ⏰ *Wed–Sun; free admission*)

Built 1919–22, the only surviving Japanese-era prison in Taiwan housed up to 300 male convicts (and 30 women in segregated facilities) until 1994. The main doors, made of extremely valuable yellow cypress from Alishan, are original. Inmates were held in three wings arranged so the corridors could be observed by a single officer from his desk. The on-site workshops in which they laboured have been preserved, as has the bathhouse where they washed together. At the time of writing, visitors could only enter at certain times (⏰ *09.30, 10.30, 13.30 & 14.30*) but this may well change. Get someone to call ahead if you'd like an English-language tour.

Cheng Huang Temple 城隍廟 (Chéng Huáng Miào) (*168 Wufeng N Rd;*

⏰ *05.30–21.00 daily*) In the late 1930s, during the Kominka Movement (see *History*, page 17), 63 of the 66 major Taoist and folk shrines then existing in Chiayi were razed or converted to other uses. This city-god temple, central to spiritual life in Chiayi since its founding in Emperor Kangxi's reign (1661–1722), was one of the three survivors. In the Qing era, government officials would reside here and take part in soul-purifying rites before assuming new posts. If you approach from Wufeng North Road, look to your left as you pass under the massive archway: you'll see two large panels inscribed with the names of those who donated money for the 1990 renovation. This list is proof of how broad a base folk religion still has in Taiwan; the nearly 3,000 names are arranged according to how much they gave, and the majority forked over what must have been at least a week's salary. To better accommodate its mini-pantheon – inside you'll find more than 630 effigies – the temple has expanded upwards. Chenghuangye, the city god, can be found right where you'd expect him to be – on the ground floor, in the very centre. High above the altar, almost lost in the gloom and soot, there's a four-character inscribed board presented to the temple on behalf of Emperor Guangxu. Dating from 1887, it reads *Táiyángxiànyòu* and means 'Protector of Taiwan and the Ocean'. It amounted to imperial recognition of the deity's power and benevolence; no other city god in Taiwan received such an accolade. Before heading upstairs, go into the rear chamber where there are icons of Mazu (in the centre) and Chenghuangye's wife (on the petitioner's right). On what locals call the second floor, go behind the Guanyin shrine and you'll find, facing out the back of the temple, a large but amateurish painting which depicts smug-faced officials taking shelter in the temple while Lin Shuang-wen's men attack the city walls. One floor up, the rear altar on the right is devoted to the Old Man Under the Moon, heaven's matchmaker. The representation here has a splendid knee-length white beard and wears a sort of 'you've no idea what you're getting yourself into' smirk. His birthday is celebrated on the second day of the sixth lunar month. Part of the fourth level is a repository for effigies which the faithful can borrow for rituals at home. The fifth floor is given over to a trio of bearded gentlemen, the Sanqing or 'Three Pure Ones' of Taoism, while the sixth and top level is unusual for a temple in that it's made largely of wood.

Every morning the streets east of the temple are a maelstrom of vendors and motorcycles. A traditional noodle-maker can be found at 159 Wenchang Street; at number 163, circular bamboo containers are used for steaming what's known in Taiwanese as *giam-guay*. This stuff – which needs to be cooked for more than four hours – looks like a light-brown cheese but is made from rice paste and crushed peanuts. Shoppers purchase big chunks which they slice and fry at home.

Chiayi Park 嘉義公園 (Jiāyì Gōngyuán) (*Minquan & Qiming rds; ⏲ 24hrs daily; free admission*)

This very pleasant suburban park wouldn't warrant a mention were it not for the adjacent arboretum and two eye-catching yet very different buildings. What's called **Shanziding Botanical Garden** 山仔頂植物園 covers 8.6ha. The mahogany and sandalwood groves are criss-crossed by shaded pathways and there's quite a bit of English-language information for the green-fingered. Rubber trees grown here from the 1920s onward supplied the Imperial Japanese Army during its Asian adventures. The tallest structure on this side of the city, **Chiayi Tower** (⏲ *09.00–17.00 Wed–Fri; 09.00–21.00 Sat; admission to the observatory NTD50/25*) is also known as Sun-Shooting Tower; an information panel inside explains the aboriginal legend behind this alternative name. If the weather's clear, do buy a ticket and ride the lift to the tenth floor for fine views. Near the tower stands the **Historical Relic Data Museum** (⏲ *09.00–17.00 Wed–Sun; free admission*), formerly part of a Shinto shrine complex. Don't bother with the displays inside – there's scant English – but the exterior is sublime.

National Palace Museum Southern Branch 故宮南部院區 (*Taibao, Chiayi County; www.npm.gov.tw; ⏲ to be announced*)

This site, within walking distance of Chiayi HSR Station but a longish bus ride from central Chiayi, was chosen in 2004. The project has been dogged by delays and controversies but the museum should be inaugurated by the end of 2015. Rather than simply provide extra exhibition space for the National Palace Museum's immense collection, it's intended to be a world-class museum of Asian art.

CHIAYI CITY TO SHIZHUO BY ROAD 159A

Road 159A is a highly attractive alternative to Highway 18 for those driving or riding towards Alishan. If you're starting from Chiayi City, get on to Minzu Road which soon becomes Daya Road. Follow the signs to Fanlu and don't panic if you find yourself on Road 159 by mistake – it joins Road 159A just before Bantianyan.

Even if you're not stopping to hike, allow at least two hours to cover the 46km between Chiayi and Shizhuo.

GETTING THERE, AWAY AND AROUND Without your own vehicle you won't make it to the most scenic parts of this road. From the station in front of Chiayi TRA Station seven buses per day go to Bantianyan (*departs ⊕ 06.20–17.20; takes 50mins; NTD60*), three of which continue on to Dahu (*takes 1¼hrs; NTD94*).

WHAT TO SEE AND DO
Bantianyan 半天巖 (Bàntiānyán) Approaching this hillside spot, 428m above sea level, you'll see thousands of persimmon trees. However, for many Taiwanese visitors the main attraction isn't fruit but **Purple Cloud Temple** (*km18.5 Rd 159A; ⊕ 05.00–21.00 daily*). Established in 1682, it's flanked by a 23m-high statue of Guanyin. At weekends there are never fewer than several hundred people in and around the temple, a good number of whom take part in Buddhist or Taoist rituals. The temple's vegetarian canteen is upstairs on the right (☏ *259 1017; ⊕ 11.30–13.00 daily; large groups & those wanting evening meals should call ahead; no EM; $*).

Three Treasures Mountain 三寶山 Past the temple the road becomes narrower and more twisting; betel-nut and persimmon groves give way to bamboo and mixed forest. Just after the roadside pavilion at km21 a large boulder bears the English words 'Dahu Community'. Here the road splits: turn right and you'll end up at Chukou on Highway 18; turn left to stay on Road 159A. The trail up Three Treasures Mountain begins with an obvious stairway, on the left and just before the km21.5 marker if you're heading inland. Allow at least three hours to get to the top of this 977m-high ridge and back to the road. Be prepared for many, many steps.

Dahu Sharp Mountain 大湖尖山 This mountain is neither the tallest nor the best-known peak in these parts, but it does offer good scenery for relatively little effort. Just past the village of Dahu 大湖, a small road veers steeply off to the right near km26: at the time of writing there was no English signpost but on the relevant Chinese sign you could see '2KM'. Getting a motorcycle or a fairly robust car right to the trailhead (exactly 1,000m above sea level) isn't difficult. From there, it's an hour or so to the peak, where a sign gives the mountain's height as 1,357m. The top and much of the trail is shaded, making this an enjoyable hike even on hot days. The effort isn't great but the rewards are generous – from the ridge you can see several higher peaks and look down on tiny settlements to the south.

Ganzizhai 柑仔宅 Past km32 tea is an important crop and landslides often damage the road. Drive slowly and not just for safety's sake: the vistas around here are superb. Ginger, runner beans and cabbages also grow well here. Just after km40, the road turns sharply right to cross the headwaters of the Bazhang river. If you take the steeper, smaller road straight ahead (which many maps leave out) you'll end up in Fenqihu. The junction is clearly marked in English.

ALISHAN NATIONAL SCENIC AREA 阿里山國家風景區 (ĂLǏSHĀN GUÓJIĀ FĒNGJǏNGQŪ) *Telephone code 05*

Alishan's fresh, cool air and mountain scenery have been drawing tourists since the Japanese era, but this little town more than 2,000m above sea level has a history quite unlike the purpose-built hill stations of the British Raj. Both the settlement and the famous narrow-gauge railway which links it to the plains were built to facilitate relentless logging. Many of the area's ancient trees were felled to provide lumber for construction and furniture-making. During the colonial era, a number of Japan's most notable temples were rebuilt using red or yellow cypress from Alishan. The Alishan National Scenic Area encompasses tea-growing areas and indigenous villages as well as the eponymous forest recreation area.

GETTING THERE AND AWAY

By car or motorcycle Highway 18 is the main artery but Road 159A (see page 236) and Local Road 129 (see opposite) are recommended for views and lighter traffic. Vehicles using Highway 18 must keep their headlights on between km29 and km96. There are petrol stations at Shizhuo and just outside the forest recreation area. All of the region's roads are vulnerable to typhoon damage, so if you plan to explore by car or motorcycle, check conditions before setting out.

By bus You can catch buses to Alishan via Shizhuo right outside Chiayi TRA Station (*10 departures per day;* ⏲ *06.10–14.10; takes 2½hrs; NTD250*). From the same station there are two services each day to Fenqihu (⏲ *07.10 & 15.10; takes 1¾hrs; NTD181*). From Chiayi HSR Station there are two direct buses to Alishan per day (⏲ *10.10 & 11.40; takes 3hrs; NTD290*) via Shizhuo (*NTD186*). The #6739 Sun Moon Lake–Alishan service leaves Shuishe at 08.00 and 09.00 each day (*takes 3½hrs; NTD350*). These buses leave Alishan for Sun Moon Lake at 13.00 and 14.00 and stop in Tataka (*NTD73*) about half an hour later.

By train If all goes to plan, the Alishan Forest Railway (see page 235) will be up and running again before the end of 2014. Trains are slower and more expensive than buses, but offer better views.

TOURIST INFORMATION

🛈 Alishan National Scenic Area Headquarters km34.2 Hwy 18; 📞259 3900; www.ali-nsa.net; ⏲ 09.00–17.00 daily

🛈 Alishan Visitor Centre Inside Alishan National Forest Recreation Area; ⏲ 08.00–17.00 daily

🏠 **WHERE TO STAY** The Greater Alishan area has lots of homestays. There's no compelling reason to stay inside the forest recreation area unless you want to see the sunrise from Zhushan.

Near Fenqihu

🏠 **Small Swiss** 小瑞士山庄 (5 rooms) 📞256 2228; **e** charlies200388882003@yahoo.com.tw; http://small-swiss.so-buy.com. The English-speaking tea farmers who run this small homestay offer various packages that include pick-up from Chiayi HSR Station & tours of the area. Don't roll up on spec; emails are much preferred to phone calls. Most of the rooms have excellent views; all have heated blankets & heated toilet seats. No meals but guests are encouraged to bring provisions & can use the refrigerator, microwave, kettle, etc. **$$$$**

🏠 **Long Yun Holiday Farm** 龍雲農場 (19 rooms) 📞256 2216; **f** 256 2106; **e** long.yun@msa.hinet.net; www.long-yun.com.tw. Located in the same homestay cluster as Small Swiss, the accommodation here is in 2 adjacent buildings. The older section has 12 straightforward rooms; the newer, higher building is an exciting piece of architecture with split-level rooms that can sleep 2–4 ppl. Some English spoken; room rates include b/fast & a dinner featuring vegetables grown by the owners. **$$$**

🏠 **Arnold Janssen Activity Centre** (14 rooms, 2 dorms) ☎ 256 1035; f 256 2271. This easy-to-find hostel is next to Fenqihu's Catholic church. English spoken; accommodation is clean & simple. The sgl & dbl rooms have no bathroom; the 4-person rooms (*NTD2,000*) do. Staying in the dorm costs NTD250 pp. No meals available but the hostel is 10mins' walk from the Historic Street. **$**

Alishan National Forest Recreation Area

🏠 **Chao Li Alishan House** (150 rooms) ☎ 267 9811; f 267 9596; e alishan-house@umail.hinet. net; www.alishanhouse.com.tw. Centrally located near the Plum Garden, Alishan House is 3 buildings stitched into 1. Rooms near the lobby are attractive & have a graceful simplicity, though perhaps not quite as much character as you'd expect given that the structure is a century-old Japanese colonial original. The sun deck on the 1960s annexe has good views of Tashan & is popular with stargazers. Business centre, gym & Wi-Fi. 3 coffee shops & an in-house restaurant serving Chinese staples (🕐 *11.30–13.30 & 18.00–20.30 daily; EM;* **$$$**). B/fast inc. **$$$$$**

🏠 **Alishan Shermuh International Tourist Hotel** (30 rooms) ☎ 267 9666; f 267 9667; www. alishan-shermuh.com/en/. Coming from the toll gate, Shermuh is the first hotel on the lower strip. It has a few advantages over its neighbours: English is spoken & its tiny sgls with bath are probably the best deal in town for solo travellers. The dbls aren't exciting in terms of furnishing but they're quite adequate. Includes Wi-Fi & b/fast at a nearby restaurant. **$$$**

✖ **WHERE TO EAT** Restaurants of varying quality are clustered around the main car park in the forest recreation area. In Fenqihu, vendors along the Historic Street serve up local snacks as well as the usual rice lunch boxes and noodle dishes.

✖ **Yongfu Tea Oil Chicken** km62.6 on Hwy 18; ☎ 256 1488; 🕐 09.30–19.30 daily. This old favourite serves very good Taiwanese home-cooking, the signature dish being chicken basted in tea seed oil (*kücháyóu jī*). A standard portion is big enough for 3 diners (*NTD350*). The vegetables (*from NTD50*) & fried river shrimp (*from NTD120*) are also excellent. No EM & no English spoken but the staff are used to foreign visitors who point to order. Solo travellers may want to order fried rice (*NTD50*) or noodles & a soup (*NTD10–30*). The restaurant takes occasional, unpredictable days off. **$$**

WHAT TO SEE AND DO

Tea plantations As soon as Highway 18 approaches 1,000m above sea level, neat plantations appear on both sides of the road, along with large buildings in which the crop is processed.

Local Road 129 At km50 on Highway 18 a side road drops southwards to three Tsou villages – **Shanmei** 山美 (*km13.5 Rd 129*), **Xinmei** 新美 (*km19 Rd 129*) and **Chashan** 茶山 (*km28.5 Rd 129*) – before hitting Highway 3 near Dapu, where there's a petrol station (*km338.5 Hwy 3;* 🕐 *07.00–19.00 daily*). Xinmei is the prettiest of the three communities but Chashan has more tourist infrastructure in the form of eateries and homestays (few have English signs, however). Despite Chashan's name ('tea mountain') not much tea is grown around here. The landscapes *en route* deserve not to be rushed.

Eryanping Trail 二延平山步道 (*km53.3 Hwy 18*) Just under 1km long but steep in places, this path leads to a ridge from where you'll get views over two drainages. It's best very early in the morning when you'll see much more of the lowlands. The viewing platform beside the highway, to the left of the trailhead, is a good alternative for lazy travellers. About 1km further along Highway 18 is **Xiding**, a farming community where tea, jelly figs and peas are grown. A century ago charcoal was an important product hereabouts. To make it, groups of local men would head into the forests for days at a time, carrying little but tools, rice, cooking oil and moonshine. During these expeditions they also hunted and foraged.

Shizhuo 石棹 (Shízhuō) (km63 Hwy 18) There's nothing really to see in Shizhuo ('stone table') but it's one of the better places to stop for supplies. Turn left for Fenqihu or Road 159A; right leads to the Tsou communities of Dabang and Lijia.

Fenqihu 奮起湖 (Fènqíhú) This little town, halfway between Chiayi City and Alishan, owes its existence to the logging railroad. Outsiders came here to work in the railway depot or hawk food to ravenous train passengers (the uphill journey used to take seven hours; replacing steam locomotives with diesel engines in the 1960s cut the journey time in half). Three engines are on display beside the railway station, including two antique units which began their working lives before World War I. Fenqihu's older buildings have walls of wood and roofs of tar paper or tin but relatively few have survived fires and redevelopment. The so-called **Historic Street**, just below the station (which is 1,405m above sea level), is a good place to search for something tasty if you've been working up an appetite on the boardwalk trails through the surrounding forests. For long-distance views, ascend 1,976m-high **Mount Dadong**. From Fenqihu it takes about an hour to walk to the trailhead where bilingual map boards show various routes, the longest of which is a five-hour loop via the peak and other features of natural interest.

Dabang and Lijia From Shizhuo it's a slow but very scenic 29km to Lijia via Dabang. The road was in good shape at the time of writing but remains vulnerable to typhoons. There are a few B&Bs along the way but getting a meal isn't easy so bring something to eat. Cyclists contemplating this route should know the road plunges to around 700m above sea level before Dabang, climbs to an elevation of almost 1,500m, then drops steeply again to Lijia.

Alishan National Forest Recreation Area 阿里山森林遊樂區 (Ālǐshān Sēnlín Yóulèqū) (km89 Hwy 18; http://recreation.forest.gov.tw; ⏰ 24hrs daily; admission NTD200/100/10 Mon–Fri, NTD150/100/10 Sat–Sun & national holidays) When people talk about Alishan, they're usually referring to this 1,400ha reserve. It's an excellent place for people who don't consider themselves hikers but want to experience mountain woodlands. Clearly signposted trails wind through sublime forest; before you know it, your gentle stroll has become a three-hour circuit that, combined with the pristine air, will do you a power of good. Come prepared for cool, wet conditions. The resort gets rain 209 days per year and heavy cloud or fog 244 days a year. During winter, the average temperature is just 2–4°C. Summertime temperatures seldom go higher than 20°C, but it can feel much warmer due to the strength of the sun. Unless you've a passion for white-pink cherry blossoms, avoid the *sakura* season in March and April when the recreation area gets packed out and room rates hit the roof. Sakura, a Japanese word adopted by the Taiwanese, means 'flowering cherry tree'. Mainland Chinese regard Alishan as a must-see, so at certain times of the year you may find yourself surrounded by PRC tour groups.

To avoid the parking fee (*NTD100 for cars, NTD20 for motorcycles*), keep going another 200m or so on Highway 18 as it veers right near the toll gate and park on the left. As soon as you enter the Recreation Area you'll see the railway station on your right and the main shopping/restaurant zone below you on the left. The information centre is in the latter. You'll need to go down some more stairs to reach the Hotel Area where Alishan's smaller inns are clustered.

Pre-dawn morning calls are standard as most tourists want to witness the sun rising from **Zhushan** 祝山, a 2,489m-high peak southeast of the resort. Some people walk – the trek takes 1½ hours and involves more than a few steps – but taking the forest railway is more fun (*takes 25mins; NTD100/50 one-way, NTD150/100 return*). The departure schedule is adjusted according to sunrise times and extra trains are organised during busy periods. Returning to Alishan on foot is highly recommended as the trail is very lovely mid-morning once the crowds disperse. The woodland it passes through isn't especially old; most of the peacock pines and cypresses were planted between 1920 and 1947. Among them you'll see stumps of giant cypresses logged during the colonial era. Most are slowly decaying and host ferns and mosses, but a few have sprung back to life.

Of the Recreation Area's several places of worship, the most interesting by far is **Tzu Yun Temple** 慈雲寺 (⏰ *06.00–19.00 daily*). With its red tin roof and white plank walls, it bears a strong resemblance to shrines in the Japanese countryside, which is hardly surprising as it was built by Japanese Buddhists in 1919. Take your shoes off before entering the main hall and try not to disturb the resident nuns.

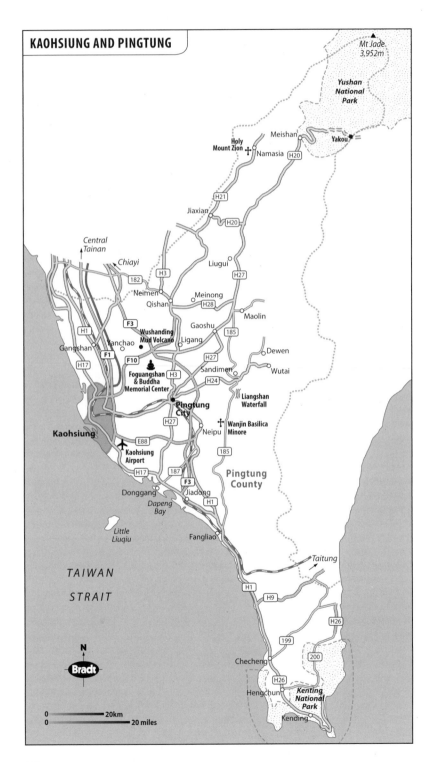

KAOHSIUNG AND PINGTUNG

Mt Jade
3,952m

Yushan
National
Park

Meishan

Holy
Mount Zion
Namasia H20 Yakou

H21

Jiaxian
H20

Central
Tainan
Chiayi   Liugui
182   H3   H27
Neimen
Meinong
Qishan   H28
Maolin
F3   Gaoshu
H1   Wushanding   185
Nanchao   Mud Volcano Ligang
Gangshan   F1   H27   Dewen
H17   F10   Sandimen   Wutai
Foguangshan   H3
& Buddha   H24
Memorial Center   Liangshan
Pingtung   Waterfall
City
H27   Wanjin Basilica
Kaohsiung   Neipu   Minore
E88
Kaohsiung   185
Airport
H17
187
Donggang   F3
Jiadong   Pingtung
Dapeng   H1   County
Bay
Little   Fangliao
Liuqiu
Taitung

TAIWAN

STRAIT
H1

H9

H26

199

N
Checcheng   200

Bradt
H26
Hengchun   Kenting
National
0   20km   Park
0   20 miles   Kending

242

8

Kaohsiung and Pingtung

Taiwan's tropical south contains much of what's great about the country: beaches, mountains, traditional villages and indigenous communities. You're more likely to see banana groves than factory chimneys and even the notoriously industrial city of Kaohsiung has become a pleasant place to stay and explore.

Kaohsiung and Pingtung's tourist sights aren't clustered like Taipei's attractions, so having a vehicle or the patience to use buses is essential if you're to make it to some of the more far-flung destinations such as the Buddhist complex at Foguangshan or the scenic but typhoon-vulnerable aboriginal districts of Maolin, Namasia and Wutai.

Kaohsiung City, which stretches all the way from the ocean to the south face of Mount Jade, has a population of 2.78 million and a land area of 2,946km². Pingtung County (population 890,000, of whom one in 12 is aboriginal; land area 2,776km²) is best known for Kenting, a national park that's an uneasy combination of beach-based hedonism and natural splendour.

If Western food and other creature comforts are important, consider basing yourself in central Kaohsiung and venturing out for day trips. Most of the destinations described in this chapter are no more than two hours from central Kaohsiung.

KAOHSIUNG 高雄 (GĀOXIÓNG) *Telephone code 07*

Kaohsiung used to feel like the place that got the polluting industries while Taipei got the investment and infrastructure. Three decades ago there was little point in visiting this oceanside conurbation unless you were doing business, but these days it's an entirely different story. In terms of life quality, Taiwan's second-largest city has almost caught up with Taipei; if blue skies and sunshine are important to you, you may well feel Kaohsiung has leapfrogged the capital. Winter days are perfect for cycling along Love River or exploring Cijin, an 11km-long island that shelters the port. In wintertime, Kaohsiung is far more pleasant than Hong Kong, which is at the same latitude.

HISTORY Like Birmingham, Los Angeles and other second cities around the world, Kaohsiung is an upstart. Two centuries ago it was nothing more than a fishing village, or rather a string of villages, one of which was located on what's now called Cijin. From 1603, Ming Dynasty admirals conducting anti-pirate sweeps referred to the region as Takau. This name, often spelled Takao and sometimes Dagou, stuck for more than three centuries, until the Japanese colonial authorities decided the written form – two Chinese characters with the literal meaning 'hit the dog' – was undignified. They replaced it with different characters meaning 'lofty hero', pronounced *Takao* in Japanese and *Gāoxióng* in Mandarin.

Kaohsiung isn't the only place in Taiwan to have had a strange name. Minxiong, a town just north of Chiayi City, was known as Damao ('hit the cat') until the Japanese colonial regime changed the written form to its current version, which means 'public hero'.

Odd toponyms can still be found in rural parts. One neighbourhood on the outskirts of Tainan is called Gourou ('dog meat') – perhaps its first resident was a butcher selling canine steaks – while in tea-growing country not far from Alishan there's a Niushihu ('cow dung lake'). Kaohsiung has a small valley marked on maps as Goushikeng ('dog faeces hole') plus a creek named Agongdian ('grandpa's shop').

The colonial regime dredged the channel between Cijin and Kaohsiung proper, widened the harbour mouth and built the first breakwater. The city's industries developed and the population of the urban core multiplied sixfold to 1.5 million between 1950 and 2010. Whereas much of Taipei's growth can be attributed to the post-World War II influx of well-heeled and well-educated mainlanders, most of the migrants who relocated to Kaohsiung in the 20th century came from the interior of the country. Country folk who preferred factory work to farm labour were joined by Hakka from Meinong, Penghu Islanders and thousands of aborigines.

Kaohsiung's international profile received a major boost in July 2009 when it hosted the Eighth World Games, an international sports gathering that features non-Olympic disciplines such as powerlifting and waterskiing. A convention centre has recently been added to the waterfront.

GETTING THERE AND AWAY
By air
Kaohsiung International Airport 高雄國際航空站 ***(Gāoxióng Guójì Hángkōngzhàn)*** (*IATA: KHH;* \ *805 7631; www.kia.gov.tw*) If you're coming from Europe via Hong Kong or Bangkok or from North America via Japan, arranging to fly into Kaohsiung rather than Taoyuan isn't difficult. Domestic routes include flights to/from Magong and Kinmen. The international and domestic terminals are linked by an elevated corridor. The international terminal has two money changers upstairs (⊕ *05.30–17.00 daily*) and a Bank of Taiwan branch downstairs (⊕ *09.00–last international flight daily*). There's a post office (*3rd flr, International Terminal;* ⊕ *08.30–16.30 Mon–Fri*) and visitor information centres with free Wi-Fi in both terminals.

Airport transfers The most popular way of getting from the airport to central Kaohsiung is **rapid-transit underground train**. Kaohsiung International Airport Station is one stop from the southern end of the Red Line. Including waiting time and short walks at both ends, allow 35 minutes to get from the airport to Kaohsiung Zuoying HSR Station (*NTD50 one-way*).

Buses to Kenting (*departs every 30mins;* ⊕ *06.25–22.15 daily; takes about 2½hrs; NTD327*) via Fangliao (*takes 1¼hrs; NTD144*) stop at road level between the terminals, so there's no need to trek into central Kaohsiung if you're heading to the beach resort or the east coast. Buy your ticket when boarding; have exact change ready.

The tiny building between the two terminals houses two **vehicle-hire companies**: Car Plus Auto Leasing (☎*801 0019;* ⊕ *08.30–21.00 daily*) and Hotai Leasing (☎*0800 024 550;* ⊕ *08.30–21.00 daily*).

Taxis are allowed to add NTD50 to what's shown on the meter, so expect to pay at least NTD400 if you're going beyond Love River.

By HSR To Taipei the bullet train takes no more than two hours (*4 departures per hr;* ⊕ *06.30–22.10; NTD1,630*). To Taichung journey time is no more than an hour (*NTD860*). Kaohsiung has an integrated HSR/TRA/rapid transit station at Zuoying. The rapid transit stop is called Zuoying but the TRA station there is called Xinzuoying.

By TRA Most expresses stop at Kaohsiung Main Station and Xinzuoying only; TRA passengers wanting to transfer to the HSR should get off at the latter. To/ from Taipei, there's at least one express per hour between dawn and mid-evening (*takes 4¾–7hrs; NTD650–843*). A few other expresses go no further than Taichung (*takes 2½–3½hrs; NTD361–469*). There are 13 services daily to Taitung (*takes on avg 2½hrs; NTD279–362*). Trains to/from Tainan are frequent and usually take under an hour (*NTD68–106*). To/from Pingtung (*NTD31–48*) takes less than half an hour.

By bus The long-distance bus stations are on your left as you leave the TRA Main Station. From the **Kuo-Kuang Bus Station** (see map, page 248) there's a bus to Taipei at least every hour around the clock (*takes 5hrs; NTD530*). To Taichung there's a bus every 40 minutes (*departs* ⊕ *05.40–22.20 daily; takes 3hrs; NTD300*). Four buses per day go to Taitung (*departs* ⊕ *03.00, 07.00, 12.30 & 17.30; takes 3½hrs; NTD443*).

Kaohsiung Bus Co Station (see map, page 248) behind the Kuo-Kuang station serves Kenting and Kaohsiung's hinterland. Around 56 buses per day go to Kenting (*#9117 & #9188;* ⊕ *06.05–22.10; takes up to 3hrs; NTD347–364*). All #9117 services stop at Donggang (*NTD115*) and Fangliao (*NTD180*). #8032 is an hourly service to Jiaxian (⊕ *06.40–20.40 daily; takes 2¼hrs; NTD231*). Three buses per day terminate at Baolai on the South Cross-Island Highway (*#8025; departs at 07.20, 13.20 & 15.20; takes 3¼hrs; NTD319*). Only one continues beyond Baolai to Taoyuan (*#8029; departs 06.15; takes 3¾hrs; NTD355*).

KAOHSIUNG'S POET ADVOCATE

Kaohsiung isn't rated highly as a literary centre, but it does count among its residents Yu Kwang-chung (b1928), a man who's been called 'arguably the most important poet writing in Chinese today... an excellent essayist, translator and critic'. Born in China and formerly resident in Hong Kong, Yu took up a teaching post in Kaohsiung in 1985 and has lived in the metropolis ever since. In his poems he balances criticisms with praise. Railing against Kaohsiung's smokestacks, Yu writes: 'They brazenly darken the blue southern sky one puff at a time / despoiling scenery that was pure and clean / They're like gangsters going after young girls / curses spewing from their mouths.' In a mellower mood, he waxes: 'The Love River divides the landscape in two / but the clouds say, it's spring / casting shadows on the water / The weather station says, no, it's summer.' Yu has translated many of his own poems into English.

For Qishan, Meinong and Foguangshan you're best off catching a bus outside Kaohsiung Zuoying HSR Station/Zuoying KMRT Station. From there Freeway Bus #10 is the quickest and cheapest service to Qishan (*departs every 20mins on w/days* ☉ *06.30–23.00 Mon–Fri, less frequent at w/ends; takes 40mins; NTD50*). Some #10 buses continue on to Meinong. For Foguangshan and the Buddha Memorial Centre, take the #8501 (*departs every 40mins;* ☉ *08.15–18.00 Mon–Fri, more frequent at w/ends; takes around 1hr; NTD63*). If the driver stops you from boarding it's because that particular bus doesn't go all the way to the monastery. Services to Kenting from the HSR station include the #9189 Kenting Express (*departs every 30mins* ☉ *07.00–19.00 daily; takes 2¼hrs; NTD383*).

By hired car There are **Car Plus Auto Leasing** counters in the HSR station and airport, plus a branch near Kaohsiung Main Station (see map, page 248) (*264 Jianguo 2nd Rd;* ☎ *236 5510; www.car-plus.com.tw*). All are open ☉ 08.30–20.30 daily.

GETTING AROUND Eating, drinking, chewing gum and smoking are prohibited on KMRT trains and city buses. Get an i-Pass stored value card from any KMRT station if you plan to spend some time in the city as it can be used on the metro, city buses, local ferries and to rent bikes.

By rapid transit The Kaohsiung Mass Rapid Transit (*www.krtco.com.tw*) has two lines, Red and Orange, which intersect at Formosa Boulevard Station (see map, page 248). KMRT trains run every 5–10 minutes, 06.00–23.00 daily. The website has fare information (*one-way journeys NTD20–65*) and travel times (*airport to Main Station takes 18mins, NTD35*). All signs and announcements are multilingual. The first part of an above-ground light-rail system, integrated with the KMRT, should be operational by 2015.

By bus The city bus hub is in front of Kaohsiung Main Station (see map, page 248). Journeys are NTD12/6 per section; few trips are more than one section. You might qualify for free bus transfers if you've just taken the KMRT; see the information inside stations for details. Destinations are shown in English on the front of each bus, and inside the name of the next stop comes up in English on an LED board above the driver. Useful services include #100 to the Talee, Hanshin and FE21' Mega department stores and #248 to Gushan Ferry Dock via Love River. Both can be caught at Kaohsiung Main Station; board #248 on the side closest to the TRA station, otherwise you'll end up in the northwestern suburbs. Both run every 15–20 minutes (*departs* ☉ *06.40–22.00 daily*).

By boat In addition to the regular ferry (*departs every 10mins;* ☉ *06.00–24.00 daily; takes 10mins; NTD15 one-way*) from Gushan Ferry Dock 鼓山輪渡站 to Cijin, there are various harbour cruises (*http://kcs.kcg.gov.tw*). Bicycles can be taken on

ONE-DAY TRAVEL PASSES

A one-day KMRT pass (*NTD200, including refundable deposit of NTD70*) is available from stations, as is the more useful One-Day Traveller's Pass (*NTD200, no deposit*). The latter is valid for unlimited rides on the KMRT, city buses and regular ferries to Cijin from when it's activated until the end of services that day, but doesn't cover the C-Bike rental system.

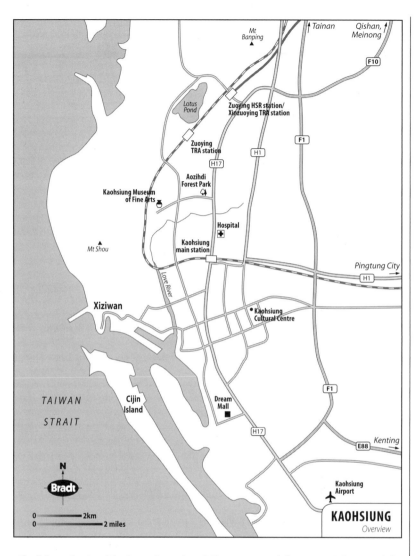

KAOHSIUNG
Overview

Map labels:

Mt Banping

Tainan

Qishan, Meinong

F10

Lotus Pond

Zuoying HSR station/ Xinzuoying TRA station

F1

Zuoying TRA station

H17

H1

Aozihdi Forest Park

Kaohsiung Museum of Fine Arts

Hospital

Mt Shou

Kaohsiung main station

Love River

Xiziwan

Kaohsiung Cultural Centre

Pingtung City

H1

F1

TAIWAN

STRAIT

Cijin Island

Dream Mall

H17

F1

E88

Kenting

N

Bradt

0 — 2km
0 — 2 miles

Kaohsiung Airport

all of these ferries. The **Love Boat** (see *What to see and do*, page 254) is good for sightseeing but, because passengers can only get on and off at one point, of no practical use.

By hired bicycle The local government is rightfully proud of what it's achieved in terms of making Kaohsiung a bike-friendly city. Bicycle-only lanes link Lotus Pond with Love River and run the length of Cijin. Bikes with baskets and lights (but without locks or helmets) can be hired through a high-tech system called **C-Bike** (*www.c-bike.com.tw*). The 50-plus rental points include Lotus Pond, the back of Kaohsiung Main Station, Kaohsiung Museum of Fine Arts and busier KMRT stations. All are automated, bilingual and accept i-Pass and credit cards (*free for the first hour then NTD20 for every 1½hrs*). Bicycles and electric mini-bikes can also be rented from **Happiness Bike** [250 B2] (*532 0969; 07.30–02.00 daily*) beside

Kaohsiung and Pingtung KAOHSIUNG

8

247

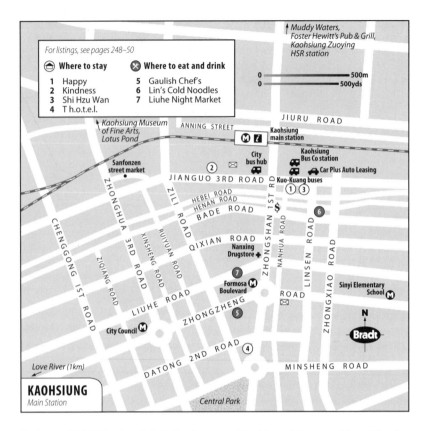

For listings, see pages 248–50

Where to stay
1 Happy
2 Kindness
3 Shi Hzu Wan
4 T h.o.t.e.l.

Where to eat and drink
5 Gaulish Chef's
6 Lin's Cold Noodles
7 Liuhe Night Market

Muddy Waters,
Foster Hewitt's Pub & Grill,
Kaohsiung Zuoying
HSR station

0 ——————— 500m
0 ——————— 500yds

JIURU ROAD

Kaohsiung Museum
of Fine Arts,
Lotus Pond

ANNING STREET

Kaohsiung
main station

City
bus hub

Kaohsiung
Bus Co station

Sanfonzen
street market

Car Plus Auto Leasing

JIANGUO 3RD ROAD

Kuo-Kuang buses

ZHONGHUA 3RD ROAD

ZILI ROAD

HEBEI ROAD
HENAN ROAD
BADE ROAD

ZHONGSHAN 1ST RD

NANHUA ROAD

LINSEN ROAD

CHENGGONG 1ST ROAD

ZIQIANG ROAD

XINSHENG ROAD

RUIYUAN ROAD

QIXIAN ROAD

Nanxing
Drugstore

ZHONGXIAO ROAD

Sinyi Elementary
School

Formosa
Boulevard

ROAD

LIUHE ROAD

ZHONGZHENG

City Council

Love River (1km)

DATONG 2ND ROAD

MINSHENG ROAD

N

KAOHSIUNG
Main Station

Central Park

Sizihwan KMRT Station Exit 1. For better and/or bigger bikes, try **Giant Bicycles** [250 E2] (*238 Qingnian 2nd Rd;* ☎ *241 3040;* ⊕ *10.00–21.30 daily*).

By taxi Handy Andy (m *0931 827 808;* e *andys_cab902@yahoo.com.tw*) speaks good English and is available for day tours in the region and shorter journeys.

TOURIST INFORMATION Kaohsiung City Government runs a website (*http://khh.travel/en/*) and a slew of visitor information centres, the most useful of which are in Kaohsiung Main Station [map, page 248] (⊕ *10.00–19.00 daily*), by Exit 2 in Kaohsiung Zuoying HSR Station (⊕ *08.30–20.30 daily*) and beside Cijin's ferry terminal [250 B3] (⊕ *10.00–20.00 Mon–Fri, 10.00–22.00 Sat–Sun*).

 WHERE TO STAY
Near Kaohsiung Main Station
All of the following hotels are shown on the map above.

⌂ **Shi Hzu Wan Hotel** (65 rooms) 241 Jianguo 2nd Rd; ☎ 236 4567; f 236 0111; e kh58888@ hotmail.com; www.westbay888.com.tw/station/. Nowhere near the part of town it's named after (Xiziwan) but close enough to the TRA & bus

stations to be very useful. Spotless, spacious guestrooms. Free self-service laundry; free parking. Rooms sometimes available for NTD2,200. B/fast inc. **$$$**

⌂ **Happy Hotel** (25 rooms) 221 Nanhua Rd; ☎ 235 8800; f 235 0975; www.happyhotel.com. tw. One of the city's best budget options, Happy Hotel has small but clean rooms & the staff are genuinely cheerful. Can arrange motorcycle rental

& it's sometimes possible to get a room & wheels for under NTD1,000. B/fast inc. **$$**

🏠 **Hotel Kindness** (103 rooms) 44 Jianguo 3rd Rd; ☏ 287 5566; f 287 8866; e h013.hotel@ msa.hinet.net; www.kindness-hotel.com.tw. Some rooms are barely bigger than the beds, but everything is kept spick & span & the location couldn't be better if you're boarding a train or bus early the next day. Midweek room rates from NTD1,400. Buffet b/fast inc & guests can borrow a bike for free. **$$**

🏠 **T h.o.t.e.l.** (42 rooms) 177 Datong 1st Rd; ☏ 231 2141; f 231 2149; e service@t-hotel. com.tw; www.t-hotel.com.tw. Popular with local businesspeople but the English-speaking staff are well able to handle visitors from afar. Room décor is monochrome with a few shades of brown thrown in. Some rooms come with jacuzzi, PC & CD player & it's well worth paying a bit more to stay in one of these. Sofas, refrigerators & big-screen LCD TVs in every room. Pool table & Wii in the basement; free self-service laundry with dryer & iron plus bike rental. Buffet b/fast inc. **$$**

Near Love River All of the following hotels are shown on the map on page 250.

🏠 **Grand Hi-Lai Hotel** (540 rooms) 266 Chenggong 1st Rd; ☏ 216 1766; f 216 1966; e rsv@grand-hilai.com.tw; www.grand-hilai. com.tw. Without doubt Kaohsiung's swankiest hotel, the Grand Hi-Lai has won a reputation for excellent service & comfort. The spacious rooms are just the right side of ostentatious; big windows mean an abundance of natural light. If you're on the southern or western sides of the building you'll pay extra for the engrossing harbour views. Book a health room if you fancy having access to your own exercise equipment. The in-bathroom TVs are tiny; rooms have separate shower cubicles & baths, but the latter are standard-size only. 13 restaurants & bars, the most popular of which is **The Harbour Buffet** (🕐 06.30–10.30, 11.30–14.30 & 17.30–

21.30; **$$$**). Sauna & squash court. Buffet b/fast inc. **$$$$$**

🏠 **Fullon Hotel Kaohsiung** (250 rooms) 45 Wufu 4th Rd; ☏ 551 1188; f 521 1166; www. fullon-hotels.com.tw. A new addition to a reliable chain, Fullon offers international-standard comfort, cleanliness & service. Two-person rooms are often less than NTD4,500. If you don't want to pay slightly more for a room on a higher floor overlooking the harbour, enjoy the view over drinks in the 26th-flr bar. Not all rooms have bathtubs so request one when booking. Sauna & gym; outdoor swimming pool open May–Oct. B/fast inc. **$$$$**

🏠 **Harmony Hotel** (31 rooms) 265 Chenggong 1st Rd; ☏ 216 6866; f 215 2628; e harmony_ hotel@xuite.net; www.harmony-hotel.com.tw. Tastefully subdued colours, sinfully thick carpets, quasi-Art Deco styling & very substantial discounts that often take even w/end prices below NTD3,000 make this hotel worth considering. PC with Wi-Fi & broadband in every room. Free parking. B/fast inc. **$$$**

🏠 **Kindness Han Shen Hotel** (43 rooms) 290 Zhonghua 4th Rd; ☏ 281 5566; f 281 5511; e h011.hotel@msa.hinet.net; www.kindness-hotel.com.tw. Very similar to its sister establishment near Kaohsiung Main Station but with significantly larger wooden-floored rooms. For NTD500 per night an extra bed can set up in your room. Free car parking, coin-operated laundry & business centre with lots of computers. Buffet b/fast inc & guests can borrow a bike for free. **$$$**

🏠 **Hotel Queen** (100 rooms) 21 Dagong Rd; ☏ 521 2211; e queenhotel@msa.hinet.net; www.5658.com.tw/queenhotel. The rooms are all of a fair size but the windows vary between cell-like apertures & huge panes that give good views of Longevity Mountain. A great location for Love River fans & barflies. A bit old-fashioned but very reasonable prices. B/fast inc. **$$**

🍴 WHERE TO EAT
Near Kaohsiung Main Station All of the following establishments are shown on the map opposite.

🍴 **Gaulish Chef's** 53 Zhongzheng 4th Rd; ☏ 241 2068; 🕐 11.30–22.00 daily. Highly

regarded by locals & expats, this restaurant serves up very good, very fresh French cuisine. The menu is nicely varied with everything from light lunches to 6-course dinners inc oysters, lobsters, escargots & steak with truffle sauce. Reservations usually necessary. EM. **$$$**

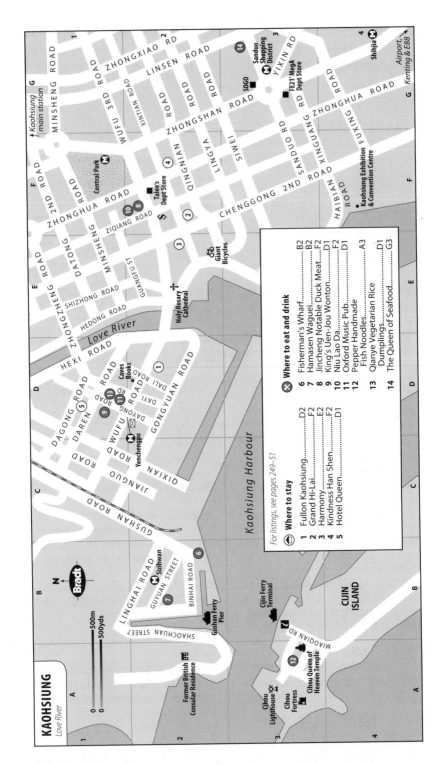

✕ **Lin's Cold Noodles** 林家涼麵 278 Linsen 1st Rd; ☎236 6759; ⊕ 08.30–19.30 Mon–Sat. Order a bowl of cold noodles with shreds of chicken (*jī sī liáng miàn*) or, if you're brave, cow's stomach cold noodles (*niú dù liáng miàn*) & wash it down with a bowl of miso soup. There are plenty of conventional hot noodle options. **$**

✕ **Liuhe Night Market** 六合夜市 Liuhe 2nd Rd; no tel; ⊕ approx 17.00–01.00 daily. Kaohsiung's most famous night market is a great place for Taiwanese snack foods, of course, but that doesn't mean it isn't international. In recent years Turkish ice cream & Pakistani dishes have been available, as have sushi, sashimi & Japanese seaweed wraps filled with salad or roe. **$**

Love River All of the following establishments are shown on the map opposite.

✕ **The Queen of Seafood** 214 Sanduo 3rd Rd; ☎335 3606; www.seafoodnet.com.tw; ⊕ 11.30–15.00, 17.30–22.00 daily. Offering both set & à la carte menus, this landmark restaurant draws both regular diners & those with something to celebrate. EM. **$$$$**

✕ **Niu Lao Da** 牛老大 18 Ziqiang 2nd Rd; ☎281 9196; ⊕ 12.00–14.00, 17.00–03.00 daily. Renowned for its fried beef & beef hot pots, Niu Lao Da sources its meat from local cattle farms. This means the beef is exceptionally fresh (less than 8hrs from slaughter to table) & you can indulge knowing you've done something to minimise food miles. The stewed rice & noodle options are good bets for solo travellers. Order with caution as the Chinese-only menu also lists cow's stomach, cow's heart & cow's lung. Local & Japanese beers available. **$$$**

✕ **Jincheng Notable Duck Meat** 金城鴨肉專門店 62 Wufu 3rd Rd; ☎241 5419; ⊕ 10.00–20.30 daily. This wildly popular eatery has expanded along the pavement & on hot days opens an AC dining room upstairs. The staff recommend you get a whole/half cold salted duck 鹽水鴨肉 (*yánshuǐ yāròu*) costing NTD420/220 so you & your friends can pull it apart with your fingers. There's every conceivable noodle option inc ban-tiao plus soups & side dishes of kimchi & tofu. Spitting bones on to the table is OK yet everything is kept very clean. **$$**

✕ **Hamasen Waguei** 59 Guyuan St; no tel; ⊕ 06.00–10.00 approx Tue–Sun. This vendor has for more than half a century been selling small bowls of what in Taiwanese is called *waguei* (NTD25). It's a wheaty, savoury concoction of mashed, steamed rice that you dig into with a fork; each bowl has half an egg & chunks of pork & comes covered with a brown sauce. **$**

✕ **King's Uen-Jou Wonton** 金溫州餛飩大王 1, Lane 163, Xinle St; ☎551 1378; ⊕ 14.00–21.00 Mon–Fri, 11.30–21.00 Sat–Sun. In business since 1954, King's is a little difficult to find (down a side street & there's no English sign) but it's earned a citywide reputation for dishes inc wonton soup noodles, beef wonton noodles & pork-rib noodles. The recipe comes from Wenzhou, a city in Fujian. Local beer available. **$**

✕ **Pepper Handmade Fish Noodles** 44 Tongshan Rd, Cijin; ☎571 1711; ⊕ 10.00–20.00 Wed–Mon. Consisting of little more than plastic stools & folding tables outside a single-storey building, this eatery has been serving delicious thick noodles made from fish dough for more than 3 decades. They're served in a broth flavoured with pork, chicken bones & seasonal greens. Crispy fried dumplings (fish or shrimp) also available & just as good. No EM so point to order. **$**

✕ **Qianye Vegetarian Rice Dumplings** 131 Dayi St; ☎521 3665; ⊕ 08.00–20.30 daily, closed 2nd & 4th Sun each month. Help yourself to salad, fried dumplings, tofu & meat-free Chinese dishes then show what you've got to the worker to find out how much you need pay (seldom more than NTD100). Come just before midday for the best pickings. Inc unlimited soup & black tea. Upstairs there's AC. No written menu. **$**

North of Kaohsiung Main Station

✕ **Muddy Waters** 417 Longde Rd; ☎522 7211; ⊕ 07.00–22.00 daily. The sandwiches (wide choice of breads, meats & dressings), pasta dishes & other Western favourites are all very good & service is faultless but portions are a tad small. Indoor & outdoor seating. The restaurant upstairs, **Mamamia** (☎522 7300; ⊕ 11.00–14.00 & 17.30–24.00 daily; **$$$**), is run by the same company (www.amy.com.tw) & puts on a good Italian spread. Both have EMs. Within walking distance of Kaohsiung Museum of Fine Arts. **$$**

WHERE TO DRINK

♀ Oxford Music Pub 111 Dayi St; ☎532 3595; ⏰ 18.00–02.00 daily. This relatively small establishment just off Wufu 4th Road is a good place to drop by if you're in the mood for English-language conversation, pub grub inc burgers & steak plus a fair choice of draught & bottled lagers. Oxford, which has been around for a good while, attracts a middle-aged clientele. Occasional live music & absolute honesty from the staff, which is more than can be said for a few bars in this neighbourhood. EM. $$$

♀ Fisherman's Wharf 漁人碼頭 Near Gushan 1st & Binhai 1st rds; ⏰ varies. Has a number of places where you can drink a beer & enjoy a bite to eat while watching the sun go down over the harbour. No EMs. $$

♀ Foster Hewitt's Pub and Grill 30 Wenzhong Rd; ☎555 0888; ⏰ 18.00–03.00 daily. With bottled & tap beers from NTD100 plus a good range of scotches & wines this Canadian-run bar is a place for top-notch Western food in addition to a fine drinking establishment. The burgers (*from NTD160*) won a prize at the 2013 Kaohsiung International Food Festival; starters, soups & salads from NTD120. Steaks start at NTD400. The EM also has Tex-Mex & Italian dishes. Min charge NTD200 pp. Easily reached from exit 2 of the KMRT's Red Line Kaohsiung Arena Station. $$

SHOPPING
Market

Sanfonzen Street Market 三鳳中街 [map, page 248] ⏰ approx 07.00–20.00 daily. Signposted Sanfong Jhong St in some places, this is a traditional shopping area somewhat like Taipei's Dihua St. There's an abundance of dried fruits & other goods – as well as photo opportunities – so if you're planning a hike this is a great place to pick up the ingredients for trail mix.

Malls and department stores

Dream Mall [map, page 247] 789 Zhonghua 5th Rd; ☎973 3888; www.dream-mall.com.tw; ⏰ 11.00–22.00 Mon–Thu, 10.30–22.30 Sat–Sun & national holidays. The biggest shopping centre in Taiwan with 400,001m² of retail space, the Dream Mall is a very broad collection of international brands & mid-price eating options. Atop the roof there's a Ferris wheel which turns slowly enough to give riders – weather permitting – value-for-money views over all of Kaohsiung & a good part of the surrounding countryside. It's best reached by bus #168 or KMRT to the Red Line's Kaisyuan Station. Take exit 3; the mall is the huge building 700m away on your left.

FE21′ MegA Department Store [250 G3] 21 Sanduo 4th Rd; ☎0800 000 563; ⏰ 11.00–22.00 daily. Incorporates a cinema & a good bookstore. Take the rapid transit to Sanduo Shopping District & leave by exit 1 to find yourself on the building's ground floor.

Hanshin Department Store [250 F2] 266-1 Chenggong Rd; ☎215 7266; ⏰ 11.00–22.00 daily. Reached by bus #100 or #168, Hanshin is directly beneath the swanky Grand Hi-Lai Hotel & has the best food court of any department store in the city.

Talee's Department Store [250 F2] 59 Wufu 3rd Rd; ☎251 6086; ⏰ 10.30–22.00 daily. The exterior is striking but inside Talee's is a fairly standard Japanese-style department store. The 7th-flr coffee shop (*drinks from NTD110*) overlooking Central Park is a good spot for a caffeine recharge.

Bookshops

Caves Books [250 D2] 76 Wufu 4th Rd; ☎561 5716; ⏰ 10.00–22.00 daily. Postcards, magazines, quite a few books in English about Taiwan & a selection of novels.

Eslite [250 G3] 17th Flr FE21′ MegA Dept Store; ☎331 3102; ⏰ 11.00–22.00 daily. Especially good for books on art & architecture in various languages & imported magazines, this branch is one of the most attractive bookshops in south Taiwan.

OTHER PRACTICALITIES
Post

✉**General Post Office** [250 D2] 177 Zhongzheng 3rd Rd; ⏰ 07.30–21.00 Mon–Fri, 08.30–16.30 Sat, 08.30–12.00 Sun

✉**Kaohsiung Main Station** [map, page 248] On your right as you leave the station's front entrance; ⏰ 08.00–17.00 Mon–Fri, 08.30–12.00 Sat

✉**Xinzuoying TRA Station** ⏰ 10.00–18.00 daily

Banks and changing money
You can change money in the GPO & the post office beside Kaohsiung Main Station. Go to the airport if you need to change cash or travellers' cheques outside normal banking hours. Useful bank branches include:

$ **Mega** 308 Zhongshan 1st Rd
$ **First Bank** 61 Wufu 3rd Rd

Medical
✚ **Kaohsiung Medical University Chung-Ho Memorial Hospital** 中和紀念醫院 100 Ziyou 1st Rd; ☎ 312 1101; www.kmuh.org.tw; ⊕ 24hrs daily
✚ **Nanxing Drugstore** [map, page 248] 173 Zhongshan 1st Rd; ⊕ 08.30–22.00 Mon–Sat

Police
Kaohsiung City Police Department 260 Zhongzheng 4th Rd; ☎ 221 5796

ENTERTAINMENT
For high-brow entertainment, see what's playing at these venues:

Kaohsiung Cultural Centre 67 Wufu 1st Rd, Lingya; ☎ 222 5136; www.khcc.gov.tw. Municipal venue for exhibitions & shows of all kinds.
Pier-2 Art Centre 1 Dayong Rd, Yancheng; ☎ 521 4899; http://pier-2.khcc.gov.tw; ⊕ 10.00–18.00 Mon–Thu, 10.00–20.00 Fri–Sun. An old harbour warehouse upcycled into an arts space, Pier-2 hosts exhibitions, rock concerts & the offices of cultural/creative businesses.

WHAT TO SEE AND DO
Around Love River (see map, page 250)

Cijin 旗津 *(Qíjīn)* Fujianese fishermen began settling on this finger of land in the 17th century and it retains some of its old, salty character. Even if you turn around and immediately return to 'mainland' Kaohsiung, the ferry (*departs every 10mins; ⊕ 06.00–24.00 daily; takes 10mins; NTD15 one-way*) from Gushan Ferry Dock to Cihou, the main settlement, is worth taking for the views you'll get of the city and the foliage-covered promontories that shelter the harbour's northwestern entrance. Cihou can be explored on foot but there are also tourist pedicabs (drivers wait outside the ferry terminal from early morning to mid-evening and charge from NTD200 for a 20-minute tour but no English spoken) and bike rentals (*from NTD50/hr*). As you would expect in what was until recently a fishing village, seafood is a speciality. Miaoqian Road, which leads from the ferry terminal to a sandy beach (swimming prohibited), is lined with restaurants. This thoroughfare's name means 'road in front of the temple', and the shrine alluded to is **Cihou Queen of Heaven Temple** [250 A3] (*93 Miaoqian Rd; ⊕ 05.30–22.00 daily*), named after and dedicated to Mazu since its founding in 1673.

More interesting than the temple are **Cihou Lighthouse** [250 A3] (*⊕ 09.00–16.00 Tue–Sun; free admission*) and **Cihou Fortress** [250 A3] (*⊕ 24hrs daily; free admission*). These two landmarks – the former was designed in the late 19th century by a British engineer and rebuilt in 1918, the latter was constructed in 1875 – stand near each other at the island's northwestern tip, atop a craggy but lush hillock the strategic importance of which is obvious. The southeastern half of Cijin is of no interest unless you've a passion for freight containers and ship-repair yards. In the 1970s, in addition to building new vessels and fixing old ones, Kaohsiung was where most of the world's ships came to die. The ship-breaking industry has since moved to countries with lower wages and more lenient environmental standards.

Former British Consular Residence 前清英國領事館 *(Qiánqīng Yīngguó Lǐngshìguǎn)* [250 A2] (☎ 525 0271; *⊕ 09.00–24.00 daily, closed 3rd Tue each month; admission NTD30/15*) A vestige of the Treaty Port era when Western powers forced China to open several towns and cities to foreign trade, this building on a

southern ridge of 354m-high Mount Shou is where British diplomats lived between 1879 and 1897. The actual consular offices were on the waterfront at the bottom of this hill and will have been turned into a museum by the time you read this.

In 1911, the British government shifted all personnel and archives to Danshui in the north. The residence and offices were sold to the Japanese government in 1925; a nearby cemetery for Westerners (marked on one of the old maps displayed inside the residence) remained in British hands but was overrun by squatters in the 1960s; traces of three of the 40-odd graves remain extant. The exhibition inside the old residence gives a broad picture of trade relations between 19th-century Taiwan and the outside world. In addition to camphor, sugar and rice, the island's exports included lumber, salt, turmeric, sesame and peanuts. Good views can be had from the on-site eatery ($\oplus$ *same as residence; EM; meals from NTD260; drinks from NTD85; waffles & floats from NTD90*).

Bus #99 leaves Yanchengpu KMRT Station (*departs every 40mins; $\oplus$ 06.00–18.00 daily; takes 15mins; NTD12*) and stops near the residence before heading north along Caishan Road. Alternatives are taking a taxi or walking about 30 minutes from Sizihwan KMRT Station (be warned: there's little shade). However, there's a short cut you can take when leaving. Look for a downhill path that starts behind the smaller of the two shrines by the residence. The neighbourhood looks poor but it's safe. Continue past three tiny temples and a disused well; finding your way to Shaochuan Street isn't difficult.

Caishan Road   From the car park below the Consular Residence it's possible to drive north through a university campus for 4.7km to where Caishan Road ends at a military base. Popular with cyclists, joggers and macaques – which sometimes dawdle on the edge of the tarmac – the road offers some agreeable ocean vistas. Consider heading up here for an afternoon coffee; some businesses open only at the weekend.

Love River   Solar-powered tourist boats ply the river's lower stretch. The **Love Boat** ($\oplus$ 15.00–22.00 Mon–Fri, 09.00–22.00 Sat–Sun; NTD120/60) sets off from a dock near where Minsheng Road reaches the river's east bank as soon as there are enough passengers. Tours last about 25 minutes and are especially popular around dusk.

Near Kaohsiung Main Station [see map, page 248]

Formosa Boulevard KMRT Station (*Zhongshan & Zhongzheng rds*) This station's four tepee-shaped glass and steel entrances call to mind the little pyramids I M Pei controversially added to the courtyard of the Louvre in the 1980s. Japanese architect Shin Takamatsu titled these creations *Prayer*, and they do resemble church spires. Not everyone is impressed, however. Nearby landowners complained about the impact on *feng shui*, saying the spires are like swords pointing into their homes. Inside the station there's a 667m² indoor ceiling installation called *The Dome of Light*. Said to be the world's largest piece of glass art, and representing 'birth, growth, honour, destruction and rebirth', it's a wash of colours and images that took Narcissus Quagliata, its Italian creator, more than 3½ years. As with any other piece of art of this size, it's worth zooming in on details, then stepping back to appreciate the overall effect. But it's not all joy and oneness with the cosmos – one section, partly obscured by a lift, features scenes of conflagration and a very messy car wreck. Perhaps the artist included the latter to impress upon people one of the reasons they should use public transport instead of driving. To learn more, take the

30-minute audio tour (*NTD50*). The station's Chinese name commemorates the Meilidao Incident of 1979 (see *History*, page 20). In the **Human Rights Learning Studio** (*near Exit 9; ⊕ 10.00–19.00 Tue–Sun*) you'll find lots of English-language materials about Taiwan's recent history.

North of Kaohsiung Main Station
Kaohsiung Museum of Fine Arts 高雄市立美術館 (✎ *555 0331; www.kmfa. gov.tw; ⊕ 09.00–17.00 Tue–Sun; free admission except for special exhibitions*) Surrounded by parkland, this museum has a good mix of local, national and international artworks, including photography and installations. A fibreglass version of *Water Buffaloes* (see page 99) is on permanent display. From Aozihdi KMRT Station (*5mins by KMRT from Kaohsiung Main Railway Station; NTD20*) it's a long (*35mins*) but pleasant walk through the not-quite-mature but very promising **Aozihdi Forest Park** (*⊕ 24hrs daily; free admission*) to the museum. Red 32 and Red 35 shuttle buses link the museum and KMRT stop.

Lotus Pond 蓮池潭 *(Liánchí Tán)* Some visitors adore this 1.3km-long lake and the colourful shrines and pagodas that surround it; others find it all a bit kitschy. Most of the pond's landmarks are near its southern end, which is easily reached by train to Zuoying TRA Station (not Xinzuoying where the HSR stops). Services are frequent from Kaohsiung Main Railway Station (*takes 8mins; NTD15*). Get a leaflet from the visitor centre (*⊕ 09.00–18.00 daily*) on the southwestern shore, then make your way to the **Dragon and Tiger Pagodas** (*⊕ 07.00–18.00 daily; free admission*) and the **Spring and Autumn Pavilions** (*⊕ 06.30–22.00 daily; free admission*). At the former it's customary to go in via the dragon's mouth and leave by the tiger's jaws. The most attractive folk shrine in the city proper is very near: **Qiming Temple** (*⊕ 06.00–21.30 daily*) has a statue of Guan Gong in the main chamber, recognisable by his burgundy complexion. Upstairs, dead-centre, there's an especially fine representation of the Jade Emperor. Instead of going all the way around the lake, consider returning to the information centre and turning right. Almost immediately you'll see the **North Gate of Fengshan Old Town** (*⊕ 24hrs daily; free admission*). Built in the 1820s, it boasts door-god images which are faded yet still august.

World Games Stadium (✎ *582 9000; www.nssac.gov.tw/english/; ⊕ for events*) So-named because it was the venue for the opening and closing ceremonies of the 2009 World Games, and alternatively known as the National Stadium, this stunning piece of eco-friendly architecture was designed by Pritzker Prize winner Toyo Ito of Japan. It's visible from and within walking distance of World Games KMRT Station (*13mins by KMRT from Kaohsiung Main Railway Station; NTD30*), one of eight Red Line stations elevated high above street level. From this part of the rapid-transit network you'll get good views over the city and **Mount Banping** 半屏山, a topographical anomaly that quarrying companies did their best to erase but which has been turned into an ecological park. Originally 223m high, the top of the hill is now around 180m above the surrounding plain.

HEADING NORTH FROM KAOHSIUNG *Telephone code 07*
WUSHANDING MUD VOLCANO 烏山頂泥火山 (WŪSHĀNDǏNG NÍHUŎSHĀN)
Nothing between Kaohsiung and Tainan justifies getting off a train but if you're in your own vehicle and curious about natural phenomena, do leave the main road

and seek out this tiny nature reserve (☉ *08.30–16.30 daily; free admission*). You may be required to sign in at the entrance. Just a few metres high, the volcano is full of warm slurry (average temperature 28°C) which bubbles and occasionally spills over the edge of the crater. It's possible to clamber up the sides and put your hand in the crater. Rivulets of mud trickle across the clearing and into the surrounding forest, where you might see snakes hunting for frogs. Near the active cone there are two dormant volcanoes that have been baked rock-hard by the sun. Close by, the **Yangnyu Mud Pools** 養女湖 are gas-belching chocolate-brown pools which sound like wave-making machines. According to scientists, the slurry has a high chlorine content while the gas is mostly methane with traces of carbon dioxide and nitrogen. Taiwan has more than a dozen mud volcanoes, the precise number changing from time to time because typhoons and seismic activity occasionally reveal new volcanoes or shut down existing ones.

Getting there and away Cars on Freeway 1 should take the Gangshan exit and follow the signs to Yanchao. Take Local Road 38 for about 5km; when you see Jinshan Elementary School on your left, turn sharp right. Stay on the main road and follow the bilingual signs for 2.8km. This route is narrow and twisting, so drive carefully.

QISHAN 旗山 AND AROUND It take a while to escape the urban sprawl but beyond central Kaohsiung there's a tremendous variety of attractions, including religious sites, ethnic minorities and ecological wonders.

Getting there and away
By car Take either north–south freeway to Freeway 10 and head northeast, then follow the signs to Qishan.

By motorcycle or bicycle If you're approaching from the coast via Highway 28, watch out for the scenic badlands around km18. From Tainan, consider Road 182 (see page 259).

By bus Qishan is easy to reach by bus from Kaohsiung HSR Station (*Freeway Bus #10 departs every 20mins* ☉ *06.30–23.00 Mon–Fri, less frequent at w/ends; takes 40mins; NTD50*). For Meinong take the #8028 (*departs every hour;* ☉ *08.05–22.45; takes 20mins; NTD32*). These buses don't stop near Foguangshan; see the entry opposite for transport information. There are also buses from Tainan to Qishan (see *Getting there*, page 259).

What to see and do
Foguangshan 佛光山 (Fóguāngshān) (✆ *656 1921; www.fgs.org.tw;* ☉ *07.00–20.00 daily; free admission*) A stop on many package tours of Taiwan and for good reason, Foguangshan is one of Taiwan's leading monasteries. Combined with the affiliated and adjacent Buddha Memorial Centre, it's an excellent place to learn about Buddhism. Its founder, Master Hsing Yun (b1927), was already well known in religious circles when he purchased this plot of land in 1967. Soon after arriving in Taiwan from the Chinese mainland in 1949, he became the first Buddhist monk in Taiwan to use radio programmes to spread his message. The propagation of Buddhism remains one of Foguangshan's main goals and the monastery now operates a television station, a worldwide network of Buddhist colleges and several publishing houses. Its charitable efforts include a children's home and a senior

citizens' home. Unlike I-Kuan Tao, Buddhism wasn't suppressed by the government during the 1960s and its followers weren't harassed. However, Buddhists were looked down on by Chiang's pro-Western pro-Christian elite, and because of this many kept their beliefs to themselves. Hsing Yun chose the name Foguangshan, which means 'The Light of Budda Mountain', because he wanted Buddhists to be explicit about their religious affiliation. Foguangshan's overseas arm is known in English as the Buddha's Light International Association (*www.blia.org*).

Monks and nuns who speak English and other foreign languages are available to guide individuals or small groups if given a few days' notice (✎ *656 1921 ext 6205;* e *fgs6205@fgs.org.tw; by donation*). If you roll up unannounced you'll be welcomed and at the very least given an English-language map. The architecture isn't remarkable, but still it's easy to spend half a day here. Three parts of the monastery are essential viewing. The **Main Shrine** (⊕ *07.00–19.00 daily*), externally grandiose, is stunning within. The three main Buddhas, each five times the height of a man, project a calming benevolence; 14,800 smaller Buddhas are ensconced in the walls. The other two must-sees appeal in very different ways. The **Cultural Exhibition Hall** (⊕ *09.00–17.00 Tue–Sun; free admission*) is a large gallery that hosts new displays every two or three months. Some of the featured artists are world class, and while the works displayed are seldom overtly Buddhist, they are in keeping with Buddhist ideals. **Pure Land Cave** (⊕ *09.00–17.00 Tue–Sun; admission by donation*) depicts the paradise described in Buddhist sutras, complete with flashing lights and animatronic figures. The most memorable tableau features zombie-like humans stumbling into the arms of a giant Buddha. Among the crowd there are Asians, Europeans and Arabs, but no-one of African descent. Pure Land Cave was opened in 1972, which perhaps explains why the Westerners are dressed like 1950s suburbanites.

At meal times, monks and nuns gather with lay people attending retreats. Before and after eating, sutras are chanted. Food is consumed in absolute silence. Casual visitors are permitted to watch and listen through the doorway. For a more conventional dining experience, head to the vegetarian tea house (⊕ *10.00–19.30 daily;* **$$**) in the basement of the Dharma Transmission Centre. The menu lists tasty rice and noodle dishes, hot pots, teas, coffees and fresh juices.

Those staying in the monastery's Pilgrims Lodge (*50 rooms;* ✎ *656 1921 ext 6205;* **$$** *no meals inc*) are welcome to watch the morning service in the main shrine at 05.50. The lodge accepts overnight guests willing to obey monastic rules – a vegetarian diet, no alcohol, no lying and no killing of living creatures. Coffee is permitted; the rooms have air conditioning and comfortable beds. Foguangshan occasionally organises English-language Buddhist retreats; for details call or email.

Getting there and away If you are travelling by **car**, take Freeway 3 then Freeway 10. Exit at Lingkou at km22 and go south on Highway 21. It's impossible to miss the memorial centre or the monastery; both are near km281. **Motorcyclists** can approach on Highway 21.

From Kaohsiung Zuoying HSR Station, **bus** #8501 goes to the Buddha Memorial Centre via Foguangshan about every half hour (⊕ *08.15–18.00 Mon–Fri; last bus back to Kaohsiung 19.15; takes 1hr; NTD63*). Services are more frequent and run a bit later into the evening at weekends. Another option is Taiwan Tourist Shuttle's Dashu route. A one-day pass costs NTD50 and on weekdays departures are hourly (⊕ *10.00–17.00; takes 1hr*) from Fengshan TRA Station (*trains from Kaohsiung Main Station take less than 10mins; NTD15–23*). At weekends Tourist Shuttles depart every half hour.

Buddha Memorial Centre 佛陀紀念館 *(Fótuó Jìniànguǎn)* (☎656 3033; www.
fgsbmc.org.tw; ⏰ 09.00–19.00 Mon–Fri, 09.00–20.00 Sat–Sun & national holidays;
free admission) This breathtaking complex, built to house a tooth believed to have
belonged to the Buddha, has a lot to offer visitors interested in Buddhism, religious
architecture and art. The tooth itself is kept out of sight in a chalice-like container
above the reclining Buddha image in the main building's Jade Buddha Shrine.
Retrieved from the ashes after the Buddha's cremation, it was taken to Tibet in the
13th century when Muslim armies destroyed many of India's Buddhist monasteries.
In 1959 the tooth returned to India in the pocket of a Tibetan lama fleeing the
Chinese Communists; he gifted it to Master Hsing Yun in 1998. Building this
complex took a decade and cost an estimated US$300 million. The eight pagodas –
four on each side of the plaza in front of the main building – represent a core part of

BATTLE-READY BUDDHISTS

Every spring, crowds pour into Neimen to watch dozens of teams take part in
a multi-day martial arts display and competition. This is the Song Jiang Battle
Array 宋江陣, one of the island's largest festivals. It's ostensibly a celebration
of Guanyin's birthday, and so takes place around the 19th day of the second
lunar month.

Rather than using karate chops to smash bricks or head-butts to break
roof tiles, the event stresses teamwork and co-ordination. Performances
feature ritualised duelling with swords, staves and pikes. Farm tools make
occasional appearances, as in olden times battle-array members had to be
able to fight using whatever was at hand, be it a hoe or even an umbrella.
Fighters carry rattan shields and wear troupe uniforms. Long dark trousers
and long-sleeved shirts are standard; participants also wear cummerbund-
like sashes of brightly coloured fabric around their waists. Many battle-array
members are senior citizens but capable of moving with the speed and grace
of ballet dancers. Musical accompaniment is provided by drums, gongs
and firecrackers.

There are three theories as to the origins of the battle array. Some think
the tradition dates from the period Koxinga and his successors controlled
southwest Taiwan (see *History*, page 12). When that regime collapsed in
1683, some anti-Qing diehards decamped to the interior, beyond the reach
of Taiwan's new rulers. Neimen was one of the places where they settled.
Because it was on the front line between the Han-dominated lowlands and
aboriginal hill districts, military knowledge was important and the frequent
drilling needed to preserve such skills was held in temple forecourts. Other
places in southwest Taiwan have battle array traditions yet nowhere have
they remained as central to community life as in Neimen.

Some claim the battle array is a vestige of the time when towns and
villages throughout Fujian maintained militias to fight off pirates. The third
explanation, which is attractive if unconvincing, is that the battle array was
inspired by one of the greats of classical Chinese literature, *The Water Margin*.
This novel recounts the adventures of a band of outlaws during the Song
Dynasty (AD960–1279) and the battle array seems to be named after the
bandits' leader. Song Jiang was a genuine historical figure: his name appears
in reports compiled by imperial officials but what happened to him after he
surrendered in 1121 is a mystery.

the Buddha's teachings, the Noble Eightfold Path. Two sets of statues deserve some of your time. One depicts the founders of the Eight Schools of Chinese Buddhism. Another shows 18 Arhats (individuals who have attained an exceptional level of enlightenment) but is unorthodox in that three members of the usual all-male lineup have been replaced with women to underscore modern Buddhism's support for gender equality. Overseeing all is a 108m-high bronze seated Buddha. The mini-mall at the front of the complex has tasteful souvenirs, places where you can get a coffee or a meal (all vegetarian). The four museums inside provide background about Foguangshan's history and founder, and feature some dazzling relics. No alcohol, tobacco or meat is allowed within the complex and visitors should dress respectfully.

Shunsian Temple 順賢宮 (*km403 Hwy 3; ⊕ 05.00–21.00 daily*) If you go inside this large Mazu temple, which was inaugurated in 2008, it's likely that one of the shrine's volunteers will beckon you over to a television screen linked to a remote-controlled camera. The camera, high up in the roof, points at a square of unpainted concrete. If you look closely, you may be able to make out the eyes, nose and chin of a matronly looking woman. This, believers claim, is an apparition of Mazu that appeared during the building of the temple. Sceptics dismiss it as nothing more than random stains and discolourations, no more convincing than the Virgin Mary appearing on a grilled cheese sandwich in Florida. The temple is a major venue for the annual Song Jiang Battle Array (see box opposite).

Jih Zhu Temple 紫竹寺 (⊕ *05.00–20.00 daily*) Neimen's most famous and most central place of worship (Jih Zhu means 'purple bamboo') has served as the battle array's headquarters, parade ground and armoury for at least 300 years. Finding it isn't difficult: from Qishan, turn left at the 7-Eleven near km400.5 on Highway 3 and within 200m you'll see the ornate gateway. This house of worship is very much on the Buddhist side of the religious spectrum and you'll see pious individuals engaging in long, personal sessions of prayer and meditation. Neimen's town god is here. Kids will enjoy the temple's classically Chinese park; note the swastika balustrades.

Road 182 From Neimen the way to Tainan is clearly marked. The scenery along the eastern half of this winding but broad 34km-long road alternates between lush bamboo forests and denuded ridges like those in Caoshan Moonscape World. At km26.5, a Chinese-only sign (on the right if you're going to Tainan) points the way to **Wujian Hiking Path 五間步道**. This short, steep concrete track is shaded by camphor and longan trees. If the weather's clear, the reward for your 30 minutes of hiking is near-360° views from the ridge. Take care not to step on the little freshwater crabs that scuttle across the path.

Getting there and away Seven #9122 services leave Tainan each day (⊕ *06.25–18.50; to Qishan takes 1½hrs; NTD153*) and take Road 182 to Neimen then Highway 3 into Qishan. Drivers can drop you near either Shunsian Temple or Jih Zhu Temple.

MEINONG 美濃 *Telephone code 07*

Taiwanese tourists associate Meinong (population: 42,000) with Hakka culture, tasty noodles and hand-painted parasols. For Western visitors, scenery and ecology

8

are the main draws. Hemmed in to the north and east by forest-covered mountains and criss-crossed by creeks and irrigation ditches, Meinong is certainly one of the south's most appealing townships. The best views and quaintest villages are some distance from the town centre so consider renting a bike if you don't have your own vehicle.

HISTORY Accounts of Meinong's founding make no mention of indigenous people. Whether or not the land was truly *terra nullius*, two brothers surnamed Lim arrived here in 1735 and started growing rice, bananas, black beans, sugarcane and vegetables. They built 24 huts and a bamboo palisade to keep bandits out.

In the 1930s a new crop revolutionised the economy: tobacco. Soon one in four families was growing this cash crop, and tobacco earnings paid for temple renovations and college educations (it's said Meinong has produced more school headmasters and PhDs relative to its population than anywhere else in Taiwan). After Taiwan joined the WTO in 2002, the island's cigarette-makers began sourcing from overseas. Tobacco is still grown in small quantities. These days the most obvious evidence of tobacco's role in Meinong's development is the hundreds of redundant curing sheds that dot the landscape.

GETTING THERE, AWAY AND AROUND
By car Freeway 10 gets you within 6km of central Meinong.

By motorcycle or bicycle None of the roads in Meinong are must-sees nor should any be avoided. A shop beside the bus station has a few bikes to rent (⊕ *07.00–20.00 daily; NTD80 per day*) but for a better choice hike the 1.4km or take a taxi to the **Lake Bike Rental Centre** (☏ *681 2433; ⊕ 08.00–17.00 daily; from NTD100 per 3hrs*).

By bus Some #10 services from Kaohsiung Zuoying HSR Station/Zuoying KMRT Station terminate in Meinong (*takes 1hr; NTD77*). From Qishan, #8028 is an hourly service (⊕ *08.05–22.45 daily; takes 20mins; NTD32*).

TOURIST INFORMATION The **Lake Bike Rental Centre** (see *Getting there, away and around*, above) will happily give you a map even if you don't rent a bike from them.

 WHERE TO STAY The following B&Bs are both shown on the map opposite.

⌂ **Jhong Jheng Lake B&B** 中正湖民宿 (33 rooms) 30 Fumei Rd; ☏ 681 2736; m 0937 622 483; www.minsu.com.tw/cc-fu/. Named after a small lake north of Meinong's old town centre, Jhong Jheng Lake B&B is located at km3 on Road 108. The blandness of the rooms doesn't matter as the views through the windows (or from the balconies that some rooms have) are excellent. Showers only, no bathtubs. Rooms in the older building are significantly cheaper; a couple can stay on a w/day for NTD1,500. B/fast by arrangement. **$$$**

⌂ **Range B&B** 人字山莊 (10 rooms) 66-5 Minquan Rd; ☏ 682 2159; m 0912 199 926; e renzjivillage@yahoo.com.tw; www.5658.com.tw/range2/. Run by a painting teacher & his wife (his works adorn the walls of every guestroom), Range is 100m south of Jhong Jheng Lake B&B & offers equally good views over the countryside. Rooms are small but pleasant & there's lots of tourist information available in the form of maps & notes left by previous guests. 2 ppl can stay here for NTD1,350 on w/days; 4 can share a room for NTD2,000. B/fast available if requested. The website is Chinese-only but shows rooms & surroundings. **$$**

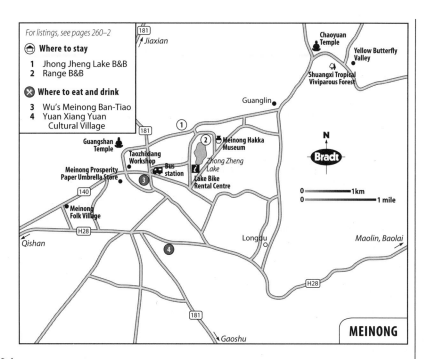

For listings, see pages 260–2

Where to stay
1 Jhong Jheng Lake B&B
2 Range B&B

Where to eat and drink
3 Wu's Meinong Ban-Tiao
4 Yuan Xiang Yuan
   Cultural Village

Jiaxian

Chaoyuan Temple

Yellow Butterfly Valley

Shuangxi Tropical Viviparous Forest

Guanglin

Guangshan Temple

Taozhixiang Workshop

Meinong Hakka Museum

Bus station

Zhong Zheng Lake

Lake Bike Rental Centre

Meinong Prosperity Paper Umbrella Store

Meinong Folk Village

Qishan

Longdu

Maolin, Baolai

Gaoshu

MEINONG

N

Bradt

0   1km
0   1 mile

✘ **WHERE TO EAT AND DRINK** The first two establishments are both shown on the map above.

✘ **Wu's Meinong Ban-Tiao** 吳美濃粄條
20 Zhongzheng Rd; ☎ 682 0188; ⏰ 08.00–
18.30 daily. Unpretentious & good value for
money, Wu's has all the usual Hakka favourites,
not only ban-tiao (see *Hakka cooking*, page 65).
Across the main road from the bus station. No
EM. **$$**

✘ **Yuan Xiang Yuan Cultural Village**
原鄉緣文化村 km36.7 Hwy 28; ☎ 681 0888;
⏰ 08.00–17.30 daily. Consider the restaurant

inside this souvenir-selling centre (*shops
⏰ 08.00–19.00 daily*) if there's 3 or more of you.
Hakka staples at reasonable prices inc ban-tiao &
pig's foot. For something different, order a portion
of bitter melon (*kǔ guā fēng*). Coffees & teas, inc *léi
chá* (here called 'pestle cereal'), are NTD100–120.
Incomplete EM. **$$**

✘ **Bafang Yunji** 11 Zhongzheng Rd Sec 1;
☎ 681 8777; ⏰ 10.30–21.00 daily. This island-
wide chain serves up a good range of boiled &

MEINONG'S CURING SHEDS

Tobacco leaves have to be cured soon after harvesting, so from 1937 onward
Meinong's farmers started building curing sheds. These slope-roof buildings
typically cover about 40m². Each has two floors and a ventilation shaft on top.
Some sheds are brick, others are concrete while a few are made of wattle and
daub. The wattle consists of slats of split bamboo; the daub is a mix of clay,
soil, rice straw, chaff and pig dung.

   The drying of the leaves was achieved by flue curing. A fire would be set
under the floor of the shed's central chamber so hot air (but neither smoke
nor sparks) would circulate around the leaves. Farmers or their wives would
stay up throughout the night to monitor the temperature.

Kaohsiung and Pingtung   MEINONG

8

261

potsticker dumplings inc curry, shrimp & spicy options. A dozen dumplings with a soup makes for a good lunch. Turn right as you leave the bus station. EM. $

SHOPPING Beautifully painted oil-paper parasols are Meinong's trademark souvenir and small ones that'll fit in your hand luggage start at NTD500. You can buy them at Yuan Xiang Yuan Cultural Village (see *Where to eat and drink*, above) and the first two listings below. All three of these places are on Road 140 between Qishan and central Meinong; none have English signs.

Meinong Folk Village 美濃民俗村 80, Lane 421, Zhongshan Rd Sec 2; 681 7508; ⏰ 08.00–17.30 daily. Kids like this place as there's space to run & play while parents browse the parasols, fans & Buddha statuettes.
Meinong Prosperity Paper Umbrella Store 美濃廣德興紙傘店 361 Zhongshan Rd Sec 1; 681 8921; ⏰ 09.00–19.00 daily. If you want to see oil-paper parasols being assembled & painted, or

if you want to order a custom-painted item (bring a photo they can work from), this is the best place to go.
Taozhixiang Workshop 陶之鄉工作室 362-1 Zhongshan Rd Sec 1; 681 3486; ⏰ 08.00–17.00 daily. The easiest to find of Meinong's pottery workshop-galleries has teapots & cups which make for good gifts. Just east of the turn-off to Guangshan Temple.

OTHER PRACTICALITIES

✉ **Post office** 39 Zhongzheng Rd Sec 1; ⏰ 08.00–17.30 Mon–Fri, 08.30–12.00 Sat

$ **Land Bank** 65 Zhongshan Rd Sec 1

WHAT TO SEE AND DO

Guangshan Temple 廣善堂 **(Guǎngshàn Táng)** Meinong's most attractive place of worship abuts the hills and is subtly different from many Taiwanese temples, the colours being more like those found in shrines established by ethnic Chinese in southeast Asia. Altars are dedicated to various deities including the Jade Emperor and Wenchang Dijun; the offices where donations are tallied and records are kept look like they've not been refurbished since the 1950s. The single-storey building (usually locked) on the right as you face the temple was a school during the colonial era.

Yongan Road and Boai Street Dozens of traditional single-storey houses can be seen on and near these two streets in central Meinong, just south of Wu's Meinong Ban-Tiao restaurant.

Meinong Hakka Museum 美濃客家文物館 (*49-3 Minzu Rd;* 681 8338; ⏰ *09.30–16.30 Tue–Fri, 09.30–17.00 Sat–Sun; admission NTD60/30*) The exterior of this museum was designed to resemble a curing shed. Inside, the entire field-to-cigarette process is explained in detail. English-language tours are sometimes available; if you're hoping for one, get a Chinese-speaker to phone a day or two before your visit.

Shuangxi Tropical Viviparous Forest 雙溪熱帶母樹林 (⏰ *24hrs daily; free admission*) Turn left at Chaoyuan Temple 朝元寺 and you'll soon come to a small car park. You can enter the forest here but if you're neither a botanist nor an arborist your stop will probably be a brief one. Nonetheless, it's worth noting the reserve's exceptional biodiversity and the reason for it. During the Japanese occupation, the colonial authorities brought in hundreds of plant and tree species from Asia, Australia and South America and nurtured them here in order to learn which species could thrive in Taiwan. A few of the exotics are the only trees of their kind anywhere in Taiwan.

Yellow Butterfly Valley 黃蝶翠谷

Between May and July this lush valley sees millions of lemon emigrants (*Catopsilia pomona*). Despite their name, these lepidopterans spend their entire lives within the watershed. During the summer you can be pretty sure of seeing small groups of butterflies lapping minerals from shallow pools; if you're lucky, you'll find yourself in a cluster of thousands. Farming and urbanisation have destroyed many of Taiwan's insect habitats, but the vast number of butterflies here is – like the diversity in Shuangxi Tropical Viviparous Forest – due to man's interfering with nature. Before World War I the colonial authorities planted hop-hornbeam trees in the area. The wood is exceptionally hard and was to be used for making railway sleepers and rifle stocks, but the leaves happen to be a favourite food of lemon emigrant larvae. More than a hundred other butterfly species can be spotted in the valley during the warmer months. Bring a picnic and spend a few hours here.

MAOLIN 茂林 *Telephone code 07*

A well-established destination that used to depend on good scenery and riverside hot springs to pull in visitors, Maolin has in recent years benefited from the growing interest in ecotourism. In this respect it has an ace to play: the Purple Butterfly Valley is one of the world's two major wintering spots for butterflies. Unlike Mexico's better-known Monarch Butterfly Valley, which attracts just one species, Maolin's Purple Butterfly Valley draws swarms of dwarf crows, chocolate tigers, striped blue crows and other lepidopterans.

Even if you've no interest in butterflies, consider visiting Maolin for its rampant birdlife and meandering creeks. Throughout the valley you'll see snakes represented in carvings and images, for Maolin is a stronghold of the Rukai tribe. The Tapakadawane (Black Rice) Festival, the tribe's main annual public celebration, is held in November or December and features tribal songs and dances.

GETTING THERE, AWAY AND AROUND

By car or motorcycle Take Highway 28 from Meinong. If you're approaching from the south, Road 185 (see page 267) is recommended. Once you reach Dajin 大津, follow Local Road 132 into the valley.

By bus There are six #8218 services per day (🕐 *06.50–16.40; takes 1hr; NTD106*) to Dajin from Pingtung. Unless you've arranged to be picked up from Dajin, you'll have to walk or hitch a ride and it's a long way to any of the attractions.

TOURIST INFORMATION The visitor information centre (🕐 *08.30–17.30 daily*) is in Dajin, obvious on the right as you head towards Maolin.

🏠 **WHERE TO STAY AND EAT** Almost all of the valley's inhabitants live in the villages of Maolin (Teldreka in Rukai), Wanshan (Oponoho) or Duona (Kungadavane). Noodles and other simple dishes are available at eateries in Maolin and Duona.

🏠 **De'en Gorge B&B** 得恩谷的民宿 (14 rooms) Near Maolin Valley; 📞 680 1539; m 0989 579 751; e yamm_juin@hotmail.com. To find this place, take the road down towards Maolin Valley but turn left instead of right after crossing the river. It's 700m up the road. Owned by an environmentally conscious Rukai family (a son speaks English & leads evening nature walks), De'en Gorge B&B has 2 kinds of room – basic but clean 4-person dorms with bath (*NTD350 pp, no b/fast*) & spacious rooms each with two dbl beds (*NTD2,500 at w/end inc*

b/fast). No AC but none needed; no TV. Dinner available but must be ordered 3 days in advance so local organic ingredients can be gathered. Camping allowed (*NTD200 pp*). **$$$**

SHOPPING

Maolin United Industry Exhibition Centre 12-4 Maolin Village; m 0985 883 756; 🕘 09.00–18.00 daily. Millet wine (*xiǎomǐ jiǔ*) made the traditional way (NTD350 for a 600cc bottle) is sold here, right next to the district office, as are glass-bead items & some other souvenirs.

Ubake 烏巴克 116 Maolin Village; ✆ 680 1035; 🕘 08.00–21.00 Sun–Fri. Ubake & his wife, who live below Maolin Village on a terrace overlooking the river, make & sell a wide range of aboriginal glass-bead & leather arts.

WHAT TO SEE AND DO

Purple Butterfly Valley 紫蝶幽谷 (Zǐdié Yōugǔ) The 'valley' isn't a single location that people can point out on a map but rather a chain of hillsides where migrating butterflies feed and rest. At times, a single tree may host well over 1,000 lepidopterans. To find the best butterflying spots, enlist the help of those who know the area very well, such as the family that runs De'en Gorge B&B (see *Where to stay*, page 263).

The four purple-crow butterfly species that winter in Maolin spend the hot season 250km to the north where it's a little cooler. Eggs are laid at both ends of the route and left to fend for themselves; because few butterflies live more than eight months, the migration is a once-in-a-lifetime journey. A bilingual exhibition about the butterflies can be found in the lobby of the **Fengshan Farmers' Association Maolin Activity Centre** (✆ 680 1115; 🕘 07.00–19.00 *daily*). There's no English sign outside but this tile-faced building is the largest structure in Maolin Village. Rooms for two people are available here (**$$**). The centre is next to the district office and faces **Maolin Ecological Park 茂林生態公園** (🕘 *24hrs daily; free admission*). During the winter you're almost guaranteed to see purple butterflies in this small hillside park. For views over the village, climb the stone steps behind the netted enclosure.

Maolin Valley Opposite the fire/ambulance station (*near km3.5 Rd 132*) a steep side road goes down to and across the river. Turn right and very soon you'll be able to drive no further. Parking and hiking up the creek is a pleasurable way to spend an hour or two.

Mei Ya Waterfall 美雅谷瀑布 Just past the village of Wanshan 萬山 (*km6.5 Rd 132*) you'll see a bilingual signpost pointing 1.9km to this scenic spot. Follow the road to its very end. The little waterfall on the left isn't the main attraction; to get to Mei Ya Waterfall you'll need to hike for around 40 minutes on a crumbling path. Don't attempt it alone.

Dragon's Head Mountain aka Mount Longtou 龍頭山 Beyond Wanshan the road crosses the river via one of the valley's post-Morakot bridges and climbs to a large viewing platform. Do stop here for a while to take in the scenery.

Duona Suspension Bridge 多納高吊橋 Tourists flock to this 232m-long bridge, which is clearly visible from Dragon's Head Mountain. For locals it's merely another part of the road network, so watch out for motorcycles and even narrow-wheelbase trucks zipping across while you dally.

Hongchen Gorge 紅塵峽谷 The road splits at km14: right leads to Duona Village, left goes down to Hongchen, where riverside hot springs were developed and soon after destroyed by Typhoon Morakot. Don't try to take a car all the way to the river but those on two wheels will do fine. At the turn-off on Local Road 132 an information board relates the discovery between 1978 and 2008 of 14 prehistoric rock carvings not far from here.

Duona Village 多納 (*km15*) This compact village, 450m above sea level, has considerable character thanks to its traditional slate homes. Admirable efforts have been made to get some of the modern buildings to fit in by covering their concrete walls with slate. If you go to the very end of the main street, which also happens to be the end of Local Road 132, you can look down over a large terrace where Duona's residents grow rice and other crops. There isn't much reason to go beyond the village unless you want to see what's left of Duona's hot springs, formerly the village's main attraction but now buried under tonnes of rock and silt.

SOUTH CROSS-ISLAND HIGHWAY *Telephone code 07*

Formerly the most spectacular way of getting from southwest Taiwan to Taitung, the high-altitude sections of this road were ravaged by Typhoon Morakot (see *History*, page 22). The highway has never properly reopened, although a few adventurous individuals in robust vehicles have made it all the way to the east. At the time of writing even that was impossible; how far you'll be allowed to proceed before being turned back at a police checkpoint depends on recent rainfall (which can trigger landslides) and whether reconstruction has progressed. Do enquire if the road is open past **Meishankou** (*km109 Hwy 20*) as the alpine vistas beyond more than justify the amount of driving involved, even if you need to eventually turn back.

If you go further than **Jiaxian** (*km58 Hwy 20*) you'll pass through a series of small settlements including: **Laonong** (*km72*), from which you can head south on Highway 27 to Maolin; **Baolai** (*km80*), a hot-springs resort fallen on hard times; and mainly Bunun villages such as **Taoyuan** (*km94*), where one bus a day from central Kaohsiung terminates (*#8029; departs 06.15; takes 3¾hrs; NTD355*). Meishankou (Mashowaru in Bunun) is 1,014m above sea level and just inside Yushan National Park. From here the highway climbs relentlessly to **Tianchi**. The highest point on Highway 20, Yakou 埡口, is just over 2,700m above sea level.

If this is impossible or too daunting, consider venturing north from Jiaxian on Highway 21. It needn't be a dead end and soon you'll see some very fine scenery.

WHAT TO SEE AND DO

Jiaxian 甲仙 The town has petrol stations, shops and a sideline in taro-flavoured ice cream. If you're approaching Jiaxian from the south, Local Road 128 is a scenic alternative that'll appeal to cyclists and others keen to avoid the heavy traffic where highways 20 and 21 meet.

Wulipu (*km223 Hwy 21*) This plateau is now home to some of those who escaped when Typhoon Morakot obliterated the village of Xiaolin. Before the calamity, Xiaolin had begun drawing the attention of scholars who realised its inhabitants had preserved a significant amount of lowland indigenous Siraya culture (see box, page 223). That said, the **Xiaolin Pingpu Culture Museum** (☎ *676 1455; ⊕ 09.00– 12.00 & 13.00 17.00 Tue–Sun; free admission*) isn't worth more than a very quick look unless you read Chinese and have a serious interest in Taiwan's aborigines.

The museum, plus homes built to house Morakot survivors, is on the right side of the road if you're approaching from Jiaxian. Just past the village on the right you'll notice **Jhen-hai Cemetery** 鎮海將軍墓 (⊕ *24hrs daily*). The 70-odd tombs date from around 1886 when imperial soldiers were deployed here to take control of the mountains and reopen long-distance trails. Dozens died of malaria and the roughly hewn gravestones are touchingly simple. On each, crudely incised characters give the deceased's name and a few other details. The graveyard's location seems to prove the adage that in Taiwan, dead folk get the best places to live.

Xiaolin Memorial Park (*km221 Hwy 21;* ⊕ *24hrs daily*) This sombre landmark commemorates the 462 Xiaolin residents who perished in the Morakot calamity. There are 181 Formosan cherry trees, one for each family, plus a simple shrine where relatives and survivors burn sticks of incense.

Holy Mount Zion 錫安山 (✆ *670 1218; http://home.ziongjcc.org/;* ⊕ *06.00–17.30 daily*) Lots of bilingual signs point the way to this Christian commune, 2.8km up a steep but safe side road. The sect based here is a non-mainstream denomination called the New Testament Church (NTC). Founded in the early 1960s by Hong Kong actress Kong Duen-Yee (1923–66), it has been led for four decades by Elijah Hong, a Taiwanese man whom some consider a fraud. According to the Church's multilingual website, Hong ('the Prophet of All Nations', as he's styled by his church), was led by God to this mountain. Believers clashed repeatedly with the authorities but 'after more than a decade of labour and toil, this wild mountain was transformed into a beautiful Eden.' These days the 300-odd residents raise rabbits and ostriches and engage in organic farming. The entire site is extremely clean and orderly; if you're not curious about alternative lifestyles, however, it's of little interest. A major annual event is the Feast of Tabernacles, celebrated 15–21 July. Non-Christian visitors, who can buy plums, aloe vera, reishi, mulberry juice and other products, are very welcome so long as they don't enter restricted areas, smoke, drink alcohol, gamble or picnic. Nor, the website warns, should they bring with them 'idols, charms, beads, incense sticks and other idol-related items'.

Namasia 那瑪夏 **(Nàmǎxià)** The name of this district reflects the indigenous heritage of the valley's inhabitants, Namasia being the Tsou name of the river that drains this beautiful valley. The villages are also known by Tsou names: Nangisaru, Maya and Takanuwa. Nowadays Tsou account for one-sixth of the population; after the tribe was decimated by epidemics in the 19th century, Bunun clans moved in from the north and eventually became the majority. You'll need local help to find the waterfalls, swimming holes, hiking trails and birdwatching spots. Rich J Matheson (m 0912 760 624; e liefintaiwan@gmail.com), a Namasia-based Canadian photographer, leads hikes in the area and can introduce local aboriginal artists and restaurants. Sometimes the side road to Chashan (see page 239) provides the only access.

HEADING EAST *Telephone code 08*

PINGTUNG CITY 屏東市 **(PÍNGDŌNG SHÌ)** There's nothing wrong with Pingtung County's capital (population: 207,000) but to describe its sights is to damn it with faint praise. Given its proximity to Maolin, Sandimen and other indigenous communities, spending more than an hour here would be a deplorable waste. Use the city as a transport base and head inland. Everything you need is within 150m of the TRA station. For long-distance and local buses, turn left as you exit the station.

To change money, walk directly away from the TRA station and keep an eye out for the bank on your right.

Getting there and away

By TRA Pingtung City is well served by trains from Kaohsiung (*about 70 departures* ⊕ *04.38–00.33 daily; takes 24–32mins; NTD31–48*). Expresses to Taitung can be boarded here (*13 departures* ⊕ *04.38–00.33 daily; takes 2–3hrs; NTD242–314*).

By bus The Kuo-Kuang station, which you'll see as soon as you exit the railway station, has services to Taipei (*#1839; departs hourly* ⊕ *24hrs daily; takes 5¼hrs; NTD570*) and Taichung (*#1873; departs hourly* ⊕ *06.30–21.30 daily; takes 3¼hrs; NTD345*).

Exploring Pingtung's hinterland by bus requires patience, but it can be done. On leaving the railway station turn left to find the local bus station. From here there are buses to Dajin for Maolin (*#8218; 6 departures daily;* ⊕ *06.50–16.40; takes 1hr; NTD106*), Donggang (*various routes; at least 50 departures daily;* ⊕ *06.00–22.00; takes about 1hr; NTD75–97*), Sandimen via Shuimen (*#8227, #8228 & #8229; about 30 departures daily;* ⊕ *06.30–21.40; takes 45mins; NTD68*) and Wanjin (*#8235; 13 departures* ⊕ *06.55–21.35 daily; takes 50mins; NTD70*).

By car or motorcycle The Jiuru (*km391*) and Changzhi (*km400*) exits on Freeway 3 are both convenient. Motorcyclists are advised to take the more scenic Highway 3 rather than the faster but far busier Highway 1. Unfortunately, the motorcycle rental businesses near Pingtung's TRA station refuse to rent to visitors who hold only international licences.

Tourist information

ℤ Pingtung County Cultural Affairs Bureau http://tour.cultural.pthg.gov.tw

ℤ Pingtung TRA Station Visitor Information Centre ⊕ 07.00–21.00 daily

Other practicalities

$ **Land Bank** 78 Fengjia Rd

ROAD 185 This north–south route hugs the base of the Central Mountain Range for 69km. Traffic is usually very light. If you're short of time, skip the southern half.

Getting there, away and around

By car If you're driving from the north, consider approaching through Meinong as Highway 28 will bring you to Dajin where you can explore Maolin before heading south along Road 185. From the Changzhi exit on Freeway 3, Highway 24 will get you to Shuimen (where there's a petrol station) quickly but be careful to follow the road as it veers left; many mistakenly continue straight on. Coming from Kenting National Park, the Road 185/Highway 1 junction is just outside Fangliao.

By motorcycle or bicycle This region is perfect for exploring on two wheels. There are few gradients on Road 185 itself but cyclists aiming for Wutai need to be in top condition.

By bus No buses run the length of Road 185. If you're using public transport, focus your energies on Sandimen.

8

Tourist Information

⏏ Maolin National Scenic Area www.maolin-nsa.gov.tw

⏏ Majia Visitor Centre km29.5 Rd 185; ⏰ 08.30–17.30 daily

⌂ Where to stay

⌂ Dream House (5 rooms) 38 Wutai Village; ☎790 2312; m 0912 786 109. Neither the owner – who like many others in this village has the Han surname Du – nor his family speak English but they're used to accommodating Western guests. The interior is filled with indigenous artefacts; room rates inc both b/fast & aboriginal-style dinner. 2 ppl can expect to pay around NTD2,500 at w/ends. For around NTD500 the owner will pick guests up from Sandimen or drive them on to Maolin. **$$**

⌂ ShaoMorLee (5 rooms) 53-1 Zaixing Rd, Zaixing Village, Ligang; m 0925 930 989; e jglamorie@hotmail.com. A 50-year-old single-storey country house converted by a

DIY/recycling enthusiast from New Zealand & his Taiwanese wife, ShaoMorLee offers a rural lowlands living experience plus proximity to Road 185's attractions. 4 rooms have a dbl bed below a deck; up to 4 guests can share for NTD2,000. The family room is charged at NTD800 pp for up to 6. All rooms have en-suite bathrooms. Inc b/fast & free use of gas barbecue & bicycles. Guests also enjoy free admission to the couple's recreational farm, DaMorLee (2.1km away) where they can learn about papercrete production & make their own pizzas. Solo travellers can use a room at the farm (*NTD1,000 inc b/fast*). The owners can pick up guests at Ligang's bus station. **$$**

✗ Where to eat

Indigenous food is easy to find in Sandimen where the main street has several places to eat, including some simple barbecue joints. Bring food if you're setting off for remote villages like Dewen or Wutai.

✗ Autumn Moon 秋月的店 km24.3 Hwy 24; ☎799 1524; ⏰ 10.00–24.00 Fri–Wed. Tourists come to this long-established Paiwan-owned restaurant, perched just above Sandimen, for the amazing views as much as the food, which is hearty rather than gourmet. It's said on some mornings you can see Little Liuqiu; even if it's hazy you'll be able to watch eagles swoop after prey. Hot dishes available 11.00–14.00 & 17.00–22.00; of meals suitable for individuals, the most authentically aboriginal is the Paiwan flavour set meal (*páiwān fēngwèi fàncān, NTD450*). Coffees & teas from NTD100; occasional live music. EM for drinks but not food. **$$$**

✗ Qingshun Mountain Cuisine 清順山產 3-2 Tongxing Rd, Yuanquan Village, Gaoshu; ☎796

1419; ⏰ 10.00–21.00 daily. A bit of a drive from any attractions but serving ultra-fresh traditional fare, this restaurant is worth seeking out if you want to try mountain rat (*shān shǔ*), muntjac (*shān qiāng*), mountain boar (*shān zhū*) or frog (*qīng wā*). Fish & freshwater shrimp are also available, as are some vegetables you're unlikely to see in lowland cities such as duck's tongue grass (*xué cài*). There's no EM but ingredients are laid out in a refrigerator so customers can see what looks good. Beer & soft drinks available; the Chinese menu doesn't list prices but reckon on spending NTD200–300 pp. No English sign; if you're heading south out of Gaoshu on Hwy 27, the restaurant is just past km34 on the left. **$$$**

Shopping

Dragonfly Beads Art Studio
蜻蜓雅築珠藝工作室 9 Zhongzheng Rd Sec 2, Sandimen; ☎799 2856; ⏰ 09.00–20.00 daily. The glass-bead jewellery which has made Dragonfly famous represents a revival of an indigenous tradition. Until well into the 20th century coloured beads were treasured by both Paiwan & Rukai ladies, as wearing them signified high social status.

The studio is on the left of the main thoroughfare just below the heart of the village. There's no English sign so look for the giant model dragonfly on the roof. Dragonfly now has more than 20 full-time employees who use Bunsen burners to soften & melt thin sticks of glass with which they decorate thimble-sized beads. Each pattern has a particular meaning such as honour or wisdom.

The peacock (*kurakuraw* in Paiwan) symbolises eternal love while the earth pattern (*cadacadaqan*) represents the acquisition of wealth. The shop's bilingual leaflet explains these motifs.

Sha Tao Zazurite Art Studio
沙滔舞琉璃藝術空間 7, Lane 37, Zhongzheng Rd Sec 2, Sandimen; ☎799 4849; ⊕ 09.00–18.00 Tue–Sun. Owned by Shatao Matilin, founder of a renowned indigenous dance troupe, this workshop/retailer is hidden in the backstreets on the left as you enter Sandimen's main village but bilingual signs point the way. Visitors are welcome to browse glass-bead art & wander into the workshop at the back where usually 3 or 4 women are busy creating necklaces, pendants & other items. Belts, shawls & CDs are also sold here; credit cards accepted.

What to see and do Sights are listed north to south.

Qingye This Rukai community is well kept and little touched by tourism. At weekends you can park outside the elementary school (follow the main road up to the police station then turn left), in the grounds of which you'll find a replica slate house. The campus also happens to be a fine picnic spot – look inland and you're sure to see crested serpent eagles circling above the forest. There are a few shops and eateries between the school and the slate- and pebble-faced Catholic chapel. The only way into the village is via a short road heading inland just north of km6 on Road 185.

Shuimen 水門 (*km25.5 Rd 185*) A gateway to points inland such as Sandimen and Majia, Shuimen is notable for its Hoklo-Hakka-indigenous ethnic mix. There are a few small hotels, eateries and shops.

Taiwan Indigenous Peoples Culture Park 原住民族委員會文化園區 ☎ *799 1219; www.tacp.gov.tw; ⊕ 08.30–17.00 daily; admission NTD150/80*) This highly regarded park is managed by the Council of Indigenous Peoples, the central government agency responsible for the welfare of Taiwan's aboriginal population. Inside there are replicas of traditional buildings and displays of handicrafts and costumes as well as the song-and-dance performances you'd expect at more commercial establishments. The park is 20 minutes' walk from bus stops in Shuimen.

Sandimen 三地門 (*Sāndìmén*) About 94% of Sandimen's 7,500 residents are indigenous and among them are Paiwan artisans who've won a reputation for crafting beautiful keepsakes using leather, wild boars' teeth and delicately coloured glass beads (see *Shopping*, opposite). The main village (which is where buses terminate) is a compact settlement laid out on a steep hillside in a way that gives almost every household an excellent view over the plains. It's a good place to see typical aboriginal families: middle-aged fathers who divide their time between building work on the plains and small farms in the hills; housewives who collect wild taros and dry them on the tarmac; and teenagers more conversant with Mandarin rap than the Austronesian language of their ancestors.

Dewen At km26.8 on Highway 24 a police checkpoint (⊕ *06.00–18.00 daily*) controls access to the mountains beyond. If the road is safe you'll be allowed to proceed after writing down some personal details; there's no need to show ID. On the left you'll very soon come to a road signposted 'Tewen 6'. This is the old spelling of the name of a Paiwan village which, during the colonial period, was reputed to grow Taiwan's best coffee. The road continues on to another Paiwan settlement,

Dashe, 13km from the turn-off. There's little reason to stop in either village but the vistas along the way are superb. After you've passed Dewen, just north of the km4 marker there's a shelter on the left from which you can look down over Dashe and the river.

Wutai The border between Sandimen and Wutai townships is also an ethnic boundary – the former is Paiwan, the latter Rukai. Indigenous culture has survived better here than in many other parts of Taiwan because the road completed by the Japanese in 1942 was abandoned after World War II and not reconstructed until 1972. Wutai is a Mandarin rendering of the indigenous toponym Vudai. In Chinese, *Wùtái* means 'fog plateau' and the valley often lives up to this name – expect sudden mists. Of the 3,100 people registered as residents of the township, fewer than 50 are Han. However, barely half of the township's population stays here year-round because jobs are scarce and the nearest high school is in Shuimen. The cluster of houses at km39 is called Shenshan. The place name means 'holy mountain' and is appropriate because it's the site of one of Taiwan's most appealing Christian places of worship, **Shenshan Roman Catholic Church** (⊕ *for services only*). The highway switchbacks through Shenshan, and the church is in the upper village. Like a lot of houses in the valley it's a squat slate-covered structure with small windows through which you'll see rows of hand-carved wooden chairs, each one made to resemble a tribesman in traditional garb.

The settlement from which the township takes its name is at km41 and it's perhaps Taiwan's most attractive village. Concrete-and-tile box houses are very much the exception; most residents live in slate-walled, slate-roofed cottages which blend in with the valley's greens and greys. On the homes that line **Wutai Art Street** you'll see certain motifs again and again: crucifixes, white lilies, boars and hundred-pacer snakes – but not clouded leopards (see page 6), which once roamed the mountains hereabouts. The nearby terraces will give you an idea of the valley's agricultural limitations; the fields of millet, corn and taro are quite tiny. Wutai's main **Presbyterian Church** (⊕ *09.00–17.30 daily*) is a slate-covered edifice with striking aboriginal features. The external staircase is adorned with a sculpture of life-size tribesmen dragging a tree trunk up a hill. Inside, the crucifix, twice the height of a man, consists of two varnished logs. The altar is a massive knot of tree roots. The bibles on the shelves are in Rukai. Underscoring the fact that this isn't a Han community, several of the grave markers in the adjacent cemetery bear not a single Chinese character, the name of the deceased being recorded solely in romanised Rukai.

Majia Between Shuimen's town centre and the petrol station on Road 185, Local Road 35 leads to a Paiwan-dominated district. If you turn right at km2.5 you'll enter **Rinari**, a new village where indigenous people resettled after Typhoon Morakot (see *History*, page 22) live in attractive, mostly wood houses. In Paiwan, *rinari* means 'let's go and live together'. Continuing uphill on Local Road 35 there are waterfalls and, at km10, a two-storey pavilion where you should stop to take in the panorama. The road is fine for normal cars as far as Majia Village at km14; only those on motorcycle, bicycle, or foot can proceed further, and then not very far and only with great caution.

Liangshan Waterfall This spot attracts hikers during the wetter months and understandably so. Park at **Majia Visitor Centre** (*km29.5 Rd 185*) and follow the signs up the surfaced road. You'll get your first sighting of the cascade after 10 minutes' walking. It's then another 20 minutes on a mostly flat and entirely gorgeous hillside trail; birdwing butterflies and blue dragonflies are numerous in autumn. The final stage is short but involves getting your feet wet and holding ropes as you clamber to the base of the fall.

Wanjin Basilica Minore (*www.catholic.org.tw/bankin/bankim/english.htm;* ⊕ *06.00–21.30 daily; free admission*) Bilingual signposts make finding Taiwan's oldest church very easy if you're coming from Road 185. When you see an army base on the left, prepare to turn right and drive about 1.5km. Located in what's probably the island's only Catholic-majority village – Marian grottos outnumber folk shrines – the current Spanish-style edifice, completed in 1870, is quite different from other churches in Taiwan. Spanish Dominican Father Fernando Sainz (1832–95) chose this village because he believed its mainly indigenous population would be more receptive to missionary work than nearby Hakka communities. He was right, making dozens of conversions in the first few years. He bought land here in 1863 but the adobe church he had built was destroyed by an earthquake two years later. In 1867 Sainz was kidnapped and held for ransom by Hakka bandits. The church suffered repeated arson attacks by anti-Christians (who alleged the Catholics made medicine out of human corpses) until 1874, when Emperor Tongzhi ordered an inscription be added to show the mission enjoyed imperial protection. The stone on which the two-character message was engraved is little bigger than a notebook but can be seen high above the main entrance. A few ecclesiastical artefacts are displayed upstairs.

Wugoushui 五溝水 (*Wŭgōushuǐ*) This splendidly preserved and extremely picturesque village, less than 2km from Wanjin, was founded in the early 18th century by Hakka settlers who dug a network of irrigation channels (Wugoushui means 'five ditches'). The most opulent structure is the **Liu Ancestral Hall** (*near the elementary school; private but visitors usually allowed into the courtyard*), built 1887–1921. The hall isn't easy to find but those who enjoy random exploring on foot or two wheels will enjoy the settlement and its surroundings. 28 Xisheng Road (*not open to the public*) used to be a school.

HEADING SOUTH *Telephone code 08*

There's no need to hug the coast if you're heading towards Kenting but if you take Freeway 3 to its southern end you'll bypass the first two of the following destinations.

DONGGANG 東港 (DŌNGGǍNG) Unless you've a passion for seafood, the only reasons to visit this sizeable harbour town (population: 49,000) are to catch a ferry to Little Liuqiu or attend the King's Ship Festival, a triennial boat-burning extravaganza that will next be held in October 2015 (see box, page 272). If your stomach is rumbling look for the dockside **Huaqiao Seafood Market**, where the day's catch is served up in small eateries (⊕ *varies;* **$$**), or more upmarket restaurants on Guangfu Road Section 2. Otherwise take a look at **Donglong Temple** (⊕ *05.30–21.30 daily*). The main object of worship in this run-of-the-mill temple is Marshal Wen, a 7th-century scholar deified for saving the life of a Tang Dynasty emperor. The temple organises the King's Ship Festival and displays the vessel in the months before the burning.

Getting there and away
By bus #9117 and #9127 from Kaohsiung stop in Donggang (*around 4 departures per hr;* ⊕ *06.05–22.00 daily; takes about 1hr; NTD115–125*). There are also buses

Ritual boat-burnings happen at several places in Taiwan's south but no event is more spectacular than Donggang's King's Ship Festival. Preparations begin more than a year ahead of the burning with divination rites to ascertain the precise dimensions of the wooden junk that's to be constructed and sacrificed. Usually about 14m long and always fantastically decorated, recent boats have cost over £250,000 each. The eight days before the actual burning feature elaborate rituals throughout the town. On the final day, volunteers push the vessel through Donggang's streets as the ship is believed to act like a supernatural magnet, drawing disease and malevolence on board.

When it returns to Donglong Temple, offerings and supplies are loaded to placate the Wang Ye spirits (see *Religion*, page 33) who've been hoodwinked into boarding. Among the items placed on board are dice for gambling, tobacco and pipes, inkstones and calligraphy brushes for writing, plus woks, food, oil and condiments for cooking. After midnight, the boat is dragged to a nearby beach; the masts are put in place, the sails unfurled and the anchors raised. Bales of joss paper (see box, page 101) are piled around the hull and, an hour before dawn, set alight with firecrackers. Flames consume the boat with surprising speed; seeing the hull blacken and collapse as the sky brightens is a truly unforgettable experience. The crowd soon thins because many locals wish to witness only the start of the conflagration. They leave as soon as they're confident the evils aboard have been consigned to another world. Stick around and by dawn you'll be able to get as close to the still-burning wreckage as the heat allows.

from Pingtung (*various routes; at least 50 departures daily;* ⊕ *06.00–22.00; takes about 1hr; NTD75–97*).

By car or motorcycle On the final night of the festival it's usually possible to park within walking distance of Donglong Temple if you get there before dusk.

DAPENG BAY 大鵬灣 Unlike some other parts of Taiwan's coast, which have been repeatedly reshaped by typhoons, Dapeng Bay has remained stable for centuries. One of Taiwan's largest lagoons (3.5km long and almost 2km wide), the bay is slowly developing into a centre for yachting and windsurfing. There's a 16.4km-long cycle path (free if you have your own bike) and artificial wetlands which attract migrant waterbirds between November and January.

Getting there, away and around Board a #9117 or #9127 bus and get off at km258 on Highway 17 (*from Kaohsiung takes 1¼hrs; NTD138*). The scenic area office is less than 100m away. Cars should take Freeway 3 to its southern end then turn right on to Highway 17 and follow the signs. Bicycles can be rented from the scenic area office (*NTD100/hr*).

Tourist information

🇮 **Dapeng Bay National Scenic Area Headquarters** km258 Hwy 17; ☎ 833 8100; www.dbnsa.gov.tw; ⊕ 08.30–18.00 daily. Bike rentals & lots of bilingual information about boat tours & local ecosystems.

JIADONG Hardly big enough to be called a town, Jiadong boasts south Taiwan's finest private mansion, **Hsiao Family Residence** (m *0936 988 376;* ⊕ *09.00–12.00 & 14.00–17.00 Tue–Sun; admission NTD50/30*). Wealthy thanks to winemaking and cloth dyeing, the Hsiao family had this complex built in stages from the 1860s to the beginning of the 20th century. Several of the craftsmen who worked on it were brought in from Fujian and much of the wood in the five halls was imported from the Chinese mainland. Hexagonal and rectangular entrances link different parts of the mansion but are deliberately unaligned; it was believed that having one doorway facing another was like setting one person's mouth in opposition to the mouth of another, and would lead to relatives arguing. The vast ceramic pot which now stands in a hallway served as a one-person air-raid shelter during World War II.

Get a Chinese-speaker to call ahead if you plan to visit on a weekday as the clan members who staff the entrance and show visitors around sometimes take extra days off.

Getting there and away
Jiadong can be reached by train (*about hourly from Pingtung* ⊕ *05.12–23.40 daily; takes 1hr; NTD48*) or Kenting-bound buses (*from Kaohsiung takes 1½hrs; NTD153*). The mansion is 400m inland of Highway 17.

MUSEUM OF MARINE BIOLOGY AND AQUARIUM 海洋生物博物館 (HǍIYÁNG SHĒNGWÙ BÓWÙGUǍN)
(☏ *882 5001;* f *882 4504; www.nmmba.gov.tw;* ⊕ *09.00–18.00 Apr–Nov, 09.00–17.00 Dec–Mar; admission NTD450/250*) This highly informative and child-friendly museum has interactive displays about coral reefs, the world's oceans and Taiwan's maritime environment. The English-language website includes a virtual tour as well as a schedule of shows and feeding times featuring whales, sharks and penguins.

Getting there and away
A few Kaohsiung–Kenting buses detour and stop right outside the museum. A taxi from Checheng costs around NTD200.

HENGCHUN 恆春 (HÉNGCHŪN)
The compact town of Hengchun ('permanent springtime') has been done up in recent years. At the same time, it's succeeded in making itself a destination in its own right rather than simply a place that feeds and waters through traffic and takes the overspill when Kenting is booked out. Coming from the north, just outside the town you'll see a model of a moon guitar, a two-stringed banjo-like instrument which features prominently in both Taiwanese opera and Hengchun folk. The latter is a traditional form of music that's been compared to Mississippi Delta Blues and which has enjoyed a minor revival in recent years. The town's main attraction is the city wall, especially the south and east gates. Bilingual signs guide those exploring on foot.

Getting there and away
All Kaohsiung–Kenting buses stop along Highway 26 in central Hengchun; from Kaohsiung journey time is at least two hours (*NTD329*). Self-drivers can approach by Highway 26 or Road 200 (see page 278).

⌂ Where to stay and eat
⌂ **Surf Shack** (5 rooms) 224 Hengnan Rd; ☏ 888 1881; e thesurfshack@yahoo.com; www.taiwansurfshack.com; restaurant ⊕ 11.30–late daily. Run by Terry, a Canadian, & E E, his Taiwanese wife, Surf Shack has basic but clean rooms. The 6-person room & the 2 dbl rooms (sometimes available for less than NTD1,000) have TV & AC; the 2 smaller rooms have little more than ceiling

fans. No private bathrooms. Small rooftop garden & barbecue facilities. Book swaps & Wi-Fi. B/fast not inc but can be requested the day before. The owners can arrange scooter rentals, peninsula tours, surf outings & snorkelling trips. The restaurant has a good selection of Western food inc highly regarded cheeseburgers & burritos. EM. **$$/$$**

KENTING NATIONAL PARK 墾丁國家公園
(KĚNDĪNG GUÓJIĀ GŌNGYUÁN) *Telephone code 08*

Taiwan's first national park, established in 1982, has been more of a tourist-industry triumph than a conservation success, its record having been marred by squabbles over beach access. However, the park authorities have made some progress in recent years, closing down undesirable businesses (such as noisy go-kart circuits) and trying to balance environmentalist ideals with the rights of human residents, some of whom have lived in the area for generations and resent being told how they can or can't use their land.

Millions of visitors pass through the park each year, occasionally jamming the coast road. If you're disappointed by the congestion and development along Kending Road – the resort's epicentre – remember that it would probably be much worse if it weren't a national park. Also, there's plenty to do without dipping your toes in the ocean. If you can, escape to the hinterland. There you'll enjoy scenes of bucolic beauty, excellent birdwatching (the region has 31 of Taiwan's 33 diurnal raptor species) and some truly pleasurable motoring. Alternatively, head out to sea and under the waves with one of Kenting's English-speaking scuba instructors.

GETTING THERE AND AWAY

By bus There are lots of buses from both Kaohsiung Zuoying HSR Station and Kaohsiung Main Station. Services to Kenting from the former include the #9189 Kenting Express (*departs every 30mins;* ⏰ *07.00–19.00 daily; takes 2¼hrs; NTD383*). From the Kaohsiung Bus Co Station near Kaohsiung Main Station there are about 56 services per day (#9117 & #9188; ⏰ *06.05–22.10; takes up to 3hrs; NTD347–364*). Some buses go beyond the main hotel/restaurant hub on Kending Road and terminate at Eluanbi Park.

By taxi Outside Kaohsiung's HSR and main stations you'll be approached by taxi drivers offering rides to Kenting for around NTD400 per person. Solo travellers may have to wait while the driver rustles up more passengers, but if you're a trio or a quartet you'll be able to leave right away, save time and be delivered direct to your hotel.

By air Hengchun Airport (*IATA: HCN;* ☏ *889 7120; www.hca.gov.tw*) has two flights each week to/from Taipei (*takes 1¼hrs; NTD2,292*). Flight times and tickets can be obtained from UNI Airways (☏ *07 791 1000; www.uniair.com.tw*). From the terminal it's a short walk to the main road where you can catch a bus to Kenting.

By TRA The train ride to Fangliao is slow (*1–2hrs from Kaohsiung; NTD89–139*) but pleasant. Walk 50m from Fangliao TRA Station, cross the main road and wave down a Kaohsiung–Kenting bus.

GETTING AROUND
By hired motorcycle Many of the smaller hotels on Kending Road can arrange scooter rentals (to guests and non-guests) and there are other rental businesses near

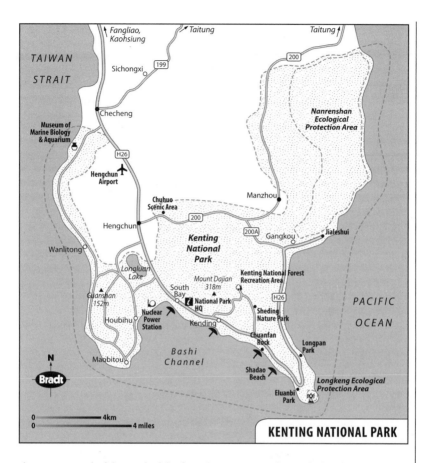

the western end of the road. If the first place you try isn't satisfied with your papers, simply try another.

By bus The buses that ply the main road until late at night mean you can hop between South Bay and Kending Road (*NTD23*) at your leisure, a useful option if you're staying at the former and want to go drinking along the latter. Short-distance buses to Sichongxi, Jialeshui and the Museum of Marine Biology and Aquarium operate from Hengchun's bus station where you can get a timetable and a one-day pass (*NTD150*).

TOURIST INFORMATION

🛈 Kenting National Park Headquarters/ Visitors Centre 596 Kending Rd; ✆ 886 1321; www.ktnp.gov.tw; ⏰ 08.10–16.50 daily, closed Lunar New Year's Eve.

LOCAL TOUR OPERATORS

U-Dive Scuba Taiwan Club m 0913 388 065; e scuba_diving1@yahoo.com; www.udive. com.tw; ⏰ hrs flexible so call ahead. Canadian-born PADI scuba instructor John Boo has lived in the Kenting area for years & can arrange equipment rentals, courses, transport & accommodation (from NTD600 pp per night; scooter rentals available for guests) in his divers' hostel in the western part of the national park.

Taiwan Dive ☎07 336 4571; m 0916 130 288; e divingintaiwan@yahoo.com.tw; www.taiwandive. com. British PADI master scuba diver trainer Andy Gray, who divides his time between Kaohsiung & Kenting, organises dives, teaches scuba courses at all levels & sells/rents/maintains scuba gear.

⌂ WHERE TO STAY

⌂ **Chateau Beach Resort** (293 rooms) 451 Kending Rd; ☎886 2345; f 886 2222; e service@ ktchateau.com.tw; http://kentingresort.com. If proximity to a beach is important, the Chateau has just what you want – a long stretch of yellow sand no more than 50m from the most popular rooms, those on the ground floor facing the ocean. Furnishings & in-room indulgences are fairly basic considering the rack rates but use of kayaks & other watersports equipment comes free. 3 pools for kids plus a deep one for adults. If you decide to stay 2 or more nights midweek either side of the summer high season, you can get some great package deals. The food served in the hotel's 3 restaurants doesn't get rave reviews, but that doesn't matter given the number of eateries nearby. Free pick-up from Hengchun Airport if arranged in advance. B/fast inc. $$$$$

⌂ **Howard Beach Resort** (405 rooms) 2 Kending Road; ☎886 2323; f 886 2359; http:// kenting.howard-hotels.com. A Kenting institution – for that reason it's revered by some, reviled by a few – the Howard has impressively large rooms with spacious balconies, plus consistently excellent buffets. Aboriginal woodcarvings enliven the long corridors, but the nearest beach, which guests access via an under-road tunnel, is a disappointment so you may spend more time around the hotel's large swimming pool. Very good midweek deals. B/fast inc. $$$$

⌂ **Bossa Nova** (4 rooms) 100 Nanwan Rd; ☎889 7137; e wavebossa@yahoo.com.tw. Located right beside & above a long-running restaurant of the same name (⌚ 11.30–23.00 daily; EM; $$), Bossa Nova's stylish Moroccan-inspired rooms make the most of limited space. 2 of the rooms share a bathroom & a small kitchen. Owners Clare & Marco speak fluent English. $$$

⌂ **Golden Ocean Azure Hotel** (21 rooms) 336 Kending Rd; ☎886 1050; e golden0933@yahoo. com.tw; www.golden-beach.com.tw/azure/. One of the lovelier of the smaller hotels along the main drag, Golden Ocean has large rooms dominated by oranges, reds & wood-browns. If there's 3 or 4 of you, request room 3A5 (w/end price NTD3,680) for its superb view of Mount Dajian & quaint if rather small bathtub. Midweek, some rooms go for NTD1,480. B/fast inc. $$$

⌂ **Kenting Yoyo Resort Hotel** (14 rooms) 212 Nanwan Rd; ☎888 2627; f 888 2617; www. yoyo-resort.idv.tw. A quiet, pleasant place to stay. The interior designer has shown some flair – most rooms have sea views, cosy balconies & wooden floors. To reserve a room, send a fax or get a Chinese-speaker to help out. B/fast inc. $$

⌂ **Wanlong Hotel** (6 rooms) 58-1 Wenhua Rd, Manzhou; ☎880 1154. Basic but clean & adequate. No toiletries provided & shared bathrooms only. One person in a room pays NTD500; when two share its NTD700. There's also a 4-person room (NTD1,500). Outside the national park but convenient if Nanrenshan or Jialeshui figure in your plans. Easy to find – just off Road 200 very near Manzhou Junior High School. $

✗ WHERE TO EAT AND DRINK
For restaurants along Kending Road (even numbers are on the inland side and lower numbers are towards the eastern end) reservations are advisable during peak season.

✗ **Amy's Cucina** 131-1 Kending Rd; ☎886 1977; www.amys-cucina.com; ⌚ 11.00–24.00 daily. A Kenting institution, Amy's EM is a straightforward list of pizzas, pasta dishes & salads. Décor is beerhouse style – hefty wooden tables & benches. The range of cocktails (NTD150–300) is impressive. $$$

✗ **Chez Papa** 142 Kending Rd; ☎886 1197; ⌚ Jul–Sep 11.00–24.00 daily, Oct–Jun 11.00– 15.00 & 18.00–22.00 daily. Cushions, benches & curtains give this a North African feel. It's a very popular place to drink (happy hour usually ⌚ 17.00–19.00 daily), but the pizzas & pastas also hit the spot. Among the more unusual options are paella dishes, lamb cumin & French classics. Beers, among them Belgian & other European brews, from NTD100. EM. $$$

✕ **Mambo** 46 Kending Rd; ✆886 2878; ⏰ 11.00–14.30, 17.00–22.30 daily. Having been around for a full decade, this large Thai restaurant has got its act together. Service is polite & rapid, the food is consistently good. Few dishes are priced more than NTD300 & there's no service charge. The music can be a bit loud, so grab one of the outside tables. Thai & local beers available. EM. $$$
✕ **Summerpoint** 252 Chashan Rd, Jialeshui; 📱 0936 160 006; ⏰ 09.00–approx 16.00 daily. The best eating option on this side of the peninsula & especially popular with surfers, Summerpoint is also a B&B with 3 nearby locations. Sandwiches (*from NTD150*), burgers (*NTD200*), salads (*NTD200*) & all-day b/fasts (*from NTD180*). Indoor & outdoor seating; EM but no English sign; located within walking distance of the Jialeshui ticket gate. $$

WHAT TO SEE AND DO Tourists interested in ecology would do well to start at the National Park Visitor Centre (see *Tourist Information*, page 275). The exhibition inside deserves the better part of an hour and is much more than a summary of the region's glories. Environmental problems such as illegal fishing, oil spills, the bleaching of coral by hot water discharged from the nuclear power station, the arrival of invasive plant species and the hunting of raptors are frankly acknowledged. There's also a good amount of human history – shipwrecks, aborigines and Japanese invaders.

Assuming you've arrive from Kaohsiung via Highway 26, you're likely to hit the sights in this order.

Longluan Lake 龍鑾潭 (⏰ *08.30–17.00 daily; free admission; parking NTD40/10*) If you're more into waterfowl than birds of prey, this 175ha body of water is the place to go. The visitor centre, on the west side of the lake and 700m from the car park, has spotting scopes. In addition to ducks and egrets, birders have a good chance of seeing the Taiwan hwamei (*Garrulax taewanus*), a grey-brown thrush-like endemic. A variety of plants thrives near the visitor centre, including sisal.

Guanshan 關山 You'll need your own vehicle to get to the top of this modest ridge, a popular sunset-viewing spot. Before the sun sinks into the Taiwan Strait, make a point of also looking east over Longluan Lake and South Bay.

South Bay 南灣 (Nánwān) This 600m-long sandy beach is one of the park's nicest, though the view is marred somewhat by the nuclear power station and wind turbines. There are shower rooms and toilets. After dark the scene here is less raucous, so some prefer to sleep here and head to Kending Road for meals.

Mount Dajian 大尖山 This 318m rock pyramid lives up to its name ('big sharp peak') and is one of the national park's most recognisable sights. Visitors are not allowed to climb the mountain, however, because of the risk they'll bring in livestock diseases that could harm the cattle which graze on its slopes.

Kenting National Forest Recreation Area 墾丁國家森林遊樂區 (Kěndīng Sēnlín Yóulèqū) (⏰ *Sep–Nov 06.00–17.00, Dec–Aug 08.00–17.00; admission NTD150/75/10 at w/ends & national holidays, NTD100/75/10 Mon–Fri; parking: cars NTD50, motorcycles NTD20*) If you've visited some of Taiwan's mid-elevation forest recreation areas, you'll immediately notice the foliage in this monsoon rainforest is quite different. The land is uplifted coral reef and the soil is relatively thin, so many of the trees have exposed root systems. Make a point of climbing the stairs in the observation tower. Unless the weather's awful, from the top you'll see the Pacific Ocean and Bashi Channel as well as the Taiwan Strait.

Sheding Nature Park 社頂自然公園 (Shèdǐng Zìrán Gōngyuán) (⊕ 24hrs daily; free admission; parking NTD40/10)

Properly exploring this hillside park takes over an hour but provides, at the very minimum, stirring views over the peninsula's east and south. The landscape is a mix of grasslands, uplifted coral reefs (including two narrow gorges you'll have lots of fun squeezing through) and mixed forest. Look closely at the trees and you'll see golf-ball-sized dark green fruit – they're wild guavas. The park is central to ongoing efforts to return Formosan sika deer (*Cervus nippon taiouanus*) to the wild, but there are usually too many people around to spot either deer or macaques. Nevertheless, you're guaranteed to see a good range of butterflies and birds such as the Himalayan tree pie (*Dendrocitta formosae*). Wear proper shoes – the trails get slippery after rain.

Chuanfan Rock 船帆石

This squarish column is said to resemble the profile of the late former US president Richard Nixon. It does, very slightly. The Chinese name, which means 'sail rock', is hardly more satisfactory, but the beach here is attractive.

Shadao Beach 砂島海灘 (km39 Hwy 26)

The foreshore here is fenced off to protect the only beach on Taiwan proper where the sand is overwhelmingly composed of crushed shells, coral and marine fossils. The **Shell Beach Exhibition Hall** (⊕ 08.30–17.00 daily; free admission) does a good job of explaining why shale turns west Taiwan's beaches dark grey, while those in the north are generally quartz sand and the south's shorelines are piled with shells and coral.

Eluanbi Park 鵝鑾鼻公園 (near km42.5; ⊕ 06.30–18.30 daily Apr–Oct, 07.00–17.30 daily Nov–Mar; admission NTD40/20; parking NTD40/10)

If you stay in a hotel near Kending Road, you'll probably notice Eluanbi's lighthouse blinking during the night. The surrounding park has geological and botanical attractions. A short distance east a side road on the right (if you're coming from Kending's main hotel area) leads to the 800m-long path to a monument marking Taiwan's southernmost point.

Longkeng Ecological Protection Area 龍坑生態保護區 (⊕ 08.00–15.00 Wed–Mon; free admission)

Only 200 people each day are allowed to enter this 62ha reserve, which has ecosystems influenced by the area's collapsed limestone cliffs and coral reefs. If you're interested in entering either of the park's ecological protection areas (the other one is Nanrenshan), visit the national park website (*www.ktnp. gov.tw*) and make an appointment at least one day and up to six weeks in advance to view a multilingual briefing video. You won't be admitted to either area if you haven't seen the video. You also need to bring ID; children under the age of seven are not allowed in for safety reasons. Both Longkeng and Nanrenshan close for at least a month each year, usually in May or June.

Longpan Park 龍磐公園 (km46 Hwy 26; ⊕ 24hrs daily; free admission)

Not a park in the urban sense of the word but a wild realm of crumbling cliffs and wind-battered grasslands. The coastline hereabouts is so windswept trees don't grow. Bushes are snapped before they can grow taller than a man, and even if there were no trampling tourists, the near constant gale would keep the grass flat. Hold on to your hat and if you're thinking of trying to clamber down to the ocean, think again – it's a very perilous scramble.

Roads 200 and 200A

Taking Road 200 inland from Hengchun, you'll soon see the entrance for **Chuhuo Scenic Area** 出火風景區 (km2.8; free admission), one of at least four places in south Taiwan where natural gas seeps out of the ground and burns throughout the year. Staying on 200 will bring you to **Manzhou** 滿州 where there are several places to eat, even though the name of this pleasant little town has a distinctly unappetising derivation. It comes from the Paiwan word *manutsuru*, meaning 'stench'. Local Paiwan used to gather here at the end of each hunt, skin their prey and discard unwanted body parts and bones. After a while, naturally, this debris stank. Manzhou is one of the best places to witness the raptor migration each October. Before you reach the centre of Manzhou, Road 200A veers southeast to Gangkou 港口. This seaside village is very popular with surfers; you can rent a kayak and paddle around the estuary.

Jialeshui 佳樂水 (🕐 *09.00–17.00 daily; admission NTD80/50 inc shuttle bus; parking NTD50/20*) The forces of erosion have given this place an extraordinary selection of wind- and wave-sculpted rocks – look for the boulders and outcrops named after and resembling a dead pig, a human face, a snail and a frog. Some self-driving tourists park outside the ticket gate to avoid the parking fee. Before doing so bear in mind it's well over 1km between the gate and where you can board an open-sided van (somewhat like a *tuk tuk*) that'll take you to the end of the paved road. The waterfall there isn't anything special but people who enjoy clambering over rocks will have lots of fun. If venturing more than 100m from the pagoda at the end of the road, take great care. Bus #8247 travels along 200 and 200A between Hengchun and Jialeshui four or five times a day (🕐 *06.20–17.15; takes 30mins; NTD53; one-day bus passes accepted*).

Nanrenshan Ecological Protection Area 南仁山生態保護區 (🕐 *08.00–15.00 Wed–Mon; free admission*) This reserve, which accounts for more than one-quarter of the national park's 18,084ha of dry land, contains some of Taiwan's last remaining low-altitude primeval forest and para-tropical rainforest. For this reason, and because Nanrenshan continues to be an important ecological research site, visitors are limited to 400 per day. More than 1,200 indigenous plant species have been identified here, plus mammals like the endemic Coxing's white-bellied rat (*Niviventer coninga*). The procedure to enter Nanrenshan is the same as that for Longkeng (see opposite). Allow four hours or more to walk from the entrance to the lake and back again.

FOLLOW BRADT

For the latest news, special offers and competitions, follow Bradt on:

🔲 www.facebook.com/BradtTravelGuides
🐦 @BradtGuides
📷 @bradtguides
📌 pinterest.com/bradtguides

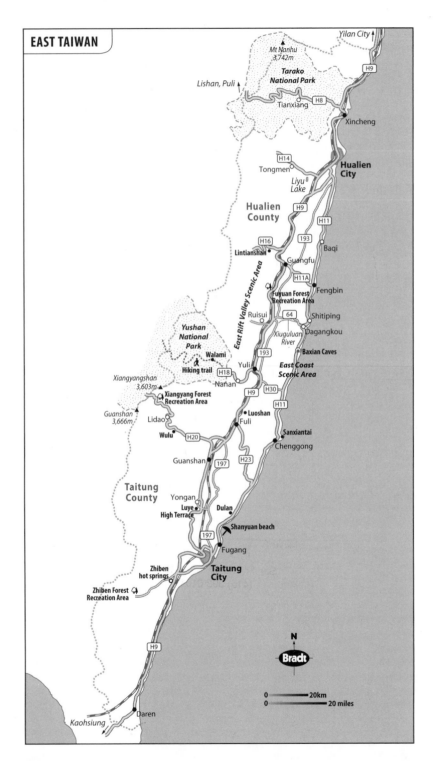

EAST TAIWAN

Yilan City

Mt Nanhu 3,742m

Tarako National Park

Lishan, Puli

H8

Tianxiang

H9

Xincheng

H14

Tongmen

Liyu Lake

Hualien City

Hualien County

H9

H11

193

Lintianshan

H16

Guangfu

Baqi

H11A

Fuyuan Forest Recreation Area

Fengbin

Ruisui

64

Shitiping

Xiuguluan River

Dagangkou

East Rift Valley Scenic Area

Baxian Caves

193

Yushan National Park

Walami

Yuli

Hiking trail

East Coast Scenic Area

H18

Xiangyangshan 3,603m

Nanan

H9

H30

Xiangyang Forest Recreation Area

H11

Guanshan 3,666m

Lidao

Luoshan

Fuli

Wulu

H20

Sanxiantai

Guanshan

197

Chenggong

H23

Taitung County

Yongan

Luye

High Terrace

Dulan

197

Shanyuan beach

Fugang

Zhiben hot springs

Taitung City

Zhiben Forest Recreation Area

H9

N

Bradt

0 — 20km
0 — 20 miles

Kaohsiung

Daren

280

9

East Taiwan

The east is many visitors' favourite region. There's wonderful scenery to gorge on and plenty of space to roam. With 559,000 people spread over 8,144km², the two counties of Hualien and Taitung have less than 3% of the ROC's population but more than a fifth of the country's land. In every sense, nature is less tamed on this side of the island. Not only are the rivers and breezes cleaner, but the typhoons are stronger and the earth tremors more frequent. Relative to the Central Mountain Range, the Coastal Range is moving northeast at up to 13cm per year. Geothermal activity near the surface has created hot springs in places like Ruisui and Zhiben.

One in four residents is Hakka and one in six indigenous. Aboriginal cultures are strong draws but it's the scenery that impresses most. The top attraction is Taroko Gorge, a stunning natural composition of immovable rock and rushing water.

Until the 1950s, the easiest way for residents of Hualien to get to Taipei was to take a boat to Keelung. Nowadays, there are fast trains and flights to both Hualien City and Taitung City. Self-driving tourists should allow an entire day to get from Taiwan's western plains because the motoring isn't always easy and there's lots to see on the way. The authorities have done a lot to make the region more accessible to travellers who depend on public transport; visitors in that category should enquire ahead of time about one-, two- and three-day passes for Taiwan Tourist Shuttle (*www.taiwantrip.com.tw*) services to Taroko Gorge, the East Rift Valley and the coast.

HUALIEN CITY 花蓮市 (HUĀLIÁN SHÌ) *Telephone code 03*

Like every other population centre in the east, Hualien City (population: 110,000) doesn't have much history. Don't expect to stumble across time-worn temples or wander through quaint alleyways. However, the city does have an appealing mix of people: the descendants of Fujianese who settled first in west Taiwan and then, a century or two later, migrated to the east coast; mainlanders who arrived in the late 1940s and the children they raised in Taiwan; Hakka families who appeared before and during the Japanese occupation; and members of the Amis, Truku and other aboriginal tribes. There's some heavy industry around the harbour but the city centre is pleasant – just bustling enough to be interesting yet almost totally free of the air pollution and traffic jams that plague west Taiwan's cities.

GETTING THERE AND AWAY

By air Hualien Airport (*IATA: HUN;* ☎ *821 0768; www.hulairport.gov.tw*) is served by five or six flights to/from Taipei Songshan Airport each day (*takes 40mins; NTD1,455*). There's one service per day to/from Kaohsiung (*takes 55mins; NTD2,095*), three per week to/from Taichung (*1hr; NTD1,921*) and a few international charters. The Taipei and Taichung flights are operated by Transasia Airways (↺ *02 4498 123; www.tna.com.tw*). A taxi from the airport to a city-centre hotel shouldn't cost more than NTD250. There are 14 buses per day between the airport and Hualien TRA Station (*departs from airport* ⊕ *08.30–19.40; takes 20mins; NTD38*).

By TRA Each day there are about 36 expresses to/from Taipei (*takes 2–3½hrs; NTD340–440*) via Yilan and six to/from Kaohsiung (*takes 4¼–5¼hrs; NTD707*) via the very scenic South Link (see *Getting there and away*, page 303) and East Rift Valley. Taitung is served by 17 expresses (*2½–3½hrs; NTD266–345*) and one local train (*4hrs; NTD222*) per day; the Hualien–Taitung line is being improved and travel times should shorten in the next few years.

By bus Hualien Bus Co operates out of an orange building next to the TRA station. Every hour there's a bus to Guangfu in the East Rift Valley (*service #1121; departs* ⊕ *06.00–22.00; takes 1¼hrs; NTD140*), three of which continue on to Ruisui (*#1122; departs* ⊕ *08.10, 11.20 & 17.00; takes 1¾hrs; NTD199*). Buses head down the coast road about once an hour (⊕ *05.30–20.30 daily*). Service #1140 terminates in Jingpu (*takes 2hrs; NTD214*) and #1145 in Chenggong (*takes 3hrs; NTD345*). Just one bus per day goes all the way to Taitung City (*#1127; departs* ⊕ *09.20; takes 4¼hrs; NTD514*). Eastern Top Transport also operates one Hualien–Taitung service each day (*departs* ⊕ *13.10; takes 4hrs; NTD494*). There's no station as such; buy your ticket from the candy-and-biscuits shop beside the stop. These buses also use Highway 11 and, like the daily Hualien Bus Co service, stop at Fugang, from where there are ferries to Green Island.

For details of buses from Hualien to Taroko Gorge National Park, see *Getting there and away* on page 288.

By boat At the time of writing the 798-passenger car ferry *Natchan Rera* was sailing daily between Suao and Hualien (*takes 2hrs; economy class NTD700 one-way*) on a trial basis. For schedule enquiries and ticket purchases, get a Chinese-speaker to contact TourKing (↺ *02 2516 9788; www.tourking.com.tw*).

By car or motorcycle Hualien can be approached from the north, south or west. The section of Highway 9 that links Suao to Xincheng is breathtaking but not much fun if you're on two wheels due to its narrowness and the number of lorries using it; that should improve in the next few years, however. Ideally, arrive via Highway 8 and Taroko Gorge and leave by going south on Highway 9 or Highway 11.

GETTING AROUND
By hired car or motorcycle

🚗 **Car Plus Auto Leasing** 117 Guolian 1st Rd; ↺831 6688; www.car-plus.com.tw; ⊕ 08.30–20.30 daily. General-use car rentals & long-term leasing.

🚗 **Pony Rent** 81 Guolian 1st Rd; ↺833 4888; ⊕ 07.00–20.00 daily. Several scooter-rental businesses operate around Hualien TRA Station but Pony is the only one which consistently accepts international licences.

By bicycle The bicycles offered by hotels to their guests aren't suitable for long-distance touring. For better bikes go to **Giant** (*35 Guoxing 1st St;* ↺ *833 6761;* ⊕ *09.00–18.00 Mon–Fri, 08.00–18.00 Sat–Sun*) where weekday rentals begin at NTD150 per day; on weekdays, you'll pay NTD200 for two hours.

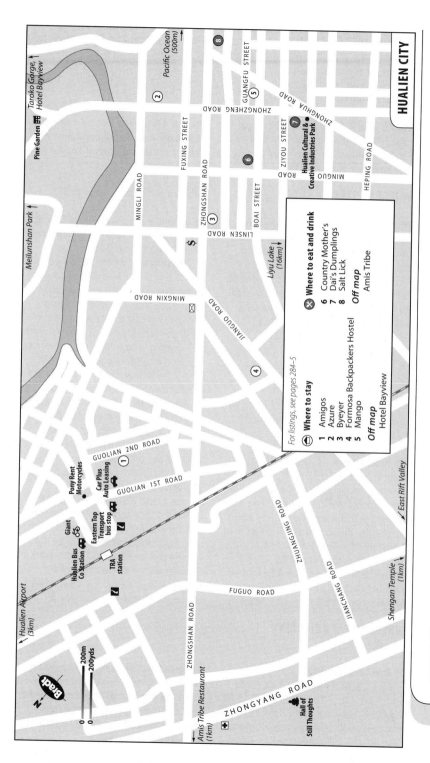

Pacific Ocean
(500m)

Taroko Gorge,
Hotel Bayview

Pine Garden

Meilunshan Park

GUANGFU STREET

ZHONGZHENG ROAD

ZHONGHUA ROAD

FUXING STREET

ZIYOU STREET

Hualien Cultural &
Creative Industries Park

MINGUO ROAD

HEPING ROAD

MINGLI ROAD

ZHONGSHAN ROAD

BOAI STREET

LINSEN ROAD

Liyu Lake
(16km)

MINGXIN ROAD

JIANGUO ROAD

For listings, see pages 284–5

Where to stay

1 Amigos
2 Azure
3 Byeyer
4 Formosa Backpackers Hostel
5 Mango
Off map
Hotel Bayview

Where to eat and drink

6 Country Mother's
7 Dai's Dumplings
8 Salt Lick
Off map
Amis Tribe

GUOLIAN 2ND ROAD

Pony Rent
Motorcycles

Car Plus
Auto Leasing

GUOLIAN 1ST ROAD

Giant

Eastern Top
Transport bus stop

Hualien Bus
Co Station

TRA
station

Hualien Airport
(3km)

ZHUANGJING ROAD

JIANCHANG ROAD

FUGUO ROAD

Shengan Temple
(1km)

East Rift Valley

ZHONGSHAN ROAD

Amis Tribe Restaurant
(1km)

ZHONGYANG ROAD

Hall of
Still Thoughts

Bradt

200m
200yds

TOURIST INFORMATION There's a visitor information centre in Hualien Airport (⊕ *08.00–17.30 daily*) and another behind the TRA station (⊕ *08.30–17.30 daily*), but by far the most useful in terms of English ability and location is the one on the left as you leave the front of the TRA station (⊕ *08.00–22.00 daily*). Also try **Hualien Tourist Service Network** (*http://tour-hualien.hl.gov.tw*).

LOCAL TOUR OPERATOR The expat-run **Hualien Outdoors** (*see advertisement, page 308; 2-16 Guolian 5th Rd*; m *0989 512 380*; e *hualienoutdoors@gmail.com; www. hualienoutdoors.org*) runs river tracing and hiking trips in and around Hualien and Taroko Gorge National Park.

🏠 **WHERE TO STAY** The following hotels are all shown on the map on page 283.

🏠 **Azure Hotel** (100 rooms) 590 Zhongzheng Rd; ☎ 833 6686; f 832 3569; e service@azurehotel. com.tw; www.azurehotel.com.tw. With dbl rooms sometimes available for less than NTD2,500, the Azure is a reasonable & reliable if slightly staid option. Each of the executive suites has a king-size-plus bed & a corner location that ensure ocean, mountain & park views. Extra bed service not available. Wi-Fi; business & fitness centres. B/fast inc. **$$$**

🏠 **Byeyer Hotel** (54 rooms) 361 Zhongshan Rd; ☎ 832 5185; f 832 5183; e byeyer@byeyer. com; www.byeyer.com. Art Deco influences are evident in Byeyer's lobby & rooms, only the most expensive of which have bathtubs. LCD TV sets are swivel-mounted so they can watched from either the bed or the sofa that's in every room. Broadband & Wi-Fi. B/fast & bike use inc. **$$$**

🏠 **Hotel Bayview** (42 rooms) 10 Mingtan St, Xincheng; ☎ 823 2345; f 823 6555; e hotelbayview@gmail.com; www.hotelbayview. com.tw. Located some distance from the city centre but very near the Qixingtan cycling/scenic area, Hotel Bayview lives up to its name if you opt for an Ocean View Deluxe Double (*NTD3,500 at w/ends*). There are also rooms for 4 ppl (*NTD5,500*). A lot of local marble has been used inside & the hotel has a reputation for quality, English-speaking service. All rooms come with b/fast, free use of bicycles &

pick-up from the airport or TRA station. Daylong excursions to Taroko Gorge & East Rift Valley can be booked through the hotel. **$$$**

🏠 **Mango Hotel** (38 rooms) 45 Guangfu St; ☎ 833 3535 f 833 8282; e service@mangohotel. com.tw; www.mangohotel.com.tw. One of the funkier establishments in east Taiwan, Mango Hotel steers very close to, but stays just the right side of, eye-straining love-motel garishness. Think plush carpeting on the walls, zebra-patterned rugs & the use of massively enlarged black-&-white photos instead of wallpaper. One of the VIP rooms has the deepest bathtub I've ever seen. **$$**

🏠 **Amigos Hostel** (2 dorms) 68 Guolian 2nd Rd; ☎ 836 2756; f 836 0243; e amigoshostel.tw@gmail. com; http://amigos-68.myweb.hinet.net/. Dorm beds are NTD450/night inc b/fast & tea or coffee throughout the day. No private rooms. Free pick-ups, internet access & kitchen use for all guests. **$**

🏠 **Formosa Backpackers Hostel** (3 dorms, 1 room) 206 Jianguo Rd; ☎ 835 2515; m 0913 810 828; e formosahostels@yahoo.com; www.freewebs/formosabackpackershostel. Beds in this highly rated hostel start at NTD380/night, while the dbl room goes for NTD1,100 midweek. Guests are welcome to browse the English-language library & use the kitchen. Bar, laundry facilities, broadband & Wi-Fi. No curfew. **$**

✕ **WHERE TO EAT AND DRINK** The following establishments are shown on the map on page 283.

✕ **Amis Tribe Restaurant**
三番兩次原住民風味餐廳 386-6 Zhongshan Rd Sec 1; ☎ 846 3131; ⊕ 11.00–14.00 & 17.00–22.00. Popular with tour groups, this aboriginal restaurant in Hualien's suburbs serves up a range of barbecued dishes (*NTD180–550*) inc fish, vegetables, delicacies

such as cold boar's skin, & meats you may not have tried before, eg: the venison-like flesh of the Reeves's muntjac 山羌 (*shān qiāng*). No EM but some English spoken; no English sign outside – it's the one with the numbers '3' & '2' on the right as you head towards the mountains. **$$$**

✗ Salt Lick 147 Zhongshan Rd; ☏833 2592; www.facebook.com/lickbbq; ⏱ 11.30–14.30 & 17.00–23.00 daily. Carnivores will love this American-managed restaurant's selection of steaks, sandwiches & barbecued delights, most priced NTD200–250. Meals come with fries & salad; side dishes of coleslaw, potato salad & US specialities like hush puppies from NTD45. Lunch specials from NTD150. 2 draft & 3 bottled beers as well as soft drinks available. Indoor & outdoor seating. EM. $$

✗ Country Mother's 156 Boai Rd; ☏831 1506; ⏱ 11.00–14.00 & 17.00–21.00 Thu–Tue. Having quickly earned a stellar reputation for its pizzas (*from NTD150*), this diner also does good calzoni, burgers (*from NTD180*), salads & several other items. Soft drinks priced from NTD25. The original branch (*34 Fuqian Rd;* ☏*823 6008;* ⏱ *06.30–14.00 Thu–Tue*), where the menu lists bagels & sandwiches (*NTD35–150*), is especially popular with tourists making an early break for Taroko Gorge. EM. $$

✗ Dai's Dumplings 120 Zhonghua Rd; ☏835 0667; ⏱ 08.00–21.00 daily. There's no menu here because the only option is soup containing 10 exquisite wonton dumplings (*NTD60*). If you've never had them before, they're egg-sized packets of ground pork, garlic, chopped onion & spices.

OTHER PRACTICALITIES

$ Land Bank 356 Zhongshan Rd

✉ Post office 408 Zhongshan Rd; ⏱ 08.00–21.00 Mon–Fri, 08.30–16.00 Sat–Sun. Money can be changed here.

✚ Buddhist Tzu Chi General Hospital 707 Zhongyang Rd Sec 2; ☏856 1825; www.tzuchi.com.tw; ⏱ 24hrs daily

WHAT TO SEE AND DO

Hall of Still Thoughts 靜思堂 **(Jìngsī Táng)** (*On the campus of Tzu Chi University;* ⏱ *09.00–17.00 daily*) This externally simple yet striking grey temple is a must-visit for those interested in learning about contemporary Buddhism's interactions with mainstream society. Upon entering you'll be invited to watch a 35-minute English-language DVD on the origins, activities and goals of the Buddhist Compassion Relief Tzu Chi Foundation (*www.tzuchi.org*), Taiwan's biggest charity in terms of membership (four million supporters out of a population of 23 million in Taiwan; another five million overseas). Tzu Chi's founder, the Venerable Dharma Master Cheng Yen (b1937), has been based in Hualien since the early 1960s. Her shift away from a purely contemplative existence into relief work was prompted by some vivid encounters with extreme poverty. Sceptics and atheists will appreciate two aspects of Tzu Chi's approach: the absence of donation boxes and the emphasis on environmental protection. Tour the very detailed bilingual exhibition before stepping inside the multilevel Buddhist chapel that's at the heart of the building. Apart from natural light coming in through skylights, the only illuminations are the hundreds of electric candles.

Meilunshan Park 美崙山公園 (⏱ *24hrs daily*) Compared with the tremendous peaks visible to the east, the small hill that gives this park its name scarcely deserves to be called *shān* ('mountain'). There are views both inland and over the Pacific to be enjoyed, and while in the area you may want to relax over a coffee at the colonial-era **Pine Garden** (*65 Songyuan St;* ⏱ *09.00–18.00 daily, closed 2nd & 4th Tue each month; admission NTD50/25*). Established during World War II by the Japanese navy as a communications post, this was where kamikaze pilots were wined and dined before setting off on their final missions. The café has hot and cold drinks (*from NTD100; no EM*) plus a few meal options.

Hualien Cultural and Creative Industries Park 創意文化園區 (*144 Zhonghua Rd; www.a-zone.com.tw; park* ⏱ *24hrs daily, display areas* ⏱ *varies*) This Japanese-era complex, a winery until 1988, now hosts exhibitions and performances; admission is often free. Finding out what's on isn't easy – the website is Chinese only – but the buildings are handsome so it's worth dropping by on the off-chance you'll find something you like.

Shengan Temple 勝安宮 (Shèngān Gōng) (🕐 *06.00–21.00 daily*) By Tainan or Lugang standards, this exceptionally colourful complex of towers, pavilions and altars has almost no past. It traces its history to precisely 06.30 on the 13th day of the sixth lunar month in 1949. At that moment, the Queen Mother of the West (a deity worshipped in China long before the emergence of Taoism) appeared in the form of a white light in a thatched hut. The cult that grew up here is now wealthy and engages in charity work in Taiwan and overseas. In an interesting reversal of Taiwanese or Chinese becoming 'rice Christians', Taiwan's media reported in 2009 that more than 50 Haitians have become disciples of the Queen Mother of the West. A comparative study of Haitian voodoo and Taiwanese folk beliefs would be interesting. Both religions have massive pantheons; followers venerate the dead and aim their prayers more often at lesser spirits than towards any supreme god.

TAROKO GORGE 太魯閣 (TÀILǓGÉ) *Telephone code 03*

Deservedly one of Taiwan's leading tourist destinations, Taroko Gorge is a true, not-to-be-missed geological spectacular. Of the many eye-popping sights, the most dramatic is the stretch where the gorge narrows from a classic V-shaped valley to a defile that turns the sky into little more than a sliver of blue, hundreds of metres above visitors' heads.

Tourists have been visiting the gorge since the 1930s, but only in meaningful numbers since the completion of the Central Cross-Island Highway in 1960. Most people spend their time gazing up at the clifftops or along the meandering Liwu River valley. Yet the boulders that rest on the riverbed are also capable of making a strong impression, and not only because of their gargantuan dimensions. The Taroko area is synonymous with marble (quarrying used to be one of this region's most important industries) but because of mineral impurities and an abundance of schists and gneiss, you'll see rocks of pure white, dark grey, cream, silver, light brown and even soft shades of gold.

Visitor and tour-coach numbers peak in the middle of the afternoon so it's best to make as early a start as possible. The good news is that there's no bad time of year to come here. During summer the Liwu and its tributaries are full of vigour, but landslides sometimes close hiking trails or even the main road. The autumn can be very lovely indeed, and even in winter there are many dry, sunny days when a good number of the national park's 144 bird species and 251 kinds of butterfly are active and visible. Springtime sees an abundance of flowers, including purple azaleas.

Hard-core mountaineers should consider Taroko National Park's other attractions, such as Mount Nanhu (3,742m), Taiwan's fifth-highest peak, or the notoriously dangerous Mount Qilai (3,605m). Permits must be obtained before you can climb either of these mountains; www.taroko.gov.tw for details.

HISTORY The geological processes that created Taroko Gorge began hundreds of millions of years ago with the accumulation of undersea sediment and volcanic lava, materials which eventually became the area's trademark layers of marble, schist and gneiss. About 6.5 million years ago, the Philippine tectonic plate collided

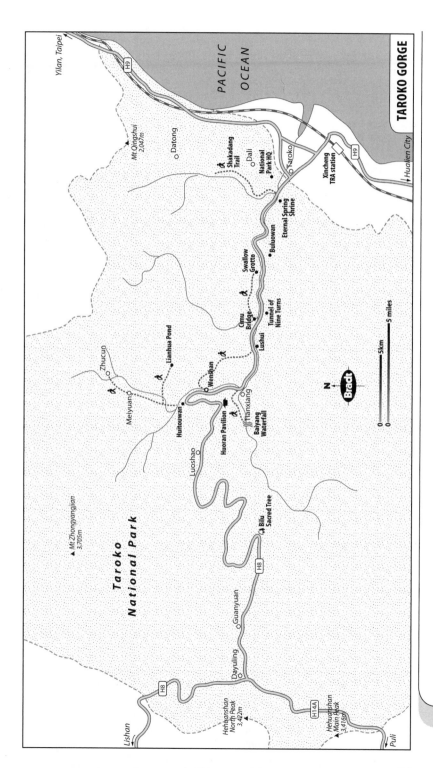

TAROKO GORGE

PACIFIC OCEAN

Yilan, Taipei

Hualien City

Mt Qingshui 2,047m

Datong

Shakadang Trail

Dali

National Park HQ

Taroko

Xincheng TRA station

Eternal Spring Shrine

Buluowan

Swallow Grotto

Cimu Bridge

Tunnel of Nine Turns

Lushui

Lianhua Pond

Wenshan

Zhucun

Meiyuan

Huitouwan

Tianxiang

Huoran Pavilion

Baiyang Waterfall

Luoshao

Mt Zhongyangjian 3,705m

Taroko National Park

Bilu Sacred Tree

Guanyuan

Dayuling

Hehuanshan North Peak 3,422m

Hehuanshan Main Peak 3,416m

Lishan

Puli

0 5km
0 5 miles

with and began to slide under the Eurasian plate. As a result, the landmass we now call Taiwan emerged from the ocean. Rivers, among them the Liwu, formed and began chiselling down through the rock. That erosion continues, but because of the tectonic uplift of the entire region the bottom of the gorge is rising by a few millimetres each year.

Austronesian people have lived on the few scraps of flat land around the gorge for at least 2,000 years. The existence of the Truku tribe, which takes its name from the gorge, can be dated from the arrival of Atayal and Sediq clans in the area three or four centuries ago. After their migration they were isolated from their brethren to the west and developed customs and a dialect of their own. Although they had some contact with the outside world – a Fujianese traveller who visited in 1697 wrote of Han Chinese mingling with the indigenous people, trading with them and panning for gold – the Truku remained the unchallenged masters of the Liwu catchment until 1914, when Japan sent a military expedition into the gorge. Once they'd taken control, they forcibly resettled many of the aborigines closer to the coast. The colonial regime built roads and began to exploit the gorge's hydro-electric potential. At the same time, they made plans for a national park which would have been triple the size of the one established by Taiwan's government in 1986. The Truku weren't recognised as a distinct ethnic group until 2004, which is why some sources still refer to the gorge's indigenous inhabitants as 'Atayal'. As of mid-2013, the tribe was 28,600 strong.

GETTING THERE AND AWAY

By car or motorcycle Taroko Gorge can be reached by Highway 9 from the coast or Highway 8 from inland. Landslides sometimes close or cause delays on the latter so checking road conditions before setting out is advised.

By TRA The nearest TRA station is Xincheng 新城. From Hualien trains take 10–20 minutes (23 *departures per day;* ⊕ *05.15–21.10; NTD24–37*). Each day about a dozen Taipei–Hualien expresses stop in Xincheng (⊕ *07.07–21.00; takes 2–3½hrs; NTD311–403*).

By bus From Hualien Bus Co Station 15 services per day go to Taroko National Park Headquarters (⊕ *05.20–21.30 daily; takes around 1hr; NTD92*) of which four continue on to Tianxiang (*takes 1¾hrs; NTD172*). One of the latter, #1141 at 08.40 (*takes 4½hrs; NTD447*), is the only daily service all the way to Lishan. All of these services reach Xincheng 30–40 minutes after departing the station in Hualien but the stop is about 600m from Xincheng TRA Station so transfers aren't convenient. Turn left when leaving Xincheng TRA Station and walk until you reach Highway 8, the first busy road. Then turn right and walk a very short distance; the bus stop for Taroko Gorge is opposite a temple.

GETTING AROUND

By bus The Taroko Tourist Shuttle is a better option than regular buses. On weekdays seven Tourist Shuttles do the Hualien TRA Station–Tianxiang run (⊕ *07.50–15.00*); at weekends there are 12 services per day (*also* ⊕ *07.50–15.00*). The one-way Hualien–Tianxiang fare is NTD172 so get an unlimited travel pass (*NTD250 for 1 day, NTD400 for 2 consecutive days*). Passes can be bought at the bus station in Hualien or the nearby visitor centre but not on the bus.

Taiwan Tour Bus (*www.taiwantourbus.com.tw*) offers a one-day Taroko excursion (*NTD1,500 pp with foreign-language guide*).

By car On Highway 8 headlights must be kept on at all times between the coast and km112. There's a petrol station (⊕ *07.00–21.00 daily*) in the built-up area just outside the park's eastern boundary and another west of the gorge at Guanyuan (*km116.8 Hwy 8; elevation: 2,374m;* ⊕ *09.00–18.00 daily*).

By hired motorcycle There's at least one rental business near Xincheng TRA Station but organising motorcycle hires is more easily done in Hualien City (see *Getting around*, page 282).

By hired bicycle Mr Rihang Su (**m** *0922 938 743;* **e** *rihangsu@gmail.com*), who also runs a homestay in Xincheng (*http://tarokolodge.blogspot.com*), rents well-maintained bicycles with locks, helmets and lights for NTD350 per day. For NTD700 per person (*inc bike; min 2 ppl*) he'll have you driven to the top of the gorge so you can spend the day freewheeling down, stopping wherever you like.

On foot Tianxiang to the park's eastern entrance is 19km but heavy traffic means walking isn't advisable. That said, the 1km-long tunnel between the national park headquarters and the start of the Shakadang Trail is safe for pedestrians.

TOURIST INFORMATION Taroko National Park Headquarters/Visitor Centre (✆ *862 1100; www.taroko.gov.tw;* ⊕ *08.30–16.45 daily, closed 2nd Mon every month*), where you can get the latest hiking and transport information, is located a few minutes' walk northeast of the junction of Highways 8 and 9. Trail and road conditions are detailed in English on the park's website.

There are service stations at Buluowan (⊕ *09.00–16.30 daily, closed 1st & 3rd Mon every month*), Lushui (⊕ *09.00–16.00 daily, closed 2nd & 4th Mon every month*) and Tianxiang (⊕ *09.00–16.00 daily, closed 2nd & 4th Mon every month*). The small bilingual exhibition at Tianxiang is worth a quick look. These service stations open on Mondays which are national holidays but close the following day instead.

WHERE TO STAY AND EAT A few places close to Tianxiang's bus stop sell hot meals and snacks (*no EMs;* **$**) but don't expect gourmet food. The restaurant in the national park headquarters (⊕ *08.00–16.30 daily; EM;* **$$**) is a much better option and has set meals for around NTD160 and hot and cold drinks NTD50–90.

🏠 **Silks Place Taroko Gorge** 太魯閣晶英酒店 (160 rooms) Tianxiang; ✆ 869 1155; **f** 869 1160; **e** rsvn@silksplace.com.tw; http://taroko.silksplace. com.tw. The only 5-star hotel inside the national park boasts a rooftop swimming pool & garden. One part is called The Resort, another The Retreat; rooms in the latter are more spacious & extra services are available. Room rates inc activities for kids, aerobics classes, demonstrations of indigenous crafts, b/fast & dinner. For non-guests the exceptionally good evening buffet is NTD800 plus 10% service charge. **$$$$$**

🏠 **Leader Village Taroko** 立德布洛灣山月村 (37 rooms) Buluowan; ✆ 861 0111; **f** 861 0191; **e** blw@leaderhotel.com; www.leaderhotel.com/ blw/leadervillage/e-homepage.html. A collection of smart, tastefully decorated wood cabins spread out on a small plateau just above the Buluowan Recreation Area, Leader Village Taroko is enjoyably remote. You can see the stars, hear the cicadas & sometimes glimpse wild animals. Every evening the mostly indigenous staff perform tribal dances. Pickup from Hualien TRA Station or airport for NTD200 pp. Midweek room rates inc b/fast start at NTD3,100 for 2 sharing; pay more for a package which inc choice of lunch or dinner – meals are usually buffet-style & very tasty with lots of meat cooked aboriginal-style (⊕ *12.00–14.00 & 18.00–20.00 daily; EM; NTD280–580+10% for non-guests*). **$$$$**

🏠 **Tienhsiang Youth Activity Centre**
天祥青年活動中心 (56 rooms) 📞869 1111; f 869 1171; e tsyac@cyc.tw; www.cyctsyac.com.tw. Not a bad option in terms of price & cleanliness, but the building wins zero points for character. All rooms have TVs, refrigerators & Wi-Fi; most have tiny balconies. The smallest dbl rooms are NTD2,200. B/fast (*NTD120 pp*) & other meals (*NTD180 pp*) available. **$$$**

🏠 **Protestant Church Hostel** (2 rooms, 3 dorms) 📞869 1203. Follow the signs to 'Tienxiang Church' & you'll soon see a small stone chapel that wouldn't look out of place in northern Europe. The hostel is on the left. The janitor doesn't speak English but is very helpful. The dbl with bath goes for NTD1,200 whether it's a w/day or national holiday, the tiny sgl (no bath) for NTD600. The dormitories, which sleep 4–8, work out around NTD400 pp. Tianxiang's Catholic church operates an equally inexpensive but less characterful hostel. **$$**

WHAT TO SEE AND DO Ecotourists will find it easy to spend three days in the gorge hiking and trying to spot resident bird species such as the little forktail (*Enicurus scouleri*) and green-backed tit (*Parus monticolus*). Whenever there's a typhoon alert, park authorities tend to close all trails immediately even if the weather seems fine. If a typhoon strikes, trails stay closed until the authorities are sure there's no likelihood of rockfalls; this may take two weeks. Visitors should therefore track weather conditions and look at the park's website before setting out for the gorge.

Shakadang Trail 砂卡礑步道 The Shakadang drains from north to south and is one of the Liwu's major tributaries. This trail, constructed during the Japanese era to facilitate the building of a small dam, follows the river closely. The route begins with a long flight of steel stairs about 30 minutes' walk from the national park headquarters. For the remainder of the trail's 4.5km length, the gradient is very gentle. Because so many people hike this trail you're unlikely to see much in the way of wildlife, but you will see Truku people tending small plots and selling bagfuls of an unusual local crop, a lettuce-type vegetable called bird's-nest fern (*Asplenium nidus*). Don't expect to reach 3D Cabin, the official end of the trail, and get back to the starting point in the 2½ hours mentioned in national park literature. If you've obtained permits in advance, it's possible to keep going to **Dali** (altitude: 915m) and **Datong** (1,128m), two old Truku settlements. Nowadays there are no permanent inhabitants, just the occasional ex-resident returning to grow crops. Getting to either of these places involves serious uphill hiking. If you plan to stay overnight contact the national park headquarters as some of the rangers have family ties to the villages. Accommodation is rudimentary; do not expect English or electricity.

Eternal Spring Shrine 長春祠 (🕐 *24hrs daily*) Dramatically positioned near the base of what looks to be a highly unstable mountain slope, this small temple is quite a sight. Water gushes through a tunnel between the two pavilions and into the Liwu River. It's possible to do an hour-long loop hike here. Walking from the Shakadang trailhead doesn't take long, but it does involve going through a tunnel that sees quite a bit of traffic.

Buluowan 布洛灣 A series of terraces 2km from and substantially higher than Highway 8, Buluowan Recreation Area has four very short but worthwhile trails, an exhibition of aboriginal weaving and basket-making, handicrafts for sale and a coffee shop. To get here, take the twisting side road that veers off to the south between km180 and km180.5 on Highway 8; Hualien–Tianxiang buses detour up this road.

Swallow Grotto 燕子口 **(Yànzǐkǒu)** This short (just under 0.5km) pathway takes you through one of the narrowest, deepest and most striking sections of the canyon. The cliff here is pock-marked as a result of abrasion by sand and grit carried downstream when the river is high; the place name refers to the birds who nest in the cavities.

Tunnel of Nine Turns 九曲洞 **(Jiǔ Qū Dòng)** If you're going to park and stretch your legs at just one point in the gorge, do it here. The 2km-long walking trail here is in fact a vestigial stretch of highway, superseded in 1996 when a long tunnel was built to straighten and broaden one of Highway 8's more dangerous sections. If you're not impressed by the dimensions of the gorge here, you're nigh impossible to please. The 'nine' in this toponym isn't literal but rather a classical Chinese way of expressing 'many'.

Zhuilu Old Road 錐麓古道 What's billed as the gorge's most challenging and rewarding hike starts from **Cimu Bridge** 慈母橋, so named ('motherly devotion') because it's where Chiang Ching-kuo had a small pavilion built as a memorial to his mother. The trail ('road' is a misnomer – it's too narrow for hikers, let alone vehicles, to pass) was cut high above the current highway by conscripted Truku labourers soon after the Japanese took control of the gorge in 1914. The views from it are superb, but it's not for casual walkers. Because hikers have to ascend from 300m above sea level to around 780m, six hours are needed to complete the 10.3km-long trail. National park notices describe the route as 'rugged [and] highly difficult' and note that the cliff section 'is narrow and dangerous and visitors are frequently hit by falling rocks'. Permits are required and should be applied for at least three days in advance.

Tianxiang 天祥 **(Tiānxiáng)** Variously spelled Tiansiang and Tienhsiang, this little settlement at km170 (elevation 480m) would amount to half a dozen households and a pair of churches if you took away the tourist industry. It's named after Wen Tianxiang, a 13th-century Chinese scholar renowned for his loyalty to the Song Dynasty as it was being crushed by Kublai Khan's invading Mongols. (This kind of patriot, unwavering in his support of a legitimate but defeated regime, had an especial appeal to Chiang Kai-shek's Nationalists.)

A number of short but challenging hikes begin in or near Tianxiang. From the Protestant church it's less than 200m (part of which is very steep) to a small plateau where you can see the ruins of a tiny Truku settlement called **Tapido**. This was a genuine indigenous community, not a resettlement village created by the Japanese or the Nationalists, and so it's almost certain there are graves here. The Truku, like many of Taiwan's indigenous tribes, practised indoor burial. When an aged person appeared close to death, he or she was moved into a sitting position. Once they'd expired, they were interred in that posture right under the house in which they had dwelt. The grave was then covered with stone slabs.

Behind the youth activity centre you'll find the start of a trail to **Huoran Pavilion**, which is on Highway 8 west of Huitouwan. There's good butterflying along both this path and the approach to Tapido.

Baiyang Trail 白楊步道 **(Báiyáng Bùdào)** In the late 1970s, just as the Interior Ministry was finalising plans for Taroko to become a national park, the Economics Ministry was pushing ahead with plans to dam the Liwu's main tributaries to produce hydro-electricity. Taipower, the state-run utility, cut a 2.1km-long road from just inland of Tianxiang to the Baiyang Waterfalls and beyond. The road, which passes through seven short tunnels, is now a beautiful hiking trail but one often closed due to typhoon damage. No permits are required but carrying a torch is advisable as some of the tunnels aren't straight. Water and snacks are a good idea as you'll be walking for at least an hour each way if you want to see the waterfalls. The spherical, basketball-sized clumps you'll notice on some of the trees are ants' nests.

Wenshan Hot Springs 文山溫泉 (Wénshān Wenquán) These riverside hot springs, 3km up the road from Tianxiang, have been known to the outside world since they were discovered by a Japanese army officer in 1914. Don't disregard the bilingual signs which warn visitors to stay away from certain spots: in 2005, a deadly rockfall brought the number of people killed by falling debris while bathing here to at least four (several others were injured) and caused the park authorities to close the entire site for six years.

What's variously called the **Wenshan Trail** or Lushui Wenshan Path leaves the highway a short distance north of the entrance to the hot springs; walk through a tunnel and look for the trailhead on your right. Local tour operator Taiwan Adventures describes it as: 'one of the tougher trails in the [park], a gem of a hike for anyone wanting to get away from the crowded more popular touristy spots.' No permit is required but check the park's website before making any plans as over the past decade the trail has been closed to the public more often than it's been open. Allow six hours one-way.

Huitouwan 迴頭彎 (km163.4) This is the jumping-off point for overnight hikes to the tiny and truly remote villages of **Meiyuan** 梅園 (meaning 'plum orchard') and **Zhucun** 竹村 ('bamboo village'). Huitouwan to Meiyuan is 5.6km; from Meiyuan to Zhucun is another 3.7km. In Meiyuan there's a small Protestant church, but no school, shop or clinic. Zhucun has a Catholic chapel. In both places, camping is the only accommodation option. The inhabitants grow high-mountain vegetables and drive slow, short-wheelbase tractors because the road is too narrow for conventional vehicles. The park authorities sometimes bar outsiders from entering if typhoons damage the track.

A side trail, which veers westward from the main track between Huitouwan and Meiyuan, usually remains open. This leads to a footbridge across the Dasha River and then on to **Lianhua Pond** 蓮花池 (elevation: 1,180m). Approaching the pond, which is just under 1ha in size, there's some uphill hiking through sublime groves of Makino bamboo.

Bilu Sacred Tree 碧綠神木 (km126.3) After Huitouwan (elevation: 720m) the road climbs steadily to this lovely spot, some 2,446m above sea level. *Bìlù* means 'greenish-blue' and is the name of the river down below, not a description of the tree, a Lunta fir (*Cunnhamia lanceolata var. konishii*) that's 50m high and more than 3,000 years old. The restaurant/shop here (⏰ *07.00–18.00 daily; EM; $$*) serves meal sets (*about NTD250 inc coffee or tea*), simpler items like soup or noodles (*about NTD90*) as well as the usual hot and cold drinks. The owner's wife, Lily Chang (m *0919 908 680;* e *chang5459@gmail.com*) was educated in the US and can update you about road conditions.

At Dayuling (2,565m), you have the choice of either going through the tunnel and on to Lishan and Shei-Pa National Park (see page 200) or heading southward to Hehuanshan and Puli (see pages 195–8).

THE EAST RIFT VALLEY

The broad and largely unspoiled expanse of lush countryside between the Central Mountain Range and the Coastal Range is indeed lovely. More than 150km long, the valley is drained by three waterways: the Hualien River flows into the ocean near the city of the same name; the majestic Xiuguluan dominates the centre; and the southward-flowing Beinan cuts through some of Taiwan's best rice-growing country. **Guangfu 光復 (Guāngfù)** is a good base for exploring the valley. Two-thirds of the township's 14,000 inhabitants are aboriginal. The substantial Hakka minority came here to work in the sugar industry, which until a few years ago dominated the local economy. The sugar refinery still stands, but most of the cane plantations are now being afforested.

The hot springs at Ruisui were developed during the Japanese era and still attract substantial numbers of Taiwanese tourists. However, for Western visitors the main draws are the valley's natural appearance and opportunities to go hiking and white-water rafting.

Because the valley is divided between Hualien County and Taitung County, telephone codes are included in all listings.

GETTING THERE AND AWAY

By TRA Most of the 17 trains linking Hualien with Guangfu each day take just over an hour (*NTD45–97*) and there's a similar number of services from Taitung (*most take 1¾hrs; NTD191–247*).

By bus Buses #1121 and #1122 link Hualien TRA Station with Guangfu (*departures hourly ⊙ 06.00–22.30 daily; takes 1¼hrs; NTD140*). Heading south, there are several buses each day from Guangfu to Yuli (*takes 1hr; NTD129*) and Fuli (*takes 1¾hrs; NTD195*). From either you can catch a bus or train to Taitung City.

By motorcycle or bicycle Two-wheelers are advised to take Highway 11 south from Hualien and then Road 193 when it veers off to the right. The first 20km of this famous cycling route have numerous twists and turns and are almost completely unpopulated (meaning there's nowhere to buy snacks or drinks) but intensely scenic. Approaching Dabalong the road becomes flatter and straighter.

TOURIST INFORMATION
☑ **East Rift Valley National Scenic Area** www.erv-nsa.gov.tw
☑ **Liyu Lake Service Station** ⊙ 08.30–17.30 daily

☑ **Xiuguluan River Rafting Centre** km89.8 Rd 193; ⊙ 08.00–17.00 daily
☑ **Luoshan Visitor Centre** km310.5 Hwy 9; ⊙ 08.30–17.30 daily

⌂ WHERE TO STAY
⌂ **Butterfly Valley Resort** (42 rooms) Fuyuan National Forest Recreation Area; ☎ 03 881 2377; f 03 881 2397; Taipei sales office: 02 2564 2070; e reservations@bvr.com.tw; www.bvr.com.tw. At first glance this looks like a very expensive place to stay – rack rates start at NTD8,000 & a 10% service charge is added to every bill. However, the rooms are very comfortable indeed & prices drop by up to 45% midweek. Inc b/fast & dinner (Westerners

who've stayed here speak highly of the food), pick-up from Hualien's airport or TRA station, entrance tickets for the forest recreation area & use of hot-springs pools. **$$$$$**
⌂ **Chief Spa Hotel** (61 rooms) Wulu, Taitung County; ☎ 089 935 075; f 089 935 085; http://chiefspa.hotel.com.tw. This long-running hotel, which has English-speaking staff & serves meals, makes for a good stop on the South Cross-Island

Highway. Guests are welcome to watch an excellent English-language video introducing the area's ecology. As well as hot-spring facilities in each bedroom, the hotel also has a public pool (*06.00–09.00 & 16.00–22.00 daily; admission for non-guests NTD250; swimsuits required*). Giving the hotel a few hours' notice that you want to use the public pool is a good idea midweek so the staff can clean it before you arrive. Inc b/fast. **$$$**

🏠 **Hualien Tourism Sugar Factory Guesthouse** (28 rooms) 19 Tangchang St, Guangfu; 03 870 5881; f 03 870 4100. No sugar has been produced at Guangfu's sugar refinery for over a decade but rather than let what used to be senior managers' official housing rot, the government-owned company which runs this site has converted the 1930s Japanese-style single-storey wooden buildings into a distinctive set of lodgings. Interiors feature tatami mats & Japanese-style bathtubs. Most rooms are for 3 ppl & cost NTD2,880–4,800 depending on season; rooms for 2 are 25% cheaper. Inc b/fast & bicycles which you'll probably use to get dinner in central Guangfu, less than 1km away. **$$$**

🏠 **Kamiyamato B&B** (5 rooms) 78 Zhongxue St, Guangfu; 03 870 6058; m 0910 224 338; e kamiyamato976@yahoo.com.tw; www. kamiyamato976.com. Run by fluent English-speaker Stephanie Liu, Kamiyamato (the old Japanese name for Guangfu) has rooms for couples, foursomes & a family room with balcony that can take up to 8 ppl. About 1km northeast of Guangfu TRA Station; free pick-up if arranged ahead of time. B/fast inc. **$$$**

🏠 **Wild Goose Homestay** (5 rooms) 5, Lane 51, Luliao Rd, Yongan; 089 550 281; m 0937 389 953; www.goose51599.com.tw. This place is a little difficult to find; once you reach Yongan, locate the elementary school. Facing the school, the homestay is less than 50m to your right. Alternatively, follow the Chinese-only signs (white characters on a red background with the owner's mobile phone number). No English spoken but the owners are very hospitable & the rooms are absolutely spotless. Reservations are essential in the summer, no doubt because of the very fair prices (*NTD2,500 for a dbl at w/ends*). B/fast inc. **$$$**

✖ WHERE TO EAT AND DRINK

✖ **Hong Wa Wu Restaurant** 紅瓦屋 FaTai'An, Guangfu; 03 870 4601; *11.00–20.00 daily*. The best known & easiest to find of FaTai'An's indigenous restaurants also goes by the name Cifadahan Café. It's a stone's throw from the wetland & often filled with tourists. The ingredients are very local & include wild vegetables & desserts made from fatai'an beans. Proprietor Na Kaw is also an artist & many of the works inside are hers. **$$**

✖ **Jianrou Villa** 劍柔山莊 FaTai'An, Guangfu; 03 870 0316; m 0920 881 089; *call to confirm*. Owner-chef Mrs Lin is an expert not only in cooking but also in the healthy properties of foods used in Amis cuisine. There's no EM; what's served varies from day to day, but may include a soup containing 8 different vegetables (some of which you've surely never eaten before), freshwater fish, salad & boar meat. No English spoken so get a Taiwanese acquaintance to call ahead to ascertain opening hours, prices & what Mrs Lin intends to cook. **$$**

WHAT TO SEE AND DO

Liyu Lake 鯉魚潭 (*24hrs daily; free admission*) Close to central Hualien and thus often quite crowded, this picturesque body of water is popular with families and couples on dates. You can rent a pedalo and cross the lake, or hire a bicycle (*from NTD100 per day*) and go around it. The path for cyclists and pedestrians is 3.5km long. The Chinese name means 'carp lake', but nature-lovers will find the tufted ducks (*Aythya fuligula*) and various herons more interesting than the piscine forms of life.

Mugua River 木瓜溪 From central Hualien, Highway 14 goes inland to a large Truku community called **Tongmen** 銅門. Less than 1km further up the Mugua River, a tributary of the Hualien River, you'll see a hydro-electric power station. You won't be allowed past the security gate without a permit; these can be obtained at the

Sometime in July or August – the precise date and exact name of the event varies from village to village – Amis clans in Hualien and Taitung counties celebrate the taking in of the harvest with singing, dancing and feasting. As with harvest festivals worldwide, these events, which tribespeople call *Ilisin*, are celebrations of abundance and expressions of gratitude for the blessings of gods and ancestors.

There's more to these festivals than revelry and gluttony. At Chishang in Taitung County, for instance, for three days the men engage in fishing while the women prepare glutinous rice, salted pork and millet liquor. On the fourth day the tribe gathers to erect bamboo watchtowers and pavilions. Traditional songs and dances can be enjoyed on the fifth and sixth days; this is when you'll see groups in traditional attire but bare feet dance with interlocked arms. On the seventh and final day the menfolk go fishing once again, hoping to close the festival with a big catch.

If you happen across one of these events, you're likely to receive a memorably warm welcome, and possibly some good-natured cajoling to get you to join in. For a detailed explanation of Amis culture and social organisation, see: www.dmtip.gov.tw/Eng/amis.htm.

small police station (⏱ *07.30–17.00 daily*) between Tongmen and the checkpoint. A maximum of 600 permits are issued each day; to boost your chances of getting one, come as early as possible on a weekday. The valley beyond Tongmen is sometimes called Mugumuyu; it's very pretty, so much so that some visitors have described it as 'Taroko II'. The road is narrow – two wheels are preferable to four.

Baibau Creek If you've an interest in ecology and how mankind can better manage the environment, you'll happily spend an hour or two here. Assuming you're approaching from the north, near km21.5 on Highway 9C (the road from Liyu Lake) you'll see English-language signs; turn right and go 4km to the very end of the surfaced road. On the same side of the creek, it's recommended that you follow a gravel path which becomes a narrow trail upstream for almost 1km; expect lots of butterflies as well as rich flora. The low, fish-friendly wooden weirs you'll see along this creek are strikingly different from the concrete barriers which disfigure many of Taiwan's waterways and which have contributed to the decline of freshwater species including the Formosan landlocked salmon (see box, page 200).

Lintianshan After World War II, when Taiwan's timber industry was in full swing, almost 400 families lived in this loggers' settlement. Decline began not with changing government policies in the late 1980s but earlier, after fires devastated nearby forests in 1972. Clusters of Japanese-style homes and offices remain in place and several have been renovated; displays about local history and exhibitions of woodcarvings make this a good place to break your journey. A short stretch of track is all that's left of a narrow-gauge railway which penetrated deep into the mountains, to an altitude of 2,600m. Trains and buses from Hualien City stop in Wanrong, 2km away.

FaTai'An Wetland 馬太鞍濕地 (Mǎtàiān Shīdì) (⏱ *24hrs daily; free admission*)
Several English-language sources refer to this ecotourism destination as Mataian,

East Taiwan THE EAST RIFT VALLEY

9

which is the Mandarin pronunciation. FaTai'An (sometimes written Fataan), the original Amis name, is also a kind of plant, the beans of which sustained the local aboriginal population during a long period of warfare with the Amis of Dabalong. This wetland is almost unique in Taiwan in that it's not on or near the coast. Unfortunately, among the 100-plus aquatic plants here are invasive species that are influencing the local ecosystem. If you come here with a guide, ask him or her to explain the traditional and quite unique *palakaw* fishing method.

To explore this area turn inland at km251.6 on Highway 9. Cross the railway tracks and look for the small bilingual signs pointing to various sites of interest as well as the area's two well-established indigenous restaurants (see *Where to eat*, page 294). Local Amis elder **Lalan Unak** (\ *03 870 0015; www.lalan-unak.com*) runs an eponymous homestay, a restaurant and short tours of FaTai'An aimed at groups of Chinese-speaking tourists.

Dabalong 太巴塱 Located east of central Guangfu near where Highway 11A crosses Road 193, the Amis of Dabalong (sometimes spelled Tafalong or Taibalang) are the traditional enemies of the Amis of FaTai'An, with whom they quarrelled and fought throughout the 19th century. You'll notice the clan's symbol, a white crab, in several places around this village, and a huge totem pole outside the elementary school. Dabalong's inhabitants are renowned for their woodcarving skills and, although almost all of the houses here are modern concrete structures, you'll certainly see a few signs of traditional Amis lifestyles, such as bouquets of millet drying in courtyards and animal skulls decorating doorways.

Fuyuan National Forest Recreation Area 富源森林遊樂區 (Fùyuán Sēnlín Yóulèqū) (\ *03 881 2377; http://recreation.forest.gov.tw;* ⊕ *08.00–22.00 daily; admission NTD100/60*) If you come to this 191ha reserve expecting an arboreal wilderness, you're in for a disappointment. The area near the visitor centre and

WHITE-WATER RAFTING IN EAST TAIWAN

Taiwan is ideal for white-water rafting. The wet season brings huge amounts of rain and the island's steep mountains mean fast rivers cut through fantastic scenery. Hualien County's Xiuguluan River is Taiwan's best-known rafting venue and every day during the summer hundreds of people board inflatables for a wild river experience.

Rivers around the world are given ratings of between one and six depending on how violent they can be. Class-one rivers are peaceful, while class-six waterways are extremely dangerous. The Xiuguluan is a relatively calm class two; even so, it has enough rapids, eddies and sudden drops to keep things exciting. It's also very scenic, though at many points during the 24km-long float you'll be too focused on staying aboard to appreciate the canyons and cliffs.

A few other places in east Taiwan, such as the Annong River in Yilan County, are trying to make their names as white-water destinations. Wherever you do it, you'll find it an exhilarating experience – but it's not for those who prefer contemplative encounters with nature. During rafting season there are often hundreds of people on the river at the same time and their behaviour can be quite boisterous. Expect screaming, shouting, water fights and deliberate collisions.

Butterfly Eco-House is more like a manicured garden than a semi-tropical forest, but if you hike the four trails (total length: 6.1km) you'll see camphor groves, wild orchids and possibly rare birds like the maroon oriole (*Oriolus traillii*). Birding here is 'great year-round', according to a Wild Bird Society of Taiwan publication. March to August is peak season for butterflies but as late as November you'll still see plenty. Fireflies are especially active from March to early May and again in October and early November. Food and accommodation can be had at the on-site Butterfly Valley Resort (see *Where to stay*, page 293). Fuyuan is south of Guangfu, several kilometres inland of Highway 9. The turn-off is between km260 and km260.5.

Ruisui 瑞穗
The busiest part of Ruisui, including the TRA station, lies east of Highway 9. West of the highway near km273 there are two neighbourhoods each with several hotels where you can soak in naturally hot, yellow carbonate water: **Ruisui Hot Springs** and, a little further inland, **Hongye Hot Springs**. Few establishments have English signs.

Saoba Monoliths
(*km275*) You'll probably spend more time gazing over groves of betel nut and pomelo trees at the mountains than at the two somewhat bland 3,000-year-old monoliths here. A bit further south there's one of Taiwan's three Tropic of Cancer monuments and, at km276.5, a small road going west. This route, Local Road 61, cuts through tiny indigenous villages before joining Road 193 between Ruisui TRA Station and the Xiuguluan River Rafting Centre.

Xiuguluan River 秀姑巒溪
Organised floats down this river (see box opposite) are possible year-round and especially popular between June and August. In peak season bookings should be made at least a day in advance; you may want to do this in person at the **Xiuguluan River Rafting Centre** (☎ *03 887 5400;* ⊕ *08.30–17.30 daily*). The centre – located where Road 193 crosses the river, 3km from Ruisui TRA Station – is also where rafting expeditions begin. In spring and autumn, provided you arrive before 09.00, it's usually possible to sign up and be on the river the same morning. All operators charge NTD750 per person; this includes life-jackets, helmets and lunch but not transport back to the centre afterwards; if you take one of the shuttle buses that return to the centre from near the river's mouth you'll need to pay an additional NTD150 per person. The centre also lends out bicycles (*free; deposit your ID*).

Walami Old Trail 瓦拉米古道
This path provides access to the ecologically rich eastern half of Yushan National Park and forms the eastern end of the Batongguan Cross-Island Old Trail (see page 206). On it you've an excellent chance of seeing troupes of Formosan macaques and small flocks of black-browed barbets (*Megalaima oorti*). After dark, you may hear the canine yapping of a short-tailed deer species no bigger than a mid-sized dog, Reeves's muntjac (*Muntiacus reevesi*). Leeches are an occasional nuisance. If you plan on going no further than **Jiaxin** 佳心, the site of a police station during the colonial era and just 4.9km past the trail entrance, you don't need any kind of permit. If you wish to go beyond Jiaxin, drop into **Nanan Visitor Centre** 南安遊客中心 (☎ *03 888 7560;* ⊕ *08.00–16.30 daily, closed 2nd Tue each month*) and register before starting your hike. At **Walami** (*14km from the trailhead; elevation: 1,060m*) there's a shelter with running water and electric lights. Accommodation is free but you should bring a sleeping bag. Because space is limited you should apply to the park authorities for a permit at least a week in advance; this can be done online. You'll also need to be self-sufficient in terms of

food and cooking equipment. If you want to hike to Walami and return the same day, you're required to register at the visitor centre before 09.00.

The nearest TRA station is Yuli, which is also served by a few buses from Taitung City. A taxi from the station to Nanan Visitor Centre costs about NTD300; all the way to the trail entrance is around NTD500.

Mount Liushidan aka Sixty Stone Mountain The uplands here are famous for one crop: day lilies. These protein-rich orange flowers are used to make soups and other dishes, but it's the sight of masses of them covering entire hillsides (as featured on this guidebook's cover) that draws tourists. The turn-off (on the left if you're heading south) is clearly marked at km308.5. At the height of day-lily season in August and part of September the mountain is closed to private vehicles; minibuses shuttle visitors up and down the mountain.

Luoshan 羅山 (*km310.5*) The main attraction here is a waterfall 4km from Highway 9. There's also a mud volcano (disappointingly flat and lifeless) very near a fish pond; at the latter, the bilingual sign telling visitors not to release animals is aimed at Buddhists who practice 'mercy release' (see box, page 10).

Highway 23 For motorists this winding and little-used road is a magnificent excellent way of cutting between the East Rift Valley and the coast. Top up your tank if coming from Highway 9 because the only gas station is at km38 (⏰ *07.00–12.00 & 13.00–16.00 daily*). The gorge-like **Taiyuan Hidden Valley** (*km40.3*) is a scenic highlight; don't give anything to the macaques who hang around here hoping to be fed.

South Cross-Island Highway (Highway 20) Even if driving all the way to the west coast isn't possible (see page 265), fans of Taiwan's highlands may still want to explore the eastern stretch of this spectacular road. The turn-off from Highway 9 is just north of Guanshan. Drivers are required to keep their headlights on between km204 and km147, a sensible precaution because thick fog is common. Do find somewhere to stop near **Wulu Canyon 霧鹿峽谷** (*km182*), where the cliffs bear yellow sulphur stains. At one time the road followed every twist and turn of the Xinwulu River but over the years tunnels have been bored to straighten out the highway. Take great care if you decide to stroll along one of the now-redundant stretches of road – they aren't maintained. For good, safe views cross the footbridge behind Chief Spa Hotel (see *Where to stay*, page 293) and follow the trail on the other side; keep going and you'll find yourself at km179.2 on Highway 20.

Beyond Wulu your best hope for a hot meal is **Lidao 利稻** (*km177 Hwy 20*), a Bunun village on a plateau 1,068m above sea level. It's a major venue of the tribe's annual Ear-shooting Festival (see *Public holidays and festivals*, page 68). From the park by the elementary school you can see the mountains very well; the artillery pieces here were made in Russia and seized by the Japanese during the Russo-Japanese War of 1904–05. In the 1920s, the colonial regime used them against truculent aborigines.

The entrance to **Xiangyang National Forest Recreation Area 向陽國家森林遊樂區** (*km154.5 Hwy 20; http://recreation.forest.gov.tw; ⏰ 08.30–16.30 daily; free admission*) is at 2,314m. Inside there are hiking trails (the longest is 1.77km) and stands of Formosan cypresses, cardinal maples and Taiwan red pines. This 362ha reserve doubles as the trailhead for several splendid high-altitude hikes, most notably to the peak of Xiangyangshan 向陽山 (3,346m) and Jiaming Lake 嘉明湖,

a sublime body of water that fills a meteor-impact crater 3,310m above sea level. If you've a week or more, the right equipment and sufficient energy and provisions, you can hike northwards across Yushan National Park to Dongpu.

Guanshan 關山 This town's 12km-long **bike path** 關山自行車道 (⊕ *24hrs daily; admission NTD50*) predates Taiwan's bicycle revolution and continues to be a major attraction. The circuit shows off the area's best scenery and deserves three or four hours. Following a gradual climb, an exhilarating downhill stretch brings you to a place where water buffalo laze in a marsh. Most of the trail is shaded by mahogany trees or betel-nut groves. Among the crops you might see along the way are millet, rapeseed, jelly figs, pears, sugarcane and oranges.

At least 20 trains per day connect Guanshan to Taitung (*most take 40mins; NTD32–69*). The conveniently located but otherwise unremarkable **Shan Shui Jyu Hotel** (*36 rooms;* ✆ *089 814 787; b/fast inc;* **$$$**), visible on the left as soon as you exit the station, rents out bicycles from NTD100 per day. Other rental businesses offering tandems and electric golf carts as well as standard bicycles can be found east of the railway line, on the road leading to **Guanshan Water Park** 關山親水公園 (⊕ *07.00–17.00 daily; free admission with the bike-path ticket*).

Luye High Terrace 鹿野高台 (Lùyě Gāo Tái) This small plateau has become one of Taiwan's top paragliding spots, and even if you're not interested in leaping off the hillside, you should come here for the excellent views up and down the East Rift Valley.

Two nearby villages are of interest. One is **Yongan 永安**, to the north. A mixed Han-aboriginal village sprawling at the base of steep mountains, there isn't much to do here except stroll through neighbourhoods separated by cornfields and banana plantations. To hike up to the terrace from the village, first find number 442 Yongan Road. Opposite that small house a one-car-wide concrete track goes down to a small creek. Cross the river, turn left and keep walking past the newly planted saplings until you see a stairway disappearing up into the forest. Take it and soon you'll be at a two-floor wooden pavilion on the northwestern edge of the terrace. Weather permitting, you'll enjoy excellent views northwards. The other village worth looking at is due south. Now called **Longtian 龍田**, it was established in 1917 to attract settlers from Japan, then as now a crowded country. Scores of hopeful immigrants arrived, but the majority, deciding life in Taiwan's cities would be easier, left within a decade. A few Japanese-style wooden bungalows are all that remain.

To reach Yongan from the south, turn inland at km348 on Highway 9 and take the twisty road going uphill to Yongan. If you're coming from the north, leave Highway 9 at km344.5 and keep driving until you see Yongan Elementary School.

HIGHWAY 11: THE COAST ROAD

There are no sights on a par with Taroko Gorge, but the coastline between the cities of Hualien and Taitung has more than enough rocky shores, steep green hills and indigenous villages to fill a day or two. Because part of this route lies within Hualien County and part within Taitung County, telephone codes are included in all listings. All km-marker numbers refer to locations on Highway 11.

GETTING THERE, AWAY AND AROUND
By car or motorcycle By Highway 11, Hualien to Taitung is 167km. Allow four hours' driving time.

By bus Whether you start from Hualien or Taitung, reaching the major sights by public transport is quite straightforward but tiring if you try to do everything in a single day. See the *Getting there and away* sections of those cities for details of bus services.

The East Coast Tourist Shuttle runs between Taitung City and Sanxiantai (*5 departures per day;* ⊕ *07.20–14.50; takes 2¼hrs; NTD188*) and can be boarded at Taitung Airport, Taitung TRA Station and Railway Art Village.

TOURIST INFORMATION

⬛ Hualien Visitor Centre km9 Hwy 11; ⊕ 08.30–17.00 daily

⬛ East Coast National Scenic Area Headquarters km124.5 Hwy 11; ☎089 841 520; ⊕ 08.30–17.00 daily; www.eastcoast-nsa.gov.tw

---

RICE FOR BREAKFAST, LUNCH AND DINNER

Rice accounts for one-fifth of all calories consumed by mankind. For many Taiwanese the proportion is even greater; affluence has brought a varied diet but even now millions of Taiwanese eat rice twice a day. Going a day without rice is unimaginable for many people. In Mandarin, the act of preparing a meal is *zhǔ fàn*, literally 'cook rice'. For breakfast, rice is served as a watery gruel with pickles, peanuts, fried eggs and dried shredded pork. Steamed rice is the basis of a typical Taiwanese lunch or dinner. Rice ground into flour is made into dumplings or noodles (most noodles, however, are made from wheat flour).

Rice grows well in Taiwan's warm climate and fields of green stalks can be seen throughout the lowlands. In recent years, average annual rice production has been about 1.08 million tonnes, meaning the island is more than 90% self-sufficient. This is an impressive achievement given the island's topography and population density, and the fact that other crops are also grown in large quantities.

Rice requires a great deal of water compared with other crops and paddy fields produce worrying amounts of methane, a greenhouse gas. However, in other respects this form of agriculture isn't too bad for the environment. Paddy networks appear to stabilise water supplies and reduce the incidence of flooding. And while paddies may look as though they support no other forms of life, they're often full of frogs, spiders and tiny moths. Unfortunately, many places are also infested by a species of snail. Known in English as golden apple snails (*Pomacea canaliculata*), these gastropods are not native to Taiwan. Introduced to the island from South America in 1979 because it was thought they'd be a popular foodstuff (they're high in protein but taste awful, even when processed), they've become a major pest because they feed on young rice shoots. Unlike their dry-land counterparts, they have tubular snorkels which enable them to stay safely submerged. They reproduce very fast: vivid pink egg masses are deposited just above the waterline to protect them from predation by fish.

As demand for organically grown food increases, more and more farmers are embracing traditional methods such as raising ducks in their rice fields. Not only do these fowl eat golden apple snails and other pests, but their feet stir the soil and their excrement is a good fertiliser. Several places in Taiwan are promoting their organic rice. Luoshan (see page 298) has been one of the most successful.

WHERE TO STAY AND EAT Between Hualien City and Taitung City the best places for eating are Chenggong and Dulan. The former has good seafood whereas the latter has a few expat-run startups.

Qi Li Xiang (6 rooms) km97.8; 089 801 118; m 0955 258 514. A sizeable property between the coast road & the ocean midway between Baxian Caves & Sanxiantai, Qi Li Xiang offers plenty of space indoors & out plus a laid-back approach which means the owners are sometimes hard to track down. 4 rooms can take 4 or more ppl. **$$$**

Sea-Hi B&B (5 rooms) km12.5; 03 867 1158; e xylemyj@yahoo.com.tw; www.seahi. idv.tw/english.php. The coast road, especially the stretch through Yanliao between km8 & km15, is dotted with homestays. Sea-Hi B&B, on the ocean side of the road, has certain advantages over many of its competitors: an easy-to-spot English sign, split-level 4-person rooms & a large garden where guests can relax, watch the waves & get Wi-Fi. Room rates NTD2,700–5,500. A little English spoken; b/fast & pick-up from Hualien airport or TRA station inc. **$$$**

WHAT TO SEE AND DO Heading south from Hualien City, the first few kilometres are somewhat bleak. However, by the time you reach Hualien Visitor Centre at km9 you'll be making frequent stops to enjoy the scenery.

Henan Temple (*km11;* 03 867 1001; *06.00–19.00 daily*) This hillside shrine was founded by a Chan master in 1967 who asked the 20 or so resident nuns to propagate the dharma through art, literature and music. It's often possible to stay overnight; calling a few days ahead is best but individuals who roll up unannounced are likely to be given a space to sleep, probably sharing a simple room with another non-monastic (*no AC; donations accepted but not solicited; b/fast available*). Guests should, of course, behave appropriately – it's a strictly vegetarian institution and once the gate is closed it's not possible to go outside until the next day.

Baqi Viewing Platform 芭崎眺望台 (*km31.5*) Because the road is so winding it's easy to miss this spot but do stop if you can to savour the view over the bay.

Fengbin 豐濱 (*km50*) This little town, where 70% of the population is Amis, is where Highway 11A from Guangfu hits the coast.

Shitiping 石梯坪 (*km65*) If you read Chinese, the place name will give you a strong clue as to what to expect. Shitiping means 'stone ladder terrace' and the coast here is dominated by rock platforms that interest both geologists and marine biologists. The local environment, which has both coral reefs and the remnants of ancient volcanic outpourings, nurtures a wide range of tropical fish, crustaceans and algae. It's possible to join whale-watching tours at the fishing harbour here.

Dagangkou 大港口 (*km66*) This is where the Xiuguluan River empties into the Pacific Ocean and where you'll disembark if you've rafted down the Xiuguluan. If you're driving, consider making a detour along Local Road 64, a lovely back-country route through the Coastal Mountain Range to Ruisui.

Baxian Caves 八仙洞 (*km77;* *09.00–17.00 daily; free admission; parking NTD50/20*) A place of tremendous archaeological importance but limited tourist interest, Baxian's 16 caves are collectively named after the Eight Immortals prominent in Taoism and Chinese mythology. Several now contain shrines but between 5,000 and 15,000 years ago humans dwelt here. Since the late 1960s tools made from stone and animal bone have been excavated here, as have fish bones left over from meals and rubbing sticks used to make fire. It's Taiwan's only confirmed Palaeolithic site. When these caves were inhabited they were much closer to the ocean; tectonic uplift has pushed the highest to 130m above sea level. Reaching them means climbing a wooden stairway which, at the time of writing, was in a state of disrepair. A few of the archaeological finds are on display in the visitor centre.

Sanxiantai aka Terraces of the Three Immortals 三仙台 (km112; free admission; parking NTD50/20)

Named after three of Taoism's Eight Immortals, what was originally a little peninsula was worn down by wind and water until it became an island that's now linked to the mainland by a distinctive eight-arch pedestrian bridge. It's the kind of place some visitors dislike with a fervid intensity (it can get crowded) but if you're here on a weekday, you may well find your stop stretches from the planned 20 minutes to over an hour.

Chenggong 成功 (km114)

Every year, in late autumn and early winter, the fishermen who are the backbone of this small town's economy head out to sea and harpoon large numbers of black marlin. Many are exported to Japan or shipped to high-end restaurants in Taipei, but some end up in local eateries, of which there's a cluster between Highway 11 and the fishing harbour. English signs or menus are unknown, alas.

WATCHED WHALES, FORGOTTEN DOLPHINS

During the summer, whale-watching boats set out from Hualien, Chenggong and some other places along the east coast. Tours usually last two to three hours and cost NTD800–1,000 per person. Bring your passport and if you're prone to seasickness, don't eat much in the hours before the tour. A broad hat and sunblock are highly recommended.

Nineteen cetacean species have been recorded off Taiwan's east coast, and if you join a whale-watching tour you're almost certain to see Risso's and Fraser's dolphins and common bottlenose dolphins. With a bit of luck, you'll spot killer whales, pygmy killers or maybe a sperm whale. If you're wondering whether a particular tour operator follows eco-friendly practices, you can check before booking by viewing the list of 'awarded boats' at Whale Watching in Taiwan (*www.whalewatching.org.tw*). Feedback for *Turumoan* (℡ 03 833 3821; *www.turumoan.com.tw*), based in Hualien City, has been especially favourable, in terms of cetaceans seen, the conduct of the crew and the level of English spoken. Ask at any visitor information centre on the coast to ascertain sailing times and other details.

One irony of these tours is that many of those on board have travelled from western Taiwan, and most of them know nothing about the west coast's beleaguered population of Indo-Pacific humpback dolphins. In recent years, the number of these pale pink legally protected creatures has dwindled to fewer than 70 (see *Conservation and Environmental Issues*, page 8). The dolphins face five major threats: pollution, land reclamation, underwater noise, interactions with fishing boats and fishing gear, and reduced freshwater flow into the estuaries within their habitat. The last is crucial because it's the fresh water flowing into salt water which creates the variable conditions that gives rise to the high fish productivity of estuaries.

Shanyuan Beach 杉原海水浴場 *(km155)* One of the east's finest beaches, this 1.5km-long stretch of sand is safe for swimming and surfing. Unfortunately, because of a hotel development of questionable legality at the southern end of the beach, the entrance there has been officially closed for some years and is likely to still be closed when you read this. However, people still use the beach, accessing it via Citong 莿桐部落, an Amis village. If you're near here you may also want to stop in **Dulan**, a mini-town which grew up on the sugar industry but is now home to artists, musicians and big-city self-exiles.

Fugang 富岡 (Fùgāng) *(km161)* This tiny fishing town between Highway 11 and the Pacific Ocean is the jumping-off point for trips to Green Island and Orchid Island (see the entries on those islands in Chapter 10 for ferry details). There are half a dozen eateries, a couple of small supermarkets and a handful of accommodation options. You'll have no problems finding any of these, or the harbour itself. It's OK to leave your vehicle in one of the free car parks near the port for a day or more. If you're coming from the East Rift Valley, approaching via Road 197 is not only scenic but also saves you the trouble of entering Taitung City. Getting here from Taitung City isn't difficult thanks to fairly frequent buses *(NTD23–38)*.

TAITUNG CITY 台東市 (TÁIDŌNG SHÌ) *Telephone code 089*

The importance of this sprawling medium-sized city lies in its location at the southern end of Highway 11. Whether you're journeying down the coast or exploring the East Rift Valley, you'll probably pass through this friendly, but not conspicuously prosperous, administrative and transport centre.

The population of 108,000 includes large aboriginal, Hakka and Hoklo communities. The last group is behind the city's best-known cultural event, the annual Han Dan procession (see box, page 307). These parades are held after dark on the 15th and 16th days of the first lunar month. Like Yanshui's Beehive Fireworks Festival, they coincide with but aren't a true part of the traditional Lantern Festival. The authorities, who initially discouraged the celebration, have in recent years latched on to Han Dan as a means of getting tourist dollars into the city. The event, which involves throwing firecrackers at a semi-naked man, certainly makes for good video clips.

Taitung is famous for its fresh fruit, custard apples being in season between December and February. If you head south from the city, you'll see fields covered with thick black netting under which betel pepper is grown. The betel pepper plant isn't related to the betel-nut palm, but its leaves are used for wrapping betel nuts before they're sold. Around the city you'll see local folk washing big baskets of these dark-green, fist-sized leaves.

GETTING THERE AND AWAY

By train The South Link rail journey from Kaohsiung (*13 expresses ⊕ 06.40–23.00 daily; takes 2¼–3¼hrs; NTD279–362*) is one of Taiwan's most scenic. In the 86km between Fangliao and Zhiben, the track crosses 158 bridges and goes through 36 tunnels, the longest of which is 8.1km. You'll see uninhabited valleys and boulder-filled riverbeds. After the 17th tunnel you'll catch glimpses of the Pacific. From Hualien there are about 17 expresses per day (*departs ⊕ 02.45–21.42 daily; takes 2½–3½hrs; NTD266–345*) and one or two slower trains each day.

By air Taitung Airport (*IATA: TTT;* ✆ *362 530; www.tta.gov.tw*) is 7km from the city centre and easy to reach by taxi or public bus. There are at least six flights to/ from Taipei Songshan Airport each day (*flight time 1hr; NTD2,238 one-way*) and three to/from Green Island (*takes 12mins; NTD1,028*). Six flights to Orchid Island (*takes 25mins; NTD1,345*) are scheduled, but cancellations are common. Departure and arrival times are listed in the English pages of the airport's website.

By bus Buses have an advantage over trains – they bring you directly to the city centre. However, journey times are slightly longer and fares a bit higher. Buses from Kaohsiung (*departs* ⊕ *03.00, 07.00, 12.30 & 17.30; takes 3½hrs; NTD443*) take Highway 9. Eastern Top Transport's inland bus station has services to towns in the East Rift Valley including Guanshan (*14 departures* ⊕ *06.10–20.20 daily; NTD110*), Chishang (*10 departures* ⊕ *07.30–20.20 daily; NTD140*) and Fuli (*departs* ⊕ *08.15, 11.30 & 16.40 daily; NTD160*). Eastern Top Transport has one bus per day to Hualien (*departs* ⊕ *06.10; takes 4hrs; NTD494*), as does Hualien Bus Co (*#1127; departs* ⊕ *14.30; takes 4¼hrs; NTD514*). Both of these Taitung–Hualien services take Highway 11 along the coast.

By car, motorcycle or bicycle The absolute best way to enter Taitung is via the South Cross-Island Highway (see page 265) but this route is may well be closed, so there's a good chance you'll approach on Highway 9 from the southeast. Be prepared to share the road with a significant number of lorries. If you're approaching from the north, both the coastal route (see pages 299–303) and the drive through the East Rift Valley (see pages 293–9) are extremely attractive.

GETTING AROUND

By bus From Eastern Top Transport's coastal bus station there are 13 #8129 buses in each direction daily between the city centre and Zhiben National Forest Recreation Area (*departs* ⊕ *06.00–21.15 daily; takes 40mins; NTD63*) via Zhiben TRA Station and the hot springs (*NTD48*). Nine services daily link Taitung TRA Station (⊕ *08.10– 18.25 daily*) with the inland station. From Eastern Top Transport's coastal station there are another 17 services daily to the railway station (⊕ *05.40–21.20 daily*), some of which go on to places like Chenggong, plus 12 to the airport (⊕ *07.20–19.40 daily*). Trips to the TRA station or the airport take about 20 minutes and cost NTD23.

By hired car

🚗 **Car Plus Auto Leasing** Beside the TRA station; ✆ 227 979; www.car-plus.com.tw;

⊕ 08.00–20.30 daily. General-use car rentals & long-term leasing.

BIKING THE EAST WITH GIANT

Taiwan-based Giant Bicycles (*www.giant-bicycles.com*), one of the world's leading bike manufacturers, offers bike-rental services at several of its shops around the island. With careful planning it's possible to pick up top-quality bikes, helmets, panniers and other equipment at certain branches in east Taiwan, use them for a few days, then return everything to a different branch. At the time of writing, Giant had yet to publish information about this facility in English, but if you send an email in English to one of the branches (*Hualien City* e *giant.d21134@msa.hinet.net; Taitung City* e *giant.d21139@msa.hinet.net*) well in advance of your arrival, it should be possible to arrange what you want.

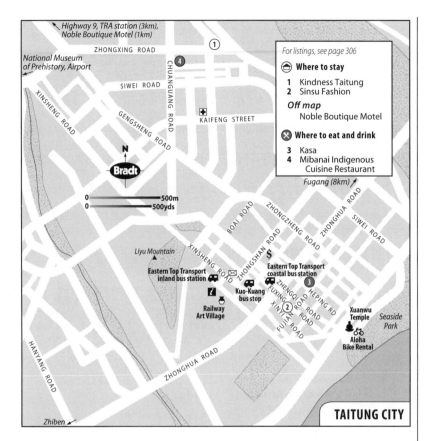

For listings, see page 306

🛏 **Where to stay**
1 Kindness Taitung
2 Sinsu Fashion
Off map
Noble Boutique Motel

❌ **Where to eat and drink**
3 Kasa
4 Mibanai Indigenous
  Cuisine Restaurant

TAITUNG CITY

By rented bicycle

🚲 **Aloha Bike Rental** 22 Nanhai Rd; ☎ 323 273; m 0953 741 055; ⏰ 08.00–19.30 daily. Located near the Seaside Park; decent, full-size bikes for NTD150 per day.

🚲 **Giant** Beside Taitung TRA Station; ☎ 235 879; ⏰ 09.00–18.00 Mon–Fri, 08.00–18.00 Sat–Sun.

By taxi Two male English-speaking taxi drivers offer tours of the Taitung area: Wang Po-chiang (m *0937 397 100*) and Allen (m *0920 928 255*). Both charge around NTD3,500 for eight-hour excursions; call well in advance to book and say which places you hope to see.

LOCAL TOUR OPERATOR

Cheryl Robbins m 0923 151 965; e cheryl@tribe-asia.com. Originally from California but now based in Taitung, this ROC-licensed tour guide & travel writer specialises in Taiwan's indigenous areas & cultures.

TOURIST INFORMATION There are visitor information centres in the airport, TRA station and Railway Art Village (all ⏰ *09.00–17.00 daily*). **Tour Taitung** (*http://tour.taitung.gov.tw*) is a useful official website.

 WHERE TO STAY There are a dozen homestays within walking distance of the train station but few have English signs. The following hotels are shown on the map above.

⌂ **Kindness Hotel Taitung** (90 rooms) 16, Lane 209, Zhongxing Rd Sec 1; ☎229 226; f 227 200; http://taidong.kindness-hotel.com.tw. This spotlessly maintained chain hotel has just one flaw & it's one that afflicts almost every hotel in the Taitung area: very little English is spoken. At least you'll have no problems getting online – in addition to the broadband & Wi-Fi throughout the buildings, there are PCs in the lobby. Guests can borrow bikes for free. Buffet b/fast, free ice cream & popcorn around the clock inc. **$$$**

⌂ **Noble Boutique Motel** (43 rooms) Km373.5, Hwy 9; ☎238 199; f 236 199; www.noblemotel. com.tw. This plush motel is conveniently located for Taitung City's airport & TRA station. Rooms (not all of which have their own integral garage) are quite spacious & tastefully decorated in pale golds & browns. All have jacuzzis, big beds & big TVs. A few scratches here & there but very clean. W/day prices go as low as NTD1,780. There's no English sign out front apart from the big illuminated word 'Motel'. B/fast inc. **$$$**

⌂ **Sinsu Fashion Hotel** (40 rooms) 243 Fujian Rd; ☎311 777; f 311 899; e sinsu311777@yahoo. com.tw; www.sinsu.com.tw. A good mid-range option in the city centre, Sinsu is notable for its attractive off-peak walk-in rates. Couples can sometimes get a room for less than NTD1,800. Massage bathtubs in some rooms & guests can use the hotel's bicycles for free. **$$**

✗ **WHERE TO EAT AND DRINK** Both of the following establishments are shown on the map on page 305.

✗ **Kasa** 卡薩 102 Heping St; m 0985 386 759; ⏱ 18.00–02.00 daily. Co-owned by a Texan & a local, Kasa has been around for some years & occupies an atmospheric old building that's ideal for a semi-outdoor restaurant-bar. Not everything listed on the EM (which has curries & Western snacks) is available every day, but usually specials plug the gaps. **$$**

✗ **Mibanai Indigenous Cuisine Restaurant** 米巴奈 470 Chuanguang Rd; ☎231 084; www. mibanai.com.tw; ⏱ 11.30–14.00 & 17.00–22.00 daily. First the bad news: there's no EM & while the workers speak a number of languages (inc Amis & Puyuma) English isn't among them. Now the good news: this long-running aboriginal restaurant is very clean & very popular with local tourists. Enlist a Mandarin-speaker or choose a set menu that fits your budget. **$$**

WHAT TO SEE AND DO

Round the City Bike Path Going anticlockwise from the Seaside Park, the first point of interest along this 21km-long track is **Railway Art Village aka Tiehua Village** (⏱ *24hrs daily, galleries* ⏱ *varies*). The public art displayed around Taitung's original railway station (trains stopped coming here in 2001) isn't likely to bowl you over but the information centre here is convenient and there's often live music (⏱ *20.00–22.00 Wed–Sat & 16.00–18.00 Sun; typical admission NTD250*). The bike path goes inland but not all the way to the National Museum of Prehistory before turning northeast and skirting the new TRA station. Pedalling onward, you'll pass within sight of the topographical oddities of **Little Huangshan** and **Liji Badlands**. The latter is somewhat like Tainan's Moonscape World. The final stretch through **Taitung Forest Park** is always pleasant.

National Museum of Prehistory 國立臺灣史前文化博物館 (Guólì Shǐqián Wénhuà Bówùguǎn) (☎ *381 166; www.nmp.gov.tw;* ⏱ *09.00–17.00 Tue–Sun; admission NTD80/50*) A long haul from the city centre, this museum is worth visiting only if you're strongly interested in Taiwan's distant past. Skim the sections about Taiwan's geological history and prehistoric animal population (which included rhinos and horses) then head downstairs to read about the prehistoric cultures which flourished in Taiwan more than 2,000 years ago. Academics have yet to determine what relationship, if any, exists between the ancient Beinan people who inhabited this part of Taiwan and modern aboriginal groups such as the

Puyuma (known in Mandarin as the *Bēinán* tribe). Traces of the Beinan culture were uncovered during the Japanese colonial era but there was no concerted effort to retrieve and catalogue the remnants until work began on Taitung's new railway

SCORCHING HAN DAN

Every year in Taitung, volunteers take turns to have firecrackers hurled at their heads and bottle rockets fired at their bodies. Wearing nothing but red shorts, gloves, goggles to protect their eyes and wet cloths over their ears and throat, these men are carried through the crowd on a bamboo-and-rattan litter which they share a doll-sized effigy of a god. Han Dan's followers agree the deity they honour was once an ordinary mortal, but details of his earthly career are in dispute. Most think he was a general who died over 3,000 years ago and who subsequently became a god of war and wealth. It's said that, because he hates the cold, he bestows good fortune on whoever warms him by showering his icons with fireworks. However, a minority believe Han Dan lived much more recently, and that he was a thug guilty of extortion and violence. Eventually, showing remorse for his crimes, he urged the people he'd terrorised to scorch him with fireworks. They did so with a vengeance – the repentant ex-gangster was blasted to death.

The ritual bombardment sounds dangerous and it is: few of the human Han Dans can endure more than ten minutes on the litter; all of them suffer wheals and minor burns. Unlike the shamans of Taiwanese folk religion, they are neither possessed by their patron deity nor in a state of trance – no wonder many swig liquor while waiting their turn. Each Han Dan wears several amulets and carries a bushy banyan branch. The latter has multiple functions: banyan leaves are said to ward off evil; the branch can be used to block incoming rockets; and when the Han Dan wants to throw in the towel, he waves the branch above his head.

According to Ho Chao-ti's superb 2006 documentary *The Gangster's God: A Film of the Taiwanese Underworld*, most of those who climb atop the litter are current or ex-mobsters. Some are new recruits; by taking part, they hope to show how tough and resolute they are, and so gain standing in criminal circles. However, her interviews with older participants revealed more complex reasons for wanting to have fireworks hurled at them: low self-esteem and a desire to suffer physical pain because they're overwhelmed with guilt about past misdeeds.

Nowadays the event is sponsored by local businesspeople who see it as a good way of getting publicity. In addition to paying for the fireworks, they present each Han Dan with cash in a red envelope and sometimes a small gold medal. There has been a complete about-face in officialdom's attitude. The ritual, first held in 1954, was banned between 1983 and 1989 because of its gang links. In recent years, however, the scorching of Han Dan has been heavily promoted by the authorities. Recent human Han Dans have included the mayor of Taitung City, an English teacher from South Africa and a local young woman.

Visitors who speak Chinese and have an especial interest in folk beliefs may want to visit **Xuanwu Temple** 玄武堂 (*9, Lane 5, Datong Rd;* ⏱ *approx 08.00–19.00 daily*). This modest shrine was established in the front room of an ordinary house near the Seaside Park so Han Dan's followers would have a place to meet and worship.

station in 1980. Some 1,523 slate coffins were found, as were the jade knives and arrowheads now displayed in the museum. The main archaeological site, 4.5km northeast of the museum, has been turned into **Beinan Culture Park** 卑南文化公園, and one of the original excavations has been preserved under a canopy (⏰ *08.30–17.00 daily; free admission*). Don't go out of your way as there's very little to see. But if you've time to kill before boarding a train (the station's 400m away), the park's a lovely place to linger.

Zhiben Hot Springs 知本溫泉 **(Zhīběn Wēnquán)** This perennially popular destination 17km southwest of the city (sometimes spelled 'Jhihben') has a decent range of hotels, some of which have public pools where you can soak for a few hours provided you have a swimsuit. That said, there are no standouts and before committing yourself to a particular establishment, you may want to ask whether it's possible to take a shower in ordinary tap water, as not every establishment offers an alternative to sulphur-tainted hot springs water. If you're here and feel like some exercise, follow the signs to **Jade Waterfall** 白玉瀑布. The trail is safe but steep; both the fall and the surroundings are very pleasant.

Zhiben National Forest Recreation Area 知本森林遊樂區 **(Zhīběn Sēnlín Yóulèqū)** (*http://recreation.forest.gov.tw*; ⏰ *07.00–17.00 Oct–Jun, 07.00–18.00 Jul–Sep; admission NTD100/50 Sat–Sun & national holidays, NTD80/50 Mon–Fri*) Some 5km past the main cluster of hotels, this 111ha reserve encompasses patches of semi-rainforest and restored mixed forest. The highest point on the trail network is a pavilion exactly 500m above sea level. The less-than-180-degree views from this spot don't really justify the exertion required by the short, steep approach – but the macaques you'll encounter *en route*, plus the giant banyan trees and numerous butterflies, certainly do. Leave enough time in your schedule for the delightful (and free) geothermal foot bath and the medicinal herbs garden.

10

Minor Islands

Each of the ROC's minor islands has its own appeal, but a few generalisations can be made. They're all thinly populated – fewer than 1% of the country's citizens live in the places described in this chapter – and apart from fishing, tourism and small-scale agriculture there's little economic activity. As a consequence, none of them suffer from industrial pollution or traffic jams.

Two kinds of Western visitor are drawn to these islands: those fanatical about watersports or birdwatching and those who want to see something quite different from 'mainland' Taiwan. Little Liuqiu and Green Island can be done as day trips, although staying overnight is recommended. The counties of Kinmen and Penghu deserve at least three days each. Both are quite different from Taiwan in terms of scenery as well as being exceptionally rich in history and architecture. The Matsu Islands and Orchid Island (the only ROC island to have an Austronesian culture) are fascinating but difficult to get to and return from. Because of transport problems, if you're heading to either give yourself at least two spare days between your planned return to Taiwan and your flight out of the country.

The ROC has two other far-flung maritime outposts. Wuqiu (population: 642) lies midway between Kinmen and Matsu, 9km from the nearest PRC-held territory. Save for the ROC servicemen posted there, very few outsiders have been able to visit Wuqiu and obtaining permission to go there is practically impossible. Pratas, a single island and two submerged atolls 400km southwest of Kaohsiung, falls under Dongsha Atoll Marine National Park. The only inhabitants are coastguard personnel and a few marine scientists but sometime in 2014 the park is expected to be ready for small environmental-education tours.

Between the KMT's retreat to Taiwan in 1949 and the 1980s, Kinmen, Matsu and Wuqiu were on the front-line of the Nationalist–Communist conflict. Now that Taipei–Beijing relations are more peaceful it's possible to travel by ferry between Kinmen and the Fujianese city of Xiamen, or from Matsu to Mawei near Fuzhou. Ironically, the easing of tensions has hurt the islands' economies. Because the ROC military presence on Kinmen, Matsu and Penghu has shrunk from more than 125,000 soldiers in the late 1950s to fewer than 20,000, local businesses like restaurants, karaoke parlours and brothels are feeling the pinch.

Taiwan's domestic airlines offer some good flight/airport pick-up/hotel packages to Penghu, Kinmen and Matsu. These can be booked online, although you'll need the help of a Taiwanese friend or local tour operator if you don't read Chinese. Changing money is easy on Penghu and Kinmen, but if you're heading to any of the other islands do carry enough cash for the entire trip.

Located on the Tropic of Cancer some 45km west of Taiwan, all but one of Penghu County's 90 islands emerged from the sea as a result of volcanic activity. When the basaltic lava pouring from the ocean bed between eight and 17 million years ago cooled, it formed the hexagonal columns which give the archipelago's cliffs and tablelands a special appearance.

Han people began settling the islands nearly a thousand years ago, but Penghu didn't become part of the Chinese empire until a Yuan Dynasty official was sent to administer them in 1281. The population grew very slowly because life was harsh. Farming was difficult and pirate raids were so frequent that in 1372 the imperial authorities commanded the inhabitants to return to the Chinese mainland. Not everyone left, it seems – in 1404 visiting officials ordered another evacuation. Again many stayed on. Dutch vessels visited in 1604 and in 1622 the VOC began building a fort. Two years later, however, the Chinese emperor ordered them to leave – and sent so many ships and soldiers the Dutch had no choice but to go. Because they couldn't set up a permanent base on Penghu, they landed at what's now Tainan (see *History*, page 11). The Dutch weren't the first Westerners to set eyes on Penghu – during the 16th century, Portuguese sailors heading for Japan came here and named the islands Pescadores, meaning 'fishermen'. Seafood has always been a staple because the climate is too dry and the soil too sandy for many crops; you'll see no rice fields. Also, farmers have to surround their vegetable patches with high walls to keep out the strong, salt-bearing winds. Along with beaches and ancient, abandoned houses, these windbreaks – usually piled-up chunks of basalt – are one of Penghu's distinctive and recurring sights. During the Japanese colonial era, one of the archipelago's few non-fish exports was lime, produced by firing a mixture of sand, coral and sea shells. More recently, the central and local governments have been saying that casinos would give the islands' economy a big boost, but when a referendum was held in 2009, county residents rejected the proposal. Many folk worried that gambling would bring crime and other social problems, and it's been argued that the islands simply don't have enough fresh water to cope with a surge in visitor numbers.

Over time, Penghu's population (currently 99,000) has been shifting away from the remoter villages and islands and towards Magong, the county's administrative centre and a city rich in historical flavour. If you arrive by plane, you'll notice the county is pretty flat. The highest point on the main island (also called Penghu) is 48m above sea level. The islands used to be almost treeless, but in recent decades government-sponsored afforestation efforts have changed this. Among the archipelago's ecological attractions are turtles and avians. The green turtles (*Chelonia mydas japonica*) that lay their eggs on Wangan Island between May and October are an endangered species protected by ROC law. Cat Island, despite its name, is a haven for seabirds.

The peak months of July and August are best avoided because of the crowds and the heat. June is a good time to come, as is September. Generally speaking, winter in the archipelago isn't much fun as chilly winds blast the landscape. However, each cold season has at least a few windows of excellent weather, each lasting several days. If you're thinking of making a special trip for watersports, check the wind forecasts on www.windguru.cz before confirming the dates.

GETTING THERE AND AWAY
By air
To Magong Extra flights are laid on during summer but to Magong Airport (*IATA: MZG;* ✎ *922 9123; www.mkport.gov.tw*) you can depend on at least 17

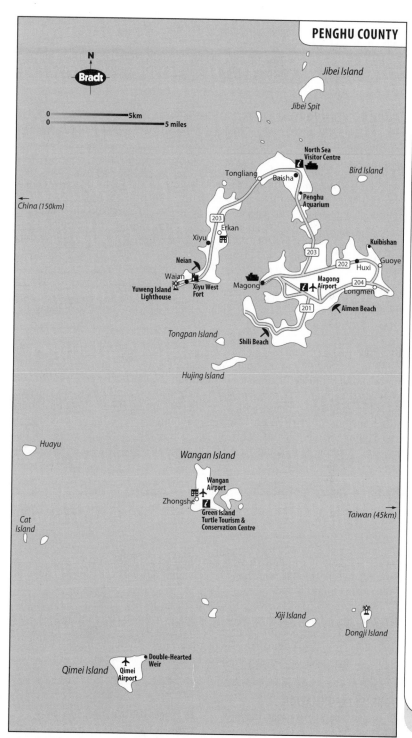

N

Bradt

0   5km
0   5 miles

Jibei Island

Jibei Spit

North Sea
Visitor Centre

Bird Island

← China (150km)

Tongliang   Baisha

Penghu
Aquarium

203

Erkan

Xiyu

Kuibishan

203

202   Huxi   Guoye

Neian

Waian

Yuweng Island
Lighthouse

Xiyu West
Fort

Magong

Magong
Airport

204

Longmen

201

Aimen Beach

Tongpan Island

Shili Beach

Hujing Island

Huayu

Wangan Island

Wangan
Airport

Zhongshe

Green Island
Turtle Tourism &
Conservation Centre

Cat
Island

Taiwan (45km) →

Xiji Island

Dongji Island

Qimei Island

Qimei
Airport

Double-Hearted
Weir

per day to/from both Taipei Songshan (*flight time: 45mins; typical one-way fare NTD2,050*) and Kaohsiung (*40mins; NTD1,718*), around 12 to/from Taichung (*35mins; NTD1,610*) and five to/from Tainan (*30mins; NTD1,562*). There are also one or two daily flights to/from Chiayi (*30mins; NTD1,596*). Most of the aircraft used are twin-propeller.

To the other islands There are one or two flights per day between Kaohsiung and Qimei Island (*flight time: 35mins; NTD1,750*) and two per week between Kaohsiung and Wangan Island (*40mins; NTD1,850*).

By boat The *Taihwa* sails from Kaohsiung to Magong year-round (*takes 4–6hrs; from NTD860 one-way*). This vessel is quite large (it carries over a thousand people plus cars and trucks) and thus more stable when the seas are rough. As with all Taiwan–Penghu ferries, you'll need a Chinese-speaker to ascertain sailing dates and confirm ticket prices (*Kaohsiung* ✆ *07 561 5313 ext 9; Magong* ✆ *06 926 4087; www. tnc-kao.com.tw*). In the warmer months there are other, faster services including one operated by All Star Co Ltd (*usually three departures per day;* ✆ *05 347 0948); takes 1½hrs; NTD1,000 one-way*) from Budai in Chiayi County.

GETTING AROUND
By air Every afternoon there's one flight in either direction between Magong and Qimei (*takes 15mins; NTD1,020*).

By boat Ferries from Magong to Wangan, Qimei and other islands to the south leave from around the South Sea Visitor Centre. The best way to confirm times and ticket prices is to go there in person the day before you want to sail; your hotel or homestay may be able to help make arrangements. In summer there are quite a few choices with many tourists opting for day-long boat tours which include short stops on Wangan and Qimei, and perhaps also Tongpan and Hujing islands (*approx NTD750 pp*). There are also some public ferries between Magong and Wangan (*NTD230 one-way*) and Hujing and Tongpan (*both NTD120 one-way*).

By hired car or motorcycle Penghu has an excellent network of broad, flat roads and there isn't much traffic. Even those who lack the courage to ride around Taiwan proper should give serious thought to using a 125cc scooter (*from NTD400 per day*) to explore outside Magong. Scooter-rental businesses can be found near the junction of Zhongzheng Road and Huian Road in central Magong. You may be turned away if you don't have a local license, so it's best to arrange car- or motorcycle-hire through your hotel or homestay. Scooters can also be rented on Wangan and Qimei islands.

By bus The service you're most likely to use is between the airport and central Magong (*23 departures per day;* ⊕ *07.10–18.55; takes 25–40mins; NTD23–51 depending on route*). With some planning you can use buses to reach most of the sights on the main islands; get a schedule from the bus station on Minzu Road in Magong.

TOURIST INFORMATION
🛈 **Penghu County Government** http://tour. penghu.gov.tw

🛈 **Penghu National Scenic Area** www. penghu-nsa.gov.tw

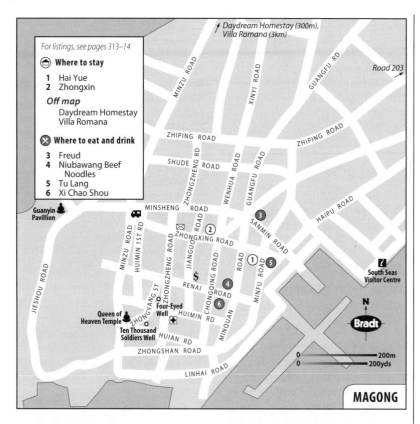

For listings, see pages 313–14

Where to stay

1 Hai Yue
2 Zhongxin

Off map
   Daydream Homestay
   Villa Romana

Where to eat and drink

3 Freud
4 Niubawang Beef
   Noodles
5 Tu Lang
6 Xi Chao Shou

MAGONG

Airport Visitor Information Centre
08.00–19.00 daily

South Sea Visitor Centre 25 Xinrong Rd;
926 4738; 06.30–21.30 daily Apr–Sep,
07.00–17.00 daily Oct–Mar

North Sea Visitor Centre Turn north off Rd
203 near km16; 993 3082; 08.00–17.30 daily

WHERE TO STAY

Magong The following hotels are all marked
on the map above.

Daydream (14 rooms) 237 Yangming Rd;
927 3371; m 0932 467 211; e daydream237@
gmail.com. An imposing villa with Mediterranean-
style décor & huge amounts of common space
indoors, Daydream also has a small swimming
pool, spacious garden & staff who speak a fair bit
of English. The location is suburban enough to be
very quiet yet near enough to the centre for night-
time sorties to Magong's restaurants & bars. B/fast
inc. **$$$**

Hai Yue Hotel (79 rooms) 75 Minfu Rd;
926 9166; e hai.yue@msa.hinet.net. This

town-centre hotel looks as if it was built in the
expectation that hordes of gamblers would be
beating a path to Penghu. The fact they're not is
good for travellers who want a degree of luxury.
Good views, large LCD TVs & broadband in every
room. Little English spoken but if you're arriving
on an off-peak day it's worth asking for a room
upgrade. Buffet b/fast inc. **$$$**

Villa Romana (4 rooms) 581 Xiwei Li; 927
7429; m 0937 604 454; e penghu.villa@gmail.
com; www.villar.com.tw. The 3rd-flr Ocean View
suite with its 2-person bathtub is many guests'
favourite but other suites also have excellent views
thanks to extra-large windows & the homestay's
isolated location at the end of a peninsula. The

entire building reflects the American co-owner's interest in the Greco-Roman period & eco-friendly architecture. Can help arrange car & scooter rental & book activities. B/fast inc. **$$$**

🏠 **Zhongxin Hotel** 中信大旅社 (20 rooms) 22 Zhongxing Rd; ☎ 927 2151. The friendly owners speak not a lick of English but budget travellers won't find a better place to stay. Don't be put off by the frayed hallways as the rooms for 2 ppl – usually priced no higher than NTD700 – are clean & come with TVs, AC & refrigerators. **$**

Outside Magong

🏠 **Be My House** (13 rooms) West of km1 Rd 204; ☎ 922 1045; f 922 1347; e ph0501.yu@msa. hinet.net; www.be-my-house.com. Easy to find & boasting stylish 2-, 3- & 4-person rooms with sofas, Be My House makes a good base for those

wanting to explore the main islands. Guests can barbecue in the garden or order meals in advance if they don't want to drive into Magong for dinner. Very little English spoken but there's an English sign out front. Every room has a refrigerator, kettle & tea/coffee. Adding an extra bed costs NTD500. B/fast inc. **$$**

🏠 **Sunrise B&B** (13 rooms) Guoye Village; ☎ 992 0818; m 0956 065 509; e sunrisebnb2005@ gmail.com; www.sunrisebb.idv.tw. Thanks to its oceanfront location & English-speaking owners, this homestay attracts many Western guests, some of whom come for windsurfing or kayaking (equipment rentals can be arranged). No rooms have balconies but there's a big deck out front. 2nd-flr rooms are especially luxurious & so priced higher. Can arrange car/motorcycle rental; airport pick-up, bike use & b/fast inc. **$$**

✕ WHERE TO EAT AND DRINK

Magong The following establishments are all marked on the map on page 313.

✕ **Freud** 2-1 Xinsheng Rd; ☎ 926 4166; ⏱ 18.00–02.30 daily. By the time you read this, Freud will be in its 3rd decade of existence. Beers from NTD90/bottle, cocktails from NTD140. Drivers will appreciate the wide range of coffees. You're bound to find something you like on the food menu (*hot dishes available* ⏱ 19.00–01.00 daily). There are lamb chops & beef stir-fry; the staff recommend a chicken dish called homemade mixed stew. **$$$**

✕ **Tu Lang Restaurant** 土銀小吃 6, Lane 38, Minfu Rd; ☎ 926 1832; ⏱ 06.00–approx 20.00 daily. The least obvious of the 5 or 6 seafood restaurants clustered around the southern end of Sanmin Rd but recommended by locals. No EM but lots of pictures of dishes on the wall. The shrimp & squid are obvious; the deep-fried balls are made with octopus & highly rated. Alternatively order by pointing at what you want in the tanks & confirm price beforehand. Local beer available. **$$$**

✕ **Xi Chao Shou** 席抄手 25 Renai Rd; ☎ 927 2899; ⏱ 10.30–15.00 & 17.00–00.30 daily. This establishment has been going for decades & serves

up a Sichuanese dish seldom seen in Taiwan – a kind of wonton called *hóng yóu chāo shŏu* 紅油抄手. Split a medium or large portion (choose the level of spiciness according to your preference) & order pork-rib noodles, beef noodles or simply a bowl of steamed white rice to round out the meal. No EM. **$$**

✕ **Niubawang Beef Noodles** 牛霸王牛肉麵 61 Minquan Rd; ☎ 926 9067; ⏱ 11.00–21.00 daily. Tired of fish & craving the flesh of land creatures? Squeeze in between the locals at this simple eatery for steamed dumplings, soups, thin rice noodles or standard noodles; the priciest dish is NTD130. No English sign (look for the bull horns among the Chinese characters) & no EM. **$**

Outside Magong

✕ **Longmen Seafood Restaurant** 58-2 Longmen Village, Huxi; ☎ 992 1277; ⏱ 11.00–20.00 daily. If you don't speak or read Chinese, ordering at a place like this can be hit or miss, as prices & quality (of the raw ingredients; there's no doubting the cook's skill) fluctuate according to weather & season. The photos on the menu help & don't be shy about examining what others are eating. **$$**

OTHER PRACTICALITIES

$ **Bank of Taiwan** 24 Renai Rd

✉ **General Post Office** 70 Zhongzheng Rd; ⏱ 08.00–18.00 Mon–Fri; 08.30–12.00 Sat–Sun. You can change money at this branch.

✚ **Penghu Hospital** 10 Zhongzheng Rd; ☎ 926 1151; ⏱ 24hrs daily

WHAT TO SEE AND DO Penghu's main island is linked by bridges and causeways to Baisha and Xiyu. If you've two or three days only, you probably won't want to venture beyond this horseshoe-shaped landmass.

Magong 馬公 (Mǎgōng)
Queen of Heaven Temple 天后宮 *(Tiānhòu Gōng)* (⊕ *08.00–18.00 daily*)
Until the 1920s, the city's name was written differently and meant 'Mazu temple harbour' – a reference to this shrine, Penghu's most famous place of worship. The temple has been around for at least 400 years and isn't especially large when compared with newer shrines in the county. Its charm lies in its obvious age and the delicacy of its finely carved wooden windows. A thorough restoration, the first since the 1920s, was completed in late 2013. Mazu, goddess of the sea and protector of fishermen, is the main object of veneration, but those interested in the history of interactions between China and the West will discover something more to their liking at the back of the temple on the right – a tall but narrow stele (a stone pillar used to make announcements) dating from 1604. The incised script on it is almost impossible to make out but the meaning is straightforward: it's a demand by a Ming Dynasty general that the Dutch expeditionary force then anchored nearby leave the islands. Those who read Chinese will notice that the stele describes the outsiders not as Dutchmen, Europeans or foreigners, but as 'red-haired barbarians'.

Ten Thousand Soldiers Well 萬軍井 The story is so much better than the reality. In 1683, Qing forces regrouped in Penghu before defeating the Ming loyalists then ruling Taiwan (see *History*, page 13). They were short of water, but their commander, Shi Lang, ordered them to dig at this spot and amazingly a spring was found. These days the well is no more than a concrete ring covered with Perspex. The little temple across the street, **Lord Shi's Shrine** 施公祠 (⊕ *07.00–20.00 daily*) is dedicated to the general.

Four-Eyed Well 四眼井 Magong's other historic well is likely older than the Queen of Heaven Temple. It gets its name from the four narrow openings through which water is drawn. There's said to be a population of goldfish proving the water is healthy; if true, they're good at hiding.

Guanyin Pavilion 觀音亭 (⊕ *06.00–19.00 daily*) After the Queen of Heaven Temple this is the Magong shrine most worth visiting. It's a timeworn place of worship with a sizeable cat population. The main focus, as you'd expect from the name, is the goddess of compassion, but among the deities worshipped in the side chambers are the lords of the North Pole Star and the South Pole Star. This duo sit next to each other. The North Pole Star Lord is a winter god in purple robes; he has a black face and a long black beard. His southern counterpart is almost albino in appearance – pale eyes and skin plus white locks and facial hair. His clothing is orange and blue. Behind the temple, which has been here since 1696, you'll find a clutch of bamboo. This evergreen, so common on Taiwan proper, is almost totally absent from Penghu.

East of Magong
Kuibishan 奎壁山 This is the name of a steep hill next to the village of Beiliao and when the tide's high and the wind is up, it's an especially dramatic location. At low tide it's possible to stroll along a basalt ledge to an islet almost 500m away. Some

maps and signposts use an alternative name, **Penghu Geopark**. When driving to or returning from Kuibishan, do spend a bit of time looking at the dozens of abandoned coral houses in the largely abandoned village of **Nanliao** 南寮 between the hill and Road 202.

Guoye 果葉 This sleepy village's location makes it a favourite with those who like to see the sun rise over the ocean. The 7km-long bike trail that starts here goes southwards to the spot where the Japanese Army first landed in Penghu in 1895. The memorial erected by the colonial regime was converted after 1945 into a monument celebrating Taiwan's return to Chinese rule. It's then a short ride into the fishing village of Longmen 龍門.

Aimen Beach 隘門沙灘 One of the longer strips of sand on the main island, Aimen Beach is just off Road 204.

Shili Beach 時裡沙灘 This 1.2km-long beach is said to be the best on the main island for swimming. There are plenty of toilets, showers and other facilities but it's not overdeveloped nor does it get uncomfortably crowded.

Baisha 白沙 (Báishā) and Xiyu 西嶼 (Xīyǔ)

Penghu Aquarium 澎湖水族館 (58 Qitou Village; ☏ 993 3006; www. penghuaquarium.com.tw; ⏰ 08.30–17.00 daily; admission NTD200/150) The exhibitions in this aquarium focus on Penghu's marine life; some turtles and other largish sea creatures which were rescued after being found sick or injured are here, and there's a shark tunnel. For children, the pools where you can handle starfish and sea cucumbers provide the most fun.

Tongliang 通梁 Located at the northeastern end of the 2.5km-long bridge linking Baisha and Xiyu, this village is notable for the massive banyan tree that sprawls in front of the Baoan Temple, some attractive ruins and vendors who sell prickly-pear ice cream 仙人掌冰淇淋 (xiān rén zhǎng bīng qí lín), a purplish concoction.

Erkan Ancient Residences 二崁古厝 (Erkǎn Gcuò) (near km30 Rd 203) This village's 50-odd enchanting traditional houses now outnumber its permanent inhabitants. The village's oldest ruin, which dates from 1690, is an interesting hodgepodge of coral, stone and mud bricks. Several of the families that used to live in Erkan established Chinese-medicine stores in Taiwan proper because local business and farming opportunities were limited. Among those who returned after making their fortunes were the two brothers who commissioned what's now called the **Chen Family Historical House** (⏰ 08.00–17.00 daily; admission NTD30/15) at number 6. Unlike most houses in the village, which face west, this 1910 Fujianese-Baroque courtyard abode looks southeast. The traditional bedsteads and washstands inside are still in excellent condition, as are the painted wall panels. The yellow-orange pomegranates depicted in one are symbols of fecundity, hundreds of seeds meaning hundreds of descendants; the pumpkin decoration is an emblem of wealth.

Daguoye Columnar Basalt 大果葉柱狀玄武岩 The far side of Erkan if you're coming from Magong, this is a miniature version of the basalt cliffs that distinguish Tongpan Island. The pond in front of the cliff is the result of quarrying; when it's full of water and the sun is shining, the cliffs reflect prettily.

Neian Recreational Area Never crowded because of its distance from Magong, this attractive bay has a decent sandy beach, boardwalks up and down the hillside, and wooden shelters where you can find some shade.

Xiyu West Fort 西嶼西台 ***(Xīyǔ Xītái)*** (☉ *07.00–18.30 daily May–Oct, 08.00–17.30 daily Nov–Apr; admission NTD30/15*) This bastion was built just after the Sino-French War of 1884–85 and equipped with four British-made Armstrong cannons. The current weapons are replicas and the massive stone-and-glutinous-rice walls have been patched up with concrete, but the views across the ocean make stopping here worthwhile. The turn-off, just beyond km34.5 on Road 203, is marked by a boulder bearing an alternative name in Chinese.

Yuweng Island Lighthouse 漁翁島燈塔 (*grounds* ☉ *09.00–16.00 Tue–Sun; free admission*) Yuweng is the old name of the island now officially named Xiyu and there's been a lighthouse on its westernmost promontory since 1778. Several of the lighthouse keepers who served here in the late 19th century were Westerners. The daughter of one died and was buried here in 1890, although it's hard to make out her name, Nelly O'Driscoll, on the grave marker. The current lighthouse is 11m high and dates from 1875; casual visitors aren't allowed inside. To see it, follow the signs and go behind the formidable-looking military installation found 2km down the turn-off from Road 203. Park on the bare earth and follow the track that goes to the right of the base. This area is battered by powerful winds all year round. One of the few plant species that can thrive around here is *Opuntia dillenii*, the cactus from which Penghu's signature prickly-pear ice cream is made. The flowers are yellow; the fruit have green skins and purple flesh.

North of the main islands
Most visitors head straight for Jibei, where there are homestays, scooter rentals and watersports.

Jibei Spit 吉貝沙嘴 ***(Jíbèi Shāzuǐ)*** The 3.1km² island of Jibei is best known for the 800m-long white spit that extends from its southern coast. Shaped like a human tongue, this sand bank is an entirely natural accumulation of tiny coral and shell fragments; it's a dazzling sight that attracts its share of coach parties. Don't ignore other parts of the island, where the beaches are less crowded and hand-built fish-trapping weirs dot the coast.

South of the main islands
It's possible to go directly to Qimei and Wangan from Taiwan; there's no need to transit through Magong.

Tongpan Island 桶盤嶼 So named because it's shaped like the lid (*pán*) of a barrel (*tǒng*), this 0.4km² islet is famous for the imposing basalt columns that face the ocean in every direction.

Hujing Island 虎井嶼 Most of this island's 400 residents live in the low-lying centre of the landmass. There are yet more basalt cliffs at the eastern and western ends and a few remnants of the Japanese military presence before and during World War II.

Wangan Island 望安島 ***(Wàngān Dǎo)*** Wangan's grassy slopes are covered by wooden stairs and walkways which make for easy exploring. In the very centre of the island, **Zhongshe Historic Village** is a place for those who adore the picturesque past. The coral and stone cottages are hugely alluring but for some visitors it's all about the windows. In many cases they're neither square nor rectangular but the shape of a flag billowing in the wind, and adorned with elaborate stone lattices behind which are traditional sliding wooden shutters. Wangan's best-known ecological attraction is the **Green Turtle Breeding Refuge**, six beach locations where during summer and early autumn female turtles wade ashore after dark to lay and bury eggs. It's possible to witness this if you apply well in advance for a permit; access to the beaches is strictly controlled and the nightly quota is just 30 people. Penghu National Scenic Area Headquarters can provide details, as can the **Green Turtle Tourism and Conservation Centre** 綠蠵龜觀光保育中心 (🕾 999 1368; ⏲ 08.30–17.00 daily). The centre, north of Wangan's ferry pier, educates visitors about the turtle population and provides information about other attractions on Wangan. A special bus service shuttles tourists between the docks and the island's points of interest (*departures as needed; tours last 2hrs; NTD150 pp*).

Qimei Island 七美嶼 *(Qīměi Yǔ)* The name of the fifth-largest island in the archipelago means 'seven beauties' and alludes to seven young women who, it's said, killed themselves by jumping down a well more than 450 years ago when Japanese pirates tried to ravish them. Don't bother with their tomb; spend your time enjoying the captivating coastal scenery. The most-photographed sight is the **Double-Hearted Weir** 雙心石滬. This fish trap on the island's northeastern side represents a massive investment of human labour but requires little maintenance. Created by piling up chunks of coral and basalt, the principle is very simple: fish swim in when the tide is high but can't escape when the tide ebbs. This particular weir isn't unique but the vast majority of the 500-odd fish-catching weirs that still exist in the archipelago are far smaller and cruder.

KINMEN COUNTY 金門縣 (JĪNMÉN XIÀN) *Telephone code 082*

When it comes to enjoying these islands, some 277km from Taiwan but within easy shelling distance of mainland China's coast, an interest in Cold War history helps but isn't essential. Here, the Chinese Civil War continued long after Chiang Kai-shek's 1949 retreat to Taiwan (see *History*, page 18). KMT forces dug into the island (quite literally – there are tunnels big enough to hide tanks and boats) and exchanged artillery fire with the Communists on the mainland until 1978. Beaches were turned into minefields and anti-paratrooper spikes were placed in farmers' fields.

Chinese civilisation here is relatively old; some local clans say they've been on the islands for almost 1,200 years. The archipelago's name translates as 'golden door' and alludes to a pair of towers built in the 15th century to keep watch for pirates. The toponym 'Quemoy', an anglicised rendering of how Kinmen is pronounced in the local dialect, is now seldom used except in the name of a local college.

Warfare has left scars but the irony is that, despite decades of conflict, Kinmen's traditional neighbourhoods are more intact than those in Taiwan, where much of the past has been bulldozed in the course of industrialisation. Between the 1950s and 1970s, Kinmenese weren't permitted to move away. The Nationalists feared the county would be depopulated. The official population is currently 115,000, but it's hard to know precisely how many people really live here as many outsiders have registered as residents so they can enjoy cheaper air tickets and discounts on kaoliang (a strong, clear sorghum-based liquor made by an immensely profitable county-owned enterprise and enjoyed throughout the ROC). There's now a regular ferry between Kinmen and the People's Republic of China, so consider making the island your final 'Free China' stop before heading to the mainland.

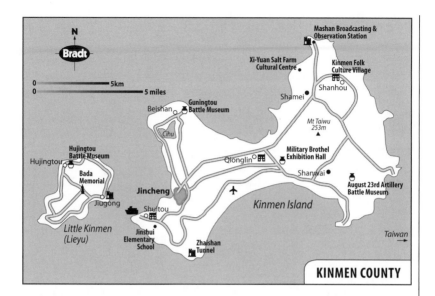

KINMEN COUNTY

Both the ROC and the PRC regard Kinmen County as part of Fujian province. Three of the 15 islands are under Beijing's control; on the ROC side only the main island and Little Kinmen (also known as Lieyu) are accessible to visitors. The land area of the ROC-controlled portion of the county is a little over 151km². The islands are mostly granite and the highest point is 253m above sea level; the main island is 19km long but just 3km across in places.

GETTING THERE AND AWAY
By air Four airlines fly between Taiwan and Kinmen and travellers can depend on at least 16 flights per day from Taipei Songshan (*NTD2,088–2,220 one-way*), eight from Kaohsiung (*NTD1,945–2,019*), six from Taichung (*NTD1,990–2,086*), two from Tainan (*NTD1,990*) and one from Chiayi (*NTD1,891*). Flight time in all cases is around an hour. Flights arrive at Kinmen Shangyi Airport (*IATA: KNH; www.kma.gov.tw*) from where you can take a taxi (*about NTD200 to Jincheng*) or a bus (*NTD12*). If you're just transiting through Kinmen ask your airline about direct buses between the airport and Shuitou Pier.

By sea More than 20 services per day link Shuitou Pier with the Chinese mainland (*takes 45–60mins; NTD650 one-way from Taiwan; RMB180 one-way from China*). There are three destinations on the Chinese side: Dongdu is near central Xiamen while Wutong is convenient for Xiamen Airport. Some boats go to Quanzhou. Sailings are occasionally cancelled because of bad weather. Coming from China, travellers eligible for visa-free entry don't need ROC visas in advance and they can change their RMB into NTD at Shuitou. However, those leaving the ROC must obtain a PRC visa before boarding the ferry; at the time of writing, visa-free transit wasn't possible.

GETTING AROUND
By hired motorcycle Hsu Hsiao-ming (m *0932 970 020*) will rent scooters (*NTD400 per day; NTD1,000 for 3 days*) to holders of international licenses. If you get a Chinese-speaker to call him a day in advance he'll meet you at the airport.

10

By hired bicycle The national park has been promoting cycling, and in many respects (cooler temperatures, little traffic, relatively short distances) Kinmen is better for exploring by bicycle than Taiwan. Bikes can be borrowed for free by anyone over 12 if they deposit ID and sign some paperwork from the following locations: Jinshui Elementary School; Shuangli Wetlands Nature Centre; Zhaishan Tunnel; and Lieyu District Rental Station. Locks and helmets are provided; bikes must be returned the same day. Alternatively, try commercial bike-rental outfits such as **San Hao** (*120 Minzu Rd, Jincheng;* \372 136; ⊕ *08.00–19.00 daily*).

By bus In addition to several conventional bus lines which are inexpensive (*NTD12 one-way*) but infrequent (*departures on most routes about hourly;* ⊕ *06.00–19.00 daily*), special sightseeing buses have been organised by the authorities. Routes and schedules change from one year to the next so ask for details at a visitor information centre.

By boat Work has started on a bridge linking the main island with Little Kinmen and it should be ready by 2017. Until then, you'll need to take a ferry from Shuitou Pier to Jiugong (*departs every ½hr from 07.00; takes 15mins; NTD60 one-way*). Not all ferries can take motorcycles (*NTD50 one-way*) and bicycles (*NTD20 one-way*). The last ferry back to Shuitou leaves Jiugong at 20.30 but the final vehicle-carrying service is at 18.00.

TOURIST INFORMATION Visitor information centres including ones at the airport (⊕ *08.00–18.00 daily*), Zhongshanlin (*on the main rd between central Jincheng & Qionglin;* ⊕ *08.30–17.00 daily*), Jiugong on Little Kinmen (⊕ *08.30–17.00 daily*), Shuitou and Juguang Tower in Jincheng. The last two (⊕ *08.30–17.00 daily*) sometimes close for an hour at lunch.

⛵ Kinmen National Park \313 100; www.kmnp.gov.tw

⛵ Kinmen County Government www.kinmen.gov.tw

LOCAL TOUR OPERATOR

Roland Zhang m 0988 426 727; e roland550727@gmail.com. Affiliated with Shanhou No. 45 Homestay but willing to help tourists wherever they're staying, this friendly English speaker can drive you from sight to sight (*from NTD2,000 per day*).

🏠 WHERE TO STAY

🏠 **Qin Inn** (7 rooms) 64 Qianshuitou, Jincheng; m 0910 395 565; e ijiaqin@gmail.com; http://qininn.tumblr.com. The best of both worlds: all the character of a splendidly preserved old building plus AC & Wi-Fi. No TV 'to allow guests to enjoy genuine historical atmosphere… & cherish spiritual exchange', according to the website. The hosts speak English well enough to provide directions to tourist attractions & restaurants. The cheapest room goes for NTD1,200. B/fast inc. **$$**

🏠 **Shanhou No. 45 Homestay** (5 rooms) 45 Shanhou, Jinsha; \353 745; m 0929 121 008. National park authorities spent over £300,000 renovating this gorgeous Southern Fujianese-style compound in Kinmen's northeast before making it available as a B&B. It's old but guests don't rough it: a lot of the original woodwork remains in place, the furnishings are gorgeous & each room has an LCD TV & Wi-Fi. W/end prices for rooms for 2, 3 or 4 ppl NTD1,800–2,400 with discounts for the second & subsequent nights. B/fast NTD80. **$$**

🏠 **Shuitou No. 37 Homestay** 水頭37號民宿 (6 rooms) 37 Qianshuitou, Jincheng; \328 131; m 0919 761 231. Occupying the rear part of one of Shuitou's finest mansions; many guests relish the chance to sleep in a traditional Chinese wooden bed. There's a conventional mattress & it's pretty comfortable but perhaps isn't for everyone.

Taiwanese b/fast inc. The largest room can take 8 ppl (*NTD4,500*). The village has more than a dozen other old-house homestays; numbers 53, 54 & 85 are also well regarded. **$$**

☝ **Six Brothers Hotel** (30 rooms) 164 Juguang Rd, Jincheng; ☎ 372 888. With rooms priced NTD800–1,800 this is a good option if you've not pre-booked a homestay or want to stay in the heart of the main town. No b/fast. **$$**

✕ WHERE TO EAT

✕ **Chiuan Min Fruit Restaurant** 28-1 Xiabao, Jinning; ☎ 324 489; ⊕ 12.00–14.00 & 18.00–21.00 Thu–Tue. Rather than having a conventional menu, the day's offerings are listed in English & Chinese on a blackboard. Set meals including dessert & fresh juice are often priced NTD600 pp; they may include lamb cooked with papaya, chicken sautéed with rosemary & apple, pork ribs served with pear or seafood dishes flavoured with pineapple. Almost all the fruit

---

LIONS THAT TAME THE WIND

For centuries, Kinmen suffered the consequences of deforestation. A lack of trees meant strong winds lifted soil from fields and dumped it in ponds, hampering agriculture and exacerbating the shortage of fresh water. Islanders have traditionally blamed Koxinga for their predicament, saying he turned their woods into the fleet which carried him and his followers to Taiwan (see *History*, page 12). In fact the problem is much older. From the 14th century onward, local people were cutting down trees so they could boil seawater to obtain salt. The problem wasn't rectified until well after World War II when soldiers were put to work planting saplings.

Because of the sandstorms bedevilling Kinmen, the archipelago's inhabitants prayed to their gods for relief and began erecting lion-spirit statues to negate the winds sometime before 1400. Several were destroyed by communist shells in the 1950s but soon replaced. Almost all take the form of a lion upright on his hind legs, ranging in height from 22cm to 3.8m.

Particularly splendid wind lions can be found in Beishan and Shanhou while the one in Guanao near Mashan has become famous on account of his large penis. The majority of Kinmen's 69 wind lions are found in the north and east parts of the main island; most are on the northeastern edge of the villages they protect and face north or northeast. It's no coincidence that this is the direction from which winds blow, almost non stop, between September and May.

Wind lions aren't found anywhere else in the ROC and they bear little resemblance to the playful-looking lions that guard the entrances of Taiwanese temples. Most are fierce-looking sentinels located in the gustiest parts of several villages. Many were hewn from granite but a few are cement or clay. Several wear superhero-type red capes, donated by the faithful who worry the lions will shiver during gales.

Over time, Kinmen's wind lions have become generalist deities. In addition to countering the wind, villagers ask them for prosperity, baby boys, abundant harvests and protection from demons believed to cause mayhem. They're also believed to repel termites, useful given the amount of wood in Kinmen's traditional buildings. Like land gods, wind lions have birthdays which are celebrated with incense and prayers. Villagers also make offerings at the end of weddings and funerals. Not surprisingly, wind-lion models are a popular souvenir.

comes from Taiwan's main island, not Kinmen. The unusual food, combined with a sleek, modern interior & fine presentation make for a special experience. Reservations required for evenings. $$$$

✗ **Jide Seafood Restaurant (Jìdé Hǎixiān Cāntīng)** 253 Minzu Rd, Jincheng; ☎324 461; ⏰ 11.00–14.00 & 17.00–23.00 daily. You'll need a Mandarin-speaker to help you order at this very central restaurant as no English is spoken & the most interesting dishes are listed in Chinese only on a bulletin board. Among Jide's signature dishes are raw crab served in a slightly spicy kaoliang-based sauce (*gāoliáng qiàng xiè*, NTD200–300 depending on portion size) & sandworms (*shā chóng*, NTD250). Also worth trying are the small but flavoursome oysters & pork ribs with yam (*yùtóu pǎigǔ*). Local beer & liquor available. $$$

✗ **California Cafe** 21, Lane 74, Zhupu S Rd, Jincheng; ☎328 743; ⏰ 11.00–21.00 Wed–Tue. A good option if you're looking for Western food, California Cafe offers a range of pizzas (*most NTD299*), salads & smaller items. Teas & coffees from NTD80. Min charge NTD150 pp. Located in the heart of Jincheng. $$

OTHER PRACTICALITIES

✉ **Post office** 4 Minsheng Rd, Jincheng; ⏰ 07.30–17.00 Mon–Fri, 08.00–11.30 Sat

$ **Land Bank** 60 Minsheng Rd, Jincheng. You can buy or sell Chinese currency at this branch.

✚ **Kinmen General Hospital** 2 Fuxing Rd, Jinhu; ☎332 547; www.kmhp.gov.tw; ⏰ 24hrs daily

WHAT TO SEE AND DO

Jincheng 金城 (Jīnchéng) Kinmen's main town is small enough to be convenient, large enough to have what you need, and sufficiently well preserved that you could spend most of a day here.

Memorial Arch to Qiu Liang-gong's Mother 邱良功母節孝坊 (*Juguang Rd Sec 1*) Commemorative stone archways of this type are called *páifāng* in Mandarin and can be found throughout the ROC. This, the largest and most ornate surviving arch anywhere in Taiwan or Fujian, is in the busiest part of Jincheng. It was built in 1812 to celebrate the loyalty and devotion Qiu Liang-gong's mother showed to the memory of his late father, who predeceased her by 28 years. Qiu, a Kinmen native who held important posts in the imperial civil service, died in 1817 and is buried in a tomb of near-imperial dimensions near Qionglin.

KINMEN CLEAVERS

If you visit Kinmen, the Taiwan-controlled archipelago that's just a few kilometres from the coast of mainland China, you'll be able to pick up a souvenir that is eminently practical and historically interesting but not something you should pack in your carry-on luggage: a meat cleaver.

Between 1949 and 1978, not a week went by without the communist forces on the mainland and the Nationalists on Kinmen exchanging artillery fire. Scavengers searched for shell casings and sold the fragments to blacksmiths, who turned the metal into cleavers and machetes. At first they were sold to locals, but when Kinmen was opened for tourism, the knives – which now come in fancy presentation boxes – proved a surprise hit. Indeed, so many have been sold that now some people wonder if the steel really is recycled war materiel.

Kinmen cleavers are available from several shops in Jincheng and also at the airport.

This neighbourhood is especially busy around breakfast time with both grocers and eateries doing a good trade. One of the best known of the latter, **Qiao Wei Xiang** (*39 Juguang Rd Sec 1;* ⏰ *07.00–19.00 daily; no EM;* **$**), has a reputation for oyster vermicelli. Also worth a quick look is **Kinmen Knife Creator** (*30 Juguang Rd Sec 1;* ⏰ *08.30–17.30 daily*). Inside the workshop you'll see shell casings which the proprietor turns into cleavers and other implements (see box opposite).

Mofan Street 模範街 This short, narrow thoroughfare is on every tour group's itinerary and while it's true the 1924 southeast Asian-style red-brick shops have a certain appeal, your visit isn't likely to exceed a quarter of an hour.

Wu River Academy 浯江書院 (*36 Zhupu N Rd;* ⏰ *08.00–17.30 daily; free admission*) This walled compound is where male youths were schooled in classical literature, calligraphy, mathematics and other disciplines. Most sources say it was founded in 1780 but some believe it could date from as early as 1687; in any case it looks far newer thanks to a loving restoration less than a decade ago. People didn't come here just to study; they also sacrificed incense to Wenchang Dijun, the patron deity for those sitting examinations, and to Zhu Zi (1130–1200), a Confucianist philosopher. As the crow flies the academy is 300m north of the memorial arch.

Juguang Tower 莒光樓 (⏰ *08.00–21.00 daily*) Located less than 1km south of central Jincheng, this quasi-classical pavilion was built in the early 1950s as a memorial to fallen soldiers. Inside there's a small exhibition about wind lions, Kinmen customs and local foodstuffs. Visitors can also watch a 20-minute multimedia introduction to Kinmen. Like the identically named Matsu township (see page 332), the tower's name reflects Chiang Kai-shek's 'retake the mainland, restore China's legitimate government' ideology.

Shuitou 水頭 *(Shuǐtóu)* Exceptionally rich in mansions built by wealthy folk who returned home after making their fortunes overseas, this village is also where you catch ferries to Lieyu or the Chinese mainland. Number 37 Qianshuitou bursts with well-kept character. The geometric patterns on the Japanese ceramic tiles that decorate the front and the shape of some of the window lintels lend the sprawl a slightly Moorish look. Looking at it today, you'd never guess that soon after it was built in 1921 by merchant Huang Shun-tu, bandits ransacked the place and kidnapped two of his relatives. When the same clan later built number 34, which also now functions as a homestay (*5 rooms;* ☎ *328 131;* **m** *0922 972 349;* **$$** *inc b/fast*), they insisted on iron-plate doors and loopholes through which the inhabitants could shoot at attackers. Number 34's white exterior contrasts with the Tuscan and terracotta reds that dominate this and other Kinmen villages.

Zhaishan Tunnel 翟山坑道 (⏰ *08.30–16.30 daily; free admission*) This 357m-long sea-level bomb shelter is a monument to what can be achieved if you've got a workforce that's healthy, strong and utterly obedient. Like the longer Jiugong Tunnel on Little Kinmen, it was chiselled out by soldiers in the early 1960s so boats could bring in reinforcements and supplies even when the shelling was at its fiercest.

Cihu 慈湖 Birdwatchers head to this man-made brackish lake in the northwest to see great cormorants and other waterbirds. October to March is the best season for twitching as the majority of the 280 bird species regularly seen in Kinmen County are winter migrants. There's more for ecotourists a very short distance to the north at the **Shuangli Wetlands Nature Centre** 雙鯉濕地 (⊕ *08.30–17.00 daily; free admission*). Displays expound on marine life as well as birds and aquatic plants; there's also a large semi-submerged window allowing you to see some of what's happening beneath the water surface.

Guningtou 古寧頭 *(Gǔníngtóu)* This is where the Nationalist Army defeated communist units in a 56-hour battle on 25–27 October 1949, establishing a line of control that hasn't to this day changed. The story is told inside the **Guningtou Battle Museum** 古寧頭戰史館 (✆ *313 274*; ⊕ *08.30–17.00 daily; free admission*). Also make a point of locating **Beishan Old Western-Style House** 北山古洋樓. It's far more interesting than its name suggests and not only because its designer blended Fujianese and 19th-century European architecture. It's riddled with bullet holes from the 1949 battle and much loved by shutterbugs.

East Kinmen For food and drink try Shamei 沙美 or Shanwai 山外.

Qionglin 瓊林 Kinmen is often described as being the shape of a dumb-bell and this ancient village is close to the narrowest part of the island. The Nationalists paid special attention to its defences, reckoning that if the Communists invaded, the attackers would try to cut the island in two here; in fact, the communist units involved in the Battle of Guningtou had intended to make their landings near Qionglin but were pushed west by the wind and current. **Qionglin Tunnel** 瓊林坑道 (⊕ *08.00–12.00 & 13.00–17.30 daily; admission NTD10*) was part of the fortification/bomb shelter system and it's fun to explore the underground corridors and chambers. The tunnel's total length is 1,355m and most of the network is around 6m underground. Near where you enter the tunnel there's an especially fine wind lion.

Military Brothel Exhibition Hall (⊕ *08.30–17.00 daily; free admission*) Between the early 1950s and 1990, the ROC's armed forces ran a network of brothels on the front-line islands and this single-floor building housed one such establishment. The bilingual displays are interesting as far as they go. Charts comparing the price of 30 minutes' sexual services and soldiers' salaries show sex was considerably cheaper in the 1980s than in the early days. However, nowhere is it made clear whether soldiers had to buy the coupons with which they paid the girls (direct payment in cash wasn't allowed) or whether coupons were sometimes given out as rewards. The displays stress that no women were forced to work in the brothels yet fail to explain the recruitment process; some Taiwanese say many of the 'volunteers' were arrestees offered a choice – trial and probably jail, or two years' working in a military brothel. Inside the hall there's a coffee shop (⊕ *10.00–17.00 daily; EM; $$*).

Xi-Yuan Salt Farm Cultural Centre 西園鹽場 (⊕ *09.00–17.00 Tue–Sun; free admission*) Producing salt by evaporating seawater is an age-old but now defunct industry along the coast of southern China and Taiwan. The ponds here were in almost constant use between the 13th century and 1995; they're now maintained as a tourist attraction and an educational site.

Mashan Broadcasting and Observation Station 馬山觀測站 (⊕ *08.00–12.00 & 13.00–17.00 daily, closed Lunar New Year's Eve & Day; free admission*) From this vantage point – a bunker reached via a narrow tunnel – you can look through telescopes at PRC fishing boats and people on the mainland going about their business. The distance to communist-controlled dry land varies between 1.8 and

2.1km, depending on the tide. From this same spot the Nationalists formerly used huge loudspeakers to make propaganda broadcasts which could be heard on the Chinese side. The observation post is part of an active army base, so take note of the rules posted at the entrance.

Kinmen Folk Culture Village 金門民俗文化村 *(Jīnmén Mínsú Wénhuà Cūn)* (*Shanhou Village;* ⊕ *08.30–17.30 daily; free admission*) Old villages in Taiwan and China tend to be higgledy-piggledy, so the symmetrical rows of perfectly maintained traditional homes that make up this very worthwhile outdoor museum come as a surprise. There are 16 residences, an ancestral shrine and a classroom where scions of the Wang clan – who built this complex after making a fortune by trading with Japan – were tutored in the Confucian classics. The exquisite swallow-tail roof ridges, which signified success in imperial civil-service examinations, were appropriate when the architects were commissioned at the very end of the 19th century. However, by the time the buildings were completed in the mid-1920s those examinations – like the empire itself – were a thing of a past. Inside you'll see some of the original furniture plus clothing from the same era.

Mount Taiwu 太武山 This isn't an imposing mountain by any standards but there's a fair bit to see around here, including a large cemetery dedicated to Nationalist soldiers who died in 1949's defensive battles, a memorial to Koxinga and Kinmen's largest freshwater lake. Beneath the mountain, protected from falling bombs by several metres of granite, there's a fully equipped hospital. You can ride a bike or motorcycle about halfway up the mountain and then continue on foot; it's a pleasant hike.

August 23rd Artillery Battle Museum 八二三戰史館 (⊕ *08.30–17.00 daily; free admission*) Named for the massive artillery campaign that began on 23 August 1958, this thorough museum is filled with and surrounded by hardware used in the battle. The bombardment didn't take the Nationalists by surprise – mainland radio stations had predicted the imminent liberation of Quemoy and intelligence-gathering overflights of communist bases on the mainland confirmed something was afoot. Nonetheless, the garrison barely survived the onslaught and would probably have been overrun had it not been for Washington's moral and material support.

Little Kinmen/Lieyu 小金門/烈嶼 (Lièyǔ)
Jiugong 九宮 You'll disembark beside a granite promontory that's not quite as solid as it looks. Five minutes' walk from the ferry dock, the entrance to **Jiugong Tunnel 九宮坑道** (⊕ *08.30–17.00 daily; free admission*) leads into Kinmen's largest underground military installation. Excavated after the 1958 artillery war, the main chamber here is 780m long, 10m high and 15m wide. Patrol boats, landing craft and small cargo vessels carrying supplies for the civilian population could moor here in safety during bombardments.

Bada Memorial 八達樓子 Located in the centre of the island, this memorial is an imitation of a tower on the Great Wall of China. The bronze statues on top celebrate seven Nationalist soldiers who died on the wall after holding back thousands of Japanese attackers for five days during a 1933 incursion.

Hujingtou 湖井頭 Unreconstructed Cold War hawks have two reasons to visit this village. Firstly, it's possible to gaze at the coast of communist China. Secondly,

Hujingtou Battle Museum 湖井頭戰史館 (🕐 *08.30–17.00 daily; free admission*), housed in a squat concrete building with crenellated walls, details some of the Nationalist Army's most heroic moments.

MATSU NATIONAL SCENIC AREA 馬祖國家風景區 (MĂZŬ GUÓJIĀ FĒNGJĬNGQŪ) *Telephone code 0836*

The northernmost outpost of the ROC is a cluster of 19 rocky islands 114 nautical miles (211km) from Taiwan. Life on the archipelago (total land area: 29.6km^2) has never been easy as there's little flat land and the growing season is short. Pirates were a scourge in the Qing Dynasty and during the 1950s and 1960s the islands were often shelled by communist forces. Gaodeng, just 9.25km from the mainland, is still off-limits to civilians because of the ROC military's presence. Nangan and Beigan have far more woodland now than before World War II. Knowing trees can hide gun emplacements, the armed forces took the business of afforestation very seriously; for a time, every conscript was assigned a sapling to care for and faced jail if his tree died.

The toponym Matsu derives from that of Mazu, the sea goddess revered throughout Taiwan and Fujian. Some believe Mazu's remains lie beneath a temple on Nangan, the largest island, and while a few Taiwanese come here for religious reasons, the majority of tourists are drawn by a combination of rugged scenery, distinctive and enduring granite cottages and military history. In June, July and August many birders come hoping to see the extremely rare Chinese crested tern, a species long believed extinct until it was rediscovered in these islands in 2000. To protect it and other avian species, eight uninhabited islands have been designated the Matsu Islands Tern Refuge.

Since 1974, the archipelago's civilian population has declined from 17,000 to just under 10,000, two thirds of whom live on Nangan. Even when servicemen are excluded, there's a serious gender imbalance: males outnumber females 58:42. Most islanders are of Fujianese descent but rather than speak Taiwanese Hokkien, the day-to-day language is Fuzhou dialect.

In a July 2012 referendum, Matsu residents voted in favour of allowing gambling resorts to be built on the islands. Opponents agree the islands need better transport links, but doubt casino developments would bring long-term economic benefits.

GETTING THERE AND AWAY Air travel between Matsu and Taiwan is often disrupted by weather conditions; allow at least one safety day if you've an international flight to catch.

By air Five or six flights per day (*departs* 🕐 *06.50–16.00*) leave Taipei Songshan Airport and land at Nangan Airport (*IATA code: LZN;* ☎ *26522*) while three (*departs* 🕐 *08.00, 13.00 & 18.10*) head for Beigan Airport (*IATA code: MFK;* ☎ *56576*). On both routes flight time is 50 minutes and one-way fare NTD1,962. There's also a daily flight from Taichung to Nangan (*departs* 🕐 *11.40; flight time: 1hr 5mins; NTD2,336 one-way*). All flights are operated by UNI Air (☎ *02 2518 5166*).

By sea The *Taima* ferry (*Keelung* ☎ *02 2424 6868; Nangan: 26655*) is the cheapest way of getting to the islands. Passengers should arrive at Pier West 2 in Keelung before 21.30 as the boat sails at 22.50. On odd days of the month the ferry's first stop is Nangan around 07.00. At 09.00 the vessel leaves for Dongyin, arriving 11.30. It then returns to Keelung, getting there seven hours later. On even days

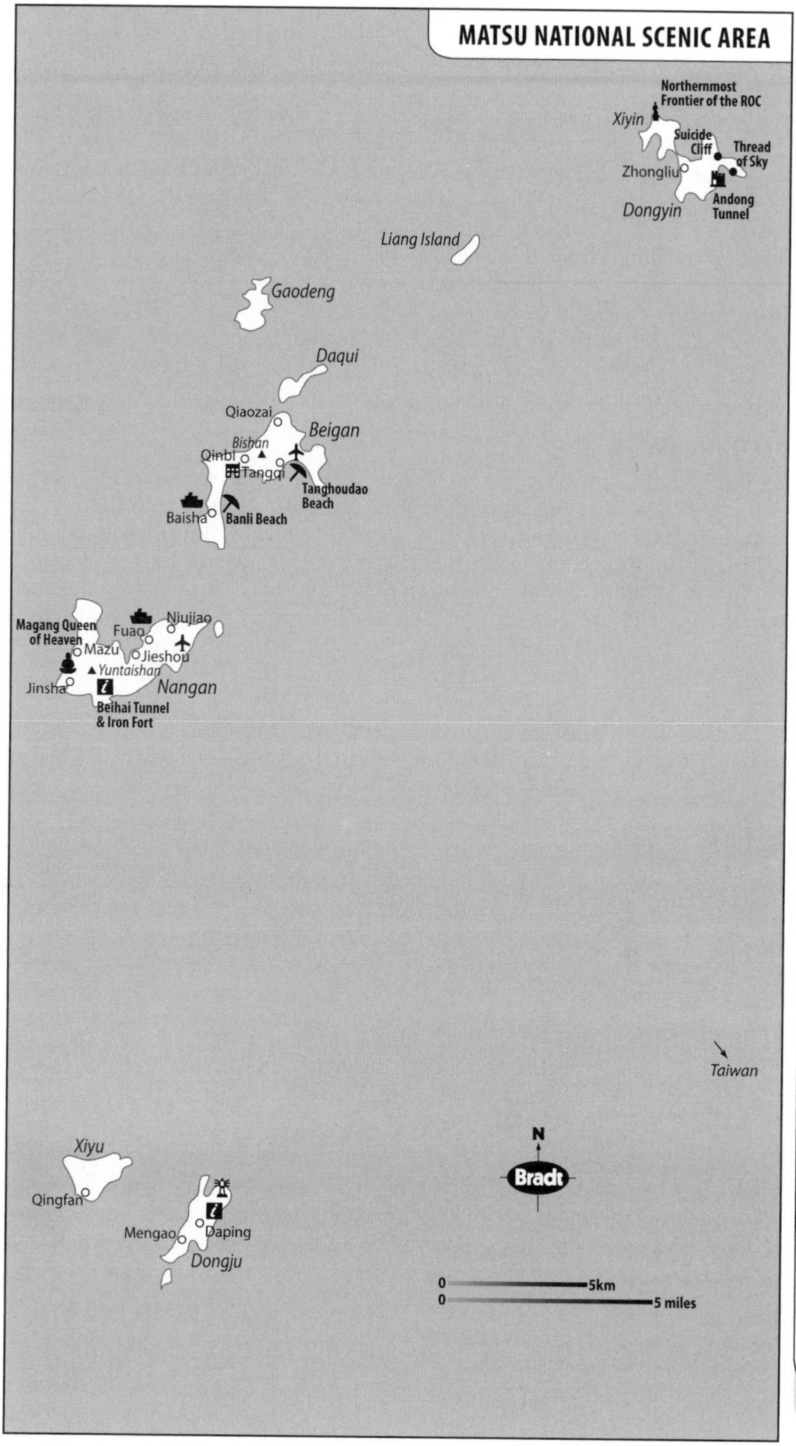

MATSU NATIONAL SCENIC AREA
Northernmost Frontier of the ROC
Xiyin
Suicide Cliff
Thread of Sky
Zhongliu
Andong Tunnel
Dongyin
Liang Island
Gaodeng
Daqui
Qiaozai
Beigan
Bishan
Qinbi
Tangqi
Tanghoudao Beach
Baisha
Banli Beach
Magang Queen of Heaven
Fuao
Niujiao
Mazu
Jieshou
Yuntaishan
Jinsha
Nangan
Beihai Tunnel & Iron Fort
Taiwan
Xiyu
Qingfan
Mengao
Daping
Dongju
N
Bradt
0 5km
0 5 miles

the ferry stops at Dongyin then Nangan before heading back to Keelung. Services are daily but on Tuesdays a smaller, less comfortable vessel takes the place of the *Taima*.

The cheapest one-way tickets entitle you to a seat in the lounge (*NTD630*) but these are only available if no bunk-bed spaces (*NTD1,050 for a single, NTD840 pp if two share a large bunk*) are available. The bunks have foam mattresses and curtains for privacy; there's a good chance you'll get some sleep. Fares are the same whether you disembark at Nangan or Dongyin; children and seniors pay half. Beer, instant noodles but not much else is available on board so bring some supplies.

There's a daily ferry between Matsu and Mawei near Fuzhou in Fujian (*departure from Nangan 14.00, from Mawei 09.15; takes 1½hrs; NTD1,300 one-way*). Tickets can be bought inside the Fuao Harbour Administration Building on Nangan. See *Getting there and away*, page 319, for more about travelling between the ROC and the PRC by sea.

GETTING AROUND

By boat Ferries leave Nangan for Beigan every hour on the hour (*departures ⏱ 07.00–17.00 daily; takes 20mins; NTD160 one-way*). At half past each hour the boat heads back to Nangan (*departs ⏱ 07.30–17.30 daily*). Three ferries per day sail from Nangan to Xiju's Qingfan Port and Dongju's Mengao Harbour (*departs ⏱ 07.00, 11.00 & 14.30; takes 50mins; NTD200 one-way*). These boats sometimes stop at Dongju before Xiju; confirm the first destination when buying your ticket. Sailing time between Xiju and Dongju is 15 minutes. Ferries return to Nangan right away. The main link between Nangan and Dongyin is the *Taima* ferry (see *Getting there and away*, page 326). One-way tickets cost NTD350/175.

During summer peak season, private operators offer boat tours to Daqiu Island, around Dongyin and out to the Tern Refuge. Details can be had from Matsu National Scenic Area Administration (see *Tourist information*, below).

By hired motorcycle Some homestays can help arrange scooter hire; ask before arriving in Matsu. The scenic area's website lists several rental businesses which may be willing to hire to visitors who have international but not ROC licenses.

By bus There are infrequent public buses on both Nangan and Beigan. Schedules can be obtained from visitor information centres.

TOURIST INFORMATION There are several visitor information centres (*most ⏱ 08.00–17.30 daily*), including one on Nangan near the entrance to Beihai Tunnel where there are free shower facilities – nice if you've just come off the *Taima* ferry – and one in Beigan opposite Banli Old House (see opposite). Useful websites include **Matsu National Scenic Area** (*http://matsu-nsa.gov.tw*) for tourist information and **Lienchiang County English Services Emblem** (*http://matsu.sp-store.com/english.html*) for details of shops, restaurants and accommodation options where English is understood.

WHERE TO STAY
Nangan

🏠 **Matsu 1st Hostel** (10 rooms) 71 Jinsha Village; ☎23353; m 0919 280 715; e admin@matsuhostel.com; www.matsuhostel.com. This picturesque option charges by person not room type;

2 ppl staying 1 night will pay NTD1,400 inc b/fast, pick-up for the airport or dock & 24hrs use of a motorcycle. Shared bathrooms only. This hostel also accepts travellers interested in working holidays; they should be willing to commit for a month & do

housekeeping, food preparation & other work in return for meals, a bed & airfare subsidy. **$$**

Beigan

🏠 **Chinbe No. 25 Guesthouse** (11 rooms) 25 Qinbi Village ☎55628; **m** 0975 421 178; **e** chinbe25@gmail.com; http://chinbe25-eng. blogspot.com. Owner Sammi Chen, who speaks good English, returned to her birthplace from Taipei in 2009 to open this tastefully furnished homestay & recently took over her father's old workshop to provide additional space. Wooden floors & stone walls give the rooms lots of character. Panoramic Sea View Suites go for NTD4,200 in peak season while smaller traditional rooms without bathrooms are just NTD2,200. Inc Matsu bagel b/fast. **$$$**

🏠 **Musi Seaview Hostel** (8 rooms) 120 Qiaozai Village; ☎55208; **f** 55372; **e** musi_ hostel@yahoo.com.tw. This is not a hostel & not all rooms in this plush new establishment have ocean views but they're well appointed. There's an outdoor area perfect for a beer or 2 at the end of the day & you're within 50m of Qiaozai's famous shrines. Heavy discounts often bring prices below NTD2,500. B/fast inc. **$$$**

🏠 **Banli Old House Homestay** (14 rooms) ☎55663; **m** 0921 801 585; **e** matsuyuansong@ gmail.com; http://tour.matsu.idv.tw/hotel_banli. php. Wooden partitions & simple furnishings mean this restored mansion (see page 330) may not be ideal for light sleepers or those who need en-suite bathrooms but it's full of character & a good place to meet backpackers. NTD500–800 pp, depending on season. Can help arrange motorcycle rental; b/fast inc. **$$**

Dongyin

🏠 **Shangrila Inn** (7 rooms) 128 Lehua Vlg; ☎76191; **m** 0919 280 767; **e** mouss0214@yahoo. com.tw; http://matsu.sp-store.com/stay10.html. Not to be confused with the high-end hotel chain, Dongyin's best accommodation choice has clean, comfortable rooms brightened by superb murals of local scenic spots. Two PCs in each room. An extra bed can be added for NTD300. Attractive prices reflect the fact that not all rooms have en-suite bathrooms. Inc b/fast & pick-up from the dock. **$$**

✖ **WHERE TO EAT** Matsu's climate and thus agriculture are quite different from Taiwan's so there are some distinct local specialities, none of which are expensive. The dish called 'fish noodles' (*yú miàn*) contains eel as well as saltwater fish. Westerners craving familiar carbohydrates enjoy 'Matsu bagels' 繼光餅 (*jì guāng bǐng*). These circular breads have long been a favourite of soldiers posted to the islands because they keep well in kitbags and make a good snack for those on sentry duty. They're baked by being stuck to the inside of a metal barrel which is then heated by fire. Several places slice them open and stuff them with egg and meat to create what many call a 'Matsu hamburger'.

OTHER PRACTICALITIES

✉ **Post office** 258 Jieshou Village, Nangan; ⊕ 08.00–17.00 Mon–Fri, 08.00–11.30 Sat

$ **Bank of Taiwan** 257 Jieshou Village, Nangan

WHAT TO SEE AND DO

Nangan 南竿 (Nángān) Sights are described in the order you'd likely tackle them if arriving by boat.

'Sleeping With Spears, Awaiting Daybreak' Approaching Fuao Harbour, you'll see four huge Chinese characters, red on a white background, up on the hillside. Read from right to left, they were installed at the behest of Chiang Kai-shek to remind everyone of his intention to retake the Chinese mainland.

Jieshou Village At the southern end of the main street in Matsu's busiest settlement there's a morning market where ready-to-eat Matsu snacks and locally caught seafood are sold. The temple overlooking the nearby cove is dedicated to

Baimazunwang ('the revered king of the white horse'), a minor deity worshipped in several shrines in Matsu but scarcely known on Taiwan proper.

Jieshou Park 介壽公園 The name of this park means 'long live Chiang Kai-shek' and inside you'll find two major buildings. One commemorates Chiang Ching-kuo, the dictator's son. The other, the **Folklore Cultural Artifacts Exhibition Hall** 民俗文物館 (⊕ 09.00–17.00 Tue–Sun; free admission) has displays about Matsu's traditional dwellings, customs and religious beliefs and multimedia introductions to the archipelago's dialect, poetry and songs.

Beihai Tunnel (⊕ at low tide only; free admission) Soldiers using pickaxes and explosives hacked out this 10m-wide, 640m-long sea-level tunnel between 1968 and 1970 so boats could resupply Nangan's garrison during bombardments. The tunnel was never used, however – high tides washed in so much silt the openings to the ocean had to be sealed. The floodlit interior is somewhat like a water-filled cathedral and the special ambience is best enjoyed if you join one of the frequent gondola tours (NTD150/person; takes around 20mins) or rent a kayak (NTD250/person; May–Oct only). Tide times are posted on the Matsu National Scenic Area's website; look for the link on the front page of the English section. Two other ex-military sites within walking distance of the tunnel are also worth visiting: **Dahan Stronghold** and **Iron Fort** (both ⊕ 08.00–17.00 daily; free admission).

Mount Yuntai On a clear day you'll see the Chinese mainland from the top of this 248m-high mountain. The exhibition room near the peak is in a military building; only Taiwan citizens are allowed inside.

Jinsha One of the archipelago's most attractive villages, Jinsha has benefited from local government subsidies to preserve and restore traditional one- and two-storey granite houses.

Magang Queen of Heaven Temple 馬港天后宮 (⊕ 24hrs daily) This mid-sized temple contains what's said to be the tomb of Lim Vo'g Niu, the Fujianese girl now revered as Mazu, the goddess of seafarers. According to one version of her life story, Lim swam out into the ocean in a bid to find her father but succumbed to exhaustion; her body washed ashore here. Some believe she was interred here while others say her remains were returned to Fujian and only her clothing was buried on Nangan. The putative grave, in front of the main altar inside the shrine, is marked by a flat granite slab covered by a sheet of glass; no excavation of the tomb was permitted when the temple was rebuilt in 2002. Effigies of Baimazunwang and his white horse are on the right. It's likely you saw the nearby Mazu statue (made of white granite and 28.8m tall) from the air or the ferry before setting foot on Nangan.

Beigan 北竿 (Běigān) Ferries from Nangan arrive at Baisha 白沙港 in the southwest; planes land at the other end of the island.

Banli 阪里 You'll find this village's standout structure, the late 19th-century **Banli Old House** (⊕ 09.00–21.00 daily; free admission), on the main street opposite the school. Built by the Wang family, it was requisitioned by the army in 1949 and only returned to its owners in 1992. From the outside you'll see stone and tiles but inside it's all wood columns and partitions. Following a government-funded restoration, most of the complex now serves as a homestay (see *Where to stay*, page 329). On the 13th day of the first lunar month, the village is the site of a unique religious ceremony which features villagers burning straw to 'feed' the spirit of Baimazunwang's faithful steed. Banli's beach is a lovely strip of clean amber-colour sand behind the visitor information centre; do be careful if you go for a swim as the waves here can be big.

Qinbi 芹壁 *(Qínbì)* The population of what could well be the ROC's most characterful village has fallen to below 200 but its distinctive stone cottages look like they'll last for eternity. The roofs, you'll notice, are covered with tiles held down by large stones. Because the tiles weren't sealed in place the houses are better ventilated than many dwellings of a similar age. Windows tend to be small and high up while walls are made of granite slabs that have been crudely squared off, or odd-shaped stones fitted together like jigsaw pieces.

Qiaozai The next village along if you're moving clockwise, Qiaozai has also suffered population outflow. It's said the village's gods now outnumber the humans. Some of the colourful shrines where the former reside are noteworthy for having flame-shaped side walls that extend beyond roof level. These are said to reduce the risk of fire.

Tangqi 塘岐 Beigan's 'capital' has a post office, a few basic hotels and the island's best eating options. The road which goes under the runway leads to **Tanghoudao Beach 塘后道沙灘**, through a small village called Houao and then up a steep road to the **War and Peace Memorial Park Exhibition Hall** (⏀ *08.30–11.50 & 13.30–17.30; free admission*). Even if you've little interest in the soldiers' uniforms and ordnance displayed inside, do walk up to this building for excellent views of the peninsula to the south. If the pro-casino lobby gets it way, these crags could be bulldozed into the ocean to make room for a gambling resort.

Dongyin 東引 (Dōngyǐn)
Just over 1,100 people live on Dongyin and fewer than a dozen on Xijin. The two islands, which are linked by a causeway, have few trees but an abundance of wild flowers. They're also still highly militarised. Don't take photos of soldiers, their equipment or army buildings and expect to be turned back at checkpoints.

Andong Tunnel 安東坑道 (⏀ *08.00–17.30 daily; free admission*) On entering this former army base you'll take 400-odd steps down a tunnel that slopes at 30 degrees then emerge halfway up a cliff face where gulls nest each summer. In addition to gun emplacements overlooking the ocean, sleeping quarters and ammunition depots the base had its own pigsty.

Dongyong Lighthouse (⏀ *08.00–16.30 daily; free admission*) If the weather's good you'll spend more time here than anywhere else on Dongyin. Reaching the lighthouse, designed by an Englishman and completed in 1904 (not 1877 as often stated), involves a little bit of walking on stone paths but the views are excellent. The cannon pointing out to sea weren't for firing at attackers but rather to warn shipping during fog.

Suicide Cliff A safe walkway leads to this dramatic viewing point where, legend has it, a fisherman's wife threw herself into the ocean rather than surrender to the pirates who'd killed her husband.

Thread of Sky 一線天 (⊕ *09.00–17.00 daily; free admission*) The name of this dramatic spot gives visitors a good idea of what to expect and the narrow opening between two cliffs doesn't disappoint. Because this part of the island is under military control you should get a permit before entering. This can be obtained free of charge from Dongyin's visitor centre (⊕ *08.00–17.30 daily*), on the hill southeast of Zhongliu.

Northernmost Frontier of the ROC 國之北疆 There's nothing here but expansive ocean views and a stone monument bearing four characters that mean 'the country's northern boundary'. The actual northernmost point is Beigu Reef, visible in good weather to the northeast.

Juguang 莒光 (Jǔguāng)

Matsu's most southerly township got its current name in the 1950s when Chiang Kai-shek made a speech comparing it to the ancient Chinese city of Ju, where more than 2,500 years ago a defeated king planned the counterattack which would restore him to the throne. The only islands of consequence are **Dongju** 東莒 and **Xiju** 西莒, similar in land area but quite different in shape. Dongju is long and thin while Xiju is much rounder and more suitable for exploring on foot. The ferry from Nangan stops at both. Dongju's ferry dock is at Mengao, just over 1km from Daping where you'll come across restaurants, homestays and scooter rentals. Continue northeast to find the visitor information centre and, at the end of the road, a lighthouse built by the British in the 1870s to ensure the safety of ships approaching Fuzhou in Fujian. On Xiju you'll disembark at Qingfan where everything is conveniently close; veer east for accommodation options.

LITTLE LIUQIU 小琉球 (XIǍO LIÚQIÚ) *Telephone code 08*

Whether you arrive at **Baisha** 白沙 or the smaller settlement of **Dafu** 大福, your first thought is likely to be that Little Liuqiu isn't very different from the rest of Taiwan. The town behind the ferry dock at Baisha is a dense collection of three-storey concrete boxes, and hundreds of tripod-shaped coastal fortifications have been piled up where the land meets the sea. Three temples are visible (Liuqiu has an amazing number of folk shrines considering its population, a mere 12,100), and the moment you step off the boat you'll find yourself in a whirligig crowd of people and motorcycles.

Don't let these initial impressions put you off. Fortunately, there's no more to Baisha than what you see from the boat – and it's the island's biggest settlement. Little Liuqiu is a jewel surrounded by clean seas. The 'little' is to distinguish it from Japan's Ryukyu Islands (now called Okinawa), the name of which was written using the same Chinese characters. The island is largely uplifted coral reef and thus unsuitable for farming. You'll see not a single rice field and very few vegetable gardens. Nonetheless, food and other necessities are no more expensive on the island than in Donggang or Kaohsiung, so there's no need to haul lots of provisions with you.

The absence of industry and the tiny number of cars mean that the sounds of nature can be heard everywhere: waves, wind and birdsong. The vibe is unusually and genuinely relaxing. No wonder, then, that some expats head here rather than Kenting when they want a get-away-from-it-all weekend. Twenty kinds of coral and 300 fish species make Liuqiu a good place for snorkelling. There's superb scuba diving but no infrastructure for divers who don't speak Chinese.

English-language sources sometimes refer to the landmass as Lamay Island because its original inhabitants were the Lamayans, an Austronesian tribe. In 1621 and again in 1631, tribesmen massacred European shipwreck survivors. The VOC attacked the tribe in 1636. Most of those fighting on the Dutch side were recruits from other Taiwanese tribes that despised the Lamayans. The climax was a siege at what's now called Black Ghost Cave. More than 300 Lamayans were massacred and the survivors were sold into slavery. After that, Little Liuqiu had no permanent human population until the ancestors of the current islanders arrived from Fujian in the late 18th century.

GETTING THERE AND AWAY

By ferry On a normal day there are eight services from Donggong to Baisha (*departs* ☉ *07.00–17.00; return fare NTD410/210*) and five to Dafu (☉ *08.00–18.45; return fare NTD380/190 inc admission to Black Ghost Cave, Meiren Cave & Mountain Pig Ditch*). Journey time on both routes is around 30 minutes. The return portion of your ticket doesn't entitle you to a seat on a particular boat; you may have to queue for the next boat if lots of people are waiting. Don't worry that you'll be stranded on the island as extra boats are laid on when needed. You can bring your bicycle on board for NTD50 one-way. Each ferry takes around 90 people.

GETTING AROUND

By motorcycle Scooters can be rented at Baisha. The standard weekday price of NTD300/day for a 125cc model includes enough fuel to get you all over the island. You won't have to look for these rental businesses – they'll find you, possibly even before you've got off the boat. Helmets are provided but few people bother to wear them. No licence needed, no deposit to be paid, no forms to be filled in.

TOURIST INFORMATION Maps of the island, which is part of **Dapeng Bay National Scenic Area** (*www.dbnsa.gov.tw*), are available inside the ferry terminal at Baisha. For more detailed information, go to the scenic area branch office (\ *861 4615;* ☉ *08.30–17.30 daily*). Turn right as you leave the harbour and you'll see it on your right just as the road begins to climb. Try also: **Little Liuqiu Township Office** (*www.liuchiu.gov.tw*).

WHERE TO STAY AND EAT Baisha has several inexpensive but characterless hotels. Except at the height of summer, if you turn up in the middle of the week you'll have no problem quickly finding somewhere to stay.

⌂ **Star Sand Homestay** (11 rooms) 173-1 Zhongshan Rd; \ 861 2101; f 861 2035; m 0920 071 671; e starsand.house@gmail.com; www.starsand.com.tw. This reliable option is within walking distance of Baisha Port & several restaurants yet very quiet. Rooms & furnishings are straightforward but there's a very pleasant courtyard area. Owner Jack Yao speaks good English. B/fast inc. **$$**

⌂ **Yucheng Hostel** (5 rooms) 19 Sanmin Rd, Yufu Village; \ 861 4891; m 0982 096 908; e agogo77772008@yahoo.com.tw. This homestay offers simple but comfortable lodgings in rooms

with wooden floors & roll-out beds. Packages which include a night's accommodation, b/fast, ferry tickets, motorbike rental & tours of the intertidal zone are priced around NTD1,700 pp for a couple. There's a lawn area where you can relax outdoors. **$$**

✕ **Baihai Restaurant** 6 Minzu Rd, Baisha; \ 861 2591; ☉ 11.30–14.00 & 17.00–20.00 daily. If you're walking from Baisha's ferry dock towards The Vase, this restaurant is the last building before you turn the corner to a temple. Surprisingly, not everything on the menu comes from the sea. Island-made pork sausages are served chopped

& mixed with lettuce. What's called a Little Liuqiu Pizza has neither tomatoes nor cheese, & is deep-fried rather than baked. However, it is circular & features seasoned prawns. There are also fish & crab dishes but you'll need language skills for the best results; no EM. $$$

WHAT TO SEE AND DO You'll have no problems finding your way around Little Liuqiu. There are plenty of bilingual maps, signs and information boards. If you turn right out of Baisha you can make the scenic area branch office your first stop and then work your way around the island clockwise.

The Vase 花瓶岩
The island's best-known and most-photographed coastal feature is shaped more like a giant mushroom than a flowerpot. Wade out towards it only if you're wearing good sandals or neoprene booties – the coral here is notoriously sharp and dangerous.

Meiren Cave 美人洞
(🕐 *08.30–18.00 daily; admission NTD120/80 inc Mountain Pig Ditch & Black Ghost Cave*) This section of coast is pleasing but not stunning, yet kids love it because it's perfect for hide-and-seek. If you walk quietly you'll likely see crabs on the footpath. Less than 1km further on, drop by **Samaji Holiday** (*28 rooms & several camping spots;* ☎ *861 4880;* f *861 4883;* e *samaji168@ gmail.com; www.samaji.com.tw;* **$$$**), on a plateau between the road and the ocean. The cabins here are a bit overpriced but there's access to the sea and good views; come late in the afternoon and you may glimpse green turtles bobbing a few metres offshore.

Mountain Pig Ditch 山豬溝
(🕐 *08.30–18.00 daily; admission inc in Meiren Cave ticket*) On the inland side of the road, this is another place where you can appreciate the island's coral-reef geology. There's lots of shade and greenery.

Fuan Temple 福安宮
(🕐 *05.00–20.00 daily*) Inside this house of worship there's a huge amount of carved wood and, in addition to the land god in the centre, a statue on the left representing a very local deity. General Shuixing – he of the bushy crimson eyebrows, bulging eyeballs and dark-green face – has been worshipped since 1987, when a team of builders working across the road found the ground-breaking spike on their excavator kept snapping, even though the land was soft. Consulting Guanyin, the foreman learned an 'infernal soldier' dwelt here. That spirit has since been assigned a legion of divine soldiers with which he protects the area from misfortune.

The shrine backs on to a small fishing harbour where you'll find the photogenic remnants of Little Liuqiu's oldest house. Known as the **Tai Mansion** (*not open to the public*), it dates from the 1820s and was the abode of one of the island's most important families. It's said building the harbour's breakwater spoiled the mansion's *feng shui* and caused the family to scatter.

Geban Bay 蛤板灣
This cove is extremely attractive but, as on most of the island's beaches, keeping your shoes on is advised because the sand contains fragments of broken coral. That said, do scoop up some grit and sift it carefully; you'll spot minute five-pointed yellow stars. These are foraminifera, the shells of organisms less than 1mm across. The scenic area administration urges visitors not to take shells, sand or foraminifera as souvenirs. During the warmer months fireflies can be seen around the bay and it's sometimes possible to witness green turtles coming ashore to lay eggs.

Black Ghost Cave 烏鬼洞 (⏱ 08.30–18.00 *daily; admission inc in Meiren Cave ticket*) The best known of the three attractions that charge admission; local people still burn incense here because of the violent events of nearly 400 years ago (see page 333). If you're squeezing into the cave itself, rent a torch (*NTD10*) from one of the vendors. There are good sea views from the platforms and stairways here. A few hundred metres off the coast you'll see fixed circular nets in the ocean used for breeding cobia (also known as black kingfish).

Guanyin Rock 觀音石 So named because of its resemblance to the Buddhist goddess, this outcrop is a short distance west of Dafu.

Dafu The island's 'second city' doesn't have much of interest to tourists, but one of the nicest spots to paddle in the water is immediately east of here. If you take the wooden stairway down to the water's edge and hunt around, you'll come across fish and crabs (including some that, in terms of size, wouldn't disgrace the table in a high-class seafood restaurant). The information board beside the road explains why this place is now so clean: formerly a landfill site, it got so noisome local people demanded something be done.

Intertidal Zones Ecotours of the rocky platforms exposed when the tide goes out have really caught on in the last few years, so much so that in 2012 the local government announced limits on the number of tourists allowed to enter these fascinating but sensitive places, which include Geban Bay and the environs of **Yufu Fishing Harbour**. Also, all groups must be accompanied by qualified guides. Almost 700 marine species – among them crabs, starfish and sea cucumbers – have been recorded in the waters around Little Liuqiu and an experienced guide should be able to show you curiosities such as sea hares which squirt out purple ink when attacked. (The ink disorientates fish and in the past was used by locals as a fishing aid.) Don't touch anything unless your guide says it's OK – rock-boring urchins and other denizens can inflict nasty stings. Nighttime tours are also engrossing, especially if greenish bioluminescent plankton sparkles just beneath the surface.

Sanlong Temple 三隆宮 (⏱ 05.30–21.00 *daily*) Once you've done a circuit of the island, explore the inland roads. From these you can get good views over the coastal villages, even though the highest point on the island is just 87m above sea level. The main attraction in the interior is this multilevel temple, the largest and perhaps most colourful place of worship on Little Liuqiu yet not the busiest. Among the deities worshipped here are the Jade Emperor (central position on what's labelled as the third floor) and Liuqiu's town god (ground floor, on the left). Unlike most other shrines around the island, visitors need not take off their shoes when entering. Every three years this temple organises a boat-burning event similar to Donggang's (see box, page 272; the next event will be October 2015).

GREEN ISLAND 綠島 (LÙ DĂO) *Telephone code 089*

No-one can dispute the aptness of the name. Green Island, created by an undersea volcanic eruption, is dominated by rich verdure and dark mossy hues that go well with the black cliffs and grey pyroclastic boulders. And it's all alone, 33km from Taiwan's shores. There's no archipelago here, just a few rocks above water at high tide to keep the island company. It's been Green Island only since 1949 – previously it was known as 'Fire-Scorched Island' because the inhabitants used to light fires on the hillsides to guide fishing vessels home. Since 1803 the islanders (current population 3,500) have been Han Chinese. Austronesian people certainly lived here a few centuries back and possibly as long as 4,000 years ago. But who exactly they were, and when and why they left, isn't known for sure. In 1951, Chiang Kai-shek's regime decided to use the island as a place of imprisonment and exile for communist agents, subversives and political opponents. Thousands of prisoners were shipped here for interrogation and re-education. Torture was routine and executions commonplace. Prisoners broke rocks on the beaches and helped build the airport. The last political convict was released in May 1990 (he's now a respected member of parliament) and visitors can tour the buildings where prisoners were held. Ordinary criminals, among them some leading mafiosi, continued to be housed in an off-limits high-security institution that's one of the island's major employers.

At high tide the island's land area is just 15km². At low tide this expands to a little over 17km² as receding waters expose coral platforms rich in marine life. The fish, crabs and other creatures that inhabit the tidal zone make snorkelling a very popular pastime, second only to soaking in one of the world's three saltwater hot springs. Local tour operators have made the snorkelling so safe even non-swimmers can join in and get a glimpse of what's beneath the surface. Because the Kuroshio Current draws fish towards the island and then traps them just offshore, there's some excellent scuba diving. Many divers prefer the winter months when underwater visibility is often 20m. For general visitors, April and May are good months as temperatures and humidity levels are lower than during the summer peak season, and the strong winds that sometimes make winter ferry crossings extremely uncomfortable are seldom a problem. If the sky isn't hazy, from the boat you'll get capital views of the mountains that abut Taiwan's east coast; you may see flying fish skim the waves and perhaps a dolphin or two. Approaching the rugged coastline in gloomy weather provokes a stirring, ends-of-the-earth sensation. For convicts and dissidents this must have exacerbated their despair. For many visitors, however, it's central to Green Island's appeal.

GETTING THERE AND AWAY

By air Daily Air (☎ *07 801 4711, 089 362 489; www.dailyair.com.tw*) flies 19-seat propeller aircraft three times each day between Taitung and Green Island (*IATA: GNI; takes 12mins; NTD1,028 one-way*). The schedule is on Taitung Airport's website (*www.tta.gov.tw*).

By boat The shipping companies that operate ferries between Fugang and Green Island (*takes about 40mins; NTD460 one-way*) have offices in the passenger terminal at Fugang's small harbour. The waiting area has air conditioning. During summer there's a boat about every two hours (*departures 07.30–15.30 daily*) but in winter there's often just one boat each way per day. The East Coast National Scenic Area Administration (☎ *841 520; www.eastcoast-nsa.gov.tw*) can provide details of upcoming sailings. Green Island Adventures, a local tour operator, books tickets. The two main ferry companies are Kaisyuan (☎ *281 047*) and Green Island Jhihsing (☎ *280 226*). Don't expect their employees to speak English.

GETTING AROUND

By motorcycle Most visitors get the use of a 125cc scooter as part of their package. Rentals can be arranged just outside the harbour. The island's only petrol station (⊕ *08.00–17.00 daily*) is between the harbour and Nanliao Village.

By bicycle Bikes can be rented from some of the motorcycle hire stores in Nanliao but Green Island is far from ideal for cycling. It can get very windy, there's not much shade and the round-island road has some steep gradients.

By bus Buses circumnavigate the island throughout the year. There's one service per hour (⏰ *08.00–11.00 & 14.00–17.00 daily*). A one-day pass costs NTD100/50 and can be purchased at Nanliao Harbour.

TOURIST INFORMATION There are bilingual displays and leaflets inside **Green Island Visitor Centre** (*outside the airport;* ☎ *672 026;* ⏰ *08.30–17.00 daily*). If you want to stay at the campsite at the southern end of Green Island, you need to make the booking here. Try also **East Coast National Scenic Area** (*www.eastcoast-nsa. gov.tw*).

LOCAL TOUR OPERATOR

Green Island Adventures m 0972 065 479; e greenislandreservations@yahoo.com ; www. greenislandadventures.com. Founder Eddie Viljoen specialises in packages that include accommodation, scuba diving, ferry or flight tickets & pick-up on both sides.

 WHERE TO STAY AND EAT These businesses are all in Nanliao Village.

🏠 **Kaishing Hotel** (80 rooms) ☎ 672 033; f 672 050. Owned by one of the ferry companies & thus often filled with tour groups, the rooms here are much nicer than the clean but dreary corridors would suggest: wooden floors & simple décor dominated by white with either blue, green or yellow. Some rooms for 4 or 6 ppl; a few rooms have balconies. Convenient location in Nanliao's 'downtown' on the inland side of the road; easy to find because of its size but little English spoken. B/fast inc. **$$$**

✕ **Monica & Marco's Seafood Restaurant** 非炒不可 m 0988 384 323; ⏰ 11.00–14.30 & 18.00–20.30 daily during peak season. If you're coming from the airport end of Nanliao, look for the sign on the left. The EM lists sashimi & 'catch of the day' plus a good range of soups. Stir fries are made around clams, shrimps & sea mushrooms. Sometimes closes in low season. Local beers & wines. **$$$**

✕ **Mr Hot Dog** ☎ 671 711; ⏰ 10.30–00.30 daily. This newish place, which attracts a young crowd, is perhaps the only restaurant in the world serving flying-fish pizza (*NTD119*). Other pizza options (*from NTD89*) inc venison & flying fish 飛魚. Pasta dishes (*from NTD149*) & hot dogs (*from NTD69*) plus salads & side dishes round out the menu. A decent selection of alcoholic (*beers from NTD100, cocktails from NTD120*) & non-alcoholic drinks. EM. **$$**

WHAT TO SEE AND DO If you arrive by ferry, turn left to reach Nanliao Village 南寮, the cluster of shops, eateries, hotels and private homes that has the island's only post office and police station. The village is also within walking distance of the airport; if you've flown in, before turning right to Nanliao, cross the road and drop into the visitor centre for maps and English-language pamphlets. It doesn't matter much which way you circumnavigate the island. The following listing goes clockwise. Near the lighthouse on the island's northwestern extremity there are some large tidal pools where you can cool off in the water; around the island there are very few spots where swimming is advisable, either because of currents or because you'll be stepping on coarse coral grit.

Green Island Human Rights Memorial Park 綠島人權紀念碑園區 (Lù Dǎo Rénquán Jìniànbēi Yuánqū) (⏰ *24hrs daily; free admission*) Occupying a large slice of the island's north coast, the memorial park's most obvious sight is the

curved semi-underground memorial wall with its immaculate lawns. Not all of the 1,000-odd names etched into the stone represent individuals incarcerated on Green Island (Annette Lu, a former vice president, is listed here even though she served her sentence in north Taiwan). Each one, however, was a political detainee during the martial-law era. Several spent two or three periods in jail and in one case the total comes to 26 years, just short of Nelson Mandela's term.

Green Island's first political jail, New Life Camp, functioned between 1952 and 1965. At times, more than 2,000 were incarcerated, including some women. Detainees left the camp to do farming and labouring work; they performed Taiwanese operas for island residents, and helped local children with their homework. Detailed information about prisoners along with photos of historical interest can be found at http://2011greenislanden.wordpress.com.

Oasis Villa 綠洲山庄 (Lùzhōu Shānzhuāng) (☉ May–Sep 08.00–18.00, Oct–Apr 08.30–17.00 daily; free admission) Hurriedly built after a prison uprising in February 1970 convinced the authorities all political detainees should be moved back to Green Island, this institution's Orwellian name won't fool anyone who looks around inside. There are four blocks, each with two floors and 52 cells; dissidents were held here, usually several to a cell, until the late 1980s.

Guanyin Cave 觀音洞 (Guānyīn Dòng) (☉ 24hrs daily; free admission) This small Buddhist grotto attracts plenty of genuine pilgrims in addition to coachloads of tourists. Inside there's a stalagmite that resembles, albeit very slightly, the goddess of mercy. The modest eatery (☉ irregular hrs; $$) by the entrance has some very tasty fare, including venison with rice (lù ròu fàn), fried rice, venison soup (lù ròu tāng), flying fish (fēi yú) but no EM or AC.

East Coast Very few people live on this side of the island, which is marked by a series of dramatic promontories. Several have been given names inspired by their shapes, among them **Cow's Head Hill** and **Pekinese Dog**. Between the road and the ocean you'll see impenetrable clusters of one of Green Island's most distinctive plants, the screwpine (also known as the fragrant pandam). Thousands have been grown as windbreaks. They bear fruit similar in size and shape to pineapples but much harder and far less delicious.

Jhaorih Hot Springs 朝日溫泉 (Zhāorì Wēnquán) (☎ 671 133; ☉ 05.00–02.00 daily; admission NTD200/100) Located in the island's southeast, these springs are a high point for many visitors who revel in watching the sun rise while soaking in sulphurous brine. Others leave disappointed because the water is often tepid or they feel the condition of the pools doesn't warrant the high admission charge (massage showers that don't work is a common complaint). Come at dusk to avoid both the sun and the crowds; the place is often packed out after dinner. Apart from two small pools very close to the waves, most of the complex – which includes indoor and outdoor pools plus changing rooms – is above the beach.

Across-Mountain Ancient Trail 過山古道 Green Island's highest point is 281m above sea level, but it's closed to the public because it's occupied by a military radar station. This hiking trail comes close and provides access to the unpopulated, unspoiled interior. Starting from near km11 on the ring road, the first quarter of the 1.85km-long path includes dozens of stone steps on which bask an incredible number and variety of lizards. A species easy to spot and recognise is Swinhoe's

Visitors to Green Island are given bilingual leaflets urging them to ride their motorcycles slowly and give way to crabs and other creatures on the road. Among the species sometimes squashed beneath tourists' wheels are the black-spectacled toad (*Duttaphrynus melanostictus*) and the coconut crab (*Birgus latro*). The latter, a nocturnal animal weighing up to 1kg, is the world's largest terrestrial arthropod. Formerly hunted for food, it's now the only crustacean species protected by Taiwan's Wildlife Conservation Law.

Green Island isn't the only place in Taiwan where road-users should take special care not to harm local fauna. Between early July and late October each year, Kenting National Park asks drivers to slow down, especially at night, because thousands of female land crabs from at least 25 species scamper across busy roads while making their way to the ocean where they lay their eggs. Around full moons, the coastal road is sometimes closed for a few hours to increase the crabs' survival chances.

japalura (*Japalura swinhonis*), sometimes called the bamboo tiger. Often more than 20cm long, including tail, it has a thick yellow stripe on either side of its trunk.

Across-Mountain Trail 過山步道 This route is of a similar length but starts from near the campsite at the island's southern tip. Like the ancient trail, it hits the concrete track that serves the radar base. From there to the visitor centre it's more than an hour of downhill walking with very little shade. Bring water, snacks and a hat.

ORCHID ISLAND 蘭嶼 (LÁNYǓ) *Telephone code 089*

Linked to Taiwan by unreliable boat and air services, Orchid Island is a spectacular escape for the relatively few visitors who get here. Some 60km due south of Green Island and 63km east of the Hengchun Peninsula, it's unique among the ROC's islands in having an Austronesian culture. Most of the islanders are members of the Tao tribe, an ethnic group whose ancestors came here about eight centuries ago and who call their 46km² homeland Pongso no Tao.

In recent decades many Orchid Islanders have moved to Taiwan for work or higher education. The official population is almost 4,900 but many adults are absent for months at a time because they earn their living elsewhere. Partly because of the geographical isolation, and partly because no tourists of any stripe were permitted to visit until 1967, the Tao have managed to preserve quite a bit of their culture. Among the most obvious manifestations of this are semi-underground typhoon-proof houses and ornate wooden fishing boats.

Tribal solidarity has been strengthened by anger over the island's use as a dumping ground for nuclear waste from Taiwan's atomic power stations. Between 1982 and 1996, almost 100,000 barrels of low- and mid-level waste were shipped to the island. For years, Taiwan's government lied to the islanders, telling them the storage facility was a fish cannery. Unusually high levels of radioactivity have been detected in the vicinity of the dump, which is at the southern end of the island, but this shouldn't deter you from visiting.

Young Tao dress no differently from other Taiwanese, yet some elderly men still go about their daily chores wearing little more than a traditional loincloth. During festivals tribal elders don rattan vests and conical helmets made of silver; the latter cover the

Minor Islands   ORCHID ISLAND

10

entire head save for narrow slits which allow the wearer to see where he's going. Before taking a photo of a man in his loincloth – or of any other islander, in fact – do ask permission. Many Tao dislike being treated as tourist attractions rather than humans. However, visitors who show tact and sensitivity speak of being warmly welcomed.

Like Green Island, Orchid Island is a nub of solidified magma pushed up by an ocean-bottom volcanic eruption. There are eight significant mountains, the highest of which reaches 552m. Despite the rugged landscape there's quite a lot of forest, some real jungle and a few small but decent beaches.

In ecological terms, the island is as close to the Philippines as it is to Taiwan. The Bataan Islands, from where the Tao are thought to have migrated, are 110km to the south. Among Orchid Island's fauna is the Formosan flying fox (*Pteropus dasymallus formosus*), a large fruit-eating bat and Taiwan endemic. Birders will hope to catch sight of the Lanyu scops owl (*Otus elegans botelensis*), an endemic subspecies of the Ryukyu scops owl. The wild orchids that gave the island its name aren't as numerous as they once were.

Orchid Island is hot and humid year-round with summer highs of almost 40°C and nasty winter storms. Annual rainfall averages 3,440mm. April is the driest month; October–November is likely the best time of year to go.

GETTING THERE AND AWAY

By air Daily Air (℡ *07 801 4711, 089 362 489; www.dailyair.com.tw*) flies 19-seat propeller aircraft six times each day between Taitung and Orchid Island (*IATA: KYD*) (*flight time: 25mins; NTD1,345*). The schedule is on Taitung Airport's website (*www.tta.gov.tw*). Flights are often booked solid, cancelled because of bad weather or delayed by military exercises.

By boat Boats leave from Fugang and there may be just one service per week (*takes about 3hrs; NTD1,000 one-way*). Boats are sometimes brought forward or delayed by a day or more to cater for large groups. A few services stop at Green Island on the outward or return leg, meaning it's theoretically possible, but very difficult in practical terms, to travel from one island to another without returning to Fugang. Be prepared for rough seas. Between April and September there are up to two ferries per day from Houbihu in Kenting National Park (*takes about 2hrs; NTD1,000*).

GETTING AROUND Hiring a scooter (*NTD500 per day*) is by far the best option, though there is a round-the-island bus service. The rental businesses (which can also provide cars and minibuses) will find you as soon as you get off the boat or leave the airport. Riders should beware of pigs and goats wandering across the road. Cars and vans can be rented in Imaorod. The airport has a small number of bicycles which tourists can use (*free; registration with ID required*). Four buses per day (*1-day pass NTD125 pp*) circle the island.

TOURIST INFORMATION Tour Taitung (*http://tour.taitung.gov.tw*) has some useful information. In Taitung you can pick up bilingual maps and leaflets about Orchid Island at visitor centres.

WHERE TO STAY AND EAT If you're visiting in the peak summer season you should make reservations. At other times, you'll likely have hotel and homestay owners greeting you on arrival. There are simple eateries in the villages but no English menus. The food supply is uneven, so don't expect everything listed on the Chinese menu to be available.

🏠 **Lamuran Homestay 魚飛浪民宿**
(6 rooms) 76 Imaorod Village; ☎732 610; m 0933
163 451; e ttung@hotmail.com. Clean, simple
accommodation but only 1 room has its own
bathroom. 4 rooms have futon beds (*max 4 ppl per
room*), 1 dbl has a king-size bed, bathroom & TV & 1
dbl is more basic. There's a deck with hammocks & sea
views. Wi-Fi; no b/fast. Tao owner Syaman Lamuran
(on Facebook under that name) speaks good English
& can collect guests from the airport. **$$**

🏠 **Mingri Homestay 明日民宿** (2 rooms,
1 dorm) 11 Iranmeylek Village; ☎732 869; m 0928
169 725; http://iranmeylek.myweb.hinet.net/

homestay_mz.htm. Basic but clean & well-located
homestay. Guests are charged according to their
numbers: NTD400 pp in the rooms (4 ppl max) &
NTD300 pp in the dorm. Can arrange round-the-
island & other excursions for groups of up to 10
ppl. No b/fast. **$**

✕ **Epicurean Restaurant-Pub 無餓不坐PUB**
77 Iratay Village; ☎731 623; ⏱ 10.00–13.00 &
18.00–22.00 Sun–Mon, 18.00–22.00 Tue. Serves
a mix of local, Taiwanese & semi-Western items.
Individual dishes from NTD150. Free internet for
customers. The family that runs this long-running
& well-liked eatery also run a homestay. **$$**

WHAT TO SEE AND DO The ring road hugs the coast and links all six villages, each of
which has a Tao name (given here with the Mandarin in parentheses). There's only
one other route suitable for vehicles, a short cut from Imaorod on the southwest
coast to Ivalion on the eastern side.

North Coast
Major features along the north and northeast coastlines have been
given names like **Crocodile Rock** and **Lovers' Archway**.

Yayo 椰油 (Yēyóu)
This village includes the ferry dock, a petrol station, a small
supermarket and Orchid Island's only high school. The beach here is said to be
good for body surfing.

Imaorod 紅頭 (Hóngtóu)
The island's airport is just north of this village, which
has a clinic and a post office.

Weather Station 氣象站
Established in 1940 by the Japanese, who needed
meteorological data for their war effort, this spick-and-span building is 322m above
sea level and surrounded by manicured lawns. The views from here are an absolute
treat. Take the short cut between Imaorod and Ivalion, then a steep side road on
the north side.

Eco-Education Trail
About 1km south of Imaorod look for the entrance
to this shortish path into a lush gully. The birding along this track is very good
with frequent reports of Japanese paradise flycatchers (*Terpsiphone atrocaudata*),
Ryukyu scops owls and other unusual avians.

Datianchi 大天池
The hike to this little lake, a volcano crater filled with rainwater
not far from Orchid Island's southern tip, can be hot and tough-going, but the trail
does get you into unspoiled evergreen broad-leaf forest.

Little Orchid Island 小蘭嶼
A little over 5km off the main island's southern tip,
Little Orchid Island has long been uninhabited. Not that long ago, Taiwan's air force
used to practise bombing runs on the island. Now it's sometimes possible to hire a
guide and a boat and visit.

Ivalion 野銀 (Yěyín)
The villages on the eastern side of the island, Ivalion in
particular, are the best places to see tribal culture and semi-underground stone

dwellings. Just like modern sustainable homes that are built into hillsides, these small Tao houses are cooler in summer and warmer in winter than the concrete boxes that fill Taiwanese towns. Because of their low profile, they're far less likely to be damaged by typhoon gusts. The downside is that the interiors are usually cramped, dark and stuffy. That doesn't matter too much because cooking, eating and socialising are done above ground on roofed platforms.

Dongqing Bay 東清灣 (Dōngqīng Wān) This broad bay has an attractive 1km-long beach where many tourists go swimming and backpackers sometimes camp. During the flying fish-catching season it's a good place to see traditional boats come and go.

Birdwing Butterfly Conservation Area 珠光鳳蝶復育園區 (Zhūguāng Fèngdié Fùyù Yuánqū) If you visit Orchid Island between April and September, you're much more likely to see Taiwan's largest butterfly than either the Lanyu scops owl or the Formosan flying fox. The wingspan of Magellan's iridescent birdwing (*Troides magellanus sonani*) often exceeds 20cm. The species, which is black and yellow with some red, is endangered because the plants it and its larvae feed on are harvested for use in Chinese traditional medicine. In this conservation area efforts are being made to provide it with a foothold where it can thrive.

Appendix 1

LANGUAGE

Many Taiwanese, possibly more than half of the population, speak Taiwanese or a blend of Taiwanese and Mandarin at home (see *Language*, pages 25–7). Except for missionaries, few Westerners have learned Taiwanese. Mandarin, the official language of both Taiwan and the People's Republic of China, is the language of education and the language most often used in television and radio broadcasts. The only Taiwanese who don't understand Mandarin are those over 60 who received very little education.

If you attempt to speak Mandarin in Taiwan, you'll get various reactions, including shock and mirth, but also lots of genuine encouragement. If you're serious about practising the language, you'll find plenty of people willing to chat.

The Mandarin words and phrases in this section (and throughout this book) have been romanised according to the *hanyu pinyin* system of spelling. That system wasn't created with English speakers in mind. For instance, the letter 'x' is pronounced something like 'sh', while 'q' approximates 'ch' and 'zh' is a bit like 'j'. If the word ends in 'o', like *wǒ* (I, me), it sounds like 'or'. The word for have (*yǒu*) is pronounced like the casual greeting 'yo!' and not like the English personal pronoun.

When reading *hanyu pinyin*, one must also take note of the four tones. First tone, marked with a horizontal line (eg: *guā*) is flat and somewhat high. Second tone is rising and marked with an acute accent (eg: *bái*). Third tone is falling then rising, indicated in this book and many other resources by a breve (eg: *guǒ*). The fourth tone is falling and its shown by a grave accent (eg: *dòu*). The seldom-used fifth tone is neutral and so doesn't have any tone marking.

It goes without saying that the best way to master Mandarin pronunciation is to listen to native speakers, imitate and practise.

Much of this section is devoted to helping readers buy food and drink because this is an important part of any Taiwan experience as well as an endeavour in which many visitors struggle.

INTRODUCING YOURSELF As soon as people know you can speak some Mandarin, they'll be asking you questions like these:

What's your name?	你叫什嗎名字?	*nǐ jiào shénme míngzi?*
My name is…	我叫…	*wǒ jiào…*
How are you?	你好嗎?	*nǐ hǎo ma?*
I'm very well	我很	*wǒ hěnhǎo*
Where are you from?	你是哪裡人?	*nǐ shì nǎlǐ de rén?*
No, not yet	還沒	*hái méi*
Bottoms up!	乾	*gān bēi*

In Mandarin, questions such as 'Are you married?' are answered affirmatively by simply repeating the verb or adjective in the question. Here are two examples: if someone asks you, 'Do you like…? (你喜歡... 嗎? /nǐ xǐ huān... ma?)', you can answer, 'like' (喜歡/xǐ huān); if they say, 'Are you happy?' (你高興嗎? /nǐ gāo xìng ma?), you can respond, 'happy!' (高興/gāo xìng).

ADDRESSING OTHERS Unlike Japanese and some other languages, in Mandarin there are very few polite/familiar forms to worry about. Titles such as Mr or Miss (there's no Ms in Mandarin) are placed after the name.

Hello, Mr Lee	你好李先生	Lǐ xiānsheng nǐ hǎo
Hello, Miss Chen	你好陳小姐	Chén xiǎojie nǐ hǎo
Goodbye!	再見	zài jiàn

ASKING FOR HELP

Excuse me/I'm sorry	對不起	duì bú qì
Where's the toilet?	廁所在哪裡	cè suǒ zài nálǐ?
Please give me…	請給我…	qǐng gěi wǒ…
I want to go online	我要上網	wǒ yào shàng wǎng
Can you speak English?	你會講英語嗎?	nǐ huì jiǎng yīngyǔ ma?
I don't understand	我聽不懂	wǒ tīng bù dǒng
Thank you	謝謝	xiè xiè
You're welcome	不用客氣	bú yòng
It doesn't matter	沒有關係	méiyǒu guānxi

SHOPPING

Do you have…?	你有沒有	nǐ yǒu méi yǒu…?
Can I see it, please?	我要看可以嗎	wǒ yào kān kěyǐ ma?
How much does it cost?	多少錢	duō shǎo qián?
It's expensive!	太貴了	tài guì le
OK, I want to buy it	我要買	wǒ yào mǎi

NUMBERS Numbers greater than ten are very easy. Eleven is shí yī, literally 'ten one', while twenty is èr shí, 'two ten'. Follow the same logic for larger numbers: 147 is yī bǎi sì shí qī – 'one hundred four ten seven'.

one	一	yī	eight	八		bā
two	二	èr	nine	九		jiǔten
three	三	sān	ten	十		shí
four	四	sì	20	二十		èr shí
five	五	wǔ	50	五十		wǔ shí
six	六	liù	100	一百		yī bǎi
seven	七	qī				

IN THE HOTEL

Do you have any vacancies?	請問有房間嗎	qǐng wèn yǒu fáng jiān ma?
I have a reservation	我有定房	wǒ yǒu dìng fáng
Room for one/two people	單人房 / 兩人房	dān rén fáng/liǎng rén fáng
How much does it cost?	多少錢	duō shǎo qián?
Does it include breakfast?	含早餐嗎?	hán zǎo cān ma?

DIRECTIONS

I want to go to…	我要去	wǒ yào qù…
… the bus station	公共汽車站	gōng gòng qì chē zhàn
… the TRA station	火車站	hǔochē zhàn
… the HSR station	高鐵站	gāo tiě zhàn
… the airport	機場	jī chǎng
… the hotel	旅館	lǚ guǎn
… the homestay	民宿	mín sù
Where is the…?	在哪裡	zài nálǐ…?
(The men's toilet will be labelled 男 (nán), the ladies' 女 (nǚ).)		
… bathroom?	廁所	cè suǒ
… post office?	郵局	yóu jú
… bank?	銀行	yín háng
… restaurant?	餐廳	cān tīng
… visitor information centre?	遊客中心	yóu kè zhōng xīn

DRIVING

I want to hire…	我要租一輛…	wǒ yào zū yī liàng…
… a car	汽車	qì chē
… a motorcycle	摩托車	mó tuō chē
… a bicycle	腳踏車	jiǎo tà chē
Can I park here?	我可以停車嗎	wǒ kěyǐ tíng chē ma?
92-octane petrol (two-star)	九二	jiǔ èr
95-octane petrol (four-star)	九五	jiǔ wǔ

EATING AND DRINKING
Meals

breakfast	早餐	zǎo cān
lunch	午餐	wǔ cān
dinner	晚餐	wǎn cān
small delicacies	小吃	xiǎo chī
snack	零食	líng shí
dim sum (Cantonese snacks)	店心	diàn xīn

Staples

steamed white rice	白飯	bái fàn
fried rice	炒飯	chǎo fàn
stewed rice; risotto	燴飯	huì fàn
gravy rice	肉燥飯	lǔ ròu fàn or ròu zǎo fàn
congee; rice porridge	粥	zhōu
breakfast rice gruel	稀飯	xī fàn
sticky rice triangles	粽子	zòng zǐ or ròu zòng
wheat noodles	麵	miàn
fried noodles	炒麵	chǎo miàn
thin rice noodles	米粉	mǐ fěn
ban-tiao (thick rice noodles)	粄條	bǎn tiáo
dry noodles with gravy	乾麵	gān miàn
sesame-paste noodles	麻醬麵	má jiàng miàn
ramen	拉麵	lā miàn
knife-cut noodles	刀削麵	dāo xuē miàn
steamed dumplings	餃子 or 水餃	jiǎo zi or shuǐ jiǎo

fried dumplings	煎餃	*jiān jiǎo*
soup-filled dumplings	小籠包	*xiǎo lóng bāo*
chicken's egg	雞蛋	*jī dàn*
hot pot	火鍋	*huǒ guō*

Flavours and condiments

spicy	辣	*là*
not spicy, please	我不要辣	*wǒ bù yào là*
salty	鹹	*xián*
black pepper	胡椒	*hú jiāo*
original flavour	原味	*yuán wèi*
tomato ketchup	番茄醬	*fān qié jiàng*
tofu	豆腐	*dòu fu*
dried tofu	豆干	*dòu gān*

Portion sizes and cooking styles

small	小	*xiǎo*
medium	中	*zhōng*
large	大	*dà*
vegetarian	素食	*sù shí*
offal cooked in gravy	滷味	*lǔ wèi*

Meats

pork	豬肉	*zhū ròu*
pork ribs	排骨	*pái gǔ*
pig's foot	豬腳	*zhū jiǎo*
ham	火腿	*huǒ tuǐ*
bacon	培根	*péi gēn*
chicken	雞肉	*jī ròu*
beef	牛肉	*niú ròu*
steak	牛排	*niú pái*
duck	鴨肉	*yā ròu*
goose	鵝肉	*é ròu*
venison	鹿肉	*lù ròu*
snake	蛇肉	*shé ròu*
barbecue	烤肉	*kǎo ròu*

Seafood

Seafood	海鮮	*hǎi xiān*
fish	魚	*yú*
squid	魷魚	*yóu yú*
octopus	章魚	*zhāng yú*
oyster	蚵	*é*
clam	蛤	*gé*
seaweed	海	*hǎi zǎo or hǎi cǎo*

Vegetables

salad	沙拉	*shā lā*
cabbage	高麗菜	*gāo lì cài*
kimchi (pickled cabbage)	泡菜	*pào cài*
fried green vegetables	炒青菜	*chǎo qīng cài*
potato	馬鈴薯	*mǎ líng shǔ*

taro	芋頭	*yù tóu*
sweet potato	地瓜	*dì guā or fān shǔ*
carrot	紅蘿蔔	*hóng luó bo*
sweetcorn	玉米	*yù mǐ*
tomato	番茄	*fān qié*
mushroom	香菇	*xiāng gū*
bitter melon	苦瓜	*kǔ guā*

Soups

soup	湯	*tāng*
thick soup, potage	羹	*gēng*
egg soup	蛋花湯	*dàn huā tāng*
miso soup	味噌湯	*wèi cēng tāng*
pork rib soup	排骨湯	*pái gǔ tāng*
wonton soup	餛飩湯	*hún tún tāng*

Hakka specialities 客家菜 *kè jiā cài*

| stir-fried pork with squid and dried tofu | 客家小炒 | *kè jiā xiǎo chǎo* |
| pig's intestine with ginger and vinegar | 薑絲炒大腸 | *jiāng sī chǎo dà cháng* |

Western foods

hamburger	漢堡	*hàn bǎo*
chips; french fries	薯條	*shǔ tiáo*
sandwich	三明治	*sān míng zhì*
cheese	起士	*qǐ shì*
spaghetti	意大利麵	*yì dà lì miàn*
pizza	比薩	*bǐ sà*

Breakfast food 早餐 *zǎo cān*

fried egg	煎蛋	*jiān dàn*
egg pancake	蛋餅	*dàn bǐng*
steamed bread	饅頭	*mán tou*
steamed roll with meat	肉包	*ròu bāo*
steamed roll with vegetables	菜包	*cài bāo*
soy milk	豆漿	*dòu jiāng*
unfilled doughnut stick	油條	*yóu tiáo*
cold (for food)	冷	*lěng*

Snacks and desserts

bread	麵包	*miàn bāo*
cake	蛋糕	*dàn gāo*
ice cream	冰淇淋	*bīng qí lín*
biscuits, cookies	餅乾	*bǐng gān*
chocolate	巧克力	*qiǎo kè lì*
sweets, candy	糖果	*táng guǒ*
chewing gum	口香糖	*kǒu xiāng táng*
pudding	布丁	*bù dīng*
soy-bean jelly	豆花	*dòu huā*

Drinks

	飲料	*yǐn liào*
boiled water	白開水	*bái kāi shuǐ*
fruit juice	果汁	*guǒ zhī*
cola	可樂	*kě lè*
coffee	咖啡	*kā fēi*
black tea	紅茶	*hóng chá*
tea with milk	奶茶	*nǎi chá*
tea with tapioca balls ('pearl milk tea')	珍珠奶茶	*zhēn zhū nǎi chá*
papaya milkshake	木瓜牛奶	*mù guā niú nǎi*
hot (for drinks and desserts)	熱	*rè*
cold; iced (for drinks)	冰	*bīng*
half sugar	半糖	*bàn táng*
no sugar	無糖	*wú táng*
less ice	少冰	*shǎo bīng*
no ice	無冰	*wú bīng*
cow's milk	牛奶	*niú nǎi*
beer	啤酒	*pí jiǔ*
kaoliang	高粱	*gāo liáng*
red wine	紅酒	*hóng jiǔ*
white wine	白葡萄酒	*bái pú tao jiǔ*

Fruits

	水果	*shuǐ guǒ*
apple	蘋果	*píng guǒ*
guava	芭樂	*bā lè*
longan	龍眼	*lóng yǎn*
lychee	荔枝	*lí zhī*
mango	芒果	*máng guǒ*
orange	橘子	*jú zǐ*
papaya	木瓜	*mù guā*
passion fruit	百香果	*bái xiāng guǒ*
pineapple	鳳梨	*fèng lí*
starfruit, carambola	楊桃	*yáng táo*
watermelon	西瓜	*xī guā*

Appendix 2

ROAD AND STREET NAMES

About a dozen road names appear again and again throughout Taiwan. Zhongshan Road honours Dr Sun Yat-sen, the founding father of the ROC, because Sun was also known as Sun Zhongshan. Zhongzheng Road does the same for Chiang Kai-shek. Minquan, Minsheng and Minzu roads are named after the three core principles of Sun's ideology, Sanminzhuyi (because of which we also have Sanmin Road). The 'Zhonghua' in Zhonghua Road means China; Aiguo equals 'patriotism'; Guangfu celebrates the return of Taiwan to Chinese rule in 1945. A few road names, including Chongqing and Nanjing, recall cities in mainland China. Heping means 'peace'; Wenhua means 'culture'; Zhongxiao is 'loyalty and filial piety'. Some road names are more prosaic: Beimen is 'north gate' while Miaoqian means 'in front of the temple'.

Academia Rd	究院路	Cisian	*see Qixian*
Aiguo E Rd	愛國東路		
Anbei Rd	安北路	Dagong Rd	大公路
Anhe Rd	安和路	Datong Rd	大同路
Anping Rd	安平路	Dihua St	迪化街
		Dongmen Rd	東門路
Bade Rd	八德路	Dunhua S Rd	敦化南路
Beian Rd	北安路		
Beimen Rd	北門路	Fuqian Rd	府前路
Binhai Rd	濱海路	Fuxing S Rd	復興南路
Boai Rd	博愛路		
		Gongyuan Rd	公園路
Changan E Rd	長安東路	Guangfu Rd	光復路
Changan W Rd	長安西路		
Chaozhou St	潮州街	Heping W Rd	和平西路
Chengde Rd	承德路	Hoping	*see Heping*
Chenggong Rd	成功路	Hsinsheng	*see Xinsheng*
Chengkung	*see Chenggong*	Huanhe N Rd	環河北路
Chienkuo	*see Jianguo*	Huanhe S Rd	環河南路
Chongqing N Rd	重慶北路	Huaxi St	華西街
Chongqing S Rd	重慶南路		
Chungcheng	*see Zhongzheng*	Jhonghua	*see Zhonghua*
Chunghsiao	*see Zhongxiao*	Jhongjheng	*see Zhongzheng*
Chunghua	*see Zhonghua*	Jhongshan	*see Zhongshan*
Chungshan	*see Zhongshan*	Jhongyi	*see Zhongyi*
Chungyi	*see Zhongyi*	Jianguo S Rd	建國南路
Cingnian	*see Qingnian*	Jianxing Rd	建行路

Jinshan S Rd	金山南路	Simen	*see Ximen*
		Sinsheng	*see Xinsheng*
Kaishan Rd	開山路	Sihwei	*see Siwei*
Keelung Rd	基隆路	Siwei Rd	四維路
Kending Rd	墾丁路	Siwei 3rd Rd	四維三路
Kuangfu	*see Guangfu*	Songjiang Rd	松江路
Linsen Rd	林森路	Taiwan Bd	台灣大道
Liuhe Rd	六合路	Tatung	*see Datong*
		Tungmen	*see Dongmen*
Meishuguan Rd	美術館路		
Miaoqian Rd	廟前路	Weixin Rd	維新路
Minchuan	*see Minquan*	Wenhua Rd	文化路
Minquan Rd	民權路	Wufei St	五妃街
Minsheng Rd	民生路	Wufu Rd	五福路
Mintsu	*see Minzu*	Wuquan Rd	五權路
Minzu Rd	民族路		
		Ximen Rd	西門路
Nanjing E Rd	南京東路	Xinle St	新樂街
Nanjing W Rd	南京西路	Xinsheng N Rd	新生北路
Nanking	*see Nanjing*	Xinsheng S Rd	新生南路
Nanmen Rd	南門路	Xinyi Rd	信義路
		Xitun Rd	西屯路
Pate	*see Bade*		
Poai	*see Boai*	Yanping S Rd	延平南路
Putou St	埔頭街	Yenping	*see Yanping*
		Yongkang St	永康街
Qingnian Rd	青年路		
Qixian Rd	七賢路	Zhonghua Rd	中華路
		Zhongshan Rd	中山路
Renai Rd	仁愛路	Zhongxiao E Rd	忠孝東路
		Zhongxiao W Rd	忠孝西路
Sanmin Rd	三民路	Zhongyang Rd	中央路
Shaochuan St	哨船街	Zhongyi Rd	忠義路
Shennong St	神農街	Zhongzheng Rd	中正路
Shuimei St	水美街		

Appendix 3

FURTHER INFORMATION

BOOKS Some of these books are impossible to find outside Taiwan or very expensive. A recently launched Taiwan-based venture, Camphor Press (*www.camphorpress.com*) has begun publishing new titles and reissuing classic Taiwan-related books in downloadable formats for popular e-readers.

Literature

Chang, Ta-chun *Wild Kids: Two Novels About Growing Up* Columbia University Press, 2002. Critically acclaimed novellas by one of Taiwan's most popular and versatile writers.

Chu, Tien-wen *Notes of a Desolate Man* Columbia University Press, 2000. Prize-winning but somewhat difficult novel narrated by a gay man.

Pai, Hsien-yung *Crystal Boys* Gay Sunshine Press, 1993. A translation of the taboo-busting novel that bolstered mainstream awareness and understanding of Taiwan's gay community. The author, who is also known as Kenneth Pai, also wrote the sublime 1971 collection of short stories *Taipei People* (sometimes titled *Taipei Characters*).

Wang Wen-hsing *Family Catastrophe* University of Hawaii, 1995. First published in Chinese in 1972, this novel examines the expectations, resentments and tensions within a typical family.

Wood, Christopher *Taiwan* Fontana, 1981. Entertaining thriller about a plot to steal priceless works from the National Palace Museum, by the man who wrote the screenplays for *Moonraker* and *The Spy Who Loved Me*.

Society

Blundell, David (editor) *Taiwan Since Martial Law: Society, Culture, Politics, Economy* National Taiwan University Press, 2012. An important collection of articles about how Taiwan has evolved over the quarter century since martial law was ended.

Caltonhill, Mark *Private Prayers and Public Parades* Taipei City Government Department of Information, 2002. An excellent book covering almost every religion – mainstream or otherwise – practised in Taiwan.

Crook, Steven *Dos and Don'ts in Taiwan* iGroup Press, 2010. A guide to modern Taiwanese customs, lifestyles and habits by the author of the Bradt Travel Guide to Taiwan.

Donnelly, Neal *Gods of Taiwan: A Collector's Account* Artist Publishing Co, 2006. Profiles of major and minor Taiwanese deities by a former US diplomat who collected god effigies during his 11 years in Taiwan, peppered with some excellent anecdotes.

Jordan, David K *Gods, Ghosts & Ancestors: Folk Religion in a Taiwanese Village* Caves Books, 2nd edition 1985. The briefest and clearest explanation of religion in Taiwan you'll find, written by an American anthropologist who did fieldwork in south Taiwan in the late 1960s. A 3rd edition ebook can be downloaded from http://weber.ucsd.edu/~dkjordan/scriptorium/gga/ggamain.html.

Nature

Brazil, Mark *Birds of East Asia* Christopher Helm, 2009. This hefty tome, which covers eastern China, Taiwan, Korea, Japan and Russia's far east, has excellent illustrations and information for almost every avian species ever recorded in Taiwan. A book by the same author and publisher devoted to Taiwan's avifauna may appear in early 2015.

Travel

Crook, Steven *Keeping Up With the War God* Yushan Publications, 2001. The author of the Bradt guide visits temples, attends traditional festivals and climbs high mountains.

Fetherling, Douglas *The Other China: Journeys around Taiwan* Arsenal Pulp Press, 1995. Slim account of two visits by a Canadian poet who was escorted around Taipei, Kinmen and Sun Moon Lake.

Goedhart, Menno & Robbins, Cheryl *The Real Taiwan and the Dutch* Taiwan Interminds Publishing, 2010. Hard to find but very useful full-colour guide to those parts of Taiwan where the Dutch East India Company interacted with the indigenous people in the 17th century.

Parfitt, Troy *Why China Will Never Rule the World: Travels in the Two Chinas* Western Hemisphere Press, 2011. Taiwan is the second of the two Chinas visited by the Canadian author, who lived near Taipei for a decade.

Robbins, Cheryl *A Foreigner's Travel Guide to Taiwan Indigenous Areas* Taiwan Interminds Publishing, 2012–14. This three-volume series, by a full-time tour guide specialising in aboriginal communities, has very useful homestay and restaurant listings plus excellent photos.

Robertson, Matt *Rock Climbing Taiwan* Climbstone, 2012. Highly practical bilingual guide to Taiwan's rock-climbing possibilities.

Saunders, Richard *The Islands of Taiwan* Community Services Centre (Taipei), 2013. A comprehensive guide to all of the ROC's minor islands.

Saunders, Richard *Taipei Escapes 1* and *Taipei Escapes 2* Community Services Centre (Taipei), 2011. Everything you need to know about reaching beautiful places in north Taiwan with an emphasis on day trips and short but spectacular hikes. The first volume covers the northeast, while the second deals with Taipei City and the northwest.

Saunders, Richard *Yangmingshan: The Guide* Community Services Centre (Taipei), 2006. A comprehensive guide to the national park on Taipei's doorstep, including history, nature and geology plus 41 suggested hikes.

Language
Books and audio materials about Mandarin Chinese available outside Taiwan tend to focus on Mandarin as it's spoken in the PRC, but this isn't a major problem (see page 25). In Taiwan, the bookshops near Taipei's National Taiwan Normal University are a good place to find language-learning materials.

McNaughton, William *Reading & Writing Chinese: A Comprehensive Guide to the Chinese Writing System* Tuttle Publishing, 2nd edition 1998. Make sure to get the original version which covers traditional characters, not the alternative simplified-character edition. The Taiwan edition by Caves Books Ltd is considerably cheaper than the one available in the UK.

Meek, Catherine, Yan, Mao, Henlan, E & Hill, Brian *Breakthrough Mandarin Chinese* Palgrave Macmillan, 1999. Pricey yet effective introduction to the language.

Qian, Kan *Colloquial Chinese* Routledge, 2nd edition 2009. Highly rated book suitable for self-study; audio materials available on CD or as MP3 files.

Easy-peasy Chinese: Mandarin Chinese Dorling Kindersley, 2007. Small and thus portable but probably contains more than enough for most travellers.

History and politics

Brown, Melissa J *Is Taiwan Chinese?* University of California Press, 2004. An academic analysis of migration and the political manipulation of culture and how they influence Taiwanese identity.

Edwards, Jack *Banzai You Bastards!* Corporate Communications (Hong Kong), 2nd edition 1996. A moving and memorable account by a Welshman captured by the Japanese in World War II and forced to labour in hellish conditions in a Taiwan mine.

Keating, Jerome F & Lin, April C J *Island in the Stream: A Quick Case Study of Taiwan's Complex History* SMC Publishing, 4th edition 2008. A comprehensive presentation of Taiwan's history from the 1500s to the present, explaining how Taiwan overcame the odds to become a free democracy, but continues to be threatened by the People's Republic of China. A 5th edition is likely in 2014.

MUSIC Pop videos by scores of Taiwanese artists have been uploaded to YouTube and can be found by searching for their English names. Particularly worth listening to are **Bobby Chen** (Chen Sheng), a versatile singer-songwriter now in his 50s, and **Biung** (Wang Hong-en), a member of the Bunun tribe whose music ranges from gentle aboriginal tunes to raucous rock. Among the most successful Taiwan-born pop stars of the past 20 years are **Jay Chou** (Zhou Jie-lun) and **A-Mei** (Zhang Hui-mei), both of whom have sold lots of albums throughout the ethnic Chinese world; the latter has also performed under her aboriginal name, **A-Mit**. Not all Taiwanese pop consists of sugary ballads; there are punk bands, death-metal acts (notably **Chthonic**, who've toured overseas) and plenty of rappers. Multi-national Taiwan-based outfit **A Moving Sound** (*www.amovingsound.com*), who describe themselves as a performance company rather than a band, have won considerable acclaim in recent years for their compositions and use of traditional Chinese instruments. Recordings of traditional indigenous polyphonic singing aren't hard to find in large CD shops. One that's especially good is *Who's Singing On Mountain* [sic] by Hualien Taiping Elementary School Chorus (Wind Records, 2004). The songs are entirely traditional and performed without any instrumental backing; liner notes in Chinese, English and Bunun explain the meaning of the lyrics.

INTERNET
Official resources

www.cwb.gov.tw Weather Bureau's bilingual site; forecasts, tide times and earthquake reports
www.ey.gov.tw Taiwan's Cabinet
www.mofa.gov.tw Ministry of Foreign Affairs
www.president.gov.tw Taiwan's Presidential Office
http://iff.immigration.gov.tw Information for foreign tourists, students and dependants
http://np.cpami.gov.tw/english/ National parks central website

Travel information

www.boca.gov.tw Visa information from Taiwan's government
www.freeway.gov.tw If you expect to spend a lot of time on the motorways, visit this site and read about traffic laws on the fast roads
www.railway.gov.tw TRA's informative but sometimes frustrating website
www.taiwanese-secrets.com Good photos and to-the-point descriptions of places around Taiwan
www.taiwanfun.com Restaurant and nightlife listings plus some travel articles
www.thsrc.com.tw High-speed rail schedules and online ticket purchasing
www.tit.com.tw Download copies of the Tourism Bureau-backed *Travel in Taiwan* magazine
www.youthtravel.net.tw Travel information for backpackers

Culture

www.culture.tw News and articles about traditional and modern culture
www.dmtip.gov.tw Digital Museum of Taiwan's Indigenous People
www.moc.gov.tw Taiwan's culture ministry
www.taoistsecret.com A commercial site with lots of information about Chinese religion
www.tribe-asia.com Handicrafts and arts made by members of Taiwan's aboriginal tribes

Taiwan blogs

http://bradttaiwan.blogspot.com Compiled by the author of this guidebook; features some sights not in the guide
http://danshuihistory.blogspot.com In-depth posts about little-known episodes in Taiwan's history
http://hikingtaiwan.wordpress.com Mouthwatering photos of Taiwan's scenery
http://hungryintaipei.blogspot.com A female foodie reviews 400+ Taipei restaurants
http://michaelturton.blogspot.com Commentary on all aspects of life in Taiwan including political, historical, educational and environmental issues
http://taiwandiscovery.wordpress.com Blog by Richard Saunders, author of several Taiwan travel books
http://taiwanincycles.blogspot.com Informative bike-oriented blog

News

www.chinapost.com.tw Pro-KMT newspaper
www.etaiwannews.com Pro-DPP newspaper
www.taipeitimes.com DPP-leaning newspaper
www.taiwantoday.tw Government website updated daily; news and some interesting features

Get involved

www.animalstaiwan.org Shelters stray dogs and runs CNR programs
www.spca.org.tw Taiwan Society for the Prevention of Cruelty to Animals
www.tahr.org.tw The website of the Taiwan Association for Human Rights, a long-established group campaigning, among other things, against the death penalty

For long-term residents

www.forumosa.com Taiwan-centric forums, lots of travel information
www.pinyin.info Scholarly resource for those intrigued by Taiwan's transliteration difficulties
www.taiwanease.com Has a comprehensive directory of Taipei eateries and other businesses
www.taiwanho.com Some useful articles and discussions

MOBILE PHONE APPS

Taiwan Adventures Mobile Guide This iOS app covers 900 hikes, hotels, hot springs and other places and has 2,000 photos.
Taiwan for Culture Vultures Written by the author of the Bradt guide, this iOS app describes temples and museums in some depth.
Tour Taiwan A free app created by Taiwan's Tourism Bureau packed with practical information. Available in iOS and Android versions.
Travel in Taiwan App version of *Travel in Taiwan* magazine.

Index

Page numbers in **bold** indicate major entries; those in *italics* indicate maps.